THE CONFLICT OF LAWS

AUSTRALIA AND NEW ZEALAND
The Law Book Company Ltd.
Sydney : Melbourne : Perth

CANADA AND U.S.A.
The Carswell Company Ltd.
Agincourt, Ontario

INDIA
N. M. Tripathi Private Ltd.
Bombay
and
Eastern Law House Private Ltd.
Calcutta and Delhi
M. P. P. House
Bangalore

ISRAEL
Steimatzky's Agency Ltd.
Jerusalem : Tel Aviv : Haifa

MALAYSIA : SINGAPORE : BRUNEI
Malayan Law Journal (Pte.) Ltd.
Singapore

PAKISTAN
Pakistan Law House
Karachi

THE
CONFLICT OF LAWS

BY

J. H. C. MORRIS, Q.C., D.C.L., LL.D., F.B.A.

Honorary Bencher of Gray's Inn,
Honorary Fellow of Magdalen College, Oxford
formerly Fellow of Gonville and Caius College, Cambridge
Emeritus Reader in the Conflict of Laws in the University of Oxford

THIRD EDITION

LONDON

STEVENS AND SONS

1984

First Edition 1971
Second Edition 1980
Third Edition 1984

Published by Stevens & Sons Limited
of 11 New Fetter Lane London.
Computerset by Promenade Graphics Limited, of Cheltenham
and printed in Scotland.

British Library Cataloguing in Publication Data
Morris, J.H.C.
    The conflict of laws.—3rd ed.
    1. Conflict of laws—England
    I. Title
    340.9   KD680

    ISBN 0–420–46890–0
    ISBN 0–420–46900–1 Pbk.

TO MY PUPILS

PREFACE

THE interval between the publication of the second and third editions of this book is much shorter than that between the first and second. This is mainly due to the Civil Jurisdiction and Judgments Act 1982 which was passed primarily to implement the EEC Convention on Jurisdiction and the Enforcement of Judgments in Civil and Commercial Matters of 1968 and the Accession Convention of 1978. These Conventions will revolutionise our law on jurisdiction in actions *in personam* and on the enforcement of foreign judgments. They have necessitated the transfer of the Part on Foreign Judgments and Arbitration to immediately after the Part on Jurisdiction of the English Court. A drawback to this new arrangement is that there is now a big gap between Chapter 2, on Domicile, and Part Four, on Family Law: but one can't have everything.

At the time of writing neither the provisions of the 1982 Act implementing the EEC Conventions nor the related amendments to the Rules of the Supreme Court (especially Order 11) have been brought into force. This is because the Conventions cannot come into force for the United Kingdom until the Accession Convention has been ratified by all six original member states of the EEC. So ratification by the United Kingdom depends on the speed of the legislative or administrative process elsewhere in the EEC. I have however written as though the whole Act and the related changes in the R.S.C. are already in force, because my information is that they are likely to be brought into force during the summer or autumn of 1984.

The 1982 Act so completely overshadows in importance all the other changes that have occurred in this subject since 1980 that there is no need to list here even the most important of these changes. Though much new material has been added to this edition, I am glad to be able to report that, by dint of judicious pruning and of rather tighter printing, it is only five pages longer than its predecessor.

My grateful thanks are due to my friends Mr. Lawrence Collins, for allowing me to make use of the material he contributed to the Supplements to *Dicey and Morris on the Conflict of Laws* on the 1982 Act; to Dr. P. M. North, for advice on what material could properly be pruned; to Professor J. D. McClean, for advice on the chapters on custody and legitimation of children; and to the publishers, for their unfailing encouragement, patience and advice and for relieving me of the tedious task of preparing the Tables and Index; and not least to my wife, for sacrificing so much of her leisure in order to read the whole book aloud to me in proof, paragraph by paragraph and footnote by footnote.

My hope is that I have stated the law as it was on October 1, 1983, but I have been able to slip in a few footnote references to changes made between then and January 1, 1984.

J.H.C.M.

Orford
January 1984

FROM THE PREFACE TO THE FIRST EDITION

LAW books are like babies: they are the greatest fun to conceive, but very laborious to deliver. The original conception of this one was that it should be a shortened version of *Dicey and Morris on The Conflict of Laws*, issued for the use of students. But it soon became a great deal more than that, because I could not rest content with merely making a précis, nor have my ideas stood still since 1967. So this has become not just potted Dicey up to date, but virtually a new book. In the main it follows the arrangement of Dicey and Morris, but there are some changes. . . . The six chapters in Part Eight appear at the end of the book and not (as in most other books) at the beginning. These chapters were originally intended to appear in the introductory Part One. But the first footnote in the chapters on Renvoi, Characterisation and the Incidental Question ended with the sentence: "The reader who finds this chapter heavy going is advised to skip it until he has finished the rest of the book." I then decided to have the courage of my convictions, and put these chapters (and three others) at the end.

I have drawn on my Oxford lectures for the occasional quip (or sally). I have tried to reduce the number and size of the footnotes in Dicey, especially by pruning the citations of Commonwealth authority; but I fear I have not been as successful as I could have wished. Still, one who writes on any branch of English law cannot expect to be taken seriously unless he cites authority for his statements. . . .

J. H. C. M.

Magdalen College,
Oxford
April 15, 1971.

CONTENTS

TABLE OF CASES

TABLE OF STATUTES

STATUTES OF THE UNITED KINGDOM PARLIAMENT

OTHER STATUTES
Australia
Commonwealth:

TABLE OF BOOKS REFERRED TO

(Only books on the Conflicts of Laws which are cited by the name of the author alone are included in this Table.)

Anton	*Private International Law: A treatise from the point of view of Scots law* (1967)
Beale	*Treatise on the Conflict of Laws* (1935)
Cavers	*The Choice of Law Process* (1965)
Cheshire and North	*Private International Law* (10th ed., 1979)
Cook	*Logical and Legal Bases of the Conflict of Laws* (1942)
Currie	*Selected Essays on the Conflict of Laws* (1963)
Dicey and Morris	*Conflict of Laws* (10th ed., 1980)
Falconbridge	*Selected Essays on the Conflict of Laws* (2nd ed., 1954)
Graveson	*Conflict of Laws* (7th ed., 1974)
Leflar	*American Conflicts Law* (3rd ed., 1977)
Lorenzen	*Selected Articles on the Conflicts of Laws* (1947)
Morse	*Torts in Private International Law* (1978)
North	*The Private International Law of Matrimonial Causes in the British Isles and the Republic of Ireland* (1977)
Nygh	*Conflict of Laws in Australia* (3rd ed., 1976)
Rabel	*Conflict of Laws: A Comparative Study* (2nd ed., 1958–1964)
Read	*Recognition and Enforcement of Foreign Judgments in the Common Law Units of the British Commonwealth* (1938)
Restatement	*American Law Institute's Restatement of the Conflict of Laws (Second)* (1971)
Robertson	*Characterisation in the Conflict of Laws* (1940)
Savigny	*Conflict of Laws* (Guthrie's translation) (2nd ed., 1880)
Schmitthoff	*English Conflict of Laws* (3rd ed., 1954)
Story	*Commentaries on the Conflict of Laws* (8th ed., 1883)
Westlake	*Private International Law* (7th ed., 1925)
Wolff	*Private International Law* (2nd ed., 1950)

Part One
INTRODUCTION

CHAPTER 1

NATURE AND SCOPE OF THE CONFLICT
OF LAWS

Introduction

THE conflict of laws is that part of the private law of a country which
deals with cases having a foreign element. By a "foreign element" is meant
simply a contact with some system of law other than English law. Such a
contact may exist, for example, because a contract was made or to be performed in a foreign country, or because a tort was committed there, or
because property was situated there, or because the parties are not English. In the conflict of laws, a foreign element and a foreign country mean a
non-English element and a country other than England. From the point of
view of the conflict of laws, Scotland and Northern Ireland are for most but
not all purposes as much foreign countries as France or Germany.

If an action is brought in an English court for damages for breach of a
contract made in England between two Englishmen and to be performed in
England, there is no foreign element, the case is not a case in the conflict of
laws, and the English court will naturally apply English internal or domestic law. But if the contract had been made in France between two
Frenchmen and was to be performed in France, then the case would be (for
an English court, but not for a French court) a case in the conflict of laws,
and an English court would apply French law to most of the matters in dispute before it,[1] just as a French court would naturally apply French law to
all such matters. If we change the facts once more and assume that the contract was made in France between an Englishman and a Frenchman but
was to be performed in England, then the case is a case in the conflict of
laws not only for an English court but also for a French court and indeed
for any court in the world in which the contract is litigated; and that court
will have to decide whether the French or the English elements are the
more significant, and apply French or English law accordingly. The significance of this distinction between these two types of case having foreign
elements will be explained later in this chapter.[2]

Public and private international law

The conflict of laws, or private international law as it is sometimes
called, has little to do with public international law. The conflict of laws is a
necessary part of the law of every country because different countries

---

[1] Not to all matters, because in an English court all matters of procedure are governed exclusively by English domestic law. See *post*, Chap. 29.

[2] *Post*, pp. 12–13.

have different legal systems containing different legal rules, while public international law seeks primarily to regulate relations between different sovereign States. Nevertheless some overlap exists; for instance, the topics of sovereign and diplomatic immunity from suit[3] and of governmental seizure of private property[4] are discussed in books on the conflict of laws as well as in books on public international law. Public international law, in theory at any rate, is the same everywhere. But the rules of the conflict of laws are different from country to country. Even between England and Scotland there are some significant differences, notably in the case of the jurisdiction of courts in actions *in personam*; while between the common law countries on the one hand and the continental European countries on the other, the differences are much more deep-rooted.

Meaning of "country"

Public international law deals mainly with relations between different States, while the conflict of laws is concerned with differences between the legal systems of different countries. A State in the sense of public international law may or may not coincide with a country (or "law district" as it is sometimes called) in the sense of the conflict of laws. Unitary States like Sweden, Italy and New Zealand, where the law is the same throughout the State, are "countries" in this sense. But public international law knows nothing of England or Scotland, New York or California, for they are merely component parts of the United Kingdom and the United States. Yet each of them is a country in the sense of the conflict of laws, because it has a separate system of law. Since the matter is of fundamental importance, it is necessary to be clear exactly what constitutes a country for the purposes of the conflict of laws. England, Scotland, Northern Ireland, the Republic of Ireland, Guernsey, Jersey and the Isle of Man is each a separate country; so is each of the American and Australian states and each of the Canadian provinces, and each colony or dependency of the United Kingdom. However, for some purposes larger units than these may constitute countries. Thus, the United Kingdom is one country for the purposes of the law of negotiable instruments,[5] Great Britain is one country for most purposes of the law of companies,[6] Australia is one country for the purposes of the law of marriage[7] and matrimonial causes,[8] and Canada is one country for the purposes of the law of divorce.[9]

On the other hand, Wales is not a country, because its system of law is the same as that of England. Nor is it necessary that a country in the sense of the conflict of laws should have a separate legislature. For instance, Scotland, the Australian Capital Territory and the District of Columbia

---

[3] *Post*, Chap. 5.
[4] *Post*, Chap. 22.
[5] Bills of Exchange Act 1882.
[6] Companies Act 1948.
[7] Marriage Act 1961.
[8] Family Law Act 1975, ss.39(3) and (4), 103.
[9] Divorce Act 1968, ss.5(1)(*a*), 14.

have no such legislature and yet they are countries; and Northern Ireland did not cease to be a country when its legislature was suspended in 1972.

Public and private law

Generally speaking, the conflict of laws is concerned much more with private than with public law. It is traditional that English books on the conflict of laws do not discuss such topics as the jurisdiction of criminal courts to try crimes committed abroad, or the extradition of persons accused of crime, or the immigration or deportation of aliens.

Jurisdiction and choice of law

The questions that do arise are of two main types: first, has the English court jurisdiction to determine this case? and secondly, if so, what law will it apply? There may sometimes be a third question, namely, will the English court recognise or enforce a foreign judgment purporting to determine the issue between the parties? Of course this third question arises only if there is a foreign judgment, and thus not in every case. But the first two questions arise in every case with foreign elements, though the answer to one of them may be so obvious that the court is in effect concerned only with the other. The law of every modern country has rules for dealing with these questions, called conflict of laws—in contrast to its domestic or internal law.

The English rules of the conflict of laws differ from those adopted in many continental European countries in one important respect. There are many situations in which, if the English court has jurisdiction, it will apply English domestic law. This is true, for example, of most issues in proceedings for divorce and separation,[10] for the guardianship, custody[11] and adoption[12] of children, and for the maintenance of wives and children.[13] Conversely, there are many situations in which, if a foreign court has jurisdiction according to English rules of the conflict of laws, its judgment or decree will be recognised or enforced in England, regardless of the grounds on which it was based or the choice of law rule which it applied.[14] Thus, in the English conflict of laws, questions of jurisdiction frequently tend to overshadow questions of choice of law. Or, to put it differently, it frequently happens that if the question of jurisdiction (whether of the English or of a foreign court) is answered satisfactorily, the question of choice of law does not arise.

Justification

What justification is there for the existence of the conflict of laws? Why should we depart from the rules of our own law and apply those of another

[10] *Post*, pp. 191–192, 206–207.
[11] *Post*, Chap. 13.
[12] *Post*, pp. 255–256.
[13] *Post*, pp. 220 *et seq*.
[14] *Post*, pp. 122, 193, 212–213.

system? This is a vital matter on which it is necessary to be clear before we proceed any further. The justification for the conflict of laws can best be seen by considering what would happen if it did not exist.

Theoretically, it would be possible for English courts to close their doors to all except English litigants.[15] But if they did so, grave injustice would be inflicted not only on foreigners but also on Englishmen. An Englishman who had made a contract with a Scotsman in Glasgow or with a Frenchman in Paris would be unable to enforce it in England; and if the courts of other countries adopted the same principle, the contract could not be enforced in any country in the world.

Theoretically, it would be possible for English courts, while opening their doors to foreigners, to apply English domestic law in all cases. But if they did so, grave injustice would again be inflicted not only on foreigners but on Englishmen. For instance, if two English people married in France in accordance with the formalities prescribed by French law, but not in accordance with the formalities prescribed by English law, the English court, if it applied English domestic law to the case, would have to treat the parties as unmarried persons and their children as illegitimate.

Theoretically, it would be possible for English courts, while opening their doors to foreigners and while ready to apply foreign law in appropriate cases, to refuse to recognise or enforce a foreign judgment determining the issue between the parties. But if they did so, grave injustice would again be inflicted not only on foreigners but also on Englishmen. For instance, if a divorce was granted in a foreign country, and afterwards one party remarried in England, he or she might be convicted of bigamy. Or if an Englishman sued a foreigner in a foreign country for damages for breach of contract or for tort, and eventually obtained a judgment in his favour, he might find that the defendant had surreptitiously removed his assets to England, and then would have to start all over again to enforce his rights.

It was at one time supposed that the doctrine of comity was a sufficient basis for the conflict of laws; and even today references to comity are sometimes found in English judgments.[16] But it is clear that English courts apply, *e.g.* French law in order to do justice between the parties, and not from any desire to show courtesy to the French Republic, nor even in the hope that if English courts apply French law in appropriate cases, French courts will be encouraged in appropriate cases to apply English law. Moreover, the doctrine of comity is quite irreconcilable with the application of the law of an enemy country in time of war, which is a commonplace when justice requires it.[17]

---

[15] Subject to any question of "denial of justice" under the rules of public international law. See Brownlie, *Principles of Public International Law*, 3rd. ed., pp. 529–531.

[16] *e.g. Igra* v. *Igra* [1951] P. 404, 412; *Travers* v. *Holley* [1953] P. 246, 257; *Garthwaite* v. *Garthwaite* [1964] P. 356, 389. For a discussion of the doctrine of comity, see *post*, pp. 505–506.

[17] *e.g. Re Francke and Rasch* [1918] 1 Ch. 470; *Re Cohn* [1945] Ch. 5.

Late development in England

Although the conflict of laws has been intensively studied by continental jurists since the thirteenth century,[18] it is of comparatively recent origin in England. A few rules of the English conflict of laws can be traced back to the seventeenth century. But the subject first came into prominence in the English courts towards the end of the eighteenth century, mainly because of conflicts between the laws of England and Scotland. In the nineteenth century its development was enormously accelerated by the rapid increase in commercial and social intercourse between England and the Continent of Europe, and by British colonisation of countries overseas. In the twentieth century this development has been still further accelerated by the mass movement of populations, stimulated by wars and their aftermath, and by technical advances in the means of transport and communications. It has not been easy for the conflict of laws to adapt itself to the changes in social and commercial life which the twentieth century has witnessed. Many of its rules were first laid down in the nineteenth century and seem better suited to nineteenth-century conditions than to those of the twentieth century. Obvious examples are furnished by the law of torts[19] and (in spite of recent statutory changes[20]) by the law of domicile, particularly the rules making it so difficult to shake off a domicile of origin.[21] Remedies for this situation (which are still in the experimental stage) have been sought in the somewhat reluctant willingness of courts to allow the law of the place where the tort was committed to be displaced in favour of the proper law of the tort in appropriate cases,[22] and in the introduction by statute of habitual residence as an alternative to domicile.[23] In the United States the reaction against nineteenth-century ideas has gone much further than it has in England. Indeed, there is an influential school of writers in the United States who believe that traditional rules of the conflict of laws have served their purpose, and that they should be scrapped and a fresh start made.[24]

Sources

The three most important sources of the English conflict of law are statutes, the decisions of the courts and the opinions of jurists. Statutes are placed first in this list (and not second as they were in the first edition of this book) because there can be no doubt that they have become, potentially at any rate, by far the most important source, and their importance seems likely to increase rather than to diminish in future. Until the middle

---

[18] For the history of the conflict of laws, see Cheshire and North, Chap. 2; Wolff, Chap. 3; Lorenzen, Chap. 7; Anton, Chap. 2; Beale, Vol. 3, pp. 1880–1975; Sack, in *Law: A Century of Progress* (1935) Vol. 3, pp. 342–454 (with special reference to the history in England); Llewelfryn Davies (1937) 18 B.Y.I.L. 49–78; De Nova (1966) *Recueil des Cours*, II, 441–477; Lipstein (1972) *Recueil des Cours*, I, 104–166.

[19] See *post*, Chap. 16.

[20] *Post*, pp. 28–30.

[21] *Post*, pp. 20–22.

[22] *Post*, pp. 314–317.

[23] *Post*, p. 35, n. 40.

[24] See *post*, pp. 516–523.

of the twentieth century, Parliamentary intervention in the conflict of laws was haphazard, sporadic and (compared with the mass of case law) slight and unimportant. Statutes were occasionally passed to remedy some glaring anomaly or injustice,[25] to facilitate the reciprocal enforcement of judgments within the United Kingdom or the Commonwealth or with such foreign States as were prepared to offer reciprocal treatment,[26] or (on one occasion only) to codify a very small part of the subject.[27] But since the middle of the twentieth century there has been an increasing spate of statutes implementing some international convention,[28] and a few very important ones prepared by the Law Commission as part of a thoroughgoing and well considered reform of the law.[29]

Of course this increasing activity of Parliament does not mean that the function of the courts is restricted to statutory interpretation. There remain large areas of the conflict of laws where case law is still the most important source, and the courts have still a creative part to play.

It is a unique feature of the conflict of laws, as compared with other branches of English law, that jurists have exerted a considerable influence on the decisions of the courts. The most influential foreign jurists have been Ulrich Huber (1636–1694), who was successively a professor of law and a judge in Friesland; Joseph Story (1779–1845), who was simultaneously a justice of the Supreme Court of the United States and a professor of law at the Harvard Law School; and the nineteenth-century German jurist Friedrich Carl von Savigny. In the twentieth century the most influential writers have been Dicey, whose *Conflict of Laws* was first published in 1896, and Cheshire, whose *Private International Law* was first published in 1935. Each of these well-known books has passed through many editions, and each is frequently cited by the courts.

Range and difficulty of the subject

Not the least interesting feature of the conflict of laws is that it is concerned with almost every branch of private law. "There is a sweep and range in it which is almost lyric in its completeness. It is the fugal music of law."[30] It is notoriously difficult—"one of the most baffling subjects of

---

[25] *e.g.* Wills Act 1861; Matrimonial Causes Act 1937, s.13; Law Reform (Miscellaneous Provisions) Act 1949, s.1; Family Allowances and National Insurance Act 1956, s.3 (all of which have since been replaced by more comprehensive enactments).

[26] *e.g.* Judgments Extension Act 1868; Maintenance Orders (Facilities for Enforcement) Act 1920; Administration of Justice Act 1920, Part II; Foreign Judgments (Reciprocal Enforcement) Act 1933; Maintenance Orders Act 1950.

[27] Bills of Exchange Act 1882, s.72.

[28] *e.g.* Carriage by Air Act 1961; Wills Act 1963; Diplomatic Privileges Act 1964; Carriage of Goods by Road Act 1965; Adoption Act 1968; Consular Relations Act 1968; International Organisations Act 1968; Carriage of Goods by Sea Act 1971; Recognition of Divorces and Legal Separations Act 1971; Maintenance Orders (Reciprocal Enforcement) Act 1972, Part II; Arbitration Act 1975; State Immunity Act 1978; Merchant Shipping Act 1979, s.14(1); Civil Jurisdiction and Judgments Act 1982.

[29] Matrimonial Proceedings (Polygamous Marriages) Act 1972, now Matrimonial Causes Act 1973, s.47; Domicile and Matrimonial Proceedings Act 1973; Foreign Limitation Periods Act 1984.

[30] Baty, *Polarized Law*, p. 5.

legal science," said the distinguished American judge Cardozo J.,[31] who also remarked on another occasion that "the average judge, when confronted by a problem in the conflict of laws, feels almost completely lost, and, like a drowning man, will grasp at a straw."[32] It is also very controversial—judges differ, and so specially do jurists. The result has sometimes seemed unedifying to those who look at the subject from the outside. "The realm of the conflict of laws," said an American writer,[33] "is a dismal swamp filled with quaking quagmires, and inhabited by learned but eccentric professors who theorise about mysterious matters in a strange and incomprehensible jargon." The apprehensive reader may rest assured that the present author is not a professor, and will strive to make the subject as comprehensible as possible.

Although the conflict of laws is highly controversial, the number of permutations and combinations arising out of any given set of facts is limited, and so is the number of possible solutions. In any given case the choice of law depends ultimately on considerations of reason, convenience and utility—*e.g.* how will the proposed choice of law work in practice, not only in this case, but also in similar cases in which a similar choice may reasonably be made? Hence in the conflict of laws, to a greater extent than in most other subjects, there is much to be learnt from the way in which similar problems have been solved in other countries with a historical and cultural background and legal tradition similar to our own. Hence no apology is needed for the occasional citation of Scottish, American and Commonwealth cases, even in a students' textbook.

Technical terms

Like any other legal subject, the conflict of laws has its technical terms (or jargon if you prefer), some of which must now be explained.

The rules of the conflict of laws are, traditionally, expressed in terms of juridical concepts or categories and localising elements or connecting factors.[34] Typical rules of the conflict of laws state that succession to immovables is governed by the *lex situs*; that the formal validity of a marriage is governed by the law of the place of celebration; and that capacity to marry is governed by the law of each party's antenuptial domicile. In these examples, succession to immovables, formal validity of marriage and capacity to marry are the categories, and *situs*, place of celebration and domicile are the connecting factors.

The *lex causae* is a convenient shorthand expression denoting the law (usually but not necessarily foreign) which governs the question. It is used in contradistinction to the *lex fori*, which always means the domestic law of the forum, *i.e.* (if the forum is English) English law. The *lex causae* may be more specifically denoted by a variety of expressions, usually in Latin,

---

[31] *Paradoxes of Legal Science*, p. 67.
[32] Cited in Cook, p. 152.
[33] Prosser (1953) 51 Mich.L.Rev. 959, 971.
[34] This expression (first suggested by Falconbridge) seems the best English equivalent of the French and German technical terms "point de rattachement" and "Anknüpfungspunkt."

such as the *lex domicilii* (law of the domicile), *lex patriae* (law of the nationality), *lex loci contractus* (law of the place where a contract is made), *lex
loci solutionis* (law of the place where a contract is to be performed or
where a debt is to be paid), *lex loci delicti* (law of the place where a tort is
committed), *lex loci celebrationis* (law of the place where a marriage is celebrated), *lex loci actus* (law of the place where a legal act takes place), *lex
situs* (law of the place where a thing is situated), *lex monetae* (law of the
country in whose currency a debt is expressed). The terms *lex loci disgra-
ziae* (law of the place where a bill of exchange is dishonoured) and *lex loci
stabuli* (law of the place where a motor car is garaged) are used only in jest.
The word "country" is also a technical term of the conflict of laws: its
meaning has already been explained.[35]

Determination of the connecting factor

A fundamental problem in the conflict of laws is whether the connecting
factor should be determined by the *lex fori* or by the *lex causae*. For
instance, domicile may mean one thing in English law and another thing in
French law: by which law, French or English, should the question of domicile be determined if it is alleged that a person is domiciled in France?
Since the determination of the *lex causae* depends on the determination of
the connecting factor, it is no longer controversial among learned writers
that the connecting factor should be determined by the *lex fori*.[36] Although
the reported cases are all concerned with domicile[37] and not with other
connecting factors, it may be assumed that English law has adopted this
prevailing opinion and that, for the purposes of an English conflict rule,
other connecting factors also will be determined by English law as the *lex
fori*.

The proposition that the *lex fori* defines the connecting factor has two
related but distinct aspects. The first is that the *lex fori* defines what it
means, *e.g.* by domicile. The second is that it also decides whether, so
defined, the connecting factor links a given issue with one legal system or
another. In an English court, English law decides what domicile means,
and also whether, in the light of this definition, a person is domiciled, *e.g.*
in England or in France. Nationality is an exception to the second of these
two aspects, but not to the first. If the *lex fori* uses nationality as a connecting factor, it must define what it means by nationality and say what is to
happen when the person concerned has two nationalities or none, or is a
national of a composite State like the United Kingdom or the United States
which comprises more than one country. But the *lex fori* can never say
whether a person is a national of a foreign state. That can only be done by
the law of the State concerned.[38] This is not an exception that has much

---

[35] *Ante*, p. 4.

[36] Most writers who discuss the determination of the connecting factor do so in connection
with their discussion of characterisation: see Cheshire and North, pp. 46–47; Robertson,
pp. 104–117; Lorenzen, pp. 97–100, 123–127. But the two questions are really quite distinct: see Wolff, s.131; Kahn-Freund (1974) *Recueil des Cours*, III, 388–395.

[37] *Post*, pp. 18–19.

[38] *Stoeck* v. *Public Trustee* [1921] 2 Ch. 67, 78, 82; *Re Chamberlain's Settlement* [1921] 2 Ch.
533; *cf. Oppenheimer* v. *Cattermole* [1976] A.C. 249.

importance in the English conflict of laws, because there are very few English conflict rules that are expressed in terms of nationality.[39]

Geographical expressions

A writer on the conflict of laws is constantly making use of certain geographical expressions which he assumes are familiar to his readers and which he endeavours always to use in the same sense. In this book, "England" includes Wales, because as we have seen[40] Wales is not a country for the purposes of the conflict of laws. "Great Britain" means England as above defined, and Scotland. The "United Kingdom" means England, Scotland and Northern Ireland. The "British Isles" or "British Islands"[41] means the United Kingdom, the Channel Islands and the Isle of Man. The "Commonwealth" is used in its widest sense to include the whole of the territories of which the Queen is recognised as the Head. It includes not only the older Dominions but also the Republics and other independent States which, for one reason or another, have ceased to be part of Her Majesty's dominions. It also includes the remaining colonies and other dependencies. But it does not include the Republic of Ireland,[42] South Africa[43] or Pakistan.[44]

The United Kingdom is of course part of the Commonwealth as above defined. But sometimes it is necessary to distinguish between the United Kingdom and the rest of the Commonwealth. This is done by referring either to "any part of the Commonwealth outside the United Kingdom" or to "the Commonwealth overseas."

General considerations

In this book, some matters of fundamental importance and great difficulty have been reserved for discussion at the end, and not discussed at the beginning as they are in most other books. The reason for this treatment is that in the author's opinion it would be daunting to the reader to inflict on him a discussion of these matters before he knows enough about the subject to understand all their implications. Its disadvantage is that the reader is left in blissful ignorance of some fundamental matters until he has reached nearly the end of the book. Therefore, by way of orientation of the reader, a few words will now be said about some of these problems, so that they may be recognised as and when they arise.

Renvoi. We have already seen[45] that there is a difference between two

---

[39] For some rare examples, see Wills Act 1963, s.1 (*post*, pp. 393–394); Recognition of Divorces and Legal Separations Act 1971, s.3(1)(*b*) (*post*, p. 197). Both these statutes implemented international conventions.

[40] *Ante*, p. 4.

[41] Southern Irishmen sometimes object to the use of this term because, as they point out, Northern Ireland is not an island and the Republic of Ireland is not British. But no better expression has yet been found; and any other would involve a cumbrous and tiresome circumlocution.

[42] Ireland Act 1949, s.1(1).

[43] South Africa Act 1962.

[44] Pakistan Act 1973.

[45] *Ante*, p. 3.

types of case with foreign elements; first, where all the significant elements are connected with one country, *e.g.* France, and the action is brought in another, *e.g.* England; and secondly, where the significant elements are divided between two countries, *e.g.* France and England. The significance of this distinction is that the first type of case is a case in the conflict of laws for an English court but not for a French court, but the second type of case is a case in the conflict of laws for any court in which it is litigated. Therefore, in the first type of case, if the English court applies French law, this must mean French domestic law, because a French court would apply no other. But in the second type of case, if the English court applies French law, because it thinks that the French elements are more significant than the English ones, it may find that a French court would apply English law, because it thinks that the English elements are the more significant. The question then arises, does "French law" mean French domestic law, or does it mean the whole of French law, including its rules of the conflict of laws? This is the famous problem of renvoi, possibly leading in this instance to a remission from French law to English law. If we change the facts and assume that the significant elements are divided, not between England and France, but between France and Germany, then an English court, if it applies French law, may find that a French court would apply German law. This also is a renvoi problem, but it leads not to a remission from French to English law, but to a transmission from French to German law, and possibly to a further reference from German to English or French law.

Suppose, for example, that a British citizen domiciled in France dies intestate leaving movables in England. In order to determine who are his next-of-kin, an English court will apply French law because he was domiciled in France; but it may find that a French court would apply English law because he was a British citizen. If the intestate had been a German national instead of a British citizen, a French court might apply German law. The problem is whether French law means French domestic law, or the whole of French law including its rules of the conflict of laws. If it means the latter, there may be a remission to English law in the first of these cases, and a transmission to German law in the second.

It may be said at once that in the vast majority of cases English courts interpret their reference to foreign law to mean its domestic rules only. But there are a few exceptional cases, to be discussed in a later chapter,[46] in which the reference has been interpreted to mean the whole of foreign law, including its rules of the conflict of laws.

Characterisation. The nature of this problem can best be shown by two examples. Suppose that a person takes a ticket in London for a railway journey to Edinburgh, and is injured in a railway accident in Scotland. Is his cause of action against the British Railways Board for breach of contract, in which case English law as the law governing the contract may apply, or for tort, in which case a combination of English and Scots law will

---

[46] *Post*, Chap. 30.

apply? By which law, English or Scottish, is this question to be answered? Or suppose that a marriage is celebrated in England between two French people domiciled in France. The marriage is valid by English law but invalid by French law because neither party has the consent of his or her parents as required by French law. If this rule of French law relates to formalities of marriage, it will not apply to a marriage celebrated in England; but if it relates to capacity to marry, it will invalidate the marriage of a French couple. By which law, French or English, is the nature of the French rule to be determined? These and other similar problems are discussed in a later chapter.[47]

The incidental question. The nature of this problem also can best be shown by two examples. Suppose that a testator domiciled in France gives movables in England to his "wife." The main question here is the succession to the movables; and it is governed by French law, because the testator was domiciled in France. But a subsidiary or incidental question may arise as to the validity of the testator's marriage: should this question be referred to the English or the French rules of the conflict of laws relating to the validity of marriages? Or suppose that the English court has to determine the capacity of a domiciled Italian to contract a second marriage after obtaining a divorce from his first wife in Switzerland. The Swiss divorce is recognised as valid in England, but not in Italy. The main question here is the question of capacity to remarry, and it is governed by Italian law, because the husband was domiciled in Italy. The incidental question is the validity of the divorce: should this question be referred to the English or the Italian rules of the conflict of laws relating to the recognition of divorces? These and other similar problems are discussed in a later chapter.[48]

The time factor. The conflict of laws deals primarily with the application of laws in space; but problems of time cannot altogether be ignored. In the conflict of laws the time factor is significant in various situations. The most important of these is when there is a retrospective change in the *lex causae* after the events have happened which gave rise to the cause of action. Should the English court apply the *lex causae* as it was when the cause of action arose, or as it is at the date of the trial? This problem and others like it are also discussed in a later chapter.[49]

---

[47] *Post*, Chap. 31.
[48] *Post*, Chap. 32.
[49] *Post*, Chap. 33.

CHAPTER 2

DOMICILE

INTRODUCTION

IN most systems of the conflict of laws, questions concerning the personal and proprietary relationships between members of a family are governed as a general rule by the personal law. In the United Kingdom, the Commonwealth and the United States, the personal law is the law of the domicile, but in most (but not all) continental European countries it is the law of the nationality.[1]

Domicile is easier to illustrate than it is to define. The root idea underlying the concept is home, the permanent home. "By domicile we mean home, the permanent home," said Lord Cranworth,[2] "and if you do not understand your permanent home, I'm afraid that no illustration drawn from foreign writers or foreign languages will very much help you to it." However, domicile cannot be equated with home, because as we shall see a person may be domiciled in a country which is not and never has been his home; a person may have two homes, but he can only have one domicile; he may be homeless, but he must have a domicile. Indeed there is often a wide gulf between the popular conception of home and the legal concept of domicile. Domicile is "an idea of law."[3] Originally it was a good idea; but the once simple concept has been so overloaded by a multitude of cases that it has been transmuted into something further and further removed from the practical realities of life.[4]

In English law, the law of the domicile exerts a strong (but not necessarily exclusive) influence on such matters as status; capacity to marry; divorce and nullity of marriage; the mutual rights and duties of husband and wife, parent and child, and guardian and ward; legitimacy, legitimation and adoption; the effect of marriage on the proprietary rights of husband and wife; and succession to movables.

There are three kinds of domicile: domicile of origin, which is the domicile assigned by law to a child when he is born; domicile of choice, which is the domicile which any independent person can acquire for himself by a combination of residence and intention; and domicile of dependency, which means that the domicile of dependent persons (children under sixteen and mentally disordered persons) is dependent on, and usually changes with, the domicile of someone else, *e.g.* the parent of a child.

---

[1] For a country by country analysis, see Rabel, Vol. I, pp. 119–129.
[2] *Whicker* v. *Hume* (1858) 7 H.L.C. 124, 160.
[3] *Bell* v. *Kennedy* (1868) L.R. 1 Sc. & Div. 307, 320, *per* Lord Westbury.
[4] Anton, p. 181.

The object of determining a person's domicile is to connect him with some legal system for certain legal purposes. To establish this connection it is sufficient to fix his domicile in some "country" in the sense of the conflict of laws, *e.g.* England or Scotland, California or New York.[5] It is not necessary to show in what part of such a country he is domiciled[6]; but it is usually insufficient to show that he is domiciled in some composite State like the United Kingdom, the United States, Australia or Canada, each of which comprises several "countries" in the conflict of laws sense. A person who emigrates, *e.g.* to the United Kingdom with the intention of settling either in England or Scotland, or to Canada with the intention of settling either in Nova Scotia or British Columbia, does not change his domicile until he has decided in which country he intends to settle and has actually settled there.[7] As a general rule, there is no such thing as a domicile in the United Kingdom, the United States, Australia or Canada. But this rule may be modified by legislation. Thus the Australian Family Law Act 1975 provides that proceedings for divorce may be instituted by a person "domiciled in Australia"[8]; and the Canadian Divorce Act 1968 similarly provides that a petition for divorce may be presented by a person "domiciled in Canada."[9] The effect of these statutes is to create an Australian or Canadian domicile for purposes of divorce.[10] This effect would no doubt be recognised in England. Hence, if a person with an English domicile of origin emigrates to Australia or Canada, with the intention of remaining permanently, but has not yet decided whether to settle in, *e.g.* Victoria or New South Wales, or Nova Scotia or British Columbia, it would seem that he would be regarded in England as domiciled in Australia or Canada for purposes of divorce, but in England for all other purposes.

GENERAL PRINCIPLES

There are four general principles to be discussed.

(1) No person can be without a domicile.[11] This rule springs from the practical necessity of connecting every person with some system of law by which a number of his legal relationships may be regulated.

> "It is a settled principle," said Lord Westbury in a leading case,[12] "that no man shall be without a domicile, and to secure this result the law attributes to every individual as soon as he is born the domicile of his father, if the child be legitimate, and the domicile of the mother if

---

[5] See, as to the meaning of "country," *ante*, p. 4.
[6] *Re Craignish* [1892] 3 Ch. 180, 192.
[7] *Bell* v. *Kennedy* (1868) L.R. 1 Sc. & Div. 307; *Att. Gen. for Alberta* v. *Cook* [1926] A.C. 444; *Gatty* v. *Att. Gen.* [1951] P. 444.
[8] s.39(3), re-enacting Matrimonial Causes Act 1959, s.23(4).
[9] s.5(1)(*a*).
[10] *Lloyd* v. *Lloyd* [1962] V.R. 70, discussed by Cowen and Mendes da Costa (1962) 78 L.Q.R. 62.
[11] Dicey and Morris, Rule 5; *Bell* v. *Kennedy* (1868) L.R. 1 Sc. & Div. 307, 320; *Udny* v. *Udny* (1869) L.R. 1 Sc. & Div. 441, 448, 453, 457.
[12] *Udny* v. *Udny, supra*, at p. 457.

illegitimate.[13] This has been called the domicile of origin, and is involuntary."

Since the domicile of the child's father may be the father's domicile of origin which itself may be derived from the father's father, it follows that a domicile of origin may be transmitted through several generations no member of which has ever lived in the country of his domicile of origin.[14]

No person can legally be without a domicile, but he may in fact be without a home. He may for instance be a wanderer or a seaman, with no home except his cabin. To meet such situations, the law has to resort to fictions; and it draws a sharp distinction between the domicile of origin and a domicile of choice.

A domicile of origin cannot be lost by mere abandonment. It can only be lost by the acquisition of a domicile of choice. Thus in *Bell* v. *Kennedy*[15]:

> Mr. Bell was born in Jamaica of Scottish parents domiciled in Jamaica. In 1828 he married in Jamaica. In 1837, at the age of 35, he left Jamaica for good and went to Scotland, where he lived with his mother-in-law and looked around for an estate on which to settle down. He found one in 1839, and from then on was admittedly domiciled in Scotland. But until then he was undecided whether to settle in Scotland or in England or elsewhere. He was dissatisfied with Scotland, mainly due to the bad weather—so different to what he was used to in Jamaica. The question was where was he domiciled in September 1838 when his wife died? The House of Lords held that he had not lost his Jamaican domicile of origin.

On the other hand, a domicile of choice can be lost by abandonment; and if it is, and a new domicile of choice is not simultaneously acquired, the domicile of origin revives to fill the gap.[16] The reasons given for this rule are not very convincing,[17] and its artificiality has often been criticised. If, for instance, an Englishman emigrates to New York at the age of twenty-five, remains there for the next forty years and then decides to retire to California, but is killed in an air crash *en route*, it does not make much sense to say that he died domiciled in England, especially as an American court would undoubtedly hold that he died domiciled in New York. Yet the opposite American rule, that a domicile of choice continues

---

[13] There is no English authority on the domicile of origin of a posthumous child or of a foundling; but it is generally assumed that the former takes the domicile of his mother and that the latter has his domicile of origin in the country where he is found. See Dicey and Morris, Rule 9(1)(*b*) and (*c*). And see *post*, pp. 29–30.

[14] See *Peal* v. *Peal* (1930) 46 T.L.R. 645; *Grant* v. *Grant*, 1931 S.C. 238.

[15] (1868) L.R. 1 Sc. & Div. 307.

[16] *Udny* v. *Udny* (1869) L.R. 1 Sc. & Div. 441; *Harrison* v. *Harrison* [1953] 1 W.L.R. 865; *Re Flynn* (*No.* 1) [1968] 1 W.L.R. 103, 117; *Tee* v. *Tee* [1974] 1 W.L.R. 213.

[17] In *Udny* v. *Udny*, *supra*, Lord Westbury said (at p. 458): "as the domicile of origin is the creature of law, and independent of the will of the party, it would be inconsistent with the principles on which it is by law created and ascribed, to suppose that it is capable of being by the act of the party entirely obliterated and extinguished."

until a new one is acquired, sometimes produces equally bizarre results. For instance, in the leading American case[18]:

> Evan Jones was born in Wales in 1850 with an English domicile of origin. In 1883 he put a Welsh girl in the family way and she threatened him with affiliation proceedings. To escape this prospect he emigrated to the United States, where he acquired a domicile of choice in Iowa, became a naturalised American citizen, and married an American wife. He was "a coal miner, an industrious, hardworking, thrifty Welshman who accumulated a considerable amount of property." In 1915, after the death of his wife, he decided to return to Wales for good and live there with his sister. He sailed from New York on May 1 in the *Lusitania,* and was drowned when she was torpedoed by a German submarine off the south coast of Ireland. He died intestate. By English law, his brothers and sisters were entitled to his property; by the law of Iowa, it went to his illegitimate daughter, from whom he had fled over thirty years ago, and with whom he had never had anything to do. The Supreme Court of Iowa held that he died domiciled in Iowa and that the daughter was entitled.

Short of holding that he died domiciled in the *Lusitania,* and therefore (since she was registered at Southampton) in England, there would appear to be no satisfactory solution to this problem. The truth is that the American rule is as much a fiction as the English one.

(2) No person can at the same time have more than one domicile, at any rate for the same purpose.[19] This rule also springs from the necessity of connecting every person with some one legal system by which a number of his legal relationships may be regulated. These relationships are very various, and so it has been suggested that the meaning of domicile may vary in accordance with the matter in question.[20] For instance, a connection between a person and a country which may make it reasonable for its courts to exercise divorce jurisdiction over him may not be sufficient for purposes of succession to movables. There is, however, no support for this suggestion in English law. The most that can be said is that, as we have seen,[21] under the Australian Family Law Act 1975 and the Canadian Divorce Act 1968, it is possible for a person to be domiciled in Australia or in Canada for purposes of divorce and elsewhere for other purposes.

(3) An existing domicile is presumed to continue until it is proved that a new domicile has been acquired. Hence the burden of proving a change of domicile lies on those who assert it.[22] Conflicting views have been expressed as to the standard of proof required to rebut the presumption.

---

[18] *Re Jones' Estate,* 192 Iowa 78, 182 N.W. 227 (1921).

[19] Dicey and Morris, Rule 6; *Udny* v. *Udny* (1869) L.R. 1 Sc. & Div. 441, 448; *Garthwaite* v. *Garthwaite* [1964] P. 356, 378–379, 393–394.

[20] *Att. Gen.* v. *Rowe* (1862) 1 H. & C. 31, 45, *per* Bramwell B.; Cook, pp. 194–210.

[21] *Ante,* p. 15.

[22] *Bell* v. *Kennedy* (1868) L.R. 1 Sc. & Div. 307, 310, 319; *Winans* v. *Att. Gen.* [1904] A.C. 287; *Ramsay* v. *Liverpool Royal Infirmary* [1930] A.C. 588; *In the Estate of Fuld (No. 3)* [1968] P. 675, 685.

According to Scarman J., the standard is that adopted in civil proceedings, proof on a balance of probabilities, not that adopted in criminal proceedings, proof beyond reasonable doubt.[23] On the other hand, according to Sir Jocelyn Simon P., "the standard of proof goes beyond a mere balance of probabilities"[24]; and as we shall see, the burden of proving that a domicile of origin has been lost is a very heavy one. Moreover, as Scarman J. himself added,[25] "two things are clear—first, that unless the judicial conscience is satisfied by evidence of change, the domicile of origin persists; and secondly, that the acquisition of a domicile of choice is a serious matter not to be lightly inferred from slight indications or casual words." The presumption of continuance of domicile varies in strength according to the kind of domicile which is alleged to continue. It is weakest when that domicile is one of dependency[26] and strongest when the domicile is one of origin, for "its character is more enduring, its hold stronger, and less easily shaken off."[27]

There is some authority for saying that it is easier to prove a change of domicile from one country to another under the same sovereign, e.g. from England to Scotland or from New South Wales to Victoria or from Manitoba to Saskatchewan, than it is to prove a change to a politically foreign country.[28] On the other hand, the view has been abandoned that in order to acquire a domicile of choice, e.g. in France, it is necessary "exuere patriam", to become a Frenchman instead of an Englishman."[29] Conversely, a person does not necessarily acquire a domicile in a country which has granted him naturalisation.[30] "It is not the law either that a change of domicile is a condition of naturalisation, or that naturalisation involves necessarily a change of domicile."[31]

(4) For the purposes of a rule of the conflict of laws, domicile means domicile in the English sense. The question where a person is domiciled is determined solely in accordance with English law.[32] Thus, persons domiciled in England often acquired a domicile of choice in France without complying with the formalities formerly required by French law for the acquisition of a French domicile.[33] Conversely, a person domiciled e.g. in

---

[23] In the Estate of Fuld (No. 3), supra, at pp. 685–686; cf. Re Flynn (No. 1) [1968] 1 W.L.R. 103, 115; Re Edwards (1969) 113 S.J. 108; Buswell v. I.R.C. [1974] 1 W.L.R. 1631, 1637.

[24] Henderson v. Henderson [1967] P. 77, 80; Steadman v. Steadman [1976] A.C. 536, 563.

[25] In the Estate of Fuld (No. 3), supra, at p. 686.

[26] Harrison v. Harrison [1953] 1 W.L.R. 865; Re Scullard [1957] Ch. 107; Henderson v. Henderson, supra, at pp. 82–83. See post, pp. 30–31.

[27] Winans v. Att. Gen. [1904] A.C. 287, 290, per Lord Macnaghten; cf. Henderson v. Henderson [1967] P. 77, 80, per Simon P.

[28] Whicker v. Hume (1858) 7 H.L.C. 124, 159; Moorhouse v. Lord (1863) 10 H.L.C. 272, 287; Winans v. Att. Gen. [1904] A.C. 287, 291; Walton v. Walton [1948] V.L.R. 487; Gunn v. Gunn (1956) 2 D.L.R. (2d) 351.

[29] Udny v. Udny (1869) L.R. 1 Sc. & Div. 441, 452, 459–460.

[30] Wahl v. Att. Gen. (1932) 147 L.T. 382 (H.L.); In the Estate of Fuld (No. 3) [1968] P. 675.

[31] Wahl v. Att. Gen., supra, per Lord Atkin at p. 385.

[32] Dicey and Morris, Rule 8.

[33] Collier v. Rivaz (1841) 2 Curt, 855; Bremer v. Freeman (1857) 10 Moo.P.C. 306; Hamilton v. Dallas (1875) 1 Ch.D. 257; Re Annesley [1926] Ch. 692. Article 13 of the Code Napoléon, which required a foreigner to obtain the authorisation of the French Government before he could establish a domicile in France, was repealed in 1927.

France may acquire an English domicile of choice regardless of whether French law would regard him as domiciled in England.[34] There is one statutory exception to this rule. Section 3(2) of the Recognition of Divorces and Legal Separations Act 1971 refers to domicile in a country in the sense of that country's law.

It is too wide a formulation to say that in an English court, domicile means domicile in the English sense. Under the renvoi doctrine,[35] English courts sometimes refer to the whole law of a foreign country, including its rules of the conflict of laws, and accept a reference back to English law either because the foreign conflict rule refers to the law of the nationality, and the *propositus* is a British citizen; or because the foreign conflict rule refers to the law of the domicile, and the foreign court regards the *propositus* as domiciled in England. In the latter case, it is not true that domicile in an English court always means domicile in the English sense; but it is still true that it means domicile in the English sense for the purpose of an English rule of the conflict of laws.

It has been suggested that the capacity of a dependent person to acquire a domicile is governed, not by English law, but by the law of his previous domicile or of his alleged new domicile.[36] But there is no sufficient English authority for this proposition, and some authority against it.[37]

ACQUISITION AND LOSS OF DOMICILE OF CHOICE

Every independent person (*i.e.* one who is not a child under sixteen or a mentally disordered person) can acquire a domicile of choice by the combination of residence and the intention of permanent or indefinite residence, but not otherwise.[38] These two factors must coincide before the law will recognise a change of domicile. Residence however long in a country will not result in the acquisition of a domicile of choice there if the necessary intention is lacking.[39] Conversely, intention however strong to change a domicile will not have that result if the necessary residence in the new country is lacking.[40] "A new domicile is not acquired until there is not only a fixed intention of establishing a permanent residence in some other country, but until also this intention has been carried out by actual residence there."[41] Hence a domicile cannot be acquired *in itinere*[42]: it is necessary not only to travel, but to arrive.

It is very difficult to keep the two requirements of residence and inten-

---

[34] *Re Martin* [1900] P. 211.
[35] *Post*, Chap. 30.
[36] Graveson (1950) 3 Int.L.Q. 149.
[37] See Dicey and Morris, p. 131; Cheshire and North, p. 182; *Re Beaumont* [1893] 3 Ch. 490 (where the child was not a dependent person by the law of her Scottish domicile); *Robinson-Scott* v. *Robinson-Scott* [1958] P. 71; *Garthwaite* v. *Garthwaite* [1964] P. 356.
[38] Dicey and Morris, Rule 10.
[39] *Jopp* v. *Wood* (1865) 4 D.J. & S. 616; *Winans* v. *Att. Gen.* [1904] A.C. 287; *Ramsay* v. *Liverpool Royal Infirmary* [1930] A.C. 588; *I.R.C.* v. *Bullock* [1976] 1 W.L.R. 1178.
[40] *In the Goods of Raffenel* (1863) 3 Sw. & Tr. 49; *Harrison* v. *Harrison* [1953] 1 W.L.R. 865; *Willar* v. *Willar*, 1954 S.C. 144, 147 ("one cannot acquire a domicile of choice by wishful thinking").
[41] *Bell* v. *Kennedy* (1868) L.R. 1 Sc. & Div. 307, 319, *per* Lord Chelmsford.
[42] *Udny* v. *Udny* (1869) L.R. 1 Sc. & Div. 441, 449–450, 453–454.

tion in watertight compartments, but in the interest of clarity of exposition they must be considered separately.

Residence

Residence is basically a question of fact; for present purposes it means very little more than physical presence. But it does mean something more, for a person passing through a country as a traveller is clearly not resident there. A person's state of mind may be relevant to the question whether he is present in a country as a traveller or as an inhabitant, but, subject to this point, residence may be established without a mental element: there is no requirement of *animus residendi*. The length of the residence is not important in itself; it is only important as evidence of intention. A person can acquire a domicile in a country, if he has the necessary intention, after residence for even part of a day.[43] Thus an immigrant can acquire a domicile in a country immediately after his arrival there. "It may be conceded that if the intention of permanently residing in a place exists, residence in pursuance of that intention, however short, will establish a domicile."[44] A domicile of choice cannot be acquired by illegal residence.[45]

In order to be resident in a country a person need not own or rent a house there. It is sufficient if he lives in an hotel[46] or in the house of a friend[47] or even in a military camp.[48]

Intention

The intention which is required for the acquisition of a domicile of choice is the intention to reside permanently or for an unlimited time in a particular country. "It must be a residence fixed not for a limited period or particular purpose, but general and indefinite in its future contemplation."[49] If a person intends to reside in a country for a fixed period, he lacks the intention necessary to acquire a domicile there, however long that period may be.[50] The same is true where a person intends to reside in a country for an indefinite time (*e.g.* until he passes an examination) but clearly intends to leave the country at some time.[51] The result of these principles is that the burden of proving a change of domicile is a very heavy one. Indeed, if we confine our attention to cases decided by the House of Lords, there appears to be an almost irrebuttable presumption against a change, because in the twelve disputed cases of domicile that have reached the House since 1860, there is only one in which it was held that a domicile

---

[43] For striking illustrations, see *White* v. *Tennant*, 31 W.Va. 790, 8 S.E. 596 (1888); *Miller* v. *Teale* (1954) 92 C.L.R. 406.
[44] *Bell* v. *Kennedy* (1868) L.R. 1 Sc. & Div. 307, 319, *per* Lord Chelmsford.
[45] *Puttick* v. *Att. Gen.* [1980] Fam. 1.
[46] *Levene* v. *I.R.C.* [1928] A.C. 217; *I.R.C.* v. *Lysaght* [1928] A.C. 234; *Matalon* v. *Matalon* [1952] P. 233.
[47] *Stone* v. *Stone* [1958] 1 W.L.R. 1287.
[48] *Willar* v. *Willar*, 1954 S.C. 144.
[49] *Udny* v. *Udny* (1869) L.R. 1 Sc. & Div. 441, 458, *per* Lord Westbury.
[50] *Att. Gen.* v. *Rowe* (1862) 1 H. & C. 31.
[51] *Jopp* v. *Wood* (1865) 4 D.J. & S. 616; *Qureshi* v. *Qureshi* [1972] Fam. 173.

of origin had been lost.[52] Two leading decisions of the House of Lords in particular have attracted much criticism. These are *Winans* v. *Att. Gen.*[53] and *Ramsay* v. *Liverpool Royal Infirmary.*[54]

In *Winans* v. *Att. Gen.*:

> Mr. Winans was a man of eccentric ideas, self-centred and strangely uncommunicative. He was born in the United States in 1823 with a domicile of origin in Maryland or New Jersey. The two ruling passions of his life were hatred of England and the care of his health. "He nursed and tended it" (*i.e.* his health, not England) "with wonderful devotion. He took his temperature several times a day. He had regular times for taking his temperature, and regular times for taking his various waters and medicines" (Lord Macnaghten).
>
> His opportunity for gratifying his hatred of England came in 1850, when he went to Russia and was employed by the Government in equipping railways and in the construction of gunboats to be used against England in the Crimean War. But nemesis overtook him in 1859, when his health broke down. He was advised by his doctors that another winter in Russia would be fatal, and that he must spend the winter in Brighton. Very reluctantly he accepted this advice, spent the winter in a Brighton hotel, and in 1860 took a lease of a house there. However, he held aloof from English people, whom he continued cordially to dislike. From then on until his death in 1897 he spent more and more time in England, living in furnished houses and hotels, and less and less time elsewhere. From 1893 until 1897 he lived entirely in England.
>
> He entertained a grandiose dream of constructing in Baltimore, Maryland, a large fleet of cigar-shaped vessels which, being proof against pitching and rolling (or so he thought), would gain for the United States the carrying trade of the world and give her naval superiority over Great Britain. He also dreamed of acquiring control of 200 acres of wharves and docks in Maryland to accommodate the cigar-shaped vessels, and a large house in which he would live and superintend the whole scheme. He was working night and day on the scheme when he died, a millionaire several times over.
>
> Mr. Winans had thus lived mainly in England for the last thirty-seven years of his life, and never revisited the United States after his departure in 1850.

On these facts, six judges held that he died domiciled in England; but a

---

[52] *Casdagli* v. *Casdagli* [1919] A.C. 145. The other cases are: *Aikman* v. *Aikman* (1861) 3 Macq. 854; *Moorhouse* v. *Lord* (1863) 10 H.L.C. 272; *Pitt* v. *Pitt* (1864) 4 Macq. 627; *Bell* v. *Kennedy* (1868) L.R. 1 Sc. & Div. 307; *Udny* v. *Udny* (1869) L.R. 1 Sc. & Div. 441; *Winans* v. *Att. Gen.* [1904] A.C. 287; *Huntly* v. *Gaskell* [1906] A.C. 56; *Lord Advocate* v. *Jaffrey* [1921] 1 A.C. 146 (where it was conceded that the husband had lost his domicile of origin, and the dispute was as to the domicile of dependency of the wife); *Ross* v. *Ross* [1930] A.C. 1; *Ramsay* v. *Liverpool Royal Infirmary* [1930] A.C. 588; *Wahl* v. *Att. Gen.* (1932) 147 L.T. 382.

[53] [1904] A.C. 287: the case of the anglophobe American millionaire.

[54] [1930] A.C. 588: the case of the human jellyfish (or sponge).

bare majority of two to one in the House of Lords held that he never lost his domicile of origin. "When he came to this country," said Lord Macnaghten,[55] he was a sojourner and a stranger, and he was I think a sojourner and a stranger in it when he died." Lord Lindley, equally robust, said[56]: "He had one and only one home, and that was in this country; and long before he died I am satisfied that he had given up all serious idea of returning to his native country." Lord Halsbury was unable to make up his mind, and fell back on the presumption of continuance.

In *Ramsay* v. *Liverpool Royal Infirmary*[57]:

> George Bowie was born in Glasgow in 1845 with a Scottish domicile of origin. In 1882, at the age of thirty-seven, he gave up his employment as a commercial traveller and did no work for the remaining forty-five years of his life. At first he lived with his mother and sisters in Glasgow. In 1892 he moved to Liverpool and sponged on his brother and another sister. He died unmarried in 1927. Thus he lived in England for the last thirty-six years of his life. During all that time he left England only twice, once on a short visit to the United States, and once on a short holiday in the Isle of Man. Though he often said he was proud to be a Glasgow man, he resolutely refused to return to Scotland, even to attend his mother's funeral. On the contrary, he expressed his determination never to set foot in Glasgow again, and arranged to be buried in Liverpool. His will, which gave the residue equally between three Glasgow charities and one Liverpool one, was formally valid if he died domiciled in Scotland, but formally invalid if he died domiciled in England.

On these facts the House of Lords, affirming both the Scottish courts below, unanimously reached the astonishing conclusion that he died domiciled in Scotland. The *ratio decidendi* evidently was that he was such a low form of life as to be incapable of forming the necessary intent to change his domicile. "The long residence of George Bowie," said Lord Thankerton,[58] "is remarkably colourless, and suggests little more than inanition."

Unfortunately, we can no longer dismiss these two cases as mere aberrations of the House of Lords, because in 1976 the Court of Appeal reached a similar decision. In *I.R.C.* v. *Bullock*[59] it was held that a Canadian with a domicile of origin in Nova Scotia who had lived mainly in England for more than forty years had not acquired an English domicile of choice, because he intended to return to Canada after the death of his English wife. Ironically, this decision meant that (as the law then stood) the wife also was domiciled in Nova Scotia at the time in question (1971–1973), although she disliked the place. On the other hand in *Re Furse*[60] the home

---

[55] At p. 298.
[56] At p. 300.
[57] [1930] A.C. 588.
[58] At p. 595.
[59] [1976] 1 W.L.R. 1178; criticised by Carter (1976–77) 48 B.Y.I.L. 362.
[60] [1980] 3 All E.R. 838.

of an American for the last thirty-nine years of his life was on a farm in England. He declared an intention to return to the United States if he became unable to lead an active physical life on the farm, where he remained until his death aged eighty. The contingency was held to be so vague and indefinite that it did not prevent the acquisition of an English domicile of choice.

Evidence of intention. Most disputes as to domicile turn on the question whether the necessary intention accompanied the residence; and this question often involves very complex and intricate issues of fact. This is because "there is no act, no circumstance in a man's life, however trivial it may be in itself, which ought to be left out of consideration in trying the question whether there was an intention to change the domicile. A trivial act might possibly be of more weight with regard to determining this question than an act which was of more importance to a man in his lifetime."[61] There is, furthermore, no circumstance or group of circumstances which furnishes any definite criterion of the existence of the intention. A circumstance which is treated as decisive in one case may be disregarded in another, or even relied upon to support a different conclusion.[62]

The questions which the court has considered include the following: where did he live and for how long? was it in a fixed place or several different places? did he build or buy a house, or live in furnished lodgings or hotels? was he accompanied by his wife and children? did he vote in elections there? was he naturalised there? did he arrange to be buried there? what churches did he attend? what clubs did he belong to? Of course this list is far from being exhaustive: a person's "tastes, habits, conduct, actions, ambitions, health, hopes and projects" are all regarded as "keys to his intention."[63] Thus the law, instead of allowing long-continued residence to speak for itself, insists on proof of a man's intention, that most elusive of all factors. The resulting uncertainty has given rise to much criticism and to proposals for reform of the law.[64]

Declarations of intention. The person whose domicile is in question may himself give evidence of his intention, but the court will view the evidence of an interested party with suspicion[65]: though in one case[66] such evidence was decisive. Declarations of intention made out of court are admissible in evidence by way of exception to the hearsay rule,[67] but they are not entitled to much weight unless supported by conduct consistent with the declaration.

---

[61] *Drevon* v. *Drevon* (1864) 34 L.J.Ch. 129, 133, *per* Kindersley V.-C.

[62] See Dicey and Morris, pp. 116–118, and cases there cited.

[63] *Casdagli* v. *Casdagli* [1919] A.C. 145, 178, *per* Lord Atkinson, commenting on *Winans* v. *Att. Gen.* [1904] A.C. 287.

[64] *Post*, p. 32.

[65] *Bell* v. *Kennedy* (1868) L.R. 1 Sc. & Div. 307, 313, 322–323; *Re Craignish* [1892] 3 Ch. 180, 190; *Qureshi* v. *Qureshi* [1972] Fam. 173, 192.

[66] *Wilson* v. *Wilson* (1872) L.R. 2 P. & M. 435. The Scottish court arrived at an opposite conclusion on the same facts: *Wilson* v. *Wilson* (1872) 10 M. 573; but the husband's evidence was not then admissible in Scotland.

[67] *Bryce* v. *Bryce* [1933] P. 83; *Scappaticci* v. *Att. Gen.* [1955] P. 47; see now Civil Evidence Act 1968, s.2(1).

"Declarations as to intention," said Lord Buckmaster,[68] "are rightly regarded in determining the question of a change of domicile, but they must be examined by considering the persons to whom, the purposes for which, and the circumstances in which they are made, and they must further be fortified and carried into effect by conduct and action consistent with the declared expression."

The courts are particularly reluctant to give effect to declarations as to domicile made by testators in their wills, since the testator himself is unlikely to understand the meaning of the word, while to allow his solicitor to determine his domicile would be to oust the jurisdiction of the court.[69]

Motive and intention. It is important to distinguish between motive and intention. As a general rule it does not matter whether a man's motive in leaving one country and living in another is good or bad: the question is, has he the requisite intention for a change of domicile? His motive may be, for instance, to enjoy the benefit of a lower rate of taxation,[70] or of a better climate, either for himself or for his troupe of performing chimpanzees,[71] to evade the rule against accumulations,[72] to get a divorce,[73] to prevent his wife from getting maintenance[74]: in none of these cases has the particular motive prevented the acquisition of a new domicile. But if the motive is suspect, the court may be reluctant to concede a change of domicile. It may conclude that there really was no change at all, but merely the appearance of a change made to secure some personal advantage.[75]

Loss of a domicile of choice

A person abandons a domicile of choice in a country by ceasing to reside there and by ceasing to intend to reside there permanently or indefinitely, and not otherwise.[76] It is not necessary to prove a positive intention not to return: it is sufficient to prove merely the absence of an intention to continue to reside.[77] A domicile of choice is lost when both the residence and the intention necessary for its acquisition are given up. It is not lost merely by giving up the residence[78] nor merely by giving up the intention.[79]

Special cases

In order that a person may acquire a domicile of choice, it has been said

---

[68] *Ross* v. *Ross* [1930] A.C. 1, 6–7. "Expression," the last word in the quotation, seems to be a misprint for "intention."

[69] *Re Steer* (1858) 3 H. & N. 594; *Re Annesley* [1926] Ch. 692; *Att. Gen.* v. *Yule* (1931) 145 L.T. 9; *Re Liddell-Grainger* (1936) 53 T.L.R. 12.

[70] *Wood* v. *Wood* [1957] P. 254.

[71] *Ibid.*

[72] *Haldane* v. *Eckford* (1869) L.R. 8 Eq. 631.

[73] *Drexel* v. *Drexel* [1916] 1 Ch. 251; *Wood* v. *Wood, supra.*

[74] *Ibid.*

[75] See *White* v. *White* [1950] 4 D.L.R. 474, affirmed [1952] 1 D.L.R. 133.

[76] Dicey and Morris, Rule 13(1); *Udny* v. *Udny* (1869) L.R. 1 Sc. & Div. 441, 450; *I.R.C.* v. *Duchess of Portland* [1982] Ch. 314.

[77] *Re Flynn (No. 1)* [1968] 1 W.L.R. 103, 113–115, criticised by Cheshire and North, p. 176; *Qureshi* v. *Qureshi* [1972] Fam. 173, 191.

[78] *Bradford* v. *Young* (1885) 29 Ch.D. 617; *Re Lloyd Evans* [1947] Ch. 695.

[79] *In the Goods of Raffenel* (1863) 3 Sw. & Tr. 49; *Zanelli* v. *Zanelli* (1948) 64 T.L.R. 556.

that "there must be a residence freely chosen, and not prescribed or dictated by any external necessity, such as the duties of office, the demands of creditors, or the relief from illness."[80] This is a somewhat misleading statement. It certainly does not mean that only a person able to exercise the most perfect freedom of choice can acquire a domicile of choice; for if it did, the acquisition of a domicile of choice would be a rare event. What it does mean can only be elucidated by examining a number of special cases. These are: persons liable to deportation; fugitives from justice; refugees; invalids; members of the armed forces; employees; and diplomats.

Persons liable to deportation. A person who resides in a country from which he is liable to be deported may lack the necessary intention because his residence is precarious. But if in fact he forms the necessary intention, he acquires a domicile of choice.[81] Once such a person has acquired a domicile of choice he does not lose it merely because a deportation order has been made against him.[82] He only loses it when he is actually deported.

Fugitives from justice. A person who leaves a country as a fugitive from criminal justice, or in order to evade his creditors, has a special motive for leaving it, but no special motive for living in any other country. In the case of a fugitive from justice, the intention to abandon his previous domicile will readily be inferred, unless perhaps the punishment which he seeks to avoid is trivial, or by the law of that country a relatively short period of prescription bars liability to punishment. In *Re Martin,*[83] a French professor committed a crime in France in connection with his professorship and fled to England, where he remained for the next twenty years. Two years after the French period of prescription had expired he returned to France. The Court of Appeal by a majority held that he had acquired an English domicile six years after his arrival in England.

Similarly, a person who leaves a country in order to evade his creditors may lose a domicile there[84]; but if he plans to return as soon as he has paid or otherwise got rid of his debts, there is no change of domicile.[85]

Refugees. If a political refugee intends to return to the country from which he has fled as soon as the political situation changes, he retains his domicile there; but if his intention is not to return to that country even when the political situation has changed, he can acquire a domicile of choice in the country to which he has fled. Thus in *Re Lloyd Evans*[86] an Englishman with a Belgian domicile of choice returned to England very reluctantly in June 1940 because of the German invasion, and lived in furnished flats in England until he died in 1944. He always intended to return to Belgium after the war. It was held that he retained his Belgian domicile.

[80] *Udny* v. *Udny* (1869) L.R. 1 Sc. & Div. 441, 458, *per* Lord Westbury.
[81] *Boldrini* v. *Boldrini* [1932] P. 9; *Zanelli* v. *Zanelli, supra*; *Szechter* v. *Szechter* [1971] P. 286, 294 G.
[82] *Cruh* v. *Cruh* [1945] 2 All E.R. 545.
[83] [1900] P. 211.
[84] *Udny* v. *Udny* (1869) L.R. 1 Sc. & Div. 441.
[85] *Re Wright's Trusts* (1856) 2 K. & J. 595; *Pitt* v. *Pitt* (1864) 4 Macq. 627.
[86] [1947] Ch. 695.

On the other hand, in *May* v. *May*[87] a Jew fled from Germany to England in 1938 to escape persecution by the Nazis. He originally intended to emigrate to the United States, but his hope of doing so was frustrated by the outbreak of war in 1939. In 1941 the idea of going to the United States gradually faded from his mind. He declared that he would never return to Germany even if the Nazis were overthrown. It was held that he had acquired an English domicile of choice by the beginning of 1942.

Invalids. If a person changes his residence for the sake of his health, does he change his domicile? Different judges have given different answers to this question. Since illnesses vary greatly in intensity, no general rule can be laid down. Each case turns on its own facts. A person who goes to a country for the temporary purpose of undergoing medical treatment there clearly lacks the necessary intention for a change of domicile. So does a person who is mortally ill and decides to move to a country to alleviate his last sufferings. On the other hand, a person who moves to a new country because he believes that he will enjoy better health there may well intend to live there permanently or indefinitely, but of course he does not necessarily have this intention.

In *Hoskins* v. *Matthews*,[88] a man whose domicile of origin was English went to Florence at the age of sixty, and lived there except for three or four months in each year in a villa that he had bought until he died twelve years later. He was suffering from an injury to the spine and left England solely because he thought that the warmer climate of Italy would benefit his health. His housekeeper deposed that he would have returned to England if he had been restored to health. Nevertheless it was held that he had acquired a domicile in Tuscany (as it then was), because he was "exercising a preference and not acting upon a necessity." On the other hand, in *Re James*[89] a man with an English domicile of origin went to South Africa in 1891 when he was thirty-eight, obtained employment there, and lived there in apartments until he died in 1905. He went to South Africa because his doctor advised him that he was not likely to live very long if he remained in Wales. Just before he left Wales he said he would never return except for a short time. He did return for six weeks in 1902, but on leaving again he said he would never return as the climate did not suit him, and that he enjoyed better health in South Africa than he ever had in Wales. On the other hand he continued to own a small farm in Wales until his death. It was held that he died domiciled in England.

Members of the armed forces. It was at one time supposed that a member of the armed forces, whether British or foreign, could not as a matter of law acquire a domicile of choice during his service, because he was bound to obey orders and go where he was sent by his superiors. But now it is clear that a member of the armed forces can, during service, acquire a

[87] [1943] 2 All E.R. 146.
[88] (1855) 8 D.M. & G. 13.
[89] (1908) 98 L.T. 438.

domicile of choice in the country in which he is stationed[90] or elsewhere,[91] provided he has established the necessary residence and formed the necessary intention. But in the great majority of cases he does not intend to make his permanent home where he is stationed, and retains the domicile which he had on entering service.[92]

Employees. A person who goes to a country in pursuance of a contract of service is in a position similar to that of a member of the armed forces in that his residence is in a sense enforced and may be precarious or for a limited time. On the other hand an employee can more easily give up his employment than a member of the armed forces can. The question whether an employee who is sent to a country intends to reside there permanently or indefinitely remains in the last resort a question of fact. There is, for this purpose, no distinction between public servants and other employees. If such persons go to a country for the temporary purpose of performing the duties of their office or employment, they do not acquire a domicile of choice there; but if they go not merely to work but also to settle, they do acquire a domicile of choice. Thus in *Att. Gen* v. *Rowe*[93] an English barrister was appointed Chief Justice of Ceylon. His intention was to hold this office until he had earned his pension and then return to England. It was held that he retained his English domicile. On the other hand, in *Gunn* v. *Gunn*[94] a man with a domicile of origin in Manitoba was employed by a corporation owning a chain of cinemas in Canada. By way of promotion he was offered, and accepted, the office of manager of a cinema in Saskatchewan. He moved to Saskatchewan with the intention of residing there for an indefinite period. It was held that he acquired a domicile of choice in Saskatchewan.

Diplomats. Diplomats are simply a special category of public servants and the same principles apply to them. It is a question of fact whether they intend to reside permanently or indefinitely in the country to which they are accredited. Generally, of course, they form no such intention[95]; but occasionally they may do so and thus acquire a domicile of choice there.[96] If a person has acquired a domicile of choice in a country, he does not lose it merely by reason of being appointed to a diplomatic post in that country.[97]

DOMICILE OF DEPENDENCY

Introduction

No dependent person can acquire a domicile of choice by his own act. As a general rule, the domicile of such persons is the same as, and changes

---

[90] *Donaldson* v. *Donaldson* [1949] P. 363; *Willar* v. *Willar*, 1954 S.C. 144.
[91] *Stone* v. *Stone* [1958] 1 W.L.R. 1287.
[92] *Cruickshanks* v. *Cruickshanks* [1957] 1 W.L.R. 564; *Sellars* v. *Sellars*, 1942 S.C. 206.
[93] (1862) 1 H. & C. 31.
[94] (1956) 2 D.L.R. (2d) 351.
[95] *Udny* v. *Udny* (1869) L.R. 1 Sc. & Div. 441; *Niboyet* v. *Niboyet* (1878) 4 P.D. 1.
[96] An instance is afforded by *Naville* v. *Naville*, 1957 (1) S.A. 280.
[97] *Att. Gen.* v. *Kent* (1862) 1 H. & C. 12; *Sharpe* v. *Crispin* (1869) L.R. 1 P. & M. 611.

with, the domicile of the person (if any) on whom he is legally dependent. The class of dependent persons was greatly reduced in size by sections 1(1) and 3(1) of the Domicile and Matrimonial Proceedings Act 1973, which came into force on January 1, 1974.[98] Section 1(1) provides that the domicile of a married woman shall, instead of being the same as her husband's by virtue only of marriage, be ascertained by reference to the same factors as in the case of any other individual capable of having an independent domicile. Section 3(1) provides that the time at which a person first becomes capable of having an independent domicile shall be when he attains the age of sixteen or marries under that age. We proceed to consider each of these enactments in turn.

Married women. Before 1974 there was an absolute rule, to which there were no exceptions, that the domicile of a married woman was the same as, and changed with, the domicile of her husband.[99] This rule reflected social conditions and attitudes of a past age; it led to serious injustice to wives especially in the matter of divorce jurisdiction[1]; it was severely criticised by almost every writer who commented on it; it was judicially described as "the last barbarous relic of a wife's servitude"[2] and as a "now completely outmoded legal concept."[3] Its abolition in 1974 was long overdue.

Section 1(1) of the Act is retrospective in the sense that it applies to women married before as well as after January 1, 1974. Hence, a transitional provision was needed. Section 1(2) provides that where immediately before that date a woman was married and then had her husband's domicile by dependence, she is to be treated as retaining that domicile (as a domicile of choice, if it is not also her domicile of origin) unless and until it is changed by acquisition of another domicile either on or after that date. In *I.R.C.* v. *Duchess of Portland,*[4] a woman with a domicile of origin in Quebec married a domiciled Englishman in 1948. She lived with her husband in England but retained links with Quebec, visiting it for ten to twelve weeks every summer, keeping a house which she owned there ready for immediate occupation and retaining Canadian citizenship. She intended to return permanently to Quebec with her husband when he retired from business, but continued to live in England. It was held that the effect of section 1(2) was that she retained her English domicile of dependency as a domicile of choice.

Section 1(1) is not retrospective in any other sense. Hence, in considering the domicile of a married woman as at any time before January 1, 1974, the old law will still apply.

Minors. Before 1974 the domicile of a minor (that is, a person under the age of eighteen) was the same as, and changed with, the domicile of the

---

[98] For a commentary on the Act, see Hartley and Karsten (1974) 37 M.L.R. 179.
[99] *Lord Advocate* v. *Jaffrey* [1921] 1 A.C. 146; *Att. Gen. for Alberta* v. *Cook* [1926] A.C. 444.
[1] See *post*, p. 189.
[2] *Gray* v. *Formosa* [1963] P. 259, 267, *per* Lord Denning M.R.
[3] *Adams* v. *Adams* [1971] P. 188, 216, *per* Simon P.
[4] [1982] Ch. 314; criticised by J. A. Wade (1983) 32 I.C.L.Q. 1 and by M.P. Thompson *ibid.* 237.

appropriate parent, that is, the father in the case of a legitimate child, and the mother in the case of an illegitimate child or a legitimate child whose father was dead.[5] The rule was not quite so strict in the case of an illegitimate or fatherless child as it was in the case of a legitimate child whose father was alive. Thus where a widow, domiciled in Scotland with her minor children, remarried and went to live with her second husband in England, taking all but one of the children with her, but leaving one behind in Scotland in the care of an aunt, it was held that the domicile of this child continued to be Scottish.[6] Although there is no authority on the point, it seems likely that the domicile of a legitimated child would be dependent on that of his father, at any rate if the legitimation was effected by the subsequent marriage of the parents.[7]

There was only one exception to the rule that the domicile of a minor was dependent on that of the appropriate parent: a female minor who married took her husband's domicile in place of her father's or mother's.

Section 3(1) of the Domicile and Matrimonial Proceedings Act 1973 provides that a child becomes capable of having an independent domicile when he attains the age of sixteen or marries under that age. In English domestic law, a marriage between persons either of whom is under sixteen is void[8]; but a child may be regarded as validly married under foreign law even if he has not attained that age.[9]

Dependent children

The rules stated above as to the domicile of minors before 1974 will continue to apply after 1973 to the domicile of dependent children (that is, children under sixteen who have not been married), but with important statutory modifications.

Section 4(1) and (2) of the Domicile and Matrimonial Proceedings Act 1973 provide that the domicile of a dependent child whose parents are alive but living apart shall be that of his mother if (a) he has his home with her and no home with his father, or (b) he has at any time had her domicile by virtue of (a) above and has not since had a home with his father. Section 4(3) provides that the domicile of a dependent child whose mother is dead shall be that which she last had before she died if at her death he had her domicile by virtue of section 4(2) above and he has not since had a home with his father. The main object of this enactment is to increase the number of cases in which the domicile of dependency of a child will be that of his mother; previously existing rules of law to that effect (*e.g.* those relating to illegitimate children and legitimate children whose fathers are dead) are expressly preserved by section 4(4).

An adopted child is now treated in law as if he had been born to the adopter or adopters in wedlock.[10] Accordingly the domicile of an adopted

---

[5] Dicey and Morris, Rule 15(1) and (3).
[6] *Re Beaumont* [1893] 3 Ch. 490.
[7] Dicey and Morris, Rule 15(2).
[8] Marriage Act 1949, s.2.
[9] *Post*, p. 165.
[10] Children Act 1975, Sched. 1, para. 3(1). Sched. 4, Part I, repeals that part of s.4(5) of the Domicile and Matrimonial Proceedings Act 1973 which deals with adopted children.

child under sixteen will be determined as if he were the legitimate child of his adopted parent or parents.

The domicile of a legitimate child whose parents are both dead, or of an illegitimate child whose mother is dead, probably cannot be changed at all.[11]

When the domicile of a dependent child is changed as a result of a change in his parents' domicile or as a result of his legitimation, the new domicile which the child gets in this way is a domicile of dependency and not a domicile of origin.[12] Hence, it is not this domicile but the one he acquired at birth which will revive if in later life he abandons one domicile of choice without at the same time acquiring another.[13] On the other hand, it would seem to follow from what has been said above about adopted children that the domicile of origin of an adopted child is deemed to be the domicile of his adoptive parent or parents at the time of his adoption. If this is correct, it is the only example in English law in which a domicile of origin can be changed.

A nice question could arise as to the domicile of origin of a legitimate child born to separated parents with different domiciles. Suppose, for example, that a husband and wife are domiciled in Scotland; they separate, and the wife comes to live in England, intending to remain permanently. Six months later, she gives birth to a child, whose father is the husband. Is the child's domicile of origin Scottish or English? Section 4 of the Domicile and Matrimonial Proceedings Act 1973 does not purport to alter the common law rule that a legitimate child takes his domicile of origin from his father. On the other hand, the domicile of the child will undoubtedly be English under section 4(1) and (2), because he has his home with his mother and no home with his father. Surely it would be artificial to hold that he took his domicile of origin from his father and then immediately changed it to his mother's domicile.

When a dependent child attains the age of sixteen he will usually retain the domicile of the appropriate parent as a domicile of choice.[14] But he now has capacity to change his domicile; and such a change may result from acts done during dependency. A nice problem arose under the old law (when minority ended at twenty-one) in *Harrison* v. *Harrison*[15]:

> Mr. Harrison was born in England in 1930 with an English domicile of origin. In 1948 his parents emigrated to South Australia, leaving him in England. In 1950 he himself emigrated to New Zealand, married a New Zealand wife, and decided to live there permanently. But three months before he attained his majority he and his wife came to England for a temporary purpose, *i.e.* the husband's business training. Two years later, the wife petitioned the English court for divorce, and the question was, where was he domiciled? It was held that he was domiciled in South Australia until he attained his majority, although

---

[11] Dicey and Morris, Rule 15(4).
[12] *Henderson* v. *Henderson* [1967] P. 77.
[13] *Ante*, p. 16.
[14] *Re Macreight* (1885) 30 Ch.D. 165.
[15] [1953] 1 W.L.R. 865. The judgment is only 11 words long.

he had never been there; that he then abandoned his South Australian domicile by intending to reside permanently in New Zealand; that he did not acquire a New Zealand domicile of choice because at no time after he attained his majority did he reside there; and that therefore his English domicile of origin revived.

Mentally disordered persons

A mentally disordered person cannot acquire a domicile of choice and, as a general rule, retains the domicile which he had when he became insane.[16] Since he cannot exercise any will, he can neither acquire nor lose a domicile. Nor can his domicile be changed by the person in charge of him.

Most of the cases which support these statements concerned persons who were "lunatics so found" by inquisition. This procedure, and the term "lunatic," are obsolete in English domestic law, which now makes provision for many kinds and degrees of mental disorder.[17] It seems unlikely that all persons who suffer from any form of mental disorder for which provision is made by English domestic law would be regarded as dependent persons for the purposes of the law of domicile. Whether or not they could form the necessary intention to acquire or lose a domicile is likely to be treated as a question of fact in each case.

There is one exception to the rule stated above that a mentally disordered person retains the domicile he had when he became insane. If a dependent child becomes insane and remains so after attaining the age of sixteen, the appropriate parent has power to change his domicile even after he attains that age. Whether the power is exercised or not is a question of fact in each case.[18]

DOMICILE OF CORPORATIONS

The English law of domicile was evolved almost entirely with individuals in mind. It can only be applied to corporations with a certain sense of strain. A corporation is not born (though it is incorporated); it cannot marry (though it can be amalgamated with or taken over by another corporation); it cannot have children (though it can have subsidiaries); it does not die (though it can be dissolved or wound up). Hence most of the occasions for determining the domicile of an individual do not arise in the case of corporations. But it may be important to know whether a so-called corporation possesses corporate personality, whether it has been amalgamated with another corporation, or whether it has been dissolved.[19] These questions are determined by the law of its domicile. A corporation is domiciled in its place of incorporation. Unlike an individual, it cannot change that domicile, not even if it carries on business elsewhere.[20]

---

[16] Dicey and Morris, Rule 16; *Bempde* v. *Johnstone* (1796) 3 Ves.198; *Urquhart* v. *Butterfield* (1887) 37 Ch.D. 357; *Crumpton's Judicial Factor* v. *Fitch-Noyes*, 1918 S.C. 378.
[17] Mental Health Act 1983.
[18] *Sharpe* v. *Crispin* (1869) L.R. 1 P. & M. 611; *Re G.* [1966] N.Z.L.R. 1028.
[19] See *post*, pp. 443–445.
[20] *Gasque* v. *I.R.C.* [1940] 2 K.B. 80.

It may be asked, if questions concerning the existence, amalgamation, or dissolution of a corporation are governed by the law of its place of incorporation, why not say so and dispense altogether with the fiction that it has a domicile? The question is unanswerable; but the difficulty is that taxing statutes sometimes refer to "a person" domiciled inside or outside the United Kingdom, and courts have held that "a person" includes a corporation,[21] thus making it necessary to decide where a corporation is domiciled for the purposes of these statutes.

The residence of a corporation is chiefly important for purposes of taxation and therefore does not require detailed discussion in a book on the conflict of laws. Briefly, it may be said that a corporation is resident in the country where its central management and control is exercised, and not necessarily in the country of its incorporation nor in the country in which its central management and control ought to be exercised. If the exercise of central management and control is divided between two or more countries, then the corporation is resident in each of those countries.[22]

PROPOSALS FOR REFORM

The English law of domicile has attracted widespread criticism. Apart from the former domicile of dependency of married women, the principal targets of this criticism are (a) the excessive importance accorded to the domicile of origin, in particular the rule that it revives to fill the gap between the abandonment of one domicile of choice and the acquisition of another,[23] and the heavy burden of proof resting on those who assert that it has been changed[24]; and (b) the excessive concentration on the element of intention as a factor in the acquisition of a domicile of choice.[25] More generally, the objections to domicile are that it is often difficult to ascertain, and that it frequently departs from the ordinary man's conception of home.

In 1954 the Private International Law Committee in their First Report[26] made various proposals for reform, which did not include the abolition of the wife's domicile of dependency. But after two abortive Bills[27] and a further examination of certain aspects of the matter by the Committee,[28] they were not proceeded with. As we have seen, important reforms concerning the domicile of married women and of dependent children were effected by the Domicile and Matrimonial Proceedings Act 1973; but the other much-criticised aspects of the law of domicile remain unreformed.

---

[21] *Gasque* v. *I.R.C., supra.*

[22] Dicey and Morris, Rule 138; *Cesena Sulphur Co. Ltd.* v. *Nicholson* (1876) 1 Ex.D. 428; *De Beers Consolidated Mines Ltd.* v. *Howe* [1906] A.C. 455; *Swedish Central Ry.* v. *Thompson* [1925] A.C. 495; *Egyptian Delta Land and Investment Co. Ltd.* v. *Todd* [1929] A.C. 1; *Unit Construction Co. Ltd.* v. *Bullock* [1960] A.C. 351.

[23] *Ante,* p. 16.

[24] *Ante,* pp. 20–22.

[25] *Ante,* pp. 23–24.

[26] Cmnd. 9068. For comments on the Report, see Graveson (1954) 70 L.Q.R. 492; Stone (1954) 17 M.L.R. 244; Cohn (1955) 71 L.Q.R. 562.

[27] For an entertaining account of the progress of these Bills through the House of Lords, see M. Mann (1969) 8 I.C.L.Q. 457.

[28] Seventh Report, Cmnd. 1955 (1963). For a critical comment on the Report, see M. Mann (1963) 12 I.C.L.Q. 1326.

In the Antipodes they have been more energetic. A uniform Domicile Act is in force in all the Australian states and territories. A similar Act is in force in New Zealand. These Acts make similar (but not identical) provision as the Domicile and Matrimonial Proceedings Act 1973 for the domicile of married women[29] and children under 18.[30] They also abolish the rule in *Udny* v. *Udny* as to the revival of the domicile of origin[31] and the rule in *Winans* v. *Att. Gen.* that stronger evidence is required to displace a domicile of origin than a domicile of choice.[32] They also define the intention required for the acquisition of a domicile of choice in a country as "the intention to make his home indefinitely in that country"[33] and provide for the domicile of persons domiciled in a "union" (*e.g.* the United Kingdom, United States, Australia and Canada) who are not domiciled in any of the countries that form the union.[34]

DOMICILE AND NATIONALITY[35]

Until the beginning of the nineteenth century domicile was universally regarded as the personal law for purposes of the conflict of laws. The change from domicile to nationality on the continent of Europe started in France with the promulgation of the Code Napoléon in 1804. One of the principal objects of the codifiers was to substitute a uniform law throughout the whole of France for the different *coutumes* of the French provinces. In matters of personal status these *coutumes* applied to persons domiciled within the province, wherever they happened to be. It was natural that the new uniform law should apply to Frenchmen everywhere, and article 3(1) of the Civil Code provided that "the laws governing the status and capacity of persons govern Frenchmen even though they are residing in foreign countries." No provision was expressly made for the converse case of foreigners residing in France, but the French courts held that in matters of status and capacity they too were governed by their national law. The provisions of the French code were adopted in Belgium and Luxembourg, and similar provisions were contained in the Austrian code of 1811 and the Dutch code of 1829.

The change from domicile to nationality on the continent of Europe was accelerated by Mancini's famous lecture delivered at the University of Turin in 1851. In his lecture he advocated the principle of nationality on the ground that laws are made more for an ascertained people than for an ascertained territory. A sovereign (he said) in framing laws for his people should consider their habits and temperament, their physical and moral qualities, and even the climate, temperature and fertility of the soil. This

---

[29] s.5 of the uniform Australian Act.
[30] ss.7 and 8.
[31] s.6.
[32] s.11.
[33] s.9.
[34] s.10.
[35] On this topic, see Cheshire and North, pp. 183–186; Anton, pp. 156–161; Nadelmann (1969) 17 Am.Jo.Comp. Law 418.

was heady wine for a people preparing to throw off a foreign yoke and unify all the small states of Italy into a new nation. Under Mancini's influence, article 6 of the Italian Civil Code (1865) provided that "the status and capacity of persons and family relations are governed by the laws of the nation to which they belong." Mancini's ideas proved extremely influential outside Italy too, and in the second half of the nineteenth century the principle of nationality replaced that of domicile in code after code in continental Europe, until today only Norway and Denmark retain the principle of domicile. The result is that the nations of the world have become divided in their definition of the personal law; and it is this fact more than any other which impedes international agreement on uniform rules of the conflict of laws. What then are the arguments in favour of nationality and domicile as the personal law?

The advocates of nationality claim that it is more stable than domicile because nationality cannot be changed without the formal consent of the State of new nationality. This is true, though it may be pointed out that the English conception of domicile of origin is in one respect more stable even than nationality, because unlike nationality it can never be destroyed: it always remains in abeyance, waiting to be revived.[36] However, as has been well said,[37] "the principle of nationality achieves stability, but by the sacrifice of a man's personal freedom to adopt the legal system of his own choice. The fundamental objection to the concept of nationality is that it may require the application to a man, against his own wishes and desires, of the laws of a country to escape from which he has perhaps risked his life."

It is also claimed that nationality is easier to ascertain than domicile because it involves a formal act of naturalisation and does not depend on the subjective intentions of the *propositus*. This is undoubtedly true, though there may be difficult cases of double nationality or of statelessness.[38] But it does not follow that the most easily ascertained law is the most appropriate law. Many immigrants who have no intention of returning to their country of origin do not trouble to apply for naturalisation. It would have been ludicrous to say that only the English courts, and not the courts of California, had jurisdiction to grant a divorce to the film actor Charlie Chaplin—or, for that matter, that only the American courts had jurisdiction to grant a divorce to Mr. Winans.

The decisive consideration for countries like the United Kingdom, the United States, Australia and Canada is that, save in a very few respects, there is no such thing as United Kingdom, American, Australian, or Canadian law. Since the object of referring matters of status and capacity to the personal law is to connect a man with some one legal system for many legal purposes, nationality breaks down altogether if the State contains more

---

[36] Cheshire and North, p. 178.
[37] Anton, p. 160.
[38] Writing in 1939, Beckett (then Second Legal Adviser to the Foreign Office) said that he had to consider three to four cases a day of disputed nationality and domicile, and that he was in doubt in about one case in twenty of nationality and in one case in four of domicile: (1939) 55 L.Q.R. 270.

than one country in the sense of the conflict of laws.[39] This is something which continental lawyers seem unable to comprehend. They sometimes speak as though the United Kingdom and the United States are as legally backward today as France was before 1804 or Italy before 1865, simply because there is a diversity of legal systems throughout the State.

DOMICILE AND RESIDENCE

Habitual residence and ordinary residence, as well as residence *simpliciter*, are sometimes used, both by Parliament[40] and by the courts,[41] as connecting or jurisdictional factors. What do these expressions mean?

Habitual residence. Habitual residence has long been a favourite expression of the Hague Conferences on Private International Law and appears in many Hague Conventions and therefore in English statutes giving effect to them; but it is increasingly used in other statutes as well. One may hazard the guess that it will be held to mean much the same thing as domicile, minus the artificial elements in that concept (*e.g.* the revival of the domicile of origin) and minus the stress now placed on the element of intention in domicile. Of course, these are very large deductions. It is greatly to be hoped that English courts will resist the temptation to define habitual residence, so that the concept may be kept free of rigid technical rules and regarded purely as a question of fact. Unfortunately the temptation was not resisted in *Cruse* v. *Chittum*,[42] where habitual residence was defined as a regular physical presence, enduring for some time.

Ordinary residence. It is not entirely clear whether ordinary residence[43] means something different from residence *simpliciter*.[44] Ordinary residence "connotes residence in a place with some degree of continuity and apart from accidental or temporary absences."[45] "If it has any definite meaning I should say it means according to the way in which a man's life is usually ordered."[46] Ordinary residence (like domicile) can be changed in a day.[47] But unlike domicile, there is nothing exclusive about residence or ordinary residence: a man can be resident and ordinarily resident in more

---

[39] See *Re O'Keefe* [1940] Ch. 124, and *post*, pp. 478–480.
[40] See, *e.g.* Wills Act 1963, s.1; Adoption Act 1968, s.11; Recognition of Divorces and Legal Separations Act 1971, s.3(1)(*a*); Domicile and Matrimonial Proceedings Act 1973, s.5(2)(3) and (4); Children Act 1975, s.24(2)(3) and (5); Unfair Contract Terms Act 1977, s.27(2)(*b*); State Immunity Act 1978, s.4(2)(*b*) and (3) (habitual residence); Bankruptcy Act 1914, s.4(1)(*d*); Carriage by Air Act 1961, Sched. 1, art. 28(1); Carriage of Goods by Road Act 1965, Sched., art. 31(1)(*a*) (ordinary residence).
[41] *Re P.* (*G.E.*) (*An Infant*) [1965] Ch. 568 (ordinary residence).
[42] [1974] 2 All E.R. 940; see Hall (1975) 24 I.C.L.Q. 1.
[43] The leading authorities on the meaning of "ordinary residence" in the Income Tax Acts are *Levene* v. *I.R.C.* [1928] A.C. 217, and *I.R.C.* v. *Lysaght* [1928] A.C. 234. These cases were followed in *R.* v. *Barnet London Borough Council, ex p. Nilish Shah* [1983] 2 A.C. 309 (entitlement to education awards).
[44] See *Levene* v. *I.R.C., supra*, at pp. 225, 232; *I.R.C.* v. *Lysaght, supra*, at pp. 243, 248; *Hopkins* v. *Hopkins* [1951] P. 116, 121–122; *Stransky* v. *Stransky* [1954] P. 428, 437.
[45] *Levene* v. *I.R.C., supra*, at p. 225, *per* Lord Cave.
[46] *Ibid.* at p. 232, *per* Lord Warrington of Clyffe.
[47] *Macrae* v. *Macrae* [1949] P. 397, 403, *per* Somervell L.J.

than one country at the same time. Thus in *I.R.C.* v. *Lysaght*,[48] a man
whose home was in the Republic of Ireland, and who came to England for
one week in every month for business reasons, during which time he stayed
in an hotel, was held to be resident and ordinarily resident in England for
income tax purposes. But clearly he was also resident and ordinarily resident in the Republic.

It has been said that a child of tender years "who cannot decide for himself where to live" is ordinarily resident in his parents' matrimonial home,
and that this ordinary residence cannot be changed by one parent without
the consent of the other. If the parents are living apart and the child is, by
agreement between them, living with one of them, he is resident in the
home of that one and his ordinary residence is not changed merely because
the other parent takes the child away from that home.[49]

It may well be that, if domicile cannot be further reformed, habitual residence as a connecting and jurisdictional factor will eventually replace it.
But this process will inevitably be a gradual one.

---

[48] [1928] A.C. 234. It would be unfair to blame the House of Lords for this extraordinary
   decision, for they felt constrained to hold that a finding by the Special Commissioners was
   one of fact and so could not be disturbed on appeal.
[49] *Re P.* (*G.E.*) (*An Infant*) [1965] Ch. 568, 585–586.

CHAPTER 3

PROOF OF FOREIGN LAW

Foreign law as fact

Paradoxical as it may sound, it has long been well established that foreign law in English courts is a matter of fact[1] which has to be pleaded and proved to the satisfaction of the judge.

The general rule is that if a party wishes to rely on a foreign law he must plead it just like any other fact on which he relies.[2] If he does not do so the court will decide a case containing foreign elements as though it were a purely English domestic case. There is one not very important exception to this principle. If a case is governed by the law of some "British territory," the court has power under the British Law Ascertainment Act 1859 to order that law to be ascertained in the manner prescribed in the Act,[3] and has sometimes exercised this power on its own motion although the foreign law was not pleaded.[4]

English courts take judicial notice of the law of England and of notorious facts, but not of foreign law.[5] Consequently, foreign law must be proved in each case (unless of course it is admitted). It cannot be deduced from previous English decisions in which the same rule of foreign law has been before the court.[6] Indeed there are cases in which different conclusions have been reached in different cases on different evidence of the same rule of foreign law.[7]

However, an appellate court which has jurisdiction to determine appeals from the courts of several countries takes judicial notice of the laws of any of those countries when it hears an appeal from a court in one of them. Thus the House of Lords, when hearing an English appeal, takes judicial notice of Scots law,[8] and when hearing a Scottish appeal, takes judicial notice of Northern Irish[9] or English law. In such cases, the foreign law,

---

[1] *Fremoult* v. *Dedire* (1718) 1 P.Wms. 429; *Mostyn* v. *Fabrigas* (1774) 1 Cowp. 161, 174; *Nelson* v. *Bridport* (1845) 8 Beav. 527.

[2] *Ascherberg* v. *Casa Musicale Sonzogno* [1971] 1 W.L.R. 173, 1128.

[3] See *post*, p. 41.

[4] *Topham* v. *Duke of Portland* (1863) 1 D.J. & S. 517.

[5] See note 1 above. In *Saxby* v. *Fulton* [1909] 2 K.B. 208, 211, Bray J. took judicial notice of the "notorious" fact that roulette is lawful in Monte Carlo. The decision has been followed in Canada: *Harold Meyers Travel Service Ltd.* v. *Magid* (1975) 60 D.L.R. (3d) 42, 44.

[6] *Lazard Brothers* v. *Midland Bank* [1933] A.C. 289. This principle was lost sight of in *Simons* v. *Simons* [1939] 1 K.B. 490, 495, and in *Re Sebba* [1959] Ch. 166.

[7] See, *e.g. Lazard Brothers* v. *Midland Bank, supra*; *Ottoman Bank* v. *Chakarian* (*No. 2*) [1938] A.C. 260.

[8] *Elliot* v. *Joicey* [1935] A.C. 209, 236; *MacShannon* v. *Rockware Glass Ltd.* [1978] A.C. 795, 815 E.

[9] *Cooper* v. *Cooper* (1888) 13 App.Cas. 88.

which was a matter of fact in the court below, becomes a matter of law on appeal.

Formerly, questions of foreign law were decided by the jury; but now by section 69(5) of the Supreme Court Act 1981[10] they are decided by the judge alone.

Although, as we have seen, foreign law is a question of fact, it is "a question of fact of a peculiar kind." Thus in *Parkasho* v. *Singh*[11] a Divisional Court reversed a manifestly erroneous decision by magistrates on a point of foreign law, while recognising that appellate courts are slow to interfere with trial courts on questions of fact.

Mode of proof

It is now well settled that foreign law must as a general rule be proved by expert evidence.[12] Foreign law cannot be proved merely by putting the text of the foreign law before the court, nor merely by citing foreign decisions or books of authority.[13] Such materials can only be brought before the court as part of the evidence of an expert witness, since without his assistance the court cannot evaluate or interpret them.

No precise or comprehensive answer can be given to the question who, for this purpose, is a competent expert. A foreign judge or legal practitioner is of course always competent. But in civil proceedings there is no longer any rule of law (if indeed there ever was) that the expert witness must have practised, or at least be entitled to practise, in the foreign country. For section 4(1) of the Civil Evidence Act 1972 provides that "it is hereby declared that in civil proceedings a person who is suitably qualified to do so on account of his knowledge or experience is competent to give expert evidence as to [foreign law], irrespective of whether he has acted or is entitled to act as a legal practitioner [in the foreign country]." This enactment renders obsolete the old case of *Bristow* v. *Sequeville*,[14] where it was held that a man who had studied law at the University of Leipzig was incompetent to prove the law of Cologne. But this ruling has been relaxed in more recent cases and section 4(1) is probably only declaratory of the law. Thus a former practitioner has been held competent.[15] So Tsar-

---

[10] Replacing earlier legislation going back to 1920. For county courts, see County Courts Act 1959, s.97. The rule applies to criminal trials: *R.* v. *Hammer* [1923] 2 K.B. 786.

[11] [1968] P. 233; approved in *Dalmia Dairy Industries Ltd.* v. *National Bank of Pakistan* [1978] 2 Lloyd's Rep. 223, 286.

[12] *Sussex Peerage Case* (1844) 11 Cl. & F. 85, 115; *Baron de Bode's Case* (1845) 8 Q.B. 208, 246–267; *Nelson* v. *Bridport* (1845) 8 Beav. 527, 536; *Castrique* v. *Imrie* (1870) L.R. 4 H.L. 414, 430.

[13] *Nelson* v. *Bridport, supra,* at p. 542; *Buerger* v. *New York Life Assurance Co.* (1926) 96 L.J.K.B. 930, 940; *cf. Callwood* v. *Callwood* [1960] A.C. 659, which contains some interesting observations on how not to prove foreign law. The principle was departed from in *Beatty* v. *Beatty* [1924] 1 K.B. 807, with unfortunate results: see *Simons* v. *Simons* [1939] 1 K.B. 490, 495, where Goddard L.J. precariously assumed that a Massachusetts maintenance order made in 1924 was final and conclusive because a New York maintenance order made in 1899 had been held to be final and conclusive in 1910.

[14] (1850) 5 Exch. 275, 277.

[15] *Re Duke of Wellington* [1947] Ch. 506, 514–515; *Re Banque des Marchands de Moscou* [1958] Ch. 182; *Rossano* v. *Manufacturers Life Insurance Co.* [1963] 2 Q.B. 352, 373.

ist lawyers who practised law in Russia before the Bolshevik revolution, but who had no practical experience of Soviet law, have often been allowed to give evidence about it.[16] A person who is entitled to practise in the foreign country, but has not yet done so, has been held competent.[17] A witness may be competent though he is not a practising lawyer at all. Any person who, by virtue of his profession or calling, has acquired a practical knowledge of foreign law may be a competent witness. Thus, the Governor of a colony,[18] an ambassador,[19] an embassy official,[20] a vice-consul,[21] a notary public,[22] the Reader in Roman-Dutch Law to the Council of Legal Education,[23] a bishop,[24] a merchant,[25] and a bank manager,[26] have all been held competent. Witnesses such as bishops, merchants and bank managers will, of course, only be regarded as experts in that part of the foreign law with which they are bound, by virtue of their profession or calling, to be familiar.

An English court will not conduct its own researches into foreign law.[27] But if an expert witness refers to foreign statutes, decisions or books, the court is entitled to look at them as part of his evidence.[28] But the court is not entitled to go beyond this: thus if a witness cites a passage from a foreign law book he does not put the whole book in evidence since he does not necessarily regard the whole book as accurate.[29] Similarly, if the witness cites a section from a foreign code or a passage from a foreign decision the court will not look at other sections of the code or at other parts of the decision without the aid of the witness, since they may have been abrogated by subsequent legislation.

If the evidence of the expert witness is uncontradicted, the court is in general bound to accept it,[30] unless the result is "extravagant"[31] or unless

---

[16] See, e.g. Russian Commercial and Industrial Bank v. Comptoire d'Escompte de Mulhouse [1925] A.C. 112; Employers Liability Co. v. Sedgwick, Collins & Co. [1927] A.C. 95; Buerger v. New York Life Assurance Co. (1926) 96 L.J.K.B. 930. But the evidence of Soviet lawyers is preferred if available: Lazard Brothers v. Midland Bank [1933] A.C. 289, 299.

[17] Barford v. Barford [1918] P. 140; Perlack Petroleum Maatschappij v. Deen [1924] 1 K.B. 111, 112; Etler v. Kertesz (1960) 26 D.L.R. (2d) 209, 212–213.

[18] Cooper-King v. Cooper-King [1900] P. 65.

[19] In the Goods of Oldenburg (1884) 9 P.D. 234.

[20] In the Goods of Dost Aly Khan (1880) 6 P.D. 6.

[21] Lacon v. Higgins (1822) Dow. & Ry.N.P. 38.

[22] In the Goods of Whitelegg [1899] P. 267.

[23] Brailey v. Rhodesia Consolidated Ltd. [1910] 2 Ch. 95.

[24] Sussex Peerage Case (1844) 11 Cl. & F. 85.

[25] Vander Donkt v. Thellusson (1849) 8 C.B. 812. But the court may refuse to admit the evidence of such a witness where that of a qualified lawyer is readily available: Direct Winters Transport Ltd. v. Duplate Canada Ltd. (1962) 32 D.L.R. (2d) 278.

[26] De Béeche v. South American Stores Ltd. [1935] A.C. 148.

[27] Di Sora v. Phillips (1863) 10 H.L.C. 624, 640.

[28] Nelson v. Bridport (1845) 8 Beav. 527, 541; Concha v. Murietta (1889) 40 Ch.D. 543; Lazard Brothers v. Midland Bank [1933] A.C. 289, 298.

[29] Nelson v. Bridport, supra, at p. 542.

[30] Buerger v. New York Life Assurance Co. (1926) 96 L.J.K.B. 930, 941; Koechlin et Cie v. Kestenbaum [1927] 1 K.B. 616, 622; Re Banque des Marchands de Moscou [1958] Ch. 182; Sharif v. Azad [1967] 1 Q.B. 605, 616.

[31] Buerger v. New York Life Assurance Co., supra.

"he says something patently absurd, or something inconsistent with the rest of his evidence."[32]

If the evidence of several expert witnesses conflicts as to the effect of foreign sources of law, the court is entitled, and indeed bound, to look at those sources in order itself to decide between the conflicting testimony.[33]

English courts give considerable weight to the decisions of foreign courts as evidence of foreign law.[34] But the court is not bound to apply a foreign decision if it is satisfied, as a result of all the evidence, that the decision does not accurately represent the foreign law.[35] Where foreign decisions conflict, the court may be asked to decide between them, even although in the foreign country the question still remains to be authoritatively settled.[36]

There are three statutes under which proof of foreign law may sometimes be dispensed with.

By the Civil Evidence Act 1972, section 4(2)–(5), where any question of foreign law has been determined in civil or criminal proceedings at first instance in the High Court, the Crown Court, certain other English courts now abolished, or in any appeal therefrom, or in the Privy Council on appeal from any court outside the United Kingdom, then any finding made or decision given on that question is admissible in evidence in any civil proceedings, and the foreign law shall be taken to be in accordance with that finding or decision unless the contrary is proved. The finding or decision as to foreign law must be reported or recorded in citable form, which means that it must be reported or recorded in writing in a report, transcript or other document which could be cited as an authority in legal proceedings in England if the question had been one of English law. The section does not apply if the subsequent proceedings are before a court which can take judicial notice of the foreign law. Thus a determination on a point of Scots law by the High Court or the Court of Appeal is not even prima facie evidence of that point in subsequent proceedings before the House of Lords. Nor is the determination prima facie binding if there are conflicting findings or decisions on the same question.

By the Evidence (Colonial Statutes) Act 1907, copies of laws made by the legislature of any "British possession,"[37] if purporting to be printed by

---

[32] *Tallina Laevauhisus A/S* v. *Estonian State SS. Line* (1947) 80 Ll.L.Rep. 99, 108; *cf. Re Valentine's Settlement* [1965] Ch. 831, 855.

[33] *Dalrymple* v. *Dalrymple* (1811) 2 Hagg.Cons. 54; *Trimbey* v. *Vignier* (1834) 1 Bing.N.C. 151; *Nelson* v. *Bridport* (1845) 8 Beav. 527, 537; *Bremer* v. *Freeman* (1857) 10 Moo.P.C. 306; *Concha* v. *Murietta* (1889) 40 Ch.D. 543; *Guaranty Trust Corporation of New York* v. *Hannay* [1918] 2 K.B. 623; *Russian Commercial and Industrial Bank* v. *Comptoire d'Escompte de Mulhouse* [1923] 2 K.B. 630, reversed [1925] A.C. 112 on the ground that the Court of Appeal had misinterpreted the foreign law; *Princess Paley Olga* v. *Weisz* [1929] 1 K.B. 718; *Re Duke of Wellington* [1947] Ch. 506; *In the Estate of Fuld (No. 3)* [1968] P. 675, 700–703.

[34] See, *e.g. Beatty* v. *Beatty* [1924] 1 K.B. 807; *Re Annesley* [1926] Ch. 692; *Bankers and Shippers Insurance Co. of New York* v. *Liverpool Marine and General Insurance Co. Ltd.* (1926) 24 Ll.L.Rep. 85 (H.L.); *In the Estate of Fuld (No. 3)* [1968] P. 675, 701–702.

[35] *Guaranty Trust Corporation of New York* v. *Hannay* [1918] 2 K.B. 623; *Callwood* v. *Callwood* [1960] A.C. 659.

[36] *Re Duke of Wellington* [1947] Ch. 506; *Breen* v. *Breen* [1964] P. 144.

[37] *i.e.* "any part of Her Majesty's dominions exclusive of the United Kingdom": s.1(3).

the government printer of the "British possession," can be received in evidence in the United Kingdom without proof that the copies were so printed. Under this Act, the text of such laws can be proved without expert witnesses[38]; but the court may require expert evidence to show that the alleged law is still in force.[39] The Act continues to apply to many Commonwealth countries which are no longer part of Her Majesty's dominions, e.g. because they have become republics.[40]

By the British Law Ascertainment Act 1859, a court in any part of Her Majesty's dominions may, if it thinks it necessary or expedient for the proper disposal of an action, state a case for the opinion of a court in any other part of Her Majesty's dominions in order to ascertain the view of that court as to the law applicable to the facts of the case stated. The Act continues to apply to many Commonwealth countries which are no longer part of Her Majesty's dominions.[41] The court has a complete discretion whether or not to state a case.[42] There are very few reported cases in which it has done so, because the procedure is expensive and involves delay. The opinion of the foreign court is not binding on the House of Lords or the Privy Council if it was given by a court over which the House of Lords or the Privy Council, as the case may be, exercises appellate jurisdiction. But subject to this the opinion of the foreign court is binding on the English court.

Burden of proof

The burden of proving foreign law lies on the party who bases his claim or defence on it.[43] If that party adduces no evidence, or insufficient evidence, of the foreign law, the court applies English law.[44] This principle is sometimes expressed in the form that foreign law is presumed to be the same as English law until the contrary is proved.[45] But this reasoning is so artificial that it seems better to abandon the terminology of presumption, and simply to say that where foreign law is not proved, the court applies English law.

---

[38] *Taylor* v. *Taylor* [1923] W.N. 65; *Waterfield* v. *Waterfield* (1929) 73 S.J. 300; *Papadopoulos* v. *Papadopoulos* [1930] P. 55.

[39] *Brown* v. *Brown* (1917) 116 L.T. 702; *R.* v. *Governor of Brixton Prison, ex p. Shuter* [1960] 2 Q.B. 89, 95–96; *Jasiewicz* v. *Jasiewicz* [1962] 1 W.L.R. 1426.

[40] Because it is commonly provided that the existing law of the United Kingdom shall continue to apply in relation to them as if they had not become republics. See, *e.g.* India (Consequential Provisions) Act 1949, s.1.

[41] For the reason given in the preceding note.

[42] *Lord* v. *Colvin* (1860) 1 Dr. & Sm. 24; *MacDougall* v. *Chitnavis,* 1937 S.C. 390, 407–408.

[43] *Dynamit A/G* v. *Rio Tinto Co.* [1918] A.C. 260, 295; *Guaranty Trust Corporation of New York* v. *Hannay* [1918] 2 K.B. 623, 655.

[44] *Lloyd* v. *Guibert* (1865) L.R. 1 Q.B. 115, 129; *Hartman* v. *Konig* (1933) 50 T.L.R. 114, 117 (H.L.).

[45] *e.g. Dynamit A/G* v. *Rio Tinto Co., supra*; *The Parchim* [1918] A.C. 157, 161; *The Colorado* [1923] P. 102, 111; *Casey* v. *Casey* [1949] P. 420, 430.

CHAPTER 4

THE EXCLUSION OF FOREIGN LAW

IN any system of the conflict of laws, and the English system is no exception, the courts retain an overriding power to refuse to enforce, and sometimes even to refuse to recognise, rights acquired under foreign law on grounds of public policy. In the English conflict of laws we need to consider first the general doctrine of public policy, which is necessarily somewhat vague; and secondly, some more specific applications of it.

PUBLIC POLICY

Introduction

The English courts will not enforce or recognise any right arising under foreign law if its enforcement or recognition would be inconsistent with the fundamental policy of English law.[1] "An English court will refuse to apply a law which outrages its sense of justice or decency. But before it exercises such power it must consider the relevant foreign law as a whole."[2]

In English domestic law it is now well settled that the doctrine of public policy "should only be invoked in clear cases in which the harm to the public is substantially incontestable, and does not depend upon the idiosyncratic inferences of a few judicial minds."[3] In the conflict of laws it is even more necessary that the doctrine should be kept within proper limits, otherwise the whole basis of the system is liable to be frustrated. As a distinguished American judge once said,[4] "the courts are not free to refuse to enforce a foreign right at the pleasure of the judges, to suit the individual notion of expediency or fairness. They do not close their doors unless help would violate some fundamental principle of justice, some prevalent conception of good morals, some deep-rooted tradition of the common weal." The doctrine of public policy has assumed far less prominence in the English conflict of laws than have corresponding doctrines in the laws of some continental European countries. One reason for this may be that English courts invariably apply English domestic law in proceedings for divorce[5] and separation,[6] for the guardianship, custody[7] and adoption[8] of minors,

---

[1] See Cheshire and North, pp. 145–155; Lloyd, *Public Policy,* Chap. 5; Kahn-Freund, *Selected Writings,* Chap. 9; Holder (1968) 17 I.C.L.Q. 926.
[2] *In the Estate of Fuld (No.* 3) [1968] P. 675, 698, *per* Scarman J.
[3] *Fender* v. *St. John Mildmay* [1938] A.C. 1, 12, *per* Lord Atkin.
[4] *Loucks* v. *Standard Oil Co.* (1918) 224 N.Y. 99, 111; 120 N.E. 198, 202, *per* Cardozo J.
[5] *Post,* pp. 191–192.
[6] *Post,* pp. 206–207.
[7] *Post,* Chap. 13.
[8] *Post,* pp. 255–256.

and for the maintenance of wives and children.[9] Thus, foreign law is inapplicable in many important departments of family law in which, in continental European countries, it is frequently excluded on grounds of public policy. Moreover, there is no room for the doctrine of public policy in actions based on foreign torts, because no such action will lie in England unless the wrong would have been actionable if committed in England.[10]

It is only on the rarest occasions that a foreign law itself can be regarded as contrary to English public policy.[11] What is usually in question is not the foreign law in the abstract, but the results of its enforcement or recognition in England in the concrete case. Thus, English courts may well regard a foreign law which permits polygamy, or the marriage of step-father and step-daughter, as unwise or even immoral. But if such a polygamous or incestuous marriage has taken place under a foreign law according to which it is valid, and especially if children have been born, it may be better to recognise it than to disturb settled family relationships by holding the marriage invalid and the children illegitimate on grounds of public policy. Everything turns on the nature of the question which arises. Thus, until 1972 no polygamously married spouse could obtain a divorce from the English courts[12]; but the spouses will be treated as married persons and thus incapable of contracting a valid marriage in England[13]; the children will be treated as legitimate[14]; and the wife will be entitled to assert rights of succession and other rights on the footing that she is a wife.[15] Again, to take an improbable but striking example, if a foreign law allowed a bachelor aged fifty to adopt a spinster aged seventeen, an English court might hesitate to give the custody of the girl to her adoptive father; but that is no reason for not allowing her to succeed to his property as his "child" on his death intestate.[16] In other words, public policy is not absolute but relative; the recognition of a foreign status is one thing, and the recognition of all its incidents another.

The doctrine of public policy may not only lead a court to refuse to enforce or recognise, *e.g.* a contract or a marriage when it would be valid under the appropriate foreign law. It may also produce the opposite effect and lead to the enforcement or recognition of, *e.g.* a contract or a marriage which under the applicable foreign law would be invalid. Thus, a foreign law which invalidates a contract or a marriage will be disregarded if it is penal, *i.e.* discriminatory.[17] On the other hand, the effect of the doctrine of public policy is always to exclude the application of foreign law which

---

[9] *Post,* pp. 220–223.

[10] *Post,* pp. 314–315. Before 1918 American courts frequently invoked the doctrine of public policy in order to deny recovery in tort for wrongful death inflicted abroad.

[11] A foreign law licensing prostitution or slavery might be an example: see *Robinson* v. *Bland* (1760) 2 Burr. 1077, 1084; *Regazzoni* v. *K.C. Sethia Ltd.* [1956] 2 Q.B. 490, 524. See, however, *Santos* v. *Illidge* (1860) 8 C.B.(N.S.) 861.

[12] *Hyde* v. *Hyde* (1866) L.R. 1 P. & D. 130; *post,* pp. 187–188.

[13] *Baindail* v. *Baindail* [1946] P. 122; *post,* pp. 181–182.

[14] *Bamgbose* v. *Daniel* [1955] A.C. 107; *post,* pp. 182–183.

[15] *Coleman* v. *Shang* [1961] A.C. 481; *Shahnaz* v. *Rizwan* [1965] 1 Q.B. 390; *Chaudhry* v. *Chaudhry* [1976] Fam. 148; *Re Sehota* [1978] 1 W.L.R. 1506; *post,* pp. 183–185.

[16] See *post,* pp. 259–260.

[17] *Post,* pp. 169–170.

would otherwise be applicable. In one case,[18] the doctrine was anomalously applied so as to invoke the application of a foreign law which would otherwise have been inapplicable; but this case has been convincingly criticised and has not been followed.[19]

The reservation of public policy in conflict of laws cases is a necessary one, but "no attempt to define the limits of that reservation has ever succeeded."[20] All that can be done, therefore, is to enumerate the cases in which the recognition or enforcement of rights arising under foreign laws has been refused on this ground. It will be found that the doctrine has been usually invoked in two classes of case, namely those involving foreign contracts; and those involving a foreign status.

Contracts

English courts have refused to enforce champertous contracts,[21] contracts in restraint of trade,[22] contracts entered into under duress or coercion,[23] or contracts involving collusive and corrupt arrangements for a divorce,[24] or trading with the enemy,[25] or breaking the laws of a friendly country.[26] On the other hand, they have enforced contracts for the loan of money to be spent on gambling abroad,[27] and for foreign loans which contravened the English Moneylenders Acts.[28] In general, it is certainly untrue that contracts governed by a foreign law will not be enforced in England if they are contrary to some imperative rule of English domestic law which the parties to an English contract cannot disregard. Thus, a foreign contract made without consideration will be enforced in England.[29]

Status

English courts will not give effect to the results of any status existing under a foreign law which is penal, *i.e.* discriminatory. Examples are the

---

[18] *Lorentzen* v. *Lydden & Co. Ltd.* [1942] 2 K.B. 202.

[19] *Bank voor Handel en Scheepvart N.V.* v. *Slatford* [1953] 1 Q.B. 248, 263–264; *post,* pp. 378–379.

[20] Westlake, p. 51.

[21] *Grell* v. *Levy* (1864) 10 C.B. (N.S.) 73, where the litigation was to take place in England. The principle would not apply to a champertous contract relating to litigation in France or the United States, where champerty is lawful: *Re Trepca Mines Ltd. (No.* 2) [1963] Ch. 199, 218. *Cf. National Surety Co.* v. *Larsen* [1929] 4 D.L.R. 918.

[22] *Rousillon* v. *Rousillon* (1880) 14 Ch.D. 351. Would the principle apply to a foreign contract in restraint of *foreign* trade?

[23] *Kaufman* v. *Gerson* [1904] 1 K.B. 591; a much-criticised decision. See Dicey and Morris, p. 807; Cheshire and North, p. 148.

[24] *Hope* v. *Hope* (1857) 8 D.M. & G. 731. Would the principle apply to a contract to procure a foreign divorce? See *Addison* v. *Brown* [1954] 1 W.L.R. 779, where it was held not to be contrary to public policy to oust the jurisdiction of a foreign court.

[25] *Dynamit A/G* v. *Rio Tinto Co.* [1918] A.C. 260.

[26] *De Wütz* v. *Hendricks* (1824) 2 Bing. 314; *Foster* v. *Driscoll* [1929] 1 K.B. 470; *Regazzoni* v. *K.C. Sethia Ltd.* [1958] A.C. 301. However, in these cases the contract was governed by English law.

[27] *Saxby* v. *Fulton* [1909] 2 K.B. 208.

[28] *Shrichand* v. *Lacon* (1906) 22 T.L.R. 245.

[29] *Re Bonacina* [1912] 2 Ch. 394. The general proposition stated in the text is now subject to an exception contained in s.27(2) of the Unfair Contract Terms Act 1977; see *post,* p. 280.

status of slavery or civil death,[30] and the disabilities or incapacities which may be imposed on priests, nuns, Protestants, Jews, persons of alien nationality,[31] coloured persons,[32] divorced persons and prodigals. Some of the disabilities referred to above are obviously imposed as a punishment, *e.g.* the inability under some systems of law of persons divorced for adultery to remarry while the innocent spouse remains single,[33] or the disabilities imposed on Jews by the Nazi régime in Germany.[34] Others equally obviously are not, *e.g.* the inability under the laws of some Catholic countries of priests and nuns to marry at all.[35] The real reason why none of these disabilities is recognised in England is that recognition would be contrary to English public policy.

There are two cases on the status of prodigals, and one on the status of "incompetents," that have been much criticised.

In *Worms* v. *De Valdor*[36]:

> A Frenchman domiciled in France sued for the delivery up and cancellation of certain bills of exchange accepted by him. Though of full age, he had been adjudicated a prodigal by a French court because of his extravagant habits, and by French law could not bring an action without the intervention of his "conseil judiciaire." Fry J. held that this was no objection to his right to sue in England. He apparently thought that there had been no change of status under French law, but that if there had been, it would not be recognised in England.

In *Re Selot's Trusts*[37]:

> A testator, presumably domiciled in England, gave a legacy to his grandson, a Frenchman domiciled in France. The trustees of the will paid the legacy into court because the grandson had been adjudicated a prodigal in France, and could not mortgage movable property without the consent of his conseil judiciaire. He charged the fund in court as security for a loan from his English solicitors without such consent. He petitioned for payment out of the fund to the solicitors. Farwell J. gave judgment in his favour, apparently because he thought the French status was penal. But was it not protective?

In *Re Langley's Settlement*[38]:

---

[30] *Re Metcalfe's Trusts* (1864) 2 D.J. & S. 122.

[31] See *Wolff* v. *Oxholm* (1817) 6 M & S. 92; *Re Fried-Krupp A/G* [1917] 2 Ch. 188; *Re Helbert Wagg & Co. Ltd.'s Claim* [1956] Ch. 323, 345–346. See *post*, p. 380.

[32] See *Sottomayor* v. *De Barros* (*No. 2*) (1879) 5 P.D. 94, 104.

[33] *Scott* v. *Att. Gen.* (1886) 11 P.D. 128, as explained in *Warter* v. *Warter* (1890) 15 P.D. 152, 155; *post*, pp. 169–170.

[34] See *Frankfurther* v. *W. L. Exner Ltd.* [1947] Ch. 629; *Novello & Co. Ltd.* v. *Hinrichsen Edition Ltd.* [1951] Ch. 595; *cf. Oppenheimer* v. *Rosenthal & Co.* [1937] 1 All E.R. 23; *Ellinger* v. *Guinness Mahon & Co.* [1939] 4 All E.R. 16.

[35] *Sottomayor* v. *De Barros* (*No. 2*) (1879) 5 P.D. 94, 104.

[36] (1880) 49 L.J.Ch. 261.

[37] [1902] 1 Ch. 488. This case and *Worms* v. *De Valdor* are criticised by Westlake, p. 48; Cheshire and North, p. 152.

[38] [1962] Ch. 541; criticised by Grodecki (1962) 11 I.C.L.Q. 578; Collier [1962] Camb.L.J. 36; Cheshire and North, pp. 152–153.

Under a settlement the proper law of which was English, the settlor was empowered to withdraw funds from the trusts thereof. The settlor acquired a domicile in California. He suffered from multiple sclerosis but was of sound mind. A Californian court declared him "incompetent" and appointed his wife as guardian of his person and property, and authorised and directed her to exercise any powers under the settlement which he could have exercised if he had been competent. The settlor and his wife purported to withdraw £20,000 from the settlement. The Court of Appeal held that this exercise of the power of withdrawal was valid and effective. They pointed out that by English law the settlor could withdraw and that by Californian law his wife could do so, and that therefore their joint withdrawal was necessarily good. They also pointed out that to deny the power of withdrawal would have penalised the settlor to the tune of £20,000.

In all these cases, English law seems to have been the *lex causae*. In *Worms* v. *De Valdor*, the question was the capacity of the plaintiff to bring an action in England, a matter of procedure governed by the *lex fori*. In *Re Selot's Trusts*, the question was the capacity of a legatee to take under the will of a testator domiciled in England. In *Re Langley's Settlement*, the question was the capacity of the settlor to exercise a power under a settlement governed by English law. It may be that the foreign incapacities would have been recognised if the foreign law had been the *lex causae*.

Public policy may sometimes require that a capacity existing under foreign law should be disregarded in England[39]; but the circumstances would have to be extreme before such a course became desirable. Thus, English courts recognise the validity of polygamous marriages (at least for some purposes[40]), of marriages by proxy,[41] and of marriages within the prohibited degrees of English law,[42] provided of course they are valid under the applicable foreign law. But they might refuse to recognise a marriage between persons so closely related that sexual intercourse between them was incestuous by English criminal law,[43] or a marriage with a child below the age of puberty.[44]

The mere fact that a foreign status or relationship is unknown to English domestic law is not a ground for refusing to recognise it.[45] Thus, legitimation by subsequent marriage was recognised and given effect to in England long before it became part of English domestic law.[46] The recognition of polygamous marriages is another example.

---

[39] *Cheni* v. *Cheni* [1965] P. 85, 98.
[40] *Post*, pp. 181–186.
[41] *Apt* v. *Apt* [1948] P. 83.
[42] *Re Bozzelli's Settlement* [1902] 1 Ch. 751 (marriage in 1880 with deceased brother's widow); *Re Pozot's Settlement* [1952] 1 All E.R. 1107, 1109 (marriage with step-daughter); *Cheni* v. *Cheni* [1965] P. 85 (marriage between uncle and niece).
[43] *Brook* v. *Brook* (1861) 9 H.L.C. 193, 227–228; *Cheni* v. *Cheni, supra,* at p. 97.
[44] In *Mohamed* v. *Knott* [1969] 1 Q.B. 1, a marriage with a girl of 13, valid by Nigerian law, was recognised as valid in England. See Karsten (1969) 32 M.L.R. 212.
[45] *Phrantzes* v. *Argenti* [1960] 2 Q.B. 19; *Shahnaz* v. *Rizwan* [1965] 1 Q.B. 390, 401.
[46] *Post*, pp. 246–247.

Other cases

Apart from cases of contract and status, examples of the exclusion of foreign law on the grounds of public policy are rare. It is not contrary to public policy to recognise foreign decrees confiscating private property,[47] but it may be otherwise if the decree is "penal" in the sense of being directed against the property of a particular individual or a particular company or a particular family or persons of a particular race or a particular alien nationality.[48] It is not contrary to public policy to recognise foreign exchange control legislation,[49] but it may be otherwise if the legislation, even though originally passed with the genuine object of protecting the State's economy, has become an instrument of oppression and discrimination.[50] The recognition of a foreign decree of divorce[51] or nullity of marriage[52] and the enforcement of a foreign judgment *in personam*[53] may be refused on grounds of public policy, but instances are extremely rare. There is no general principle that the application of a foreign law is contrary to public policy merely because it operates retrospectively.[54]

"Residual discretion"

In recent years English judges have stated that the courts possess a "residual discretion" to refuse to recognise a foreign status[55] conferred or imposed upon a person by the law of his domicile, or a foreign decree of divorce or nullity of marriage,[56] if the recognition would be improper or unjust or unconscionable in the circumstances of the particular case. In the first of the cases in which these statements were made, it is probable that the court intended to do no more than call attention to the distinction between the recognition of a status and the recognition of its incidents. In the later cases it may be that the courts intended to do no more than refer to the doctrine of public policy and to the analogous doctrine that foreign decrees of divorce and nullity will not be recognised in England if recognition would be contrary to natural justice.[57] But if the courts intended to reduce the whole of the conflict of laws, or even that part of it which is concerned with status, to the level of judicial discretion, it is submitted that this is contrary both to principle and to authority. For, as has been well said, "to state the law in terms of judicial discretion . . . is to admit that

---

[47] *Luther* v. *Sagor* [1921] 3 K.B. 532, 559; *Princess Paley Olga* v. *Weisz* [1929] 1 K.B. 718.
[48] *Post*, p. 380.
[49] *Kahler* v. *Midland Bank* [1950] A.C. 24; *Zivnostenska Banka* v. *Frankman* [1950] A.C. 57.
[50] *Re Helbert Wagg & Co. Ltd.'s Claim* [1956] Ch. 323, 352.
[51] *Post*, pp. 202–203.
[52] *Post*, p. 214.
[53] *Post*, pp. 119–120.
[54] *Post*, p. 499.
[55] *Re Langley's Settlement* [1962] Ch. 541, 555, 557–558; *Russ* v. *Russ* [1963] P. 87, 100; [1964] P. 315, 327–328, 334, 335; *Cheni* v. *Cheni* [1965] P. 85, 98; *Qureshi* v. *Qureshi* [1972] Fam. 173, 201.
[56] *Gray* v. *Formosa* [1963] P. 259, 269, 270, 271; *Lepre* v. *Lepre* [1965] P. 52, 63. As to divorce, see now Recognition of Divorces and Legal Separations Act 1971, s.8(2), and *post*, pp. 201, 203.
[57] *Post*, pp. 202–203, 213–214.

no certainty or predictability is attainable in this matter."[58] And again: "the courts might just as well abandon any attempt to formulate and apply defined rules of law if these can be overridden by an indefinable discretion."[59] And, as Lord Hodson said in *Boys* v. *Chaplin*,[60] "rules of law should be defined and adhered to as closely as possible lest they lose themselves in a field of judicial discretion where no secure foothold is to be found by litigants or their advisers."

PENAL LAWS

It is well settled that English courts will not directly or indirectly enforce a foreign penal law. "The courts of no country execute the penal laws of another,"[61] said Chief Justice Marshall of the United States. The reason has been thus explained by the Privy Council[62]:

> "The rule has its foundation in the well-recognised principle that crimes, including in that term all breaches of public law punishable by pecuniary mulct or otherwise, at the instance of the State Government, or of someone representing the public, are local in this sense, that they are only cognisable and punishable in the country where they were committed. Accordingly no proceeding, even in the shape of a civil suit, which has for its object the enforcement by the State, whether directly or indirectly, of punishment imposed for such breaches by the *lex fori*, ought to be admitted in the courts of any other country."

A "penal" law within the meaning of this rule is a criminal law imposing a penalty recoverable at the instance of the State or of an official duly authorised to prosecute on its behalf.[63] The word "penal" in this rule has quite a different meaning from that which it bears in the rule considered in the previous section of this chapter,[64] that English courts will not give effect to the results of any foreign status which is penal; for in that rule "penal" means merely discriminatory.

It is for the English court to determine for itself whether the foreign law in question is a penal law, and it is not bound by the interpretation placed upon the law by the courts of the foreign country.[65]

Since "the essential nature and real foundation of a cause of action are not changed by recovering judgment upon it,"[66] the court will not enforce a foreign judgment based upon a foreign penal law.[67]

---

[58] Grodecki (1962) 11 I.C.L.Q. 578, 582.
[59] Nygh (1964) 13 I.C.L.Q. 39, 51.
[60] [1971] A.C. 356, 378.
[61] *The Antelope* (1825) 10 Wheat. 66, 123.
[62] *Huntington* v. *Attrill* [1893] A.C. 150, 156.
[63] *Ibid.* at pp. 157–158.
[64] *Ante*, pp. 44–45.
[65] *Huntington* v. *Attrill, supra.*
[66] *Wisconsin* v. *Pelican Insurance Co.* (1888) 127 U.S. 265, 292.
[67] *Huntington* v. *Attrill, supra.*

The leading case on the enforcement of foreign penal laws is *Huntington* v. *Attrill*[68]:

> Under a New York statute, the directors of a company who signed certificates which were false in any material representation became personally liable for the debts of the company contracted while they were directors. The defendant was a director of a New York company. He signed a certificate which stated falsely that the whole of its capital stock had been paid up. The plaintiff, who had lent money to the company, sued the defendant in New York under the statute for the unpaid balance of his loan, and obtained judgment for over 100,000 dollars. The judgment remained unsatisfied, and the plaintiff brought an action on it in Ontario. The Privy Council, reversing the courts below, held that the statute was not a penal law and that the plaintiff could recover.

Another striking illustration of the rule is afforded by *Banco de Vizcaya* v. *Don Alfonso de Borbon y Austria*[69]:

> The King of Spain deposited securities with the Westminster Bank in London. A decree of the Constituent Cortes of Spain declared the ex-King to be guilty of high treason, and ordered all his properties, rights and grounds of action to be seized for its own benefit by the Spanish State. An action by a nominee of the State to recover the securities was dismissed.

The rule under discussion is limited to the *enforcement* of foreign penal laws. It does not extend to their recognition. Thus a contract which is illegal because of a penal rule of its proper law will be treated as invalid and will not be enforced in England.[70]

REVENUE LAWS

"No country ever takes notice of the revenue laws of another," said Lord Mansfield in *Holman* v. *Johnson*[71]; and though (as will be seen below) this proposition is too widely stated, it has ever since been assumed by English lawyers that foreign revenue laws will not be enforced in England. Authority for this more limited proposition was sparse[72] until the decision of the House of Lords in *Government of India* v. *Taylor*[73] placed the matter beyond doubt. The reason for non-enforcement is that "tax-gathering is not a matter of contract but of authority and administration as between the State and those within its jurisdiction."

A foreign revenue law is a law requiring a non-contractual payment of money to the State or some department or sub-division thereof. It includes

---

[68] [1893] A.C. 150. *Cf.* the similar decision of the Supreme Court of the United States in *Huntington* v. *Attrill* (1892) 146 U.S. 657.
[69] [1935] 1 K.B. 140.
[70] *Post*, p. 289.
[71] (1775) 1 Cowp. 341, 343.
[72] *Municipal Council of Sydney* v. *Bull* [1909] 1 K.B. 7; *Re Visser* [1928] Ch. 877.
[73] [1955] A.C. 491, 514.

income tax,[74] capital gains tax,[75] customs duty,[76] death duties,[77] local rates,[78] compulsory contributions to a State insurance scheme[79] and a profits levy.[80]

English courts will not enforce foreign revenue laws either directly or indirectly. Direct enforcement occurs when a foreign State or its nominee seeks to recover the tax by action in England. Indirect enforcement occurs, *e.g.* where a company in liquidation seeks to recover from one of its directors assets under his control which the liquidator would use to pay foreign taxes due from the company,[81] or where a debtor pleads that the debt has been attached by a foreign garnishee order obtained by a foreign State claiming a tax,[82] or where an ancillary administrator has assets in his hands which, if sent to the principal administrator in the country of the deceased's domicile, would be used to pay death duties,[83] or where a foreign government asserts a lien over goods situated in England in respect of unpaid tax.[84] But where neither direct nor indirect enforcement arises, foreign revenue laws are freely recognised.[85] Thus Lord Mansfield's proposition that "no country ever takes notice of the revenue laws of another" is now seen to be too widely stated.[86] The difference between enforcement and recognition was thus explained by Lord Simonds in *Regazzoni* v. *K. C. Sethia Ltd.*[87]:

> "It does not follow from the fact that today the court will not enforce a revenue law at the suit of a foreign State that today it will enforce a contract which requires the doing of an act in a foreign country which violates the revenue law of that country. The two things are not complementary or co-extensive. This may be seen if for revenue law penal law is substituted. For an English court will not enforce a penal law at the suit of a foreign State, yet it would be surprising if it would enforce a contract which required the commission of a crime in that State."

OTHER PUBLIC LAWS

Dicey and Morris[88] say that English courts will not enforce other public

---

[74] *U.S.A.* v. *Harden* (1963) 41 D.L.R. (2d) 721 (Supreme Court of Canada).
[75] *Government of India* v. *Taylor, supra.*
[76] *Att. Gen. for Canada* v. *Schulze* (1901) 9 S.L.T. 4.
[77] *Re Visser* [1928] Ch. 877.
[78] *Municipal Council of Sydney* v. *Bull* [1909] 1 K.B. 7.
[79] *Metal Industries (Salvage) Ltd.* v. *Owners of S.T. Harle,* 1962 S.L.T. 114; *cf. The Acrux* [1965] p. 391, where the point was overlooked.
[80] *Peter Buchanan Ltd.* v. *McVey* [1954] I.R. 89.
[81] *Ibid.*
[82] *Rossano* v. *Manufacturers Life Insurance Co. Ltd.* [1963] 2 Q.B. 352.
[83] *Jones* v. *Borland,* 1969 (4) S.A. 29; *cf. Bath* v. *British and Malayan Trustees Ltd.* [1969] 2 N.S.W.R. 114; *Re Lord Cable* [1977] 1 W.L.R. 7, 25–26.
[84] *Brokaw* v. *Seatrain U.K. Ltd.* [1971] 2 Q.B. 476.
[85] *Re Emery's Investment Trusts* [1959] Ch. 410; *Regazzoni* v. *K. C. Sethia Ltd.* [1958] A.C. 301.
[86] *Regazzoni* v. *K. C. Sethia Ltd.* [1956] 2 Q.B. 490, 515, 520, 524; [1958] A.C. 301, 322, 328, 330.
[87] [1958] A.C. 301, 322.
[88] Rule 3.

laws of a foreign State; and in *Att. Gen. of New Zealand* v. *Ortiz*[89] Lord Denning M.R. held that they are right. He defined a public law for this purpose as an exercise by a foreign government of its sovereign authority over property outside its territory. In that case the defendant brought an ancient Maori carving from New Zealand to England in contravention of a New Zealand statute which provided that historic articles knowingly exported or attempted to be exported should be forfeited to the Crown. This was interpreted to mean "shall be liable to be forfeited." The Government of New Zealand brought an action in England for the return and delivery up of the carving. It was held that the action failed, *per* Lord Denning M.R. because the New Zealand statute was a public law, *per* Ackner and O'Connor L.JJ. because it was a penal law. But it is difficult to see how the location of the property at the material time can be relevant in determining whether a foreign law is either a public or a penal law. This decision was affirmed by the House of Lords,[90] but only on the ground that the Court of Appeal were right in their interpretation of the New Zealand statute. The House expressed no opinion on whether it was a penal or public law. On the contrary, they said that this part of the judgments of the Court of Appeal was *obiter*.

[89] [1984] A.C. 1.
[90] *Ibid*. p. 41.

Part Two

JURISDICTION OF THE ENGLISH COURT

CHAPTER 5

SOVEREIGN AND DIPLOMATIC IMMUNITY

THE courts of England are, generally speaking, open to the whole world. In particular, nobody is prevented from being a plaintiff or a defendant because he is of foreign nationality. It is quite common for English courts to try disputes between foreigners which have no connection whatsoever with England. This is because the parties have agreed to litigate in England, attracted no doubt by the high reputation for impartiality which English justice enjoys among those who can afford it. England is of course not the only country in the world whose courts have a reputation for impartiality; in particular the Swiss courts also have such a reputation.

Although, as has just been said, the foreign nationality of the parties does not deny them access to the English courts, it is true that, speaking very generally, the matrimonial jurisdiction of the court depends on the domicile or habitual residence of the petitioner or respondent[1]; and that the jurisdiction of the court in actions *in personam* depends primarily on the presence of the defendant in England when the writ is served, or, if he is resident within the EEC, on his residence in England at that time.[2]

There is, however, one class of persons who cannot sue, namely alien enemies, and three classes of persons who cannot as a general rule be sued, namely foreign sovereign States; foreign diplomats; and international organisations and their members. These latter will now be discussed.

Foreign States

Introduction. At common law, no foreign sovereign State could be sued in the English courts without its consent.[3] The immunity was derived ultimately from the rules of public international law and from the maxim of that law, *par in parem non habet imperium.* These rules of public international law became part of the English common law.[4]

In the nineteenth century and for most of the twentieth century the "absolute" rule of immunity prevailed, whereby foreign sovereign States were accorded immunity for all activities, whether governmental or commercial. But the increase in State trading in the twentieth century led a number of States (including the United States) to develop a distinction, generally known as the "restrictive" theory, between acts of government, *acta jure imperii,* and acts of a commercial nature, *acta jure gestionis.* Under the restrictive theory, States were immune in respect of acts of

---

[1] *Post,* Chap. 12.
[2] *Post,* Chap. 6.
[3] *Duke of Brunswick* v. *King of Hanover* (1844) 6 Beav. 1; (1848) 2 H.L.C.1.
[4] *The Cristina* [1938] A.C. 485, 490, *per* Lord Atkin.

government but not in respect of commercial acts. In the United Kingdom the courts applied, until comparatively recently, the absolute theory both in relation to actions *in rem* against trading ships[5] and actions *in personam* involving trading activities.[6] The results proved unfortunate and led to widespread criticism. It was even said that "the English courts accord to foreign States immunity to an extent to which no other State would accord immunity either to this country or to any other State."[7] However, in 1975 the Privy Council held that a foreign government was not entitled to immunity in an action *in rem* against a ship used for trading purposes,[8] and in 1977 the Court of Appeal held, by a majority, that a State was not entitled to immunity in respect of commercial transactions.[9]

The Brussels Convention on the Immunity of State-owned Ships (1926) attempted to exclude immunity in the case of ships and cargoes owned or operated by States for commercial purposes; but it achieved only limited support, and was not ratified by the United Kingdom until 1979. In 1972 a much more comprehensive European Convention on State Immunity, severely restricting the scope of the doctrine, was concluded under the auspices of the Council of Europe and came into force in 1976.[10]

State Immunity Act 1978. The law of sovereign immunity in the United Kingdom is now regulated by the State Immunity Act 1978, which was designed in part to implement the European Convention, but is world-wide in effect. The Act goes considerably further than the Convention in restricting immunity. It applies to any foreign or Commonwealth State other than the United Kingdom, and it applies not only to the State itself but also to the sovereign of the State in his public capacity,[11] to the government of the State, and any department of its government.[12] Provision is made for the application of the Act by Order in Council to the constituent territories of a federal State.[13] At common law a difficult question which often arose was whether a State corporation or agency could claim to be an emanation of the foreign State and thus entitled to immunity. The Act deals with this problem through the concept of a "separate entity." A separate entity which is distinct from the executive organs of the foreign government and is capable of suing and being sued is not entitled to immunity unless the proceedings relate to something done by it in the exercise of sovereign authority and the circumstances are such that the State would have been immune.[14] It may still be difficult for the courts to deter-

---

[5] *The Porto Alexandre* [1920] P. 30; *The Cristina, supra, per* Lord Atkin at p. 490, and Lord Wright at p. 512.
[6] *Kahan* v. *Pakistan Federation* [1951] 2 K.B. 1003; *Baccus S.R.L.* v. *Servicio National del Trigo* [1957] 1 Q.B. 438.
[7] Cohn (1958) 34 B.Y.I.L. 260.
[8] *The Philippine Admiral* [1977] A.C. 373. *Cf. The I Congreso del Partido* [1983] 1 A.C. 244; see Hazel Fox (1982) 98 L.Q.R. 94.
[9] *Trendtex Trading Corporation* v. *Central Bank of Nigeria* [1977] Q.B. 529.
[10] The text of the Convention is printed in Cmnd. 5081. For a commentary, see Sinclair (1973) 22 I.C.L.Q. 254.
[11] In his personal capacity he is assimilated to an ambassador: s.20. See *post*, p. 61.
[12] s.14(1).
[13] s.14(5).
[14] s.14(1) and (2).

mine whether a "separate entity" was acting "in the exercise of sovereign authority."

Section 1 of the Act lays down what is still the general rule, namely that a State is immune from the jurisdiction of the courts of the United Kingdom, and that they must give effect to this immunity even though the State does not appear. The next ten sections lay down exceptions to this general rule. It is important to bear in mind that none of these exceptions (except the first) confers jurisdiction on the English courts which otherwise they would not have: they merely remove an immunity which otherwise would exist. It may still be necessary to obtain leave to serve notice of the writ out of the jurisdiction under Order 11 of the Rules of the Supreme Court,[15] if the defendant does not submit to the jurisdiction and cannot be served here with a writ.

A State is not immune in the following types of proceedings:

(1) Proceedings in respect of which the State has submitted to the jurisdiction of the courts of the United Kingdom.[16] At common law, sovereign immunity could be waived by or on behalf of the foreign State, but the doctrine was confined within very narrow limits. Waiver had to take place at the time when the court was asked to exercise jurisidction[17]; it could not be inferred from a prior contract to submit to the jurisdiction of the court[18] or to arbitration.[19] The Act has made a far-reaching and welcome change by providing that a State may submit after the dispute has arisen, or by a prior written agreement.[20] It will also be deemed to have submitted if it institutes the proceedings, or intervenes or takes any step in the proceedings, unless the intervention was solely for the purpose of claiming immunity, or unless it was in reasonable ignorance of facts entitling it to immunity and immunity is claimed as soon as reasonably practical.[21] A submission in respect of any proceedings extends to an appeal, but not to a counterclaim unless it arises out of the same legal relationship or facts as the claim.[22] A written submission to arbitration by a State is submission to proceedings in the courts of the United Kingdom relating to the arbitration, unless contrary provision is made or the arbitration agreement is between States.[23]

(2) Proceedings relating to a commercial transaction entered into by the State.[24] This exception is extremely important and is much wider than the corresponding provision in the European Convention. "Commercial transaction" is defined to mean (a) any contract for the supply of goods or ser-

---

[15] *Post*, pp. 68–76.
[16] s.2(1).
[17] *Mighell* v. *Sultan of Johore* [1894] 1 Q.B. 149.
[18] *Kahan* v. *Pakistan Federation* [1951] 2 K.B. 1003; *Baccus S.R.L.* v. *Servicio Nacional del Trigo* [1957] 1 Q.B. 438.
[19] *Duff Development Co.* v. *Government of Kelantan* [1924] A.C. 797.
[20] s.2(2).
[21] s.2(3), (4) and (5).
[22] s.2(6).
[23] s.9.
[24] s.3(1)(*a*). This confirms the decision of the Court of Appeal in *Trendtex Trading Corporation* v. *Central Bank of Nigeria* [1977] Q.B. 529.

vices; (b) any loan or other transaction for the provision of finance (and any guarantee or indemnity in respect thereof or of any other financial obligation); and (c) any other transaction or activity (whether of a commercial, industrial, financial, professional or other similar character) into which a State enters otherwise than in the exercise of sovereign authority.[25] But it does not include a contract of employment: that is made a separate exception.[26]

(3) Proceedings relating to an obligation of the State which by virtue of a contract (whether a commercial transaction or not) falls to be performed wholly or partly in the United Kingdom.[27] This would include contracts made in the exercise of sovereign authority provided they are to be performed here.

(4) Proceedings relating to a contract of employment between the State and an individual where (a) the contract was made in the United Kingdom or (b) the work is to be wholly or partly performed there.[28] This exception does not apply if either (a) at the time when the proceedings are brought, the employee is a national of the foreign State, or (b) at the time when the contract was made, the employee was neither a national of nor habitually resident in the United Kingdom.[29] But it does apply in each of these cases if the work is for an office, agency or establishment maintained by the State in the United Kingdom for commercial purposes, unless the employee was, at the time when the contract was made, habitually resident in the foreign State.[30] Nor does the exception apply to proceedings concerning the employment of members of a diplomatic mission or consular post.[31]

(5) Proceedings in respect of death or personal injury, or damage to or loss of tangible property, caused by an act or omission in the United Kingdom.[32]

(6) Proceedings relating to any interest of the State in, or its possession or use of, immovable property in the United Kingdom, or any obligation of the State arising therefrom.[33]

(7) Proceedings relating to any interest of the State in movable or immovable property by way of succession, gift or *bona vacantia*.[34] Further, the fact that a State claims an interest in any property does not preclude the court from exercising any jurisdiction relating to the estates of deceased persons or persons of unsound mind or to insolvency, the winding up of companies or the administration of trusts.[35]

(8) Proceedings relating to United Kingdom patents, trade marks and

[25] s.3(3). See *Alcom Ltd.* v. *Republic of Colombia* [1983] 3 W.L.R. 906.
[26] Exception (4), *post*.
[27] s.3(1)(*b*).
[28] s.4(1).
[29] s.4(2). For the meaning of "national of the United Kingdom," see s.4(5) as amended by British Nationality Act 1981, Sched. 7.
[30] s.4(3).
[31] s.16(1)(*a*).
[32] s.5.
[33] s.6(1). See *Intro Properties (U.K.) Ltd.* v. *Sauvel* [1983] Q.B. 1019.
[34] s.6(2).
[35] *Ibid*.

similar rights belonging to the State, or to the alleged infringement by the State in the United Kingdom of any such rights, including copyright.[36]

(9) Proceedings relating to the State's membership of a corporate or unincorporated body or a partnership which has members other than States and is incorporated or constituted under the law of the United Kingdom or is controlled from or has its principal place of business in the United Kingdom.[37]

(10) Actions *in rem* against a ship belonging to the State, or actions *in personam* for enforcing a claim in connection with such a ship, if at the time when the cause of action arose the ship was in use or intended for use for commercial purposes.[38] A similar provision applies to actions *in rem* against a cargo belonging to the State if both the cargo and the ship were in use or intended for use for commercial purposes, and to actions *in personam* for enforcing a claim in connection with such a cargo.[39]

(11) Proceedings relating to a State's liability for value added tax, customs duty, agricultural levy, or rates in respect of premises occupied by it for commercial purposes.[40]

Indirect impleading. So far we have assumed (except in exception (10) above) that the question of sovereign immunity arises in proceedings in which the State is named as defendant in an action *in personam, i.e.* direct impleading. But at common law the doctrine of sovereign immunity protected a foreign State not only in direct proceedings against it but also in indirect proceedings against property in its possession or control or in which it claims an interest. Thus if a foreign State has an interest in property situated in England, whether proprietary, possessory or of some lesser nature, an action which affects its interest would be stayed, even though it was not brought against it personally but was, *e.g.* an action *in rem* against a ship[41] or an action *in personam* against its bailee[42] or agent.[43] The rule was not limited to ownership, and applied to lesser interests which might not merely be not proprietary but not even possessory, so that it applied to property under the control of the foreign State[44] and perhaps also to property in respect of which it had no beneficial interest but only the legal title.[45] The Act implicitly assumes that these rules of the common law will continue to apply.[46] Moreover, it specifically provides that the court may entertain proceedings against a person other than a State notwithstanding

[36] s.7.
[37] s.8.
[38] s.10(1) and (2). This confirms the decision of the Privy Council in *The Philippine Admiral* [1977] A.C. 373. "Commercial purposes" are defined in s.17(1).
[39] s.10(4).
[40] s.11.
[41] *The Parlement Belge* (1880) 5 P.D. 197; *The Jupiter* [1924] P. 236; *The Cristina* [1938] A.C. 485; *The Arantzazu Mendi* [1939] A.C. 256.
[42] *U.S.A. and Republic of France* v. *Dollfus Mieg et Cie, and Bank of England* [1952] A.C. 582.
[43] *Rahimtoola* v. *Nizam of Hyderabad* [1958] A.C. 379.
[44] *The Cristina, supra; The Arantzazu Mendi, supra.*
[45] *Rahimtoola* v. *Nizam of Hyderabad, supra*, at p. 403.
[46] See ss.2(4)(b), 6 and 10.

that the proceedings relate to property in its possession or control, or in which it claims an interest, if the State would not have been immune had the proceedings been brought against it, or, in the case where the State merely claims an interest, if the claim is neither admitted nor supported by prima facie evidence.[47]

Execution. In general, even if a State is not immune under one of the exceptions, its property is not subject to execution for the enforcement of a judgment or arbitration award.[48] This is subject to two important exceptions: execution is allowed if (a) the State consents in writing, or (b) the property is for the time being in use or intended for use for commercial purposes.[49] A central bank is accorded special treatment under the Act. If (as is likely) it is a "separate entity," its property is immune from execution, even if it is not entitled to immunity from suit; and its property is not regarded as in use or intended for use for commercial purposes.[50] In practice, therefore, the property of a State's central bank will only be liable to execution if it has waived, in writing, its immunity from execution.

Service of process. The Act provides for a method of service on a State by transmission of the writ through the Foreign and Commonwealth Office to the State's Ministry of Foreign Affairs.[51] A State which appears in proceedings cannot thereafter object that service was not properly effected upon it.[52] Service by transmission of the writ through the Foreign and Commonwealth Office is not necessary if the State has agreed to a different method of service.[53]

Miscellaneous. Provision may be made by Order in Council to restrict or extend the immunities of a State under the Act. If they exceed those accorded by the law of that State in relation to the United Kingdom, they may be restricted. If they are less than those required by any treaty or convention to which that State and the United Kingdom are parties, they can be extended.[54]

A certificate from the Secretary of State is conclusive evidence on any question whether any country is a State, whether any territory is a constituent territory of a federal State, or as to the person or persons to be regarded as the head or government of a State.[55]

Foreign diplomats

Before 1964, the immunity from suit of foreign ambassadors and members of their staffs was secured by the common law as reinforced by the Diplomatic Privileges Act 1708, which has always been treated as declara-

---

[47] s.6(4). See *Juan Ysmael & Co. Inc.* v. *Indonesian Government* [1955] A.C. 75; *Rahimtoola* v. *Nizam of Hyderabad, supra,* at p. 410.
[48] s.13(2)(*b*).
[49] s.13(3) and (4). "Commercial purposes" are defined in s.17(1).
[50] s.14(4).
[51] s.12(1).
[52] s.12(3).
[53] s.12(6).
[54] s.15.
[55] s.21(*a*).

tory of the common law. That Act was passed in the following remarkable circumstances[56]:

> The Russian ambassador to the Court of St. James was arrested and removed from his coach in London for non-payment of a debt of £50. The Czar Peter the Great resented this affront so highly that he demanded that the Sheriff of Middlesex and all others concerned in the arrest should be punished with instant death. But, to the amazement of the Czar's despotic court, Queen Anne informed him "that she could inflict no punishment upon the meanest of her subjects, unless it was warranted by the law of the land; and therefore she was persuaded that he would not insist upon impossibilities." To appease the wrath of Peter, a Bill was brought into Parliament and duly passed. A copy of this Act, elegantly engrossed and illuminated, accompanied by a letter from the Queen, was then sent to Moscow by ambassador extraordinary.

The Act of 1708 has now been repealed and replaced by the Diplomatic Privileges Act 1964, which gives effect to the Vienna Convention on Diplomatic Relations 1961.[57] Section 1 of the Act provides that the following provisions of the Act shall have effect in substitution for any previous enactment or rule of law; and section 2 enacts those articles of the Convention which are set out in the First Schedule as part of the law of the United Kingdom. Hence, much of the old case law is now only of historical interest.

The most important single change effected by the Convention in the law of the United Kingdom is that it abolishes the principle of absolute immunity: diplomatic immunity, even that of the ambassador himself, is now only qualified. The Convention divides persons entitled to diplomatic immunity into three categories[58]: (1) "diplomatic agents," namely, the head of the mission and members of his diplomatic staff; (2) "members of the administrative and technical staff," *i.e.* persons employed in secretarial, clerical, communications and public relations duties, such as typists, translators, coding clerks and press and cultural representatives; and (3) "members of the service staff," namely, members of the staff of the mission in its domestic service, such as cooks, cleaners, porters and chauffeurs. These three classes are each entitled to differing degrees of immunity from civil and criminal jurisdiction.

Foreign consuls. Foreign consuls and members of their staffs are not within the terms of the Vienna Convention on Diplomatic Relations. It appears to be accepted that they are entitled to immunity from suit at common law in respect of their official acts, but not in respect of their private acts.[59] This is confirmed by the Consular Relations Act 1968, which enacts

[56] *Taylor* v. *Best* (1854) 14 C.B. 487, 491–493.
[57] The full text of the Convention is printed in (1961) 10 I.C.L.Q. 600. For a commentary on the Act and the Convention, see Margaret Buckley (1965–66) 41 B.Y.I.L. 321.
[58] Diplomatic Privileges Act 1964, Sched. 1, Art. 1.
[59] *Engelke* v. *Musman* [1928] A.C. 433, 437–438; Oppenheim, *International Law*, 8th ed., Vol. I. p. 841; Beckett (1944) 21 B.Y.I.L. 34.

as part of the law of the United Kingdom those articles of the Vienna Convention on Consular Relations 1963 which are set out in the First Schedule.[60] Under that Convention, consular officers and consular employees[61] are not amenable to jurisdiction in respect of acts performed in the exercise of consular functions, with some exceptions in civil actions.

Evidence. If in any proceedings any question arises whether or not any person is entitled to immunity from suit, a certificate issued by or under the authority of the Secretary of State stating any fact relating to that question is conclusive evidence of that fact.[62]

Waiver. Diplomatic and consular immunity may be waived by the sending State.[63] A waiver by the head or acting head of a diplomatic mission is deemed to be a waiver by that State.[64] Waiver must always be express, except that the initiation of proceedings precludes the plaintiff from invoking immunity from jurisdiction in respect of any counterclaim directly connected with the principal claim.[65] There is no requirement that waiver must take place in the face of the court, as in waiver of sovereign immunity at common law.[66] Waiver of immunity from jurisdiction in civil or administrative proceedings does not imply waiver of immunity in respect of execution of the judgment, for which a separate waiver is required.[67]

International organisations, etc.

The International Organisations Act 1968 empowers the Crown by Order in Council to confer various degrees of immunity from suit and legal process upon any international organisation of which the United Kingdom is a member[68]; on representatives to the organisation or representatives on, or members of, any of its organs, committees or sub-committees, on specified high officers of the organisation, and persons employed by or serving as experts or as persons engaged on missions for the organisation[69]; and on specified subordinate officers or servants of the organisation.[70] No such immunity may be conferred on any person as the representative of the United Kingdom or as a member of his staff.[71]

The Act also empowers the Crown by Order in Council to confer

---

[60] s.1(1). The full text of the Convention is printed in (1964) 13 I.C.L.Q. 1214.
[61] For definitions, see Sched. 1, Art 1(d) and (e).
[62] Diplomatic Privileges Act 1964, s.4; Consular Relations Act 1968, s.11.
[63] Diplomatic Privileges Act 1964, Sched. 1, Art 32(1); Consular Relations Act 1968, Sched. 1, Art. 45(1).
[64] Diplomatic Privileges Act 1964, s.2(3); Consular Relations Act 1968, s.1(5).
[65] Diplomatic Privileges Act 1964, Sched. 1, Art. 32(2) and (3); Consular Relations Act 1968, Sched. 1, Art. 45(2) and (3). See *High Commissioner for India* v. *Ghosh* [1960] 1 Q.B. 134.
[66] *Ante*, p. 57.
[67] Art. 32(4) of Sched. 1 of the 1964 Act; Art 45(4) of Sched. 1 of the 1968 Act.
[68] s.1(1), (2)(b), and Sched. 1, Part I, para. 1. The International Organisations Act 1981, s.2 extends this to international commodity organisations of which the United Kingdom is not a member.
[69] s.1(2)(c), (3), and Sched. 1, Part II, para. 9.
[70] s.1(2)(d) and Sched. 1, Part III, para. 14.
[71] s.1(6)(b).

immunity from suit on the judges, registrars or other officers of any international tribunal, on parties to any proceedings before any such tribunal, and their advocates and witnesses[72]; and on representatives of foreign States and their official staffs attending conferences in the United Kingdom.[73]

If in any proceedings a question arises whether any person is or is not entitled to any immunity, a certificate issued by or under the authority of the Secretary of State stating any fact relating to that question is conclusive evidence of that fact.[74]

Orders in Council have been made under this and earlier Acts conferring immunity from suit on a large number of international organisations and (in most cases) on their representatives, officers and staffs. These organisations range from the United Nations Organisation to the International Coffee, Cocoa and Sugar Organisations. The possibility of waiver of the immunities thereby conferred is specifically provided for by these Orders in Council; but the term is not defined.

---

[72] s.5(1), (2).
[73] s.6.
[74] s.8. See also *Zoernsch* v. *Waldock* [1964] 1 W.L.R. 675.

CHAPTER 6

JURISDICTION IN ACTIONS *IN PERSONAM*

AN action *in personam* is an action brought against a person to compel him to do a particular thing, *e.g.* the payment of a debt or of damages for breach of contract or for tort, or the specific performance of a contract; or to compel him not to do something, *e.g.* when an injunction is sought. It does not include Admiralty actions *in rem*, probate actions, administration actions, petitions in matrimonial causes, or for guardianship or custody of children, or proceedings in bankruptcy or for the winding up of companies.

This Chapter is divided into two parts, depending on whether or not the defendant is "domiciled"[1] in the EEC. If he is not, then the old law still applies whereby an action *in personam* can be brought against a person who is present in England and served there with the writ or who voluntarily submits to the jurisdiction of the court, or, with the leave of the court, in certain cases mentioned in Order 11 of the Rules of the Supreme Court, if he is not present in England and has not submitted to the jurisdiction. But if he is "domiciled" in the EEC the old law does not apply and special jurisdictional rules laid down by the Civil Jurisdiction and Judgments Act 1982 apply instead.

1. *WHERE THE DEFENDANT IS NOT "DOMICILED" IN THE EEC*

Under this head we need to consider first the presence of the defendant in England; secondly the submission of the defendant to the jurisdiction; and thirdly the extended jurisdiction under the Rules of the Supreme Court.

PRESENCE

Every action in the High Court commences with the issue of a writ[2]; and the service of the writ, or something equivalent thereto,[3] is essential as the foundation of the court's jurisdiction. When a writ cannot legally be served on a defendant, the court can exercise no jurisdiction over him; conversely, when a defendant can be legally served with a writ, the court can exercise jurisdiction. A defendant who is in England can, generally speaking, always be legally served with a writ, unless he is "domiciled" in the EEC (including of course the United Kingdom). Hence any person who is in England and served there with the writ is subject to the *in personam* juris-

---

[1] For the meaning of "domicile" in this context, see *post*, pp. 79–81.
[2] Or, sometimes, as originating summons: see R.S.C. Ord. 5. But this makes no difference to the jurisdiction of the court.
[3] See, *e.g.* Ord. 10, r. 1(4) (defendant's solicitor accepting service on his behalf); r. 1(5) (acknowledgment of service); r. 3 (contract containing a term that the High Court shall have jurisdiction); Ord. 10, r. 1(2) (service by post).

diction of the court. The application of this principle differs according as the defendant is an individual, a partnership firm, or a corporation.

Individuals

Any individual who is present in England is liable to be served with a writ in an action *in personam*, however short may be the period for which he is present in England, and irrespective of his nationality, or domicile, or usual place of residence, provided it is outside the EEC, or of the nature of the cause of action. Thus in *Maharanee of Baroda* v. *Wildenstein*,[4] an Indian princess residing in France brought an action against an American art dealer also residing in France for rescission of a contract to sell her a picture. The contract was made in France and governed by French law. The writ was served on the defendant at Ascot races during a temporary visit to England. It was held that the court had jurisdiction.

As a general rule, the writ must be served personally on the defendant by the plaintiff or his agent.[5] But, if it appears to the court that it is impracticable to serve the writ personally, the court may make an order for substituted service, that is, by taking such steps as the court may direct to bring the writ to the defendant's notice.[6]

Partnerships

A writ can be served as of right on any individual member of a partnership firm who is present in England at the time of service. But before June 1891, a writ could not be served as of right on the firm itself, even if it carried on business in England, unless the partners were present in England or submitted to the jurisdiction.[7] This caused much inconvenience, and in that month the Rules of the Supreme Court were altered accordingly. The present rule[8] now reads as follows:

> "Any two or more persons claiming to be entitled, or alleged to be liable, as partners in respect of a cause of action and carrying on business within the jurisdiction may sue, or be sued, in the name of the firm (if any) of which they were partners at the time when the cause of action accrued."

The writ may be served at the principal place of business of the partnership in England on any person having the control or management of the part-

---

[4] [1972] 2 Q.B. 283. The actual decision would now be different because of the defendant's residence in France. *Cf. Colt Industries Inc.* v. *Sarlie* [1966] 1 W.L.R. 440.

[5] Ord. 10, r. 1(1). Some exceptions are stated in r. 1(2)(4) and (5) and r. 3, see note 3 above. As to what amounts to personal service, see Ord. 65, r. 2.

[6] Ord. 65, r. 4. As to when substituted service will be allowed, see *Field* v. *Bennett* (1886) 3 T.L.R. 239; *Fry* v. *Moore* (1889) 23 Q.B.D. 395; *Wilding* v. *Bean* [1891] 1 Q.B.100; *Jay* v. *Budd* [1898] 1 Q.B. 12; *Porter* v. *Freudenberg* [1915] 1 K.B. 857, 887–888; *Laurie* v. *Carroll* (1958) 98 C.L.R. 310.

[7] *Russell* v. *Cambefort* (1889) 23 Q.B.D. 526; *Western National Bank* v. *Perez* [1891] 1 Q.B. 304.

[8] Ord. 81, r. 1.

nership business there; and the writ is deemed to have been duly served on the firm, even if all the individual partners are abroad,[9] and even if they are all foreigners.[10] If the firm is duly served in England under this rule, leave may be given to serve a partner abroad under Order 11, r. 1(1)(c), on the ground that he is a necessary or proper party to the action.[11] Execution of the judgment can only issue against the property in England of the partnership or of individual partners who are served in England or (with leave) abroad, or who submit to the jurisdiction.[12]

Corporations

When is a corporation "present" in England? The presence of a corporation, like its nationality or domicile or residence, is to some extent a fiction; but under the Companies Act 1948 a corporation is deemed to be present in England for purposes of service of process in a number of situations.

If the company is registered in England under the Companies Act 1948 or any other Act, it is present in England, even if it only carries on business abroad, and service of a writ can always be effected by leaving it at, or sending it by post to, the company's registered office in England.[13] Similarly, if a company registered in Scotland carries on business in England, a writ may be served on it by leaving it at, or sending it by post to, the company's principal place of business in England, with a copy to the company's registered office in Scotland.[14]

If the company is incorporated outside Great Britain and establishes a place of business in Great Britain, it must file with the Registrar of Companies the name and address of a person resident in Great Britain who is authorised to accept service of process on behalf of the company.[15] In that case, any process is sufficiently served if it is addressed to the person whose name has been delivered to the Registrar and left at or sent by post to the address which has been so delivered,[16] even though the company no longer carries on business in Great Britain.[17] If the company defaults in this obligation, or if the person named dies or ceases to reside in Great Britain or refuses to accept service on behalf of the company or for any reason cannot be served, process may be served by leaving it at, or sending it by post to, any place of business established by the company in Great Britain,[18] so long as the company still carries on business from that place.[19]

---

[9] Ord. 81, r. 3.
[10] *Worcester etc. Banking Co.* v. *Firbank* [1894] 1 Q.B. 784. Contrast *Von Hellfield* v. *Rechnitzer* [1914 1 Ch. 748, where the firm did not carry on business in England.
[11] *West of England Steamship Owners Association* v. *John Holman & Sons* [1957] 3 All E.R. 421. Alternatively, the plaintiff may sue all the partners individually "trading as . . . " (the firm name): *ibid.* For Ord. 11, r. 1(1)(c), see *post*, p. 70.
[12] Ord. 81, r. 5.
[13] Companies Act 1948, s.437(1).
[14] *Ibid.* s.437(2) and (3).
[15] *Ibid.* s.407(1)(c).
[16] *Ibid.* s.412.
[17] *Sabatier* v. *Trading Co.* [1927] 1 Ch. 495.
[18] Companies Act 1948, s.412, proviso.
[19] *Deverall* v. *Grant Advertising Inc.* [1955] Ch. 111.

The earliest of these statutory provisions for serving process on corporations incorporated outside England was first enacted in 1907. They seem to cover the ground adequately. However, there is a line of cases dating from 1872 to 1936, under which a foreign corporation could at common law be treated as being present in England for the purposes of jurisdiction *in personam* if it carried on business in England. Order 65, r. 3, of the Rules of the Supreme Court[20] provides that service of the writ may be effected by leaving a copy with the chairman, president, secretary, treasurer or other similar officer of the corporation, unless provision for service of the writ is otherwise made by any enactment. It was under this rule that foreign companies carrying on business in England could be served with process.

When in 1907 foreign corporations were first compelled to file with the Registrar of Companies the name and address of a person authorised to accept service of process on behalf of the corporation if they established a place of business in Great Britain,[21] it might have been expected that Order 65, r. 3, would cease to apply to such corporations, and that the cases on what constitutes carrying on business at common law would become obsolete. But, curiously enough, the point seems never to have been argued until 1977, when it was held that Order 65, r. 3 does not apply if it is possible to proceed under the Companies Act 1948.[22] So we have probably heard the last of the cases on carrying on business in England at common law.

SUBMISSION

A person who would not otherwise be subject to the jurisdiction of the court in an action *in personam* may preclude himself by his own conduct from objecting to the jurisdiction, and thus give the court jurisdiction over him which, but for his submission, it would not possess.

This submission may take place in various ways. A person who begins an action as plaintiff in general gives the court jurisdiction to entertain a counterclaim by the defendant in some related matter, but not an action on an independent ground.[23] A person who appears voluntarily as defendant submits to the jurisdiction even though he is out of England at the time of issue and service of the writ. He may, for instance, instruct his solicitor to accept service on his behalf; and if his solicitor indorses on the writ a statement that he accepts service on behalf of the defendant, the writ is deemed to have been duly served on him.[24] Or he may acknowledge service, in which case also the writ is deemed to have been duly served on him.[25] But

---

[20] Formerly Ord. 9, r. 8, which in turn re-enacted s.16 of the Common Law Procedure Act 1852.
[21] Companies Act 1907, s.35; now Companies Act 1948, s.407(1)(c); *ante*, p. 66.
[22] *The Theodohos* [1977] 2 Lloyd's Rep. 428; followed in *The Vrontados* [1982] 2 Lloyd's Rep. 241.
[23] *South African Republic* v. *Compagnie Franco-Belge du Chemin de Fer du Nord* [1897] 2 Ch. 487; [1898] 1 Ch. 190; *Factories Insurance Co.* v. *Anglo-Scottish Insurance Co.* (1913) 29 T.L.R. 312; *High Commissioner for India* v. *Ghosh* [1960] 1 Q.B. 134.
[24] Ord. 10, r. 1(4).
[25] Ord. 10, r. 1(5).

a person who appears merely to contest the jurisdiction of the court does not submit thereto.[26]

Submission may also be inferred from the terms of a contract. A contract may provide that the English court shall have jurisdiction to hear and determine any action in respect of the contract, and that process may be served on the defendant or on his agent to accept service. If the agent is present in England, the defendant is deemed to submit to the jurisdiction, and service may be effected on the agent as of right.[27] But if the agent is abroad, then leave must be obtained for service out of the jurisdiction under the provisions of Order 11, r. 1(1) of the Rules of the Supreme Court[28], unless service is permitted without leave under Order 11, r. 1(2).

Finally, it must be emphasised that the principle of submission only applies to actions *in personam*: it does not apply, for instance, to petitions for a decree of divorce or nullity of marriage.[29]

EXTENDED JURISDICTION UNDER THE RULES OF THE SUPREME COURT

If the defendant is not in England and served there with the writ and does not submit to the jurisdiction, the court has no jurisdiction at common law to entertain an action *in personam* against him. Sections 18 and 19 of the Common Law Procedure Act 1852 modified this principle of the common law and gave the court a discretionary power to permit service out of the jurisdiction. The power to do so is now contained mainly in Order 11, r. 1(1) of the Rules of the Supreme Court, made by the judges under statutory authority. Before we consider the specific cases in which this discretionary power may be exercised, certain principles of general application must first be stated.[30]

(1) There is an essential difference between cases where the defendant is in England and served there with the writ, or where he submits to the jurisdiction, and the cases about to be considered. If he is in England, or submits to the jurisdiction, the plaintiff may proceed as of right; but under Order 11, r. 1(1) the jurisdiction of the court is essentially discretionary, and will only be exercised in a proper case. Four cardinal points have been emphasised in the decided cases as to how this jurisdiction should be exercised. First, the court ought to be exceedingly careful before it allows a writ to be served on a foreigner out of England. Secondly, if there is any doubt in the construction of any of the sub-heads of Order 11, r. 1(1), that doubt ought to be resolved in favour of the defendant. Thirdly, since applications for leave are made *ex parte*, that is to say, in the absence of the defendant, the plaintiff must make a full and fair disclosure of all the facts of the

---

[26] *Re Dulle's Settlement (No. 2)* [1951] Ch. 842.
[27] *Tharsis Sulphur Co.* v. *Société des Métaux* (1889) 58 L.J.Q.B. 435; *Montgomery, Jones & Co.* v. *Liebenthal & Co.* [1898] 1 Q.B. 487; Ord. 10, r. 3(1).
[28] Ord. 10, r. 3(2).
[29] Domicile and Matrimonial Proceedings Act 1973, s.5(2) and (3); *post*, pp. 190, 208.
[30] See generally Collins (1972) 21 I.C.L.Q. 656.

case.[31] Fourthly, the court will refuse leave if the case is within the letter but outside the spirit of the rule.[32]

(2) In exercising its jurisdiction under Order 11, r. 1(1), the court will consider whether England is the *forum conveniens*,[33] where the witnesses are and what law governs. If the parties have agreed that the dispute between them shall be referred to the exclusive jurisdiction of a foreign court, leave will usually be refused.[34]

(3) An action may fall within more than one of the sub-heads of Order 11, r. 1(1).

(4) It is also provided that leave to serve the writ out of the jurisdiction shall not be granted unless it is made "sufficiently to appear" to the court that the case is a proper one for such service.[35] This means that the plaintiff must do more than make out a prima facie case; but it does not mean that he must satisfy the court beyond all reasonable doubt that he has a good case and that it can be brought within one of the sub-heads of the rule.[36] At this interlocutory stage it is not the function of the court to try the merits.

We now proceed to state, and comment on where necessary, the various sub-heads of Order 11, r. 1(1). Some of these sub-heads were amended in 1983 in consequence of the Civil Jurisdiction and Judgments Act 1982. The opportunity was taken to amend some others whose interpretation had caused difficulty, and to re-arrange them all in a more logical and scientific order.

General

(a) If relief is sought against a person domiciled within the jurisdiction.[37]

"Domicile" here and throughout Order 11, rule 1 is to be determined not in accordance with the strict rules of common law but in accordance with the provisions of sections 41–46 of the Civil Jurisdiction and Judgments Acts 1982.[38]

(b) If an injunction is sought ordering the defendant to do or refrain from doing anything within the jurisdiction (whether or not

---

[31] *Société Générale de Paris* v. *Dreyfus Bros.* (1885) 29 Ch.D. 239; 242–243; (1887) 37 Ch.D. 215; 224–225; *The Hagen* [1908] P. 189, 201; *Re Schintz* [1926] Ch. 710, 716–717.
[32] *Johnson* v. *Taylor Bros.* [1920] A.C. 144, 153; *Rosler* v. *Hilbery* [1925] Ch. 250, 259–260; *George Monro Ltd.* v. *American Cyanamid Corporation* [1944] K.B. 432, 437, 442; *Beck* v. *Value Capital Ltd.* (*No. 2*) [1978] 1 W.L.R. 6.
[33] *Société Générale de Paris* v. *Dreyfus Bros.*, *supra*; *Rosler* v. *Hilbery*, *supra*; *Kroch* v. *Rossell* [1937] 1 All E.R. 725.
[34] *Re Schintz* [1926] Ch. 710; *Mackender* v. *Feldia* [1967] 2 Q.B. 590; contrast *Evans Marshall & Co. Ltd.* v. *Bertola S.A.* [1973] 1 W.L.R. 349.
[35] Ord. 11, r. 4(2).
[36] *Hemelryck* v. *William Lyall Shipbuilding Co.* [1921] 1 A.C. 698; *The Brabo* [1949] A.C. 326; *Vitkovice Horni, etc.* v. *Korner* [1951] A.C. 869.
[37] Ord. 11, r. 1(1)(a).
[38] Ord. 11, r. 1(4). See *post*, pp. 79–81.

damages are also claimed in respect of a failure to do or the doing of that thing).[39]

The injunction need not be the only relief sought, but it must be the substantial relief sought: leave will be refused if the claim for an injunction is not made bona fide, but merely to bring the case within the sub-head.[40] Leave will also be refused if a foreign court can more conveniently deal with the question,[41] or if there is no real ground to anticipate repetition of the action complained of,[42] or if the injunction cannot be made effective in England.[43]

The Court of Appeal has recently developed a practice whereby the court may grant an interlocutory injunction (known as a *Mareva* injunction)[44] to restrain a defendant from removing his assets out of the jurisdiction. This power cannot be exercised if the defendant is not amenable to the jurisdiction of the court independently of the claim for an injunction. If he is not served with a writ in England and does not submit, the plaintiff must bring his case within one of the other sub-heads of Order 11, r. 1(1); it is not sufficient for him merely to rely on the claim for an injunction to give the court jurisdiction under this sub-head.[45]

(c) If the claim is brought against a person duly served within or out of the jurisdiction, and a person out of the jurisdiction is a necessary or proper party thereto.[46]

This sub-head is very important, and has given rise to much litigation. It has been amended so as to remove the requirement that the first defendant must be duly served within the jurisdiction, which caused some difficulty. The most obvious cases to which it applies are cases where joint debtors or joint tortfeasors are alleged to be liable to the plaintiff[47]; or where the plaintiff has alternative claims against two persons, *e.g.* a claim against a principal for breach of contract, and against an agent for breach of warranty of authority.[48] It enables the court to assume jurisdiction against an absent defendant over whom, if the action had been brought against him alone, the court would have no jurisdiction,[49] *e.g.* an action for a tort committed abroad.[50] The plaintiff or his solicitor must state in his affidavit the

---

[39] Ord. 11, r. 1(1)(*b*).

[40] *De Bernales* v. *New York Herald* 1893 2 Q.B. 97n.; *Watson* v. *Daily Record* [1907] 1 K.B. 853; contrast *Dunlop Rubber Co. Ltd.* v. *Dunlop* [1921] 1 A.C. 367.

[41] *Société Générale de Paris* v. *Dreyfus Bros.* (1887) 37 Ch.D. 215; *Rosler* v. *Hilbery* [1925] Ch. 250.

[42] *De Bernales* v. *New York Herald* [1893] 2 Q.B. 97n.; *Watson* v. *Daily Record* [1907] 1 K.B. 853.

[43] *Marshall* v. *Marshall* (1888) 38 Ch.D. 330.

[44] After *Mareva Compania Naviera S.A.* v. *International Bulkcarriers S.A.* [1975] 2 Lloyd's Rep. 509.

[45] *The Siskina* v. *Distos Compania Naviera S.A.* [1979] A.C. 210. But for cases where the defendant is "domiciled" within the EEC, see Civil Jurisdiction and Judgments Act 1982, s.25, and *post*, p. 88.

[46] Ord. 11, r. 1(1)(*c*).

[47] *Williams* v. *Cartwright* [1895] 1 Q.B. 142.

[48] *Massey* v. *Heynes* (1888) 21 Q.B.D. 330.

[49] *Williams* v. *Cartwright* [1895] 1 Q.B. 142.

[50] *The Duc d'Aumale* [1903] P. 18.

grounds for his belief that there is as between the plaintiff and the persons on whom the writ has been served a real issue which the plaintiff may reasonably ask the court to try.[51] If it is clear that the action against the first defendant is bound to fail, leave will be refused.[52]

The person whom it is sought to serve out of the jurisdiction must be a necessary or proper party to the action. These terms are alternative, and a person may be a proper party although he is not a necessary party. The question whether B is a proper party to an action against A is simply answered: suppose both A and B had been in England, would they both have been proper parties to the action? If they would, and only one of them, A, is in England, then B is a proper party, and leave may be given to serve him out of the jurisdiction.[53] For instance, if defective goods are manufactured by B abroad, and supplied to A in England, and by him sold to the plaintiff, he can bring an action for breach of contract against A and for the tort of negligence against B.[54]

Contract

(d) If the claim is brought to enforce, rescind, dissolve, annul, or otherwise affect a contract,[55] or to recover damages or obtain other relief in respect of the breach of a contract, being (in either case) a contract which
  (i) was made within the jurisdiction, or
  (ii) was made by or through an agent trading or residing within the jurisdiction on behalf of a principal trading or residing out of the jurisdiction, or
  (iii) is by its terms or by implication governed by English law; or
  (iv) contains a term to the effect that the High Court shall have jurisdiction to hear any action in respect of the contract.[56]

This sub-head is very important: and its four branches require separate discussion.

(i) A contract concluded by postal correspondence is made where the letter of acceptance is posted.[57] The same is the case if the contract is made by telegram.[58] But if the parties use "instantaneous" means of communica-

---

[51] Ord. 11, r. 4(1)(d).
[52] The Brabo [1949] A.C. 326.
[53] Massey v. Heynes (1888) 21 Q.B.D. 330, 338; The Elton [1891] P. 265; Osterreichische Export etc. Co. v. British Indemnity Co. Ltd. [1914] 2 K.B. 747.
[54] Cf. The Manchester Courage [1973] 1 Lloyd's Rep. 386; Adastra Aviation Ltd. v. Airparts (N.Z.) Ltd. [1964] N.Z.L.R. 393; Pratt v. Rural Aviation Ltd. [1969] N.Z.L.R. 46.
[55] An action for a declaration that a contract has been frustrated is a claim which "otherwise affects" a contract within the meaning of this sub-head: B.P. Exploration (Libya) Ltd. v. Hunt [1976] 1 W.L.R. 788.
[56] Ord. 11, r. 1(1)(d).
[57] Wansborough Paper Co. Ltd. v. Laughland [1920] W.N. 344; Benaim v. Debono [1924] A.C. 514, 520; Clarke v. Harper and Robinson [1938] N.Ir. 162.
[58] Cowen v. O'Connor (1888) 20 Q.B.D. 640; Lewis Construction Co. Ltd. v. M. Tichauer S.A. [1966] V.R. 341.

72 JURISDICTION IN ACTIONS IN PERSONAM

tion, *e.g.* telephone or telex, the contract is made where the acceptance is communicated to the offeror.[59]

(ii) This includes not only contracts made by agents but also contracts made through agents who have no authority to make contracts, but only to obtain orders and transmit them to the foreign principal for acceptance or rejection.[60] Order 10, r. 2, provides an alternative method of service if the conditions laid down in (ii) are satisfied and also two further conditions, namely that the contract was made in England, and that the agent's authority has not been determined and he is still in business relations with his principal. The method is to issue the writ against the principal and serve it with leave of the court on the agent in England.

(iii) This means that English law is the proper law of the contract. The rules for ascertaining the proper law of a contract are fully considered elsewhere in this book[61] and there is no need to repeat here what is there said, except to point out that if the plaintiff has alternative remedies in contract and tort upon the same facts, he can choose his remedy. Thus, where the plaintiff was employed abroad under a contract governed by English law, and sustained personal injuries abroad in the course of his employment there, he was allowed to serve the writ on his employers out of the jurisdiction in an action for breach of an implied term in the contract, even though the facts also gave rise to a claim in tort, for which leave would have been refused because the tort was not committed in England.[62]

(iv) We have already seen[63] that submission to the jurisdiction of the court may be inferred from the terms of a contract; and that, if one party to a contract nominates a person who is in England as his agent to accept service of process on his behalf, service may be effected on the agent as of right.[64] But if the nominated agent is abroad, service can only be effected on him with the leave of the court under this sub-head.[65]

(e) If the claim is brought in respect of a breach committed within the jurisdiction of a contract made within or out of the jurisdiction, and irrespective of the fact, if such be the case, that the breach was preceded or accompanied by a breach committed out of the jurisdiction that rendered impossible the performance of so much of the contract as ought to have been performed within the jurisdiction.[66]

---

[59] *Entores Ltd.* v. *Miles Far East Corporation* [1955] 2 Q.B. 327; approved by the House of Lords in *Brinkibon Ltd.* v. *Stahag Stahl G.m.b.H.* [1982] 2 A.C. 34, at least as a general rule.

[60] *National Mortgage and Agency Co. of New Zealand* v. *Gosselin* (1922) 38 T.L.R. 832.

[61] *Post*, Chap. 15.

[62] *Matthews* v. *Kuwait Bechtel Corporation* [1959] 2 Q.B. 57.

[63] *Ante*, p. 68.

[64] Ord. 10, r. 3(1).

[65] See *Unterweser Reederi G.m.b.H.* v. *Zapata Offshore Co.* [1968] 2 Lloyd's Rep. 158. For the sequel in the American courts, see *M/S Bremen* v. *Zapata Offshore Co.* 407 U.S. 1 (1972), where the English jurisdiction clause was upheld. See on this case Collins (1971) 20 I.C.L.Q. 530; (1973) 22 I.C.L.Q. 329; Kahn-Freund (1977) 26 I.C.L.Q. 825, 836–837.

[66] Ord. 11, r. 1(1)(*e*). The last words of the sub-head, from "and irrespective of the fact" onwards, were added in 1921 to overcome the decision of the House of Lords in *Johnson* v. *Taylor* [1920] A.C. 144. See *post*, p. 74.

This sub-head is also very important, and has given rise to much litigation.

A contract may be broken in one of three ways, namely by express repudiation, implied repudiation, or failure to perform.

Breach by express repudiation occurs when one party informs the other that he no longer intends to perform the contract. If X who is abroad writes a letter of repudiation to A in England, the breach is not committed in England.[67] On the other hand, if X who is abroad sends his agent to England, or writes to his agent who is in England, instructing him to repudiate a contract with A who is in England, and the agent does so, e.g. by letter posted in England, then the breach is committed in England.[68]

Breach by implied repudiation occurs when one party does an act which is inconsistent with the contract, for instance, when X promises to sell a house to A but sells it to B instead. Although there is no authority on the point, the breach in such a case presumably occurs where the inconsistent act is done.

The normal form of breach is the failure by one party to perform one or more of his obligations under the contract. In such a case it is not necessary that the whole contract was to be performed in England by both parties thereto, but it is necessary that some part of it was to be performed in England and that there has been a breach of that part.[69] It is not sufficient if the contract or part of it might be performed either in England or abroad; it is necessary that the contract or part of it was to be performed in England and not elsewhere.[70] The contract need not contain an express term providing for performance in England.[71] It is enough if the court can gather that this was the intention of the parties by construing the contract in the light of the surrounding circumstances, including the course of dealing between the parties.[72] In most of the reported cases, the breach complained of was the failure to pay money, a matter in which it is especially difficult to determine the place of performance in the absence of an express term in the contract. "The general rule is that where no place of payment is specified, either expressly or by implication, the debtor must seek out his creditor."[73] But this is only a general rule and, as stated, it only applies where no place of payment is expressed or implied in the contract. It certainly does not mean that a creditor can confer jurisdiction on the English

---

[67] *Cherry v. Thompson* (1872) L.R. 7 Q.B. 573, 579; *Holland v. Bennett* [1902] 1 K.B. 867, both approved by the Privy Council in *Martin v. Stout* [1925] A.C. 359, 368–369; but see *Cooper v. Knight* (1901) 17 T.L.R. 299.

[68] *Mutzenbecher v. La Aseguradora Espanola* [1906] 1 K.B. 254; *Oppenheimer v. Louis Rosenthal & Co. A/G* [1937] 1 All E.R. 23.

[69] *Rein v. Stein* [1892] 1 Q.B. 753.

[70] *Bell & Co. v. Antwerp London and Brazil Line* [1891] 1 Q.B. 103; *The Eider* [1893] P. 119; *Comber v. Leyland* [1898] A.C. 524; *Cuban Atlantic Sugar Sales Corporation v. Compania de Vapores San Elefterio Lda.* [1960] 1 Q.B. 187.

[71] *Reynolds v. Coleman* (1887) 36 Ch.D. 453.

[72] *Rein v. Stein* [1892] 1 Q.B. 753; *Fry & Co. v. Raggio* (1891) 40 W.R. 120; *Charles Duval & Co. Ltd. v. Gans* [1904] 2 K.B. 685.

[73] *The Eider* [1893] P. 119, 136–137, *per* Bowen L.J.

court merely by taking up residence in England after the making of the contract, thus making England the place of performance.[74]

In a contract of employment, wages or salary would normally be payable where the service is to be performed, in the absence of an express or implied term in the contract.[75] But if the employee is employed in only a nominal or consultative capacity, and is free to reside where he likes, his salary may be payable in England, if that is where he decides to live.[76] In a contract for services, it may be possible to infer that the fee or commission is payable at the contractor's usual place of business in England, even if the work is to be performed abroad.[77]

In a contract for the sale of goods by a seller in England to a buyer abroad, it will, in the absence of a contractual term to the contrary, be easy to infer that the buyer's obligation was to pay for the goods in England.[78] The same is the case if a principal in England sends goods to an agent abroad to be sold by him on commission.[79] But it is otherwise if, on the true construction of the contract, the only duty of the foreign agent is to sell the goods and remit the proceeds to England from abroad in a specified manner, because it will be inferred that his duty is at an end when he makes the remittance.[80] If a foreign principal appoints an agent in England to sell his goods on commission, it is usually inferred that the commission is payable in England.[81]

The duties of the seller of goods under a c.i.f. contract are to ship the goods and deliver the shipping documents to the buyer. It is not his duty to deliver the goods to the buyer. Consequently, if a foreign seller under such a contract ships goods which are found to be defective when they arrive in England,[82] or if he fails to ship them at all, the breach is not committed in England. In *Johnson* v. *Taylor*,[83] the English buyer sought to bring the foreign seller within the sub-head by alleging a failure to deliver the shipping documents in respect of goods which the seller had failed to ship. The House of Lords refused leave to serve notice of the writ out of the jurisdiction, because the substantial breach complained of was the failure to ship the goods, and this had occurred abroad. But this eminently reasonable decision was reversed by the concluding words of the sub-head, which were added in the following year.

---

[74] *Malik* v. *Narodni Banka Ceskoslovenska* [1946] 2 All E.R. 663.
[75] See *Malik* v. *Narodni Banka Ceskoslovenska, supra.*
[76] *Vitkovice Horni etc.* v. *Korner* [1951] A.C. 869.
[77] *Thompson* v. *Palmer* [1893] 2 Q.B. 80; *International Power and Engineering Consultants Ltd.* v. *Clark* (1964) 43 D.L.R. (2d) 394.
[78] *Robey & Co.* v. *Snaefell Mining Co. Ltd.* (1887) 20 Q.B.D. 152; *Fry & Co.* v. *Raggio* (1891) 40 W.R. 120.
[79] *Rein* v. *Stein* [1892] 1 Q.B. 753; *Charles Duval & Co. Ltd.* v. *Gans* [1904] 2 K.B. 685.
[80] *Comber* v. *Leyland* [1898] A.C. 524, a case "of a somewhat special character," *per* Stirling L.J. in *Charles Duval & Co. Ltd.* v. *Gans, supra,* at p. 691.
[81] *Hoerter* v. *Hanover etc. Works* (1893) 10 T.L.R. 103; *International Corporation Ltd.* v. *Besser Manufacturing Co.* [1950] 1 K.B. 488.
[82] *Crozier Stephens & Co.* v. *Auerbach* [1908] 2 K.B. 161; *Cordova Land Co. Ltd.* v. *Victor Bros. Inc.* [1966] 1 .L.R. 793.
[83] [1920] A.C. 144.

Tort

(f) If the claim is founded on a tort and the damage was sustained, or resulted from an act committed, within the jurisdiction.[84]

This sub-head formerly required that the tort should have been committed in England. Difficulties arose in interpreting this requirement, *e.g.* in cases where a negligent act was committed abroad and the resulting damage was sustained in England. These difficulties are removed by the altered wording of the sub-head, under which the courts are likely to reach the same result as the European Court reached on the interpretation of article 5(3) of the Brussels Convention on jurisdiction and the enforcement of judgments.[85]

As we have seen, if the plaintiff has alternative causes of action in contract and tort on the same facts, he may choose to rely on sub-heads (d), (e) or (f), at his option.[86]

Property

(g) If the whole subject-matter of the action is land situate within the jurisdiction (with or without rents or profits) or the perpetuation of testimony relating to land so situated.[87]

(h) If the claim is brought to construe, rectify, set aside or enforce an act, deed, will, contract, obligation or liability affecting land situate within the jurisdiction.[88]

There was at one time a tendency to construe this sub-head somewhat narrowly, but it now seems clear that "enforced" does not mean merely "specifically performed" but that the sub-head applies, *e.g.* to an action to recover rent due under a lease of land, or damages for breach of covenant.[89]

(i) If the claim is made for a debt secured on immovable property or is made to assert, declare or determine proprietary or possessory rights, or rights of security, in or over movable property, or to obtain authority to dispose of movable property, situate within the jurisdiction.[90]

This sub-head is new; it is a wider version of former rule 1(1)(*k*) and is modelled on article 5(8) of Schedule 4 to the Civil Jurisdiction and Judgments Act 1982.[91]

(j) If the claim is brought to execute the trusts of a written instrument, being trusts that ought to be executed according to English law and

---

[84] Ord. 11, r. 1(1)(*f*).
[85] Case 21/76 *Bier* v. *Mines de Potasse d'Alsace* [1976] E.C.R. 1735, *post*, pp. 82–83.
[86] *Matthews* v. *Kuwait Bechtel Corporation* [1959] 2 Q.B. 57; *ante*, p. 72.
[87] Ord. 11, r. 1(1)(*g*).
[88] Ord. 11, r. 1(1)(*h*).
[89] See *Agnew* v. *Usher* (1884) 14 Q.B.D. 78; *Kaye* v. *Sutherland* (1887) 20 Q.B.D. 147; *Tassell* v. *Hallen* [1892] 1 Q.B. 321; *Official Solicitor* v. *Stype Investments Ltd.* [1983] 1 W.L.R. 214.
[90] Ord. 11, r. 1(1)(*i*).
[91] *Post*, p. 88.

of which the person to be served with the writ is a trustee, or is for any relief or remedy which might be obtained in any such action.[92]

This sub-head has been amended so as to omit the requirement that the trust property must be situate in England. That requirement caused difficulty where a trustee sold the trust property and absconded abroad with the proceeds.[93]

    (k) If the claim is made for the administration of the estate of a person who died domiciled within the jurisdiction, or is for any relief or remedy which might be obtained in any such action.[94]

    (l) If the claim is brought in a probate action within the meaning of Order 76.[95]

Foreign judgments and arbitration awards

    (m) If the claim is brought to enforce any judgment or arbitration award.[95a]

This sub-head fills a lacuna in Order 11, rule 1(1) by enabling leave to be granted in a common law action on a foreign judgment or arbitration award against a debtor who remains out of England but has assets in England. This sub-head is all the more necessary now that section 34 of the Civil Jurisdiction and Judgments Act 1982 has abolished the rule that the original cause of action does not merge in a foreign judgment.[96] Section 34 thus prevents the plaintiff from bringing a fresh action in England on the original cause of action.

Taxation

    (n) If the claim is brought against a defendant not domiciled in Scotland or Northern Ireland in respect of a claim by the Commissioners of Inland Revenue for or in relation to any of the duties or taxes which have been, or are for the time being, placed under their care and management.[97]

Service abroad without leave

Order 11, rule 1(2)(a) provides that service of a writ out of the jurisdiction without the leave of the court is permissible provided that each claim made by the writ is a claim which by virtue of the Civil Jurisdiction and Judgments Act 1982 the court has power to hear and determine. Rule

---

[92] Ord. 11, r. 1(1)(j).
[93] *Winter* v. *Winter* [1894] 1 Ch. 421.
[94] Ord. 11, r. 1(1)(k).
[95] Ord. 11, r. 1(1)(l).
[95a] Ord. 11, r. 1(1)(m).
[96] *Post*, p. 107.
[97] Ord. 11, r. 1(1)(n).

1(2)(*b*) provides that service out of the jurisdiction without the leave of the court is also permissible provided that each claim made by the writ is a claim which by virtue of any enactment the High Court has power to hear and determine notwithstanding that the person against whom the claim is made is not in England or that the wrongful act, neglect or default giving rise to the claim did not take place in England. The enactments referred to include the Carriage by Air Act 1961, the Carriage by Air (Supplementary Provisions) Act 1962, the Carriage of Road Act 1965 (all of which implement international conventions) and section 6 of the Protection of Trading Interests Act 1980.[98] All these statutes were formerly listed in a sub-head of Order 11, rule 1(1). But it was thought that if, *e.g.* an international convention gave a plaintiff the right to sue a defendant who is not in England, that right ought not to be subject to the court's discretion.

2. *WHERE THE DEFENDANT IS "DOMICILED" IN THE EEC*

Introductory

In accordance with article 220 of the Treaty of Rome, a Convention on jurisdiction and the enforcement of judgments in civil and commercial matters was signed by the six original Member States of the EEC in September 1968 and came into force between them on February 1, 1973, together with a Protocol on Interpretation of 1971. Article 63 of the Convention declares that any State which becomes a Member of the EEC must accept the Convention (with or without adjustments), and this was a term of the United Kingdom's accession to the EEC in 1972. Negotiations between the original six and the three new Member States (the United Kingdom, the Republic of Ireland and Denmark) proceeded for six years in Brussels and resulted in an Accession Convention which was signed in October 1978. The accession of Greece was agreed in October 1982 with a minimum of amendments.

The United Kingdom of course took no part in drafting the original Convention, which reflects concepts and attitudes peculiar to the civil law, and parts of which are characterised by a rigidity which is quite alien to the spirit of the common law. Many changes designed to make it more palatable for United Kingdom consumption were effected in the Accession Convention, but not so many as the United Kingdom would have wished.

Part I of the Civil Jurisdiction and Judgments Act 1982 gives effect in the law of the United Kingdom to the Brussels Convention of 1968 as amended by the Accession Convention of 1978 ("the Convention"). The Act sets out in Schedule 1 the English text of the Convention and its Protocol, and in Schedule 2 the English text of the 1971 Protocol on Interpretation, both of which are to have the force of law in the United Kingdom.[99] Here we are concerned with the scope of the Convention (Title I) and with its provisions on jurisdiction (Title II). Its provisions on the recognition and enforcement of judgments (Title III) are considered in a later chapter.[1]

---

[98] *Post*, p. 122.
[99] s.2(1).
[1] *Post,* p. 130.

Interpretation

The Act provides that any question as to the meaning or effect of the Convention shall, if not referred to the European Court, be determined in accordance with the principles laid down by that court, of which judicial notice shall be taken.[2] The reports of Mr. Jenard on the original Convention and of Professor Schlosser on that Convention as amended by the Accession Convention may be considered by United Kingdom courts in interpreting the Convention.[3] They are published in the *Official Journal of the European Communities*.[4] The Jenard Report has had great influence on the interpretation of the Convention in national courts and in the European Court. The Schlosser Report will no doubt have a similar influence. It has great significance for the United Kingdom because many of the amendments sought by the United Kingdom during the accession negotiations were given effect to by "understandings" recorded in the Report and not by formal amendments to the Convention.

The 1971 Protocol sets out the conditions under which references may be made to the European Court for a preliminary ruling on the interpretation of the Convention where a national court considers that a decision on the question is necessary to enable it to give judgment.[5] In England, a court sitting in an appellate capacity *may* make such a reference, and the House of Lords *must* do so.

Courts of the original six Contracting States have referred several cases on the Convention to the European Court, which has given judgment in some 30 cases. An important question which has arisen several times is whether the Court should interpret the Convention according to an independent Convention concept or according to national law, *i.e.* according to the law of the national court requesting the preliminary ruling. The Court has nearly always preferred the former alternative.[6] It is obvious that this is the only way in which the Convention can be made to mean the same thing in all Contracting States. Only in one case has the court preferred to interpret the Convention in accordance with national law.[7]

Scope of the Convention

The scope of the Convention is very wide. It applies almost to the whole range of "civil and commercial matters," with a few exceptions listed in Article 1. These are as follows:

(1) the status or legal capacity of natural persons, rights in property arising out of a matrimonial relationship, wills and succession[8]; (2) bankruptcy and winding-up of insolvent companies[9]; (3) social security; (4) arbitration.

---

[2] s.3(1) and (2).
[3] s.3(3).
[4] O.J. 1979 No. C. 59 at pp. 1 and 71 respectively.
[5] Sched. 2, art. 3.
[6] See Case 29/76 *LTU* v. *Eurocontrol* [1976] E.C.R. 1541, which is the leading case. There are many others.
[7] Case 12/76 *Tessili* v. *Dunlop AG* [1976] E.C.R. 1473.
[8] See Case 143/78 *De Cavel* v. *De Cavel* (*No.* 1) [1979] E.C.R. 1055; Case 120/79 *De Cavel* v. *De Cavel* (*No.* 2) [1980] E.C.R. 731; Case 25/81 *W.* v. *H.* [1982] E.C.R. 1189.
[9] See Case 133/78 *Gourdain* v. *Nadler* [1979] E.C.R. 733.

The exception for arbitration means that such matters as judicial control over arbitrators, the enforcement of arbitration awards and (in the view of the British Government) the validity and effect of arbitration agreements are not within the Convention.[10]

General scheme of the Convention

The primary basis of jurisdiction is the "domicile" of the defendant within the Contracting State. In addition there are other special bases of jurisdiction; and there are certain cases where specified courts have exclusive jurisdiction regardless of domicile. Provision is also made for submission to the jurisdiction by contract or appearance, and for certain other procedural matters, including *lis alibi pendens* and jurisdiction to order provisional or protective measures. As a general rule the domicile of the plaintiff is irrelevant; he need not even be domiciled in a Contracting State.[11]

The jurisdictional rules of the Convention make two important departures of principle from English law as it was before the Act came into force. First, English courts cannot exercise jurisdiction over defendants domiciled in another Contracting State merely by virtue of the temporary presence of the defendant in England at the time of service of the writ. Secondly, where a defendant is outside England at that time and the English court has jurisdiction under the Convention, service of the writ outside England is no longer a matter for the discretion of the court but a matter of right.[12]

Domicile

Individuals. The Convention made no attempt to define "domicile" although it is the primary basis of jurisdiction. Article 52(1) provides that in order to determine whether a party is domiciled in the Contracting State whose courts are seised of the matter, the court shall apply its internal law. The traditional concept of domicile in English law would have been a quite unsuitable criterion for jurisdiction under the Convention, not only because it is sometimes so artificial and so difficult to ascertain, but also because it differs so much from the concept of domicile in the six original Contracting States, where it generally means something much the same as habitual residence. So section 41 of the Act provides a new definition of domicile which applies only for the purpose of the Act and the Convention. The effect is broadly as follows: an individual is domiciled in the United Kingdom (or a part of it) if he is resident in and has a substantial connection with the United Kingdom (or that part); if he is resident in the United Kingdom but has no substantial connection with any part of the United Kingdom he is domiciled in that part in which he is resident. Substantial connection is presumed from residence for three months or more, unless the contrary is proved.

It will only be rarely that domicile in a "place" within the United King-

---

[10] See Schlosser, para. 61.
[11] There are exceptions in articles 5(2), 8(1)(2), and 14(1).
[12] See R.S.C. Ord. 11, r. 1(2)(*a*), *ante*, p. 76.

dom will be relevant.[13] Section 41(4) provides that an individual is domiciled in a particular place in the United Kingdom if he is domiciled in the part of the United Kingdom in which that place is situated and is resident in that place.

If the defendant is not domiciled in any part of the United Kingdom, the English court may have to decide whether he is domiciled in another Contracting State in order to determine whether the Convention applies. The effect of article 52(2) is that in such circumstances the English court is to apply the law of that other State. But if the party is not domiciled in that other State by its law, or is alleged to be domiciled in a non-Contracting State, then his domicile will be determined by English law as the *lex fori*, which for this purpose is set out in section 41(7) of the Act. This provides that an individual is domiciled in a state other than a Contracting State if he is resident in, and has a substantial connection with, that state. There is no presumption from length of residence.

It would perhaps have been better to have defined domicile for the purposes of the Act and the Convention simply as habitual residence. That would have avoided the need for the rather complicated definitions in section 41. It would also have avoided adding one more jurisdictional factor to those already used by English law, *i.e.* domicile in the traditional sense, ordinary residence and habitual residence. It is true that the Convention sometimes contemplates that domicile differs from habitual residence.[14] But this has not prevented the European Court from using the two terms as if they were synonymous.[15]

Corporations and associations. Article 53(1) provides that the "seat" of a company or other legal person or association shall be treated as its domicile, and that in order to determine that seat the court shall apply its rules of private international law. Because the "seat" of a corporation is a term unknown in the law of the United Kingdom, section 42(3) and (4) of the Act provide for the determination of the seat of corporations and associations. The effect is that a corporation or association has its seat in the United Kingdom if (a) it was incorporated or formed under the law of a part of the United Kingdom and has its registered office or some other official address in the United Kingdom, or (b) its central management and control is exercised in the United Kingdom. It has its seat in a particular part of the United Kingdom if it has its seat in the United Kingdom and (a) it has its registered office or some other official address in that part; or (b) its central management and control is exercised in that part; or (c) it has a place of business in that part. This means that a company registered under the Companies Acts with its registered office in England may have its seat not only in England but also in Scotland if its central management and control is exercised there, and also in Northern Ireland if it has a place of business there. Section 42(5) provides for those cases where it is necessary to determine the "place" of the seat.

[13] See, *e.g.* arts. 5(2) (maintenance); 6(1) (co-defendants); 8(2) (insurance).
[14] *e.g.* in arts. 5(2), 15(3) and 59.
[15] Case 166/80 *Klomps* v. *Michel* [1981] E.C.R. 1593.

In order to determine the seat of a corporation or association which does not have its seat in the United Kingdom, section 42(6) provides that a corporation or association has its seat in a state other than the United Kingdom if (a) it was incorporated or formed under the law of that state and has its registered office or some other official address there, or (b) its central management and control is exercised in that state. But it does not have its seat in another Contracting State if the courts of that state would not regard it as having its seat there.[16]

Trusts. Article 52(3) provides that in determining the domicile of a trust the court shall apply its rules of private international law. Section 45 of the Act provides that a trust is domiciled in a part of the United Kingdom if the system of law of that part is the system of law with which the trust has its closest and most real connection. Of course it is artificial and novel to speak of the domicile of a trust at all. But it is a convenient form of shorthand.

General jurisdiction

Section 1 of Title II of the Convention (articles 2–4) sets out the general rule of jurisdiction. First, persons domiciled in a Contracting State should be sued in that State, and may be sued in another Contracting State only by virtue of the special rules in Sections 2–6.[17] Secondly, the Convention expressly blacklists certain "exorbitant" bases of jurisdiction which may not be used against persons domiciled in a Contracting State.[18] These include the rule of French law which enables French nationals to sue any defendant in France, and the rule of English law which enables persons temporarily present in England to be served there with a writ. But as against a person not domiciled in a Contracting State, the jurisdiction of the courts of each Contracting State is, apart from the exclusive jurisdictional provisions of article 16, subject to national law.[19] This means that as against, *e.g.* a New York resident, the rule of jurisdiction based on temporary presence in England and the rules in Order 11 will continue to apply.

Special jurisdiction

Section 2 (articles 5 and 6) sets out the special bases of jurisdiction under the Convention. These are additional to the primary basis of domicile. They only apply if the defendant is domiciled in a Contracting State other than the one in which he is sued. For if he is domiciled in that State, jurisdiction will be derived from his domicile there under article 2, and there is no need for any special jurisdiction; while if he is not domiciled in any Contracting State, the Convention does not apply and jurisdiction depends on national law, *i.e.* in England on service of the writ on the defendant during his temporary presence in England or on the rules in Order 11. Article

---

[16] s.42(7).
[17] Arts. 2(1), 3(1).
[18] Art. 3(2).
[19] Art. 4.

5 provides that a person domiciled in one Contracting State may be sued in another in the following cases:

(1) *Contract.* In matters relating to a contract, the courts for the place of performance of the obligation in question have jurisdiction. This very important head has given rise to great difficulty in interpretation, partly because there were significant discrepancies between the different language versions, all of them equally authentic, but mainly because it is not drafted with sufficient precision. In Case 14/76 *De Bloos* v. *Bouyer*[20] the European Court held, in the context of an exclusive sales and distribution agreement, that "the obligation in question" meant the obligation which is the basis of the plaintiff's claim. But in Case 133/81 *Ivenel* v. *Schwab*[21] the Court adopted a different approach in the context of a contract of employment. The Court, much influenced by the doctrine of "characteristic performance" in the EEC Convention on the Law Applicable to Contractual Obligations,[22] though it is not yet in force, held that the obligation in question was the one which was characteristic of the contract, namely the obligation to work.

In Case 12/76 *Tessili* v. *Dunlop AG*[23] the Court held that it was for the national court, applying its own rules of the conflict of laws, to determine where the obligation is to be performed. But this case was the first case on the Convention to reach the European Court, and the Court preferred to interpret the Convention in accordance with national law and not in accordance with an independent Convention concept. Since then the current of authority has flowed strongly in the opposite direction, and it may be that the Court will one day depart from its ruling in *Tessili* v. *Dunlop AG*.

If the parties agree on the place of performance, whether in writing or orally, that agreement will be effective to confer jurisdiction, provided at least that the agreement is not a sham.[24]

This head of jurisdiction applies even if the defendant denies the existence of the contract.[25]

(2) *Maintenance.* In matters relating to maintenance, the courts for the place where the maintenance creditor is domiciled or habitually resident will have jurisdiction.[26] This is considered in a later chapter.[27]

(3) *Tort.* In matters relating to tort, delict or quasi-delict, the courts for the place where the harmful act occurred have jurisdiction. The place where the harmful act occurred is, at the option of the plaintiff, either the

---

[20] [1976] E.C.R. 1497.
[21] [1982] E.C.R. 1891.
[22] *Post*, p. 299.
[23] [1976] E.C.R. 1473.
[24] Case 54/79 *Zelger* v. *Salinitri* [1980] E.C.R. 89.
[25] Case 38/81 *Effer* v. *Kantner* [1982] E.C.R. 825.
[26] Art. 5(2).
[27] *Post*, pp. 223–224.

place where the wrongful act occurred or the place where the damage was suffered.[28]

(4) *Civil claims in criminal proceedings.* As regards a civil claim for damages or restitution which is based on an act giving rise to criminal proceedings, the court seised of those proceedings has jurisdiction to the extent that it has jurisdiction under its own law.[29] So the English court hearing a criminal charge against a defendant domiciled in another Contracting State has jurisdiction to order him to make restitution under the Criminal Justice Act 1972.

(5) *Branches and agencies.* As regards a dispute arising out of the operations of a branch, agency or other establishment, the courts for the place where the branch, etc., is situated have jurisdiction.[30] The tests for determining whether an entity is a branch or agency are whether it is subject to the direction and control of the parent body and has the appearance of permanence.[31] The dispute must arise out of the operations of the branch, such as contracts into which it has entered.[32] This head of jurisdiction was intended to apply to disputes between the branch and third parties, not to disputes between the branch and the parent body.[33]

(6) *Trusts.* The courts of the Contracting State in which the trust is domiciled have jurisdiction in an action against a person in his capacity as settlor, trustee or beneficiary.[34] The trust must have been created by statute or by a written instrument; resulting or constructive trusts are not included. Nor are trusts arising under wills or intestacies, because wills and intestacies are outside the scope of the Convention.[35] Article 5(6) applies to disputes relating to the internal relationships of the trust, such as disputes between beneficiaries or between trustees and beneficiaries, and not to disputes relating to its external relations, such as the enforcement by third parties of contracts made by trustees.[36]

(7) *Co-defendants.* A person domiciled in another Contracting State may also be sued, where he is one of a number of defendants, in the courts for the place where any one of them is domiciled.[37] This jurisdiction is analogous to the "necessary and proper party" provisions of Order 11, rule 1(1)(c). But there is no room for discretion under article 6(1), and it allows a plaintiff to sue a foreign defendant in the domicile of another, less important, defendant. There must however be a connection between the claims made against each of the defendants.[38]

[28] Case 21/76 *Bier* v. *Mines de Potasse d'Alsace* [1976] E.C.R. 1735; [1978] Q.B. 708.
[29] Art. 5(4).
[30] Art. 5(5).
[31] Case 14/76 *De Bloos* v. *Bouyer* [1976] E.C.R. 1497; Case 139/80 *Blanckaert & Willems* v. *Trost* [1981] E.C.R. 819.
[32] Case 33/78 *Somafer* v. *Saar-Ferngas AG* [1978] E.C.R. 2183.
[33] *De Bloos* v. *Bouyer, supra,* at 1519.
[34] Art. 5(6).
[35] Art. 1; Schlosser, para. 52.
[36] Schlosser, para. 120. As to the domicile of a trust, see *ante,* p. 81.
[37] Art. 6(1).
[38] Jenard, p. 26.

(8) *Third parties*. A person sued as a third party in an action on a warranty or guarantee or in any other third party proceedings may be sued in the court seised of the original proceedings, unless these were instituted solely with the object of removing him from the jurisdiction of the court which would be competent in his case.[39]

(9) *Counterclaims*. In a counterclaim arising from the same contract or facts on which the original claim was based, the court in which the original claim is pending has jurisdiction.[40]

Jurisdiction in matters relating to insurance

The original Convention made special provision in Section 3 (articles 7–12) for jurisdiction in matters of insurance in order to protect the policy-holder, the supposedly weaker party. As Schlosser says,[41] the accession of the United Kingdom introduced a totally new dimension to the insurance business as it had hitherto been practised within the EEC. This was because the London insurance market has such a large share of world-wide insurance business, particularly in the international insurance of large risks. In such business the policy-holder is likely to be a powerful multi-national corporation which does not need the protection which the original Convention sought to give to an individual policy-holder insuring his house, his car or his life.

During the accession negotiations the United Kingdom sought to adapt the Convention to meet the new situation, and some changes were made. The result is the very complicated law contained in articles 7–12A, which have to be read with section 44 of the Act. These provisions are exclusive except that they are without prejudice to articles 4 and 5(5). The rules are still weighted heavily in favour of the policy-holder. He can sue the insurer in the courts for the place where he is domiciled as well as in the courts of the insurer's domicile.[42] In liability insurance or the insurance of a house or its contents, he can also sue in the courts for the place where the harmful event occurred.[43] But the policy-holder may be sued only in the courts of the Contracting State in which he is domiciled.[44] Moreover article 12(1)–(3) severely restricts the power of the parties (*i.e.* in practice the insurer) to contract out of these rules by means of a jurisdiction agreement in the contract of insurance. Article 12(4) and (5) (which were added by the Accession Convention) relax these restrictions if the policy-holder is not domiciled in a Contracting State, or in the case of the large risks listed in article 12A.

Jurisdiction over consumer contracts

Section 4 (articles 13–15) of the Convention contains special provisions for jurisdiction over consumer contracts in order to protect consumers, the

---

[39] Art. 6(2).
[40] Art. 6(3).
[41] Para. 136.
[42] Art. 8.
[43] Art. 9.
[44] Art. 11.

economically weaker party. These provisions are exclusive except that they are without prejudice to articles 4 and 5(5). "Consumer" and "consumer contracts" are defined in article 13(1). The effect of articles 13(2) and 14 (which have to be read with section 44 of the Act) is broadly that the consumer can only be sued in the Contracting State in which he is domiciled; but the consumer can sue the other party in the courts of his domicile or in the courts of the defendant's domicile, or in the courts for the place where the defendant has a branch or agency and the dispute arises out of the operations of the branch. Article 15 severely restricts the power of the parties (in practice the seller or lender) to contract out of these rules by means of a jurisdiction agreement in the contract.

Exclusive jurisdiction

Article 16 of the Convention provides for cases where courts in Contracting States are to have exclusive jurisdiction, regardless of the parties' domicile. This exclusive jurisdiction applies even if the defendant is not domiciled in a Contracting State.[45] The two most important cases of exclusive jurisdiction listed in article 16 are as follows:

(1) *Immovable property*. In proceedings which have as their object rights *in rem* or tenancies of immovable property, the courts of the Contracting State in which the property is situated have exclusive jurisdiction.[46] Such proceedings are those involving title or possession, and not those for damage caused to an immovable, nor do they include actions on the purely contractual aspects of a property transaction.[47] As to leases or tenancies, article 16(1) would include actions for forfeiture or possession and disputes between lessors and lessees as to the existence or interpretation of a lease[48]; but probably not actions for rent.[49]

(2) *Corporations*. In proceedings which have as their object the validity of the constitution, the nullity or the dissolution of companies or associations, or the decisions of their organs, the courts of the Contracting State in which the company or association has its seat have exclusive jurisdiction.[50] This head of jurisdiction does not include proceedings for the winding-up of insolvent companies, which are outside the scope of the Convention.[51] But it does include proceedings for the winding-up or reconstruction of solvent companies.[52] Section 43 of the Act provides for the determination of the seat of a company or association for the purposes of article 16(2). It has its seat in the United Kingdom (or a part of the United Kingdom) if (a) it was incorporated or formed under the law of a part of

---

[45] Art. 4.
[46] Art. 16(1).
[47] Schlosser, paras. 163, 167–172.
[48] Case 73/77 *Sanders* v. *Van der Putte* [1977] E.C.R. 2383.
[49] Jenard, p. 35.
[50] Art. 16(2).
[51] Art. 1.
[52] Schlosser, paras. 57–58.

the United Kingdom, or (b) its central management and control is exercised in a part of the United Kingdom.

Jurisdiction agreements

Article 17 deals with jurisdiction agreements. These are considered in the next chapter.[53]

Submission

Article 18 provides that apart from jurisdiction derived from other provisions of the Convention, a court of a Contracting State before whom a defendant enters an appearance shall have jurisdiction. This rule does not apply where appearance was entered solely to contest the jurisdiction, or where another court has exclusive jurisdiction under article 16. But it does apply where the parties have chosen another court under article 17.[54] Thus the provisions of article 18 prevail over those of article 17 in case of conflict.

Examination as to jurisdiction

Articles 19 and 20 require national courts to investigate of their own motion whether they have jurisdiction under the Convention if the case is principally concerned with a matter over which the courts of another Contracting State have exclusive jurisdiction under article 16, or if the defendant is domiciled in another Contracting State and does not enter an appearance. Moreover, the court must stay the proceedings if it is not shown that the defendant had been able to receive the document instituting the proceedings in sufficient time to enable him to arrange for his defence. This last provision is to be replaced by article 15 of the Hague Convention of 1965 on the Service Abroad of Judicial and Extra-Judicial Documents in Civil and Commercial Matters. This Convention is in force between the United Kingdom and all other Member States of the EEC except the Republic of Ireland. It is implemented in England by R.S.C. Order 11, rule 5.

The requirement that the court must act on its own motion is a novelty in English law with its adversarial procedure. It has had to be implemented by detailed Rules of Court.[55]

Lis alibi pendens and related actions

Articles 21–23 deal with these matters; they are considered in the next chapter.[56]

Provisional and protective measures

Article 24 provides that application may be made to the courts of a Contracting State for such provisional, including protective, measures as may

---

[53] *Post,* p. 100.
[54] Case 150/80 *Elefanten Schuh* v. *Jacqmain* [1981] E.C.R. 1671.
[55] See S.I. 1983 No. 1181 amending R.S.C. Ord. 6, r. 7 and adding Ord. 13, r. 7B.
[56] *Post,* p. 98.

be available under the law of that State, even if, under the Convention, the courts of another Contracting State have jurisdiction as to the substance of the matter. This article applies only to provisional measures in cases within the scope of the Convention.[57]

Typical of the protective measures contemplated by article 24 is the *saisie conservatoire* of French law, under which French courts have drastic powers to seize the defendant's property, put it under seal or freeze his banking account, even when the property or account is situated outside France. In that case of course the order of the French court, to be effective, would need to be enforced in the State where the property or account is situated. The courts of all the other original Member States have similar powers. The efficacy of such protective measures frequently depends on the element of surprise, so that they are often made *ex parte* and without notice to the defendant. But then they cannot be enforced under the Convention in other Contracting States, because article 27(2) provides that a judgment shall not be recognised if it was given in default of appearance, if the defendant was not duly served with the document instituting the proceedings in sufficient time for him to arrange for his defence.[58] Article 24 meets this situation by enabling protective measures to be applied for in, *e.g.* the courts of the State where the property is situated. It may be important in the interests of the plaintiff to achieve a surprise effect; but it is equally important in the interests of the defendant (and of third parties) that such measures should be rapidly brought to the notice of all concerned and that they should have the opportunity to take immediate countermeasures.

From our point of view, perhaps the most important "protective measures" known to English law are Anton Piller orders[59] and Mareva injunctions,[60] both of which are of recent origin. An Anton Piller order is an order for the inspection of premises to discover important documents or valuable chattels to which the plaintiff may be entitled. Such an order has been made even where the premises were situated abroad.[61] The Mareva injunction was invented by the Court of Appeal in 1975 and subsequently developed and refined. It is an interlocutory injunction restraining a defendant from removing his assets out of the jurisdiction pending trial. But it was held by the House of Lords in *The Siskina*[62] that a Mareva injunction could not be granted where the defendant is not amenable to the jurisdiction of the court independently of the claim for an injunction.

Strictly speaking there was no need to alter English law as laid down by the House of Lords in this case, for article 24 only applies to "such protective measures as may be available under the law of" the State applied to. But it would have been contrary to the spirit of the Convention, and would

---

[57] Case 25/81 *W.* v. *H.* [1982] E.C.R. 1189.
[58] See Case 123/79 *Denilauler* v. *Couchet Frères* [1980] E.C.R. 1553, where article 27(2) was applied to orders for protective measures.
[59] After *Anton Piller KG.* v. *Manufacturing Processes* [1976] Ch. 55.
[60] After *Mareva Compania S.A.* v. *International Bulkcarriers S.A.* [1975] 2 Lloyd's Rep. 509.
[61] *Cook Industries Inc.* v. *Galliher* [1979] Ch. 439.
[62] [1979] A.C. 210.

have looked extremely odd, if English (and Irish) courts were the only ones in the EEC which had no power to order protective measures unless they had jurisdiction in the main action. Accordingly section 25 of the Act provides that the High Court shall have power to grant interim relief where proceedings have been or are to be commenced in another Contracting State or another part of the United Kingdom, and these proceedings are or will be proceedings whose subject-matter is within the scope of the Convention. This in effect reverses the decision of the House of Lords in *The Siskina* and restores that of the Court of Appeal. Section 24 deals with cases where the jurisdiction of the court is doubtful, rather than non-existent.

Jurisdiction within the United Kingdom

Section 16 of the Act applies a modified form of the jurisdictional provisions of the Convention as between the different parts of the United Kingdom. This is set out in Schedule 4. It applies where (a) the subject-matter of the proceedings is within the scope of the Convention and (b) the defendant is domiciled in the United Kingdom or the proceedings are of a kind mentioned in article 16 (*i.e.* exclusive jurisdiction).[63] In interpreting any provision in Schedule 4 the court is to have regard to any relevant principles laid down by the European Court on Title II of the Convention and to the Jenard and Schlosser reports.[64]

The principal differences between the rules set out in Schedule 4 and those of the Convention set out in Schedule 1 Title II are as follows:

(1) The version of article 5(3) in Schedule 4 makes it clear that the jurisdiction applies where the tort is merely threatened.

(2) There is a new article 5(8), the effect of which is to give the English court jurisdiction in proceedings to enforce a debt secured on immovable property or to determine proprietary or possessory rights or rights of security in or over movable property, in each case where the property is situated in England.

(3) There is a new article 5A which confers jurisdiction, in proceedings which have as their object a decision of an organ of a company or association, on the courts of that part of the United Kingdom in which the company or association has its seat. The seat will be determined in accordance with section 43 of the Act.[65]

(4) There is no provision for insurance contracts, which therefore come within the general rule of domicile or the special provisions of article 5(1) (contract) or 5(5) (branch or agency).

(5) Article 13 (consumer contracts) is modified so as to exclude the references to advertising, and so as to make it clear that it does not apply to insurance.

(6) In article 17 (jurisdiction agreements) there is no requirement as to writing.

[63] s.16(1).
[64] s.16(3).
[65] *Ante,* p. 85.

(7) The provisions relating to *lis pendens* and related actions (articles 21–23) are omitted.

The effect of Schedule 4 article 3 is that English courts can no longer exercise jurisdiction based on the temporary presence in England of the defendant or on Order 11, if the defendant is domiciled in Scotland or Northern Ireland.

Section 10 of the Act deals with two miscellaneous allocations of jurisdiction in proceedings brought in the United Kingdom by virtue of article 5(6) (trust domiciled in the United Kingdom) or of article 14(1) (consumer domiciled in the United Kingdom).

CHAPTER 7

JURISDICTION IN ACTIONS *IN REM*

THE only action *in rem* known to English law is an Admiralty action[1] against a ship or other *res*, such as cargo or freight, connected with a ship, or against an aircraft or hovercraft.[2] Its primary object is to satisfy the plaintiff's claim out of the *res*. For the essence of the procedure *in rem* is that the *res* may be arrested by the Admiralty marshal, and sold by the court to meet the plaintiff's claim, provided it is proved to the satisfaction of the court. It does not follow that the successful plaintiff will recover the full amount of his claim, for this may exceed the amount of the proceeds of sale of the *res*, or there may be other claimants with a higher priority. But in most actions *in rem* no arrest in fact takes place, because the owner of the *res* arranges for bail or for some other security to be given. This cannot be done unless the owner acknowledges service and thereby submits to the jurisdiction,[3] in which case the action proceeds as an action *in personam* and the defendant's liability is not limited either to the amount of the bail or to the value of the *res*.[4] Hence, the threat of arrest often constitutes the occasion of, or inducement for, submission to jurisdiction *in personam* by the owner of the *res*.

A writ by which an action *in rem* is begun must be served on the property against which the action is brought.[5] If the action is brought against a ship, the writ must be affixed for a short time on any mast of the ship or on the outside of any suitable part of the ship's superstructure, and when the writ is removed, a copy must be left affixed on a sheltered, conspicuous part of the ship.[6] If the writ is served in any other way, *e.g.* by leaving a copy with the master, the service is invalid and will be set aside,[7] because other persons with an interest in the ship would not be sufficiently notified of the proceedings.

Unlike a writ beginning an action *in personam*, a writ beginning an action *in rem* cannot be served out of the jurisdiction. Therefore, as a general rule, the *res* must be in England at the time when the writ is

---

[1] A list of Admiralty actions is given in s.20 of the Supreme Court Act 1981.

[2] Actions *in rem* against aircraft are practically unknown, but an instance is afforded by *The Glider Standard Austria S.H. 1964* [1965] P. 463.

[3] See *ante*, p. 67.

[4] *The Dictator* [1892] P. 304; *The Gemma* [1899] P. 285; *The Dupleix* [1912] P. 8; *The August 8* [1983] 2 W.L.R. 419(P.C.).

[5] R.S.C., Ord 75, r. 8(1): unless the owner's solicitor endorses on the writ a statement that he accepts service of the writ on behalf of the owner, or the owner acknowledges service, in either of which cases the writ is deemed to have been duly served on him: Ord. 10, r. 1(4) and (5).

[6] Ord. 75, r. 11(1).

[7] *The Prins Bernhard* [1964] P. 117, 130–132.

served,[8] though it need not be in England at the time when the writ is issued. It is immaterial that the ship leaves the jurisdiction after the service of the writ but before the execution of the warrant of arrest.[9]

Before 1956 an action *in rem* could not be brought against any ship other than the one in respect of which the cause of action arose.[10] But under section 21(4) of the Supreme Court Act 1981, re-enacting section 3(4) of the Administration of Justice Act 1956, which was passed to implement the Brussels Convention of 1952 on the Arrest of Seagoing Ships,[11] such an action may be brought against a sister ship owned (at the time of the issue of the writ) by the person who (at the time when the cause of action arose) would have been liable on the claim in an action *in personam*.[12] There is no requirement that the sister ship must have been owned by that person at the time when the cause of action arose. But the action may be brought against one ship only, either against the one in respect of which the cause of action arose, or against a sister ship, but not both.[13] However, this does not prevent the plaintiff from issuing a writ against the ship in respect of which the cause of action arose and against several sister ships in the same ownership, and then serving it on one ship as soon as one whose value is sufficient to satisfy his claim comes within the jurisdiction.[14] The writ will expire unless it is renewed not later than twelve months after the date when it was issued.[15] The court has a discretionary power to renew the writ[16]; and Brandon J. has given guide-lines as to how the discretion should be exercised in the circumstances here envisaged.[17]

The Brussels Convention of 1968 on Jurisdiction and the Enforcement of Judgments, as amended and set out in Schedule 1 to the Civil Jurisdiction and Judgments Act 1982, will have only a minimal effect on the Admiralty jurisdiction *in rem*, for the following reasons. The most important part of the jurisdiction is derived from an international convention, the Brussels Convention of 1952 on the Arrest of Seagoing Ships. Article 57 of the Brussels Convention of 1968 provides that the Convention shall not affect any convention to which the Contracting States are or will be parties and which, in relation to particular matters, govern jurisdiction or the recognition or enforcement of judgments. Article 25(2) of the Accession Convention (printed immediately after article 57 in Schedule 1 to the Act) provides that the 1968 Convention as amended shall not prevent a court of a Contracting State which is a party to a convention on a particular matter from assuming jurisdiction in accordance with that convention, even where

---

[8] *Castrique* v. *Imrie* (1870) L.R. 4 H.L. 414, 448. This again is subject to the two exceptions noted in note 5 above.

[9] *The Nautik* [1895] P. 121.

[10] *The Beldis* [1936] P. 51.

[11] Cmnd. 8954 (1953). The text is printed in *British Shipping Laws*, Vol. 8, pp. 1438–1443.

[12] See *The St. Elefterio* [1957] P. 179; *The St. Merriel* [1963] P. 247; *The Andrea Ursula* [1973] Q.B. 265; *The I Congreso del Partido* [1978] Q.B. 500, 537–542, reversed [1983] 1 A.C. 244, but not on this point.

[13] *The Banco* [1971] P. 137.

[14] *The Berny* [1979] Q.B. 80; Supreme Court Act 1981, s.21(8).

[15] Ord. 6, r. 8(1).

[16] Ord. 6, r. 8(2).

[17] *The Berny, supra.*

the defendant is domiciled in another Contracting State which is not a party to that convention. Therefore English courts can continue to exercise the jurisdiction *in rem* conferred by the Brussels Arrest Convention of 1952, even if the owner of the ship is domiciled in a Contracting State which is not a party to that convention. But the Arrest Convention, as its name implies, applies only to ships. Accordingly, article 5(7) of the 1968 Convention (added by the Accession Convention) provides that claims for remuneration for the salvage of cargo or freight may be brought in the court under whose authority the cargo or freight (a) has been arrested or (b) could have been arrested, but bail or other security has been given: provided that the defendant has an interest in the cargo or freight or had such an interest at the time of the salvage.

The net result is therefore that the only types of Admiralty jurisdiction *in rem* which can no longer be exercised in cases where the owner of the *res* is domiciled in a Contracting State are (i) claims (other than claims for salvage) against cargo or freight; and (ii) claims against aircraft or hovercraft. All of these are extremely rare.

CHAPTER 8

STAYING ACTIONS—*LIS ALIBI PENDENS* AND FOREIGN JURISDICTION CLAUSES

THE court has an inherent jurisdiction, reinforced now by statute,[1] to stay an action in England or to restrain by injunction the institution or continuation of proceedings in a foreign court, whenever it is necessary to do so in order to prevent injustice. This jurisdiction is highly discretionary and is exercised with extreme caution.[2] The jurisdiction extends to all types of proceedings, including Admiralty actions *in rem*,[3] petitions in matrimonial causes[4] and probate or administration proceedings[5] as well as actions *in personam.*

The most common grounds for the intervention of the court are, first, that simultaneous actions are pending in England and in a foreign country between the same parties and involving the same or similar issues (*lis alibi pendens*); and, secondly, that the parties to a contract have agreed that all disputes between them shall be referred to the exclusive jurisdiction of a foreign court (foreign jurisdiction clause). But, as we shall see, the jurisdiction is not limited to these two heads. They will now be discussed in turn.

LIS ALIBI PENDENS

The court may be asked to stay an action in England, or to enjoin an action abroad, in two distinct situations: first, where the same plaintiff sues the same defendant in England and abroad; and, secondly, where the plaintiff in England is defendant abroad, or vice versa. The principles applicable to these two situations are the same, but their application differs in that, as we shall see, it requires a stronger case to induce the court to interfere in the second situation than it does in the first. It is therefore surprising that the power of the court to interfere in the second situation was established

---

[1] Supreme Court Act 1981, s.49(3); Civil Jurisdiction and Judgments Act 1982, s.49; *cf.* R.S.C. Ord. 18, r. 19.

[2] *McHenry* v. *Lewis* (1882) 22 Ch.D. 397, 406; *Peruvian Guano Co.* v. *Bockwoldt* (1883) 23 Ch.D. 225, 232; *Logan* v. *Bank of Scotland (No. 2)* [1906] 1 K.B. 141, 150; *Re Norton's Settlement* [1908] 1 Ch. 471, 479; *Cohen* v. *Rothfield* [1919] 1 K.B. 410, 413; *Sealey* v. *Callan* [1953] P. 135, 146; *Settlement Corporation* v. *Hochschild* [1966] Ch. 10, 15.

[3] *The Christianborg* (1885) 10 P.D. 141; *The Cap Blanco* [1913] P. 130; *The Marinero* [1955] P. 68; *The Soya Margareta* [1961] 1 W.L.R. 709; *The Abidin Daver* [1984] 2 W.L.R. 196 (H.L.).

[4] *Thornton* v. *Thornton* (1886) 11 P.D. 176; *Orr-Lewis* v. *Orr-Lewis* [1949] P. 347; *Sealey* v. *Callan* [1953] P. 135. But in matrimonial causes the court's inherent power to stay (though not abolished) is now reinforced by its statutory power (and sometimes duty) to stay in defined circumstances: see *post*, pp. 217–220.

[5] *Re Bonnefoi* [1912] P. 233.

as early as 1821,[6] but in the first situation not until 1882.[7] The court may stay the English proceedings, or restrain the foreign proceedings by injunction, or require the plaintiff to elect which proceedings he will pursue.[8]

When a court thus restrains foreign proceedings by injunction, it is not attempting to dictate to the foreign court, for "the injunction was not to the court, but to the party."[9] But as the effect of granting an injunction is to interfere with proceedings in another jurisdiction, "this power should be exercised with great caution to avoid even the appearance of undue interference with another court."[10] And since an injunction restraining proceedings in a foreign court may often be difficult to enforce, "there is no doubt that where the court has stayed one of the actions it has been most usually that in the English court."[11]

Before 1973, when as we shall see the House of Lords introduced a radical change into English law, the mere fact that the same plaintiff started proceedings against the same defendant in respect of the same cause of action in England and in a foreign country was not a ground for staying the English proceedings or restraining the foreign proceedings. In order to justify a stay, the defendant had to show that allowing both actions to continue would cause injustice to him and that staying or enjoining one of them would not cause injustice to the plaintiff. It was said that the court would be very slow to grant a stay because it could not tell what advantage there might be in preferring one court to another.[12] The result was that it was very difficult to obtain a stay. But now it is much easier, and it has been said that judicial chauvinism has given way to judicial comity.[12a]

If the plaintiff in England is defendant abroad, or the defendant in England is plaintiff abroad, the court was even more reluctant to stay the English proceedings, or to restrain the foreign proceedings, than it was where the same person is plaintiff in both countries.[13] This was said to be because the result of a stay or of an injunction would be to confine the party stayed

---

[6] *Bushby* v. *Munday* (1821) 5 Madd. 297; *Beckford* v. *Kemble* (1822) 1 S. & St. 7. See McClean (1969) 18 I.C.L.Q. 931.

[7] *McHenry* v. *Lewis* (1882) 22 Ch.D. 397.

[8] *The Christianborg* (1885) 10 P.D. 141, 152–153, *per* Baggallay L.J.

[9] *Love* v. *Baker* (1665) 1 Cas. in Ch. 67; *Bushby* v. *Munday* (1821) 5 Madd. 297, 306–307.

[10] *Cohen* v. *Rothfield* [1919] 1 K.B. 410, 413; *Settlement Corporation* v. *Hochschild* [1966] Ch. 10, 15.

[11] *The Christianborg* (1885) 10 P.D. 141, 153.

[12] *McHenry* v. *Lewis* (1882) 22 Ch.D. 397; *Peruvian Guano Co.* v. *Bockwoldt* (1883) 23 Ch.D. 225, 232; *Hyman* v. *Helm* (1883) 24 Ch.D. 531, 544; *St. Pierre* v. *South American Stores Ltd.* [1936] 1 K.B. 382; *Ionian Bank Ltd.* v. *Couvreur* [1969] 1 W.L.R. 781.

[12a] *The Abidin Daver* [1984] 2 W.L.R. 196, 203.

[13] *Hyman* v. *Helm* (1883) 24 Ch.D. 531; *Cohen* v. *Rothfield* [1919] 1 K.B. 410; *The Janera* [1928] P. 55; *The London* [1931] P. 14; *The Madrid* [1937] P. 40; *St. Pierre* v. *South American Stores Ltd.* [1936] 1 K.B. 382. Contrast *Smith Kline and French Laboratories Ltd.* v. *Bloch* [1983] 1 W.L.R. 730; and *British Airways Board* v. *Laker Airways Ltd.* [1984] Q.B. 142, where the foreign proceedings were restrained; and *The Abidin Daver, supra,* where the English proceedings were stayed.

or enjoined to the role of defendant in an action over which he would not have equal control.[14]

In 1936, Scott L.J. stated the principles on which the court acts in words which were much quoted and universally followed down to 1973:

> "(1) A mere balance of convenience is not a sufficient ground for depriving a plaintiff of the advantages of prosecuting his action in an English court if it is otherwise properly brought. The right of access to the King's court must not be lightly refused. (2) In order to justify a stay two conditions must be satisfied, one positive and the other negative: (a) the defendant must satisfy the court that the continuance of the action would work an injustice because it would be oppressive or vexatious to him or would be an abuse of the process of the court in some other way; and (b) the stay must not cause an injustice to the plaintiff. In both, the burden of proof is on the defendant."[15]

In 1973 however a bare majority of the House of Lords in *The Atlantic Star*,[16] reversing both the courts below, held that Scott L.J.'s formulation needed to be interpreted more flexibly. In that case, a collision occurred in dense fog in Belgian internal waters between the *Atlantic Star*, a Dutch ship owned by the defendants, and two barges, one Dutch, the other Belgian. Proceedings were brought in a Belgian court by the owners of the Belgian barge, the owners of cargo laden therein, the dependants of two deceased members of her crew, and by the owners of cargo laden in the Dutch barge. The owners of the Dutch barge issued a writ *in rem* in England and served it on the *Atlantic Star* when she called at an English port. They thought that their chances of success would be greater in England than in Belgium, because the Belgian court would be unlikely to overturn a surveyor's report which tended to exonerate the *Atlantic Star* from blame. The House of Lords by a majority ordered a stay. The House was invited to introduce into English law the Scottish doctrine of *forum non conveniens*, but unanimously decided not to do so. Instead, the majority relaxed the rules about staying by holding that Scott L.J.'s test of "vexation or oppression" should be interpreted more liberally in future.

In 1978, a differently constituted House of Lords in *MacShannon* v. *Rockware Glass Ltd.*[17] went considerably further and stayed an action in England although there was no *lis alibi pendens* at all. All except Lord Keith were in favour of discontinuing the use of the words "vexation and oppression" altogether on the ground, stated by Lord Salmon, that "the real test of stay or no stay depends upon what the court in its discretion considers that justice demands. I prefer this test to the test of whether the plaintiff has behaved 'vexatiously' or 'oppressively' on a so-called liberal interpretation of those words. I do not, with respect, believe that it is poss-

---

[14] *Cohen* v. *Rothfield, supra,* at p. 414.
[15] *St. Pierre* v. *South American Stores Ltd.* [1936] 1 K.B. 382, 398.
[16] [1974] A.C. 436.
[17] [1978] A.C. 795.

ible to interpret them liberally without emasculating them and completely destroying their true meaning."[18]

In *MacShannon's* case the plaintiff was a Scotsman resident in Scotland. He was injured in an accident at work in a factory in Scotland owned by his employers, a company registered in England. On the advice of the English solicitors to his London-based trade union, he brought his action in England and not in the natural forum (Scotland), because his solicitors believed that he would get higher damages in England and that proceedings in Scotland would take longer to come to trial. But when it was shown that medical and other expert witnesses were equally available in Scotland, and that therefore the comparative cost and inconvenience of a trial in England would be appreciably greater than those of a trial in Scotland, the House of Lords, reversing the majority decision of the Court of Appeal, unanimously ordered the English action to be stayed. If at the date when the writ was issued the plaintiff's home had been in England, or even in France,[19] the result might well have been different.

Lord Diplock restated the second of Scott L.J.'s two propositions as follows:

> "In order to justify a stay two conditions must be satisfied, one positive and the other negative: (a) the defendant must satisfy the court that there is another forum to whose jurisdiction he is amenable in which justice can be done between the parties at substantially less inconvenience and expense, and (b) the stay must not deprive the plaintiff of a legitimate personal or juridical advantage which would be available to him if he invoked the jurisdiction of the English court."[20]

The fact that the plaintiff will probably recover higher damages abroad than he would do in England may be a legitimate advantage to him if the foreign forum is a natural one.[21]

When "vexation or oppression" was the test, it was a subjective one: a bona fide belief by the plaintiff or his legal advisers that he would have an advantage in suing in England was sufficient. But under the new formulation the advantage must be a real one. It must be shown objectively to exist. A mere bona fide belief, however genuinely it may be held, is not enough.[22]

A defendant in England may be restrained from proceeding abroad even where there is no alternative forum in England.[23]

---

[18] At p. 819B.
[19] Cf. *Devine* v. *Cementation Co. Ltd.* [1963] N.Ir. 65, where the Court of Appeal refused to stay an action in Northern Ireland by a plaintiff whose home was in the Republic of Ireland, near the border, against his employers, an English company, for damages for personal injuries sustained in an accident at work in their factory in Scotland.
[20] At p. 812A-B.
[21] *Castanho* v. *Brown and Root Ltd.* [1981] A.C. 557; contrast *Smith Kline and French Laboratories Ltd.* v. *Bloch* [1983] 1 W.L.R. 730.
[22] *MacShannon* v. *Rockware Glass Ltd.* [1978] A.C. 795, *per* Lord Diplock at p. 812F-H; *cf. per* Lord Salmon at pp. 820E, 821A, and *per* Lord Keith at p. 829D-E.
[23] *Castanho* v. *Brown and Root Ltd.*, *supra*; *British Airways Board* v. *Laker Airways Ltd.* [1983] 3 W.L.R. 544.

One fundamental question remains: have the House of Lords in *Mac-Shannon* v. *Rockware Glass Ltd.* introduced into English law the Scottish doctrine of *forum non conveniens* which five years earlier in *The Atlantic Star* they unanimously refused to do? Before we can answer this question, we must first consider to what extent (if any) this doctrine is already part of English law.

First, there are a few reported cases in which leave to serve notice of the writ out of the jurisdiction under Order 11, r. 1(1) of the Rules of the Supreme Court has been refused because a foreign court could more conveniently deal with the matter.[24] But, as we have seen,[25] there is an essential difference between cases where the defendant is in England and served there with the writ, and cases under the highly discretionary jurisdiction conferred by Order 11.

Secondly, there are three reported cases, all decided within the three years 1906–1908, in which the court stayed an English action which it undoubtedly had jurisdiction to entertain (because the defendant was served with a writ in England), even in the absence of a *lis alibi pendens*. The best known of these cases is *Logan* v. *Bank of Scotland (No. 2)*,[26] where a Scottish schoolmaster brought an action in England against two directors of a Scottish company claiming £50 damages for misrepresentation alleged to have been made in the prospectus of the company. The two directors were both undischarged bankrupts and neither of them appeared. The plaintiff joined the Bank of Scotland as defendant on the ground that its name appeared on the prospectus as the company's bankers. The bank had its head office and most of its branch offices in Scotland and one branch in London. The decision of the case depended wholly on Scots law and mainly on the evidence of witnesses resident in Scotland. The inconvenience and extra expense of a trial in England would thus have been extreme; and not surprisingly the Court of Appeal stayed the action.

Evidently, this case (like its two companions) was of a very special character, and affords no justification for the suggestion[27] that English law has a doctrine of *forum non conveniens* comparable in scope and vitality to the Scottish and American doctrines.[28] Any such suggestion is quite inconsistent with cases like *Maharanee of Baroda* v. *Wildenstein*[29] and with the refusal of the House of Lords in *The Atlantic Star*[30] to introduce such a doctrine into English law.

But the question remains, did the House of Lords do so in *MacShannon* v. *Rockware Glass Ltd.*? They certainly had no such intention. Lord Salmon said: "This doctrine has never been part of the law of England. And, in my opinion, it is now far too late for it to be made so save by Act of Par-

---

[24] *Ante,* p.70.
[25] *Ante,* p.68.
[26] [1906] 1 K.B. 141. The other cases are *Egbert* v. *Short* [1907] 2 Ch. 205 and *Re Norton's Settlement* [1908] 1 Ch. 471.
[27] Inglis (1965) 81 L.Q.R. 380. *Cf.* McClean (1969) 18 I.C.L.Q. 931, 945–948.
[28] For the Scottish doctrine, see Anton, pp. 148–154. For the American doctrine, see Leflar, s.51.
[29] [1972] 2 Q.B. 283; *ante*, p.65.
[30] [1974] A.C. 436.

liament."[31] Lord Diplock said: "It would not be consonant with the traditional way in which judicial precedent has played its part in the development of the common law of England to attempt to incorporate holus-bolus from some other system of law, even so close as that of Scotland, doctrines or legal concepts that have hitherto been unrecognised in English common law."[32] But, after reformulating Scott L.J.'s second proposition as quoted above,[33] he added these significant words: "If the distinction between this restatement of the English law and the Scottish doctrine of *forum non conveniens* might on examination prove to be a fine one, I cannot think that it is any the worse for that."[34] And Lord Fraser said that the two tests "differ more in theoretical approach than in practical substance."[35]

Article 21 of the Brussels Convention on Jurisdiction and the Enforcement of Judgments provides that where proceedings involving the same cause of action and between the same parties are brought in the courts of different Contracting States, any court other than the court first seised shall of its own motion decline jurisdiction in favour of that court. Article 22 provides that where related actions are brought in the courts of different Contracting States, any court other than the court first seised may stay its proceedings. For the purposes of the article, actions are deemed to be related if they are so closely connected that it is expedient to hear and determine them together to avoid the risk of irreconcilable judgments resulting from separate proceedings. These two articles have no counterpart in Schedule 4 of the Civil Jurisdiction and Judgments Act 1982, which applies a modified version of the Convention as between the different parts of the United Kingdom.

FOREIGN JURISDICTION CLAUSES

In international business it is common for a contract to provide that all disputes between the parties arising out of the contract shall be referred to the exclusive jurisdiction of a foreign court. In such a case the court will stay proceedings brought in England in breach of such an agreement,[36] unless the plaintiff proves that it is just and proper to allow them to continue.[37] The burden of proof is on the plaintiff, and not, as in cases of *lis alibi pendens,* on the defendant. This is because the ground on which a stay is

---

[31] [1978] A.C. 795, at p. 817B.
[32] At p. 811B.
[33] *Ante*, p.96.
[34] At p. 812B. *Cf. The Abidin Daver* [1984] 2 W.L.R. 196, 203, *per* Lord Diplock.
[35] At p. 822G.
[36] *Law* v. *Garrett* (1878) 8 Ch.D. 26; *Austrian Lloyd S.S. Co.* v. *Gresham Life Insurance Society Ltd.* [1903] 1 K.B. 249; *Kirchner & Co.* v. *Gruban* [1909] 1 Ch. 413; *The Cap Blanco* [1913] P. 130; *The Eleftheria* [1970] P. 94; *Trendtex Trading Corporation* v. *Credit Suisse* [1982] A.C. 679. See Pryles (1976) 25 I.C.L.Q. 543; Kahn-Freund (1977) 26 I.C.L.Q. 825.
[37] *The Athenee* (1922) 11 Ll.L.R. 6; *The Fehmarn* [1958] 1 W.L.R. 159; *Evans Marshall & Co. Ltd.* v. *Bertola S.A.* [1973] 1 W.L.R. 349; *The Adolph Warski* [1976] 2 Lloyd's Rep. 241; *Carvalho* v. *Hull, Blyth (Angola) Ltd.* [1979] 1 W.L.R. 228 (where owing to a revolution in the foreign country the foreign court was a different court from that contemplated by the parties).

granted is not so much that there is injustice as that the court makes people abide by their contracts. If the plaintiff seeks leave to serve the writ out of the jurisdiction in disregard of a foreign jurisdiction clause, the burden of proof on him is of course much heavier. But even in this situation the court will sometimes grant leave and disregard the foreign jurisdiction clause.[38]

The validity of a foreign jurisdiction clause is a matter for the proper law of the contract of which it forms part, and so is its interpretation, in particular whether it provides for the exclusive jurisdiction of the foreign court, or merely that the parties will not object to the exercise of jurisdiction by that court,[39] and whether it covers claims in tort as well as claims in contract.[40] The proper law of the contract will usually, but not invariably, be the law of the country of the chosen foreign court.[41] On the other hand, the effect of the foreign jurisdiction clause is a matter for the *lex fori*. If in that law there is a prohibition against ousting the jurisdiction of the court in a particular context,[42] or lessening the liability of one of the parties,[43] no foreign jurisdiction clause can prevail against it. In English domestic law an example of the first type of statutory prohibition is section 141 of the Consumer Credit Act 1974, which provides that the county court shall have jurisdiction to hear and determine any action by the creditor or owner to enforce a consumer credit agreement, and that such an action shall not be brought in any other court. An example of the second type is article III paragraph 8 of the Hague-Visby Rules scheduled to the Carriage of Goods by Sea Act 1971.

In exercising its discretion whether or not to grant a stay, the court takes into account all the circumstances of the case, and in particular (1) in which country the evidence is available, and the effect of that on the relevant convenience and expense of a trial in England or abroad; (2) whether the contract is governed by the law of the foreign country in question, and if so, whether it differs from English law in any material respect; (3) with what country either party is connected, and how closely; (4) whether the defendants genuinely desire trial in the foreign country, or are only seeking procedural advantages; (5) whether the plaintiffs would be prejudiced by having to sue in the foreign court because they would be deprived of security for their claim, or be unable to enforce the judgment in their favour, or be faced with a time-bar not applicable in England, or for political, racial, religious or other reasons be unlikely to get a fair trial.[44]

Two contrasting cases (which are not easy to reconcile) illustrate the application of these principles. In *The Fehmarn*[45]:

---

[38] *e.g. Ellinger* v. *Guinness Mahon & Co.* [1939] 4 All E.R. 16; *Evans Marshall & Co. Ltd* v. *Bertola S.A., supra.*
[39] *Hoerter* v. *Hanover etc. Works* (1893) 10 T.L.R. 103; *Evans Marshall & Co. Ltd.* v. *Bertola S.A., supra.*
[40] *The Sindh* [1975] 1 Lloyd's Rep. 372; *The Makefjell* [1976] 2 Lloyd's Rep. 29.
[41] *Post*, p. 275.
[42] *Messageries Maritimes* v. *Wilson* (1954) 94 C.L.R. 577.
[43] *The Hollandia* [1983] 1 A.C. 565.
[44] *The Eleftheria* [1970] P. 94, 100, *per* Brandon J.
[45] [1958] 1 W.L.R. 159, criticised by Webb (1958) 7 I.C.L.Q. 599; Kahn-Freund (1977) 26 I.C.L.Q. 825, 851n.; Cheshire and North, p. 114n.

Under a Russian contract, turpentine was shipped from a Russian port to London in a German ship. The bill of lading contained a clause providing that all disputes should be judged in the U.S.S.R. according to Russian law. An English company, as holders of the bill of lading, brought an action *in rem* against the ship in England, alleging that the turpentine was contaminated on delivery. All the plaintiff's proposed witnesses resided in England. The German ship regularly traded to England and all the owners' proposed witnesses could conveniently be examined in England, except certain witnesses as to the condition of the railway wagons in which the turpentine was delivered to the ship. The Court of Appeal declined to stay the action.

On the other hand, in *The Eleftheria*[46]:

Plywood was shipped from a Roumanian port to England on board a Greek ship. The bills of lading provided that disputes should be decided in Greece according to Greek law. An English company, as holders of the bills of lading, brought an action *in rem* against the ship in England, claiming damages for breach of contract. Most of the evidence was available in England, but Greek law differed materially from English law in the relevant respects. The factors tending to rebut and reinforce the prima facie case for a stay were nicely balanced. Brandon J. stayed the action.

Even if the plaintiff alleges that the contract containing the foreign jurisdiction clause (*e.g.* an insurance contract) is voidable for non-disclosure of a material fact and that therefore the clause is not binding on him, the court will prima facie stay the English action[47]; but it might be otherwise if the contract is void, *e.g.* for mistake.[48]

Article 17 of the Brussels Convention on Jurisdiction and the Enforcement of Judgments deals with the formal validity and effect of jurisdiction clauses. The agreement must be either in writing or evidenced in writing or, in international trade or commerce, in a form which accords with practices in that trade or commerce of which the parties are or ought to have been aware.

If one or more of the parties is domiciled in a Contracting State and they have chosen the jurisdiction of a court in a Contracting State, that court has exclusive jurisdiction. If none of the parties is domiciled in a Contracting State, the courts of other Contracting States have no jurisdiction unless the chosen court declines jurisdiction. Similar provision is made for jurisdiction clauses in trust instruments.

Article 17 applies if the courts of more than one Contracting State are chosen by the parties.[49]

---

[46] [1970] P. 94.
[47] *Mackender* v. *Feldia* [1967] 2 Q.B. 590.
[48] *Ibid.*, at p. 598.
[49] Case 23/78 *Meeth* v. *Glacetal* [1978] E.C.R. 2133.

National law may not invalidate agreements by requiring additional formalities to those prescribed by article 17.[50]

The defendant may waive the clause, *e.g.* by submitting to the jurisdiction of another court.[51]

The version of article 17 contained in Schedule 4 of the Civil Jurisdiction and Judgments Act 1982 (dealing with cases where the defendant is domiciled in the United Kingdom) omits the requirement as to writing.

---

[50] Case 25/79 *Sanicentral* v. *Collin* [1979] E.C.R. 3423; Case 150/80 *Elefanten Schuh* v. *Jacqmain* [1981] E.C.R. 1671.

[51] *Elefanten Schuh* v. *Jacqmain, supra.*

Part Three

FOREIGN JUDGMENTS AND ARBITRATION

CHAPTER 9

FOREIGN JUDGMENTS

UNSATISFIED foreign judgments give rise to difficult and delicate questions in the conflict of laws.[1] The plaintiff, for example, brings an action against the defendant in Switzerland for damages for breach of contract or for tort, and eventually obtains judgment, only to discover that the defendant has surreptitiously removed his assets to England, so that the Swiss judgment cannot be enforced against him in Switzerland. The plaintiff cannot call upon English officials to enforce the Swiss judgment in England, because at common law a foreign judgment has no direct operation in England. Still less can he call upon Swiss officials to do so. Must he then begin all over again and bring a fresh action against the defendant in England? Until recently he was certainly entitled to do this, because a foreign judgment, unlike an English judgment, did not extinguish the original cause of action.[2] But a far better course has nearly always been to bring an action in England at common law, not on the original cause of action, but on the foreign judgment; or to register the foreign judgment under statute in the High Court.

This Chapter is divided into two parts, depending on whether the foreign judgment was rendered outside or inside the EEC. In the former case the common law still applies, amended and reinforced by statute. In the latter case recognition and enforcement of the foreign judgment are governed exclusively by the Civil Jurisdiction and Judgments Act 1982.

1. *JUDGMENTS RENDERED OUTSIDE THE EEC*

INTRODUCTION

The distinction between recognition and enforcement

It is plain that, while a court must recognise every foreign judgment which it enforces, it need not enforce every foreign judgment which it recognises. Some foreign judgments do not lend themselves to enforcement, but only to recognition. Examples are a judgment dismissing a claim (unless it orders the unsuccessful plaintiff to pay costs, as it frequently does); or a declaratory judgment; or a decree of divorce or nullity. But there may be orders ancillary to such decrees which, because they order the payment of money, are capable of enforcement: *e.g.* an order that the husband should pay maintenance to the wife, or that the unsuccessful party should pay the other's costs. A foreign judgment *in rem* decreeing the sale

---

[1] See, generally, Read, *Recognition and Enforcement of Foreign Judgments* (1938); Dicey and Morris, Chap. 33; Cheshire and North, Chap. 19; Anton, Chap. 26.

[2] See *post*, p.107.

of a ship or other chattel to meet the plaintiff's claim does not normally require enforcement in England, because the plaintiff's claim can usually be satisfied out of the proceeds of sale of the *res*, or out of the bail or other security which the owner gave to avoid the arrest of the *res*.[3] There are indeed only two reported cases of a foreign judgment *in rem* being enforced in England by an action *in rem*.[4]

The recognition in England of foreign decrees of divorce and nullity will be discussed in a later chapter.[5] This chapter is concerned only with the enforcement of foreign judgments *in personam*, and with their recognition for defensive purposes in cases where the foreign judgment was in favour of the defendant.

The basis of enforcement and recognition

English courts have recognised and enforced foreign judgments from the seventeenth century onwards.[6] It was at one time supposed that the basis of this enforcement was to be found in the doctrine of comity. English judges believed that the law of nations required the courts of one country to assist those of any other, and they feared that if foreign judgments were not enforced in England, English judgments would not be enforced abroad.[7] But later this theory was superseded by what is called the doctrine of obligation, which was stated by Parke B. in *Russell* v. *Smyth*[8] and *Williams* v. *Jones*[9] and approved by Blackburn J. a generation later in *Godard* v. *Gray*[10] and *Schibsby* v. *Westenholz*[11] in the following words:

> "We think that . . . the true principle on which the judgments of foreign tribunals are enforced in England is . . . that the judgment of a court of competent jurisdiction over the defendant imposes a duty or obligation on the defendant to pay the sum for which judgment is given, which the courts in this country are bound to enforce; and consequently that anything which negatives that duty, or forms a legal excuse for not performing it, is a defence to the action."

And in *Godard* v. *Gray* Blackburn J. categorically denied that it was an admitted principle of the law of nations that a State is bound to enforce foreign judgments in its courts.

During the eighteenth and the first part of the nineteenth century it was much debated whether a foreign judgment given by a court of competent jurisdiction could be re-examined on the merits when recognition or

---

[3] See *ante*, Chap. 7.
[4] *The City of Mecca* (1879) 5 P.D. 28; reversed on other grounds (1881) 6 P.D. 106; *The Despina G.K.* [1983] Q.B. 214.
[5] *Post*, Chap. 12.
[6] See Sack in *Law, A Century of Progress, 1835–1935* (1937) Vol. 3, pp. 342, 382–384.
[7] See *Roach* v. *Garvan* (1748) 1 Ves.Sen. 157, 159; *Wright* v. *Simpson* (1802) 6 Ves. 714, 730; *Alves* v. *Bunbury* (1814) 4 Camp. 28.
[8] (1842) 9 M. & W. 810, 819.
[9] (1845) 13 M. & W. 628, 633.
[10] (1870) L.R. 6 Q.B. 139, 148–150.
[11] (1870) L.R. 6 Q.B. 155, 159.

enforcement of that judgment was sought in England. It is perhaps significant that the conclusiveness of foreign judgments in favour of defendants[12] was established several years before the conclusiveness of foreign judgments in favour of plaintiffs. As late as 1834 Lord Brougham said in the House of Lords "a foreign judgment is only prima facie, not conclusive, evidence of a debt."[13] But when the doctrine of comity was superseded by the doctrine of obligation, it became clear that a foreign judgment in favour of the plaintiff given by a court of competent jurisdiction was conclusive in England. This was established in *Godard* v. *Gray*,[14] and has never been doubted since.

It is important to realise that this doctrine of obligation is quite different from the theory of vested rights which Dicey in England and Beale in the United States regarded as the foundation of the whole of the conflict of laws, and which has gone out of fashion since their deaths.[15] The foreign judgment creditor does not come to the English court asking it to enforce a foreign-created right. The right enforced is the creature of English law. For, in the first place, it is essential that the foreign court should have had jurisdiction, not in the sense of the foreign law, but in the sense of the English rules of the conflict of laws. Secondly, the defences that may be pleaded in an action on a foreign judgment are all created exclusively by English law. Hence the English court enforces an English-created, not a foreign-created, right.

Abolition of the non-merger rule

Until 1982 a foreign judgment, unlike an English judgment,[16] did not extinguish the original cause of action.[17] So if the plaintiff obtained a foreign judgment for a debt, and the judgment was not satisfied, he could either sue the defendant in England on the judgment, or he could bring an action on the debt, in which case the judgment was merely available as evidence of the debt. But, though well established by early cases, this rule rested on no sound basis of principle. Like the now exploded doctrine that a foreign judgment is merely evidence of a debt and therefore impeachable upon the merits, it was derived from the technical rule that a foreign court is not in the eyes of English law a court of record. Whereas one branch of that rule was exploded in the latter half of the nineteenth century, the other remained as an illogical anomaly, in conflict with the general policy of the law *ut sit finis litium*. In *Carl Zeiss Stiftung* v. *Rayner & Keeler* (*No. 2*),[18] Lord Wilberforce regarded it as "illogical" and its continued existence as "precarious." It has now been abolished by section 34 of the Civil Jurisdiction and Judgments Act 1982.

[12] *Ricardo* v. *Garcias* (1845) 12 Cl. & F. 368.
[13] *Houlditch* v. *Donegal* (1834) 2 Cl. & F. 470, 477. *Cf. Smith* v. *Nicolls* (1839) 5 Bing.N.C. 208, 221.
[14] (1870) L.R. 6 Q.B. 139. *Cf. Castrique* v. *Imrie* (1870) L.R. 4 H.L. 414.
[15] See *post*, pp. 507–511.
[16] *King* v. *Hoare* (1844) 13 M.& W. 494, 504; *Ex p. Bank of England* [1895] 1 Ch. 37.
[17] *Hall* v. *Odber* (1809) 11 East 118; *Smith* v. *Nicolls* (1839) 5 Bing.N.C. 208; *Bank of Australasia* v. *Harding* (1850) 9 C.B. 661.
[18] [1967] 1 A.C. 853, 966F-G

Enforcement at common law

A judgment creditor seeking to enforce a foreign judgment in England at common law cannot do so by direct execution of the judgment. He must bring an action on the foreign judgment. But he can apply for summary judgment under Order 14 of the Rules of the Supreme Court on the ground that the defendant has no defence to the claim[19]; and if his application is successful, the defendant will not be allowed to defend at all. The speed and simplicity of this procedure, coupled with the tendency of English judges narrowly to circumscribe the defences that may be pleaded to an action on a foreign judgment, mean that foreign judgments are in practice enforceable in England much more easily than they are in many civil law countries, where enforcement is easy in theory but difficult in practice because of the tendency of the courts to enlarge the scope of the defence that enforcement would be contrary to *ordre public* or public policy.[20] Thus it came about that foreign judgments are more easily enforceable in England than are English judgments in some foreign countries.[21]

Enforcement under statute

A foreign judgment under which a sum of money is payable may be enforceable in England under statute by a slightly more direct process of registration. The two most important statutes are the Administration of Justice Act 1920, and the Foreign Judgments (Reciprocal Enforcement) Act 1933.

Part II of the Administration of Justice Act 1920 provides for the reciprocal enforcement by registration of judgments of superior courts in the United Kingdom on the one hand, and judgments of superior courts in the Commonwealth overseas on the other. The Act has been extended by Order in Council to numerous countries of the Commonwealth; but before an Order is made, it is essential for Her Majesty to be satisfied that reciprocal provisions have been made in the country concerned for the enforcement there of United Kingdom judgments.[22] Registration is discretionary and not as of right, since it can be refused unless the registering court "in all the circumstances of the case . . . thinks it just and convenient that the judgment should be enforced in the United Kingdom."[23] Moreover, registration may not be ordered if the original court acted without jurisdiction (though no attempt is made to elucidate the meaning of this term), or if the defendant establishes any of a limited number of defences which are very similar to those available at common law.[24]

The Foreign Judgments (Reciprocal Enforcement) Act 1933 provides for the reciprocal enforcement by registration of judgments of courts in the United Kingdom on the one hand, and judgments of courts in politically

---

[19] *Grant* v. *Easton* (1883) 13 Q.B.D. 302.
[20] See Gutteridge (1932) 13 B.Y.I.L. 49; Graupner (1963) 12 I.C.L.Q. 367.
[21] See the Report of the Foreign Judgments (Reciprocal Enforcement) Committee, Cmd. 4213 (1932), paras. 2, 9, 10, 14.
[22] s.14.
[23] s.9(1).
[24] s.9(2).

foreign countries, and also in countries of the Commonwealth outside the United Kingdom, on the other. (The reason for including Commonwealth judgments was that it was hoped that the régime of the Act of 1933 would gradually replace that of the Act of 1920.) Like the Act of 1920, the Act of 1933 can only be extended by Order in Council to a country if Her Majesty is satisfied that substantial reciprocity of treatment will be assured therein for United Kingdom judgments.[25] The Act now extends to five politically foreign countries, and to six countries in the Commonwealth. However, it is much more important than the Act of 1920. This is because it is drafted in much more detail, and contains specific rules on when foreign courts are deemed to have jurisdiction for the purposes of the Act, and on what defences the defendant may set up in opposition to an application to register a foreign judgment. These rules are modelled very closely on those of the common law. Registration of a judgment under the Act is available as of right instead of merely at discretion as under the Act of 1920.

Sections 18 and 19 of the State Immunity Act 1978 provide for the recognition (but not the enforcement) of judgments rendered against the United Kingdom in States which are parties to the European Convention on State Immunity.

Common law and statute

The Acts of 1920 and 1933 are of limited geographical application and the judgments of very many foreign countries are not within their scope. There thus remains a considerable area within which enforcement of a foreign judgment at common law is the only process possible. The provisions of the Act of 1933 were deliberately framed so as to reproduce the rules of the common law as closely as possible,[26] though, as the Foreign Judgments (Reciprocal Enforcement) Committee conceded, it was found desirable to make one or two very slight departures from the common law in order to secure international agreements which would be likely to operate satisfactorily in practice.[27] The question therefore arises whether the provisions of the Act as to the jurisdiction of foreign courts, and as to the scope of the defences, can legitimately be invoked by a court which is asked to enforce a foreign judgment at common law, even though the Act has not been extended by Order in Council to the foreign country in question. After some fluctuation of opinion among judges of first instance,[28] it has now been laid down by the Court of Appeal that "one cannot ascertain what the common law is by arguing backwards from the provisions of the Act."[29]

---

[25] s.1(1).

[26] Report of the Foreign Judgments (Reciprocal Enforcement) Committee, Cmd. 4213 (1932), paras. 2, 16, 18 and Annex V, para. 7.

[27] *Ibid.* Annex V, para.7.

[28] See *Re Trepca Mines Ltd.* [1960] 1 W.L.R. 1273, 1282; *Rossano* v. *Manufacturers Life Insurance Co. Ltd.* [1963] 2 Q.B. 352, 383; contrast *Société Co-opérative Sidmetal* v. *Titan International Ltd.* [1966] 1 Q.B. 828, 845–846; *Vogel* v. *R. A. Kohnstamm Ltd.* [1973] 1 Q.B. 133, 134.

[29] *Henry* v. *Geoprosco International Ltd.* [1976] Q.B. 726, 751.

JURISDICTION OF THE FOREIGN COURT[30]

Introduction

The most fundamental of all requirements for the recognition or enforcement of foreign judgments in England (whether at common law or under the Administration of Justice Act 1920 or the Foreign Judgments (Reciprocal Enforcement) Act 1933) is that the foreign court should have had jurisdiction according to the English rules of the conflict of laws. Thus in a famous leading case[31]:

> The plaintiff brought an action in England on a judgment of a court in the island of Tobago. The defendant had never been in the island, nor had he submitted to its jurisdiction. There had been a substituted service, valid by the law of Tobago, effected by nailing a copy of the writ to the courthouse door. Lord Ellenborough refused to enforce the judgment. He said: "Can the Island of Tobago pass a law to bind the rights of the whole world? Would the world submit to such an assumed jurisdiction?"

The most frequently quoted judicial statement of the bases of jurisdiction at common law is the following statement of Buckley L.J. in *Emanuel* v. *Symon*[32]:

> "In actions *in personam* there are five cases in which the courts of this country will enforce a foreign judgment: (1) where the defendant is a subject of the foreign country in which the judgment has been obtained; (2) where he was resident in the foreign country when the action began; (3) where the defendant in the character of plaintiff has selected the forum in which he is afterwards sued[33]; (4) where he has voluntarily appeared; and (5) where he has contracted to submit himself to the forum in which the judgment was obtained."

As Read observes,[34] "little objection can be taken to this as a starting point so long as it is realised (a) that these are dicta; (b) that the enumeration is not necessarily exhaustive; and (c) that they are not to be accepted uncritically or without elaboration or qualification." As will be seen later,[35] the first case mentioned in Buckley L.J.'s statement (the nationality of the defendant) can no longer be relied upon. His second case, residence, is the most common basis for conceding jurisdiction to foreign courts in actions *in personam*. His third, fourth and fifth cases are variations on the single

---

[30] Since as we have seen the Administration of Justice Act 1920 contains no rules on jurisdiction, and the rules in the Foreign Judgments (Reciprocal Enforcement) Act 1933 were modelled closely on those of the common law, it is convenient to consider these Acts together with the common law, pointing out differences when they occur.

[31] *Buchanan* v. *Rucker* (1809) 9 East 192. *Cf. Sirdar Gurdyal Singh* v. *Rajah of Faridkote* [1894] A.C. 670, 683–684, *per* Lord Selborne.

[32] [1908] 1 K.B. 302, 309. *Cf. Schibsby* v. *Westenholz* (1870) L.R. 6 Q.B. 155, 161; *Rousillon* v. *Rousillon* (1880) 14 Ch.D. 351, 371.

[33] Presumably a slip for "selected the forum as the one in which he would sue."

[34] Read, p. 147.

[35] *Post,* p. 115.

theme of submission. Residence and submission will therefore be discussed first. Lastly, consideration will be given to various factors which do not give the foreign court jurisdiction.

Where jurisdiction exists

Residence. Actor sequitur forum rei is the time-honoured maxim; hence it is natural for the plaintiff to sue in the country where the defendant resides, and it is well settled that this is sufficient for jurisdiction.[36] What is doubtful is whether the mere temporary presence of the defendant in a foreign country is enough. As we have seen,[37] it is settled that the temporary presence of the defendant in England gives the English court jurisdiction over him at common law; and *Carrick* v. *Hancock*[38] is usually cited for the proposition that the same is true for foreign courts. But though the dicta in that case are very definite, the actual decision might just as well have been based on the defendant's submission as on his presence. For he duly appeared to the writ, and though he did not personally remain in the foreign country, he was represented throughout the subsequent proceedings, put in a defence and counterclaim, and on three separate occasions took his opponent to the Court of Appeal. Casual presence, as distinct from residence, hardly seems a desirable basis of jurisdiction if the cause of action arose outside the foreign country concerned. For the court is not a convenient one for either of the parties, nor is it in a favourable position to deal intelligently either with the facts or with the law. It will be remembered that Buckley L.J. in *Emanuel* v. *Symon* said "residence," not "presence"; so does the Foreign Judgments (Reciprocal Enforcement) Act 1933.[39]

If the defendant is a corporation, neither its residence nor its presence has any real meaning; the only practical test is, does it carry on business in the foreign country? There is a long line of cases dealing with the question whether a foreign corporation does or does not carry on business in England so as to render itself amenable to the jurisdiction of the English courts at common law.[40] The principle of these cases applies also to the question whether a corporation is resident in a foreign country so as to give its courts jurisdiction over it. Hence a foreign court is recognised as having jurisdiction over a corporation if it is engaged in "some carrying on of business at a definite and, to some reasonable extent, permanent place" within the foreign country. The mere presence there of a representative of the corporation will not suffice.[41] Nor is it sufficient if the corporation has a representative resident there who has authority to elicit orders from customers but not to make contracts on its behalf.[42] The Foreign Judgments

[36] *Schibsby* v. *Westenholz* (1870) L.R. 6 Q.B. 155, 161.
[37] *Ante*, p. 65.
[38] (1895) 12 T.L.R. 59.
[39] s.4(2)(*a*)(iv).
[40] *Ante*, p. 67.
[41] *Littauer Glove Corporation* v. *F. W. Millington Ltd.* (1928) 44 T.L.R. 746.
[42] *Vogel* v. *R. A. Kohnstamm Ltd.* [1973] 1 Q.B. 133. *Cf. Sfeir & Co.* v. *National Insurance Co. of New Zealand Ltd.* [1964] 1 Lloyd's Rep. 330, a case on the Administration of Justice Act 1920.

(Reciprocal Enforcement) Act 1933 requires that the corporation must have its *principal* place of business (and not merely carry on business) in the foreign country.[43] The Act also provides that the foreign court is deemed to have jurisdiction for the purposes of the Act if the defendant (not necessarily a corporation) had an office or place of business in the foreign country and the proceedings were in respect of a transaction effected through or at that office or place.[44] There does not appear to be any authority for this basis of jurisdiction at common law; but the Foreign Judgments (Reciprocal Enforcement) Committee regarded it as a rational extension of the common law rules.[45]

Section 32 of the Civil Jurisdiction and Judgments Act 1982 provides that a judgment given by a court of an overseas country shall not be recognised or enforced in the United Kingdom if (a) the bringing of the proceedings in the foreign court was contrary to a valid agreement under which the dispute was to be settled otherwise than by proceedings in the courts of that country; and (b) the judgment debtor did not agree to the bringing of those proceedings, counterclaim or otherwise submit to the jurisdiction of that court.[46] The United Kingdom court is not bound by any decision of the overseas court relating to these matters.[47] But the section does not affect the recognition or enforcement in the United Kingdom of a judgment which is required to be recognised under the Brussels Convention 1968. Under that Convention, the fact that a judgment was given in defiance of a choice of jurisdiction clause is not a ground on which its recognition or enforcement can be refused in other Contracting States.[48] But unless and until the European Court decides otherwise, a judgment in an EEC State given in defiance of an arbitration clause will come within section 32, because arbitration is one of the matters specifically excluded from the scope of the Convention by article 1.[49]

Submission. Submission to the jurisdiction of a foreign court can take place in various ways. The most obvious is where the plaintiff himself invokes the jurisdiction and thereby renders himself liable to a judgment for the defendant in respect of a counterclaim, cross-action or costs.[50]

If the defendant voluntarily appears and pleads to the merits, he clearly submits to the jurisdiction of the court; and this is so even if he also contests the jurisdiction.[51] But what if he appears merely to contest the jurisdiction? Although the Court of Appeal in *Henry* v. *Geoprosco*

---

[43] s.4(2)(*a*)(iv).
[44] s.4(2)(*a*)(v).
[45] Cmd. 4213 (1932), Annex V, para. 8.
[46] There was a similar provision (now repealed as redundant) in s.4(3)(*b*) of the Foreign Judgments (Reciprocal Enforcement) Act 1933, but no authority at common law.
[47] See *Tracomin S.A.* v. *Sudan Oil Seeds Ltd.* [1983] 1 W.L.R. 662, 1026.
[48] Article 27; *post*, p.132.
[49] *Ante*, pp. 78–79.
[50] *Schibsby* v. *Westenholz* (1870) L.R. 6 Q.B. 155, 161; *Burpee* v. *Burpee* [1929] 3 D.L.R. 18; Foreign Judgments (Reciprocal Enforcement) Act 1933, s.4(2)(*a*)(ii).
[51] *Boissière & Co.* v. *Brockner* (1889) 6 T.L.R. 85, criticised by Clarence Smith (1953) 2 I.C.L.Q. 510, 517–520.

International Ltd.[52] left this question open, they did hold that if a defendant appears before a foreign court and invites it in its discretion not to exercise the jurisdiction which it had under its local law, then he voluntarily submits to the jurisdiction. Furthermore, they indicated that if the defendant's protest against the jurisdiction of the foreign court took the form of what in England used to be regarded as a conditional appearance, the entry of the conditional appearance would be a voluntary submission.

A similar difficulty arises when the defendant appears solely in order to protect his property in the foreign country which the foreign court is about to seize, whether to found jurisdiction or in execution of a default judgment. Is this a voluntary appearance? The cases all say yes[53]; but they suggest that it might be different if the defendant appears to obtain the release of property already seized by the foreign court.[54] In *Guiard* v. *De Clermont*,[55] for instance:

> The defendants were sued for breach of contract in the Tribunal de Commerce of the Seine which gave judgment against them in default of appearance for the equivalent of £525. The defendants were not resident or present in France when the writ was issued, nor had they yet submitted to the jurisdiction. But they had a small sum of £4 or £8 standing to their credit in a French bank; and the thought of losing this trifling sum was apparently so agonising that they foolishly filed an "opposition" to the Tribunal de Commerce asking that the default judgment should be reopened. The Tribunal de Commerce allowed the opposition, heard the case on its merits and gave judgment for the defendants. But the Court of Appeal in Paris held that the defendants' opposition was out of time, and restored the original judgment of the Tribunal de Commerce. It was held that this judgment could be enforced against the defendants in England. Moral: greed does not pay.

These two cases have been reversed by section 33 of the Civil Jurisdiction and Judgments Act 1982, which provides that the defendant shall not be regarded as having submitted to the jurisdiction of an overseas court (unless the judgment must be recognised under the Brussels Convention 1968) if he appeared (a) to contest the jurisdiction of the court; (b) to ask the court to dismiss or stay the proceedings on the ground that the dispute should be submitted to arbitration or to the determination of the courts of another country; or (c) to protect or obtain the release of property seized or threatened with seizure in the proceedings.[56]

---

[52] [1976] Q.B. 726. *Cf. Harris* v. *Taylor* [1915] 2 K.B. 580. The decision in *Henry* v. *Geoprosco* has been heavily criticised by academic writers : see Collins (1976) 92 L.Q.R. 268; Solomons (1976) 25 I.C.L.Q. 665; Carter (1974–75) 47 B.Y.I.L. 379; Cheshire and North, pp. 638–641.

[53] *De Cosse Brissac* v. *Rathbone* (1861) 6 H. & N. 301 (the third plea); *Voinet* v. *Barrett* (1885) 55 L.J.Q.B. 39; *Guiard* v. *De Clermont* [1914] 3 K.B. 145.

[54] *Ibid.* and see *Henry* v. *Geoprosco International Ltd.* [1976] Q.B. 726, 746–747.

[55] *Supra.*

[56] See *Tracomin S.A.* v. *Sudan Oil Seeds Co. Ltd.* [1983] 1 W.L.R. 662, 1026. There was a similar provision (now partially repealed as redundant) in s.4(2)(a)(i) of the Foreign Judgments (Reciprocal Enforcement) Act 1933.

Another example of submission is where a contract provides that all disputes between the parties shall be referred to the exclusive jurisdiction of a foreign tribunal. In such a case the foreign court is deemed to have jurisdiction over the parties.[57] An agreement to submit may also take the form of an agreement to accept service of process at a designated address. Thus, if a person takes shares in a foreign company, the articles of association of which provide that all disputes shall be submitted to the jurisdiction of a foreign court, and that every shareholder must "elect a domicile" at a particular place for service of process, and that in default the officers of the company may do so for him, then he is deemed to have agreed to submit to the jurisdiction of the foreign court, even if he never does elect a domicile.[58] And a member of a foreign company is bound by a statute enacted in the country of its incorporation providing that the particular company may sue and be sued in the name of its chairman and that execution on any judgment against the company may be issued against the property of any member in like manner as if the judgment had been obtained against him personally.[59] But English courts have stopped short of inferring an agreement to submit from a mere general provision in the foreign law (and not in a statute specifically referring to the particular company) that the shareholder must "elect a domicile" for the service of process,[60] unless he does in fact elect such a domicile.[61]

As a general rule, an agreement to submit to the jurisdiction of a foreign court must be express; it cannot be implied.[62] If the parties agree, expressly or by implication, that their contract shall be governed by a particular foreign law, it does not follow that they agree to submit to the jurisdiction of the courts which apply it.[63] Nor can any such agreement be implied from the fact that the cause of action arose in a foreign country, nor from the additional fact that the defendant was present there when the cause of action arose.[64] In *Emanuel* v. *Symon*,[65] the Court of Appeal held that a defendant did not submit to the courts of a foreign country merely because he became a member of a partnership firm which carried on business there. But in *Blohn* v. *Desser*,[66] Diplock J. held that where a person resident in England became a sleeping partner in an Austrian firm she did

---

[57] *Feyerick* v. *Hubbard* (1902) 71 L.J.K.B. 509; *Jeannot* v. *Fuerst* (1909) 25 T.L.R. 424; Foreign Judgments (Reciprocal Enforcement) Act 1933, s.4(2)(*a*)(iii).

[58] *Copin* v. *Adamson* (1874) L.R. 9 Ex. 345; (1875) 1 Ex. D. 17 (the first replication).

[59] *Bank of Australasia* v. *Harding* (1850) 9 C.B. 661; *Bank of Australasia* v. *Nias* (1851) 16 Q.B. 717; *Kelsall* v. *Marshall* (1856) 1 C.B.(N.S.) 241.

[60] *Copin* v. *Adamson* (1874) L.R. 9 Ex. 345 (the second replication). The point was reserved in the Court of Appeal: see 1 Ex.D. 17, 19.

[61] *Vallee* v. *Dumergue* (1849) 4 Exch. 290.

[62] *Sirdar Gurdyal Singh* v. *Rajah of Faridkote* [1894] A.C. 670; *Emanuel* v. *Symon* [1908] 1 K.B. 302; *Vogel* v. *R. A. Kohnstamm Ltd.* [1973] 1 Q.B. 133, not following dicta in *Blohn* v. *Desser* [1962] 2 Q.B. 116, 123, and in *Sfeir & Co.* v. *National Insurance Co. of New Zealand Ltd.* [1964] 1 Lloyd's Rep. 330, 339–340.

[63] *Mattar and Saba* v. *Public Trustee* [1952] 3 D.L.R. 399; *Dunbee Ltd.* v. *Gilman & Co. Ltd.* [1968] 2 Lloyd's Rep. 394.

[64] *Sirdar Gurdyal Singh* v. *Rajah of Faridkote* [1894] A.C. 670; *Emanuel* v. *Symon* [1908] 1 K.B. 302.

[65] *Supra.*

[66] [1962] 2 Q.B. 116.

submit to the jurisdiction of the Austrian courts. These cases can perhaps be reconciled on the basis that *Emanuel* v. *Symon* was concerned with the liability of the partners *inter se*, whereas *Blohn* v. *Desser* was concerned with the liability of a partner to an outside creditor. In other words, there was an element of holding out in *Blohn* v. *Desser* which was absent from *Emanuel* v. *Symon*. But *Blohn* v. *Desser* has been severely criticised extra-judicially[67] and has subsequently not been followed,[68] and it is submitted that on this point it cannot be supported.

Where jurisdiction does not exist

The provisions of the Foreign Judgments (Reciprocal Enforcement) Act 1933 as to the jurisdiction of foreign courts are exclusive. That is to say, no judgment can be registered under the Act unless the jurisdiction of the foreign court can be brought under one of the five heads of section 4(2)(*a*).[69] But the rules of common law as to jurisdiction are not necessarily exclusive. Like any other common law rules, they are no doubt capable of judicious expansion to meet the changing needs of society. However, it seems reasonably clear that none of the bases of jurisdiction about to be discussed are sufficient at common law, though some of them are quite often relied upon by foreign courts. None of them is mentioned in the Foreign Judgments (Reciprocal Enforcement) Act 1933. They are as follows:

Possession of property in the foreign country. This is relied upon in Scotland,[70] but has been rejected in England.[71]

Presence of the defendant in the foreign country at the time when the cause of action arose. Though a tentative dictum of Blackburn J. favours this head,[72] the Privy Council and the Court of Appeal have since rejected it.[73]

Nationality. There is a long chain of dicta extending from 1828 to 1948 suggesting that the courts of a country might have jurisdiction over a defendant if he was a national of that country.[74] But there is no actual decision to this effect. On the contrary, nationality as a basis of jurisdiction has more recently been doubted by three High Court judges,[75] and definitely rejected by the Irish High Court.[76] It cannot, therefore, safely be relied

---

[67] Lewis (1961) 10 I.C.L.Q. 910; Cohn (1962) 11 I.C.L.Q. 583; Carter (1962) 38 B.Y.I.L. 493.

[68] *Vogel* v. *R. A. Kohnstamm Ltd.* [1973] 1 Q.B. 133.

[69] *Société Co-opérative Sidmetal* v. *Titan International Ltd.* [1966] 1 Q.B. 828. For the five heads of s.4(2)(*a*), see *ante*, notes 39, 44, 50, 56, 57, 61.

[70] See Anton, pp. 106–114; Civil Jurisdiction and Judgments Act 1982, Sched. 8, para. 2(8).

[71] *Emanuel* v. *Symon* [1908] 1 K.B. 302.

[72] *Schibsby* v. *Westenholz* (1870) L.R. 6 Q.B. 155, 161.

[73] *Sirdar Gurdyal Singh* v. *Rajah of Faridkote* [1894] A.C. 670; *Emanuel* v. *Symon, supra.*

[74] *Douglas* v. *Forrest* (1828) 4 Bing. 686; *Schibsby* v. *Westenholz, supra,* at p. 161; *Rousillon* v. *Rousillon* (1880) 14 Ch.D. 351, 371; *Emanuel* v. *Symon, supra,* at p. 309; *Gavin Gibson & Co.* v. *Gibson* [1913] 3 K.B. 379, 388; *Harris* v. *Taylor* [1915] 2 K.B. 580, 591; *Forsyth* v. *Forsyth* [1948] P. 125, 132.

[75] *Blohn* v. *Desser* [1962] 2 Q.B. 116, 123, *per* Diplock J.; *Rossano* v. *Manufacturers Life Insurance Co. Ltd.* [1963] 2 Q.B. 352, 382–383, *per* McNair J., *Vogel* v. *R. A. Kohnstamm Ltd.* [1973] 1 Q.B. 133, 141, *per* Ashworth J.

[76] *Rainford* v. *Newell-Roberts* [1962] I.R. 95.

upon today. It is obviously inappropriate when the defendant is a Commonwealth citizen[77] or an American citizen, since in neither case does the political unit (or State) coincide with the law district (or country).

Domicile. There are dicta in English cases[78] which suggest (though rather faintly) the recognition of domicile as a basis of jurisdiction; but no English decision supports this, though one Canadian decision does.[79] Despite this decision, Read (a Canadian writer) concludes that "domicile alone, unaccompanied by either residence or presence, will not yet suffice."[80]

Reciprocity. Will the jurisdiction of the foreign court be recognised if the situation is such that, *mutatis mutandis*, the English court might have assumed jurisdiction, *e.g.* under Order 11, r. 1(1) of the Rules of the Supreme Court?[81] Almost certainly it will not.

In *Schibsby* v. *Westenholz*,[82] the plaintiff brought an action in England on a French judgment. The defendant was not in France when the writ was issued (it was served on him in England), nor did he appear or submit to the jurisdiction. The Court of Queen's Bench was much pressed with the argument that, under what were then sections 18 and 19 of the Common Law Procedure Act 1852 and is now Order 11, r. 1(1) of the Rules of the Supreme Court, the English court would have had power to order service out of the jurisdiction on converse facts, and therefore it should enforce the French judgment. In rejecting this argument, Blackburn J. said:

> "If the principle on which foreign judgments were enforced was that which is loosely called 'comity,' we could hardly decline to enforce a foreign judgment given in France against a resident in Great Britain under circumstances hardly, if at all, distinguishable from those under which we, *mutatis mutandis*, might give judgment against a resident in France; but it is quite different if the principle be that which we have just laid down" (*i.e.* the doctrine of obligation, quoted earlier in this chapter[83]).

This decision was followed in *Turnbull* v. *Walker*,[84] where Wright J. refused to enforce a New Zealand judgment based on provisions for the service of writs out of the jurisdiction which were identical with the English provisions.

In spite of these decisions, it was suggested (*obiter*) by Denning L.J.[85]

[77] *Gavin Gibson & Co.* v. *Gibson, supra.*
[78] *Turnbull* v. *Walker* (1892) 67 L.T. 767, 769; *Emanuel* v. *Symon* [1908] 1 K.B. 302, 308, 314; *Jaffer* v. *Williams* (1908) 25 T.L.R. 12, 13; *Gavin Gibson & Co.* v. *Gibson* [1913] 3 K.B. 379, 385.
[79] *Marshall* v. *Houghton* [1923] 2 W.W.R. 553.
[80] Read, p. 160. *Cf.* Cheshire and North, p. 642.
[81] *Ante,* pp. 68–76.
[82] (1870) L.R. 6 Q.B. 155, 159.
[83] *Ante,* p. 106.
[84] (1892) 67 L.T. 767.
[85] *Re Dulles' Settlement (No. 2)* [1951] Ch. 842, 851.

that an English court would recognise that a court in the Isle of Man had jurisdiction to give a judgment based on service of the writ out of the jurisdiction if the English court would have assumed jurisdiction in converse circumstances. And in *Travers* v. *Holley*[86] the Court of Appeal recognised a New South Wales divorce granted in the absence of domicile on the ground that "it would be contrary to principle and inconsistent with comity if the courts of this country were to refuse to recognise a jurisdiction which *mutatis mutandis* they claimed for themselves." The width and generality of this statement led to extrajudicial suggestions that the principle of reciprocity might be applicable to foreign judgments *in personam*.[87] But it has since been held, with manifest correctness, that this is not so and that English courts do not concede jurisdiction *in personam* to foreign courts merely because English courts would, in converse circumstances, have power to order service out of the jurisdiction.[88] "The decision in *Travers* v. *Holley* was a decision limited to a judgment *in rem* in a matter affecting matrimonial status, and it has not been followed in any case except a matrimonial case."[89] This means, of course, that in actions *in personam* English courts claim a wider jurisdiction than they concede to foreign courts. But any other decision would have meant abandoning the doctrine of obligation as the basis on which foreign judgments are enforced in favour of the long-exploded doctrine of comity. For since the power of the English court to order service out of the jurisdiction is discretionary, so also (if the principle of reciprocity had prevailed) would have been its recognition of foreign judgments based on similar jurisdictional grounds.

DEFENCES

Introduction

The most usual defence pleaded to an action on a foreign judgment at common law is that the foreign court had no jurisdiction to give the judgment according to English rules of the conflict of laws. It is sometimes said that a foreign judgment rendered without jurisdiction in this sense is a complete nullity in England. But this is probably an over-statement, since money paid in pursuance of the judgment could probably not be recovered back.[90] What is true is that such a judgment will not be recognised or enforced in England.

The remaining defences now about to be discussed are (a) that the judgment was obtained by fraud; (b) that the enforcement or recognition of the

---

[86] [1953] P. 246, 257, *per* Hodson L.J. See *post*, p. 194.
[87] Kennedy (1954) 32 Can. Bar Rev. 359, 373–383; (1957) 35 *ibid.* 123; Cheshire, 7th ed. pp. 557–558; contrast Cheshire and North, pp. 643–644.
[88] *Re Trepca Mines Ltd.* [1960] 1 W.L.R. 1273, 1280–1282; *Société Co-opérative Sidmetal* v. *Titan International Ltd.* [1966] 1 Q.B. 828; *Sharps Commercials Ltd.* v. *Gas Turbines Ltd.* [1956] N.Z.L.R. 819, 823; *Crick* v. *Hennessy* [1973] W.A.R. 74.
[89] *Re Trepca Mines Ltd., supra,* at pp. 1281–1282, *per* Hodson L.J. *Cf. Indyka* v. *Indyka* [1969] 1 A.C. 33, *per* Lord Reid at p. 58E, *per* Lord Wilberforce at p. 106D; *Henry* v. *Geoprosco International Ltd.* [1976] Q.B. 726, 745.
[90] Nussbaum, *Principles of Private International Law*, p. 247. Contrast Read, p. 125.

judgment would be contrary to English public policy; (c) that the proceedings in which the judgment was obtained were opposed to natural justice; and (d) that the judgment was for multiple damages. In considering these defences, it should be borne in mind that, unless otherwise stated, they may be pleaded as a defence to an action on the judgment at common law, or used as grounds for refusing to register the judgment under the Administration of Justice Act 1920 or for setting aside the registration of the judgment under the Foreign Judgments (Reciprocal Enforcement) Act 1933, or pleaded by the plaintiff if the defendant sets up a foreign judgment in his favour as a defence to a claim on the original cause of action. In this last case they are not strictly defences but replications.

After these four defences have been discussed, we shall next consider certain matters which cannot be relied upon as defences to foreign judgments.

What are defences

Fraud. It is settled that a foreign judgment, like any other, can be impeached for fraud.[91] Such fraud may be either fraud on the part of the court, as where it is interested in the subject-matter of the suit[92]; or fraud on the part of the successful party, as where he suppresses evidence or produces forged or perjured evidence; or fraud on the part of both court and party, as where one party bribes the court.

The difficult question is whether a foreign judgment can be impeached for fraud if, in order to prove the fraud, it is necessary to reopen the merits which have already been decided by the foreign court. Two principles are here in conflict, the principle that foreign judgments are impeachable for fraud, and the principle that the merits cannot be reopened. In this situation, three decisions of the Court of Appeal lay down in the clearest terms that it is the former principle which prevails.[93]

In the first of these cases, *Abouloff* v. *Oppenheimer*,[94] the defendant argued unsuccessfully in the foreign court that the plaintiff was deceiving it: but the court gave judgment for the plaintiff. In an action on the judgment in England, the defendant pleaded fraud, and the plaintiff demurred. She thereby conceded that the foreign judgment had been obtained by fraud, so that it was unnecessary to prove the fraud by evidence. The Court of Appeal allowed the defendant's plea and overruled the demurrer. The court had some difficulty in reconciling its decision with the then recently established principle that foreign judgments are conclusive on the merits and cannot be impeached for errors of fact or law.[95] Lord Coleridge C.J.

---

[91] *Ochsenbein* v. *Papelier* (1873) L.R. 8 Ch.App. 695; Administration of Justice Act 1920, s.9(2)(*d*); Foreign Judgments (Reciprocal Enforcement) Act 1933, s.4(1)(*a*)(iv); and cases cited in note 93, *infra.*

[92] See *Price* v. *Dewhurst* (1837) 8 Sim. 279.

[93] *Abouloff* v. *Oppenheimer* (1882) 10 Q.B.D. 295; *Vadala* v. *Lawes* (1890) 25 Q.B.D. 310; *Syal* v. *Heyward* [1948] 2 K.B. 443; *cf. Elllerman Lines Ltd.* v. *Read* [1928] 2 K.B. 144 (judgment *in rem*).

[94] *Supra.*

[95] *Godard* v. *Gray* (1870) L.R. 6 Q.B. 139; *Castrique* v. *Imrie* (1870) L.R. 4 H.L. 414; *ante,* pp. 106–107.

and Brett L.J. solved the difficulty by holding that the issue whether a foreign court had been deliberately misled was not, and never could be, one on which that court had passed.[96] Hence to examine the judgment in subsequent proceedings in England was not to reopen the merits of the foreign judgment.

The technical nature of this reasoning was admitted in *Vadala* v. *Lawes*,[97] where again the defendant argued unsuccessfully in the foreign court that the plaintiff was deceiving it, but the court gave judgment for the plaintiff. This time the plaintiff did not demur to the defendant's plea of fraud in an action in England on the foreign judgment, so that it was necessary for the defendant, in order to establish the fraud, to adduce precisely the same evidence as that which had been rejected by the foreign court. The Court of Appeal allowed him to do so. Lindley L.J. refused to "fritter away" the judgment in *Abouloff* v. *Oppenheimer*; and he said:

> "If the fraud upon the foreign court consists in the fact that the plaintiff has induced that court to come to a wrong conclusion, you can reopen the whole case even although you will have in this court to go into the very facts which were investigated and which were in issue in the foreign court."

In *Syal* v. *Heyward*,[98] the defendants knew at the time of the foreign proceedings that the plaintiff was deceiving the foreign court, but they did nothing and allowed judgment to go against them in default of appearance. Yet they were successful in an application to set aside the registration of the foreign judgment under the Foreign Judgments (Reciprocal Enforcement) Act 1933 on the ground of fraud. Thus the conclusion seems inescapable that foreign judgments can be impeached for fraud more easily than can English judgments, since English judgments can only be set aside on this ground if evidence newly discovered since the trial can be produced.[99]

Contrary to public policy. A foreign judgment can be impeached if its enforcement or recognition in England would be contrary to public policy[1]: but there are very few reported cases in which such a plea has been successful.

In *Re Macartney*,[2] a Maltese judgment ordering the personal representatives of a deceased putative father to pay perpetual maintenance to the mother of his illegitimate child was refused enforcement in England on three grounds: (1) it was contrary to public policy to enforce an affiliation

[96] At pp. 302, 306.
[97] (1890) 25 Q.B.D. 310, 316–317.
[98] [1948] 2 K.B. 443; criticised by Cowen (1949) 65 L.Q.R. 82; followed in *Svirskis* v. *Gibson* [1977] 2 N.Z.L.R.4.
[99] See *Flower* v. *Lloyd* (*No.* 1) (1877) 6 Ch.D. 297; (*No.* 2) (1879) 10 Ch.D. 327; *Boswell* v. *Coaks* (1894) 86 L.T. 365 n.; *Birch* v. *Birch* [1902] P. 130; D. M. Gordon (1961) 77 L.Q.R. 358, especially at pp. 376–377.
[1] See Administration of Justice Act 1920, s.9(2)(f); Foreign Judgments (Reciprocal Enforcement) Act 1933, s.4(1)(a)(v). For public policy generally, see *ante,* Chap. 4.
[2] [1921] 1 Ch. 522.

order not limited to the child's minority[3]; (2) the cause of action—a posthumous affiliation order—was unknown to English domestic law; and (3) the judgment was not final and conclusive, because the Maltese court could vary the amount of the payments.[4] The third ground by itself would have been sufficient to dispose of the case. Under the second ground, the court relied heavily on an American case[5] in which a French judgment awarding maintenance to a French son-in-law against his American father-in-law and mother-in-law was refused enforcement in the United States.

This American case and *Re Macartney* were disapproved or distinguished in two later cases, one Canadian, the other English. In *Burchell* v. *Burchell*,[6] an Ontario court enforced a judgment of an Ohio divorce court ordering a wife to make a lump-sum payment to her husband, although by the law of Ontario a wife was not bound to support her husband. In *Phrantzes* v. *Argenti*[7] (which was not a case on a foreign judgment), Lord Parker C.J. refused to enforce a claim by a Greek daughter against her father for the provision of a dowry on her marriage as required by Greek law. But his ground for doing so was not that the cause of action was unknown to English domestic law, but that English law had no remedy for awarding a dowry, the amount of which in Greek law was within the discretion of the court and varied in accordance with the wealth and social position of the father and the number of his children. Therefore, it is probably going too far to say (as was said in *Re Macartney*) that a foreign judgment based on a cause of action unknown to English domestic law cannot be enforced in England.

On the other hand, the Supreme Court of the Republic of Ireland has refused to enforce an English order for costs which was ancillary to a divorce decree.[8] The grounds of this decision were partly that the cause of action was unknown to the law of the Republic (where divorce is not allowed), and partly that to enforce an order ancillary to a divorce decree was contrary to Irish public policy.

It is not contrary to public policy to enforce a foreign judgment for what in England would be called exemplary damages.[9]

Contrary to natural justice. At common law, a foreign judgment can be impeached on the ground that the proceedings were opposed to natural justice; but the limits of this defence are even vaguer than those of public policy, and reported cases in which it has been successfully raised are even rarer. The proceedings are not opposed to natural justice merely because the judgment is manifestly wrong.[10] The objection frequently takes the

---

[3] The notion was that it was undesirable that the illegitimate daughter should spend her whole life in idleness basking in the Mediterranean sunshine, while father toiled and moiled in cloudy England to support her.
[4] See, as to this, *post*, p. 126.
[5] *De Brimont* v. *Penniman* (1873) 10 Blatchford Circuit Court Reports 436.
[6] [1926] 2 D.L.R. 595.
[7] [1960] 2 Q.B. 19, 31–34.
[8] *Mayo-Perrott* v. *Mayo-Perrott* [1958] I.R. 336.
[9] *S. A. Consortium General Textiles* v. *Sun and Sand Agencies Ltd.* [1978] Q.B. 279, 300.
[10] *Godard* v. *Gray* (1870) L.R. 6 Q.B. 139; *Castrique* v. *Imrie* (1870) L.R. 4 H.L. 414; *Robinson* v. *Fenner* [1913] 3 K.B. 835, 842.

form that one party was prevented from putting his case to the foreign court. But the proceedings are not opposed to natural justice merely because the court admitted evidence which is inadmissible in England,[11] or did not admit evidence which is admissible in England,[12] for the admissibility of evidence is a matter of procedure and so governed by the *lex fori*.[13] Nor are they opposed to natural justice if the objection could have been or was taken before the foreign court. Thus in *Jacobson* v. *Frachon*[14]:

> A merchant of Lyons contracted to sell silk to a merchant of London. A dispute arose about the quality of the silk. The Frenchman brought an action against the Englishman in a French court. The court appointed an expert to examine the goods and report on their quality. The expert made no proper examination of the goods; he refused to listen to the Englishman's witnesses; and his report (described by the English court as "the erroneous and uncandid production of a biased and prejudiced mind") was wholly in favour of the Frenchman. The French court gave judgment in favour of the Frenchman. The Englishman then sued the Frenchman in England on the contract. The Frenchman pleaded the French judgment in his favour as a defence. The Court of Appeal held that the judgment was not impeachable, because the French court was not obliged to accept the report, and because the Englishman had attacked it unsuccessfully in France.

The objection sometimes takes the form that the defendant did not receive notice of the proceedings in sufficient time to enable him to defend them. It is at this point that the defence that the proceedings were opposed to natural justice tends to become confused with the defence that the foreign court had no jurisdiction. If the defendant was resident in the foreign country when the proceedings were begun, or if he voluntarily appeared, it would seem impossible for him to take the objection that he did not receive sufficient notice, for in such circumstances any notice is sufficient which is in accordance with the law of the foreign country.[15] If the defendant agreed in advance to submit to the jurisdiction of the foreign court, it is invariably held that he cannot complain if he received insufficient notice[16]; his agreement to submit to the jurisdiction of the foreign court is deemed to include an agreement to submit to its rules of procedure. "It is not contrary to natural justice that a man who has agreed to receive a particular mode of notification of legal proceedings should be bound by a judgment in which that particular mode of notification has been followed, even though he may not have had actual notice of them."[17]

---

[11] *De Cosse Brissac* v. *Rathbone* (1861) 6 H. & N. 301 (the sixth plea).

[12] *Scarpetta* v. *Lowenfeld* (1911) 27 T.L.R. 509; *Robinson* v. *Fenner, supra*.

[13] *Post*, Chap. 29.

[14] (1927) 138 L.T. 386.

[15] Dicey and Morris, pp. 1089–1090.

[16] *Vallée* v. *Dumergue* (1849) 4 Exch. 290; *Bank of Australasia* v. *Harding* (1850) 9 C.B. 661; *Bank of Australasia* v. *Nias* (1851) 16 Q.B. 717; *Copin* v. *Adamson* (1875) 1 Ex.D. 17; *Feyerick* v. *Hubbard* (1902) 71 L.J.K.B. 509; *Jeannot* v. *Fuerst* (1909) 25 T.L.R. 424; *Batavia Times Publishing Co.* v. *Davis* (1979) 102 D.L.R. (3d) 192.

[17] *Vallée* v. *Dumergue, supra*, at p. 303, *per* Alderson B.

Neither the Administration of Justice Act 1920 nor the Foreign Judgments (Reciprocal Enforcement) Act 1933 mentions the defence that the proceedings were opposed to natural justice. Instead, the former Act provides that no judgment may be registered thereunder if the defendant was not duly served with the process of the court and did not appear[18]; and the latter provides that the registration of a judgment must be set aside if the defendant did not receive notice of the proceedings in sufficient time to enable him to defend them and he did not appear.[19] These grounds for refusing to register or for setting aside the registration of a judgment are quite independent of and distinct from the ground that the foreign court had no jurisdiction. Hence it follows that the common law authorities establishing that a defendant who agrees to submit to the jurisdiction of a foreign court also agrees to waive notice of the proceedings do not apply to foreign judgments registrable under those Acts.

Judgments for multiple damages. Section 5 of the Protection of Trading Interests Act 1980 prohibits the enforcement in the United Kingdom of judgments for multiple damages or any judgment specified by the Secretary of State as concerned with the prohibition of restrictive trade practices. Section 6 goes much further and gives United Kingdom citizens, corporations incorporated in the United Kingdom and persons carrying on business in the United Kingdom against whom multiple damages have been awarded, the right to recover so much of the damages as exceeds the sum assessed by the foreign court as compensation for the loss or damage sustained. This section contains the unusual provision that proceedings under it may be brought notwithstanding that the plaintiff in the foreign proceedings is not within the jurisdiction of the United Kingdom court. These two sections are aimed primarily at the tendency of American courts to interpret United States anti-trust legislation in such a way as to infringe the sovereignty of the United Kingdom and other States.

What are not defences

The title to this subsection is somewhat more dogmatic that the cases warrant. It is certain that the first matter about to be discussed is not by itself a defence; but the other two are much more doubtful.

Errors of fact or law. It is no defence that the foreign judgment is manifestly wrong either on the facts or on the law.[20] The merits cannot be reopened in England. But, as we have seen,[21] this rule does not apply if it is alleged that the judgment was obtained by fraud.

In *Godard* v. *Gray*,[22] it was held to be no defence that the foreign court, purporting to apply English domestic law, made an obvious mistake in

---

[18] s.9(2)(c).
[19] s.4(1)(a)(iii).
[20] *Godard* v. *Gray* (1870) L.R. 6 Q.B. 139; *Castrique* v. *Imrie* (1870) L.R. 4 H.L. 414.
[21] *Ante,* pp. 118–119.
[22] *Supra.*

doing so. It would seem to follow that it is no defence that the foreign court applied its own domestic law when according to English rules of the conflict of laws it should have applied English domestic law. In *Simpson* v. *Fogo*,[23] however, Page-Wood V.-C. refused to recognise a Louisiana judgment on the ground that it showed on its face "a perverse and deliberate refusal to recognise the law of England."[24] However, this decision has since been doubted,[25] and is now only of historical interest.

Lack of internal competence. Is it a defence that though the foreign court had jurisdiction in the sense of the English rules of the conflict of laws, it lacked competence in the sense of its own domestic law? This is a difficult question, and the authorities are in a state of some confusion.

In *Vanquelin* v *Bouard*,[26] the defendant was sued in England on a French judgment in respect of a bill of exchange. The French court had jurisdiction according to the English rules of the conflict of laws; and the subject-matter of the action (bills of exchange) was within its internal competence. But the defendant pleaded that this particular French court had no internal competence over him because he was not a trader. This plea was held bad.

On the other hand, in *Castrique* v. *Imrie*,[27] a case on a foreign judgment *in rem*, Blackburn J. regarded it as material "whether the sovereign authority of that State has conferred on the court jurisdiction to decide as to the disposition of the thing, and the court has acted within its jurisdiction." This could be taken to mean that a foreign judgment *in rem*, in order to be recognised in England, must have been pronounced by a court having internal competence as well as international jurisdiction. Further, in *Papadopoulos* v *Papadopoulos*,[28] one reason for refusing to recognise a Cypriot decree of nullity was that the Cypriot court had no internal competence to annul a marriage under the Order in Council which established it. And in *Adams* v. *Adams*,[29] a Rhodesian divorce was not recognised because the judge who pronounced it had not taken the oath of allegiance and the judicial oath in the prescribed form.

In *Macalpine* v. *Macalpine*,[30] there was some discussion whether fraud rendered a Wyoming decree of divorce void or merely voidable. It is believed that this distinction furnishes the key to the problem here dis-

---

[23] (1863) 1 H. & M. 195

[24] If Page-Wood V.-C. felt so strongly he should perhaps have asked Palmerston to send a gun-boat to bombard New Orleans. He was a man of strong views. He was accustomed to say that he "would rather hear of 300,000 Frenchmen having landed at Dover than that the Deceased Wife's Sister's Marriage Bill had passed into law" (Atlay, *Lives of the Victorian Chancellors,* Vol. 2, p. 355).

[25] By Scrutton L.J. in *Luther* v. *Sagor* [1921] 3 K.B. 532, 538, and Lords Reid and Wilberforce in *Carl Zeiss Stiftung* v. *Rayner & Keeler (No.* 2) [1967] 1 A.C. 853, 917–918, 922, 978.

[26] (1863) 15 C.B. (N.S.) 341; approved in *Pemberton* v. *Hughes* [1899] 1 Ch. 781, 791.

[27] (1870) L.R. 4 H.L. 414, 429. Blackburn J.'s statement was approved by Lord Chelmsford at p. 448.

[28] [1930] P. 55.

[29] [1971] P. 188.

[30] [1958] P. 35, 41, 45; *cf. Merker* v. *Merker* [1963] P. 283, 297–299. See *post,* p. 202, for discussion of a similar problem in the recognition of foreign divorces.

cussed. If the foreign judgment is merely irregular, *i.e.* valid until set aside, it will be held valid in England unless and until it is set aside in the foreign country.[31] If on the other hand the foreign judgment is a complete nullity by the law of the foreign country, then it will be held invalid in England. A foreign judgment is, of course, much more likely to be irregular than void. Hence the practical result is that lack of internal competence is hardly ever a good defence.

Discovery of fresh evidence. As a general rule, the defendant must take all available defences in the foreign court; if he does not do so, he cannot be allowed to plead them afterwards in England.[32] But, as we have seen,[33] this rule does not apply if it is alleged that the judgment was obtained by fraud, though it does apply if it is alleged that the proceedings were opposed to natural justice.

But what is the position if, when neither of these defences is alleged, the defendant since the date of the judgment discovers fresh evidence which he could not with reasonable diligence have discovered earlier and which shows that the judgment is erroneous? For example, the plaintiff sues for a debt in a foreign court; the defendant pleads that he has paid the debt but lost the receipt; the court disbelieves him and gives judgment for the plaintiff. The defendant later discovers the missing receipt, but it is now too late for him to get the foreign judgment set aside in the foreign country. Can he resist its enforcement by action in England?

In *De Cosse Brissac* v. *Rathbone*,[34] a similar plea was held to be no defence. Since no judgments were delivered, it is hard to know whether this was a decision on the question of law, or merely a decision on the sufficiency of the particular plea. The latter answer seems preferable, for two reasons. First, the plea was much less precise than a statement of claim would have to be in an action to review an English judgment on this ground; it did not even allege that if the fresh evidence had been produced to the foreign court, it must have led to an opposite result.[35] Secondly, since an English judgment can be set aside, even in the absence of fraud, if the unsuccessful party discovers new and material evidence after the trial,[36] there seems no reason why a foreign judgment should be in a better position.

ENFORCEMENT

A foreign judgment can be enforced in England by action at common law or, in cases to which they apply, by registration under the Administration

---

[31] See, to this effect, *S. A. Consortium General Textiles* v. *Sun and Sand Agencies Ltd.* [1978] Q.B. 279, 297, 307.

[32] *Henderson* v. *Henderson* (1844) 6 Q.B. 288; *Ellis* v. *M'Henry* (1871) L.R. 6 C.P. 228.

[33] *Ante,* pp. 118–119.

[34] (1861) 6 H. & N. 301 (the fifth plea).

[35] *Boswell* v. *Coaks* (1894) 86 L.T. 365 n., 366 n.; D. M. Gordon (1961) 77 L.Q.R. 358, 533, especially at pp. 549–554.

[36] Halsbury's *Laws of England,* 4th ed., Vol. 26, para. 561; D. M. Gordon (1961) 77 L.Q.R. 358, 533, especially at pp. 371, 536.

of Justice Act 1920, or the Foreign Judgments (Reciprocal Enforcement) Act 1933.

At common law

A foreign judgment *in personam*, given by a court having jurisdiction according to English rules of the conflict of laws, may be enforced by action in England, provided (a) it is for a debt, or definite sum of money, (b) it is not a judgment for taxes or penalties, and (c) it is "final and conclusive."

The judgment must be for a debt, or definite[37] sum of money (including damages and costs[38]), and not, *e.g.* a judgment ordering the defendant specifically to perform a contract.[39]

It must not be for taxes[40] or penalties.[41] It is well settled that an English court will not entertain an action for the enforcement, either directly or indirectly, of a foreign penal or revenue law.[42] Hence it will not enforce, either directly or indirectly, a foreign judgment ordering the payment of taxes or penalties. However, if the foreign judgment imposes a fine on the defendant and also orders him to pay compensation to the injured party (called the *"partie civile"* in French proceedings), the latter part of the judgment can be severed from the former and enforced in England. Thus in *Raulin* v. *Fischer*[43]:

> D, a young American lady, while recklessly galloping her horse in the Bois de Boulogne, Paris, ran into P, an elderly French colonel, and seriously injured him. D was prosecuted for her criminal negligence by the French authorities, and P intervened in the proceedings and claimed damages from D as allowed by French law. The court convicted D, fined her 100 francs, and ordered her to pay 15,000 francs to P by way of damages, and also costs. It was held that P could recover the sterling equivalent of the damages and costs in England.

The judgment must be "final and conclusive" in the court which rendered it.[44] "It must be shown that in the court by which it was pronounced, it conclusively, finally and for ever established the existence of the debt of which it is sought to be made conclusive evidence in this country, so as to make it *res judicata* between the parties."[45] So a summary judgment in which only a limited number of defences can be pleaded, and which is liable to be upset by the unsuccessful party in plenary proceedings where all defences may be set up, is not final and conclusive.[46] However, at common law a foreign judgment may be final and conclusive even though it is

---

[37] See *Sadler* v. *Robins* (1808) 1 Camp. 253.
[38] *Russell* v. *Smyth* (1842) 9 M. & W. 810.
[39] See *Duke* v. *Andler* [1932] 4 D.L.R. 529.
[40] *Government of India* v. *Taylor* [1955] A.C. 491, 514; *Rossano* v. *Manufacturers Life Insurance Co. Ltd.* [1963] 2 Q.B. 352, 376–378; *U.S.A.* v. *Harden* (1963) 41 D.L.R. (2d) 721 (Supreme Court of Canada). See Stoel (1967) 16 I.C.L.Q. 663.
[41] *Huntington* v. *Attrill* [1893] A.C. 150.
[42] *Ante,* Chap. 4.
[43] [1911] 2 K.B. 93.
[44] *Nouvion* v. *Freeman* (1889) 15 App.Cas. 1; *Blohn* v. *Desser* [1962] 2 Q.B. 116.
[45] *Nouvion* v. *Freeman, supra,* at p. 9, *per* Lord Herschell.
[46] *Ibid.*

subject to an appeal, and even though an appeal is actually pending in the foreign country where it was given.[47] But in a proper case a stay of execution would no doubt be ordered pending a possible appeal.[48]

The requirement that the foreign judgment must be final and conclusive usually makes it impossible to enforce a foreign maintenance order in England at common law, because the foreign court usually has power to vary the amount of the payments.[49] If, however, the foreign court has power to vary the amount of future payments, but not that of past payments, then an action may be brought in England to recover the arrears.[50] And as we shall see,[51] provision is made by statute for the reciprocal enforcement in one part of the United Kingdom of maintenance orders made in another part, and for the reciprocal enforcement in England of maintenance orders made in the Commonwealth overseas and certain foreign countries and vice versa.

Under the Administration of Justice Act 1920

When Part II of this Act has been extended by Order in Council to any part of the Commonwealth outside the United Kingdom, a judgment creditor who has obtained a judgment in a superior court in that part of the Commonwealth may, if a sum of money is payable under the judgment, apply to the High Court in England or Northern Ireland or to the Court of Session in Scotland at any time within twelve months of the date of the judgment to have the judgment registered in that court; and the court may order the judgment to be registered accordingly,[52] in which case the judgment will be of the same force and effect as if it were a judgment of the court in which it is registered.[53]

This Act was the outcome of proposals for the reciprocal enforcement of judgments and arbitral awards throughout the British Empire which were brought forward at the Imperial Conference of 1911. No Order in Council may be made extending the Act to any country unless Her Majesty is satisfied that reciprocal provisions have been made by the legislature of that country for the enforcement there of United Kingdom judgments.[54] Orders in Council have been made extending the Act to all the Australian states (but not the Capital Territory), to New Zealand, Newfoundland, Saskatchewan and a large number of colonies and former colonies.[55]

Registration of a judgment under the Act is not as of right, but discretionary; for the Act provides that the court *may* order the judgment to be registered if the court thinks it just and convenient that the judgment

---

[47] *Scott* v. *Pilkington* (1862) 2 B. & S. 11; *Colt Industries Inc.* v. *Sarlie (No. 2)* [1966] 1 W.L.R. 1287.
[48] *Ibid.*
[49] *Harrop* v. *Harrop* [1920] 3 K.B. 386; *Re Macartney* [1921] 1 Ch. 522. The rule is criticised by Grodecki (1959) 8 I.C.L.Q. 18, 32–40.
[50] *Beatty* v. *Beatty* [1924] 1 K.B. 807.
[51] *Post*, pp. 225–226.
[52] s.9(1).
[53] s.9(3)(*a*).
[54] s.14.
[55] For a full list, see Halsbury, *Laws of England,* 4th ed., Vol. 8, para. 752, n.4.

should be enforced in the United Kingdom.[56] Moreover, registration may not be ordered if the original court acted without jurisdiction, or if the defendant establishes any one of a limited number of defences.[57] These accord very closely with those available at common law, except that no judgment can be registered if the judgment debtor satisfies the court either that an appeal is pending, or that he is entitled and intends to appeal against the judgment.[58]

The judgment creditor remains free to bring an action on the foreign judgment in the ordinary way; but if he does, he will usually be deprived of his costs.[59]

It was intended that the régime created by the Act of 1920 should gradually be replaced by that of the Foreign Judgments (Reciprocal Enforcement) Act 1933. Under section 7 of that Act the Crown may apply Part I of the Act to "His Majesty's dominions outside the United Kingdom." The Order in Council made under this section prevents the further extension of the Act of 1920 to any part of the Commonwealth. But it does not automatically apply the scheme of the Act of 1933 in substitution for that of the Act of 1920. For that to be done a further and specific Order in Council is required.[60] As will be seen, a few such Orders have been made; but the replacement of the scheme of the Act of 1920 by that of the Act of 1933 is proceeding much more slowly than was anticipated.

Under the Foreign Judgments (Reciprocal Enforcement) Act 1933

When Part I of this Act has been extended by Order in Council to any foreign country outside the United Kingdom, a judgment creditor under a judgment to which the Act applies may apply to the High Court in England or Northern Ireland or to the Court of Session in Scotland at any time within six years of the date of the judgment to have the judgment registered in that court, and on any such application the court must (not may) order the judgment to be registered.[61] A registered judgment has the same force and effect as if it had been a judgment originally given in the registering court.[62] The Act applies to any judgment of a court (not necessarily a superior court) of a country to which Part I extends if it is final and conclusive as between the parties thereto, and there is payable thereunder a sum of money, not being a sum payable in respect of taxes or in respect of a fine or other penalty.[63] As at common law, a judgment is deemed to be final and conclusive notwithstanding that an appeal is pending against it.[64] But

---

[56] s.9(1)
[57] s.9(2)
[58] s.9(2)(e).
[59] s.9(5).
[60] *Yukon Consolidated Gold Corporation* v. *Clark* [1938] 2 K.B. 241.
[61] ss. 2(1), 12(a), 13(a).
[62] s.2(2). Hence a stay of execution will not be ordered merely because an English action is pending between the same parties and raising similar issues: *Wagner* v. *Laubscher Bros. & Co.* [1970] 2 Q.B. 313.
[63] s.1(2), as amended by Civil Jurisdiction and Judgments Act 1982, Sched. 10, para. 1. A sum payable by way of exemplary damages is not a penalty: *S. A. Consortium General Textiles* v. *Sun and Sand Agencies Ltd.* [1978] Q.B. 279, 299–300, 305–306.
[64] s.1(3).

the court has a discretionary power to set aside the registration of a judgment on such terms as it thinks fit, if the defendant satisfies the court that
an appeal is pending, or that he is entitled and intends to appeal.[65]

No Order in Council may be made extending the Act to any country
unless Her Majesty is satisfied that substantial reciprocity of treatment will
be assured to United Kingdom judgments in that country.[66] The Act now
extends only to Austria, Israel, Norway, Pakistan and Surinam among
politically foreign countries,[67] and to Guernsey, Jersey, the Isle of Man,
India, the Australian Capital Territory and Tonga among countries of the
Commonwealth.[68]

Registration *must* be set aside if the original court had no jurisdiction, or
if the defendant establishes any one of a limited number of defences which
accord very closely with those available at common law.[69] Registration
may be set aside if the matter in dispute had, before the foreign judgment
was given, been the subject of a final and conclusive judgment by a court
having jurisdiction in the matter.[70] For instance, if a plaintiff sues a defendant in Switzerland and in Austria, and both courts have jurisdiction, and
the Swiss court dismisses the action, but the Austrian court gives judgment
for the plaintiff, the English court *may* set aside the registration of the Austrian judgment.

Unlike the Administration of Justice Act 1920, the Act of 1933 prevents
the judgment creditor from bringing an action in England on the foreign
judgment.[71] Nor can he sue on the original cause of action.[72]

Under the State Immunity Act 1978

The European Convention on State Immunity (1972) provides that a
Contracting State shall give effect to a final judgment given against it by a
court of another Contracting State if, under the rules of the Convention,
the State could not claim immunity from jurisdiction.[73] Accordingly, section 18 of the State Immunity Act 1978 provides that a judgment given
against the United Kingdom by a court in another Contracting State[74] shall
be recognised in any court in the United Kingdom as conclusive between
the parties thereto in all proceedings founded on the same cause of action,
and may be relied on by way of defence or counter-claim in such proceedings. This only applies if the United Kingdom was not entitled to immunity

---

[65] s.5.

[66] s.1(1).

[67] It formerly extended also to Belgium, France, Italy and the Federal Republic of Germany,
but the bilateral conventions with those countries have been superseded by the Brussels
Convention 1968: see Civil Jurisdiction and Judgments Act 1982, Sched. 1, art. 56.

[68] The Act has also been extended to countries which are parties to certain international conventions, but only in relation to proceedings arising out of those conventions. See Dicey
and Morris, pp. 1107–1108.

[69] s.4(1)(*a*).

[70] s.4(1)(*b*).

[71] s.6.

[72] Civil Jurisdiction and Judgments Act 1982, s.34; *ante*, p. 107.

[73] Cmnd. 5081, art. 20. See Sinclair (1973) 22 I.C.L.Q. 254, 266–267, 273–276. For State
Immunity, see *ante*, pp. 56–60.

[74] s.21(*c*) of the Act provides that a certificate from the Secretary of State shall be conclusive
evidence on any question whether a State is a party to the Convention.

under the rules of the Convention (*i.e.* under sections 2–11 of the Act[75]) and only to final judgments, *i.e.* those no longer subject to appeal or, if given in default of appearance, liable to be set aside. Section 19, in accordance with the Convention, states certain exceptions in which the judgment need not be recognised. These are: (1) if recognition would be manifestly contrary to public policy or if any party to the proceedings had no adequate opportunity to present his case; (2) if service of process was not in accordance with the Convention (*i.e.* with section 12 of the Act[76]); (3) if proceedings between the same parties and based on the same facts and having the same purpose are pending before a court in the United Kingdom or in another Contracting State and were the first to be instituted; (4) if the judgment is inconsistent with a prior judgment given by a court in the United Kingdom or in another Contracting State in proceedings between the same parties; or (5) in the case of a judgment concerning the interest of the United Kingdom in movable or immovable property by way of succession, gift or *bona vacantia*, if the foreign court would not have had jurisdiction under rules equivalent to the United Kingdom rules applicable to such matters, or if the foreign court applied a law other than that which would have been applied by a United Kingdom court and would have reached a different result if it had applied that law.

Section 31 of the Civil Jurisdiction and Judgments Act 1982 makes similar provision for the recognition and enforcement of foreign judgments against States other than the United Kingdom or the State to which the foreign court belongs.

RECOGNITION AS DEFENCE

A foreign judgment *in personam* in favour of the defendant given by a court having jurisdiction may be relied upon for defensive purposes by the defendant if the plaintiff sues him in England on the original cause of action. A foreign judgment in favour of the defendant is a conclusive answer to an action in England on the original cause of action.[77] But the judgment must be "final and conclusive" in the court which rendered it[78]; this requirement applies when the judgment is relied upon as a defence just as it does when the plaintiff seeks to enforce it.[79] The foreign judgment is not a defence if the action was brought against a different party.[80] Nor is it a defence unless it was given on the merits. Thus in *Harris* v. *Quine*[81]:

A brought an action against B in the Isle of Man to recover a debt.

---

[75] *Ante*, pp. 57–59.
[76] *Ante*, p. 60.
[77] *Ricardo* v. *Garcias* (1845) 12 Cl. & F. 368; *Jacobson* v. *Frachon* (1927) 138 L.T. 386. *Cf.* Foreign Judgments (Reciprocal Enforcement) Act 1933, s.8.
[78] *Plummer* v. *Woodburne* (1825) 4 B. & C. 625; *Frayes* v. *Worms* (1861) 10 C.B.(N.I.) 149; *Carl Zeiss Stiftung* v. *Rayner & Keeler Ltd.* (*No.* 2) [1967] 1 A.C. 853.
[79] *Ante*, p. 125.
[80] *Carl Zeiss Stiftung* v. *Rayner & Keeler Ltd.* (*No.* 2) [1967] 1 A.C. 853, 910A–911F, 928C–929A, 936C–937F, 944B–946A.
[81] (1869) L.R. 4 Q.B. 653.

Under a Manx statute no action could be brought to recover a debt more that three years after it accrued. The Manx court gave judgment for B on the ground that the debt was statute barred. Later A sued B to recover the debt in England. It was held that the Manx judgment was no defence. It would have been otherwise if the judgment had held that the Manx statute extinguished the debt.

The position is the same under section 8 of the Foreign Judgments (Reciprocal Enforcement) Act 1933.[82]

Section 3 of the Foreign Limitation Periods Act 1984 provides (on the recommendation of the Law Commission[83]) that where a court of a foreign country has determined any matter by reference to the law relating to limitation of that or any other country (including England), the court shall be deemed to have determined that matter on its merits.

2. JUDGMENTS RENDERED INSIDE THE EEC

Introduction

The jurisdictional provisions of the Brussels Convention on Jurisdiction and the Enforcement of Judgments were discussed in Chapter 6.[84] Here we are concerned with its provisions on the recognition and enforcement of judgments.

For reasons of clarity of exposition, the provisions of the Convention on jurisdiction and on the recognition and enforcement of judgments are dealt with in different chapters. But it cannot be stressed too strongly that the Convention is one and indivisible and should be considered as a whole. Its provisions on recognition and enforcement are intended to mesh with its provisions on jurisdiction. The latter provide ample guarantees for the defendant: as a general rule he can only be sued in the courts of his domicile[85]; his right to defend himself is safeguarded[86]; if he does not enter an appearance the court itself must protect him by declaring of its own motion that it has no jurisdiction, unless its jurisdiction is derived from the provisions of the Convention[87]; the court must stay the proceedings unless satisfied that the defendant had an opportunity to be heard.[88] The strictness of these provisions has its counterpart in the extreme liberality of the provisions on recognition and enforcement, which are designed to allow judgments given in one Contracting State to run freely throughout the Community.

Of course the provisions on recognition and enforcement only apply to judgments within the scope of the Convention as defined in article 1. But

---

[82] *Black-Clawson International Ltd.* v. *Papierwerke Waldhof-Aschaffenburg A/G* [1975] A.C. 591.
[83] Law Com. No. 114 (1982).
[84] *Ante,* pp. 77–89.
[85] Arts. 2 and 3.
[86] Art. 18.
[87] Art. 20 (1).
[88] Art. 20 (2).

subject to that, "judgment" includes any judgment given by a court or tribunal of a Contracting State, whatever it may be called.[89]

The Convention makes two important departures of principle from the English rules for recognition and enforcement at common law and under the Foreign Judgments (Reciprocal Enforcement) Act 1933. First, the Convention is not limited to money judgments, but extends also to, e.g. injunctions and orders for specific performance. Secondly, as a general rule (but subject to some limitations) the court in which enforcement is sought may not investigate the jurisdiction of the court which gave the judgment. The scheme of the Convention is that, in general, it is for the original court to determine that it has jurisdiction; once it has so determined, the court in which enforcement is sought cannot, in general, question its decision.

It is important to note that under the Convention the enforcement procedures apply to all judgments within its scope, whether or not they are against persons domiciled in a Contracting State. Thus an English judgment against a New York resident where the jurisdiction of the English court was based on the temporary presence of the defendant in England is enforceable in France; and a French judgment against a New York resident where the jurisdiction of the French court was based on the French nationality of the plaintiff under article 14 of the French Civil Code is enforceable in England. But article 59 of the Convention allows a Contracting State to assume in relation to a non-Contracting State the obligation not to recognise judgments given in other Contracting States against defendants domiciled or habitually resident in the third State where the basis of jurisdiction could only be one of the so-called "exorbitant" bases of jurisdiction listed in article 3(2). Negotiations for such a bilateral convention between the United Kingdom and the United States did not proceed to a conclusion. Negotiations are continuing between the United Kingdom and Canada and Australia.

Mode of enforcement

The enforcement of EEC judgments in the United Kingdom is by way of registration under section 4 of the Civil Jurisdiction and Judgments Act 1982 and article 31(2) of the Convention. It is implicit in the decision of the European Court in Case 42/76 *De Wolf* v. *Cox*[90] that no other mode of enforcement is available, e.g. an action on the judgment at common law. Registration is to be in the High Court.[91] The application for registration must be made *ex parte* in the first instance.[92] At this stage in the proceedings the defendant has no right to be heard, or even to be informed of the application for registration. This is intended to preserve the element of surprise and to prevent him from removing his assets out of the State where enforcement is sought. If enforcement is authorised, the defendant may then apply to the High Court to set aside the registration: thereafter he

[89] Art. 25.
[90] [1976] E.C.R. 1759.
[91] s.4(1) and art. 32.
[92] Art. 34(1).

may appeal once only on a point of law.[93] If enforcement is refused, the plaintiff may re-apply to the High Court[94] and there is a further right of appeal by either party, but once only on a point of law.[95] The single appeal on a point of law under articles 37 and 41 is to the Court of Appeal or, under the "leap-frog" procedure of the Administration of Justice Act 1969, to the House of Lords.[96]

Provisional or protective orders are enforceable[97]; but not if they are granted *ex parte* without the defendant being given an opportunity to be heard.[98]

The Convention does not deal with interest on money judgments, *i.e.* interest for the period after judgment. This is dealt with in section 7 of the Act.

Grounds on which recognition or enforcement may be refused

The grounds on which recognition may be refused are set out in article 27. These apply equally to enforcement.[99] They are as follows: (1) if recognition is contrary to public policy; (2) if the judgment was given in default of appearance and the defendant was not duly served with the writ in sufficient time to enable him to arrange for his defence (but the court in which recognition is sought is not bound by the findings of the original court on this point[1]); (3) if the judgment is irreconcilable with a judgment given in a dispute between the same parties in the State in which recognition is sought; (4) if the original court has decided a preliminary question concerning the status or legal capacity of natural persons, rights in property arising out of a matrimonial relationship, wills or succession in a way which conflicts with a rule of private international law of the State in which recognition is sought, unless the same result would have been reached by the application of the rules of private international law of that State (this is specially relevant to claims for maintenance[2]); or (5) if the judgment is irreconcilable with an earlier judgment given in a non-Contracting State involving the same cause of action and between the same parties, provided that the earlier judgment is entitled to recognition in the State addressed. It will be noted that article 27 does not include the fact that the judgment was obtained by fraud. This is because in continental law this ground for refusal is included in the head of public policy. English courts have had no difficulty in deciding that a foreign divorce obtained by fraud need not be recognised in England since recognition would be contrary to public policy.[3]

The court in which enforcement is sought is not entitled to review the

---

[93] Arts. 36 and 37.
[94] Art. 40.
[95] Art. 41.
[96] s.6(1) and (2).
[97] Case 143/78 *De Cavel* v. *De Cavel* (*No.* 1) [1979] E.C.R. 1055.
[98] Case 123/79 *Denilauler* v. *Couchet Frères* [1980] E.C.R. 1553.
[99] Art. 34(2).
[1] Case 228/81 *Pendy Plastic Products BV* v. *Pluspunkt* [1982] E.C.R. 2723; *cf.* Case 166/80 *Klomps* v. *Michel* [1981] E.C.R. 1593.
[2] *Post*, p.226.
[3] *Kendall* v. *Kendall* [1977] Fam. 208; *post*, p. 203.

merits of the judgment.[4] Nor can it question the jurisdiction of the court which gave the judgment, except where it conflicts with the provisions of articles 7–12A (insurance), 13–15 (consumer contracts) or 16 (exclusive jurisdiction).[5] But even in these cases, the court in which enforcement is sought is bound by the findings of fact on which the original court based its jurisdiction. However, the court in which enforcement is sought is not bound by the findings of the original court as to whether the case is within the scope of the Convention.[6]

Reciprocal enforcement within the United Kingdom

The reciprocal enforcement of judgments within the United Kingdom now depends on section 18 and Schedules 6 and 7 of the Civil Jurisdiction and Judgments Act 1982, which replace the Judgments Extension Act 1868 and the Inferior Courts Judgments Extension Act 1882. The principal difference between the 1982 Act and those which it replaces is that the former applies equally to money and non-money judgments. Thus under the 1982 Act injunctions and orders for specific performance granted or made in one part of the United Kingdom are enforceable in other parts. Section 18 does not apply to judgments in proceedings other than civil proceedings, nor to maintenance orders or orders concerning the legal capacity of an individual, including judicial separation, guardianship and custody, nor to judgments in bankruptcy, winding up of companies or administration of the estate of a deceased person.[7]

Enforcement is by way of registration in the court in which enforcement is sought of a certificate granted by the court which gave the judgment. Registration (even of certificates of judgments of inferior courts) is in superior courts only, *i.e.* the High Court in England or Northern Ireland, or the Court of Session in Scotland. Schedule 6 contains the procedure for enforcement of certificates of money judgments, and Schedule 7 for enforcement of certificates of non-money judgments. Registration of a certificate *must* be set aside if the registration was contrary to the provisions of the Schedules, and *may* be set aside if the registering court is satisfied that the matter in dispute had previously been the subject of a judgment by another court having jurisdiction in the matter.[8] But, as under the 1868 and 1882 Acts, it is not a ground for setting registration aside that the original court had no jurisdiction over the defendant, or that the judgment was obtained by fraud, or that its enforcement would be contrary to public policy, or that the proceedings were opposed to natural justice.

The judgment may not be enforced except by registration under Schedules 6 or 7.[9]

Section 19 contains provisions for the recognition, as opposed to enforcement, of judgments to which section 18 applies.

---

[4] Arts. 29, 34 (3).
[5] Art. 28.
[6] Case 29/76 *LTU* v. *Eurocontrol* [1976] E.C.R. 1541.
[7] s.18(3), (5) and (6).
[8] Sched. 6 para. 10; Sched. 7 para. 9.
[9] s.18(8).

CHAPTER 10

ARBITRATION

FOREIGN arbitration awards can be enforced in England in various ways. First, they can be enforced by action at common law. Secondly, if they come within the Geneva Convention for the Execution of Foreign Arbitral Awards (1927), they can be enforced under Part II of the Arbitration Act 1950 under conditions very similar to, but not precisely identical with, those obtaining at common law. Thirdly, if they come within the New York Convention on the Recognition and Enforcement of Foreign Arbitral Awards (1958), they can be enforced under the Arbitration Act 1975 in a similar manner to those coming under the Geneva Convention. Fourthly, arbitration awards made in countries of the Commonwealth outside the United Kingdom to which Part II of the Administration of Justice Act 1920 extends or in countries to which Part I of the Foreign Judgments (Reciprocal Enforcement) Act 1933 extends can be enforced in England as if they were judgments, *i.e.* by registration.[1] Fifthly, arbitration awards made in one part of the United Kingdom can be enforced in other parts by registration under the Civil Jurisdiction and Judgments Act 1982.

Very often the plaintiff can choose between different methods of enforcement. Thus, if the award is one which the Geneva Convention applies, the plaintiff may enforce it under Part II of the Arbitration Act 1950 or, if he prefers, by action at common law.[2] If the award is one to which the New York Convention applies, he may enforce it under the Arbitration Act 1975 or by action at common law.[3] If the award is enforceable as a judgment under the Administration of Justice Act 1920, the Foreign Judgments (Reciprocal Enforcement) Act 1933 or the Civil Jurisdiction and Judgments Act 1982, the plaintiff can enforce it if he prefers under the summary procedure of section 26 of the Arbitration Act 1950 or by action at common law. The mode of enforcement by action at common law is thus always available; this mode is therefore still the most important.

AT COMMON LAW

Introduction

The enforcement of foreign arbitration awards sometimes raises even more delicate questions than does the enforcement of foreign judgments.

---

[1] Certain arbitration awards made in pursuance of a contract for the international carriage of goods can also be enforced by registration under this Act: Carriage of Goods by Road Act 1965, ss.4(1), 7(1). See Dicey and Morris, pp. 1156–1157. See also the Arbitration (International Investment Disputes) Act 1966.

[2] Arbitration Act 1950, s.40(*a*), which saves the right to enforce such awards at common law.

[3] Arbitration Act 1975, s.6, which saves the right to enforce such awards at common law.

Moreover, the enforcement of foreign arbitration awards may be required more frequently than the enforcement of foreign judgments. This is because actions *in personam* are usually brought in the country where the defendant resides and keeps his assets, so that the need for enforcement elsewhere is the exception rather than the rule. But there is an increasing tendency for contracts between businessmen residing in different countries to provide for arbitration in a third or "neutral" country, where neither resides or keeps his assets, so that the need for enforcement is the rule rather than the exception. On the other hand, business men may perhaps be more inclined to obey the award of a tribunal of their own choice than they are to obey the decision of a court.

Although English courts have enforced foreign judgments from the seventeenth century onwards,[4] it is only since 1927[5] (so far as one can judge from reported cases) that they have enforced foreign arbitration awards, and so authority is relatively scanty. This is no doubt because arbitration is so ancient and well-developed an institution in England that for many years most disputes that had any connection with England, and many that had none,[6] were referred to arbitration in England, and so the enforcement of the award in England was a purely domestic matter.

A foreign arbitration award can be enforced by action in England at common law if (1) the parties submitted to the arbitration by an agreement which is valid by its proper law, and (2) the award is valid and final according to the law which governs the arbitration proceedings.[7]

Validity of the agreement to arbitrate

In the eyes of an English court, the jurisdiction of the arbitrators is derived from the agreement of the parties to arbitrate. Such an agreement may assume one of two forms, in that it may submit present or future disputes to arbitration.[8] A contract may contain an arbitration clause by which the parties agree that if disputes arise under the contract they shall be referred to arbitration. Or parties may agree to submit a particular dispute between them (which need not necessarily stem from a contract) to the decision of a particular arbitrator. In both cases the validity, interpretation and effect of the agreement to arbitrate are governed by the proper law of the agreement. In the first type of case, there is a very strong presumption that the proper law of the contract is the law of the country where the arbitration is to be held.[9] But the presumption, though strong, can be

---

[4] *Ante*, p. 106.

[5] *Norske Atlas Insurance Co. Ltd.* v. *London General Insurance Co. Ltd.* (1927) 43 T.L.R. 541.

[6] For a striking and well-known example, see *Gilbert* v. *Burnstine* (1931) 255 N.Y. 348, 174 N.E. 706, where the New York Court of Appeals enforced an English award made in pursuance of an arbitration clause in a contract made and to be performed in New York between two residents of that state. See also Kerr J. (1978) 41 M.L.R. 1, 5–6.

[7] Dicey and Morris, Rule 199.

[8] See Arbitration Act 1950, s.32; Sched. 1, art. 1; Sched. 2, art. 1; *Russell on Arbitration*, 20th ed., p. 44.

[9] *Hamlyn* v. *Talisker Distillery* [1894] A.C. 202; *Spurrier* v. *La Cloche* [1902] A.C. 466; *Norske Atlas Insurance Co.Ltd.* v. *London General Insurance Co. Ltd.* (1927) 43 T.L.R. 541; *Tzortzis* v. *Monark Line A/B* [1968] 1 W.L.R. 406.

rebutted; for the House of Lords has emphasised that an arbitration clause is only one of several circumstances to be considered in determining the proper law of a contract.[10]

The presumption does not apply if the parties cannot agree on the place of arbitration and their contract provides that the arbitrator is to be appointed by, *e.g.* the President of the International Court of Justice, or of a Chamber of Commerce, or of a trade or professional association. In such cases the proper law of the contract has to be ascertained in the ordinary way by a consideration of all the surrounding circumstances.[11]

When the agreement is to refer an existing dispute to a particular arbitrator, the law of the country where the arbitration is to be held is even more likely to be the proper law of the contract, because the arbitration is the sole object of the agreement.

The law governing the arbitration proceedings

The parties can not only choose the law which governs their agreement to arbitrate but also the law which governs the arbitration proceedings. Normally the parties exercise this power by determining the country in which the arbitration is to take place, the law of which then usually becomes the proper law of the contract. But if the parties to an English contract provide for arbitration in Switzerland, English law would govern the validity, interpretation and effect of the arbitration clause (including the scope of the arbitrators' jurisdiction), but the arbitration proceedings (including the extent to which they are subject to judicial control) would be governed by Swiss law. Where the parties fail to choose the law governing the arbitration proceedings, those proceedings will almost certainly be governed by the law of the country in which the arbitration takes place, on the ground that it is the country most closely connected with the proceedings. Thus in *Whitworth Street Estates Ltd.* v. *James Miller and Partners Ltd.*[12]:

> A & Co., a Scottish firm of builders, agreed to carry out conversion work at the factory in Scotland of B & Co., an English company. The contract contained an arbitration clause providing for the appointment of an arbitrator by the President of the Royal Institute of British Architects. The President appointed a Scottish architect as arbitrator and the arbitration proceedings took place in Scotland. The House of Lords held (by a majority of 3 to 2) that the proper law of the contract was English law, and (unanimously) that the arbitration proceedings were governed by Scots law, so that the High Court had no power to order the arbitrator to state his award in the form of a special case.

However, if there is no law governing the arbitration proceedings, because they have not yet begun, the proper law of the contract (in default

---

[10] *Compagnie Tunisienne de Navigation S.A.* v. *Compagnie d'Armement Maritime S.A.* [1971] A.C. 572, disapproving dicta in *Tzortzis* v. *Monark Line A/B, supra.*
[11] *Whitworth Street Estates Ltd.* v. *James Miller and Partners Ltd.* [1970] A.C. 583.
[12] [1970] A.C. 583.

of any other) will have to determine such questions as whether the court has power to extend the time during which arbitration must be begun.[13]

Validity of the award

To be enforceable in England, the award must be valid by the law governing the arbitration proceedings, *i.e.* normally the law of the country in which the arbitration is held. That law will determine how the arbitrators are to be appointed, in so far as this is not regulated by the arbitration agreement; the effect of one party's failure to appoint an arbitrator,[14] *e.g.* whether an arbitrator may be appointed by the court, or whether the arbitration can proceed before the sole arbitrator appointed by the other party; and whether the authority of an arbitrator can be revoked. That law will also determine what law the arbitrators are to apply, and whether they can decide *ex aequo et bono*. Provided the award is valid by the law governing the arbitration proceedings, none of these matters is of any concern to the English court which is asked to enforce the award. It is true that, in English domestic law, arbitrators must apply some fixed and recognisable system of law, whether English or foreign.[15] This is because it is contrary to public policy for the parties to oust the jurisdiction of the court to control the proceedings under sections 22 to 25 of the Arbitration Act 1950. But there is no reason, so far as English law is concerned, why the parties should not be allowed to oust the jurisdiction of a foreign court.[16]

Finality of the award

To be enforceable in England, the award must be final and binding on the parties in the English sense, *i.e.* it must fulfil one of the conditions for the enforcement of foreign judgments *in personam*.[17] Whether the award is final in the English sense depends on the law governing the arbitration proceedings. The question to be answered is "Has it become final, as we understand that phrase, in the country in which it was made? Of course the question whether it is final in [that country] will depend no doubt upon [the foreign] law, but the [foreign] law is directed to showing whether it is final as that word is understood in English."[18] These remarks were made in a case where the award was enforced under Part II of the Arbitration Act 1950, but it is thought that they are equally applicable to the enforcement of awards at common law.

---

[13] *International Tank and Pipe S.A.K.* v. *Kuwait Aviation Fuelling Co. K.S.C.* [1975] Q.B. 224.

[14] *Bankers and Shippers Insurance Co. of New York* v. *Liverpool Marine and General Insurance Co. Ltd.* (1926) 24 Ll.L.R. 85 (H.L.); *Norske Atlas Insurance Co. Ltd.* v. *London and General Insurance Co. Ltd.* (1927) 43 T.L.R. 541; *cf. Oppenheim & Co.* v. *Mahomed Haneef* [1922] 1 A.C. 482.

[15] *Orion Compania Espanola de Seguros* v. *Belfort Maatschappij* [1962] 2 Lloyd's Rep. 257; but see *Eagle Star Ins. Co.* v. *Yuval Ins. Co.* [1978] 1 Lloyd's Rep. 357, 362.

[16] *Addison* v. *Brown* [1954] 1 W.L.R. 779.

[17] See Arbitration Act 1950, s.16, and *ante*, p. 125.

[18] *Union Nationale des Cooperatives Agricoles* v. *Catterall* [1959] 2 Q.B. 44, 53, *per* Lord Evershed M.R.

Mode of enforcement

In order to enforce an arbitration award in England it is necessary to obtain an enforcement title from an English court. A plaintiff seeking to enforce an English award can choose between bringing an action on it and applying for leave to enforce it under section 26 of the Arbitration Act 1950.[19] This summary procedure is also available for the enforcement of a foreign award.[20] But it should only be used where the validity of the award or the right to proceed upon it is "reasonably clear."[21]

An award may be expressed in foreign currency, and such an award can be enforced under section 26.[22] But, whether enforced by action or under section 26, it must be converted into sterling before it can be enforced in England by any process of execution. The date for conversion will be the date when the court authorises enforcement of the judgment or when leave to enforce the award in sterling under section 26 is given.[23]

A foreign arbitration award may be enforced in England whether or not the law governing the arbitration proceedings requires a judgment or order of the foreign court to make the award enforceable.[24] Provided the award is final in the English sense by the law governing the arbitration proceedings, it can be enforced in England even though by that law it is not enforceable in the foreign country until a judgment of a court has been obtained. If the English court insisted on a foreign judgment in order to make the award enforceable in England, it would not be enforcing the award but the judgment, and the foreign award as such would be deprived of all effect in England. All doubts concerning this important principle were dispelled by the decision of the Court of Appeal in *Union Nationale des Cooperatives Agricoles* v. *Catterall*.[25] That case was decided under Part II of the Arbitration Act 1950, but it is thought that the principle applies with equal force to enforcement at common law.

However, if the party in whose favour a foreign award is made obtains a judgment on it in the country where it was rendered, he can enforce that judgment in England in accordance with the principles on which foreign judgments *in personam* are enforced.[26] By submitting to arbitration in a

---

[19] The application can be made *ex parte* by affidavit unless the court otherwise directs, in which case it is made by originating summons; R.S.C., Ord. 73, r. 10.

[20] *Dalmia Cement Ltd.* v. *National Bank of Pakistan* [1975] Q.B. 9, 19–23.

[21] *Re Boks & Co. and Peters, Rushton & Co. Ltd.* [1919] 1 K. B. 491; but see *Middlemiss and Gould* v. *Hartlepool Corporation* [1972] 1 W.L.R. 1643, 1647. In *Union Nationale des Cooperatives Agricoles* v. *Catterall* [1959] 2 Q.B. 44, 52, this test was adopted and applied to the enforcement of a foreign award under Part II of the Arbitration Act 1950. S.36(1) of the Act makes the summary procedure under s.26 specifically applicable to the enforcement of foreign awards which comes within Part II. See *post*, p. 141.

[22] *Jugoslavenska Oceanska Plovidba* v. *Castle Investment Co.* [1974] Q.B. 272. See *post*, pp. 462–463.

[23] *Miliangos* v. *George Frank (Textiles) Ltd.* [1976] A. C. 443, 469D, *per* Lord Wilberforce.

[24] *Union Nationale des Cooperatives Agricoles* v. *Catterall* [1959] 2 Q.B. 44; Dicey and Morris, p. 1135, where it is suggested that the earlier and much-criticised decision to the contrary of Eve J. in *Merrifield Ziegler & Co.* v. *Liverpool Cotton Association* (1911) 105 L.T. 97 would not now be followed. See, to this effect, *Dalmia Dairy Industries Ltd.* v. *National Bank of Pakistan* [1978] 2 Lloyd's Rep. 223, 249.

[25] [1959] 2 Q.B. 44.

[26] *East India Trading Co. Inc.* v. *Carmel Exporters and Importers Ltd.* [1952] 2 Q.B. 439; *International Alltex Corporation* v. *Lawler Creations Ltd.* [1965] I.R. 264.

foreign country, the parties also submit to the jurisdiction of the foreign court which declares the award enforceable.[27]

Recognition as defence

The conditions under which a foreign arbitration award may be enforced in England at common law presumably apply also to its recognition as a defence to an action on the original cause of action. A valid English award duly made in pursuance of a valid agreement to arbitrate is a defence to an action on the original cause of action,[28] and there seems no reason why the same should not be true of a foreign award. But it is doubtful whether this would apply if the foreign award was not based on the merits but, e.g. on the ground that the arbitration was out of time.[29]

Defences to actions on foreign awards

There is very little authority on the grounds on which a foreign award can be challenged in England, notwithstanding that it was made in accordance with a valid agreement to arbitrate, and is valid and final according to the law governing the arbitration proceedings. But it can hardly be supposed that foreign arbitration awards will be more readily enforced or recognised in England than are foreign judgments. Hence the existence of the following grounds of challenge can probably be taken for granted:

(a) that under the agreement to arbitrate the arbitrators had no jurisdiction to make the award[30];

(b) that the award was obtained by fraud[31];

(c) that the enforcement or recognition of the award would be contrary to English public policy[32]; and

(d) that the proceedings in which the award was obtained were opposed to natural justice.

UNDER PART II OF THE ARBITRATION ACT 1950

The Geneva Convention

Efforts to promote the international enforcement and recognition of commercial arbitration awards have on a number of occasions been made by means of multilateral international conventions. The United Kingdom is a party to the Protocol on Arbitration Clauses (1923) and to the Geneva Convention on the Execution of Foreign Arbitral Awards (1927). Part II of the Arbitration Act 1950 (repealing and replacing earlier legislation)

---

[27] *International Alltex Corporation* v. *Lawler Creations Ltd., supra.*

[28] *Ayscough* v. *Sheed, Thomson & Co. Ltd.* (1924) 40 T.L.R. 707 (H.L.).

[29] Compare *Ayscough* v. *Sheed, Thomson & Co. Ltd., supra* (action barred by English award holding that arbitration was out of time) with *Harris* v. *Quine* (1869) L.R. 4 Q.B. 653 and *Black-Clawson International Ltd.* v. *Papierwerke Waldhof-Aschaffenburg A/G* [1975] A.C. 591 (action not barred by foreign judgment dismissing claim as statute-barred). See *ante,* p. 130.

[30] See *Kianta Osakeyhtio* v. *Britain and Overseas Trading Co. Ltd.* [1953] 2 Lloyd's Rep. 569; [1954] 1 Lloyd's Rep. 247; *Dalmia Dairy Industries Ltd.* v. *National Bank of Pakistan* [1978] 2 Lloyd's Rep. 223.

[31] See *Oppenheim & Co.* v. *Mahomed Haneef* [1922] 1 A.C. 482, 487.

[32] See *Dalmia Dairy Industries Ltd.* v. *National Bank of Pakistan, supra.*

enacts the Protocol of 1923 as supplemented by the Convention of 1927 as part of the law of the United Kingdom.

Scope of application

Part II of the Act is limited to awards (other than awards made in pursuance of an arbitration agreement governed by English law)[33] made between persons who are subject to the jurisdiction of different States, both of which are parties to the Protocol of 1923 and both of which have, by reason of reciprocity, been declared by Order in Council to be parties to the Convention of 1927.[34] The meaning of the somewhat obscure phrase "subject to the jurisdiction" has occasioned much speculation. It has been held to mean not that the parties must have different nationalities, but that (i) they must reside or carry on business in two different contracting States, and (ii) that the contract containing the submission to arbitration must have resulted from business so conducted.[35]

The award must further have been made in a territory specified by Order in Council, that is to say, the territory of a Contracting State.[36] But this State need not be one of which either party is a citizen or in which either party resides. Thus a Danish award made between English and French parties is within Part II, because the United Kingdom, France and Denmark are all Contracting States.[37]

Conditions of enforceability

The conditions under which foreign awards within Part II can be enforced or recognised in England are very similar to those applicable at common law. They are as follows.[38] The award must have

(a) been made in pursuance of an agreement for arbitration which was valid under the law by which it was governed[39];

(b) been made by the tribunal provided for in the agreement or constituted in manner agreed upon by the parties;

(c) been made in conformity with the law governing the arbitration procedure;

(d) become final in the country in which it was made[40];

(e) been in respect of a matter which may lawfully be referred to arbitration under the law of England;

and its enforcement must not be against the public policy or the law of England.

---

[33] Arbitration Act 1950, s.40(b).
[34] s.35(1)(b). For a list of States which have been declared to be parties to the Convention, see S.I. 1978 No. 186 and S.I. 1979 No. 304.
[35] *Brazendale & Co. Ltd.* v. *Saint Freres S.A.* [1970] 2 Lloyd's Rep. 34. *Cf. Union Nationale des Cooperatives Agricoles* v. *Catterall* [1959] 2 Q.B. 44, 50, *per* Lord Evershed M.R.
[36] Arbitration Act 1950, s.35(1)(c).
[37] *Union Nationale des Cooperatives Agricoles* v. *Catterall, supra.*
[38] Arbitration Act 1950, s.37(1).
[39] See *Kianta Osakeyhtio* v. *Britain and Overseas Trading Co. Ltd.* [1954] 1 Lloyd's Rep. 247.
[40] See *Union Nationale des Cooperatives Agricoles* v. *Catterall* [1959] 2 Q.B. 44, and *ante*, p. 139.

An award is not deemed final if any proceedings for contesting its validity are pending in the country in which it was made.[41]

An award will not be enforceable if it does not deal with all the questions referred or contains decisions on matters beyond the scope of the agreement for arbitration, or if the party against whom it is sought to enforce the award was not given notice of the arbitration proceedings in sufficient time to enable him to present his case, or was under some legal incapacity and was not properly represented.[42] Except to this limited extent, it is no defence that the proceedings were opposed to natural justice, nor is it a defence that the award was obtained by fraud.

Mode of enforcement

A party who has obtained an award which is within Part II of the Act may, at his option, enforce it by action or by an application for leave to enforce the award under section 26 of the Act.[43] But the latter procedure should only be used in "reasonably clear cases."[44] Alternatively, he may enforce it by action at common law.[45]

UNDER THE ARBITRATION ACT 1975

This Act was passed to enable the United Kingdom to accede to the New York Convention on the Recognition and Enforcement of Foreign Arbitral Awards of 1958.[46] The main differences between the New York and Geneva Conventions are as follows:

(1) The definition of awards to which the former applies is much simpler. The award need only be made in a State, other than the United Kingdom, which is a party to the Convention.[47] There is no requirement that the parties to the award must be "subject to the jurisdiction" of different Contracting States, nor that the arbitration agreement should not be governed by English law.

(2) The burden of proof is differently distributed. The plaintiff seeking enforcement merely has to produce the original award or a certified copy of it, the original arbitration agreement or a certified copy of it, and (where the award or agreement is in a foreign language) a certified translation.[48] The burden is then on the defendant resisting enforcement to prove any of the following substantive defences:

---

[41] Arbitration Act 1950, s.39.
[42] s.37(2).
[43] s.36(1).
[44] *Union Nationale des Cooperatives Agricoles* v. *Catterall* [1959] 2 Q.B. 44, 52, where the test laid down in *Re Boks & Co. and Peters, Rushton & Co. Ltd.* [1919] 1 K.B. 491 was approved and applied. See also *Middlemiss and Gould* v. *Hartlepool Corporation* [1972] 1 W.L.R. 1643, 1647B.
[45] Arbitration Act, 1950, s.40(*a*).
[46] For a commentary on the Act, see Lew (1975) 24 I. C.L.Q. 870. For the text of the Convention, see Fifth Report of the Private International Law Committee, Cmnd. 1515 (1961).
[47] For a list of parties to the Convention, see S.I. 1979 No. 304.
[48] Arbitration Act 1975, s.4.

(a) that a party to the arbitration agreement was (under the law applicable to him) under some incapacity;

(b) that the arbitration agreement was not valid under the law to which the parties subjected it, or, failing any indication thereon, under the law of the country where the award was made;

(c) that he was not given proper notice of the appointment of the arbitrator or of the arbitration proceedings or was otherwise unable to present his case;

(d) that the award deals with a difference not contemplated by or not falling within the terms of the submission to arbitration or contains decisions on matters beyond the scope of the submission to arbitration (unless they can be separated);

(e) that the composition of the arbitral authority or the arbitral procedure was not in accordance with the agreement of the parties, or, failing such agreement, with the law of the country where the arbitration took place; or

(f) that the award has not yet become binding on the parties, or has been set aside or suspended by a competent authority of the country in which, or under the law of which, it was made.[49]

Recognition or enforcement of an award may also be refused if the award is in respect of a matter which is not capable of settlement by arbitration, or if it would be contrary to public policy to recognise or enforce the award.[50] In these two cases the point can be taken either by the defendant or by the court on its own motion. Recognition or enforcement may not be refused except in the cases mentioned above.[51]

(3) The defences to enforcement are drafted with greater precision than they are in the Geneva Convention, and thus provide fewer opportunities for obstruction by a defendant resisting enforcement.

(4) If the defendant proves any of these defences, refusal to enforce the award is within the discretion of the court, and not mandatory as it generally is under the Geneva Convention.

A party who has obtained a "Convention award" may, at his option, enforce it either by action or by an application for leave to enforce the award summarily under section 26 of the Arbitration Act 1950.[52] The award may also be relied upon as a defence to an action on the original cause of action.[53]

Article VII. 2 of the New York Convention provides that the Geneva Convention shall cease to have effect between Contracting States on their becoming bound by this Convention. The Arbitration Act 1975 implements this provision not by repealing Part II of the Arbitration Act 1950 (because it may still be required as between the United Kingdom and States which are parties to the Geneva Convention but not to the New

---

[49] s.5(2) and (4).
[50] s.5(3).
[51] s.5(1).
[52] ss.3(1)(a), 6. See *ante*, pp. 138, 141.
[53] s.3(2).

York Convention), but by the enactment in section 2 that where a "Convention award" would, but for that section, be also a "foreign award" within the meaning of Part II of the Arbitration Act 1950, that Part shall not apply to it.

UNDER PART II OF THE ADMINISTRATION OF JUSTICE ACT 1920 OR PART I OF THE FOREIGN JUDGMENTS (RECIPROCAL ENFORCEMENT) ACT 1933

As we have seen,[54] the Administration of Justice Act 1920 provides for the direct enforcement in the United Kingdom of judgments of superior courts of countries of the Commonwealth overseas to which the Act has been extended by Order in Council.[55] The Act provides that any such judgment may be registered in the High Court in England, if that court thinks it is just and convenient that the judgment should be enforced in the United Kingdom[56]; and that a judgment so registered shall be of the same force and effect as if it had been a judgment of the High Court.[57] The Act defines a judgment so as to include an arbitration award if the award has, in pursuance of the law in force in the place where it was made, become enforceable in the same manner as a judgment given by a court in that place.[58] The plaintiff remains free to bring an action on the award at common law, but he may be deprived of his costs.[59]

The Foreign Judgments (Reciprocal Enforcement) Act 1933 also provides[60] that the provisions of the Act, except sections 1(5) and 6, apply to an arbitration award which has become enforceable in the same manner as a judgment in the place where it was made. The effect of the exception for section 6 is that such an award can be enforced at the option of the plaintiff either by registration under the Act or under the summary procedure of section 26 of the Arbitration Act 1950 or by action at common law.

UNDER THE CIVIL JURISDICTION AND JUDGMENTS ACT 1982

For the purposes of section 18 of the Civil Jurisdiction and Judgments Act 1982, which provides for the reciprocal enforcement of judgments within the United Kingdom,[61] "judgment" is defined so as to include an arbitration award which has become enforceable in the part of the United Kingdom in which it was given in the same manner as a judgment given by a court of law in that part.[62] The Act thus provides machinery for the reciprocal enforcement of such awards within the United Kingdom. Such

---

[54] *Ante*, pp. 126–127.
[55] For a list of such countries, see Halsbury, *Laws of England*, 4th ed., Vol. 8, para. 752, n. 4.
[56] Administration of Justice Act 1920, s.9(1).
[57] s.9(3)(*a*).
[58] s.12(1).
[59] s.9(5).
[60] s.10A, added by Civil Jurisdiction and Judgments Act 1982, Sched. 10, para. 4.
[61] *Ante*, p. 133.
[62] s.18(2)(*e*).

awards made in Scotland or Northern Ireland can be enforced in England under Schedule 6 of the Act (if they order payment of a sum of money) or under Schedule 7 (if they order any relief or remedy not requiring payment of a sum of money). But registration under these Schedules is not the only way in which such awards can be enforced, as it is with judgments. They can also be enforced in England at the option of the plaintiff under the summary procedure of section 26 of the Arbitration Act 1950 or by action at common law.[63] But for some obscure reason the provisions of section 19 as to recognition as opposed to enforcement do not apply to arbitration awards.

STAYING OF ENGLISH ACTIONS

Under section 4(1) of the Arbitration Act 1950, re-enacting earlier legislation going back to section 11 of the Common Law Procedure Act 1854, the court has a discretionary power to stay proceedings brought in England in breach of an agreement to refer the dispute to arbitration. This subsection provides the machinery for indirect specific performance of arbitration agreements. But, if the submission to arbitration was made in pursuance of an agreement to which the Protocol of 1923 applied, the court had a mandatory duty under section 4(2) to stay the proceedings, unless the court was satisfied that the agreement or arbitration had become inoperative or could not proceed or that there was not in fact any dispute between the parties with regard to the matter agreed to be referred. Section 4(2) is now repealed by section 8(2)(a) of the Arbitration Act 1975.

The New York Convention of 1958 contains an extraordinary provision (article II) which says that the court must stay proceedings brought in breach of a written arbitration agreement. This is not confined to agreements leading to awards capable of recognition or enforcement under the Convention, nor even to agreements having some foreign element. Had it been implemented without modification, it would have been necessary to repeal not only section 4(2) of the Arbitration Act 1950 but also section 4(1) and to surrender the discretion which English courts have long exercised. The Private International Law Committee recommended[64] that the New York Convention should not be implemented by the United Kingdom unless some means could be found of restricting article II to foreign agreements in such a way as not to expose the United Kingdom to the charge of breaking its treaty obligations.

Accordingly, section 1 of the Arbitration Act 1975 provides that the court must stay any proceedings brought in breach of an arbitration agreement which is not a domestic arbitration agreement. A domestic arbitration agreement means an arbitration agreement which does not provide for arbitration in a State other than the United Kingdom and to which neither (a) an individual who is a national of or habitually resident in any State other than the United Kingdom, nor (b) a body corporate which is incorporated in, or whose central management and control is exercised in,

---

[63] s.18(8).
[64] Fifth Report, Cmnd. 1515, paras. 18–21.

any State other than the United Kingdom, is a party. So, if the arbitration agreement provides for arbitration in the United Kingdom and both parties thereto are United Kingdom parties as above defined, the agreement is a domestic arbitration agreement and the duty to stay does not arise.

The court need not stay the proceedings if satisfied (a) that the arbitration agreement is null and void, inoperative or incapable of being performed, or (b) that there is not in fact any dispute between the parties with regard to the matter agreed to be referred. Condition (a) above is taken from the Convention. The fact that the defendant would be financially incapable of satisfying the award in full does not mean that the agreement is incapable of being performed and is therefore no reason for refusing a stay.[65] Condition (b) is a gloss on the Convention taken over from section 4(2) of the Arbitration Act 1950 on the advice of the Private International Law Committee.[66] Relying on this provision of the Act, the House of Lords has held that a claim on a bill of exchange will not be stayed if there is a counterclaim for unliquidated damages to which an arbitration agreement applies.[67] On the other hand, the court has no power under the Act to give judgment for part of a claim and refer the balance to arbitration, unless it is possible to quantify the amount of the claim indisputably due.[68]

In addition to its statutory power and duty to stay English proceedings brought in disregard of an arbitration clause, the court has an inherent but discretionary power to restrain by injunction the bringing of proceedings in a foreign court in disregard of an arbitration clause.[69]

---

[65] *The Rena K* [1979] Q.B. 377, 391–393.
[66] Fifth Report, Cmnd. 1515, Appendix 3, comment (3).
[67] *Nova (Jersey) Knit Ltd.* v. *Kamngarn Spinnerei G.m.b.H.* [1977] 1 W.L.R. 713.
[68] *Associated Bulk Carriers Ltd.* v. *Koch Shipping Inc.* [1978] 2 All E.R. 254.
[69] *Pena Copper Mines Ltd.* v. *Rio Tinto Co. Ltd.* (1912) 105 L.T. 846; *Tracomin S.A.* v. *Sudan Oil Seeds Co. Ltd. (No. 2)* [1983] 1 W. L. R. 1026.

Part Four

FAMILY LAW

CHAPTER 11

MARRIAGE

Introduction

MARRIAGE is a contract in the sense that there can be no valid marriage unless each party consents to marry the other. But it is a contract of a very special kind.[1] It can only be concluded (at least as a general rule) by a formal, public act, and not, *e.g.* by an exchange of letters or over the telephone; no action for damages will lie for breach of the fundamental obligation to love, honour and obey; the contract cannot be rescinded by the mutual consent of the parties: it can only be dissolved (if at all) by a formal, public act, usually the decree of a divorce court. Marriage is a contract in the limited sense indicated above, but it is far more than a contract: it creates a status, something of interest to the community as well as to the parties. As Lord Westbury said in *Shaw* v. *Gould*,[2] "marriage is the very foundation of civil society, and no part of the laws and institutions of a country can be of more vital importance to its subjects than those which regulate the manner and conditions of forming, and if necessary of dissolving, the marriage contract."

It would be difficult to overestimate the importance of the question, what law governs the validity of a marriage. The validity of a marriage may arise in almost any conceivable context, and not merely in judicial proceedings in which it is directly in issue. In no department of the conflict of laws is there a greater need for certainty in the choice of law rule. Unfortunately the English rules of the conflict of laws exhibit an alarming state of uncertainty on this matter.

The original rule was that the validity of a marriage depended on the law of the place of celebration (*lex loci celebrationis*). In 1861 the House of Lords drew a distinction between the formalities of marriage, governed by the *lex loci celebrationis*, and capacity to marry, governed by the law of each party's antenuptial domicile.[3] In 1866 Sir J. P. Wilde (later Lord Penzance) said that "marriage is the voluntary union for life of one man and one woman to the exclusion of all others."[4] He thus stressed that marriage is a consensual transaction; and seemed at first sight to deny that polygamous marriages can be recognised by English law, at least for certain purposes.

---

[1] See *Mordaunt* v. *Mordaunt* (1870) L.R. 2 P. & M. 109, 126–127, *per* Lord Penzance.
[2] (1868) L.R. 3 H.L. 55, 82.
[3] *Brook* v. *Brook* (1861) 9 H.L.C. 193. The distinction was adumbrated by Dr. Lushington in *Conway* v. *Beazley* (1831) 3 Hagg.Ecc. 639, 647, 652; *cf.* the Irish case, *Steele* v. *Braddell* (1838) Milw. 1.
[4] *Hyde* v. *Hyde* (1866) L.R. 1 P. & M. 130, 133.

We need to consider, therefore, first, formalities; secondly, capacity to marry; thirdly, consent of parties; and fourthly, polygamous marriages.

FORMALITIES OF MARRIAGE

It has been settled law since 1752[5] that the formalities of marriage are governed by the *lex loci celebrationis*. It is sufficient to comply with the formalities prescribed by that law; and as a general rule it is necessary to do so. *Locus regit actum* is the maxim; and in this context the maximum is imperative, not merely facultative.

The leading modern case is *Berthiaume* v. *Dastous*,[6] where two Roman Catholics domiciled in Quebec were married in France in a Roman Catholic church. Owing to the carelessness of the priest who married them, there was no civil ceremony as required by French law. The Privy Council held that the marriage was void; and Lord Dunedin said:

> "If there is one question better settled than any other in international law, it is that as regards marriage—putting aside the question of capacity—*locus regit actum*. If a marriage is good by the laws of the country where it is effected, it is good all the world over, no matter whether the proceeding or ceremony which constituted marriage according to the law of the place would or would not constitute marriage in the country of the domicile of one or other of the spouses. If the so-called marriage is no marriage in the place where it is celebrated, there is no marriage anywhere, although the ceremony or proceeding if conducted in the place of the parties' domicile would be considered a good marriage."

So well established is the principle that compliance with the local form is sufficient, that it applies even though the marriage, originally invalid by the local law, has been subsequently validated by retrospective legislation in the *locus celebrationis*, and even though the legislation does not take effect until after the parties have acquired an English domicile. Thus, in *Starkowski* v. *Att. Gen.*[7] two Roman Catholics domiciled in Poland were married without civil ceremony in a Roman Catholic church in Austria in May 1945. At that time Austrian law did not recognise marriages without a civil ceremony; but a few weeks later a law was passed in Austria retrospectively validating such marriages if they were duly registered. By some oversight the marriage in question was not registered until 1949, by which time the parties had acquired an English domicile, and separated. In 1950 the wife married another man in England. The House of Lords held that the Austrian marriage was valid and therefore the English ceremony was bigamous and void. Their Lordships expressly left open the question what

---

[5] *Scrimshire* v. *Scrimshire* (1752) 2 Hagg. Con. 395; *Dalrymple* v. *Dalrymple* (1811) 2 Hagg. Con. 54; *Simonin* v. *Mallac* (1860) 2 Sw. & Tr. 67; *Berthiaume* v. *Dastous* [1930] A.C. 79; *Apt* v. *Apt* [1948] P. 83; *Kenward* v. *Kenward* [1951] P. 124.
[6] [1930] A.C. 79, 83.
[7] [1954] A.C. 155.

the position would have been if the English ceremony had preceded the registration of the Austrian marriage. It is thought that, in that case, the English ceremony would be held valid and the Austrian marriage void, because foreign retrospective legislation would hardly be held to invalidate a valid marriage celebrated in the country of the parties' domicile. There is Canadian authority which indirectly supports this view.[8]

There is some reason to think that if the marriage is formally invalid by the domestic law of the place of celebration, but formally valid by the system of law referred to by its conflict rules, the marriage would be held valid in England under the doctrine of renvoi.[9] In *Taczanowska* v. *Taczanowski*,[10] two Polish nationals domiciled in Poland were married in Italy in a form which did not constitute a valid marriage by Italian domestic law. There was evidence that the Italian courts would recognise a marriage celebrated in Italy in accordance with the forms prescribed by the law of the parties' common nationality. But the marriage was not formally valid by Polish domestic law, and so it was not held valid on this ground in England. (It was held valid on another ground which is discussed later.[11]) It seems a safe deduction that it would have been held valid if it had been valid by Polish domestic law. Otherwise there would have been no point in admitting and discussing the evidence of the Italian conflict rule.

What do we mean by the formalities of marriage? Obviously, the term includes such questions as whether a civil ceremony, or any ceremony at all, is required, the number of witnesses necessary, the permitted hours during which marriages can be celebrated, whether publication of banns is necessary, and so on. In *Apt* v. *Apt*[12] the Court of Appeal held that the question whether proxy marriages are valid is a question of formalities. They distinguished between the method of giving consent and the fact of consent, and upheld a marriage celebrated by proxy in Argentina between a man domiciled and resident there and a woman domiciled and resident in England, since it appeared that proxy marriages are valid by Argentine law, though they are not valid by English law.

The most controversial question is whether lack of parental consent relates to the formalities of marriage or to capacity to marry. The answer appears to be that it relates to formalities, whether the requirement is imposed by English law or foreign law, and in the latter case no matter how stringently the requirement is expressed: but the cases have been much criticised.

English law requires parental consent to the marriages of minors; and there is some historical justification for treating this requirement as a formality. It was first imposed by Lord Hardwicke's Marriage Act of 1753. That Act also dealt with licences and publication of banns, matters which no one doubts are formalities. A marriage celebrated without parental con-

---

[8] *Ambrose* v. *Ambrose* (1961) 25 D.L.R. (2d) 1. See *post*, pp. 502–503.
[9] For renvoi, see *post*, Chap. 30.
[10] [1957] P. 301, 305, 318.
[11] *Post*, pp. 155–156.
[12] [1948] P. 83.

sent is not invalid in English domestic law. The Act applied to England
only and not to Scotland. Hence the practice arose of eloping English
couples marrying without parental consent and without formal ceremony
at Gretna Green, just across the border in Scotland.[13] The validity of such
marriages was established in a series of eighteenth-century cases[14] which
were decided at a time when English courts did not distinguish between the
formalities of marriage and capacity to marry, but referred both aspects to
the *lex loci celebrationis*. When that distinction was introduced in 1861, the
Gretna Green cases were explained away as having turned on the formalities of marriage.[15]

Of course it did not follow from this that foreign requirements of parental consent could also be treated as formalities. Those imposed by French
law, for instance, are much more stringent than those imposed by English
law. They expressly apply to the marriages of Frenchmen and French-
women, no matter where celebrated; and if they are not complied with, the
marriage is voidable at the instance of the party who needed parental consent, or of his or her parents. Yet in *Simonin* v. *Mallac*,[16] they were treated
as inapplicable to a marriage between French persons celebrated in England. In that case a Frenchman aged twenty-nine married a Frenchwoman
aged twenty-two in England. The marriage was valid by English domestic
law, but voidable by French law because neither party had obtained the
consent of his or her parents as required by what was then article 151 of the
French Civil Code. This article required the parties to demand their
parents' consent by a respectful and formal act, but article 152 provided
that the marriage could lawfully take place if consent was not forthcoming
after three months' formal asking. Although the marriage was annulled in
France,[17] the country of the parties' domicile, it was held valid in England.
The ground of the decision was that the validity of marriage generally is
governed by the *lex loci celebrationis*; but it was subsequently explained as
having turned on formalities.[18] The court intimated[19] that article 148 of the
French Civil Code, which imposed an absolute and not merely a qualified
prohibition on marriages without parental consent, might receive a different interpretation.

However, the suggested distinction was ignored in *Ogden* v. *Ogden*,[20]
where a domiciled Frenchman aged nineteen married in England a domi-

---

[13] The ease with which English couples could get married in Scotland without publicity or parental consent was much reduced by the Marriage (Scotland) Act 1856, s.1, which required
residence of one of the parties in Scotland for 21 days prior to the ceremony; and by the
Marriage (Scotland) Act 1939, s.5, which prohibited marriages in Scotland without formal
ceremony.
[14] The leading case is *Compton* v. *Bearcroft* (1769) 2 Hagg.Con. 444, n.
[15] *Brook* v. *Brook* (1861) 9 H.L.C. 193, 215, 228–229, 236.
[16] (1860) 2 Sw. & Tr. 67.
[17] The French nullity decree would now be recognised in England because it was rendered by
the courts of the country where both parties were domiciled. See *post*, p. 211.
[18] *Brook* v. *Brook* (1861) 9 H.L.C. 193, 218; *Sottomayor* v. *De Barros* (*No. 1*) (1877) 3 P.D.
1, 7.
[19] At p. 77.
[20] [1908] P. 46. This case affords a striking example of characterisation in accordance with the
lex fori; see *post*, Chap. 31.

ciled Englishwoman without the consent of his parents as required by article 148 of the French Civil Code. This article provided that a son who had not attained the age of twenty-five years could not contract marriage without the consent of his parents. The parties lived together in England for a few months, after which the husband returned to France, leaving the wife in England, and obtained a nullity decree from the French court on the ground of lack of parental consent. The Court of Appeal held that nevertheless the marriage was valid in England, because (among other reasons) the requirement of parental consent was a mere formality.[21] The consequences of this decision were extremely awkward for the English-woman, for both parties had remarried on the strength of the French nullity decree, but she was left married to a man who by the law of his domicile was not only not her husband but was the husband of someone else. She could not as the law then stood get a divorce in England, since her husband was domiciled in France; and the Court of Appeal also held that the French nullity decree would not be recognised in England.[22]

No case in the English conflict of laws has been criticised more heavily than *Ogden* v. *Ogden*.[23] A very pertinent criticism is that of Falconbridge, who says that the requirement of parental consent "cannot be character-ised in the abstract and for all cases either as a matter of formalities of cel-ebration or as a matter of capacity to marry, but that in the law of one country it may by its terms and in the light of its context in that law be a matter of capacity, and in the law of another country it may by its terms and in the light of its context in that law be a matter of formalities." But in spite of these criticisms, *Ogden* v. *Ogden* has since been followed in Scot-land[24] and England.[25]

The Gretna Green cases and *Simonin* v. *Mallac* make it plain that English law has no common law doctrine of evasion of law, or *fraude à la loi* as the French call it.[26] Though the parties travelled to Scotland and England respectively in order to evade the requirements of the law of their domicile as to parental consent, the marriages were nevertheless held valid.

There is no exception to the proposition that a marriage, formally valid by the *lex loci celebrationis*, is formally valid in England. But there are four real or apparent exceptions to the converse proposition that a marriage, formally invalid by the *lex loci celebrationis*, is formally invalid in England. They are as follows: first, when it is impossible for the parties to use the local form; secondly, marriages in countries under belligerent occupation; thirdly, marriages of members of H.M. Forces serving abroad; and fourthly, marriages under the Foreign Marriage Act 1892.

---

[21] At pp. 57, 75. The other reasons relate to capacity to marry and are considered *post*, p. 166.

[22] It would now be recognised because the husband was domiciled in France. See *post*, p. 211.

[23] See Cheshire and North, pp. 49–52; Beckett (1934) 15 B.Y.I.L. 46, 77–81; Robertson, pp. 28–29, 239–242; Dicey and Morris, pp. 267–268; Falconbridge, pp. 74–76.

[24] *Bliersbach* v. *McEwen*, 1959 S.C. 43.

[25] *Lodge* v. *Lodge* (1963) 107 S.J. 437.

[26] s.27(2) of the Unfair Contract Terms Act 1977 does introduce such a doctrine into the law of contract. See *post*, p. 280.

Use of the local form impossible

If there is an insuperable difficulty in using the local form, *e.g.* because the parties are Christians and wish to marry in a heathen country, or on a desert island, or in some Muslim country where no civil or Christian form of marriage is provided, the marriage will be formally valid if it is celebrated in accordance with the requirements of English common law. This means English law as it stood before Lord Hardwicke's Marriage Act 1753. That is to say, the marriage need not be celebrated in church, and no licence or publication of banns or witnesses are necessary: it is sufficient if the parties take each other as husband and wife. At one time it was supposed that it was essential to the validity of an English common law marriage that it should be celebrated in the presence of an episcopally ordained clergyman. But the two decisions of the House of Lords[27] which laid down this rule have since been confined to marriages celebrated in England or Ireland[28]; and of course the principle under consideration could hardly apply to such a marriage, for ample facilities are provided for civil marriages in both countries, with or without such religious ceremony as the parties see fit to adopt. Hence a common law marriage celebrated abroad may be valid if celebrated before a clergyman who is not episcopally ordained,[29] or before a layman,[30] or (presumably) before no one.

In many cases marriages which have been held valid under this principle are not real exceptions to the general rule that the *lex loci celebrationis* must be complied with. For their validity depends on the principle that the English common law, or so much of it as is applicable in the circumstances, applies to British subjects in a settled colony and also in some other colonies and places where Her Majesty once exercised extra-territorial jurisdiction.[31] Hence this law becomes, by a fiction of law, part of the *lex loci* itself.[32] But there are other situations in which this is not so, *e.g.* when the marriage is celebrated in an independent non-Christian country where no civil form of marriage is provided and to which the Foreign Marriage Act 1892 does not extend. The principle is not confined to the marriages of British subjects. It has been suggested[33] that the marriage of parties who are not British subjects would be valid, if there was an insuperable difficulty in complying with the local law, if it was in the form recognised as sufficient in the circumstances by the law of their common domicile. But this view has been rejected by the courts on the ground that it would encounter

---

[27] *R.* v. *Millis* (1844) 10 Cl. & F. 534; *Beamish* v. *Beamish* (1861) 9 H.L.C. 274. These two decisions have been much criticised, and on historical grounds they seem indefensible: see Pollock and Maitland, *History of English Law*, Vol. 2, pp. 370–372; Lord Hodson (1958) 7 I.C.L.Q. 205, 208–209; *Catterall* v. *Catterall* (1847) 1 Rob.Ecc. 580; *Merker* v. *Merker* [1963] P. 283, 294, *per* Sir Jocelyn Simon P.

[28] *Wolfenden* v. *Wolfenden* [1946] P. 61; approved by the Court of Appeal in *Apt* v. *Apt* [1948] P. 83, 86, and by the Privy Council in *Penhas* v. *Tan Soo Eng* [1953] A.C, 304, 319.

[29] *Wolfenden* v. *Wolfenden, supra.*

[30] *Penhas* v. *Tan Soo Eng, supra.*

[31] *Catterall* v. *Catterall* (1847) 1 Rob.Ecc. 580; *Wolfenden* v. *Wolfenden, supra*; *Penhas* v. *Tan Soo Eng, supra.*

[32] *Taczanowska* v. *Taczanowski* [1957] P. 301, 328, 329.

[33] Dicey, 6th ed., p. 772; *Kochanski* v. *Kochanska* [1958] P. 147, 153–155.

difficulties if the parties were domiciled in different countries.[34] The difficulty does not seem insuperable, however; it could easily be overcome by applying the law of each party's domicile cumulatively,[35] as is done as a matter of course when capacity to marry is in question.[36]

There is no English authority on the validity of marriages celebrated in merchant ships on the high seas. It is thought that such a marriage would be held valid if celebrated in accordance with the formalities prescribed by the law of the ship's port of registration; and that, if this was English law, it would suffice if the parties took each other for husband and wife,[37] provided the court was satisfied that it was impracticable for them to wait until the ship reached a port where sufficient facilities were available either by the *lex loci* or under the Foreign Marriage Act 1892. There would be no such element of emergency if the ship was lying in a foreign port, unless there was an insuperable difficulty in marrying ashore in compliance with the *lex loci* or the Foreign Marriage Act. However, a marriage celebrated in a British warship lying off Cyprus has been upheld.[38] The parties were British subjects domiciled in England and the ceremony was performed by the ship's chaplain in the presence of the captain, though without banns or licence. Marriages on board British warships are now regulated by section 22 of the Foreign Marriage Act 1892 as amended in 1947.[39]

Marriages in countries under belligerent occupation

During the concluding weeks of the Second World War and its immediate aftermath, many thousands of marriages were celebrated in Germany and Italy between Roman Catholics or Jews domiciled in Poland and other eastern European countries. These marriages were not valid by the local law either because there was no civil ceremony or because some formality required by the local law was omitted. The validity of these marriages has been tested in a number of cases, and they have been held valid if they were celebrated in the form required by English common law and the husband was a member of belligerent occupying forces,[40] or of forces associated with them,[41] or (perhaps) of an organised body of escaped prisoners of war.[42] The status of the wife seems to be immaterial.[43] The leading case

---

[34] *Taczanowska* v. *Taczanowski, supra,* at pp. 326, 331; *Preston* v. *Preston* [1963] P. 141, 152–153.

[35] See Mendes da Costa (1958) 7 I.C.L.Q. 217, 247–250.

[36] *Post,* pp. 162–165.

[37] In the Irish case, *Du Moulin* v. *Druitt* (1860) 13 Ir.C.L. 212, it was held, following *R.* v. *Millis* (1844) 10 Cl. & F. 534, that the presence of an episcopally ordained clergyman was necessary. But since *Wolfenden* v. *Wolfenden* [1946] P. 61, *Du Moulin* v. *Druitt* is no longer a safe guide.

[38] *Culling* v. *Culling* [1896] P. 116.

[39] See *post,* p. 157.

[40] *Taczanowska* v. *Taczanowski* [1957] P. 301.

[41] *Preston* v. *Preston* [1963] P. 141, 411.

[42] *Merker* v. *Merker* [1963] P. 283, 295.

[43] *Taczanowska* v. *Taczanowski, supra*; *Preston* v. *Preston, supra,* at pp. 425, 430.

is *Taczanowska* v. *Taczanowski*,[44] where the Court of Appeal upheld the validity of a marriage celebrated in 1946 in an Italian church by a Roman Catholic priest serving as a Polish Army chaplain; the husband was an officer of the Polish forces serving with the British Army in Italy and the wife a Polish civilian. The marriage was formally invalid by Italian law and also by Polish law. It was not valid under the previous exception (because there was no insuperable difficulty in complying with the local law), nor under the next exception (because the chaplain was not acting under the orders of the British Commander-in-Chief). The main ground of the decision appears to have been that as the husband was not in Italy from choice but under the orders of his military superiors, he was exempt from the operation of the local law unless he submitted to it of his own volition. Widely construed, this ratio could be taken to include ordinary civilians who are present in a country from necessity and not from choice. But it is now clear that the principle does not extend to them.[45]

The decision in *Taczanowska* v. *Taczanowski* has been followed[46] and distinguished[47] and has been heavily criticised by academic writers.[48] It is indeed a remarkable proposition that a marriage celebrated in a foreign country between persons domiciled in another foreign country who have never visited England in their lives, and may never do so, can derive formal validity from compliance with the requirements of English domestic law as it existed 200 years before the marriage. It cannot be supposed that such parties ever intended to submit to English common law. If the *lex loci* is inapplicable for any reason, it would seem more sensible to refer the formal validity of the marriage to the law of the parties' domicile: but this, as we have seen,[49] the courts decline to do.

Marriages of members of H.M. Forces serving abroad

Such marriages were formerly regulated by section 22 of the Foreign Marriage Act 1892, which was repealed and replaced by a new section 22 by the Foreign Marriage Act 1947. This provides that marriages between persons of whom at least one is a member of Her Majesty's Forces serving in foreign territory, or otherwise employed in such territory as may be specified by Order in Council, may be celebrated by a chaplain serving with

---

[44] [1957] P. 301. According to contemporary press reports, this was a test case involving the validity of some 3,000–4,000 similar marriages. The reader is invited to compare the anxiety of the Court of Appeal to uphold the marriage in this case, with its anxiety to pick holes in the marriage in *Kenward* v. *Kenward* [1951] P. 124, and then to reflect on the maxim "hard cases make bad law."

[45] *Preston* v. *Preston* [1963] P. 411, 426–427, 434–435, disapproving *Kochanski* v. *Kochanska* [1958] P. 147, where the principle was extended to the marriage of inmates of a Polish displaced persons' camp in Germany: but in *Preston* v. *Preston*, *supra*, the same camp was held to be a military one.

[46] *Kochanski* v. *Kochanska* [1958] P. 147; *Merker* v. *Merker* [1963] P. 283; *Preston* v. *Preston* [1963] P. 141, 411. It is a pity that the husband's conduct in this last case was so reprehensible that the Court of Appeal refused him leave to appeal to the House of Lords.

[47] *Lazarewicz* v. *Lazarewicz* [1962] P. 171.

[48] Cheshire and North, pp. 323–327; Dicey and Morris, p. 273; Mendes da Costa (1958) 7 I.C.L.Q. 217, 226–235; Andrews (1959) 22 M.L.R. 396, 403–407.

[49] *Ante*, p. 155.

the naval, military or air forces in such territory or by anyone authorised by the commanding officer of such forces. Such marriages are as valid in law as if solemnised in the United Kingdom with a due observance of all forms required by law. The section does not apply to Dominion Forces,[50] but there is no requirement that either party must be a British citizen.[51] The term "foreign territory" does not include any part of the Commonwealth,[52] but it does include a ship in foreign waters.[53] The operation of the section depends very largely on Orders in Council.[54] Like the original section 22 of the Foreign Marriage Act 1892, and unlike the rest of that Act, the new section 22 is largely declaratory of the common law. It is a real exception to the principle that compliance with the formalities prescribed by the local law is necessary to the validity of a marriage; but of course its scope is limited.

Marriages under the Foreign Marriage Act 1892

A marriage solemnised in the manner provided by section 8 of the Foreign Marriage Act 1892, in any foreign[55] country or place, by or before a "marriage officer," between parties of whom one at least is a British citizen, is as valid in law as if it had been solemnised in the United Kingdom with a due observance of all the forms required by law.[56]

"Marriage officers" under the Act are British consuls and ambassadors and members of their diplomatic staff, provided in all cases that they hold a marriage warrant from the Secretary of State.[57] There is thus complete discretion to exclude any foreign country from the operation of the Act; and in some countries the marriage officers are only authorised to celebrate marriages between two British citizens.[58]

Section 8 provides that every marriage under the Act must be solemnised at the official house of the marriage officer, with open doors, between the hours of 8 a.m. and 6 p.m., in the presence of two or more witnesses. The ceremony may be according to the rites of the Church of England, or in such other form as the parties see fit to adopt, in which case they must at some stage declare that they know of no lawful impediment to the marriage and utter the statutory words of consent.

The Act contains requirements as to notice of intended marriage,[59] the filing and entering of such notice,[60] parental consent,[61] the taking of an

---

[50] Foreign Marriage Act 1947, s.3.

[51] *Taczanowska* v. *Taczanowski* [1957] P. 301, 319–320 (with reference to the original s.22).

[52] subs. (2) of the new s.22.

[53] subs. (3) of the new s.22.

[54] See the Foreign Marriage (Armed Forces) Order, S.I. 1964 No. 1000, as amended by S.I. 1965 No. 137.

[55] A "foreign" country or place in the Act means one outside the Commonwealth.

[56] Foreign Marriage Act 1892, s.1.

[57] *Ibid*. s.11. The solemnisation of marriages under the Act is regarded primarily as a consular function, and warrants are only issued to ambassadors or members of their diplomatic staff in exceptional circumstances.

[58] A list of the countries to which the Act extends is given in Halsbury, *Laws of England*, 4th ed., Vol. 8, para. 454, n. 2.

[59] s.2.

[60] s.3.

[61] s.4.

oath,[62] and the registration of the marriage.[63] But all these requirements are directory only and not mandatory; even if none of them is
complied with, the marriage will still be valid provided the requirements of section 8 (which is the crucial section) have been met.[64]
Moreover, the solemnisation of the marriage precludes subsequent
inquiry as to whether the parties resided within the district of the marriage officer for the requisite three weeks, or whether parental consent
was given[65]; and the solemnisation and registration of the marriage
precludes subsequent inquiry as to the authority of the marriage officer.[66]

A marriage celebrated under the Act is valid in England as regards form
(but not necessarily valid in other respects, *e.g.* capacity), though it may be
invalid under the *lex loci*.[67] But although it may appear at first sight that
the parties need not concern themselves with the formal requirements of
the local law, in practice it is often essential that these requirements should
be observed. For before a marriage is solemnised under the Act, the marriage officer must be satisfied (a) that at least one of the parties is a British
citizen; (b) that the local authorities will not object to the solemnisation of
the marriage; (c) that insufficient facilities exist for the marriage under the
local law; and (d) that the parties will be regarded as validly married by the
law of the country to which each party belongs.[68] Moreover, the marriage
officer need not solemnise a marriage, or allow one to be solemnised in his
presence, if in his opinion the solemnisation thereof would be inconsistent
with international law or the comity of nations.[69] It is impossible to say
what this imprecise phrase means; but it can hardly mean that the invalidity
of the marriage by the local law is a sufficient ground for refusing to solemnise it.

Thus, in many cases, the advantage of the Act is not that it permits the
parties to disregard the *lex loci* but that it enables them to obtain a certificate which will be evidence of the marriage in England.

Nothing in the Act is to confirm or impair or affect the validity of any
marriage solemnised beyond the seas otherwise than as therein provided.[70]
Hence, any marriage which is valid under the other exceptions discussed
above remains valid.[71]

---

[62] s.7.
[63] s.9.
[64] *Collett* v. *Collett* [1968] P. 482.
[65] Foreign Marriage Act 1892, s.13(1).
[66] *Ibid.* s.13(2).
[67] *Hay* v. *Northcote* [1900] 2 Ch. 262, where a marriage celebrated in accordance with the
    Consular Marriage Act 1849 was held valid although it had been annulled by the courts of
    the parties' domicile. But such a decree of nullity would now be recognised in England: see
    post, p. 211.
[68] Foreign Marriage Order, S.I. 1970 No. 1539, para. 3 (1).
[69] Foreign Marriage Act 1892, s.19.
[70] *Ibid.* s.23.
[71] See *Wolfenden* v. *Wolfenden* [1945] 2 All E.R. 539, 543C–D.

CAPACITY TO MARRY

Introduction

Traditionally, this rubric (sometimes called essential validity) includes the impediments of the prohibited degrees of consanguinity and affinity and lack of age; but there seems no reason why it should not also include the impediments of lack of parental consent, in so far as that is not treated as a mere formality; previous marriage; and physical incapacity: in short, all impediments to marriage, other than formal ones, which have already been considered, and lack of consent of parties, which is reserved for later discussion.[72] This has the advantage of avoiding a multiplicity of categories: but it should be borne in mind that the social and policy reasons for the various impediments are not always the same, and that this may possibly justify the application of different conflict rules.

The rival theories. English textwriters have canvassed two theories as to what law governs capacity to marry. The theory of Dicey, which may be called the orthodox view, is that capacity to marry is governed by the law of each party's antenuptial domicile.[73] The theory of Cheshire is that the basic presumption is that capacity to marry is governed by the law of the husband's domicile at the time of the marriage, but that this presumption is rebutted if it can be inferred that the parties at the time of the marriage intended to establish their home in a certain country and that they did in fact establish it there within a reasonable time.[74] The difference between the two theories is that an incapacity imposed by the law of the wife's antenuptial domicile will invalidate the marriage according to Dicey, but will not generally invalidate it according to Cheshire. Thus, as a general rule, more marriages will be valid under Cheshire's theory than under Dicey's; but this is not invariably the case.[75]

Dicey's view is based on the idea that the community to which each party belongs is interested in his or her status, and that in these days of sex equality no preference should be shown to the laws of one community rather than to the laws of the other.

Cheshire's view is based on the idea that the community to which the parties belong *after* their marriage is more interested in their status than the communities to which they belonged before. At first sign this is a plausible view, but on closer examination it seems to prove too much. Suppose that a man domiciled in country A marries a woman domiciled in country B, and that at the time of the marriage the parties intend to establish their

---

[72] *Post*, p. 173.

[73] Dicey and Morris, Rule 33. For other views, see Hartley (1972) 35 M.L.R. 571; Jaffey (1978) 41 M.L.R. 38.

[74] Cheshire and North, p. 331. It should be noted (a) that Cheshire's views have been virtually abandoned in the more recent editions edited by Dr. North; and (b) that neither Dicey and Morris nor Cheshire and North are discussing physical incapacity.

[75] A case in point is *Schwebel* v. *Ungar* (1964) 48 D.L.R. (2d) 644; *post*, p. 169. There the validity of the marriage could only be sustained by an exclusive reference to the law of the wife's antenuptial domicile.

home in country C and do in fact establish it there within a reasonable time. According to Cheshire, the law of C is more interested in the status of these parties than the laws of A and B, and therefore the law of C and no other should determine whether they had capacity to marry. But now suppose that, ten years after the marriage, the parties abandon their domicile and matrimonial home in C and establish another in country D. By the same token, the law of D is now more interested in their status than any other law, and it alone should determine whether they had capacity to marry. Of course, nobody seriously suggests that the validity of a marriage should be reassessed every time the parties change their domicile: that would be unjust as well as quite impracticable.

Cheshire says that "whether the intermarriage of two persons should be prohibited for social, religious, eugenic or other like reason is a question that affects the community in which the parties live together as man and wife,"[76] i.e. the intended matrimonial home. This may be true of the prohibited degrees of consanguinity, for the prohibition is based mainly on considerations of eugenics, and arguably this is a post-matrimonial matter. But it certainly is not true of the prohibited degrees of affinity, for such prohibitions can only be justified (if at all)[77] by religious or moral considerations, and this is a pre-matrimonial matter. It would therefore be anomalous for English law to give effect to the religious or moral principles prevailing in a particular country when the man is domiciled there, but to ignore them in the case of a woman.

Cheshire says that principle supports the view that capacity to marry should be governed by the law of the intended matrimonial home, because capacity to make a commercial contract is governed by the system of law with which the transaction has the most substantial connection.[78] There is, however, all the difference in the world between a marriage (which as we have seen[79] is like a contract only in the sense that it is a consensual transaction) and an ordinary commercial contract. To argue from one to the other seems quite unjustifiable.

Very serious practical difficulties are likely to arise if the validity of a marriage has to remain in suspense while we wait and see (for an unspecified period) whether or not the parties implement their (unexpressed) antenuptial intention to acquire another domicile.[80] This is especially true if interests in property depend on the validity of a marriage, as, for instance, where a widow's pension ceases on her remarriage.

We must now abandon theory and see how English courts have approached the question of what law governs capacity to marry. We shall see that (apart from physical incapacity) with one exception[81] the cases

[76] Cheshire and North, p. 332.
[77] See *Padolecchia* v. *Padolecchia* [1968] P. 314, 340, where Simon P. ingeniously pointed out that the deceased wife's sister might not necessarily be born when the wife died.
[78] Cheshire and North, p.333. For capacity to make a commercial contract, see *post*, p. 285.
[79] *Ante*, p. 149.
[80] This is now conceded in Cheshire and North, p. 334.
[81] *Sottomayor* v. *De Barros* (*No. 2*) (1879) 5 P.D. 94; *post*, p. 163.

strongly support Dicey's view, and that the most recent ones[82] expressly approve it.

Consanguinity and affinity

Introductory: changes in English domestic law. Before 1835, a marriage between persons within the prohibited degrees of consanguinity or affinity was only voidable in English domestic law. This meant that the validity of the marriage could only be attacked during the joint lives of the parties, and then only by one party in a nullity suit against the other; and that, in the absence of a decree of nullity pronounced by a court of competent jurisdiction, the marriage was valid, the children were legitimate, and the devolution of property was not affected by the circumstance that the parties were married within the prohibited degrees. In 1835, however, Lord Lyndhurst's Marriage Act rendered such marriages not merely voidable, but void. This meant that the validity of the marriage could be attacked at any time, even after the death of the parties, by any person, in any proceedings; that if the marriage was void the children were illegitimate; and that the devolution of property often went awry. The Chancery reports of the Victorian and Edwardian reigns are full of cases in which gifts to children failed because their parents were married within the prohibited degrees.

The prohibited degrees of English law were, as a general rule, stricter than those of neighbouring European countries. For example, in English law a man could not marry his deceased wife's sister, nor a woman her deceased husband's brother, while in many European countries such marriages were and are valid. It therefore became the practice for English couples within the English prohibited degrees to marry during a temporary visit to some European country where the marriage was valid. Just as English couples in the eighteenth century managed to escape from the provisions of Lord Hardwicke's Marriage Act 1753 by getting married in Scotland,[83] so their successors hoped to escape from the rigours of Lord Lyndhurst's Marriage Act 1835 by getting married in some suitable European country.

This practice was ended, with disastrous results for the family concerned, by the decision of the House of Lords in *Brook* v. *Brook*.[84] In that case a man and his deceased wife's sister, both British subjects domiciled in England, went through a ceremony of marriage during a temporary visit to Denmark, by whose law the marriage was valid. The husband, the wife, and one of the infant children of the marriage died within a few days of each other in an epidemic of cholera. It was held that the marriage was void, that the children were illegitimate, and that therefore the dead child's

---

[82] *Padolecchia* v. *Padolecchia* [1968] P. 314, 336; *R.* v. *Brentwood Marriage Registrar* [1968] 2 Q.B. 956, 968; *Szechter* v. *Szechter* [1971] P. 286, 295B. See however *Radwan* v. *Radwan* (*No. 2*) [1973] Fam. 35, discussed *post*, p. 180.

[83] *Ante*, p. 152.

[84] (1861) 9 H.L.C. 193.

one-fifth share of the family property passed to the Crown as *bona vacantia* and not to his natural brothers and sisters.[85]

In the decade which followed the decision in *Brook* v. *Brook*, attempts to induce Parliament to legalise marriages between a man and his deceased wife's sister were almost annual events[86]; but it was not until 1907 that such marriages became lawful,[87] and not until 1921 that a marriage between a woman and her deceased husband's brother was legalised.[88] (It is hardly surprising that the suffragette movement reached its height mid-way between these dates.) Marriages between a man and his deceased wife's niece or aunt, or between a woman and her deceased husband's nephew or uncle, were legalised in 1931.[89] But marriages between a man and his *divorced* wife's sister, niece or aunt, or between a woman and her *divorced* husband's brother, nephew or uncle, remained invalid until 1960.[90]

The combined effect of these statutes was greatly to reduce the discrepancy between English law and the laws of neighbouring European countries, and thus to reduce the practical importance of the English conflict rules about to be discussed. However, these rules still have some importance because, for example, a marriage between uncle and niece is void by English law but valid by the laws of many other countries, and on the other hand a marriage between first cousins is valid in English law but invalid by the laws of some Catholic countries.

The conflict of laws. In *Brook* v. *Brook*,[91] the facts of which have already been stated, the House of Lords finally established that a distinction must be drawn between the formalities of marriage, governed by the *lex loci celebrationis*, and capacity to marry, governed by the law of each party's antenuptial domicile. At about the same time it was held in *Mette* v. *Mette*[92] that a marriage in Frankfurt between a man domiciled in England and a woman domiciled in Frankfurt was void because they were within the prohibited degrees of English law, although the marriage was valid by the law of Frankfurt. It was subsequently held in *Re Paine*[93] that a marriage in

---

[85] The husband made a will on his deathbed in which he gave his property to his five infant children by name. The case thus demonstrates the dangers involved in giving property to infants, who may die intestate before they can make a will.

[86] Students of Gilbert and Sullivan will recall that in *Iolanthe* (first produced in 1882), Strephon, whose mother was a fairy and whose father was a Lord Chancellor, was sent into Parliament by the Queen of the Fairies; and that one of the predictions she made about his career was:

> "He shall prick that annual blister
> Marriage with deceased wife's sister."

[87] Deceased Wife's Sister's Marriage Act 1907.

[88] Deceased Brother's Widow's Marriage Act 1921.

[89] Marriage (Prohibited Degrees of Relationship) Act 1931. These three statutes are now consolidated in s.1 of the Marriage (Enabling) Act 1960.

[90] Marriage (Enabling) Act 1960.

[91] (1861) 9 H.L.C. 193; ante, p. 161. *Cf. Re De Wilton* [1900] 2 Ch. 481, which was a decision to the like effect.

[92] (1859) 1 Sw. & Tr. 416. The *ratio decidendi* was "There can be no valid contract unless each was competent to contract with the other" (p. 423).

[93] [1940] Ch. 46. It is perhaps unfortunate that Dr. Cheshire's book (first published in 1935) was not cited to the court in this case.

Germany between a man domiciled in Germany and a woman domiciled in England was void because they were within the prohibited degrees of English law, although the marriage was valid by the law of Germany.

In *Sottomayor* v. *De Barros* (*No.* 1),[94] two first cousins supposedly domiciled in Portugal married in England. The marriage was valid by English law, but invalid by the law of Portugal, under which first cousins could not marry without papal dispensation. The parties were very young—the boy was aged sixteen and the girl fourteen-and-a-half. The marriage was one of convenience only, arranged for them by their parents; and though they lived together in the same house in England for six years, the marriage was never consummated. The girl then petitioned for a decree of nullity on the ground of consanguinity. The suit was undefended, but the Queen's Proctor intervened and alleged[95] (*inter alia*) that the parties were domiciled in England and not in Portugal; that they intended at the time of the marriage to live together in England and did so live for six years; and that the validity of the marriage was to be determined by English domestic law. The somewhat inconvenient course was taken of ordering that the question of law should be argued before the questions of fact. On the assumption, then, that the parties were both domiciled in Portugal at the time of the marriage, the Court of Appeal held that the marriage was void, because "as in other contracts, so in that of marriage, personal capacity must depend on the law of the domicile."[96] This seems a clear decision against the law of the intended matrimonial home.

The case was then remitted to the Divorce Division in order that the questions of fact raised by the Queen's Proctor's pleas might be determined. When it appeared that the husband's domicile at the time of the marriage was not Portuguese but English, Sir James Hannen P. pronounced the marriage valid[97] in reliance on a dictum in the judgment of the Court of Appeal that "Our opinion on this appeal is confined to the case where both the contracting parties are, at the time of their marriage, domiciled in a country the laws of which prohibit their marriage."[98] The judgment of Hannen P. seems to be based on the theory that capacity to marry is governed by the *lex loci celebrationis*, which is, to put it mildly, difficult to reconcile with *Brook* v. *Brook* and *Sottomayor* v. *De Barros* (*No.* 1).

There is obvious difficulty in reconciling this decision with the other cases, and especially with *Mette* v. *Mette*[99] and *Re Paine*.[1] Of the various attempts at reconciliation,[2] the most significant are (a) that an incapacity imposed by English law is more important than an incapacity imposed by foreign law; and (b) that an incapacity imposed by the law of the husband's domicile is more important than an incapacity imposed by the law of the

[94] (1877) 3 P.D. 1.
[95] See the report of the case in the court below: 2 P.D. 81, 82.
[96] (1877) 3 P.D. 1, 5.
[97] *Sottomayor* v. *De Barros* (*No.* 2) (1879) 5 P.D. 94.
[98] (1877) 3 P.D. 1, 6–7.
[99] (1859) 1 Sw. & Tr. 416; *ante*, p. 162.
[1] [1940] Ch. 46; *ante*, pp. 162–163.
[2] See Falconbridge, pp. 640–643.

wife's domicile. Neither of these is satisfactory. Cheshire[3] used the decision (while disregarding its reasoning) as support for his theory that capacity to marry is governed by the law of the intended matrimonial home. Dicey[4] found it necessary to make an exception to his general rule that capacity to marry is governed by the law of each party's antenuptial domicile, which exception he formulated as follows:

"The validity of a marriage celebrated in England between persons of whom the one has an English, and the other a foreign, domicile is not affected by any incapacity which, though existing under the law of such foreign domicile, does not exist under the law of England."

This exception is admittedly illogical, but it has been approved by the Court of Appeal,[5] and until *Sottomayor* v. *De Barros* (*No.* 2) is overruled, it must be taken to represent the law. But, as we shall see,[6] its scope is reduced by the Marriage (Enabling) Act 1960.

If the marriage is celebrated abroad and is valid by the law of each party's domicile, it will be held valid in England, though the parties were within the prohibited degrees of English law.[7] At any rate this is true if the parties are not so closely related that intercourse between them would be incestuous by English criminal law.[8] On this ground, marriages celebrated in Italy between a woman and her deceased husband's brother,[9] and in Egypt between an uncle and niece,[10] have been held valid, even though the parties were within the prohibited degrees of English law.

Must the parties have capacity to marry by the *lex loci celebrationis* as well as by the laws of their antenuptial domiciles? There is singularly little authority on this question. On principle it would seem that if the marriage is celebrated in England, the answer must be yes, because the English court could hardly disregard its own law on such a vital matter and hold valid a marriage which that law prohibited, even if it was valid by the law of the parties' domicile. If the marriage is celebrated abroad, the question is more difficult. There is no English authority,[11] but there is one early Australian case and one modern Canadian case, in each of which the marriage was held valid, despite the lack of capacity by the *lex loci*. In *Will of Swan*,[12] it was held that a will had been revoked by the testator's marriage in Scotland to his deceased wife's niece. The marriage was void by Scots law, but voidable in his lifetime by the Victorian law of his domicile, since

[3] Cheshire, 7th ed., p. 285. His views have been much watered down in the 10th ed., pp. 341–342.
[4] See Dicey and Morris, p. 301, Exception 3 to Rule 33.
[5] *Ogden* v. *Ogden* [1908] P. 46, 74–77.
[6] *Post*, p. 165.
[7] *Re Bozzelli's Settlement* [1902] 1 Ch. 751; *Cheni* v. *Cheni* [1965] P. 85.
[8] *Cheni* v. *Cheni, supra*, at p. 97.
[9] *Re Bozzelli's Settlement, supra*.
[10] *Cheni* v. *Cheni, supra*.
[11] But see *Breen* v. *Breen* [1964] P. 144 (*post*, p. 168), where, in the different context of bigamy, Karminski J. was prepared to hold that incapacity by the *lex loci* was fatal to the validity of a marriage.
[12] (1871) 2 V.R. (I.E. & M.) 47.

Lord Lyndhurst's Marriage Act 1835 had not then been adopted in Victoria. Similarly, in *Reed* v. *Reed*,[13] two first cousins domiciled in British Columbia wished to marry. The girl, who was aged eighteen, was unable to obtain the consent of her parents as required by the law of British Columbia. So the parties got married in the state of Washington, where such consent was not required. But unknown to them, first cousins were incapable of marriage by the law of Washington, though they were capable by the law of British Columbia. The marriage was held valid.

Section 1 of the Marriage (Enabling) Act 1960 permits a marriage between a man and his former wife's sister, aunt or niece, or between a woman and her former husband's brother, uncle or nephew. Section 1(3) of the Act provides that the section does not validate a marriage if either party is at the time of the marriage domiciled in a country under whose law there cannot be a valid marriage between the parties. Hence the section impliedly accepts Dicey's view on capacity to marry and rejects that of Cheshire. The reference to "either party" means that neither Cheshire's intended matrimonial home theory nor Dicey's exception based on *Sottomayor* v. *De Barros* (*No.* 2)[14] can apply to any marriage mentioned in section 1, if one party was domiciled in England at the time of the marriage.

Lack of age

Section 2 of the Marriage Act 1949 (re-enacting the Age of Marriage Act 1929) provides that a marriage between persons either of whom is under the age of sixteen is void. In other systems, the minimum age for marriage may be higher or lower. There is only one reported English case in which the law governing this impediment has been considered. In *Pugh* v. *Pugh*,[15] a marriage was celebrated in Austria between a British officer domiciled in England but stationed in Austria, and a girl of fifteen domiciled in Hungary. Four years later the parties came to England in accordance with their antenuptial intention, but parted almost at once. The marriage was valid by Austrian and Hungarian law, but it was held void. It therefore appears that no marriage is valid if either party is under sixteen, if either party (not necessarily the party under age) is domiciled in England. This seems anomalous: was it really the object of the statute to protect middle-aged English colonels from the wiles of designing Hungarian teenagers? The law is different in Scotland, where section 1(1) of the Marriage (Scotland) Act 1977 provides that "no person domiciled in Scotland may marry before he attains the age of 16."

The court in *Pugh* v. *Pugh* relied on *Brook* v. *Brook*[16] and the other cases on the prohibited degrees which have already been considered; and this seems sufficient justification for treating lack of age as coming under capacity to marry.

---

[13] (1969) 6 D.L.R. (3d) 617.
[14] (1879) 5 P.D. 94; *ante*, p. 164.
[15] [1951] P. 482. *Cf. Mohamed* v. *Knott* [1969] 1 Q.B. 1, where the girl was only 13, but the marriage was held valid because it was valid by the law of each party's antenuptial domicile. The Domicile and Matrimonial Proceedings Act 1973, s.3(1), impliedly assumes that parties may be validly married under foreign law below the age of 16: see *ante*, p. 29.
[16] (1861) 9 H.L.C. 193; *ante*, p. 161.

It is thought that a marriage celebrated in England would be held void if one party was under sixteen, regardless of the domicile of the parties: and there is a dictum to this effect in *Pugh* v. *Pugh*.[17]

Lack of parental consent

As we have seen,[18] English courts seem committed to the view that lack of parental consent, whether imposed by English or by foreign law, and no matter how stringently the requirement is expressed, is a mere formality and therefore incapable of invalidating a marriage celebrated in England. In *Ogden* v. *Ogden*,[19] however, the facts of which have already been stated, this was not the only ground of the decision. Other grounds were (a) that capacity to marry is governed by the *lex loci celebrationis* and not by the law of the parties' domicile[20]; and (b) that a marriage celebrated in England between a person domiciled in England and a person domiciled abroad is not invalidated by any incapacity which, though existing under the foreign law, does not exist in English law.[21] The first of these grounds is manifestly inconsistent with the decisions of the House of Lords in *Brook* v. *Brook*[22] and of the Court of Appeal in *Sottomayor* v. *De Barros* (*No. 1*).[23] The second reflects the illogical exception to the general rule on capacity to marry which was introduced by *Sottomayor* v. *De Barros* (*No. 2*).[24]

These two additional grounds leave open the possibility that a foreign requirement of parental consent may one day be characterised as relating to capacity to marry and not to the formalities of marriage.

Although the decision in *Ogden* v. *Ogden* has been heavily criticised,[25] it can be defended on policy grounds. It is a strong thing to hold a marriage, celebrated in England and valid by English law, to be invalid because of its failure to comply with foreign law. Of course the decision left the woman in an unfortunate position, and for this reason it has been described as "grotesque from the social point of view."[26] But it was really fortuitous that she had remarried: the decision might not have seemed so grotesque if she had been seeking to uphold the marriage, *e.g.* by claiming maintenance from her French husband.

Previous marriage

It is submitted with some confidence that this impediment can properly

---

[17] [1951] P. 482, 491–492. The possible scope of the English statute is discussed by Beckett (1934) 15 B.Y.I.L. 46, 64–65, and Morris (1946) 62 L.Q.R. 170–171. The law in Scotland is the same, for s.1(2) of the Marriage (Scotland) Act 1977 provides that "a marriage solemnised in Scotland between persons either of whom is under the age of 16 shall be void."

[18] *Ante*, pp. 151–153.

[19] [1908] P. 46; *ante*, pp. 152–153.

[20] At pp. 58–62.

[21] At pp. 75–77.

[22] (1861) 9 H.L.C. 193; *ante*, p. 161.

[23] (1877) 3 P.D. 1; *ante*, p. 163.

[24] (1879) 5 P.D. 94; *ante*, p. 163.

[25] *Ante*, p. 153, n. 23.

[26] Falconbridge, p. 74.

be included under the heading of capacity to marry. There is high authority for placing it under this rubric[27]; nor does it seem an abuse of language to say that a monogamously married man or woman has no capacity to contract a second marriage until the first is dissolved. If this is correct, the authority of the House of Lords can be cited for the proposition that capacity to marry is governed by the law of each party's antenuptial domicile and not by the law of the husband's domicile or of the intended matrimonial home. In *Shaw* v. *Gould*,[28] a man and a woman, both domiciled in England, married there and separated soon afterwards. The marriage was dissolved by the Court of Session in Scotland, and the woman then married a domiciled Scotsman and lived with him in Scotland. The divorce was not recognised in England because the first husband never lost his English domicile of origin. The House of Lords held that the second marriage was void, although it was valid by the law of the second husband's domicile and by the law of the intended matrimonial home. Lord Cranworth said[29]: "If the first marriage here was not dissolved there could not have been a second marriage. Till the first was dissolved there was no capacity to contract a second." It is submitted that this type of case demonstrates the impossibility of accepting any other view than that capacity to marry is governed by the law of each party's antenuptial domicile.

Again, in *Padolecchia* v. *Padolecchia*[30] a man domiciled in Italy was divorced from his first wife in Mexico. This divorce was not recognised in Italy. He went to live in Denmark and, during a one-day visit to England, went through a ceremony of marriage with a woman domiciled in Denmark. They both returned to Denmark to live, and later the man (still domiciled in Italy) petitioned the English court for a decree of nullity on the ground of his own bigamy. Sir Jocelyn Simon P. held that since the Mexican divorce was not recognised in Italy, the man had no capacity to marry by the law of his domicile; and he expressly approved Dicey's Rule 33.[31] He declined to consider the possibility that the marriage might be valid by the law of the intended matrimonial home. This decision is thus a strong authority in favour of the orthodox view.

Three situations need to be discussed in greater detail. The first is where the remarriage of a person whose marriage has been validly dissolved or annulled has been held invalid. The second is where the remarriage has been held valid notwithstanding an invalid decree of divorce. The third is where the law of the country where a divorce was granted imposes some restriction on the right of a divorced person to remarry.

---

[27] See, *e.g. Conway* v. *Beazley* (1831) 3 Hagg.Ecc. 639, 647, 652, *per* Dr. Lushington; *Brook* v. *Brook* (1861) 9 H.L.C. 193, 211–212, *per* Lord Campbell; *Shaw* v. *Gould* (1868) L.R. 3 H.L. 55, 71, *per* Lord Cranworth; *Padolecchia* v. *Padolecchia* [1968] P. 314, 336, *per* Simon P.

[28] (1868) L.R. 3 H.L. 55.

[29] At p. 71.

[30] [1968] P. 314.

[31] At p. 336.

Remarriage after valid foreign divorce or nullity decree. In *R*. v. *Brentwood Marriage Registrar*,[32] an Italian husband married a Swiss wife and later obtained a divorce from her in Switzerland, where they were domiciled. This decree was recognised in England but not in Italy. After the divorce the wife remarried. The husband wanted to marry in England a Spanish national domiciled in Switzerland. But the registrar refused to marry them because in his view there was an impediment. By Swiss law, his capacity to marry was governed by the law of his nationality. The Divisional Court upheld the registrar's objection to the remarriage.

The actual decision in this case would now be different, because section 7 of the Recognition of Divorces and Legal Separations Act 1971 (as amended by section 15(2) of the Domicile and Matrimonial Proceedings Act 1973) provides that where a foreign divorce is entitled to recognition under the Act, neither spouse shall be precluded from remarrying in the United Kingdom on the ground that the divorce would not be recognised in any other country. But the principle of the decision would still apply to remarriages outside the United Kingdom, or to remarriages anywhere after a foreign decree of nullity recognised by English law, but not by the law of the husband's domicile. However, in *Perrini* v. *Perrini*[33] an Italian husband married in Italy a woman domiciled in New Jersey. She obtained a decree of nullity from the New Jersey court on the ground of want of consummation. This decree was recognised in England but not in Italy. Later the husband, still domiciled in Italy, went through a ceremony of marriage in England with an English woman. It was held that the remarriage was valid. The decision may be right in the result, but the reasoning leaves much to be desired.[34] The decision seems right because the second wife had capacity to marry the husband by the English law of her domicile; the marriage was celebrated in England; therefore the situation was a *Sottomayor* v. *De Barros* (*No.* 2)[35] one, and the law of the husband's Italian domicile was irrelevant.

Similar problems could arise even after an English divorce, because in *Breen* v. *Breen*[36] Karminski J. was prepared to hold that one party to an English divorce might be unable to contract a valid marriage in the Republic of Ireland if Irish law refused to recognise the English divorce. Thus if spouses domiciled in the Republic of Ireland are habitually resident in England, and one of them obtains a divorce in England and then remarries in the Republic of Ireland, the remarriage would appear to be invalid, since the divorce would not be recognised in the country of his or her domicile. The position would be the same if the remarriage took place in England. The paradoxical result would then be that a foreign decree of divorce might have a greater effect in England than an English decree. This is

---

[32] [1968] 2 Q.B. 956; discussed by Chesterman (1969) 32 M.L.R. 84. This case is an example of that form of renvoi known as transmission (see *post*, Chap. 30) and also of the incidental question (see *post*, Chap. 32).

[33] [1979] Fam. 84.

[34] See Collier [1979] Camb.L.J. 289.

[35] (1879) 5 P.D. 94; *ante*, p. 163.

[36] [1964] P. 144; criticised by Unger (1961) 24 M.L.R. 784, and Webb (1962) 11 I.C.L.Q. 251.

because the validity of a remarriage in the United Kingdom after a foreign decree of divorce is preserved by section 7 of the Recognition of Divorces and Legal Separations Act 1971 (as amended), while that of a remarriage in the United Kingdom after an English decree of divorce is not.

Another consequence of the decision in *Breen* v. *Breen* is that in bigamy cases (unlike cases on the prohibited degrees of consanguinity and affinity),[37] an incapacity imposed by a foreign *lex loci celebrationis* is apparently fatal to the validity of a marriage.

Remarriage after void foreign divorce. The converse situation to that in the *Brentwood* and *Perrini* cases arose in the Canadian case of *Schwebel* v. *Ungar*.[38] A husband and wife, both Jews, were domiciled in Hungary. They decided to emigrate to Israel. While en route to Israel they were divorced by a Jewish ghet (or extra-judicial divorce) in Italy. They then separately acquired domiciles of choice in Israel. The wife married a man domiciled in Ontario during a temporary visit to that province. The ghet was ineffective to dissolve the marriage by the law of Hungary (where they were domiciled at the time of the ghet) but was effective to do so by the law of Israel (where they were domiciled at the time of the remarriage). It was not recognised as a valid divorce in Ontario, since the parties were not domiciled in Israel when it was delivered. Nevertheless, the remarriage was held valid, because immediately prior to the remarriage the wife's status by the law of her domicile was that of a single woman.

The Law Commission's proposals. The Law Commission and the Scottish Law Commission provisionally recommend[39] that section 7 of the Recognition of Divorces and Legal Separations Act 1971 should be widened so as to provide that where a decree of divorce or nullity is entitled to recognition in the United Kingdom, neither spouse should be regarded as incapable of remarrying, whether in the United Kingdom or elsewhere, on the ground that the decree would not be recognised in any other country. They also recommend that a person whose marriage is dissolved or annulled in the United Kingdom should be regarded as free to remarry, whether in the United Kingdom or elsewhere, notwithstanding that the law of his domicile would not recognise the decree. A third recommendation is that a person whose foreign divorce or annulment is not recognised in the United Kingdom should not be regarded here as free to remarry. This would reverse the decision in *Schwebel* v. *Ungar*.

Restrictions on the remarriage of divorced persons. Such restrictions are imposed for three main reasons: first, to punish the guilty party; secondly, to safeguard the unsuccessful party's right to appeal; and thirdly, to pre-

---

[37] *Ante*, p. 164.

[38] (1963) 42 D.L.R. (2d) 622 (Ontario Court of Appeal); (1964) 48 D.L.R. (2d) 644 (Supreme Court of Canada); discussed by Lysyk (1965) 43 Can. Bar Rev. 363; approved by Simon P. in *Padolecchia* v. *Padolecchia* [1968] P. 314, 339. The case is a good example of the so-called incidental question: see *post*, Chap. 32.

[39] Unpublished Consultation Paper circulated to a selected audience in May 1983.

vent disputes about the paternity of children subsequently born to the woman.[40]

In *Scott* v. *Att. Gen.*,[41] a husband obtained a divorce in Cape Colony, where he was domiciled, on the ground of his wife's adultery. By the law of the Cape, a person divorced for adultery was prohibited from remarrying so long as the injured party remained unmarried. After the divorce the wife came to England and married the co-respondent, who was domiciled in England. It was held that her remarriage was valid, because after the divorce she was a single woman and therefore free to acquire an English domicile separate from that of her first husband. But in the later case of *Warter* v. *Warter*,[42] the same judge (Sir James Hannen P.) explained *Scott* v. *Att. Gen.* on the different ground that the prohibition on remarriage attached only to the guilty party and could therefore be disregarded in England because it was penal, *i.e.* discriminatory. The implication is that the remarriage in England would have been held valid even if the wife had remained domiciled in Cape Colony.

In *Warter* v. *Warter*, a husband, domiciled in England but resident in India, divorced his wife in India for adultery.[43] She married in England a man domiciled in England less than six months after the decree absolute. Section 57 of the Indian Divorce Act 1869 provided that it should be lawful for the parties to remarry when six months from the date of the decree absolute had expired and no appeal had been presented, but not sooner. It was held that the remarriage was invalid.

The result of these two cases appears to be that if the restriction on remarriage imposed by the foreign law is an integral part of the proceedings by which alone both parties can be released from their incapacity to contract a fresh marriage, it will receive effect in England; but if the restriction on remarriage is imposed on one party only, it will be disregarded as penal.[44]

Physical incapacity

In English domestic law, a marriage is voidable at common law if one of the parties is incapable of consummating it,[45] or by statute if it has not been consummated owing to the wilful refusal of the respondent to consummate

[40] See Hartley (1967) 16 I.C.L.Q. 680, 694–699. As to the third reason, see *Lundgren* v. *O'Brien (No.* 2) [1921] V.L.R. 361.
[41] (1886) 11 P.D. 128.
[42] (1890) 15 P.D. 152, 155. The decision in *Warter* v. *Warter* was followed in *Miller* v. *Teale* (1954) 92 C.L.R. 406 (High Court of Australia) and *Hellens* v. *Densmore* (1957) 10 D.L.R. (2d) 561 (Supreme Court of Canada), but distinguished in *Buckle* v. *Buckle* [1956] P. 181, which was decided under the Indian and Colonial Divorce Jurisdiction Act 1926 (see next note).
[43] At that time it was supposed that the Indian courts had jurisdiction to grant divorces to persons domiciled in England and resident in India. In *Keyes* v. *Keyes* [1921] P. 204 it was decided that they had not. Their jurisdiction to do so was restored by the Indian and Colonial Divorce Jurisdiction Act 1926, which, however, no longer applies to India after independence.
[44] Dicey and Morris, p. 295.
[45] Matrimonial Causes Act 1973, s.12(*a*).

it.[46] Wilful refusal is more likely than impotence to produce problems in the conflict of laws, because impotence renders a marriage invalid nearly everywhere,[47] whereas wilful refusal is sometimes a ground for nullity, as in England, sometimes a ground for divorce, as in Canada,[48] and is sometimes not an independent ground for relief at all, as in Scotland[49] and Australia.[50]

English courts have always applied English domestic law when deciding whether to grant divorces. Until 1947, it was assumed that the same applied to the annulment of marriages on the grounds of impotence and wilful refusal: and it may well be that this is still the law. For example, in two cases decided in 1944,[51] marriages were annulled on the ground of the wife's wilful refusal to consummate, although in each case the husband was domiciled abroad and there was no evidence that by the law of his domicile this was a ground for annulment. In neither case was foreign law pleaded.

In 1947, in *Robert* v. *Robert*,[52] the possible application of foreign law to this question was considered for the first time. The marriage was celebrated in Guernsey, between parties there domiciled; and Barnard J. held that the question whether it should be annulled for wilful refusal to consummate must be decided by the law of Guernsey, either because "wilful refusal to consummate a marriage . . . must be considered as a defect in marriage, an error in the quality of the respondent" (a matter for the *lex loci celebrationis*)[53] or else because a question of capacity was involved, with the result that the law of the parties' domicile must be applied in accordance with the decision in *Sottomayor* v. *De Barros (No. 1)*.[54] But *Robert* v. *Robert* is not a very impressive authority for the application of foreign law, for not only did the *lex loci celebrationis* and the law of the parties' domicile coincide, but also no difference was shown to exist between the law of Guernsey and the law of England. Moreover, *Robert* v. *Robert* was overruled in *De Reneville* v. *De Reneville*[55] on the question of jurisdiction, although it was not expressly dissented from on the question of choice of law.

In the Northern Irish case of *Addison* v. *Addison*,[56] Lord MacDermott

---

[46] *Ibid.* s.12(*b*). This was first made a ground for nullity by s.7 of the Matrimonial Causes Act 1937.

[47] But not, *e.g.* in France or Australia.

[48] Divorce Act 1968, s.4(1)(*d*).

[49] Report of the Royal Commission on Marriage and Divorce (1956), Cmd. 9678, paras. 288–289, 294; Clive and Wilson, *Law of Husband and Wife in Scotland*, p. 48. Contrast the remarks of Willmer J. in *Ramsay-Fairfax* v. *Ramsay-Fairfax* [1956] P. 115, 125, which are (it is thought) wrong.

[50] s.51(1) of the Family Law Act 1975 abolished proceedings (other than pending proceedings) for the annulment of a voidable marriage.

[51] *Easterbrook* v. *Easterbrook* [1944] P. 10; *Hutter* v. *Hutter* [1944] P. 95.

[52] [1947] P. 164.

[53] At pp. 167–168. There is some difficulty in accepting Barnard J's view that wilful refusal as a ground for nullity depends upon error, for there is no requirement in s.13(3) of the Matrimonial Causes Act 1973 or its predecessors that the petitioner was at the time of the marriage ignorant of the facts alleged. Moreover, as we shall see (post, p. 174) the effect of mistake is not a matter for the *lex loci celebrationis*.

[54] (1877) 3 P.D. 1; *ante*, p. 163.

[55] [1948] P. 100, 118.

[56] [1955] N.Ir. 1, 30.

"very much doubted if the question of capacity to marry which is to be determined by the law of the domicile has to do with more than juristic capacity. Whether a contracting party is capable in the physical sense of discharging the obligations of matrimony seems to be so linked with the nature and quality of those obligations as to be, naturally and aptly, a matter for the *lex loci contractus*." Again, this is not a very impressive authority, for there was no difference between the *lex loci celebrationis* (Northern Irish law) and the law of the domicile (English law) on wilful refusal to consummate; and *Addison* v. *Addison* was overruled by the House of Lords in *Ross Smith* v. *Ross Smith*[57] on the question of jurisdiction, though not expressly dissented from on the question of choice of law.

In *Ponticelli* v. *Ponticelli*,[58] Sachs J. held that English law, which was the *lex fori* and the law of the husband's domicile, and not Italian law, which was the *lex loci celebrationis* and the law of the wife's antenuptial domicile, determined the question of wilful refusal to consummate. Had it been necessary to choose between the law of the husband's domicile and the *lex fori*, he would have preferred the former.

On the other hand, in *Ross Smith* v. *Ross Smith*[59] the House of Lords held that the English court had no jurisdiction to annul a marriage for wilful refusal to consummate merely because it had been celebrated in England. Lord Reid[60] and Lord Morris[61] both gave as one of their reasons for declining jurisdiction the undesirability of granting relief on grounds unknown to the law of the parties' domicile. This could be taken to imply that, had jurisdiction been held to exist, the *lex fori* would have been applied. And in *Magnier* v. *Magnier*,[62] a marriage was annulled for wilful refusal without reference to the law of the husband's domicile: but foreign law was not pleaded.

In this confusing state of the authorities, it is very much an open question what law governs impotence and wilful refusal. The application of the law of the husband's domicile at the date of the marriage is supported by *Robert* v. *Robert*[63] and *Ponticelli* v. *Ponticelli*.[64] The application of the *lex loci celebrationis* is supported by *Robert* v. *Robert* and *Addison* v. *Addison*.[65] The application of the *lex fori* is supported by *Easterbrook* v. *Easterbrook*,[66] *Hutter* v. *Hutter*,[67] *Magnier* v. *Magnier*[68] and (perhaps) by *Ross Smith* v. *Ross Smith*.[69] It has been plausibly suggested[70] that the

[57] [1963] A.C. 280, 307, 312, 348.
[58] [1958] P. 204, following *Way* v. *Way* [1950] P. 71 (*post*, p. 174), and not following *Robert* v. *Robert* [1947] P. 164 *supra*.
[59] [1963] A.C. 280.
[60] At p. 306.
[51] At pp. 313, 322.
[62] (1968) 112 S.J. 233.
[63] [1947] P. 164.
[64] [1958] P. 204.
[65] [1955] N.Ir. 1.
[66] [1944] P. 10.
[67] [1944] P. 95.
[68] (1968) 112 S.J. 233.
[69] [1963] A.C. 280, 306, 313, 322.
[70] Bishop (1978) 41 M.L.R. 512.

applicable law should be the law of the petitioner's domicile at the date of the marriage, on the ground that if the petitioner has no ground of complaint under his or her personal law, he or she ought not to be granted a decree. Certainly it seems that reliance on the law of the husband's domicile as such cannot survive section 1 of the Domicile and Matrimonial Proceedings Act 1973, which as we have seen provides that a wife can have a domicile different from that of her husband.

There is however no reported case in which the court has applied a foreign law which differed from English domestic law. So far as wilful refusal is concerned, the whole problem would admit of a simple and rational solution if wilful refusal were made a ground for divorce and not for nullity. It is hard to justify the existence of wilful refusal as a ground for nullity, because it is necessarily a post-matrimonial matter.

Although a decree annulling a voidable marriage formerly declared the marriage to be and to have been absolutely void to all intents and purposes, nevertheless it seems that if the *lex fori* is applicable, it must be applied as it is at the date of the trial, and not as it was at the date of the marriage. For marriages have been annulled for wilful refusal to consummate even though they were celebrated before 1938,[71] when this first became a ground for annulment in English law.

CONSENT OF PARTIES

Marriage is a voluntary union; there can be no valid marriage unless each party consented to marry the other. The question of consent is often a question of fact, but sometimes it may be a question of law. Of course the laws of foreign countries may differ widely from English law, for instance, as to the effect of fraud, as to the distinction between mistake as to the identity of the other party and mistake as to attributes, or between mistake as to the nature of the ceremony and mistake as to its effects, or the question whether duress or fear must emanate from the other party or can be extraneous.

In English law it was formerly a disputed question whether lack of consent rendered a marriage void or voidable. The question is set at rest (so far as marriages taking place after July 31, 1971, are concerned) by section 12(c) of the Matrimonial Causes Act 1973, which provides that a marriage shall be voidable if either party did not consent to it, whether in consequence of duress, mistake, unsoundness of mind or otherwise. In addition to these common law instances of lack of consent, there are three situations where by statute a marriage is voidable on this ground. The first is where at the time of the marriage either party, though capable of giving a valid consent, was suffering from mental disorder within the meaning of the Mental Health Act 1983 of such a kind or to such an extent as to be unfitted

---

[71] *Cowen* v. *Cowen* [1946] P. 36, overruled in *Baxter* v. *Baxter* [1948] A.C. 274, but not on this point: see at p. 282; *Dredge* v. *Dredge* [1947] 1 All E.R. 29; but in none of these cases was the point argued. They none of them had anything to do with the conflict of laws. *Cf. De Reneville* v. *De Reneville* [1948] P. 100, where the marriage was celebrated in 1935.

for marriage. The second is where the respondent was at the time of the marriage suffering from venereal disease in a communicable form. The third is where the respondent was at the time of the marriage pregnant by some person other than the petitioner.[72] In the second and third cases it is provided that the court shall not grant a decree of nullity unless it is satisfied that the petitioner was at the time of the marriage ignorant of the facts alleged[73]; and this is why they are properly characterised as instances of lack of consent. They are cases of mistake as to the attributes of the other party—a kind of mistake which was inoperative at common law.

There are a few reported cases which suggest, but do not conclusively answer, the question what system of law governs the requirement of consent. In *Apt* v. *Apt*,[74] where it was held that the validity of proxy marriages was a question of formalities, the Court of Appeal drew a distinction between the method of giving consent and the fact of consent. This observation enabled Hodson J. in *Way* v. *Way*[75] to hold that "questions of consent are to be dealt with by reference to the personal law of the parties rather than by reference to the law of the place where the contract was made. But this case is not a clear-cut authority because no difference was shown to exist between English law (which was the law of the husband's domicile) and Russian law (which was the law of the wife's domicile and also the *lex loci celebrationis*). It was followed in *Szechter* v. *Szechter*,[76] where a Polish professor divorced his wife and married his secretary in order to rescue her from prison and enable her to escape to the West; and Sir Jocelyn Simon P. applied Polish law as the law of each party's antenuptial domicile. But this case also is not a clear-cut authority because the law of the parties' domicile and the *lex loci celebrationis* coincided, and because, before pronouncing a decree, the learned President held that the marriage was also invalid by English domestic law.

On the other hand, the *lex loci celebrationis* was applied in *Parojcic* v. *Parojcic*[77]; but the decision would have been the same if the law of each party's antenuptial domicile had been applied, because they had lost their Yugoslav domicile of origin and acquired an English domicile of choice before their marriage in England. Moreover, it so happens that in all the reported cases,[78] English domestic law has been applied, either alone or cumulatively with the law of the domicile as in *Szechter* v. *Szechter*, even where the marriage was celebrated abroad and both parties were domiciled

---

[72] Matrimonial Causes Act 1973, s.12(*d*), (*e*) and (*f*).

[73] *Ibid*. s.13(3).

[74] [1948] P. 83, 88.

[75] [1950] P. 71, 78. His judgment was reversed by the Court of Appeal, *sub nom. Kenward* v. *Kenward* [1951] P. 124, but not on this point. Sir Raymond Evershed M.R. at p. 133 was prepared to assume that Hodson J.'s view on the law governing consent was correct.

[76] [1971] P. 286.

[77] [1958] 1 W.L.R. 1280; criticised by Webb (1959) 22 M.L.R. 198.

[78] See, in addition to the cases cited in notes 75, 76, 77 and 79, *Cooper* v. *Crane* [1891] P. 369; *Valier* v. *Valier* (1925) 133 L.T. 830; *Hussein* v. *Hussein* [1938] P. 159 (in each of which the marriage was celebrated in England); and *Mehta* v. *Mehta* [1945] 2 All E.R. 690; *Silver* v. *Silver* [1955] 2 All E.R. 614; *Kassim* v. *Kassim* [1962] P. 224 (in each of which the marriage was celebrated abroad).

abroad at the time of their marriage[79]: but this may have been because there was no evidence, or insufficient evidence, of the foreign law. It cannot be said, therefore, that the question is finally settled. But it is submitted that the best rule is that no marriage is valid if by the law of either party's domicile he or she does not consent to marry the other.[80]

It may be that the rule in *Sottomayor* v. *De Barros* (*No.* 2)[81] applies to consent of parties as it applies to capacity to marry.[82]

POLYGAMOUS MARRIAGES[83]

Introduction

Even if the marriage complies with the *lex loci celebrationis* as regards formalities and with the law of each party's antenuptial domicile as regards capacity to marry and consent of parties, it will, for certain limited purposes only, not be regarded as a valid marriage in England, if it is actually or potentially polygamous. The importance of this topic is now much reduced because the former hostility of English law to polygamous marriages has largely broken down and because the two chief targets for criticism (denial of matrimonial relief[84] and denial of social security benefits[85]) have been removed by legislation.

It is not often that an undefended divorce case becomes a leading case, not only in England but wherever the common law prevails: but such has been the fate of *Hyde* v. *Hyde*.[86] The petitioner was an Englishman by birth, and in 1847, when he was about sixteen years old, he joined a congregation of Mormons in London, and was soon afterwards ordained a priest of that faith. In London he met the respondent and her family, all of whom were Mormons, and became engaged to her. In 1850 the respondent and her mother emigrated to Salt Lake City, in the Territory of Utah, in the United States, and in 1853 the petitioner joined them there. They were married in 1853, the marriage being celebrated by Brigham Young, the president of the Mormon church, and governor of the territory. They lived together in Utah until 1856, when the petitioner went on a mission to the Sandwich Islands (now called Hawaii), leaving the respondent in Utah. On his arrival in the islands the scales fell from his eyes and he renounced

---

[79] *H.* v. *H.* [1954] P. 258, discussed by Woodhouse (1954) 3 I.C.L.Q. 454; *Buckland* v. *Buckland* [1968] P. 296.

[80] Dicey and Morris, Rule 34.

[81] (1879) 5 P.D. 94; *ante*, p. 163.

[82] *Vervaeke* v. *Smith* [1981] Fam. 77. The House of Lords made no comment on this proposition: [1983] 1 A.C. 145.

[83] See Dicey and Morris, pp. 308–328; Cheshire and North, pp. 296–312; Fitzpatrick (1900) 2 Jo.Comp.Leg. (2nd series) 359; Beckett (1932) 48 L.Q.R. 341; Morris (1953) 66 Harv.L. Rev. 961; Sinclair (1954) 31 B.Y.I.L. 248; Mendes da Costa (1966) 44 Can. Bar Rev. 293; Hartley (1969) 32 M.L.R. 155; Poulter (1976) 25 I.C.L.Q. 475; Jaffey (1978) 41 M.L.R. 38.

[84] *Post*, p. 187.

[85] *Post*, p. 184.

[86] (1866) L.R. 1 P. & M. 130.

the Mormon faith and preached against it. A sentence of excommunication was pronounced against him in Utah in December 1856 and his wife was declared free to marry again, which she did in 1859 or 1860. In 1857 the petitioner resumed his domicile in England, where he became the minister of a dissenting chapel at Derby. He petitioned for divorce on the ground of his wife's adultery.

Lord Penzance refused to adjudicate on his petition on the ground that "marriage, as understood in Christendom, may for this purpose be defined as the voluntary union for life of one man and one woman to the exclusion of all others,"[87] and that this Mormon marriage was no marriage which the English Divorce Court could recognise, because there was evidence that polygamy was a part of the Mormon doctrine, and was the common custom in Utah. "It is obvious," he said, "that the matrimonial law of this country is adapted to the Christian marriage, and is wholly inapplicable to polygamy."[88] He pointed out that to divorce a husband at the suit of his first wife on the ground of his bigamy and adultery with the second, or to annul the second marriage on the ground that it was bigamous, would be "creating conjugal duties, not enforcing them, and furnishing remedies when there was no offence."[89]

It will be observed that the marriage in *Hyde* v. *Hyde* was not actually but only potentially polygamous because the petitioner never married more than one wife.

At the end of his judgment Lord Penzance made the following important reservation[90]:

> "This court does not profess to decide upon the rights of succession or legitimacy which it might be proper to accord to the issue of polygamous unions, or upon the rights or obligations in relation to third persons which people living under the sanction of such unions may have created for themselves. All that is intended to be here decided is that as between each other they are not entitled to the remedies, the adjudication, or the relief of the matrimonial law of England."

What is a polygamous marriage?

What English law means by a polygamous marriage can best be gathered from the following six propositions:

(1) It is immaterial that the husband never exercised his privilege of taking more than one wife and that he never intended to do so.[91] A potentially polygamous marriage is thus in the same category as an actually polygamous one. Moreover, if the husband does take more than one wife, no distinction can be drawn between them.

(2) If the husband's personal law does not permit him to take more than

---

[87] At p. 133.
[88] At p. 135. *Cf. Baindail* v. *Baindail* [1946] P. 122, 125, *per* Lord Greene M.R.
[89] At pp. 135, 136–137.
[90] At p. 138.
[91] *Hyde* v. *Hyde* (1866) L.R. 1 P. & M. 130; *Sowa* v. *Sowa* [1961] P. 70.

one wife, but does permit him to take concubines, a marriage celebrated under such a law is polygamous, at any rate if concubinage is a status recognised by that law.[92]

(3) On the other hand, in spite of the distinction drawn in *Warrender* v. *Warrender*[93] and *Hyde* v. *Hyde*[94] between "Christian" and "infidel" marriages, a marriage may be monogamous although neither party is a Christian. The crucial question is whether the law under which the marriage is celebrated permits polygamy; if it does not, the marriage is monogamous. On this ground Japanese marriages[95] and Jewish marriages[96] have been treated as monogamous, and so has a composite ceremony at Singapore in mixed Chinese and Jewish form.[97]

(4) A marriage may be monogamous although under the *lex loci celebrationis* it can be dissolved by mutual consent or at the will of either party, with merely formal conditions of official registration. On this ground a Russian marriage celebrated in 1924 was treated as monogamous.[98]

(5) The nature of the ceremony according to the *lex loci celebrationis*, and not the personal law of either party, determines whether a marriage is monogamous or polygamous. Or, to adopt a more sophisticated statement, it is for the *lex loci celebrationis* to determine the nature and incidents of the union and then for English law to decide whether the union is a monogamous or polygamous marriage.[99] Hence, if a domiciled Englishman[1] or Englishwoman[2] goes through a ceremony of marriage in polygamous form in a country where polygamy is lawful, he or she contracts a polygamous marriage.[3] Conversely, if a Muslim domiciled, *e.g.* in India or Pakistan, goes through a ceremony of marriage in an English register office, he contracts a monogamous marriage.[4] This may not be very logical,[5] but if the personal law of the husband had been applied, the effect would have been to deny English matrimonial relief to English girls marrying Muslims in England. However, it seems that for the purposes of section 11(*d*) of the Matrimonial Causes Act 1973,[6] a marriage is not potentially polygamous, even though celebrated in polygamous form, if neither spouse can under

---

[92] *Lee* v. *Lau* [1967] P. 14.
[93] (1835) 2 Cl. & F. 488, 532, *per* Lord Brougham.
[94] (1866) L.R. 1 P. & M. 130, 133–136.
[95] *Brinkley* v. *Att. Gen.* (1890) 15 P.D. 76.
[96] *Spivack* v. *Spivack* (1930) 46 T.L.R. 243.
[97] *Penhas* v. *Tan Soo Eng* [1953] A.C. 304.
[98] *Nachimson* v. *Nachimson* [1930] P. 217.
[99] *Lee* v. *Lau* [1967] P. 14, 20.
[1] *Re Bethell* (1887) 38 Ch.D. 220; *cf. Hyde* v. *Hyde* (1866) L.R. 1 P. & M. 130, where, however, the husband had probably acquired a domicile of choice in Utah before the ceremony.
[2] *Risk* v. *Risk* [1951] P. 50.
[3] It does not follow that the marriage is valid. This question is discussed *post*, p. 180.
[4] *Chetti* v. *Chetti* [1909] P. 67; *R.* v. *Hammersmith Marriage Registrar* [1917] 1 K.B. 634; *Srini Vasan* v. *Srini Vasan* [1946] P. 67; *Baindail* v. *Baindail* [1946] P. 122; *Maher* v. *Maher* [1951] P. 342; *Ohochuku* v. *Ohochuku* [1960] 1 W.L.R. 183; *Russ* v. *Russ* [1964] P. 315; *Qureshi* v. *Qureshi* [1972] Fam. 173. The law in Scotland is the same: *MacDougall* v. *Chitnavis*, 1937 S.C. 390.
[5] See Cheshire and North, pp. 299–302.
[6] *Post*, p. 180.

his or her personal law take another spouse during the subsistence of the marriage.[7]

(6) It was at one time supposed that the monogamous or polygamous character of the marriage had to be determined once and for all at its inception.[8] But now it is clear that a potentially polygamous marriage may become monogamous by reason of subsequent events. This may happen if, for instance, the parties (being domiciled in an eastern country like India, Pakistan or Sri Lanka) change their religion from one which permits polygamy to one which does not[9]; or if the husband changes his domicile from a country whose law permits polygamy to a country whose law does not[10]; or if the law under which the marriage is celebrated subsequently prohibits polygamy[11]; or (perhaps) if the parties, having gone through a polygamous ceremony in a country whose law permits polygamy, subsequently go through a monogamous ceremony in England[12]; or (under some systems of law) if a child is born.[13] But it seems that the event relied upon to produce this result must take place before the cause of action arises.[14]

The proposition laid down in *Ali* v. *Ali*[15] that a potentially polygamous marriage may become monogamous if the parties acquire an English domicile is a far-reaching one. It means that all those now living in England who are parties to a potentially polygamous marriage became entitled to English matrimonial relief as soon as they formed the intention to remain here permanently or indefinitely. The result may not be very logical and is difficult to reconcile with prior authority, notably with *Hyde* v. *Hyde* itself.[16] But it is to be welcomed on practical grounds because it narrowed the scope of that decision.[17]

In all these cases of conversion, the marriage was only potentially polygamous; but there seems no reason why their principle should not be equally effective to convert an actually polygamous marriage into a monogamous one, after the number of wives has been reduced to one by death or divorce.

There is no English authority on the converse problem, namely, when does a monogamous marriage become polygamous.[18] The answer may be

---

[7] *Hussain* v. *Hussain* [1983] Fam. 26.
[8] *Hyde* v. *Hyde* (1866) L.R. 1 P. & M. 130; *Mehta* v. *Mehta* [1945] 2 All E.R. 690.
[9] *The Sinha Peerage Claim* (1939) 171 *Lords' Journals* 350; [1946] 1 All E.R. 348n., as explained in *Cheni* v. *Cheni* [1965] P. 85, 90–91, and in *Parkasho* v. *Singh* [1968] P. 233, 243, 253.
[10] *Ali* v. *Ali* [1968] P. 564; *R.* v. *Sagoo* [1975] Q.B. 885. It is otherwise if the wife changes her domicile: *Onobrauche* v. *Onobrauche* (1978) 122 S.J. 210.
[11] *Parkasho* v. *Singh, supra*; *R.* v. *Sagoo, supra*.
[12] *Ohochuku* v. *Ohochuku* [1960] 1 W.L.R. 183. But, as was pointed out in *Ali* v. *Ali, supra*, at p. 578, if the polygamous marrage was valid, it is difficult to see how the registrar succeeded in marrying the parties again in England.
[13] *Cheni* v. *Cheni* [1965] P. 85. This is the leading case on the conversion of a potentially polygamous marriage into a monogamous one.
[14] *Ali* v. *Ali* [1968] P. 564.
[15] *Supra.*
[16] See Tolstoy (1968) 17 I.C.L.Q. 721.
[17] See Morris (1968) 17 I.C.L.Q. 1014.
[18] The case of *Att. Gen of Ceylon* v. *Reid* [1965] A.C. 720 was concerned solely with the law of Ceylon.

that the marriage has, so to speak, the benefit of the doubt: if it is monogamous at its inception, it remains monogamous although a change of religion or of domicile may entitle the husband to take another wife; if it is polygamous at its inception, it may become monogamous by reason of a change of religion, of domicile, or of law before the happening of the events which give rise to the proceedings.[19] Since a marriage celebrated in England in monogamous form between parties whose personal law permits polygamy is a monogamous marriage, it is difficult to see how a change of religion or of domicile could convert a monogamous marriage into a polygamous one. It is uncertain what the effect on such a marriage would be if the husband entered into a valid polygamous marriage abroad.

The Law Commission has provisionally recommended that no marriage should be regarded as polygamous, irrespective of the form of the ceremony and of the effect of such marriage under the *lex loci celebrationis*, unless it is actually polygamous.[20]

Validity of polygamous marriages celebrated in England

A marriage celebrated in England in accordance with polygamous forms and without any civil ceremony as required by English law is invalid, whatever the domicile of the parties.[21] There is no direct authority for this proposition,[22] but it must be correct on principle. The formal validity of marriages celebrated in England is entirely a matter of statute law. There is no longer any room in which the principles of the common law can operate. There is no provision in the Marriage Act 1949 which could conceivably validate a "marriage" celebrated in England in accordance with polygamous forms and without civil ceremony, *e.g.* a "marriage" performed in a private house or other unregistered building.

It is otherwise of course if a civil ceremony in an English register office is followed by a religious ceremony in an unregistered building, or if there is a combined religious and civil ceremony in a registered building, *e.g.* a Muslim mosque registered under section 41 of the Act. In the former case the religious ceremony does not supersede or invalidate the prior civil ceremony and is not registered as a marriage in any marriage register book[23]; the religious ceremony is a nullity so far as English law is concerned and the civil ceremony is the only marriage which English law can recognise.[24] In the latter case the marriage is no doubt not only valid but also monogamous.

---

[19] See Dicey and Morris, p. 313, approved by Simon P. in *Cheni* v. *Cheni* [1965] P. 85, 90.
[20] Working Paper No. 83 (1982).
[21] Dicey and Morris, Rule 36.
[22] The nearest indirect one is *R.* v. *Bham* [1966] 1 Q.B. 159, where the accused, a Muslim, was prosecuted for knowingly and wilfully solemnising a marriage in an unregisterd building contrary to s.75(2) of the Marriage Act 1949. The "marriage" was celebrated in accordance with Muslim rites; the "wife" was an Englishwoman and the "husband" a Muslim. It was held that he could not be convicted of an offence under the section because it applied only to marriages in a form known to and recognised by English law as capable of producing a valid monogamous marriage.
[23] Marriage Act 1949, s.46(2).
[24] *Qureshi* v. *Qureshi* [1972] Fam. 173, 186.

Capacity of persons domiciled in England to contract polygamous marriages

Capacity to marry is, as we have seen,[25] governed by the law of each party's antenuptial domicile. Hence it seems to follow that a man or woman whose personal law does not permit polygamy has no capacity to contract a valid polygamous marriage.[26] This is to some extent confirmed by section 11(d) of the Matrimonial Causes Act 1973,[27] which provides that an actually or potentially polygamous marriage entered into outside England after July 31, 1971 by a person domiciled in England is void.

In *Radwan* v. *Radwan (No.* 2),[28] Cumming-Bruce J. (but with the current of authority against him) held that a woman domiciled in England had capacity to contract an actually polygamous marriage with a man domiciled in Egypt at the Egyptian Consulate-General in Paris, because the parties intended to live together and did live together for some years in Egypt. He based this conclusion on some early dicta on capacity to marry in general which stressed the intended matrimonial residence,[29] and refused to follow the more recent authorities holding that each party must have capacity to marry the other by the law of his or her antenuptial domicile.[30] In this case the marriage was not within the statutory provision mentioned above, because it was celebrated in 1951. But it appears that even if it had been, the result might still have been the same, because Cumming-Bruce J. suggested[31] that the plain words of what is now section 11(d) of the Matrimonial Causes Act 1973 might be neutralised by section 14(1), which contains a saving for the rules of private international law. But, as he conceded, this would deprive section 11(d) of all meaning.

Radwan v. *Radwan (No.* 2) has been heavily criticised by academic writers,[32] and it is submitted that the case was wrongly decided. The

---

[25] *Ante*, pp. 161–170.

[26] Dicey and Morris, Rule 37; *Re Bethell* (1887) 38 Ch.D. 220; *Risk* v. *Risk* [1951] P. 50; *Ali* v. *Ali* [1968] P. 564; *Crowe* v. *Kader* [1968] W.A.R. 122; *contra, Kenward* v. *Kenward* [1951] P. 124, 145, *per* Denning L.J.; *Radwan* v. *Radwan (No.* 2) [1973] Fam. 35. Rule 37 in Dicey and Morris is stated in terms of "personal law" and not in terms of "domicile" because in many eastern countries the personal law is often a religious law. Hence a domiciled Englishman or Englishwoman who acquired a domicile of choice in, *e.g.*, India, Pakistan or Sri Lanka could not contract a valid polygamous marriage without a change of religion to Islam.

[27] Re-enacting s.4 of the Matrimonial Proceedings (Polygamous Marriages) Act 1972, which added a new para. (*d*) to s.1 of the Nullity of Marriage Act 1971. S.4 of the Act of 1972 was not included in the Law Commission's draft Bill, but was introduced therein by the Bill's sponsors in order to dispel Parliamentary opposition based on the erroneous supposition that the Bill legalised polygamous marriages.

[28] [1973] Fam. 35.

[29] *Warrender* v. *Warrender* (1835) 2 Cl. & F. 488, 535–536, *per* Lord Brougham; *Brook* v. *Brook* (1861) 9 H.L.C. 193, 207, *per* Lord Campbell.

[30] *Re Paine* [1940] Ch. 46; *Pugh* v. *Pugh* [1951] P. 482; *Padolecchia* v. *Padolecchia* [1968] P. 314; see *ante*, pp. 162–163, 165, 167. At the end of his judgment in *Radwan*, Cumming-Bruce J. said: "Nothing in this judgment bears upon the capacity of minors, the law of affinity, or the effect of bigamy upon capacity to enter into a monogamous union." Hence it has not been thought necessary to modify any of the views on capacity to marry expressed in the earlier part of this chapter.

[31] At pp. 51–52.

[32] Karsten (1973) 36 M.L.R. 291; Pearl [1973] Camb.L.J. 43; J. A. Wade (1973) 22 I.C.L.Q. 571; Dicey and Morris, pp. 318–319; Cheshire and North, pp. 349–350; Halsbury, *Laws of England*, 4th ed., Vol. 8, para. 477. It is defended by Jaffey (1978) 41 M.L.R. 38.

learned judge's anxiety to uphold the marriage after the parties had lived together for nineteen years and had had eight children is understandable. But hard cases make bad law.

In *Hussain* v. *Hussain*[33] the Court of Appeal placed a very narrow interpretation on section 11(*d*). They held that it did not invalidate a potentially polygamous marriage celebrated in Pakistan between a Muslim man domiciled in England and a Muslim woman domiciled in Pakistan, since the man could not lawfully take another wife under English law and the woman could not lawfully take another husband under the law of Pakistan. Had the woman been domiciled in England and the man in Pakistan, the decision would have been different.

The Law Commission has provisionally recommended that section 11(*d*) should be amended so that it would apply only to actually polygamous marriages.[34]

Recognition of valid polygamous marriages in England

We come now to the important question, to what extent will English law recognise a valid polygamous marriage? It must be borne in mind that we are dealing with marriages that are both polygamous and valid, *e.g.* a marriage celebrated in India or Pakistan between Muslims there domiciled. We are not dealing with marriages celebrated in England, or with marriages celebrated anywhere either party to which is domiciled in England.

The present law can be summarised by saying that a polygamous marriage will be recognised in England as a valid marriage, even if it is actually polygamous, unless there is some strong reason to the contrary.[35] In spite of Lord Penzance's emphatic statement in *Hyde* v. *Hyde*[36] that his decision was limited to the question of matrimonial relief (a question which is reserved for consideration in the next chapter), there was for many years a tendency to assume that all polygamous marriages were wholly unrecognised by English law.[37] However, since 1939[38] it has become clear that they are recognised for many purposes. We proceed to consider some typical situations.

(1) *Whether a bar to a subsequent monogamous marriage.* A valid polygamous marriage will be recognised to the extent that it constitutes a bar to a subsequent monogamous marriage in England, and so entitles the second "wife" (or the husband) to a decree of nullity on the ground of bigamy.[39] Otherwise the husband would be validly married to his first wife

---

[33] *Hussain* v. *Hussain* [1983] Fam. 26. See Schuz (1983) 46 M.L.R. 652.

[34] Working Paper No. 83 (1982).

[35] Dicey and Morris, Rule 38, approved by Winn J. in *Shahnaz* v. *Rizwan* [1965] 1 Q.B. 390, 397 and by Lord Parker C.J. in *Mohamed* v. *Knott* [1969] 1 Q.B. 1, 13–14.

[36] (1866) L.R. 1 P. & M. 130, 138; quoted *ante*, p. 176.

[37] See *Harvey* v. *Farnie* (1880) 6 P.D. 35, 53; *Re Bethell* (1887) 38 Ch.D. 220; *R.* v. *Hammersmith Marriage Registrar* [1917] 1 K.B. 634, 647; *R.* v. *Naguib* [1917] 1 K.B. 359, 360.

[38] *The Sinha Peerage Claim* (1939) 171 *Lords' Journals* 350; [1946] 1 All E.R. 348n., is usually considered to mark the turning point.

[39] *Srini Vasan* v. *Srini Vasan* [1946] P. 67; *Baindail* v. *Baindail* [1946] P. 122; *Hashmi* v. *Hashmi* [1972] Fam. 36; see Hartley (1969) 16 I.C.L.Q. 680, 691–694.

in the country where he married her and to his second wife in England—a state of affairs which would encourage rather than discourage polygamy.

(2) *Bigamy*. The question whether a valid polygamous marriage is a sufficient first marriage to support an indictment for bigamy was expressly left open in *Baindail* v. *Baindail*.[40] It has subsequently been held by a court of quarter sessions not to be sufficient.[41] However, there seems no reason why a polygamously married man should not be convicted of perjury under section 3 of the Perjury Act 1911 if he obtained a certificate for an English marriage ceremony by falsely stating that he was an unmarried man and that he knew of no impediment to his marriage. (The maximum penalty for this offence is the same as that for bigamy.) It is one thing for a polygamist to marry two wives, and quite another thing for him to pose as an unmarried man.

(3) *Legitimacy of and succession by children*. "It cannot, I think, be doubted now," said Lord Maugham, delivering the opinion of the Committee of Privileges of the House of Lords in *The Sinha Peerage Claim*,[42] "(notwithstanding some earlier dicta by eminent judges[43]) that a Hindu marriage between persons domiciled in India[44] is recognised by our courts, that the issue are legitimate, and that such issue can succeed to property in this country, with a possible exception which will be referred to later." Provided the marriages are valid by the *lex loci celebrationis* and by the personal law of the parties, it is immaterial that the husband married more than one wife or that the succession is governed by English law. Thus, in *Bamgbose* v. *Daniel*,[45] children of no less than nine polygamous marriages celebrated in Nigeria between persons there domiciled were held entitled to succeed to their father's property on his death intestate, although by a Nigerian Marriage Ordinance of 1884 the property was distributable in accordance with the English Statute of Distribution 1670. Therefore, the word "children" in that statute (and presumably the word "issue" in the Administration of Estates Act 1925) is wide enough to cover the children of a valid polygamous marriage. If this is so, it is tempting to assume that the decision in *Bamgbose* v. *Daniel* would have been the same if the father had acquired an English domicile after the celebration of his marriages and before his death, and if the case had come before the Chancery Division and not (as it did) before the Privy Council.[46]

[40] *Supra*, at p. 130.
[41] *R*. v. *Sarwan Singh* [1962] 3 All E.R. 612. This case was overruled in *R*. v. *Sagoo* [1975] Q.B. 885, but only on the ground that the marriage had become monogamous under the principles stated *ante*, p. 178. The principle of the decision was not doubted.
[42] (1939) 171 *Lords' Journals* 350; [1946] 1 All E.R. 348n. *Cf. Baindail* v. *Baindail* [1946] P. 122, 127, *per* Lord Greene M.R.
[43] The reference is apparently to the decision of Stirling J. in *Re Bethell* (1887) 38 Ch.D. 220, which is usually explained away on the ground that the husband was domiciled in England and therefore lacked capacity to contract a valid polygamous marriage.
[44] The Hindu Marriage Act 1955 abolished polygamy among Hindus in India; but the principle stated by Lord Maugham is no doubt still applicable to Muslim marriages between persons domiciled in India or elsewhere.
[45] [1955] A.C. 107.
[46] The practical importance of the question here discussed is reduced by ss.14 and 15 of the Family Law Reform Act 1969. See *post*, pp. 244–245.

It has even been held that if a Muslim domiciled in Pakistan enters into a potentially polygamous marriage there and then, during the subsistence of that marriage, goes through a ceremony of marriage with an English-woman in an English register office, the children of the second "marriage" are legitimate although the marriage itself is void.[47] The ground for this decision was that the second marriage was a valid polygamous marriage by Pakistani law. It seems manifestly wrong, because if the second marriage was valid, why was it annulled, and if it was polygamous, how did the court have jurisdiction to annul it?

The "possible exception" referred to by Lord Maugham in *The Sinha Peerage Claim* is the right to succeed as heir to real estate in England (which after 1925 is restricted to succession to entailed property and one or two other exceptional cases[48]). This exception was considered necessary because it was thought that difficulties might arise if there was a contest between the first-born son of the second wife and the later-born son of the first wife, each claiming to be the heir.

(4) *Succession by wives.* It seems that the surviving wife of a polygamous marriage could succeed to the husband's property on his death intestate, whether he married one wife or several, and whether he died domiciled in a country whose law permits polygamy or in England. In *Coleman* v. *Shang*[49] the widow of a potentially polygamous marriage celebrated in Ghana between parties there domiciled was held entitled to a grant of let-ters of administration to the husband's estate on his death intestate, although by a Ghana Marriage Ordinance of 1884 two-thirds of the prop-erty was distributable in accordance with the English Statute of Distribu-tion 1670. Therefore, the word "wife" in that statute (and presumably the word "spouse" in the Administration of Estates Act 1925) is wide enough to cover the wife of a polygamous marriage, at any rate if there is only one. Once again it is tempting to assume that the decision in *Coleman* v. *Shang* would have been the same if the husband had acquired an English domicile after the celebration of the marriage and before his death and if the case had come before the Chancery Division and not (as it did) before the Privy Council.[50]

In *Coleman* v. *Shang*[51] the Privy Council said:

"Difficulties may no doubt arise in the application of this decision in cases where there is more than one widow, both in dealing with applications for the grant of letters of administration and in the distri-bution of the estate, but they can be dealt with as and when they arise."

In *Re Sehota*,[52] one of two surviving widows of a polygamous marriage was

---

[47] *Hashmi* v. *Hashmi* [1972] Fam. 36.
[48] Law of Property Act 1925, ss.131, 132; Administration of Estates Act 1925, s.51(2).
[49] [1961] A.C. 481; *cf. Baindail* v. *Baindail* [1946] P. 122, 127, *per* Lord Greene M.R.
[50] If there was only one wife the marriage would become monogamous under the rule in *Ali* v. *Ali* [1968] P. 564, *ante*, p. 178.
[51] [1961] A.C. 481, 495.
[52] [1978] 1 W.L.R. 1506.

held to be a "wife" within the meaning of section 1(1)(*a*) of the Inheritance (Provision for Family and Dependants) Act 1975 and as such entitled to apply for financial provision under that Act. Moreover, the Privy Council has, without apparent difficulty, adopted the practice, in dealing with the estates of deceased Chinese who died domiciled in Malaya, of assigning the one-third share of the widow under the Statute of Distribution equally between the several widows.[53] And there is Canadian and Rhodesian authority for the proposition that gifts by will to a surviving wife attract succession duty at the lower rate applicable to a spouse, even if there is more than one wife.[54]

(5) *Social security legislation.* It was held in a number of decisions of Commissioners under the National Insurance Acts that the polygamously married wife of a contributor was not entitled to, *e.g.* maternity benefit or widow's benefit under those Acts, even if the marriage was only potentially polygamous.[55] The reason given was that "the question whether the words 'marriage,' 'husband,' 'wife' and 'widow' when used in an Act of Parliament or statutory instrument are intended to include polygamous marriages and the parties thereto must be decided in the light of the language of the Act or instrument in question taken as a whole, and of its manifest scope and purpose." It was thought that it could not have been the intention to allow several wives of one contributor to claim benefits under the Acts. But it was obviously unjust to deny such benefits to the one and only wife of a man who was compelled to pay contributions because of his employment in this country, simply because his marriage was potentially polygamous. Accordingly, regulations[56] made under section 162(*b*) of the Social Security Act 1975 (re-enacting and extending earlier legislation dating back to 1956[57]) provide in general terms that a polygamous marriage shall for the purposes of that Act and the Family Allowances Act 1965 (and any enactment construed as one with them) be treated as having the same consequences as a monogamous marriage for any day, but only for any day, throughout which it is in fact monogamous.[58]

Some curious anomalies were revealed by the case of *Imam Din* v. *National Assistance Board*[59]:

The husband married his second wife in Pakistan in 1948 when both

---

[53] *Cheang Thye Phin* v. *Tan Ah Loy* [1920] A.C. 369; *cf. The Six Widows' Case* (1908) 12 Straits Settlements L.R. 120.
[54] *Yew* v. *Att. Gen. for British Columbia* [1924] 1 D.L.R. 1166 (British Columbia Court of Appeal); *Estate Mehta* v. *Acting Master*, 1958 (4) S.A. 252 (Supreme Court of the Federation of Rhodesia and Nyasaland). In the latter case there was only one wife, but reliance on this fact was expressly disclaimed (at p. 262).
[55] Decisions Nos. R(G) 18/52, 11/53, 3/55, 7/55.
[56] Social Security and Family Allowances (Polygamous Marriages) Regulations 1975, S.I. 1975 No. 561.
[57] Family Allowances and National Insurance Act 1956, s.3. Under this section, a potentially polygamous marriage was treated as monogamous if, but only if, it had at all times been monogamous.
[58] There are additional provisions relating to the right to a retirement pension under the Social Security Act 1975.
[59] [1967] 2 Q.B. 213.

were Muslims domiciled there. The first wife was still alive but she died in the following year. In 1961 the husband and his second wife came to England, where the husband abandoned the wife and four of their children, leaving them destitute. The wife obtained assistance from the Board, which preferred a claim against the husband under section 43 of the National Assistance Act 1948, alleging that he was liable to maintain the wife under section 42(1)(a), which provided that "a man shall be liable to maintain his wife and children." The Divisional Court held that the claim succeeded because common sense and justice required that the word "wife" in section 42(1)(a) should include the wife of a polygamous marriage.

No one will quarrel with this conclusion. But the somewhat odd result was that, although the wife could not obtain maintenance in direct proceedings against her husband, even though the marriage was only potentially polygamous,[60] the husband could, indirectly, be made to pay for her maintenance if she had been in receipt of supplementary benefit, even if the marriage was at one time actually polygamous. This result is hardly likely to increase the layman's respect for the law. Moreover, it should be noted that the second Mrs. Imam Din would not have been entitled to any social security benefits under the law as it then stood, because her marriage was not in fact at all times monogamous.

(6) *Miscellaneous cases.* The Divisional Court has recognised a potentially polygamous marriage celebrated in Nigeria between a man and a girl of thirteen domiciled there, and revoked a "fit person" order made in respect of the girl under section 62 of the Children and Young Persons Act 1933.[61] The Privy Council has held that a husband and wife whose marriage is potentially polygamous cannot be guilty of a criminal conspiracy.[62] The wife of a potentially polygamous marriage has been allowed to assert a contractual claim against her husband for "deferred dower" under a marriage contract governed by Muslim law.[63] There is American authority for the proposition that the surviving spouse of a valid polygamous marriage can recover workmen's compensation for the death of her husband in an accident arising in the course of his employment.[64] If this case is followed in England, it would mean that the surviving spouse of a valid polygamous marriage would rank as a dependant under the Fatal Accidents Act 1976 and could recover damages for the tortiously-inflicted death of her husband. In the law of immigration, the word "wife" includes each of two or more wives for the purposes of deportation.[65] There is no reason to doubt that the polygamously-married wife of a British citizen would be entitled to claim such citizenship by registration under section 8 of the British

[60] *Sowa* v. *Sowa* [1961] P. 70.
[61] *Mohamed* v. *Knott* [1969] 1 Q.B. 1.
[62] *Mawji* v. *The Queen* [1957] A.C. 126.
[63] *Shahnaz* v. *Rizwan* [1965] 1 Q.B. 390; *Qureshi* v. *Qureshi* [1972] Fam. 173.
[64] *Royal* v. *Cudahy Packing Co.* 195 Iowa 759, 190 N.W. 427 (1922).
[65] Immigration Act 1971, s.5(4).

Nationality Act 1981. The summary remedy provided by section 17 of the Married Women's Property Act 1882 applies to the spouses of a valid polygamous marriage.[66] The Matrimonial Homes Act 1983 is not confined to monogamously-married spouses.[67] A man who maintains his wife under a polygamous marriage is entitled to a deduction of tax under section 8(1) of the Income and Corporation Taxes Act 1970, even if there is more than one wife.[68]

Thus, a great deal of water has flowed under the bridges since 1866, when Lord Penzance denied matrimonial relief to the unfortunate Mr. Hyde. It is now clear that English law does recognise valid polygamous marriages unless there is some strong reason to the contrary. The previous pages have shown that this reason has to be very strong indeed before recognition will be denied. This is just as well now that England has become a multi-racial society. For it would not facilitate the integration of immigrants into English society if they were to be denied the elementary rights which native-born English people enjoy as of course.

---

[66] *Chaudhry* v. *Chaudhry* [1976] Fam. 148.
[67] s.10(2).
[68] *Nabi* v. *Heaton* [1981] 1 W.L.R. 1052; appeal allowed by consent [1983] 1 W.L.R. 626.

CHAPTER 12

MATRIMONIAL CAUSES

INTRODUCTION: POLYGAMOUS MARRIAGES

Matrimonial causes defined. Matrimonial causes are generally considered to include petitions for divorce, nullity of marriage, judicial separation, presumption of death and dissolution of marriage and for a declaration as to status.

Before 1858 jurisdiction over matrimonial causes (except divorce) was vested in the ecclesiastical courts, of which there was one in every diocese. Their jurisdiction depended on the residence of the respondent within the diocese. They had no power to dissolve a marriage; that could only be done by private Act of Parliament. In 1857 the Matrimonial Causes Act transferred the matrimonial jurisdiction of the ecclesiastical courts to a new Court for Divorce and Matrimonial Causes, and gave it power to dissolve a marriage. The new court did not last long, for in 1875 its jurisdiction was transferred to the Probate, Divorce and Admiralty Division of the new High Court, whence it was transferred in 1971 to the new Family Division of that court.[1] Since 1968, undefended matrimonial causes have also been heard in county courts designated by the Lord Chancellor.[2]

Polygamous marriages. As we have seen,[3] it was held in *Hyde* v. *Hyde*[4] that the parties to a polygamous marriage, even if it was valid by the law of the place of celebration and of each party's domicile, and even if it was only potentially polygamous, were not entitled to the remedies, the adjudication or the relief of the matrimonial law of England.

The rule in *Hyde* v. *Hyde* led to increasing hardship, especially after the influx of Commonwealth immigrants into the United Kingdom in the 1950s and 1960s. English judges did their best to mitigate its severity and restrict its scope by various devices, *e.g.* by holding that a marriage celebrated in monogamous form in England is a monogamous marriage, whatever the domicile of the parties, and that a potentially polygamous marriage could be converted into a monogamous one by subsequent events.[5] Finally, the rule was abolished (on the recommendation of the Law Commission)[6] by section 1 of the Matrimonial Proceedings (Polygamous Marriages) Act 1972, now re-enacted as section 47 of the Matrimonial Causes Act 1973, which provides that English courts are not precluded from granting matri-

---

[1] See now Supreme Court Act 1981, Sched. 1, para. 3.
[2] Matrimonial Causes Act 1967, s.1(1).
[3] *Ante,* p. 176.
[4] (1866) L.R. 1 P. & M. 130.
[5] See *ante,* pp. 177–178.
[6] See Law Com. No. 42 (1971).

monial relief or making a declaration concerning the validity of a marriage by reason only that the marriage was entered into under a law which permits polygamy.[7] This applies whether the marriage is potentially or actually polygamous; in the latter case, rules of court may require notice of the proceedings to be served on any other spouse, and may give him or her the right to be heard.[8]

"Matrimonial relief" is widely defined[9] so as to include decrees of divorce, nullity of marriage, judicial separation, presumption of death and dissolution of marriage, and orders for financial provision under section 27 of the Act,[10] variation of maintenance agreements, ancillary relief[11] or orders under Part I of the Domestic Proceedings and Magistrates' Courts Act 1978.[12] A "declaration concerning the validity of a marriage" is defined[13] to mean a declaration as to status under Order 15, r. 16, of the Rules of the Supreme Court[14] or under section 45 of the Matrimonial Causes Act 1973.[15]

This enactment does not mean that a polygamously married wife could get a divorce on the ground of her husband's adultery with another wife, because adultery means "consensual sexual intercourse between a married person and a person of the opposite sex, *not the other spouse*, during the subsistence of the marriage."[16] Since *ex hypothesi* the marriages are both valid and the other wife is a "spouse," the husband cannot commit adultery with her.[17] Nor does it mean that a later wife could get a decree of nullity on the ground of bigamy, because the earlier marriage is *ex hypothesi* valid.

DIVORCE

Jurisdiction of the English courts

The Matrimonial Causes Act 1857 was silent as to the jurisdiction of the new court to grant the new remedy; nor were there any precedents in the ecclesiastical courts, for they had no power to dissolve a marriage. The judges were thus left to navigate an uncharted sea without a compass; and naturally their early experiments relied on some jurisdictional criteria which seem strange today, *e.g.* nationality[18] and submission.[19] After a long

---

[7] For Scotland, see s.2 of the Act of 1972; for Northern Ireland, see Matrimonial Causes (Northern Ireland) Order, S.I. 1978 No. 1045, art. 50.

[8] s.47(4). See Matrimonial Causes Rules 1977, r. 108.

[9] s.47(2).

[10] *Post*, p. 221.

[11] *i.e.*, for financial relief (*post*, pp. 220–221) or custody of children (*post*, p. 231). See *Chaudhry* v. *Chaudhry* [1976] Fam. 148, 151.

[12] Sched. 2, para. 39. See *post*, p. 221.

[13] s.47(3) of the Act of 1973.

[14] *Post*, p. 216.

[15] *Post*, pp. 244, 251.

[16] Rayden, *Divorce*, 14th ed., p. 204.

[17] *Onobrauche* v. *Onobrauche* (1978) 122 S.J. 210.

[18] *Deck* v. *Deck* (1860) 2 Sw. & Tr. 90.

[19] *Callwell* v. *Callwell* (1860) 3 Sw. & Tr. 259; *Zycklinski* v. *Zycklinski* (1862) 2 Sw. & Tr. 420.

period of uncertainty during which the courts wavered between domicile and residence,[20] it was eventually laid down by the Privy Council in *Le Mesurier* v. *Le Mesurier*[21] that "according to international law, the domicile for the time being of the married pair affords the only true test of jurisdiction to dissolve their marriage." The essence of the rule in *Le Mesurier* v. *Le Mesurier* was that there should be only one test of jurisdiction and only one court capable of dissolving a particular marriage—the court of the parties' domicile.[22] As the domicile of the wife during marriage was the same as that of her husband,[23] this meant that the court had no jurisdiction to grant her a divorce unless the husband was domiciled in England at the commencement of the proceedings. This resulted in hardship to a wife whose husband deserted her and acquired or resumed a foreign domicile. Judicial attempts to mitigate this hardship proved unavailing[24]; and so Parliament was compelled to intervene.

The Matrimonial Causes Act 1937, s.13, provided that the court should have jurisdiction to grant a divorce, in proceedings by a wife, notwithstanding that the husband was not domiciled in England, if she had been deserted by her husband, or the husband had been deported from the United Kingdom, and the husband was immediately before the desertion or deportation domiciled in England. This was last re-enacted as section 46(1)(*a*) of the Matrimonial Causes Act 1973.[25]

This reform was found not to go far enough. So the Law Reform (Miscellaneous Provisions) Act 1949, s.1, provided that the court should also have jurisdiction to grant a divorce, in proceedings by a wife, notwithstanding that the husband was not domiciled in England, if she had been ordinarily resident in England for a period of three years immediately preceding the commencement of the proceedings, and the husband was not domiciled in any other part of the United Kingdom or in the Channel Islands or the Isle of Man. This was last re-enacted as section 46(1)(*b*) of the Matrimonial Causes Act 1973.[25]

Both these enactments were confined to proceedings by a wife. They did not extend to cross-petitions by a respondent husband.[26] This could cause injustice to the husband, because attack is often the best form of defence.

In 1972 the Law Commission made far-reaching proposals for reform of the law concerning the English courts' jurisdiction in matrimonial causes.[27] These proposals were translated into law by the Domicile and Matrimonial Proceedings Act 1973,[28] which came into force on January 1, 1974. Section

---

[20] See *Wilson* v. *Wilson* (1872) L.R. 1 P. & D. 435, 442 (domicile); *Niboyet* v. *Niboyet* (1878) 4 P.D. 1 (residence).
[21] [1895] A.C. 517, 540.
[22] *Indyka* v. *Indyka* [1969] 1 A.C. 33, 65–66, *per* Lord Reid.
[23] *Ante*, p. 28.
[24] See *Stathatos* v. *Stathatos* [1913] P. 46; *De Montaigu* v. *De Montaigu* [1913] P. 154; *H.* v. *H.* [1928] P. 206; *Herd* v. *Herd* [1936] P. 205.
[25] Now repealed by s.17(2) of and Sched. 6 to the Domicile and Matrimonial Proceedings Act 1973.
[26] *Levett* v. *Levett and Smith* [1957] P. 156; *Russell* v. *Russell and Roebuck* [1957] P. 375.
[27] Law Com. No. 48 (1972).
[28] For a commentary on the Act, see Hartley and Karsten (1974) 37 M.L.R. 179.

1 provides, as we have seen,[29] that a wife can have a domicile different from that of her husband. Section 5(2) provides that English courts have jurisdiction to entertain proceedings for divorce and judicial separation if (and, subject to section 5(5), only if) either of the parties to the marriage (a) is domiciled in England on the date when the proceedings are begun, or (b) was habitually resident in England throughout the period of one year ending with that date. The domicile or the habitual residence for one year of either spouse, whether husband or wife, petitioner or respondent, are now the only bases for jurisdiction. Thus, the new rules treat both spouses equally; the scales are not tilted in favour of the husband, as they were between 1895 and 1938, nor in favour of the wife, as they were between 1949 and 1974.

Section 5(5) of the Act provides that the court also has jurisdiction to entertain proceedings for divorce, judicial separation or nullity of marriage, notwithstanding that the jurisdictional requirements of the section are not satisfied, if they are begun at a time when proceedings which the court has jurisdiction to entertain by virtue of subsections (2), (3) or (5) are pending in respect of the same marriage for divorce, judicial separation or nullity of marriage. This subsection contemplates (a) supplemental petitions by the petitioner for the same relief on a different ground, or for a different form of relief, and (b) cross-petitions by the respondent. The court will have jurisdiction to entertain the supplemental or cross-petition, even though neither party is domiciled or habitually resident in England, provided it had jurisdiction to entertain the original petition and that petition is still pending. The effect of section 5(5) may be illustrated by an example. H is domiciled and habitually resident in France. W is domiciled in England and has been habitually resident there for one year when she petitions for judicial separation. She then abandons her domicile and habitual residence in England. H then cross-petitions for nullity of marriage. The court has jurisdiction to entertain H's cross-petition under section 5(5), provided W's petition is still pending. W then withdraws her petition for judicial separation and presents a supplemental petition for divorce. The court has jurisdiction to entertain W's supplemental petition under section 5(5), provided H's cross-petition is still pending, even though neither H nor W is now domiciled or habitually resident in England.

The exercise of the English courts' jurisdiction in proceedings for divorce is subject to rules requiring or enabling the court to stay those proceedings in certain circumstances. These rules are considered later in this chapter.[30]

Service of petition. The divorce petition may be served on the respondent out of the jurisdiction without leave of the court.[31] The court has power to dispense with service altogether in appropriate cases,[32] but is reluctant to

---

[29] *Ante*, p. 28.
[30] *Post*, pp. 217–220.
[31] Matrimonial Causes Rules 1977, r. 117(1).
[32] *Ibid.* r. 14(11).

do so except in most exceptional circumstances. It will not do so merely because the respondent is unable to communicate, *e.g.* because he or she is resident in enemy territory in time of war[33] or detained as a political prisoner.[34] But it may do so in a proper case if satisfied that all reasonable steps have been taken to notify the respondent and that he or she must have realised that proceedings are contemplated[35] or is indifferent to their result.[36]

Choice of law

The question of choice of law has never been prominent in the English rules of the conflict of laws relating to divorce, which has always been treated as primarily a jurisdictional question. On the one hand, as we shall see,[37] English courts when deciding whether to recognise foreign divorces have never examined the grounds on which the decree was granted in order to see whether they were sufficient by English domestic law. On the other hand, when English courts have themselves assumed jurisdiction, they have never applied any other law than that of England. In marked contrast, courts on the continent of Europe have, since the beginning of this century, often applied foreign law, usually the law of the parties' nationality. This has sometimes involved them in very complicated problems, especially when the parties are of different nationalities.[38]

In English law the only possible alternative to the *lex fori* would be the law of the domicile. No difference between them could exist before 1938, because English courts did not exercise jurisdiction unless the parties were domiciled in England. The Matrimonial Causes Act 1937, by allowing a deserted wife to petition for divorce although her husband was domiciled abroad, introduced the possibility that the law of the parties' domicile might no longer be English law. The Court of Appeal assumed without discussion that nevertheless English law was still applicable[39]; and this has since been confirmed by section 46(2) of the Matrimonial Causes Act 1973.[40] This provided that in any proceedings in which the court had jurisdiction by virtue of that section, the issues should be determined in accordance with the law which would be applicable thereto if both parties were domiciled in England at the time of the proceedings, *i.e.* English law. This subsection has now been repealed,[41] but this was not intended to alter the law.[42] Hence, if a spouse habitually resident in England but domiciled abroad petitions for divorce on a ground recognised by the law of his domi-

---

[33] *Luccioni* v. *Luccioni* [1943] P. 49; *cf. Read* v. *Read* [1942] 2 All E.R. 423.

[34] *Spalenkova* v. *Spalenkova* [1954] P. 141, where the cases are considered.

[35] *Weighman* v. *Weighman* [1947] 2 All E.R. 852; *Heath* v. *Heath* [1950] P. 193.

[36] *Paolantonio* v. *Paolantonio* [1950] 2 All E.R. 404. For the strange consequences which sometimes ensue, see *Whitehead* v. *Whitehead* [1963] P. 117.

[37] *Post*, p. 193.

[38] See the celebrated *Arrêt Rivière* (1953) 42 *Revue Critique* 412 in the French Cour de Cassation.

[39] *Zanelli* v. *Zanelli* (1948) 64 T.L.R. 556.

[40] Re-enacting earlier legislation going back to s.1(4) of the Law Reform (Miscellaneous Provisions) Act 1949.

[41] By s.17(2) of and Sched. 6 to the Domicile and Matrimonial Proceedings Act 1973.

[42] Law Com. No. 48, para. 103–108.

cile but not by English law, the court has no power to grant a decree. Conversely, if he petitions for divorce on a ground recognised by English law, it is immaterial that the ground is not recognised by the law of the domicile.

The rule may be justified on the ground that it would be highly inconvenient and undesirable from the practical point of view to apply foreign law in English divorce suits. For instance, to require the petitioner to lead evidence of foreign law in an undefended case (and 95 per cent. of divorce cases are undefended) would be a serious obstacle to the swift and inexpensive administration of justice. Again, to require English courts to dissolve marriages on exotic foreign grounds would be distasteful to the judges and unacceptable to public opinion.

Recognition of divorces granted in the British Isles

Judicial divorce has been available in Scotland since the sixteenth century, but in England only since 1858[43] and in Northern Ireland only since 1939.[44] The question whether English courts would recognise foreign divorces first arose early in the nineteenth century in connection with Scottish divorces. In *R.* v. *Lolley*[45] the accused, who was married and domiciled in England, induced his wife to divorce him in Scotland after a residence there of forty days. He then returned to England and went through a ceremony of marriage with another woman. He was convicted of bigamy and sentenced to transportation for seven years[46]; and all the judges resolved that no sentence of any foreign country could dissolve an English marriage.

It became increasingly difficult to determine what constituted an "English marriage" within the meaning of this resolution. In a series of cases decided by the House of Lords, it was gradually settled that a Scottish divorce would be recognised in England if the parties were domiciled in Scotland at the date of the institution of the proceedings,[47] but not otherwise.[48]

The Recognition of Divorces and Legal Separations Act 1971, which came into force on January 1, 1972, was passed to implement a Hague Convention on these matters. On the recommendation of the two Law Commissions,[49] the opportunity was taken to provide for the automatic recognition throughout the United Kingdom of decrees of divorce granted after December 31, 1971, under the law of any part of the British Isles.[50] Thus, no such divorce can be questioned in the United Kingdom on any ground of lack of jurisdiction. It can only be questioned if according to English or (as the case may be) Scottish or Northern Irish rules of the con-

---

[43] Matrimonial Causes Act 1857.
[44] Matrimonial Causes Act (N.I.) 1939.
[45] (1812) Russ. & Ry. 237.
[46] The sentence was remitted after one or two years: 2 Cl. & F. 570.
[47] *Harvey* v. *Farnie* (1882) 8 App.Cas. 43; *cf. Warrender* v. *Warrender* (1835) 2 Cl. & F. 488.
[48] *Dolphin* v. *Robins* (1859) 7 H.L.C. 390; *Shaw* v. *Gould* (1868) L.R. 3 H.L. 55.
[49] Law Com. No. 34 (Scot. Law Com. No. 16) (1970), para. 51.
[50] Recognition of Divorces and Legal Separations Act 1971, s.1, as amended by s.15(2) of the Domicile and Matrimonial Proceedings Act 1973. So far as the recognition of such divorces in Northern Ireland is concerned, the date is December 31, 1973: 1973 Act, ss.15(3), 17(5). All this is, of course, outside the scope of the Hague Convention, which applies to the recognition of divorces obtained in politically foreign countries.

flict of laws there was no subsisting marriage between the parties,[51] *e.g.* because there never was such a marriage or because it had been validly dissolved or annulled. Thus the wheel has turned full circle since *Lolley's* case in 1812.

It should be noted that section 1 of the Act refers to a "decree" of divorce granted "under the law of" (not "in") any part of the British Isles. The significance of this is that extra-judicial divorces are not included. They are considered in a later part of this chapter.[52]

Unlike the rest of the Act, section 1 is not retrospective: it only applies to the recognition in the United Kingdom of decrees of divorce granted under the law of any part of the British Isles after December 31, 1971.[53] The recognition of divorces granted under the law of any part of the British Isles before that date will continue to depend on the common law rules.[54] These are summarised in the pages that immediately follow. As will be seen, some of them have been abolished in relation to divorces obtained outside the British Isles, but they have not been abolished in relation to decrees granted before 1972 within the British Isles. In applying the rule in *Travers* v. *Holley*[55] to these divorces, it must be remembered that that rule applied regardless of the basis on which the foreign court assumed jurisdiction,[56] and even if the divorce was granted before the jurisdiction of the English court was enlarged by statute.[57] Therefore, it would seem to follow that if the validity of, *e.g.* a Scottish divorce granted before 1972 falls to be decided in England after 1973, it will be recognised if in fact either spouse had been habitually resident in Scotland throughout the period of one year ending with the date when the proceedings were begun, even though the Scottish court assumed jurisdiction on some other ground, and even though English courts did not have jurisdiction to grant divorces on a similar basis until January 1, 1974.[58]

Recognition of divorces obtained outside the British Isles

Introduction. Before 1972, English judges had developed the following rules for the recognition of foreign divorces. In all of them, the basis on which the foreign court assumed jurisdiction,[59] and the grounds on which it pronounced a divorce,[60] were both equally irrelevant.

---

[51] 1971 Act, s.8(1).
[52] *Post,* pp. 203–206.
[53] So far as recognition in Northern Ireland is concerned the date is December 31, 1973: see note 50, *supra.*
[54] Except that Scottish divorces granted under s.2 of the Law Reform (Miscellaneous Provisions) Act 1949, which made provision for Scotland corresponding to that which s.1 made for England (see *ante,* p. 189) will be recognised in England by force of the statute. See, to this effect, *Indyka* v. *Indyka* [1969] 1 A.C. 33, 59 F–G, *per* Lord Reid.
[55] [1953] P. 246; *post,* p. 194.
[56] *Robinson-Scott* v. *Robinson-Scott* [1958] P. 71.
[57] *Indyka* v. *Indyka, supra.*
[58] See North, pp. 169–170. Dr. North's ingenious argument seems unanswerable.
[59] *Robinson-Scott v. Robinson-Scott* [1958] P. 71, 88; *Indyka* v. *Indyka* [1969] 1 A.C. 33, 66 C.
[60] *Bater* v. *Bater* [1906] P. 209; *Wood* v. *Wood* [1957] P. 254; *Indyka* v. *Indyka, supra.*

(1) Under what is sometimes called the rule in *Le Mesurier* v. *Le Mesurier*,[61] a foreign divorce was recognised in England if the parties were domiciled in the foreign country at the commencement of the proceedings.

(2) Under the rule in *Armitage* v. *Att. Gen.*,[62] a foreign divorce was recognised in England if it would be recognised by the courts of the country in which the parties were domiciled.[63] The justification for this rule was that if the status of the parties is changed *or recognised as having been changed* in the country of their domicile, the change of status should be recognised in England. The rule enabled a great many divorces granted in the United States and in continental European countries to be recognised in England, although the parties were not domiciled in the particular American state or the particular European country where the divorce was granted.[64]

(3) Under the rule in *Travers* v. *Holley*,[65] a foreign divorce obtained by a wife (or by husband and wife jointly[66]) was recognised in England if the English court would, *mutatis mutandis*, have had jurisdiction to grant her a divorce under section 46(1)(*a*) or (*b*) of the Matrimonial Causes Act 1973 or its predecessors,[67] *e.g.* because she had been ordinarily resident in the foreign country for three years. The justification for this rule was that "it would be contrary to principle and inconsistent with comity if the courts of this country were to refuse to recognise a jurisdiction which *mutatis mutandis* they claim for themselves."[68] The rule applied regardless of the basis on which the foreign court assumed jurisdiction. Thus, if the wife had in fact been ordinarily resident in the foreign country for three years, the divorce was recognised even though the foreign court assumed jurisdiction on some basis then unknown to English law, *e.g.* the wife's separate domicile.[69] The rule applied even if the divorce was granted before the relevant part of section 46(1) of the Matrimonial Causes Act 1973 was first enacted in England: thus that section and its predecessors, while prospective so far as the English jurisdictional rules were concerned, had a retrospective effect on the English recognition rules.[70]

---

[61] [1895] A.C. 517. The label may be inaccurate, unless one assumes that the Privy Council were intending to lay down a general rule for divorce recognition as well as for divorce jurisdiction. But it is convenient.

[62] [1906] P. 135.

[63] There is no English authority on whether this means domiciled at the date of the commencement of the proceedings or domiciled at the date of the decree.

[64] As to when a divorce granted in one American state must be recognised in another under the full faith and credit clause of the American Constitution, see Griswold (1951) 25 A.L.J. 248, 255–259, reprinted in (1951) 65 Harv.L.Rev. 193, 208–217; Morris (1952) 29 B.Y.I.L. 283, 290–301, Restatement, ss.70–73.

[65] [1953] P. 246.

[66] *Tijanic* v. *Tijanic* [1968] P. 181. But not a divorce obtained by a husband, even on a cross-petition; *Levett* v. *Levett and Smith* [1957] P. 156.

[67] *Ante.* p. 189.

[68] *Travers* v. *Holley* [1953] P. 246, 257, *per* Hodson L.J.

[69] *Robinson-Scott* v. *Robinson-Scott* [1958] P. 71.

[70] *Indyka* v. *Indyka* [1969] 1 A.C. 33. But see the powerful arguments to the contrary adduced by Latey J. at first instance and Russell L.J. (dissenting) in the C.A.: [1967] P. 233, 244–245, 262–263. To these arguments the House of Lords gave (it is submitted) no adequate answer.

(4) Under the rule in *Indyka* v. *Indyka*,[71] a foreign divorce was recognised in England if there was a "real and substantial connection" between the petitioner or the respondent[72] and the foreign country where the divorce was obtained, *e.g.* because of nationality or residence or both.

Before 1967, when *Indyka* v. *Indyka* was decided, the recognition of foreign divorces in England depended on the answers to some relatively simple questions: were the parties domiciled in the foreign country? if not, would the divorce be recognised by the courts of their domicile? if not, would the English court (*mutatis mutandis*) have had jurisdiction to grant the wife a divorce? After 1967, the courts were left to grope their way as best they could through the uncertainties of what constituted a "real and substantial connection"; and large numbers of people simply did not know whether or not they were married, and if so, to whom. It therefore became obvious that the new criterion was not specific enough to provide a basis for recognition without the necessity for constant recourse to the courts.

In 1968, the Hague Conference on Private International Law produced a Convention on the recognition of divorces and legal separations[73] which is implemented by the Recognition of Divorces and Legal Separations Act 1971.[74] The Act retains the liberality of the *Indyka* rules while at the same time injecting some much-needed certainty into the law. In two respects, it is more liberal than the Convention. First, the Act applies to all divorces and legal separations obtained in any country outside the British Isles, and not merely to divorces and legal separations obtained in countries which are parties to the Convention. For it would have been an unnecessary complication to have one set of rules applicable to Convention countries and another set of rules applicable to the rest of the world. Secondly, the Convention requires that its two main bases of recognition—habitual residence and nationality—should be reinforced by other factors designed to discourage "forum-shopping," which occurs when the petitioner brings suit not in the natural forum, but in what for him is a more favourable forum. The Act abandons these complicated reinforcing factors in the interests of simplicity and because, as the Law Commissions cogently pointed out,[75] the stage when recognition is sought is not the appropriate stage at which to discourage forum-shopping. At that stage the forum-shopping, if any, has already taken place, and the real problem is to prevent limping marriages. This abandonment of the reinforcing factors is in accordance with the Convention, article 17 of which provides that it does not prevent a Contracting

---

[71] [1969] 1 A.C. 33. In this case, the House of Lords subjected the English rules for the recognition of foreign divorces to a searching analysis. Although many views were canvassed, the *ratio decidendi* is believed to be as stated in the text.

[72] *Mayfield* v. *Mayfield* [1969] P. 119; *Turczak* v. *Turczak* [1970] P. 198.

[73] For the text of the Convention and comment thereon by Anton, see (1969) 18 I.C.L.Q. 620–643, 657–664. The text and a commentary also appear in Law Com. No. 34 (Scot. Law Com. No. 16) (1970).

[74] For a commentary on the Act, see Karsten (1972) 35 M.L.R. 299. The Act applied originally only to England and Scotland. It now applies also to Northern Ireland: Domicile and Matrimonial Proceedings Act 1973, s.15. The Convention may be looked at as an aid to the interpretation of the Act in so far as the Act is ambiguous.

[75] Law Com. No. 34. para 29(a).

State from applying recognition rules more favourable than those of the Convention.

Apart from section 1, which has already been considered,[76] the Act is retrospective: it applies to the recognition of divorces and legal separations obtained outside the British Isles before as well as after January 1, 1972, the date when it came into force.[77] There are two exceptions to this rule of retrospective operation.[78] Section 10(4)(b) provides that the provisions of the Act do not affect any property rights to which any person became entitled before January 1, 1972, and do not apply where the validity of the divorce or legal separation has been decided by any competent court in the British Isles before that date. The intention no doubt was that the English court should follow the decision of the other court in the British Isles and refuse to recognise the divorce. But this is not what the Act says; it says that the provisions of the Act "do not apply." These provisions include section 6, which abolishes the rules in *Travers* v. *Holley*[79] and *Indyka* v. *Indyka*.[80] Therefore, if, *e.g.* a Scottish court decided before January 1, 1972, not to recognise a foreign divorce obtained outside the British Isles, and the question of its validity arose in England after that date, it is not clear whether the English court should follow the decision of the Scottish court and refuse to recognise the divorce, or apply its own pre-1972 rules and recognise it. The marriage is bound to "limp" whatever the English court decides. If it adopts the first alternative mentioned above the marriage will limp as between England (and Scotland) and the country where the divorce was obtained. If it adopts the second alternative, the marriage will limp as between England and Scotland.

The Act saves the common law rules in *Le Mesurier* v. *Le Mesurier*[81] and *Armitage* v. *Att. Gen.*[82] and the statutory rules contained in "any enactment other than this Act."[83] But subject to this it provides that no divorce or legal separation obtained outside the British Isles shall be recognised as valid in the United Kingdom except as provided in the Act.[84] The effect of this important provision is retrospectively to abolish the rules in *Travers* v. *Holley* and *Indyka* v. *Indyka* so far as divorces obtained outside the British Isles are concerned, and also to preclude the courts from developing further judge-made rules of recognition.

The Act is at first sight deceptively short and simple in appearance, but

---

[76] *Ante*, p. 192.

[77] s.10(4).

[78] They do not exhaust the difficulties to which a retrospective change in the recognition rules can give rise: see the remarkable case of *Hornett* v. *Hornett* [1971] P. 255, where a French divorce obtained in 1924 was recognised in England, although it could not have been recognised before 1967 when *Indyka* v. *Indyka* [1969] 1 A.C. 33 was decided. See further on this case *post*, pp. 494–495.

[79] [1953] P. 246; *ante*, p. 194.

[80] [1969] 1 A.C. 33; *ante*, p. 195.

[81] [1895] A.C. 517; *ante*, p. 194.

[82] [1906] P. 135; *ante*, p. 195.

[83] The reference is to the recognition of Hong Kong divorces under the Colonial and Other Territories (Divorce Jurisdiction) Acts 1926–1950, on which see Dicey and Morris, Rule 42(3) and pp. 352–353.

[84] s.6(5), as substituted by s.2(2) of the Domicile and Matrimonial Proceedings Act 1973.

its interpretation gives rise to at least one problem of very great difficulty. The key to understanding it is to realise that it draws a distinction between "overseas divorces" and "other divorces obtained outside the British Isles," though we have to wait until section 10(4) before this distinction is actually spelt out in so many words. The former are divorces recognised under sections 2 to 5 of the Act, implementing the Hague Convention. The latter are divorces not within the Hague Convention but recognised under the two common law rules saved by section 6 of the Act. These two kinds of divorces will now be separately considered.

Overseas divorces. Section 2 of the Act provides that sections 3 to 5 shall have effect, subject to section 8,[85] as respects the recognition in the United Kingdom of the validity of overseas divorces, that is to say, divorces which (a) have been obtained by means of judicial[86] or other proceedings in any country outside the British Isles, and (b) are effective under the law of that country. So it is clear at the outset that no overseas divorce can be recognised under sections 3 to 5 unless it falls within this definition. What does "effective under the law of that country" mean? A divorce would presumably not be effective if there was some procedural or other irregularity (not amounting to want of notice to the respondent or want of opportunity to take part in the proceedings[87]) in obtaining the decree,[88] or if the foreign court had no internal competence under its own law to grant it.[89] If the foreign decree is not final until a specified period of time has elapsed, or until a decree absolute is pronounced, or while an appeal is pending, it is not effective under the law of the foreign country and will not be recognised in England as an overseas divorce.[90] Further, the requirement of effectiveness may have important repercussions on the recognition in England of divorces granted in federal States where divorce is a matter for state as opposed to federal law, *e.g.* the United States. This problem is considered below.[91]

Section 3(1) provides for the recognition of overseas divorces if at the date of the institution of the proceedings (a) either spouse was habitually resident in the foreign country, or (b) either spouse was a national of that country.[92] Section 3(2) provides that in relation to a country which uses the concept of domicile as a ground of divorce jurisdiction, section 3(1)(a) shall have effect as if the reference to habitual residence included a reference to domicile *within the meaning of that law.* Hence, in contrast to the normal rule,[93] a divorce obtained in a country which uses domicile as a ground of jurisdiction will be recognised if either spouse was domiciled there in the sense of that country's law. (If either spouse was domiciled

[85] The provisions of s.8 are considered *post*, pp. 201–202.
[86] Extra-judicial divorces are considered *post*, pp. 203–206.
[87] These are covered by s.8(2)(a) of the Act and are considered *post*, p. 202.
[88] As in *Pemberton* v. *Hughes* [1899] 1 Ch. 781, where the divorce was recognised.
[89] As in *Adams* v. *Adams* [1971] P. 188, where the divorce was not recognised.
[90] *Torok* v. *Torok* [1973] 1 W.L.R. 1066.
[91] *Post*, pp. 198–199.
[92] See *Torok* v. *Torok, supra.* As to nationals of British colonies or other dependent territories, see s.10(3) of the Act.
[93] *Ante*, pp. 18–19.

there in the sense of English law, the divorce would be recognised under section 6 below.) Section 3(3) provides that in relation to a country comprising territories in which different systems of law are in force in matters of divorce, the foregoing provisions of the section (except those relating to nationality) shall have effect as if each territory were a separate country. Hence, subject to what is said below about the effect of section 2, a Nevada divorce will be recognised in England if either spouse was habitually resident in Nevada, or was domiciled there in the sense of its law, or was an American citizen.

If there are cross-petitions for divorce, it is sufficient if the jurisdictional tests were satisfied at the date of the institution either of the original proceedings or of the cross-proceedings, and it is immaterial which of them led to the decree.[94]

In some countries, a legal separation can be converted into a divorce after a prescribed period, e.g. one year. The Act provides that in such a case the divorce is entitled to recognition if the legal separation was so entitled.[95] It is immaterial that, before the legal separation was converted into a divorce in the country where the separation was obtained, the spouses ceased to be habitually resident or domiciled in or nationals of that country.

If the foreign court makes a finding of fact (including a finding that either spouse was habitually resident or domiciled in or a national of the foreign country), whether expressly or by implication, on the basis of which jurisdiction was assumed, that finding is conclusive evidence of that fact if both spouses took part in the proceedings, and in any other case is sufficient proof of that fact unless the contrary is shown.[96] If the proceedings are judicial in character, entering an appearance counts as taking part therein.[97]

If a divorce is obtained in a federal State like the United States, it is far from clear whether, in order to be recognised in the United Kingdom, it has to be effective under the law of the particular state where it was obtained, or whether it has to be effective under the law of the United States. Section 2 says it must be "effective under the law of that country." The Act does not define "country" except to say that it includes a colony or other dependent territory of the United Kingdom.[98] As we have seen,[99] section 3(3) provides that in relation to a country comprising territories in which different systems of law are in force in matters of divorce, the foregoing provisions of the section (except those relating to nationality) shall have effect as if each territory were a separate country. Hence, it is apparent that section 3 is using the word "country" not in its usual conflict of laws sense of "law district" (e.g. an American state or a Canadian prov-

---

[94] s.4(1).
[95] s.4(2).
[96] s.5(1). But the Act does not require the recognition of any finding of fault made by the foreign court: s.8(3).
[97] s.5(2).
[98] s.10(3).
[99] Supra.

ince) but in the sense of "State," *i.e.* a political unit known to public inter-national law.[1] Section 3(3) obviously means that, in the case of political units like the United States or Canada, the "country" is the United States or Canada and the separate states or provinces are "territories." The ques-tion is whether "country" has the same meaning in section 2, which is closely linked with section 3. If it has, it follows that no divorce can be recognised under section 3 unless it was effective under the law of the pol-itical unit (or State) in which it was obtained. This would be in accordance with article 1 of the Convention, which provides that the Convention applies to the recognition in one Contracting State of divorces and legal separations obtained in another Contracting State which are legally effec-tive there. It is true that article 13 provides that in the application of the Convention to divorces or legal separations obtained in Contracting States having, in matters of divorce or legal separation, two or more legal systems applying in different territorial units, any reference to the law of the State of origin shall be construed as referring to the law of the territory in which the divorce or separation was obtained. But the phrase "law of the State of origin" does not appear in article 1, so it is hard to see how article 13 can affect its construction.

The better opinion would appear to be that no American divorce can be recognised as an "overseas divorce" under section 3 of the Act unless it is "effective under the law of that country," *i.e.* the United States.[2] "Effec-tive under the law of the United States" presumably means that the divorce is entitled to full faith and credit under the American Constitution in all the other states.[3] At first sight it may seem to be an inconvenient construction of the Act to require an examination of the American Constitution before, *e.g.* a Nevada divorce can be recognised in England. But this is precisely what had to be done at common law under the rule in *Armitage* v. *Att. Gen.*[4] and what still has to be done under section 6 of the Act. On the other hand, the opposite construction would mean that a Nevada divorce might have to be recognised in England, even though it would not be recognised in any other American state. Which is absurd.

These difficulties do not arise in relation to the recognition in England of Australian or Canadian divorces, because in Australia and Canada divorce is now a federal matter regulated by federal statutes, and the law of each Australian state and of each Canadian province is the same.[5]

---

[1] For the difference between "country" and "State" as those terms are used in this book, see *ante*, p. 4.

[2] Morris (1975) 24 I.C.L.Q. 635; North, pp. 173–176; Cheshire and North, pp. 374–375; Dicey and Morris, pp. 349–351; *contra*, Clive, Book Review of North, 1978 S.L.T. 186–187.

[3] As to when an American divorce is entitled to full faith and credit in the other states, see *ante*, p. 194, n.64. In *Cruse* v. *Chittum* [1974] 2 All E.R. 940, a Mississippi divorce was recognised under s.3(1)(*a*) of the Act without any evidence that it was entitled to full faith and credit in the other states. But the proceedings in England were undefended, and the significance of s.2 was not perceived by counsel or court.

[4] [1906] P. 135; *ante*, p. 194. And also under the rule in *Indyka* v. *Indyka* [1969] 1 A.C. 33 when combined (as it could be) with the rule in *Armitage* v. *Att. Gen.*: see *Messina* v. *Smith* [1971] P. 322.

[5] Divorce Act 1968 (Canada); Family Law Act 1975 (Australia).

Other divorces obtained outside the British Isles. Section 6 of the Act deals with the recognition in the United Kingdom of other divorces obtained outside the British Isles. Unlike sections 2 to 5, section 6 has nothing to do with implementing the Hague Convention. Its object is to preserve the first two common law rules for divorce recognition mentioned above, namely the rule in *Le Mesurier* v. *Le Mesurier*[6] and the rule in *Armitage* v. *Att. Gen.*[7] In cases falling within section 6, the provisions of section 2 of the Act do not apply, so there is no requirement that the divorce must be effective under the law of the foreign State where it was obtained.[8] Nor do the provisions of the Act about cross-petitions,[9] conversion of legal separations into divorces[10] or findings of fact[11] apply. In section 6, domicile means domicile in the sense of English law, not in the sense of the foreign law.

A new section 6 had to be substituted for the original one by section 2(2) of the Domicile and Matrimonial Proceedings Act 1973 in consequence of the enactment in section 1 of that Act that a wife can have a domicile different from that of her husband. The new section 6 is somewhat tortuously drafted, but its effect is as follows. A divorce obtained outside the British Isles will be recognised in the United Kingdom if (a) both spouses were domiciled at the date of the institution of the proceedings in the country where it was obtained, or one of them was domiciled there at that date and the divorce was recognised as valid under the law of the other spouse's domicile; or (b) the divorce was recognised as valid under the law of the spouse's common domicile, or (where they had no common domicile) under the law of each spouse's domicile.

It seems curious that an overseas divorce can be recognised under section 3 of the Act if one spouse was habitually resident in, or a national of, a country outside the British Isles, or domiciled there in the sense of that country's law, regardless of whether it would be recognised in the country where the other spouse was habitually resident, or of which he was a national, or where he was domiciled in the sense of that country's law; whereas a divorce cannot be recognised under section 6 if one spouse was domiciled in the foreign country in the sense of English law unless it would be recognised in the country where the other spouse was domiciled in that sense. This means that if one spouse is domiciled in England, a divorce cannot be recognised under section 6 at all, because recognition would involve circular reasoning.

The Law Commission and the Scottish Law Commission have identified some defects in the Act which they provisionally recommend[12] should be abolished. First they recommend that the confusing and unnecessary distinction between "overseas divorces" and "other divorces obtained outside

---

[6] [1895] A.C. 517; *ante* p. 194.
[7] [1906] P. 135; *ante*, p. 194.
[8] *Ante*, pp. 197, 199.
[9] s.4(1); *ante*, p. 198.
[10] s.4(2); *ante*, p. 198.
[11] s.5; *ante*, pp. 198.
[12] Unpublished Consultation Paper circulated in May 1983.

the British Isles" should be abolished, and that sections 4 and 5 of the Act should apply to all divorces obtained outside the British Isles. Secondly, they recommend that section 6 should be amended so that if the divorce was granted or recognised in the domicile of one party it should be recognised in the United Kingdom even if it would not be recognised in the domicile of the other party. Surprisingly, there is no mention of the problems which arise from the ambiguity of the phrase "effective under the law of that country" in section 2.[13]

Grounds on which foreign divorces may be attacked

A foreign divorce granted by a court having jurisdiction according to English rules of the conflict of laws may nevertheless be attacked on a number of grounds, such as want of notice to the respondent. Before 1972, when the Recognition of Divorces and Legal Separations Act 1971 came into force, English courts had shown a distinct tendency to confine these grounds within narrow limits. There can be no doubt that this attitude was a wise one. "A decree of divorce," said Lindley M.R.,[14] "altering as it does the status of the parties and affecting, as it may do, the legitimacy of their after-born children, is much more like a judgment *in rem* than a judgment *in personam.*" Since the decree binds all the world, it logically follows that anyone can be heard to say why the decree does not bind him. Hence these grounds of attack may be taken not only by the respondent to the divorce proceedings, but also by third parties, *e.g.* a second spouse[15] or a person interested in property on the footing that the divorce is invalid in England.[16] This would open up a prospect of grave uncertainty in family relationships, since the validity of a remarriage by either party to the divorce, and the legitimacy of the children thereof, would be imperilled. In a statement which has often been cited with approval, Lindley M.R. said[17]: "English courts never investigate the propriety of the proceedings in a foreign court, unless they offend against English views of substantial justice. When no substantial justice, according to English notions, is offended, all that English courts look to is the finality of the judgment and the jurisdiction of the court." On the other hand, English judges have claimed a "residual discretion" to refuse to recognise divorces which offended their sense of justice,[18] and have occasionally exercised it.[19]

Section 8 of the Recognition of Divorces and Legal Separations Act 1971 contains provisions some of which require and some of which empower the court to refuse recognition to foreign divorces. These provisions apply not only to "overseas divorces" which would otherwise be recognised under

---

[13] *Ante*, pp. 197, 198–199.
[14] *Pemberton* v. *Hughes* [1899] 1 Ch. 781, 793.
[15] *Brown* v. *Brown* [1963] N.S.W.L.R. 1371; *Powell* v. *Cockburn* (1976) 68 D.L.R. (3d) 700.
[16] *Pemberton* v. *Hughes, supra.*
[17] *Ibid.* at p. 790.
[18] See *Russ* v. *Russ* [1964] P. 315, 327–328, 334, 335; *Hornett* v. *Hornett* [1971] P. 255, 260–261; *Qureshi* v. *Qureshi* [1972] Fam. 173, 201. *Cf.* the nullity cases, *Gray* v. *Formosa* [1963] P. 259; *Lepre* v. *Lepre* [1965] P. 52, *post*, p. 214. And see *ante*, pp. 47–48.
[19] *Middleton* v. *Middleton* [1967] P. 62, criticised by Unger (1966) 29 M.L.R. 327; Lipstein [1966] Camb.L.J. 181; Carter (1966) 41 B.Y.I.L. 445; *Re Meyer* [1971] P. 298, with which contrast *Igra* v. *Igra* [1951] P. 404.

sections 2 to 5 of the Act but also to other divorces obtained outside the British Isles which would otherwise be recognised under section 6. Section 8(1) provides that a divorce obtained outside the British Isles (and thus including an "overseas divorce") *must* be refused recognition if at the time when it was obtained there was according to English rules of the conflict of laws no subsisting marriage between the parties, *e.g.* because there never was such a marriage or because it had been validly dissolved or annulled.[20] Section 8(2) provides that a divorce obtained outside the British Isles (and thus including an "overseas divorce") *may* be refused recognition in three situations, and in no others. The first is where it was obtained by one spouse without such steps having been taken for giving notice of the proceedings to the other spouse as, having regard to the nature of the proceedings and all the circumstances, should reasonably have been taken. The second is where it was obtained by one spouse without the other spouse having been given such opportunity to take part in the proceedings as, having regard to the matters aforesaid, he should reasonably have been given. The third is where its recognition would be manifestly contrary to public policy. These three grounds (all of which are discretionary) will now be separately discussed.

(a) *Want of notice to the respondent.* This ground has long been familiar to English judges; and since non-recognition on this ground is discretionary under the Act, some assistance may still be derived from the case law before the Act. The most recent cases clearly hold that a divorce can be recognised if the respondent received no notice of the proceedings until after they were over.[21] But in *Macalpine* v. *Macalpine*[22] it was held that a divorce would be refused recognition on this ground if it was combined with fraud on the part of the petitioner, as where he falsely told the foreign court that he did not know the respondent's address.

(b) *Want of opportunity to take part.* There are very few reported cases in which a party to a foreign divorce, while receiving notice of the proceedings, was denied an opportunity to take part. In *Newmarch* v. *Newmarch*,[23] the wife's English solicitors at her request instructed Australian solicitors to file an answer to her husband's divorce petition, but they failed to do so, with the result that the suit went undefended and a divorce was granted. This was treated as a ground for not recognising the divorce under this head: but in all the circumstances the divorce was recognised.

(c) *Recognition manifestly contrary to public policy.* The word "manifestly" appears in section 8(2) of the Act because it appears in article 10 of the Convention, where it was inserted to discourage the excessive reliance by the courts of some countries on alleged grounds of public

---

[20] This applies also to divorces granted in the British Isles: see *ante*, pp. 192–193.

[21] *Boettcher* v. *Boettcher* [1949] W.N. 83; *Igra* v. *Igra* [1951] P. 404; *Arnold* v. *Arnold* [1957] P. 237; *Wood* v. *Wood* [1957] P. 254, 296; *Hornett* v. *Hornett* [1971] P. 255. But want of notice may have an important effect on whether an English maintenance order should be allowed to survive a foreign divorce; see *post*, p. 227.

[22] [1958] P. 35.

[23] [1978] Fam. 79. *Cf. Joyce* v. *Joyce* [1979] Fam. 93.

policy. There are very few reported cases in which a foreign divorce has been refused recognition in England on this ground. In *Kendall* v. *Kendall*,[24] the wife was deceived by her husband's Bolivian lawyers into applying for a divorce which she did not want in a language which she did not understand. It was held that recognition would be refused in England on the ground of public policy.

The Act appears to have abolished the "residual discretion" referred to above; any such divorces could now be refused recognition only on one of the three grounds just mentioned. The difference may be purely verbal. Apart from this, section 8(2) of the Act does not seem to effect any significant change in English law.

Recognition of extra-judicial divorces

Some religious laws, *e.g.* the Jewish and Muslim, allow one party to a marriage (usually but not necessarily the husband) to divorce the other by his own unilateral act, by a process called in Muslim law a talak and in Jewish law a ghet. In Jewish law the ghet is granted by a Rabbinical court, but the proceedings are "in no sense a judicial investigation."[25] In the ancient Muslim law which is still in force in the Sudan and other parts of east Africa, the husband can divorce his wife by simply saying "I divorce you" three times. No reasons need be given, the presence of the wife is not necessary, nor need notice be given to her. But in Egypt the divorce is usually registered with a court, though this is not essential for its validity.[26] And under the Pakistani Muslim Family Laws Ordinance 1961, the effect of the talak is suspended for 90 days to allow conciliation proceedings to take place before an arbitration council on which the wife is represented.[27] These conciliation proceedings may take place either in Pakistan or in a Pakistani embassy abroad.

The question arose whether these extra-judicial divorces would be recognised in England. Despite an early decision of the Court of Appeal to the contrary,[28] it gradually became clear that they would,[29] even though the ghet was obtained or the talak was delivered in England,[30] provided of course that the parties were domiciled in a country (*e.g.* Israel or Pakistan) the laws of which permit such a method. The reason was that if the cause for divorce is immaterial, so should the method be.

Section 2 of the Recognition of Divorces and Legal Separations Act 1971 applies the provisions of section 3 to divorces which have been obtained by judicial or other proceedings in any country outside the British Isles and

---

[24] [1977] Fam. 208. *Cf. Joyce* v. *Joyce* [1979] Fam. 93.

[25] *Har-Shefi* v. *Har-Shefi* (*No.* 2) [1953] P. 220, 222.

[26] See the expert evidence given in *Russ* v. *Russ* [1963] P. 87, 95; [1964] P. 315, 321–322.

[27] See *Qureshi* v. *Qureshi* [1972] Fam. 173; *R.* v. *Registrar General of Births, Deaths and Marriages, ex. p. Minhas* [1977] Q.B.1; *Quazi* v. *Quazi* [1980] A.C. 744.

[28] *R.* v. *Hammersmith Marriage Registrar* [1917] 1 K.B. 634. This decision was distinguished out of existence by Scarman J. and the C.A. in *Russ* v. *Russ, supra.*

[29] *Sasson* v. *Sasson* [1924] A.C. 1007 (P.C.); *Har-Shefi* v. *Har-Shefi* (*No.* 2) [1953] P. 220; *Russ* v. *Russ, supra*; *Lee* v. *Lau* [1967] P. 14; *Qureshi* v. *Qureshi* [1972] Fam. 173; *Quazi* v. *Quazi, supra.*

[30] *Har-Shefi* v. *Har-Shefi* (*No.* 2), *supra*; *Qureshi* v. *Qureshi, supra.*

which are effective under the law of that country. It thus to some extent confirms the English cases mentioned above. But the application of the Act (as amended by the Domicile and Matrimonial Proceedings Act 1973) to extra-judicial divorces is extremely complicated,[31] and no less than five situations have to be distinguished.

(1) An "overseas" extra-judicial divorce will be recognised in England under section 3 of the Act if either spouse was habitually resident in or a national of the country outside the British Isles where it was obtained,[32] provided it was effective under the law of that country and provided it was obtained by some kind of "proceedings." This term is not defined in the Act or in the Convention. It probably means that there must be some kind of formality external to the parties, e.g. appearance before a Rabbinical court,[33] registration of the divorce with some kind of authority, or notification to the chairman of the appropriate arbitration council as provided by the Pakistan Muslim Family Laws Ordinance 1961: even though there may be no power to prevent the husband from insisting on a divorce. In *Quazi* v. *Quazi*[34] the House of Lords held that Pakistani talaks are included, because notification to the chairman of the arbitration council amounted to proceedings officially recognised in Pakistan and effective there within the meaning of article 1 of the Convention, and therefore within section 2 of the Act. The House left open the question whether purely informal talaks, or other forms of Muslim divorces by mutual consent such as khulas, would be included. This question is still not satisfactorily settled.[35]

Section 8(2) of the Act[36] requires that there must be such notice to the other spouse and opportunity to take part as are reasonable, having regard to the nature of the proceedings. It does not seem likely that section 8(2) will be very strictly interpreted in relation to extra-judicial divorces, because no amount of notice would enable the wife successfully to contest the husband's unilateral divorce, and therefore it would be pointless to insist on an empty formality.[37]

(2) If both spouses were domiciled in the country outside the British Isles where the extra-judicial divorce was obtained, or if one of them was domiciled there and the divorce was recognised as valid under the law of the other spouse's domicile, it will be recognised in England under section 6 of the Act (as substituted by section 2(2) of the Domicile and Matrimonial Proceedings Act 1973). It will also be recognised in England (under the

---

[31] See Dicey and Morris, pp. 359–365; Cheshire and North, pp. 378–384; North, Chap. 11; Karsten (1980) 43 M.L.R. 202.

[32] In *R.* v. *Registrar General of Births, Deaths and Marriages, ex. p. Minhas* (1977) Q.B. 1, it was held that a divorce by talak is "obtained" where the husband writes the words "I divorce you" and not where the wife receives the communication, nor where the conciliation proceedings (if any) take place. To the same effect is *R.* v. *Immigration Appeal Tribunal* [1984] 2 W.L.R. 36.

[33] See *Broit* v. *Broit*, 1972 S.C. 192.

[34] [1980] A.C. 744.

[35] *Sharif* v. *Sharif* (1980) 10 Fam. Law 216. *Cf. Zaal* v. *Zaal* (1983) 4 F.L.R. 284; *Chaudhary* v. *Chaudhary*, (1983) 13 Fam. Law 177; *R.* v. *Immigration Appeal Tribunal, supra*, p. 40.

[36] *Ante*, p. 202.

[37] See *Maher* v. *Maher* [1951] P. 342, 345. But see *Zaal* v. *Zaal, supra*.

same section) if it was recognised as valid under the law of the spouses' common domicile, or (where they had no common domicile) under the law of each spouse's domicile. It will be recalled that no divorce can be recognised under section 6 if at the date when it was obtained one spouse was domiciled in England.[38] Section 2 of the Act does not apply to divorces recognised under section 6. There is therefore no requirement that there should be any proceedings or that the divorce should be effective under the law of the country where it was obtained. But the provisions of section 8(2) about notice and opportunity to be heard would apply.

(3) If the extra-judicial divorce was obtained in the British Isles (including a foreign embassy or consulate[39]) before January 1, 1974, it cannot be recognised under the Act at all: not under section 1, because it was not "granted under the law of any part of the British Isles," nor under section 3 or section 6, because it was not "obtained outside the British Isles." However, for the same reason the divorce would not fall within section 6(5) of the Act, which provides that no divorce obtained outside the British Isles shall be recognised as valid except as provided in the Act. Therefore the divorce could be recognised at common law under the rule in *Armitage* v. *Att. Gen.*[40] if it was recognised as valid under the law of the spouses' common domicile.[41] There would be no need for any proceedings, nor would section 8(2) of the Act apply. But the court would have a residual discretion not to recognise the divorce if justice so required, though this discretion would be sparingly exercised.[42]

(4) In *Qureshi* v. *Qureshi*,[43] Sir Jocelyn Simon P. recognised a talak that had been delivered in England by a husband domiciled in Pakistan; but he expressed misgivings as to the possible mischief that might arise when the safeguards inherent in a judicially pronounced divorce were thus by-passed. In consequence of this, section 16(1) of the Domicile and Matrimonial Proceedings Act 1973 provides that no proceeding in the United Kingdom, the Channel Islands or the Isle of Man on or after January 1, 1974, shall be regarded as validly dissolving a marriage unless instituted in the courts of law of one of those countries. There is no difference between "proceeding" in section 16 of the 1973 Act and "proceedings" in section 2 of the 1971 Act.[44] Section 16(1) perhaps leaves the door just open for the recognition (under the rule in *Armitage* v. *Att. Gen.*)[45] of a purely informal talak obtained in the British Isles on or after that date and recognised as valid under the law of the parties' domicile. If so, the paradoxical result is that the more informal and primitive the divorce, the more likely it is to be recognised. It is difficult to suppose that Parliament intended any such result.

---

[38] *Ante*, p. 200.
[39] *Radwan* v. *Radwan* [1973] Fam. 24; *Chaudhry* v. *Chaudhry* [1976] Fam. 148.
[40] [1906] P. 135, *ante*, p. 194.
[41] See, to this effect, *Chaudhry* v. *Chaudhry, supra*, at p. 150. Before 1974 the spouses could not have different domiciles.
[42] *Qureshi* v. *Qureshi* [1972] Fam. 173, 201.
[43] [1972] Fam. 173, 199A.
[44] *Quazi* v. *Quazi* [1980] A.C. 744, 823.
[45] [1906] P. 135; *ante*, p. 194.

(5) In order to prevent the parties from evading section 16(1) of the 1973 Act by making a short trip, *e.g.* to France and delivering the talak there, section 16(2) provides that any divorce obtained outside the British Isles on or after January 1, 1974, by means of a proceeding other than a proceeding in a court of law will not be regarded as validly dissolving a marriage if both parties were habitually resident in the United Kingdom throughout the preceding year, unless the divorce is required to be recognised as valid by any of the provisions of sections 2 to 5 of the Act of 1971.[46] Again, the door is perhaps left open for the recognition of a purely informal talak without any "proceeding" at all. The reason for distinguishing between recognition under sections 2 to 5 and recognition under section 6 of the Act of 1971 is that the former sections implement the Hague Convention, while the latter does not. So, unless the distinction had been drawn, the United Kingdom might have been in breach of its treaty obligations under the Convention. The distinction may be illustrated thus. H and W are both domiciled in and citizens of Israel. They have been habitually resident in England for one year when H obtains an extra-judicial divorce from W in Israel. If Jewish ghets are obtained by "proceedings", as they almost certainly are, this divorce must be recognised in England, because recognition is required under section 3(1)(*b*) of the Act of 1971 by reason of H and W's citizenship of Israel. But if H and W had not been citizens of Israel, the extra-judicial divorce would not be recognised in England, because recognition is not required under sections 2 to 5 of the Act but only under section 6.

There can be no doubt that English courts would recognise a foreign divorce obtained by legislative or by administrative as opposed to judicial process.[47] Such a method would clearly fall within the words "judicial or other proceedings" in section 2 of the Act.

JUDICIAL SEPARATION

Unlike divorce *a vinculo matrimonii*, judicial separation (or legal separation as it is called on the continent of Europe) was a remedy granted by the ecclesiastical courts before 1858. There it was called divorce *a mensa et thoro* (divorce from bed and board). The principal effect of a decree was (and is) to entitle the petitioner to live apart from the respondent, but not to dissolve their marriage nor enable either party to remarry. Comparatively few petitions are presented today; the remedy is sought chiefly by persons who have religious scruples about divorce.

With a few minor exceptions, all that is said in the previous section of this chapter about divorce applies equally to judicial separation. In particular, section 5(2) of the Domicile and Matrimonial Proceedings Act 1973 (dealing with the jurisdiction of the English courts) applies to judicial separation as it applies to divorce; so does the Recognition of Divorces and Legal Separations Act 1971. Nor has it ever been doubted that the English courts will apply English domestic law and no other, even if the parties are

---

[46] s.16(2) originated as an amendment to the Bill proposed by Lord Simon of Glaisdale (as he had since become).

[47] See *Manning* v. *Manning* [1958] P. 112.

domiciled abroad. The few exceptions are as follows. (1) Before 1972 the jurisdiction of the English courts was different in judicial separation from what it was in divorce. The main basis of jurisdiction in judicial separation (inherited from the ecclesiastical courts) was the residence of the respondent in England.[48] Other bases were the domicile of both parties in England,[49] and section 46(1)(a) but not (b) of the Matrimonial Causes Act 1973 and its predecessors.[50] (2) The Colonial and Other Territories (Divorce Jurisdiction) Acts 1926–1950 do not apply to judicial separation.[51] (3) There is no special problem about the recognition of extra-judicial separations, for these no longer exist.

An English decree of judicial separation has other effects besides the basic one mentioned above. It does not prevent either party from petitioning for divorce on the same grounds as those on which the decree of judicial separation was granted; in such a petition for divorce, the court may treat the decree of judicial separation as sufficient proof of any adultery, desertion or other fact by reference to which it was granted; and a period of desertion immediately preceding the institution of the proceedings for judicial separation will be deemed immediately to precede the presentation of the petition for divorce, if the parties have not resumed cohabitation and the decree of judicial separation has been continuously in force since it was granted.[52] There appears to be only one reported case in which a foreign decree of judicial separation has been recognised in England. In *Tursi* v. *Tursi*,[53] an Italian decree granted by the court of the parties' domicile was recognised. It was held that the foreign decree had the same effect in England as an English decree and that it did not bar subsequent proceedings in England for divorce, because the words "decree of judicial separation" in what is now section 4(3) of the Matrimonial Causes Act 1973 are wide enough to cover foreign as well as English decrees.

Another effect of an English decree of judicial separation is that while the decree is in force and the separation is continuing, if either party to the marriage dies intestate, his property devolves as if the other party were dead.[54] Presumably the effect of a foreign decree would be the same, even if it did not have this effect under the foreign law.

NULLITY OF MARRIAGE

Jurisdiction of the English courts

Before 1974 the jurisdiction of the English courts to entertain petitions for nullity of marriage was one of the most vexed and difficult questions in the whole of the English conflict of laws. An enormous simplification of the

---

[48] *Armytage* v. *Armytage* [1898] P. 178; *Anghinelli* v. *Anghinelli* [1918] P. 247; *Raeburn* v. *Raeburn* (1928) 44 T.L.R. 394; *Sim* v. *Sim* [1944] P. 87; *Sinclair* v. *Sinclair* [1968] P. 189.
[49] *Eustace* v. *Eustace* [1924] P.45.
[50] *Ante*, p. 189.
[51] *Ante*, p. 170, n. 43; p. 196, n. 83.
[52] Matrimonial Causes Act 1973, s.4.
[53] [1958] P. 54.
[54] Matrimonial Causes Act 1973, s.18(3).

law was effected by section 5(3) of the Domicile and Matrimonial Proceedings Act 1973.[55] This provides that English courts have jurisdiction to entertain such petitions if (and, subject to section 5(5), only if) either of the parties to the marriage (a) is domiciled in England on the date when the proceedings are begun, or (b) was habitually resident in England throughout the period of one year ending with that date, or (c) dies before that date and either was at death domiciled in England, or had been habitually resident in England throughout the period of one year ending with the date of death. The third limb of this subsection is intended to cover the rare but still theoretically possible case where a person with sufficient interest petitions for a decree that a marriage is void after the death of one or both of the parties thereto. In theory, he can also do so during the lives of the parties. With this insignificant exception, the bases for jurisdiction in nullity are now the same as in divorce and judicial separation. A voidable marriage no longer confers the husband's domicile on the wife as a matter of law.[56] Again with this insignificant exception, the bases for jurisdiction are now the same whether the marriage is alleged to be void or voidable. It is therefore no longer necessary to consult foreign law (the law of the husband's domicile at the date of the marriage[57]) in order to discover into which of these two categories the marriage falls, at any rate for jurisdictional purposes. It is just possible that the court might still refer to foreign law in order to determine whether the decree should be retrospective, as it is in English law in the case of a void marriage, or prospective, as it is in English law in the case of a voidable marriage.[58] But it seems more likely that this will be treated as a procedural matter, and so governed by the *lex fori*.

The provisions of section 5(5) of the Act on jurisdiction to entertain supplemental or cross-petitions apply to nullity of marriage as they apply to divorce and judicial separation. There is therefore no need to repeat here the earlier discussion.[59]

The exercise of the English courts' jurisdiction in proceedings for nullity of marriage is subject to rules enabling the court to stay those proceedings in certain circumstances. These rules are considered later in this chapter.[60]

One effect of the new English jurisdictional rules for nullity of marriage is to reverse two of the leading cases at common law: the decision of the Court of Appeal in *De Reneville* v. *De Reneville*[61] and the decision of the House of Lords in *Ross Smith* v. *Ross Smith*.[62] In each of these cases jurisdiction was declined; but in each case it would now be held that the petitioning wife was domiciled or habitually resident in England.

---

[55] Implementing the recommendations of the Law Commission: Law Com. No. 48 (1972), paras. 49–62.
[56] Domicile and Matrimonial Proceedings Act 1973, s.1.
[57] *De Reneville* v. *De Reneville* [1948] P. 100.
[58] Matrimonial Causes Act 1973, s.16.
[59] *Ante*, p. 190.
[60] *Post*, pp. 217–220.
[61] [1948] P. 100.
[62] [1963] A.C. 280.

Choice of law

The question what law governs the validity of a marriage was considered in the previous chapter. It was there pointed out that the formal validity of a marriage is governed (in general) by the law of the place of celebration,[63] and capacity to marry (in general) by the law of each party's antenuptial domicile.[64] There is more doubt about physical incapacity, which may be governed by the *lex fori* or possibly by the law of the petitioner's domicile,[65] and consent of parties, which may be governed by the law of each party's antenuptial domicile or possibly by the *lex fori*.[66] There is no need to repeat the former discussion of these matters in this chapter. But something should be said on the question whether a marriage could be annulled in England on some ground unknown to English law.

The grounds on which a marriage is void or voidable in English law are clearly set out in sections 11 and 12 respectively of the Matrimonial Causes Act 1973, and the bars to relief in the case of voidable marriages in section 13. Section 14(1) provides that where, apart from the Act, any matter affecting the validity of a marriage would under the rules of private international law fall to be determined by reference to the law of a foreign country, nothing in sections 11, 12 or 13(1) shall preclude the determination of that matter by that foreign law, or require the application to the marriage of the grounds or bar to relief there mentioned. This subsection seems to leave open the question with which we are concerned.

Of course a marriage could be annulled for failure to comply with the formalities prescribed by the law of the place of celebration, however much those formalities might differ from those of English domestic law.[67] And a marriage could be annulled if the parties were within the prohibited degrees of the law of their antenuptial domicile, even though they might have capacity to marry by English domestic law.[68] But could a marriage be annulled in England on some ground quite unknown to English domestic law, *e.g.* lack of parental consent[69] or mistake as to the attributes of the other spouse?[70] In the former case it is possible that the English court might fall back on tradition, characterise the impediment as a formality, and treat it as immaterial if the marriage was celebrated in England[71] or Scotland[72] but as invalidating the marriage if it was celebrated in the country by whose law the requirement of parental consent was imposed. But, as we have seen,[73] there are grave objections to this course. In the latter case the impediment could not by any stretch of the imagination be characterised as a formality, and the court would be squarely faced with

---

[63] *Ante*, pp. 150–158.

[64] *Ante*, pp. 159–170.

[65] *Ante*, pp. 170–173.

[66] *Ante*, pp. 173–175.

[67] See, *e.g. Berthiaume* v. *Dastous* [1930] A.C. 79 (marriage in church without civil ceremony).

[68] *Sottomayor* v. *De Barros (No. 1)* (1877) 3 P.D. 1 (first cousins).

[69] See *Ogden* v. *Ogden* [1908] P. 46 (French law).

[70] See *Mitford* v. *Mitford* [1923] P. 130 (German law).

[71] *Simonin* v. *Mallac* (1860) 2 Sw. & Tr. 67; *Ogden* v. *Ogden, supra.*

[72] *Lodge* v. *Lodge* (1963) 107 S.J. 437.

[73] *Ante*, pp. 151–153.

the question whether a marriage could be annulled on some ground unknown to English law. There is no English authority on this question. All that can be said is that there is no reported case in which a marriage has been annulled on any such ground.

In *Vervaeke* v. *Smith*,[74] the House of Lords refused to recognise a foreign decree annulling a marriage celebrated in England on the ground (unknown to English law) that it was a mock marriage. The implication is that the English court would not annul a marriage on such a ground.

Recognition of foreign decrees

Unlike the English rules for the recognition of foreign divorces, the rules for the recognition of foreign nullity decrees still depend on the common law, and draw no distinction between decrees obtained inside and outside the British Isles. Although English courts have recognised foreign divorces since 1882,[75] it was not until 1923 that they recognised foreign decrees of nullity as such,[76] and not merely as evidence that the marriage was invalid by foreign law.[77] Because of its later development, and of the much smaller number of nullity decrees than of divorce decrees, the law is still in a relatively imperfect state of development. In particular, the new statutory rules for the jurisdiction of the English courts to grant decrees of nullity have so far had no impact on the recognition rules, nor have the new statutory rules for divorce recognition. In considering the cases, it must be remembered that until 1974 a marriage that was valid or voidable conferred the man's domicile on the woman as a matter of law, while a void marriage did not have this effect.[78]

The leading case is *Von Lorang* v. *Administrator of Austrian Property*,[79] where the facts were as follows:

> In 1897 a marriage was celebrated in France between an Austrian subject and a woman who before her marriage was a British subject domiciled in Scotland. They lived together at Wiesbaden in Germany and acquired a domicile there. In 1923 the Administrator claimed the wife's movable property in Scotland under the Treaty of Peace (Austria) Order 1921, on the ground that she became an Austrian national

[74] [1983] 1 A.C. 145.
[75] *Harvey* v. *Farnie* (1882) 8 App.Cas. 43.
[76] *Mitford* v. *Mitford* [1923] P. 130.
[77] As in *Scrimshire* v. *Scrimshire* (1752) 2 Hagg.Cons. 395 and *Sinclair* v. *Sinclair* (1798) 1 Hagg.Cons. 294.
[78] *Ante*, p. 28.
[79] [1927] A.C. 641. The case is usually cited (even by Scottish Law Lords) as *Salvesen* v. *Administrator of Austrian Property*. But the author was informed by Lord Keith of Avonholm that it is just as much a solecism to cite the case in this way as it would be to cite *Donoghue* v. *Stevenson* [1932] A.C. 562 as *M'Allister* v. *Stevenson*, or *Bourhill* v. *Young* [1943] A.C. 92 as *Hay* v. *Young*: even though the result of the case was to declare that the appellant was and always had been Miss Salvesen and had never become Frau von Lorang. Lord Reid (in a letter to the author) defended the usual mode of citation on the ground that "the Salvesens are a very well-known Scottish family"; but (with great respect) this does not seem very convincing. So let us be correct, even if everybody else (except Falconbridge and Anton) is out of step.

by her marriage. The wife then took steps to discard her Austrian nationality. She petitioned the Wiesbaden court for a decree of nullity on the ground that the ceremony was formally invalid by French law. In 1924 the Wiesbaden court annulled the marriage on this ground.

The House of Lords held that the German decree must be recognised in Scotland because it was rendered by the court of the parties' common domicile. It will be seen that it was essential for the success of the appellant that the decree should be retrospective and that it should operate *in rem*, since otherwise the Administrator, who was not a party to the nullity proceedings, would not have been bound by the decree. This decision means that a number of earlier cases,[80] in which nullity decrees rendered in the common domicile of the parties were not recognised in England, must be taken to be overruled.[81]

Subsequent cases make it clear that the result is the same if the marriage was celebrated in England with all the formalities required by English law, and then annulled in the parties' common domicile on the ground of failure to comply with the formalities imposed by that law.[82] But what is the position if the decree is pronounced in the domicile of only one of the parties? This problem has arisen in three English cases where the recognition of Maltese nullity decrees was in question. In all three cases the facts were, irrelevant details apart, the same: a man domiciled in Malta married a woman domiciled in England at an English register office. Subsequently the man obtained a nullity decree from the Maltese court on the ground that no Roman Catholic priest was present at the ceremony as required by the Canon law in force in Malta. Two conflicting judicial attitudes to this situation are discernible. One view is that the Maltese decree should not be recognised in England, because "by its very terms it destroys the one and only ground on which the claim to exercise jurisdiction over the wife could be based,"[83] that is, her domicile of dependence in Malta. The other view is that the Maltese decree should be recognised in England because, the marriage being valid by English law, the woman acquired the domicile of the man by operation of law and therefore Malta was the common domicile of both parties; alternatively, because the marriage was only voidable by Maltese law and so again Malta was the common domicile of both par-

---

[80] *Simonin* v. *Mallac* (1860) 2 Sw. & Tr. 67; *Hay* v. *Northcote* [1900] 2 Ch. 262; *Ogden* v. *Ogden* [1908] P. 46.

[81] See, to this effect, *Ross Smith* v. *Ross Smith* [1963] A.C. 280, 345, with regard to *Simonin* v. *Mallac, supra*; *Merker* v. *Merker* [1963] P. 283, 299, with regard to *Hay* v. *Northcote, supra*; and *Lepre* v. *Lepre* [1965] P. 52, 62, with regard to *Ogden* v. *Ogden, supra*.

[82] *De Massa* v. *De Massa* [1939] 2 All E.R. 150, n.; *Galene* v. *Galene* [1939] P. 237. It must now be taken that in these two cases the court was wrong in pronouncing a decree of nullity, since, if the foreign decree was recognised, there was no marriage left to annul. The proper course would have been to dismiss the petition on this ground: see *Turner* v. *Thompson* (1887) 13 P.D. 37.

[83] *Chapelle* v. *Chapelle* [1950] P. 134, 144, approved (*obiter*) by Lord Denning M.R. and Donovan L.J. in *Gray* v. *Formosa* [1963] P. 259, 268–271. *Chapelle* v. *Chapelle* has been heavily criticised by academic writers: see Cheshire and North, pp. 407–408; Graveson, pp. 334–335; Cross (1950) 3 Int.L.Q. 247; Lipstein (1949) 26 B.Y.I.L. 472; Jackson (1950) 28 Can. Bar Rev. 679; Fleming (1953) 2 I.C.L.Q. 453; Grodecki (1958) 74 L.Q.R. 230–234. Moreover, an opposite result was reached, on facts hardly distinguishable, in *De Bono* v. *De Bono*, 1948 (2) S.A. 802 and *Vassallo* v. *Vassallo* [1952] S.A.S.R. 129.

ties; alternatively, even if the marriage was void by Maltese law, so that only the man was domiciled in Malta, still the decree should be recognised in England, because English courts should concede to foreign courts a jurisdiction which they themselves claim.[84] It is submitted that this second view is much to be preferred. But since a valid or voidable marriage no longer confers the man's domicile on the woman as a matter of law, only the last of these arguments remains available. Despite the analogy of divorce,[85] it is submitted that a nullity decree granted by the courts of one party's domicile should be recognised in England, even if it would not be recognised by the courts of the other party's domicile.

On the analogy of the rule in divorce,[86] it was held in *Abate* v. *Abate*[87] that English courts will recognise a decree of nullity pronounced by the courts of the country where the parties were not domiciled if it would be recognised by the courts of their common domicile. Presumably the result would be the same if the decree was recognised in the separate domiciles of each of the parties. It remains to be seen what the position would be if the decree was recognised in the domicile of one of the parties but not in the domicile of the other. Despite the analogy of divorce,[85] it is submitted that it should be recognised in England.

A foreign decree of nullity will also be recognised in England if both parties were resident in the foreign country at the commencement of the proceedings.[88] It may be that, on the analogy of the new rule for the jurisdiction of English courts to grant decrees of nullity, a foreign decree will also be recognised if it was granted in the country where only one party was habitually resident.

On the analogy of the common law rule in divorce,[89] it was held in *Law* v. *Gustin*[90] that English courts will recognise a foreign decree of nullity if there was a real and substantial connection between the petitioner and the foreign country where the decree was pronounced. But this decision would now probably be based on the ground that the petitioning wife had a separate domicile in the foreign country when she petitioned for nullity.

There is no decision as to whether the rule in *Travers* v. *Holley*[91] applies to the recognition of foreign nullity decrees. There are dicta in *Merker* v. *Merker*[92] and *Lepre* v. *Lepre*[93] suggesting that it might.

As in the case of divorce, the ground on which the foreign court annulled the marriage is irrelevant to the recognition of the foreign decree in Eng-

---

[84] *Gray* v. *Formosa* [1963] P. 259, 271–273, *per* Pearson L.J., and (in more detail) *Lepre* v. *Lepre* [1965] P. 52, 58–63, *per* Simon P.

[85] *Ante*, p. 200.

[86] *Armitage* v. *Att. Gen.* [1906] P. 135; *ante*, p. 194.

[87] [1961] P. 29.

[88] *Mitford* v. *Mitford* [1923] P. 130; *Corbett* v. *Corbett* [1957] 1 W.L.R. 486; *Merker* v. *Merker* [1963] P. 283.

[89] *Indyka* v. *Indyka* [1969] 1 A.C. 33; *ante*, p. 195.

[90] [1976] Fam. 155. The decree was obtained in 1968, and the petitioning wife therefore had a domicile of dependence with her husband in England. The case was followed in *Perrini* v. *Perrini* [1979] Fam. 84.

[91] [1953] P. 246; *ante*, p. 194.

[92] [1963] P. 283, 296.

[93] [1965] P. 52, 61–62.

land, unless its recognition would be contrary to public policy or to natural justice. "It is well established that if the English courts recognise the jurisdiction of a foreign court to annul a marriage, the ground on which that marriage was annulled by the foreign court is wholly immaterial."[94]

The Law Commission and the Scottish Law Commission provisionally recommend[95] that the rules for the recognition of foreign nullity decrees should be reduced to statutory form and assimilated as nearly as possible to the amended statutory rules for the recognition of foreign divorces.[96] That is to say, a decree of nullity granted under the law of any part of the British Isles should be entitled to automatic recognition throughout the United Kingdom; and decrees of nullity obtained outside the British Isles by judicial or other proceedings should be recognised in the United Kingdom on the same grounds and to the same extent as decrees of divorce are recognised under section 3 of the Recognition of Divorces and Legal Separations Act 1971 or the amended section 6.

Grounds on which foreign nullity decrees may be attacked

As we have seen,[97] English courts have confined within narrow limits the grounds on which a foreign divorce, granted by a court having jurisdiction according to English rules of the conflict of laws, can be attacked in England. For to multiply the grounds of attack (many of which might be open to third parties) would introduce grave uncertainty into family relationships, for example, if either party remarried on the strength of the decree and had children. Precisely the same considerations apply to collateral attack on foreign decrees of nullity. Yet it seems that English courts have scrutinised foreign nullity decrees with more care than they have scrutinised foreign divorces, and shown themselves more willing to allow such decrees to be attacked on grounds other than jurisdictional grounds. The following grounds of attack have been considered in English cases.

Fraud. A foreign nullity decree can probably be attacked for fraud or collusion. In *Von Lorang's* case[98] the House of Lords was careful to point out that the foreign decree had not been obtained by these means; and Lord Phillimore said that if it had been, it would not have been recognised.

Procedural defects. A foreign decree of nullity is not open to attack on the ground of a mere defect of procedure in the foreign proceedings. Thus a German decree declaring a marriage celebrated in Germany to be null and void for lack of form was recognised in England, although by German law the decree was a nullity because it should have declared the marriage to be non-existent.[99]

---

[94] *Corbett* v. *Corbett* [1957] 1 W.L.R. 486, 490. Contrast *Vervaeke* v. *Smith* [1983] 1 A.C. 145.
[95] Unpublished Consultation Paper (May 1983).
[96] *Ante*, pp. 192, 197–201.
[97] *Ante*, p. 201.
[98] [1927] A.C. 641, 652, 663, 671–672.
[99] *Merker* v. *Merker* [1963] P. 283.

Res judicata. A foreign nullity decree will not be recognised in England if it is inconsistent with a prior English judgment which is final and conclusive.[1]

Recognition contrary to public policy. A foreign nullity decree will not be recognised in England if recognition would be contrary to public policy.[2]

Recognition contrary to natural justice. In *Gray* v. *Formosa*,[3] a Maltese decree annulling a marriage validly celebrated in England on the ground that no Roman Catholic priest was present at the ceremony was refused recognition in England on the ground that it offended against English ideas of natural justice. In *Lepre* v. *Lepre*,[4] Sir Jocelyn Simon P. felt constrained to follow this decision, but he did so with understandable reluctance. The result of the cases appears to be that it is not contrary to natural justice to recognise a foreign decree if the respondent could not be personally heard owing to war conditions,[5] nor to recognise a decree based on the ground that a Christian cannot marry a Jewess,[6] or on the ground that there was no civil ceremony[7]; but it is contrary to natural justice to recognise a decree based on the ground that there was no religious ceremony.[8] These distinctions are not creditable to English law.

PRESUMPTION OF DEATH AND DISSOLUTION OF MARRIAGE

Jurisdiction of the English courts

Proceedings for presumption of death and dissolution of marriage were first introduced into English law by section 8 of the Matrimonial Causes Act 1937 and are now regulated by section 19 of the Matrimonial Causes Act 1973. The relief provided is not primarily or in essence dissolution of marriage. Its object is to enable the petitioner to obtain a declaration that the other spouse is presumed to be dead. But a safeguard is added to guard against the awkward situation which would otherwise arise if the presumption turned out to be wrong. This safeguard takes the form of joining to the decree of presumption of death a decree of dissolution. But this is merely

---

[1] *Vervaeke* v. *Smith, supra.*
[2] *Ibid.*
[3] [1963] P. 259; criticised by Carter (1962) 38 B.Y.I.L. 497; North, p. 264; Cheshire and North, pp. 414–415. Lord Denning's judgment in this case seems to have been delivered *quasi in furore*; and he seems to have overlooked the possible application of s.2 of the Legitimacy Act 1959, now s.1 of the Legitimacy Act 1976 (*post*, p. 243), which would have prevented at least two of the children from being bastardised, even if the Maltese decree had been recognised, and even if by Maltese law the effect of the decree was to bastardise the children.
[4] [1965] P. 52.
[5] *Mitford* v. *Mitford* [1923] P. 130.
[6] *Corbett* v. *Corbett* [1957] 1 W.L.R. 486.
[7] *Merker* v. *Merker* [1963] P. 283.
[8] *Gray* v. *Formosa* [1963] P. 259; *Lepre* v. *Lepre* [1965] P. 52.

ancillary to the former decree and does not alter its essential character. The subject receives separate treatment here not because it is particularly important but because of the clear doctrinal distinction drawn in *Wall* v. *Wall*[9] between ordinary divorce decrees and decrees of presumption of death and dissolution of marriage.

Section 5(4) of the Domicile and Matrimonial Proceedings Act 1973 provides that English courts have jurisdiction to entertain proceedings for presumption of death and dissolution of marriage if (and only if) the petitioner (a) is domiciled in England on the date when the proceedings are begun, or (b) was habitually resident in England throughout the period of one year ending with that date.[10] The bases for jurisdiction are thus the same as in divorce and judicial separation, except that the domicile and habitual residence of the petitioner alone are relevant.[11]

Choice of law

Section 19(5) of the Matrimonial Causes Act 1973 (re-enacting earlier legislation) provided that the issues should be determined in accordance with the law which would be applicable if both parties to the marriage were domiciled in England at the time of the proceedings, *i.e.* English law. This subsection has now been repealed,[12] but this was not intended to alter the law.[13]

Recognition of foreign decrees

English courts are not bound to treat as conclusive a decree of presumption of death made by a foreign court, even a court of the domicile,[14] unless it is accompanied by an order vesting the deceased's property in someone, *e.g.* an administrator,[15] or (perhaps) by a decree of dissolution of marriage. But they will probably do so in order to avoid a limping marriage if the foreign court is that of the domicile, or if (*mutatis mutandis*) the English court would have had jurisdiction in the circumstances. Thus in *Szemik* v. *Gryla*[16] the husband and wife were Polish nationals domiciled in Poland where they married in 1936. In 1947 the wife obtained a declaration from a Polish court that the husband died in 1942 and she remarried in 1953. By Polish law the declaration entitled the wife to remarry and her

---

[9] [1950] P. 112.
[10] For dispensing with service of the petition, see Matrimonial Causes Rules 1977, r. 14 (11), and *N.* v. *N.*, *L.* v. *L.*, *C.* v. *C.* [1957] P. 385. For the strange consequences which sometimes ensue, see *Deacock* v. *Deacock* [1958] P. 230, where a wife who was judicially presumed to be dead was subsequently awarded maintenance.
[11] In Scotland, the domicile or habitual residence for one year in Scotland of the missing person on the date when he was last known to have been alive are also bases for jurisdiction: Presumption of Death (Scotland) Act 1977, s.1(3)(a).
[12] By s.17(2) of and Sched. 6 to the Domicile and Matrimonial Proceedings Act 1973.
[13] See Law Com. No. 48 (1972), para. 108.
[14] *In the Goods of Wolf* [1948] P. 66.
[15] *In the Goods of Spenceley* [1892] P. 255; *In the Goods of Schulhof* [1948] P. 66; *In the Goods of Dowds* [1948] P. 256.
[16] (1965) 109 S.J. 175.

remarriage dissolved her first marriage. In fact the husband was not dead but was living in England where he had acquired an English domicile in 1946. Scarman J. recognised the Polish declaration and remarriage as having dissolved the first marriage.

In Scotland, a decree of a foreign court declaring that a person has died or is presumed to have died is sufficient evidence of the facts so declared if the person was domiciled or habitually resident in the foreign country on the date when he was last known to be alive.[17]

DECLARATIONS AS TO STATUS

Order 15, r. 16 of the Rules of the Supreme Court provides that "no action or other proceeding shall be open to objection on the ground that a merely declaratory judgment or order is sought thereby, and the court may make binding declarations of right whether or not any consequential relief is or could be claimed." In *Har-Shefi* v. *Har-Shefi* (*No.* 1)[18] the Court of Appeal held that the court has power under this rule to make a declaration as to the petitioner's status, even though no other relief is sought. This has been found to be a very convenient mode of testing whether a foreign decree of divorce or nullity will be recognised in England, and it has been frequently resorted to. There are a few reported cases in which the court's jurisdiction to make such a declaration has been discussed. The result of these cases appears to be that the High Court[19] has jurisdiction to make such a declaration if at the commencement of the proceedings (a) the petitioner is domiciled in England[20] or (b) both parties are resident in England[21] or (c) if there is an alternative prayer for divorce which the court has jurisdiction to entertain.[22] The reason for (c) is that the court cannot grant a decree of divorce without first being satisfied that there is a subsisting marriage to dissolve. If the petitioner is the wife, and the husband is domiciled and resident abroad, there was formerly a difficulty in that her domicile depended on the very matter in controversy, namely the validity of the foreign decree of divorce or nullity.[23] But this difficulty has disappeared now that a wife can have a domicile different from that of her husband. The jurisdiction under Order 15, r. 16 is discretionary and it will not be exercised where the statutory procedure under section 45 of the Matrimonial Causes Act 1973[24] is available since the latter involves safeguards for third parties not to be found in the former.[25]

---

[17] Presumption of Death (Scotland) Act 1977, s.10.

[18] [1953] P. 161.

[19] Not a divorce county court: *Practice Direction* [1971] 1 W.L.R. 29; Matrimonial Causes Rules 1977, rr. 12 (1), 109.

[20] *Har-Shefi* v. *Har-Shefi* (*No.* 1), *supra*; *Merker* v. *Merker* [1963] P. 283; *Garthwaite* v. *Garthwaite* [1964] P. 356; *Lee* v. *Lau* [1967] P. 14. See North (1965) 14 I.C.L.Q. 579.

[21] *Qureshi* v. *Qureshi* [1972] Fam. 173, 193–194, following dicta in *Garthwaite* v. *Garthwaite*, *supra*, at pp. 384, 397.

[22] *Lepre* v. *Lepre* [1965] P. 52, 56–58.

[23] See, *e.g. Har-Shefi* v. *Har-Shefi* (*No.* 1) [1953] P. 161; *Garthwaite* v. *Garthwaite*, *supra*; *Lepre* v. *Lepre*, *supra*.

[24] *Post*, p. 244.

[25] *Kassim* v. *Kassim* [1962] P. 224; *Collett* v. *Collett* [1968] P. 482; *Aldrich* v. *Att. Gen.* [1968] P. 281; *Vervaeke* v. *Smith* [1981] Fam. 77, approved by Lord Simon [1983] 1 A.C. 145, 167.

The jurisdiction can be invoked even if the other spouse is dead and the petitioner is the only party.[26] But there is no jurisdiction under this rule to make a declaration that a marriage is void *ab initio*; that can only be done in a properly constituted petition for nullity.[27] Nor is there any jurisdiction under this rule to make a declaration that a marriage is valid *ab initio*,[28] or to make a declaration as to legitimacy[29]; that can only be done in properly constituted proceedings under section 45(1) of the Matrimonial Causes Act 1973.[30] Nor is there any jurisdiction to make an order that the respondent shall pay maintenance to the petitioner.[31] But there is jurisdiction to order him to pay her deferred dower under a contract governed by Muslim law.[32]

The exercise of the court's jurisdiction to make a declaration as to status is subject to rules enabling the court to stay those proceedings in certain circumstances. These rules are considered in the pages that follow.

STAYING OF MATRIMONIAL PROCEEDINGS

Introduction

As we have seen, section 5 of the Domicile and Matrimonial Proceedings Act 1973 greatly extended the jurisdiction of the English courts to entertain proceedings for divorce (and also for judicial separation and nullity of marriage). Sections 7 and 13 extended the jurisdiction of the Scottish and Northern Irish courts respectively.[33] The Act thus increased the risk that the courts of more than one country might have jurisdiction to dissolve the same marriage. Thus, one spouse might be domiciled in England and habitually resident in Scotland, while the other might be domiciled in Jersey and habitually resident in France. In such a case, so far as the law of the United Kingdom is concerned, the courts of four countries might each have jurisdiction to dissolve the marriage. Evidently, we have come a long way since 1895, when "the essence of the rule in *Le Mesurier* v. *Le Mesurier*[34] was that there should be only one test of jurisdiction and only one court capable of dissolving a particular marriage—the court of the parties' domicile."[35]

When the two Law Commissions were considering what should be the bases of jurisdiction of the English and Scottish courts in matrimonial causes, the Scottish Law Commission was much concerned lest people domiciled in Scotland might gravitate to England and petition there for divorce, tempted perhaps by what was then a more liberal English divorce law[36] and by what was then, and still is, a more generous attitude to the

---

[26] *Re Meyer* [1971] P. 298.
[27] *Kassim* v. *Kassim, supra.*
[28] *Collett* v. *Collett, supra.*
[29] *Aldrich* v. *Att. Gen., supra.*
[30] See *post*, p. 244.
[31] *Qureshi* v. *Qureshi* [1972] Fam. 173, 194, 200.
[32] *Qureshi* v. *Qureshi, supra*, at p. 195.
[33] s.13 is now replaced by art. 49 of the Matrimonial Causes (Northern Ireland) Order, S.I. 1978 No. 1045.
[34] [1895] A.C. 517; *ante*, p. 194.
[35] *Indyka* v. *Indyka* [1969] 1 A.C. 33, 65–66, *per* Lord Reid.
[36] See now Divorce (Scotland) Act 1976.

granting of financial provision for the wife and children of the marriage. The two Commissions were agreed that the jurisdiction of the English and Scottish courts should, *mutatis mutandis*, be the same; but for a long time they disagreed as to how best to prevent the danger which the Scottish Law Commission feared. The English Law Commission preferred to give the courts of either country a discretionary power to stay proceedings if the courts of the other seemed more appropriate. But unfortunately the Scottish Law Commission insisted on a mandatory duty to stay in specifically defined circumstances.[37] Eventually a compromise was hammered out (heavily weighted in favour of the Scottish Law Commission's view) and the result is to be found in the somewhat tortuously worded provisions of Schedule 1 to the Domicile and Matrimonial Proceedings Act 1973.[38] These proposals were never canvassed in the Working Paper[39] which preceded the Report, and were thus never submitted to expert public scrutiny as the Law Commission's proposals usually are.

We need to distinguish between obligatory stays and discretionary stays. The former only apply to proceedings for divorce and then only when proceedings for divorce or nullity of marriage have been started elsewhere in the British Isles. The latter are not confined to proceedings for divorce and extend to cases where other matrimonial proceedings have been started inside or outside the British Isles.

Obligatory stays

Where before the beginning of the trial or first trial in any proceedings for divorce which are continuing in an English court it appears to the court:

    (a) that proceedings for divorce or nullity of marriage in respect of that marriage are continuing in another jurisdiction in the British Isles; and

    (b) that the parties to the marriage have resided together after its celebration; and

    (c) that the place where they resided together when the proceedings in the English court were begun, or last resided together before those proceedings were begun, is in that other jurisdiction; and

    (d) that either of the parties was habitually resident in that jurisdiction throughout the year ending with the date on which they last resided together before the date on which the proceedings in the English court were begun,

the English court must order the proceedings to be stayed.[40] The object of this provision was to give jurisdictional priority to the country most closely connected with the marriage, that is to say to the country to which the marriage may be said to "belong."[41] In most cases it will no doubt do so. But it is not difficult to imagine cases where it will not, *e.g.* where the parties

---

[37] See Law Com. No. 48 (1972), paras. 75–102.
[38] Sched. 3 makes similar provision for Scotland and Sched. 1 of the Matrimonial Causes (Northern Ireland) Order 1978 makes similar provision for Northern Ireland.
[39] Working Paper No. 28 (1970), paras. 70–80.
[40] Domicile and Matrimonial Proceedings Act 1973, Sched. 1, para. 8. See Matrimonial Causes Rules 1977, r. 36 (1).
[41] Law Com. No. 48 (1972), para. 85.

are domiciled in England, lived together in England for years, and one spouse is habitually resident in England, and yet the English proceedings must be stayed, merely because they last lived together for a week in Scotland and the other spouse is now habitually resident in Scotland.[42]

The obligatory duty to stay only applies to proceedings in the English court for divorce, and only arises on the application of a party to the marriage, not on the court's own motion.

Discretionary stays

Where before the beginning of the trial or first trial in any proceedings for divorce, judicial separation, nullity of marriage or a declaration as to the validity or subsistence of the petitioner's marriage it appears to the English court

  (a) that any proceedings in respect of that marriage or capable of affecting its validity or subsistence are continuing in another jurisdiction outside England; and

  (b) that the balance of fairness and convenience between the parties to the marriage is such that it is appropriate for the proceedings in that other jurisdiction to be disposed of before further steps are taken in the proceedings in the English court,

the English court may if it thinks fit order that the proceedings before it be stayed.[43] This reinforces the court's inherent but seldom used power to stay matrimonial proceedings on the ground of *lis alibi pendens*.[44] The new discretionary power to stay applies to a wider range of proceedings in the English court than the obligatory duty to stay discussed above, nor need the other jurisdiction be within the British Isles. The power may be exercised on the court's own motion as well as on the application of a party to the marriage. In considering the balance of fairness and convenience, the court must have regard to all factors appearing to be relevant, including the convenience of witnesses and any delay or expense which may result from the proceedings being stayed, or not being stayed.

General

While proceedings for divorce, judicial separation, nullity of marriage or a declaration as to the validity or subsistence of the petitioner's marriage are pending in the English court, and the trial or first trial of those proceedings has not begun, it is the duty of the petitioner, or of a cross-petitioning respondent, to furnish particulars of any proceedings which he knows to be continuing in a jurisdiction other than England and which are in respect of the same marriage or capable of affecting its validity or subsistence.[45] If the

---

[42] See Dicey and Morris, p. 421, Illustration 3.

[43] Domicile and Matrimonial Proceedings Act 1973, Sched. 1, para. 9. See Matrimonial Causes Rules 1977, r. 36 (2); *Mytton* v. *Mytton* (1977) 7 Fam.Law 244; *Shemshadfard* v. *Shemshadfard* [1981] 1 All E.R. 726.

[44] See, *e.g. Thornton* v. *Thornton* (1886) 11 P.D. 176; *Orr-Lewis* v. *Orr-Lewis* [1949] P. 347; *Sealey* v. *Callan* [1953] P. 135. S.5(6)(*b*) of the Act preserves this inherent power to stay.

[45] Domicile and Matrimonial Proceedings Act 1973, Sched. 1, para. 7.

court is satisfied that a person has failed to perform this duty, it may exercise its discretionary power to order a stay even after the beginning of the trial or first trial.[46]

An obligatory or discretionary stay may be discharged on the application of any party to the proceedings if it appears to the court that the other proceedings by reference to which the stay was ordered are themselves stayed or concluded, or that a party to those proceedings has delayed unreasonably in prosecuting them. Once an obligatory stay has been discharged, no further obligatory stay may be imposed.[47]

There are elaborate provisions restricting the powers of the English court to grant ancillary relief when English proceedings for divorce, judicial separation or nullity of marriage are stayed because of proceedings in another jurisdiction in the British Isles for any of those forms of relief.[48]

FINANCIAL RELIEF

Jurisdiction of the English courts

Ancillary relief. On granting a decree of divorce, judicial separation or nullity of marriage or at any time thereafter, English courts have wide powers of making orders that either party to the marriage (usually but not necessarily the husband) shall make financial provision for the other or for the children of the family. The orders that can be made are the following: an order that either party shall make periodical payments (secured or unsecured) to the other or for the benefit of a child of the family[49]; an order that he shall pay a lump sum to the other or for the benefit of a child of the family[50]; an order that he shall transfer property to the other or for the benefit of a child of the family[51]; an order that he shall settle property for the benefit of the other and of the children of the family[52]; an order varying any antenuptial or postnuptial settlement made on the parties to the marriage[53]; an order extinguishing or reducing the interest of either party to the marriage under any such settlement[54]; and an order for the sale of property.[55]

The court has jurisdiction to make any of these so-called ancillary orders whenever it has jurisdiction in the main suit.[56] Thus it will make an order for periodical payments by a husband even though he is domiciled and resident abroad and has no assets in England.[57] It will vary a settlement which

---

[46] *Ibid.* para. 9 (4).
[47] *Ibid.* para. 10.
[48] *Ibid.* para. 11.
[49] Matrimonial Causes Act 1973, s.23(1)(*a*), (*b*), (*d*) and (*e*). "Child of the family" is defined in s.52(1).
[50] s.23(1)(*c*) and (*f*).
[51] s.24(1)(*a*).
[52] s.24(1)(*b*).
[53] s.24(1)(*c*).
[54] s.24(1)(*d*).
[55] Matrimonial Causes Act 1973, s.24A, added by Matrimonial Homes and Property Act 1981, s.7.
[56] Dicey and Morris, Rule 50 (1).
[57] *Cammell* v. *Cammell* [1965] P. 467.

comprises property situated abroad and is governed by foreign law and the trustees of which reside abroad.[58] It will order a settlement of a party's English property, although he is domiciled and resident abroad.[59] But it will decline to exercise its powers in cases where any order that it might make would be wholly ineffective.[60] This jurisdiction (unlike all those that follow) is unaffected by the Civil Jurisdiction and Judgments Act 1982.

Failure to maintain. Under section 27 of the Matrimonial Causes Act 1973,[61] the court has power to order either party to the marriage to make periodical payments (secured or unsecured) or pay a lump sum to the other or for the benefit of a child of the family on the ground that he has failed to provide reasonable maintenance for the applicant or has failed to provide, or to make a proper contribution towards, reasonable maintenance for any child of the family. This power is exercisable although no relief in the form of divorce, judicial separation or nullity of marriage is asked for. The court has jurisdiction under this section if (a) the applicant or the respondent is domiciled in England on the date of the application, or (b) the applicant has been habitually resident in England throughout the period of one year ending with that date, or (c) the respondent is resident in England on that date.[62]

Maintenance in magistrates' courts. Under Part I of the Domestic Proceedings and Magistrates' Courts Act 1978, re-enacting earlier legislation, magistrates' courts have power, on various grounds set out in section 1 of the Act, to order one party to a marriage to make payments (by way of periodical payments or as a lump sum) to the other party or for the benefit of a child of the family[63] under the age of eighteen.[64] The court has jurisdiction to make such an order if at the date of the application either the applicant or the respondent ordinarily resides within the commission area for which the court is appointed.[65] If the respondent resides in Scotland or Northern Ireland, the court has jurisdiction if the applicant resides in England and the parties last ordinarily resided together as man and wife in England.[66] The domicile of either party is irrelevant.[67] But if the respondent is resident outside the United Kingdom and the EEC, the court has no jurisdiction to make an order under this Act, even if he submits to the juris-

---

[58] *Nunneley* v. *Nunneley* (1890) 15 P.D. 186; *Forsyth* v. *Forsyth* [1891] P. 363.

[59] *Hunter* v. *Hunter and Waddington* [1962] P. 1.

[60] *Tallack* v. *Tallack* [1927] P. 211; *Goff* v. *Goff* [1934] P. 107; *Wyler* v. *Lyons* [1963] P. 274.

[61] As amended by s.63 of the Domestic Proceedings and Magistrates' Courts Act 1978.

[62] Matrimonial Causes Act 1973, s.27(2), as amended by s.6(1) of the Domicile and Matrimonial Proceedings Act 1973. The section says "if and only if," but the jurisdiction of the court is enlarged if the respondent is domiciled (in the sense of the Civil Jurisdiction and Judgments Act 1982) in another EEC State or another part of the United Kingdom. See *post*, pp. 223–224.

[63] Defined in s.88(1). The definition is the same as that in s.52(1) of the Matrimonial Causes Act 1973.

[64] Or, in certain circumstances, over that age: s.5(3).

[65] s.30(1).

[66] s.30(3)(*a*). "Ordinarily resided together as man and wife" seems to mean little more than, in plain English, "copulated": see *Lowry* v. *Lowry* [1952] P. 252.

[67] s.30(5).

diction of the court.[68] This is because the principle of submission[69] has no application to courts of inferior jurisdiction which derive their jurisdiction from statute. "If such an inferior court lacks jurisdiction, parties cannot, by agreement or otherwise, confer jurisdiction upon it."[70]

However, if the respondent resides in any part of the Commonwealth to which the Maintenance Orders (Facilities for Enforcement) Act 1920 has been extended by Order in Council,[71] machinery is provided by section 3 of the Act whereby a wife resident in England can get a provisional maintenance order[72] from a magistrates' court in England, which will be enforceable against the husband if and when it is confirmed by a court in the country where he resides. It is immaterial that the applicant's cause for complaint did not arise in England.[73] Section 4 of the Act provides reciprocal machinery whereby a provisional order made in the absence of the husband in a country to which the Act extends may be confirmed by a magistrates' court in England if the husband resides there and has been served with a summons. Thus there are two hearings, one in the absence of the husband, and the other in the absence of the wife. The husband may raise any defence that he might have raised in the original proceedings, but no other defence. It is entirely within the discretion of the court whether to confirm the order with or without modifications, or refuse to confirm it, or remit the case to the court which made the order for the purpose of taking further evidence. This machinery is sometimes known as the "shuttlecock" procedure.[74] Of course the machinery is defective, in that the wife at the first hearing cannot be cross-examined on behalf of the husband, and the husband at the second hearing cannot be cross-examined on behalf of the wife. But it is better than no machinery at all.

Part I of the Maintenance Orders (Reciprocal Enforcement) Act 1972, which is intended ultimately to replace the Act of 1920,[75] makes similar and more elaborate provision for the reciprocal enforcement of maintenance orders, not confined to cases where the defendant is resident in any part of the Commonwealth. Part I of the Act differs from the Act of 1920 in several respects, of which the following are the most important:

(1) It applies to Scotland as well as to England and Northern Ireland.

---

[68] *Forsyth* v. *Forsyth* [1948] P. 125.
[69] *Ante*, p. 67.
[70] *Forsyth* v. *Forsyth*, *supra*, at p. 132, *per* Tucker L.J.
[71] The Act has been extended to a large number of Commonwealth countries: see the Maintenance Orders (Facilities for Enforcement) Order 1959, S.I. 1959 No. 377, as amended by S.I. 1974 No. 557, S.I. 1975 No. 2188 and S.I. 1979 No. 116. The Act still extends to South Africa although it has ceased to be part of the Commonwealth: South Africa Act 1962, s.2(1) and Sched. 2, para. 2. But it no longer extends to Pakistan except as regards orders registered or confirmed by a court in England or Northern Ireland before September 1, 1973: Pakistan Act 1973, s.4(4).
[72] A "maintenance order" is defined by s.10 of the Act as an order (other than an affiliation order) for the periodical payments of sums of money towards the maintenance of the wife or other dependants of the person against whom the order is made. "Dependants" are defined to mean such persons as he is liable to maintain according to the law in force where the order was made.
[73] *Collister* v. *Collister* [1972] 1 W.L.R. 54.
[74] See *Pilcher* v. *Pilcher* [1955] P. 318, 330.
[75] See s.22(2)(*a*), which repeals the Act of 1920. This subs. is not yet in force.

(2) It can be extended to any country outside the United Kingdom which is prepared to grant reciprocal treatment to United Kingdom orders (called in the Act a "reciprocating country"[76]) and not merely to any part of the Commonwealth outside the United Kingdom.

(3) It defines a maintenance order so as to include an affiliation order,[77] which the Act of 1920 did not.

(4) The "shuttlecock" procedure applies to orders varying or revoking maintenance orders.[78] The provisions of the Act of 1920 in this respect were found to be defective.[79]

(5) It defines a maintenance order so as to include an order for the payment of a lump sum,[80] which the Act of 1920 did not.

Since the general scheme of Part I of the Act is the same as that of the Act of 1920, there is no need to give a detailed exegesis here.

Part II of the Maintenance Orders (Reciprocal Enforcement) Act 1972 gives effect to the United Nations Convention on the Recovery of Maintenance Abroad (1956). Spurning the accumulated experience of the Commonwealth with the "shuttlecock" procedure under the Act of 1920, the United Nations in its wisdom devised a procedure under which there is only one hearing, in the country where the defendant resides. Section 26 of the Act provides that where a person (usually a woman) in the United Kingdom claims maintenance from a person "subject to the jurisdiction of" (*i.e.* presumably resident in) a convention country,[81] she may go to the clerk of the magistrates' court for the area in which she resides. The clerk assists her to complete an application and supporting documents which will comply with the law of the foreign country, and transmits the application through diplomatic channels to the appropriate authority in the foreign country. Conversely, section 27 provides that where an application by a person in a convention country for maintenance from another person residing in England or Northern Ireland[82] is received through diplomatic channels by the clerk for the magistrates' court for the area in which that other person resides, it shall be treated as if it were a complaint; the court must proceed as if the complainant were before the court, and if it makes an order it must be registered in that court.[83]

The Brussels Convention. The Brussels Convention of 1968 on Jurisdiction and the Enforcement of Judgments applies to claims for maintenance, including payment of a lump sum. It will be remembered that article 3 pro-

---

[76] s.1. The countries which have been designated as "reciprocating countries" (usually with a restricted definition of "maintenance orders") are listed in S.I. 1974 No. 566, S.I. 1975 No. 2187 and S.I. 1979 No. 115. A version of Part I of the Act has been applied under s.40 (with considerable modifications) to the Republic of Ireland: S.I. 1974 No. 2140. Another version has been applied to Hague Convention countries: S.I. 1979 No. 1317 as amended by S.I. 1981 Nos. 837, 1545 and 1674 and by S.I. 1983 Nos. 885 and 1523.
[77] s.21.
[78] ss.5, 9.
[79] See *Pilcher* v. *Pilcher* [1955] P. 318.
[80] s.21(1)(*a*), as amended by Civil Jurisdiction and Judgments Act 1982, Sched. 11, para. 4.
[81] For a list of convention countries, see S.I. 1975 No. 423, as amended by S.I. 1978 No. 279.
[82] For Scotland, see s.31.
[83] A version of Part II of the Act has been applied under s.40 to most states of the U.S.A.: S.I. 1979 No. 1314 as amended by S.I. 1981 No. 606.

vides that a person domiciled (in the sense of the Civil Jurisdiction and Judgments Act 1982) in a Contracting State may be sued in the courts of another Contracting State only by virtue of the rules set out in Sections 2 to 6 of Title II; and that Schedule 4, article 3 of the Act makes similar provision for persons domiciled (in that sense) in a part of the United Kingdom.[84] Article 5(2) of the Convention provides that a person domiciled in a Contracting State may in matters relating to maintenance be sued in the courts for the place where the maintenance creditor is domiciled or habitually resident, or, if the matter is ancillary to proceedings concerning the status of a person, in the court which, according to its own law, has jurisdiction to entertain those proceedings, unless that jurisdiction is based solely on the nationality of one of the parties. Article 5(2) of Schedule 4 makes similar provision for persons domiciled in a part of the United Kingdom. Hence, English courts have no jurisdiction to make a maintenance order if the respondent is domiciled in another EEC State or in another part of the United Kingdom, unless the maintenance creditor is domiciled or habitually resident in England or unless the respondent enters an appearance within the meaning of article 18.[85] The only exception to this proposition is that they have jurisdiction to make ancillary orders in proceedings for divorce, nullity of marriage or judicial separation whenever they have jurisdiction in the main suit. Such orders are "ancillary to proceedings concerning the status of a person" within the meaning of article 5(2). The exception at the end of article 5(2) has no relevance for English courts, because they do not exercise jurisdiction in divorce, nullity of marriage or judicial separation on the basis of nationality.[86]

"Maintenance" in article 5(2) means maintenance imposed by law and not maintenance payable under an agreement between the parties. Such agreements therefore come within article 5(1) (contract) and not within article 5(2).[87]

Enforcement of foreign maintenance orders

A foreign maintenance order for periodical payments ranks at common law as a foreign judgment *in personam*. If, as is usually the case, the foreign court has power to vary the amount of the payments, the foreign order cannot be enforced in England at common law, because it is not "final and conclusive."[88] However, if the foreign court has power to vary the amount of future payments, but not that of past payments, then the arrears may be recovered in England by an action on the foreign judgment.[89]

This is the position at common law, and it usually prevents the enforcement of foreign maintenance orders in England. But the common law has been radically altered by statutes which provide for the reciprocal enforce-

---

[84] *Ante*, pp. 81, 89.
[85] *Ante*, p. 86.
[86] Domicile and Matrimonial Proceedings Act 1973, s.5; *ante*, pp. 190, 208.
[87] Schlosser, para. 92.
[88] *Harrop* v. *Harrop* [1920] 3 K.B. 386; *Re Macartney* [1921] 1 Ch. 522. See *ante*, p. 126. The rule is criticised by Grodecki (1959) 8 I.C.L.Q. 18, 32–40; but it is well established.
[89] *Beatty* v. *Beatty* [1924] 1 K.B. 807.

ment of maintenance orders within the United Kingdom, and also between England (and Northern Ireland) and countries of the Commonwealth overseas, and between the United Kingdom and designated countries overseas.

Under Part II of the Maintenance Orders Act 1950, a maintenance order made in one part of the United Kingdom may be registered in a court in another part of the United Kingdom if the person liable to make the payments resides there and it is convenient that the order should be enforceable there.[90] The registration of the order is therefore within the discretion of the court; but this discretion vests in the court which made the order and not in the court which is asked to register it.[91] These provisions apply to orders made by the High Court in England or Northern Ireland, by the Court of Session in Scotland, by county courts or sheriff courts, and magistrates' courts.[92] An order so registered in a court in any part of the United Kingdom may be enforced in that part of the United Kingdom in all respects as if it had been made by that court and as if that court had had jurisdiction to make it.[93] The power to vary or discharge a registered order belongs to the court which made it and not to the court in which it is registered,[94] except that a variation in the rate of payments due under an order made by a magistrates' court or a sheriff court may be made by the court in which it is registered and not by the court which made it.[95]

Under section 1 of the Maintenance Orders (Facilities for Enforcement) Act 1920, a maintenance order[96] made in a country to which the Act extends may be registered in England or Northern Ireland. Section 2 provides reciprocal machinery whereby a maintenance order made in England or Northern Ireland may be registered in a country to which the Act extends. Unlike sections 3 and 4 of the Act, which have already been considered,[97] these two sections presuppose that the court which made the order had jurisdiction to make it, e.g. because the husband was resident in the country where the court was sitting, but that, apart from the Act, there would be difficulty in enforcing the order, e.g. because the husband has subsequently changed his residence from England or Northern Ireland to a Commonwealth country, or vice versa. Unlike sections 3 and 4, sections 1 and 2 apply to orders made by the High Court or by county courts as well as to orders made by magistrates' courts. When an order has been registered, it has the same force and effect as if it had been an order originally obtained in the court in which it is registered. The court has no discretion to refuse to register an order, nor has the husband any right to be heard to show cause against the registration, or to appeal against it. Unlike the confirmation of a provisional order, the registration of an existing order is thus a purely ministerial process.

[90] ss.16(1), 17 (2). See R.S.C., Ord. 104.
[91] s.17(2), (4).
[92] The orders to which the Act applies are set out in s.16(2) of the Act. This subs. has frequently been amended.
[93] Maintenance Orders Act 1950, s.18(1).
[94] *Ibid.* ss.21(1), 22(4).
[95] *Ibid.* s.22(1), (4).
[96] For definition, see *ante*, p. 222, n. 72.
[97] *Ante*, p. 222.

Part I of the Maintenance Orders (Reciprocal Enforcement) Act 1972 make similar but more elaborate provision for the registration in the United Kingdom of maintenance orders made in reciprocating countries and vice versa.

The Recognition of Divorces and Legal Separations Act 1971 does not require the recognition of any maintenance or other ancillary orders made by a foreign court.[98]

Under the Civil Jurisdiction and Judgments Act 1982, maintenance judgments given in another EEC State, in order to be enforced in England, are sent, not to the High Court like other judgments, but to the Secretary of State (*i.e.* the Home Secretary) so that he can transmit them to the appropriate magistrates' court for registration.[99] The application for registration must be made *ex parte* in the first instance.[1] The application will be determined in the first instance by the prescribed officer of the court, almost certainly the clerk to the justices. If enforcement is authorised, the respondent may then appeal to the magistrates' court to set aside the registration; thereafter he may appeal once only on a point of law.[2] If enforcement is refused, the applicant may appeal to the magistrates' court[3] and there is a further right of appeal by either party, but once only on a point of law.[4] The single appeal on a point of law under articles 37 and 41 is to the High Court by way of case stated.[5]

The grounds on which recognition may be refused are set out in article 27[6] and need not be repeated here. They apply equally to enforcement.[7] Article 27(4) provides a ground of refusal which is of special relevance to maintenance orders. Its effect is that if, *e.g.* a French divorce court orders a man to pay maintenance to a woman on the footing that she is his wife, but by English rules of the conflict of laws she is not his wife, the order cannot be enforced in England.

Conversion of foreign currencies into sterling is governed by section 8 of the Act.[8]

Maintenance orders made in Scotland or Northern Ireland are enforced in England under Part II of the Maintenance Orders Act 1950.[9]

Effect of foreign divorce on English maintenance order

It was held in *Bragg* v. *Bragg*[10] that a magistrates' court's order for the maintenance of a wife does not automatically lapse if the marriage is subsequently dissolved in England, but that the magistrates' court has a dis-

---

[98] s.8(3).
[99] Sched. 1 arts. 31(2) and 32, s.5.
[1] Art. 34(1). For the reasons for this, see *ante*, p. 131.
[2] Arts. 36 and 37.
[3] Art. 40.
[4] Art. 41.
[5] s.6(3)(*a*).
[6] *Ante*, p. 132.
[7] Art. 34(2).
[8] See *post*, p. 463.
[9] s.18(5)(*a*); *ante*, p. 225.
[10] [1925] P. 20.

cretion to discharge or vary the order, or keep it alive. In *Wood* v. *Wood*[11] the Court of Appeal held that the same principle applies if the marriage is validly dissolved by a foreign court having jurisdiction under English rules of the conflict of laws. Thus a foreign divorce may be effective for the purpose of restoring the parties to the status of single persons, and yet may not terminate the former husband's duty to support his former wife. Any other decision would have meant that a foreign divorce was more efficacious in England than an English divorce.

As we have seen,[12] the mere fact that a foreign divorce was granted on a ground insufficient for divorce in English law is irrelevant when the status of the parties is in issue in England; and the fact that the respondent received no notice of the proceedings is not decisive. But both these matters are very relevant when the English court is exercising its discretion whether or not to keep alive a maintenance order in favour of a wife.[13] If the wife actively participates in the foreign divorce proceedings, and especially if she unsuccessfully litigates the question of maintenance in the foreign court, the case for keeping the order alive is very much weaker.[14]

The principle of *Wood* v. *Wood* is not limited to orders made by magistrates' courts. It extends to orders for periodical payments made by the High Court or a divorce county court on granting a decree of judicial separation or under section 27 of the Matrimonial Causes Act 1973 (as amended).[15] The Act expressly contemplates that such orders may continue in force after a decree of divorce.[16]

On the other hand, the principle of *Wood* v. *Wood* is limited to cases where the wife's right to support has crystallised in a court order before the foreign divorce. If there is no such order, none can be made after a valid foreign divorce. This is because sections 23 and 24 of the Matrimonial Causes Act are limited to English divorces,[17] and section 27 of that Act and Part I of the Domestic Proceedings and Magistrates' Courts Act 1978 presuppose that the parties are husband and wife.[18] Now that the English rules for the recognition of foreign divorces have become so liberal, this poses a serious threat to the financial security of wives.

Accordingly the Law Commission recommend[19] that the High Court should have a discretionary power to make orders for financial relief after a foreign decree of divorce, nullity of marriage or judicial separation which is entitled to recognition in England, subject to certain jurisdictional safe-

---

[11] [1957] P. 254; followed in *Qureshi* v. *Qureshi* [1972] Fam. 173, where the divorce was extra-judicial.
[12] *Ante*, pp. 193, 202.
[13] *Wood* v. *Wood* [1957] P. 254, 283–284, 290, 296, 298, 299.
[14] *Cf. Pastre* v. *Pastre* [1930] P. 80; *Mezger* v. *Mezger* [1937] P. 19 and *Kirk* v. *Kirk* [1947] 2 All E.R. 118, as explained in *Wood* v. *Wood, supra*.
[15] See *ante*, p. 221.
[16] s.28(2). See also *Newmarch* v. *Newmarch* [1978] Fam. 79.
[17] See *Moore* v. *Bull* [1891] P. 279; *Torok* v. *Torok* [1973] 1 W.L.R. 1066. Contrast *P.* v. *P.* [1971] P. 318, where an order was made under s.23(2)(*b*) of the Act in favour of a child.
[18] *Turczak* v. *Turczak* [1970] P. 198; criticised by Cretney (1969) 119 New L.J. 1121, and Karsten (1970) 33 M.L.R. 205.
[19] Law Com. No. 117 (1982). This recommendation is implemented by Part III of the Matrimonial and Family Proceedings Bill now before Parliament.

guards. These are that one party must be domiciled in England either at the date of the application or at the date when the foreign divorce took effect in the foreign country; or one party must have been habitually resident in England throughout the period of one year before either of those dates; or one or both parties must have at the date of the application a beneficial interest in a dwelling-house in England which was at some time during the marriage their matrimonial home.

CHAPTER 13

GUARDIANSHIP AND CUSTODY OF MINORS

Introduction

Traditionally the sovereign as *parens patriae* is interested in the welfare of his minor subjects who because of tender years are incapable of looking after themselves. The duty to protect their interests was delegated to the Lord Chancellor from whom it passed to the Court of Chancery and thence in 1875 to the Chancery Division of the High Court, whence it was transferred in 1971 to the new Family Division.[1] This is the origin of the inherent jurisdiction of the High Court over minors; and the court also has a statutory jurisdiction under the Guardianship of Minors Act 1971.[2] The inherent jurisdiction may be invoked even though no application is made under section 41 of the Supreme Court Act 1981 to make the minor a ward of court.[3]

The power to make a minor a ward of court is by no means limited to orphans: it can be exercised even though one or both parents are alive. The object is usually to give the applicant parent a tactical advantage over the other in a struggle for custody, or to prevent the minor from associating with undesirable people or contracting an undesirable marriage. Once a minor is made a ward of court, the court has very extensive powers in relation to him: it can, *e.g.* restrain him (more usually her) from marrying without the court's consent, prevent him from leaving the country, or send him abroad to be looked after by a foreign guardian. Anyone who disregards an order of the court about a ward of court is liable to severe penalties for contempt of court.

The Family Division of the High Court and divorce county courts can also make custody orders in the exercise of their matrimonial jurisdiction. The county courts and magistrates' courts also have power to make guardianship and custody orders.[4]

One dominant principle, now enshrined in statute, underlies the whole of the law concerning guardianship and custody of minors. It is stated in section 1 of the Guardianship of Minors Act 1971, which runs as follows:

> "Where in any proceeding before any court . . . the legal custody or upbringing of a minor . . . is in question, the court, in deciding that question, shall regard the welfare of the minor as the first and paramount consideration. . . . "

[1] See now Supreme Court Act 1981, Sched. 1, para. 3. See generally, Mr. Justice Cross (1967) 83 L.Q.R. 200; Lowe and White, *Wards of Court* (1979).
[2] s.15(1)(*a*).
[3] *Re N.* [1967] Ch. 512, 529–531, *per* Stamp J.; *L.* v. *L.* [1969] P. 25, 27, *per* Simon P., doubting *Re E.* [1956] Ch. 23 on this point.
[4] Guardianship of Minors Act 1971, s.15.

This section applies whatever the nature of the dispute before the court, *i.e.* not only to disputes between parents but also to disputes between parents and strangers and between strangers.[5] It applies not only in domestic English cases but also in cases with a foreign element, where it may take precedence even over a guardianship or custody order made by a foreign court.[6] It should therefore be regarded as a rule of public policy applicable notwithstanding any rule of the conflict of laws.

Jurisdiction of the English court

Guardianship of minors is the one department of the English conflict of laws in which allegiance has assumed prominence in the jurisdictional rules of the English court. This is because the inherent jurisdiction over minors is, as we have seen, derived from the sovereign as *parens patriae*. The sovereign accords protection to all who owe him allegiance; and those who owe him allegiance (and need his protection) include not only British citizens but also those who are present in England. Hence the High Court has jurisdiction to appoint a guardian for a minor if he is present in England, even though he is domiciled abroad and owns no property in England and even though guardians have already been appointed for him by the courts of his domicile.[7] The court also has jurisdiction to appoint a guardian for a minor if he is a British citizen, even though he is not present in England.[8] This jurisdiction was asserted in very emphatic terms in 1854[9]; but today the circumstances would have to be exceptional before jurisdiction was exercised on this basis.[10]

The High Court also has jurisdiction to appoint a guardian for a minor if he is ordinarily resident in England, even though he is an alien and physically absent from the country. This was decided in *Re P.*,[11] where a husband and wife, both stateless persons, lived separately in England. They had a son aged six who by arrangement spent five days a week with his mother and week-ends with his father. One week-end the father failed to return him to the mother, but instead flew with him to Israel. The mother sought to make the child a ward of court. Jurisdiction could not be invoked on the basis of presence, nor of nationality. Domicile was rejected as a basis on the ground, stated by Russell L.J.,[12] that "the whole trend of English authority on the parental jurisdiction of the Crown over infants bases the jurisdiction on protection as a corollary of allegiance in some shape or form. Domicile is an artificial concept which may well involve no possible

---

[5] *J. v. C.* [1970] A.C. 668.
[6] *Re B.'s Settlement* [1940] Ch. 54; *McKee v. McKee* [1951] A.C. 352; *post*, pp. 234–236.
[7] *Johnstone v. Beattie* (1843) 10 Cl. & F. 42; *Stuart v. Marquis of Bute* (1861) 9 H.L.C. 440; *Nugent v. Vetzera* (1866) L.R. 2 Eq. 704; *Re D.* [1943] Ch. 305; *J. v. C.* [1970] A.C. 688, 720; *Re A.* [1970] Ch. 665.
[8] *Hope v. Hope* (1854) 4 D.M. & G. 328; *Re Willoughby* (1885) 30 Ch.D. 324; *Harben v. Harben* [1957] 1 W.L.R. 261.
[9] *Hope v. Hope, supra.*
[10] *Re P.* [1965] Ch. 568, 582, 587–588.
[11] *Supra.*
[12] At p. 592. *Cf.* Lord Denning M.R. at p. 583.

connection with allegiance." Jurisdiction was therefore assumed on the basis of ordinary residence; and it was held that the child was still ordinarily resident in England, though he had been physically present in Israel for the last two years.

There is no jurisdiction to appoint a guardian for a minor merely because he owns property in England.[13]

The High Court has jurisdiction to make a custody order in respect of a minor whenever it would have jurisdiction under the principles stated above to appoint a guardian for him.[14] The High Court or a divorce county court may also make an order for the custody of any minor child of the family when it has jurisdiction to pronounce a decree of divorce, nullity of marriage or judicial separation[15] or when it makes an order for financial provision on the ground of failure to provide reasonable maintenance.[16] It will exercise these statutory powers even though the minor is abroad.[17] This is in accordance with the general principle that the court has jurisdiction to make any ancillary orders in matrimonial proceedings whenever it has jurisdiction in the main suit.[18]

The exercise of jurisdiction is in the highest degree discretionary, so much so that Harman L.J. once said "I never heard of binding authority in an infant case before."[19] This is at it should be, for ideas of what the welfare of the minor requires are apt to change with improving knowledge of child psychology. For the same reason, appellate courts are very slow to interfere with the trial judge's exercise of discretion in a guardianship or custody case, provided it was exercised on proper principles.

The High Court, county courts and magistrates' courts also have jurisdiction under the Guardianship of Minors Act 1971 to appoint a guardian for a minor or to make a custody order in respect of a minor. A county court or magistrates' court has jurisdiction if the applicant or the respondent or the minor resides in the area of the court's district.[20] But these courts cannot exercise jurisdiction if the respondent resides in Scotland or Northern Ireland[21] unless a summons is served upon him in England; though magistrates' courts can make an order giving the custody of a minor to a person resident in England if one parent and the minor reside in England, even if the other parent resides in Scotland or Northern Ireland.[22]

Conflicts of jurisdiction in the United Kingdom

In Scotland, there is no wardship procedure, and there are no wards of court; nor is any parental consent needed for the marriage of children over sixteen. The domicile of the child is the main test of jurisdiction to make

---

[13] *Brown* v. *Collins* (1883) 25 Ch.D. 56; *cf. Re Bourgoise* (1889) 41 Ch.D. 310.
[14] Dicey and Morris, Rule 56(1).
[15] Matrimonial Causes Act 1973, s.42(1). "Child of the family" is defined in s.52(1).
[16] s.42(2).
[17] *Philips* v. *Philips* (1944) 60 T.L.R. 395; *Harben* v. *Harben* [1957] 1 W.L.R. 261.
[18] *Ante*, pp. 220–221.
[19] *Re H.* [1966] 1 W.L.R. 381, 402.
[20] s.15(1)(*b*)(*c*).
[21] s.15(3)(*b*).
[22] s.15(4) as amended by Guardianship Act 1973, Sched. 2.

a custody order.[23] In England, as we have seen, children may be made wards of court up to the age of eighteen (formerly twenty-one) if they are present in England. These differences have led to some sharp conflicts of jurisdiction in the case of children domiciled in Scotland but present in England.

In *Johnstone* v. *Beattie*,[24] a father domiciled in Scotland by will appointed his wife and eight other persons, all domiciled and resident in Scotland, to be tutors and curators for his newly-born daughter. After his death the mother took the child to England with their consent and died five years later. By her will, made two months before she died, she expressed the earnest prayer and hope that the child would be allowed to reside in England with her maternal grandfather and great-aunt. The grandfather filed a bill in Chancery for the sole purpose of making the child, now aged six, a ward of court and preventing her removal to the care of the Scottish tutors and curators. A contest for guardianship developed between the Scottish tutors and curators and the grandfather. The House of Lords, by a majority of three to two, decided in favour of the grandfather.

This decision has been much criticised; but surely no court could fail to give weight to the mother's dying wish. It caused much resentment in Scotland on the ground that the rights of the duly-appointed Scottish tutors and curators were entirely disregarded in England. This resentment was hardly appeased by the later decision of the House of Lords in *Stuart* v. *Marquis of Bute*.[25] In that case the orphan child was domiciled in Scotland but present in England and the Court of Chancery appointed guardians for him. The House of Lords, reversing the Court of Session, held that that court must not ignore the rights of the English guardians in Scotland.

In *Re X's Settlement*[26] there was a contest for custody between an English mother, who made her children wards of court in England, and a Scottish father, who petitioned for divorce in Scotland. He sought the leave of the Chancery Division to ask for custody in his Scottish divorce proceedings, since otherwise the Court of Session might feel a difficulty in exercising jurisdiction over English wards. Vaisey J. refused him leave on the ground that it was unnecessary. "Conflict between those two courts," he said, "is entirely out of the question. Each acts in the manner which it considers right as occasion arises. Neither court is avid of jurisdiction, and neither court will disclaim the jurisdiction with which it is entrusted."

But despite these soothing words, conflicts of jurisdiction continue to occur. In *Babington* v. *Babington*,[27] for instance, a husband and wife were domiciled in Scotland, where their matrimonial home was. Differences arose, and the wife went to live in England, taking the eleven-year-old daughter of the marriage with her. The wife made the child a ward of court in England. The husband petitioned the Court of Session for custody and

---

[23] *Ponder* v. *Ponder*, 1932 S.C. 233; *McLean* v. *McLean*, 1947 S.C. 79; *Babington* v. *Babington*, 1955 S.C. 115.
[24] (1843) 10 Cl. & F. 42.
[25] (1861) 9 H.L.C. 440.
[26] [1945] Ch. 44, 47.
[27] 1955 S.C. 115. Further facts are taken from Cmnd. 842 (1959), para. 39.

was awarded interim access to the child (who was at an English boarding school) during the Christmas holidays. The husband then applied to the English court for leave to take the child to Scotland for the short period of the Scottish order. The wife opposed the application and sought an order for leave to take the child to Switzerland for a holiday. The English court refused the husband's application and granted the wife's application. When the husband's petition to the Court of Session for custody came on for hearing the wife asked for a stay of proceedings. It is hardly surprising that it was refused, on the ground that in the opinion of the Court of Session the court of the domicile is pre-eminent in matters of custody.

This case caused almost as much misgiving in Scotland as *Johnstone* v. *Beattie* had done over a century before. It is certainly not in the interests of children that they should become bones of contention, not only between struggling parents, but also between struggling courts. It is not edifying that such struggles should occur within the United Kingdom. Yet they continue. In *Hoy* v. *Hoy*,[28] the mother of a sixteen-year-old girl domiciled in England but temporarily resident in Scotland made her a ward of court in England and obtained an order restraining her from marrying a domiciled Scotsman with whom she was living. The mother then applied to the Court of Session for an interdict (injunction) restraining the couple from marrying in Scotland. Although the Scottish courts have repeatedly declared that the courts of the domicile are pre-eminent in matters of guardianship and custody, the mother's application was refused on the grounds that "the writ of the Chancery Court does not run in Scotland" and that "the English order is clearly one which the Court of Chancery had no jurisdiction to pronounce against either respondent."

It is pleasant to record that a more neighbourly attitude was shown by the English courts in *Re G.*[29] and *Re S.*[30] In both these cases the court took the unusual step of removing a very young child (aged three in each case) from the custody of its mother in order that the Court of Session (where divorce proceedings were pending at the instance of the Scottish father) could decide the question of custody, on the ground that in all the circumstances that court was the more convenient forum and that it was undesirable that the child should be shuttled backwards and forwards from one parent to another.

Attempts to settle by legislation this question of conflicting jurisdictions within the United Kingdom have so far proved abortive. In 1959 a Committee under the chairmanship of Lord Hodson recommended[31] that pre-eminent jurisdiction should belong to the courts of that part of the United Kingdom in which the child is ordinarily resident; and that custody orders should be reciprocally enforceable within the United Kingdom, just as maintenance orders now are. But one member of the Committee vigorously dissented from the former recommendation, and no action has been

---

[28] 1968 S.C. 179.
[29] [1969] 1 W.L.R. 1001.
[30] [1971] Ch. 621.
[31] Cmnd. 842 (1959). For comments on the Report, see Kahn-Freund (1960) 23 M.L.R. 64; Gareth Jones (1960) 9 I.C.L.Q. 15.

taken to implement the Committee's Report. In 1976 the Law Commission and the Scottish Law Commission published a Working Paper recommending that the principal test of jurisdiction should be the habitual residence of the child at the date of commencement of the proceedings.[32] It is understood that publication of the final recommendations of the two Law Commissions is imminent.

Effect of foreign guardianship orders in England

It has never been decided which foreign court has jurisdiction to appoint a guardian for a child. The English courts would presumably concede jurisdiction to the courts of the country where the minor was present, or of which he was a national, or in which he was ordinarily resident, since these are the three bases on which English courts exercise jurisdiction. So long as the position of the foreign guardian is not challenged, he can exercise any of the powers of an English guardian in England without hindrance. But, as we have seen,[33] the fact that a foreign guardian has been appointed does not prevent the English court from appointing one if it has jurisdiction to do so. If an English guardian has been appointed, and especially if the child has been made a ward of court, then the foreign guardian must move much more circumspectly. Undoubtedly the welfare of the child would be the first and paramount consideration today in any contest for custody between a foreign and an English guardian[34]; and some older cases in which the welfare of the child was lost sight of would not now be followed.[35]

If a foreign guardian seeks payment out to himself of a fund in court belonging to his ward, the court will not necessarily order payment out, even though the guardian is entitled to it under the foreign law, but may require evidence that it will be applied for the benefit of the ward.[36]

Effect of foreign custody orders in England

A custody order made by a foreign court does not prevent the English court from making such custody orders in England with respect to the minor as, having regard to his welfare, it thinks fit.[37] A striking illustration of this principle is afforded by *McKee* v. *McKee*,[38] decided by the Privy Council:

A husband and wife, American citizens resident in the United

---

[32] Working Paper No. 68 (Memorandum No. 23), paras. 3.74–3.78.
[33] *Ante*, p. 230.
[34] Guardianship of Minors Act 1971, s.1; quoted *ante*, p. 229.
[35] *e.g. Nugent* v. *Vetzera* (1866) L.R. 2 Eq. 704; *Di Savini* v. *Lousada* (1870) 18 W.R. 425. See, as to these cases, *Re B.'s Settlement* [1940] Ch. 54, 59–63; *McKee* v. *McKee* [1951] A.C. 352, 365–366.
[36] *Re Chatard's Settlement* [1899] 1 Ch. 712.
[37] Dicey and Morris, Rule 58; approved in *J.* v. *C.* [1970] A.C. 668, 700, *per* Lord Guest; *Re B.'s Settlement* [1940] Ch. 54; *McKee* v. *McKee* [1951] A.C. 352; *Re Kernot* [1965] Ch. 217; *Re T.* [1969] 1 W.L.R. 1608; *Re R.* (1981) 2 F.L.R. 416.
[38] *Supra*.

States, separated and agreed that neither should remove their minor son out of the United States without the written consent of the other. In 1945, in divorce proceedings in California, custody of the boy was awarded to the mother, and the father was allowed access. At that time the boy was living with the father under a previous custody order of the Californian court. On Christmas Eve 1946, when he heard that his last appeal against the custody order had failed, the father, in breach of his agreement and without the knowledge or consent of the mother, took the boy to Ontario and settled with him there. The mother then began habeas corpus proceedings in Ontario. In 1947, after a hearing lasting eleven days, the Ontario judge awarded the custody of the boy to the father. His decision was affirmed by a majority of the Ontario Court of Appeal, reversed by a majority of the Supreme Court of Canada, but restored by the Privy Council.

The two grounds for this decision were first, that a custody order by its nature is not final and is at all times subject to review by the court which made it; moreover, its persuasive effect is diminished by the passage of time[39]; and secondly, that in Ontario as in England the welfare of the minor is the first and paramount consideration.

Although the principle that the welfare of the child is the first and paramount consideration governs in all cases, as was held by the House of Lords in *J.* v. *C.*[40] and in later cases by the Court of Appeal,[41] the courts must, in applying it, have regard to all the circumstances of the case. This is well illustrated by the so-called "kidnapping" cases, where one parent kidnaps a child from the custody of the other and spirits him away by air[42] to England, perhaps many thousands of miles away. (*McKee* v. *McKee* was not strictly a kidnapping case, because the child was lawfully in the custody of the father when he took him to Ontario; nor was *J.* v. *C.*). In many cases the kidnapping is in defiance of a custody order made by a foreign court,[43] but the same principles apply to any unilateral kidnapping of a child by one parent from the other.[44] English judges disapprove of such behaviour, and are prepared to send the child back to the country from which he was kidnapped without making a full examination of the merits of the dispute, provided they are satisfied that that would be in the best interests of the child.

---

[39] As to the effect of this, see *Re T.* [1969] 1 W.L.R. 1608.

[40] [1970] A.C. 668.

[41] *Re L.* [1974] 1 W.L.R. 250; *Re R.* (1981) 2 F.L.R. 416.

[42] Although the kidnapping of children is facilitated by modern means of travel, it is by no means exclusively a 20th century phenomenon. In 1860, for instance, one testamentary guardian kidnapped the 13-year-old Marquis of Bute from the home of the other. Lord Campbell waxed indignant: "She clandestinely, and furtively, and fraudulently removed the infant from the jurisdiction of the Court of Chancery, and was prepared to set the Court of Chancery at defiance. She carried the infant with her to the railway station at King's Cross, and conducted him by rail, under the cloud of night, from London across the border between England and Scotland, and next morning deposited him at the Granton Hotel near Edinburgh": *Stuart* v. *Marquis of Bute* (1861) 9 H.L.C. 440, 459.

[43] *Re H.* [1966] 1 W.L.R. 381; *Re E.* [1967] Ch. 287, 761; *Re C.* [1978] Fam. 105; *Re R.* (1981) 2 F.L.R. 416.

[44] *Re T.* [1968] Ch. 704, distinguished in *Re A.* [1970] Ch. 665; *Re L.* [1974] 1 W.L.R. 250.

Otherwise, the innocent parent would suffer a grave injustice, for it would take a long time for the English court to decide the merits, because much of the evidence would have to come from abroad; and during that time the child might have developed roots in England. But in the last resort the welfare of the child always outweighs other considerations such as the conduct of the parents and the respect due to any order of a foreign court.[45] As was said in a recent case, the strength of an application for a summary order for the return of a child rests not on the so-called kidnapping of the child, or on an order of a foreign court, but on the assessment of the best interests of the child.[46]

International conventions

There is a Council of Europe convention on the recognition and enforcement of custody orders and a Hague Convention on Child Abduction,[47] both adopted and opened for signature in 1980. The former has been signed by the United Kingdom and fourteen other states, but not yet ratified by the United Kingdom. The latter has been signed by eight states, but not yet by the United Kingdom. It is understood that active consideration is being given to the question whether one or both of these conventions are acceptable to the United Kingdom and should be ratified.

The Council of Europe convention deals with the recognition and enforcement in one contracting state of custody orders made in other contracting states in relation to a child under the age of sixteen. Each state has to establish a central authority to which application can be made by any person who has obtained a custody order in a contracting state. The duty of the central authority applied to is then to discover the whereabouts of the child, to secure the enforcement of the foreign custody order and then to deliver the child to the applicant (art. 5). If the child was improperly removed (*i.e.* removed across an international frontier in breach of a custody order), then the central authority must cause steps to be taken forthwith for the return of the child, provided (a) that the child and its parents were all nationals of the state where the custody order was made and the child was habitually resident there, and (b) that the application is made within six months of the improper removal (art. 8). In such a case there are no grounds for refusing enforcement. In other cases of improper removal, there is a limited number of grounds on which enforcement may be refused (art. 9). If the removal is not improper but enforcement of the order is sought in a state other than that which granted it, enforcement may also be refused on a wider range of grounds listed in article 10. These grounds include the fact that by reason of a change of circumstances (including the passage of time) the original custody order is manifestly no longer in accordance with the welfare of the child. The United Kingdom has exer-

---

[45] *Re L., supra; Re C., supra; Re R., supra.*

[46] *Re R., supra.*

[47] For a commentary on the Council of Europe convention, see Jones (1980) 30 I.C.L.Q. 467, and for a commentary on the Hague Convention, see Anton, *ib.* 536. The most important articles in both conventions are printed in Morris and North, *Cases and Materials on Private International Law* (1984), Chap. 12.

cised the power of reservation contained in article 17 to apply this principle to cases of improper removal under articles 8 and 9.

The Hague Convention applies only to cases of wrongful removal or retention of a child under sixteen habitually resident in a contracting state, but removal or retention is wrongful not only if it is in breach of a custody order but also if it is in breach of rights of custody in the state of the child's habitual residence. The machinery of the Hague Convention is similar to that of the Council of Europe convention in that applications for the return of the child are to be made through central authorities established in each contracting state. There are a number of grounds on which the return of the child may be refused, but they are narrower than those in the Council of Europe convention.

In summary, the Council of Europe convention is concerned with the recognition of all foreign custody orders, whether or not improper removal is involved; the Hague Convention is concerned with the restoration of children who have been wrongly removed or retained, whether or not in breach of a foreign custody order.

CHAPTER 14

LEGITIMACY, LEGITIMATION AND ADOPTION

INTRODUCTION

LET us begin by defining our terms.

Legitimacy means the status which a legitimate child acquires at the time of his birth. Legitimation means that a child who is illegitimate at the time of his birth becomes legitimate by reason of subsequent events. (The most important of these subsequent events, and the only one which has a legitimating effect in English domestic law, is the subsequent marriage of the child's parents; but in other systems other events may legitimate an illegitimate child, *e.g.* parental recognition.) Adoption is an act whereby the relationship of parent and child is created between persons who are not necessarily so related by nature.

It is very important to distinguish between the question whether a child is legitimate or has been legitimated or adopted, and the question whether such a child can succeed to property.[1] The former is a question of recognising a status and is governed (speaking very generally) by the law of the father's domicile. The latter is a question of construction, governed in the case of intestate succession to immovables by the *lex situs*; in the case of intestate succession to movables by the law of the deceased's domicile at the time of his death; in the case of succession to movables or immovables under a will, presumably by the law of the testator's domicile at the time of making his will; and in the case of *inter vivos* trusts or settlements by the proper law of the trust or settlement. It is a question of what the settlor or testator meant when he used expressions like "children," and what Parliament meant when it used expressions like "issue" in the Administration of Estates Act 1925. It does not necessarily follow that, because a child has been legitimated or adopted under foreign law, therefore he can succeed to property under a settlement, a will or an intestacy; nor does it follow that, because a child is illegitimate, therefore he cannot succeed to property as a "child." For the law governing the succession, whether English or foreign, may accord different rights of succession to different classes of children. If the law governing the succession says that a child can succeed to property whether he is legitimate or illegitimate,[2] there is no need to inquire whether he is legitimate; conversely, if the law governing the succession says that in no circumstances can an adopted child succeed as a

---

[1] The distinction between the two questions is very clearly pointed out by F. A. Mann (1941) 57 L.Q.R. 112, 128–141; by Falconbridge, pp. 755–758; and by Lord Denning M.R. in *Re Valentine's Settlement* [1965] Ch. 831, 839.

[2] The Law Commission has recommended that all the disadvantages of illegitimacy should be removed so far as they affect the illegitimate child: Law Com. No. 118 (1982).

"child" to the property of his adoptive parent, there is no point in inquiring whether the foreign adoption would be recognised in England. It so happens that in all the reported cases, the succession has been governed by English domestic law: and this has tended to obscure the fact that two distinct questions are involved.

Succession to property is not the only context in which it is necessary to determine whether a child is legitimate, or has been legitimated or adopted, under foreign law. But it is the most important context, and nearly all the reported cases are cases on succession.

Our discussion of legitimacy, legitimation and adoption will therefore deal separately with the recognition of the status and the child's rights of succession.

LEGITIMACY

Recognition of the status

Here we are confronted not by the familiar question, what is the English conflict rule, but by the more fundamental question, is there an English conflict rule at all? Three theories have been canvassed by English writers. None is completely satisfactory.

According to the first and oldest theory, a child is legitimate if (and only if) he is born or conceived in lawful wedlock, *i.e.* a marriage which is valid by English rules of the conflict of laws.[3] Down to 1959 this was the traditional test of legitimacy in English domestic law; and the theory under discussion projects that test into the conflict of laws. According to this theory, English law has no conflict rule for legitimacy, only a conflict rule for the validity of marriage.[4] This theory is supported by all the English reported cases down to 1947, including two in the House of Lords.[5] But the difficulty is that according to some systems of law, including now English domestic law, a child may be legitimate even though his parents were not, and could not be, validly married. This is the doctrine of putative marriage, invented by the canon lawyers in order to preserve the legitimacy of the children when they multiplied the grounds on which a marriage could be annulled. From the canon law it passed into the law of most continental European countries, and a variation of it was, as we shall see,[6] enacted in England by section 2 of the Legitimacy Act 1959 (now section 1 of the Legitimacy Act 1976). Obviously, it is a defect in a conflict rule that it cannot be applied to many foreign systems of law. It is an even greater defect that it fails to take account of the domestic law of the forum.

According to a second theory, much canvassed by distinguished English textwriters,[7] the legitimacy of a child depends on the law of his domicile of

---

[3] See Dicey, 3rd ed., pp. 520–521; Westlake, pp. 101–103.
[4] For the validity of marriage, see *ante*, Chap. 11.
[5] *Brook* v. *Brook* (1861) 9 H.L.C. 193; *Shaw* v. *Gould* (1868) L.R. 3 H.L. 55.
[6] *Post*, p. 243.
[7] Cheshire and North, pp. 440–451; Wolff, pp. 109, 382; Graveson, pp. 363, 367–369; Schmitthoff, pp. 282–284.

origin. Dicta favouring this view can be quoted,[8] but they were all delivered in cases on legitimation by subsequent marriage, to which (as we shall see[9]) different considerations apply. The objection to this theory is, as Westlake pointed out long ago,[10] that since the child's domicile of origin is that of his father if he is legitimate and that of his mother if he is illegitimate,[11] the legitimacy of the child cannot depend on the law of his domicile of origin if his domicile of origin depends on his legitimacy—not, at any rate, if the child's father and mother had different domiciles at the time of the child's birth. This difficulty is not a mere academic one: it was felt in at least two of the reported cases, one of them a decision of the House of Lords.[12] The vicious circle can be broken, somewhat arbitrarily,[13] by disregarding the domicile of the mother and saying that the law of the father's domicile at the time of the child's birth determines whether the child is legitimate or not. But this formulation, besides raising difficulties in the case of a posthumous child, is quite inconsistent with the authorities.

According to a third theory, the question whether a child is legitimate or not is a question of construction of words like "children" or "issue" in deeds, wills and statutes.[14] But the difficulty is that this view disregards the fact that, as previously pointed out,[15] two questions are involved, first the recognition of the status, and secondly whether the child can succeed to property. Moreover, it would furnish no guidance to a court if the question of legitimacy arose in its own right as an abstract question, as it can do under section 45(1) of the Matrimonial Causes Act 1973,[16] or if the question arose in some context other than that of succession.

We must now abandon theory and see how the English courts have dealt with the question of legitimacy of children under a foreign law.

In *Brook* v. *Brook*,[17] a man and a woman, both domiciled in England, went through a ceremony of marriage in Denmark and immediately afterwards returned to England. The marriage was valid by Danish law but void by English domestic law because the woman was the sister of the man's deceased wife. A child of the marriage died intestate and unmarried, domiciled in England. The House of Lords held that the marriage was void, that the child was illegitimate, and that his brothers and sisters could not succeed to his property, which went to the Crown as *bona vacantia*. The actual decision is no doubt consistent with all three theories discussed above. But

---

[8] *Birtwhistle* v. *Vardill* (1835) 2 Cl. & F. 571, 573–574; *Re Don's Estate* (1857) 4 Drew. 194, 197; *Re Goodman's Trusts* (1881) 17 Ch.D. 266, 291, 292; *Re Andros* (1883) 24 Ch.D. 637, 638.

[9] *Post*, pp. 247–248.

[10] Westlake, pp. 101, 231.

[11] *Ante*, pp. 15–16.

[12] *Shaw* v. *Gould* (1868) L.R. 3 H.L. 55; *Re Paine* [1940] Ch. 46. Cf. *Smijth* v. *Smijth* (1918) 1 S.L.T. 156.

[13] Wolff, pp. 109, 382, denies that it is arbitrary, but his reasons are not convincing; see Welsh (1947) 63 L.Q.R. 71–73; Dicey and Morris, p. 458, n. 39.

[14] Welsh (1947) 63 L.Q.R. 65.

[15] *Ante*, pp. 238–239.

[16] *Post*, p. 244.

[17] (1861) 9 H.L.C. 193. Cf. *Re De Wilton* [1900] 2 Ch. 481.

the *ratio decidendi* is consistent only with the first theory, since the validity of the marriage was the only question discussed by the House of Lords.

In the famous case of *Shaw* v. *Gould*,[18] which is still the leading authority, a testator domiciled in England devised land in England on trust for the sons lawfully begotten of his great-niece Elizabeth Hickson, and bequeathed movables on trust for her children. Elizabeth, while domiciled in England, and aged sixteen, was induced by the fraud of Thomas Buxton (also domiciled in England) to go through a ceremony of marriage with him. The marriage was valid by English law, and at that time could only have been dissolved by private Act of Parliament; but it was never consummated, and Buxton was sent to prison for fraud. Some years later, Elizabeth (like all nice girls) fell in love with a law student, one John Shaw, who was eating his dinners at Gray's Inn. Her still subsisting marriage with Buxton was of course an impediment to their union. So Buxton was persuaded to go to Scotland and stay there for forty days so that Elizabeth could divorce him in the Court of Session. After the divorce Elizabeth married John Shaw, who was now domiciled in Scotland, lived with him in Scotland and had children by him. The House of Lords held that these children were illegitimate, and could take neither the land nor the movables under the testator's will, because the marriage of their parents was void, because the Scottish divorce could not be recognised in England, since Buxton (and therefore Elizabeth) was domiciled in England. "Whether the appellants answer the descriptions respectively of 'sons lawfully begotten' and of 'children,' " said Lord Chelmsford,[19] "depends upon whether their parents were lawfully married; and this again depends upon the effect of a divorce in Scotland dissolving the marriage of their mother with Thomas Buxton."

The decision seems clear enough, and so does the *ratio decidendi*. Of course it is a major obstacle confronting those who believe that the legitimacy of a child depends on the law of his father's domicile at the time of the child's birth (since the Shaw children were undoubtedly legitimate by the law of their father's Scottish domicile), or on the law of the child's domicile of origin (since it is impossible to determine the Shaw children's domicile of origin unless one first decides whether or not they were legitimate). The textwriters who hold these views have treated the decision with scant respect. Thus Cheshire goes so far as to say: "The House of Lords lost its direction through its persistent concentration upon one general principle to the exclusion of others."[20] Elsewhere he calls it "an abnormal decision and one to be interpreted in the light of the exceptional circumstances involved."[21] This, of course, is a more or less polite way of saying that in the writer's opinion the decision is wrong.

In *Re Paine*,[22] a testatrix domiciled in England gave securities on trust for her daughter Ada absolutely if Ada should leave any child or children

---

[18] (1868) L.R. 3 H.L. 55. *Cf. Re Stirling* [1908] 2 Ch. 344.
[19] At pp. 72–73. *Cf.* Lord Cranworth at p. 69: "The whole, therefore, turns on the validity of the divorce."
[20] Cheshire and North, p. 443.
[21] *Ibid.* p. 444.
[22] [1940] Ch. 46.

surviving her, with a gift over if she should not. In 1875 Ada, who was domiciled in England, went through a ceremony of marriage in Germany with a man who never lost his German domicile of origin. She lived with him in England and had three children, one of whom survived her. The marriage was valid by German law but void by English domestic law because Ada was the sister of the man's deceased wife. Bennett J. held that the marriage was void, that the children were therefore illegitimate, and that the gift over took effect. Like *Shaw* v. *Gould*, the decision seems quite inconsistent with the view that legitimacy depends on the law of the child's domicile of origin or with the view that it depends on the law of the father's domicile at the time of the child's birth.

Down to this point there appears to be no reported English case in which a child not born or conceived in lawful wedlock was held to be legitimate. But in *Re Bischoffsheim*[23] Romer J. laid down the following proposition:

"Where succession to personal property depends on the legitimacy of the claimant, the status of legitimacy conferred on him by his domicile of origin (*i.e.* the domicile of his parents at his birth) will be recognised by our courts, and if that legitimacy be established, the validity of his parents' marriage should not be entertained as a relevant subject for investigation."

In that case a testator, presumably domiciled in England, gave a share of residue to the children of his granddaughter Nesta. In 1917 Nesta, whose domicile of origin was English, was married in New York to the brother of her first husband, and in 1920 she had a son, Richard. The marriage was valid by the law of New York, but void by English domestic law. Romer J. was unable to hold that Nesta and her second husband had acquired a New York domicile by 1917, when they were married, but he did decide that they had acquired a New York domicile by 1920, when Richard was born: and he held that Richard was entitled to share with Nesta's children by her first marriage in the testator's residuary estate.

This decision seems difficult to reconcile with *Re Paine*, which was not cited, and with *Shaw* v. *Gould*, which was distinguished on three very unsatisfactory grounds:

(1) In *Shaw* v. *Gould* the children's domicile of origin was English, because Elizabeth's domicile remained that of Thomas Buxton, her lawful husband, since the Scottish divorce was not recognised in England. This is true, but it is arguing in a circle, because it was impossible to decide that the children's domicile of origin was English without first deciding that they were illegitimate—the very point in issue.

(2) "The relevance of the Scottish proceedings and of the decree which resulted therefrom appears to me to have been a matter rather of assumption by the House of Lords than one of direct decision."[24] This is a bold argument. It treats as *obiter* nearly every word spoken by every Lord who gave judgment in *Shaw* v. *Gould*.

---

[23] [1948] Ch. 79, 92; approved by the Privy Council in *Bamgbose* v. *Daniel* [1955] A.C. 107, 120; criticised by Dicey and Morris, pp. 460–462.
[24] [1948] Ch. 79, 91.

(3) "The claims under consideration (in *Shaw* v. *Gould*) were not confined to personal estate in England, for there was a claim to English real estate as well; and this may have had some effect on the line which was adopted both in the argument and in their Lordships' opinions."[25] This is a reference to the rule in *Birtwhistle* v. *Vardill*,[26] under which (as we shall see[27]) a child who is recognised in England as having been legitimated under foreign law could not succeed as heir to real estate in England. But here Romer J. seems to fall into elementary error, for it has been held that the rule in *Birtwhistle* v. *Vardill* "relates only to the case of descent of land upon an intestacy, and does not affect the case of a devise in a will to children."[28]

Re Bischoffsheim can perhaps be reconciled with the previous decisions by saying that a child not born or conceived in lawful wedlock is legitimate in England if, and only if, he is legitimate by the law of the domicile of each of his parents at the time of his birth.

Section 1(1) of the Legitimacy Act 1976 (re-enacting section 2(1) of the Legitimacy Act 1959) alters English law by providing that the child of a void marriage[29] shall be treated as the legitimate child of his parents if at the time of his conception (or at the time of the celebration of the marriage if later) both or either of his parents reasonably believed that the marriage was valid. This enactment is retrospective as to status but not as to rights of succession.[30] By section 1(2) of the Act, the section only applies where the father of the child was domiciled in England at the time of the birth, or, if he died before the birth, was so domiciled immediately before his death. This very restrictive provision seems nicely calculated to ensure that, if the facts of *Shaw* v. *Gould* were to recur, the children would still be illegitimate in England, since their father was not domiciled in England at the time when they were born. In Australia, the very similar section 91 of the Marriage Act 1961 provides that the section applies if either parent was domiciled in Australia at the time of the birth. This seems much more liberal and sensible than section 1(2) of the Legitimacy Act 1976. The divergence between the laws of the two countries, which does not reflect any difference of policy, could lead to unfortunate results. Suppose, for instance, that a man domiciled in Australia goes through a ceremony of marriage with a woman domiciled in England, and has children by her. The marriage is void, but both parties reasonably believe that it is valid. The children are legitimate in Australia, but illegitimate in England.

---

[25] *Ibid.*
[26] (1840) 7 Cl. & F. 895.
[27] *Post*, p. 252.
[28] *Re Grey's Trusts* [1892] 3 Ch. 88, 93.
[29] s.10(1) defines a void marriage (somewhat obscurely) as "a marriage, not being voidable only, in respect of which the High Court has or had jurisdiction to grant a decree of nullity, or would have or would have had such jurisdiction if the parties were domiciled in England." This probably means no more than that there must have been some sort of ceremony. The parties (or one of them) must believe that the marriage was valid, not merely that they are validly married.
[30] Legitimacy Act 1976, Sched. 1, para. 3.

Matrimonial Causes Act 1973, *section* 45(1). This subsection provides a convenient method whereby a person can obtain an authoritative declaration from the High Court that he is the legitimate child of his parents. It provides that any person who is a British subject,[31] or whose right to be deemed a British subject depends wholly or in part on his legitimacy or on the validity of any marriage, may, if he is domiciled in England or Northern Ireland or claims any real or personal estate situated in England, apply by petition to the court for a decree declaring that he is the legitimate child of his parents, or that the marriage of his father and mother, or of his grandfather and grandmother, or his own marriage, was a valid marriage. The subsection re-enacts earlier legislation going back to the Legitimacy Declaration Act 1858. The Attorney-General must be supplied with a copy of the petition and of supporting affidavits and he will be a respondent on the hearing of the petition.[32] The decree of the court is binding on the Crown and on all other persons, provided they have been given notice of the application or made parties to the proceedings, unless it was obtained by fraud or collusion.[33] There is no jurisdiction under this subsection to make a declaration as to the legitimacy of any person other than the petitioner.[34]

Succession by legitimate persons

A person who is recognised as legitimate in England under the principles discussed above can succeed to property under English deeds, wills or intestacies in like manner as if he were legitimate by English domestic law.[35] Conversely, a person who is not recognised as legitimate in England under the principles discussed above has no greater rights of succession under English deeds, wills or intestacies than he would have had if he were illegitimate by English domestic law.[36]

Sections 14 and 15 of the Family Law Reform Act 1969, which came into operation on January 1, 1970, enormously enhance the succession rights of illegitimate children in English domestic law, and consequently reduce the significance of legitimacy, whether under English or foreign law, in relation to succession under English deeds, wills or intestacies.

Before 1970, an illegitimate child could not (with one exception) take any interest in the intestacy of any person other than his spouse or children, nor (with one exception) could any person except his spouse or children take any interest in the intestacy of an illegitimate person. The one exception was that under section 9 of the Legitimacy Act 1926, illegitimate children and their mothers were given mutual rights of succession on their respective deaths intestate, provided that, if the mother died intestate, she left no legitimate child surviving her.

---

[31] This now means Commonwealth citizen: British Nationality Act 1981, s.51(1). For the meaning of Commonwealth citizen, see s.37(1).

[32] s.45(6).

[33] s.45(5). See *The Ampthill Peerage* [1977] A.C. 547.

[34] *Aldrich* v. *Att. Gen.* [1968] P. 281.

[35] *Re Bozzelli's Settlement* [1902] 1 Ch. 751; *Re Bischoffsheim* [1948] Ch. 79.

[36] *Brook* v. *Brook* (1861) 9 H.L.C. 193; *Shaw* v. *Gould* (1868) L.R. 3 H.L. 55; *Re De Wilton* [1900] 2 Ch. 481; *Re Stirling* [1908] 2 Ch. 344.

Before 1970, the general rule of construction was that gifts to "children," "issue," "descendants," "sons," etc., in deeds and wills went to legitimate children only, unless (a) it was impossible from the surrounding circumstances that any legitimate children could take under the gift, *e.g.* because the parent of the children was dead or incapable of having children and he left illegitimate children only; or (b) it appeared from the language of the deed or will that illegitimate children were intended to take, *e.g.* when the testator gave property to "the natural children of my daughter" or to "the reputed children of my son."[37] Furthermore, there was a rule of public policy under which illegitimate children born after the death of the testator, or after the execution of a deed, could not take under gifts to children, however clear the intention was to benefit them.[38]

Now, by section 14 of the Family Law Reform Act 1969, where either parent of an illegitimate child dies intestate, the illegitimate child or, if he is dead, his issue, is entitled to take any interest in the property to which he or his issue would have been entitled if he had been born legitimate[39]; and where an illegitimate child dies intestate, each of his parents, if surviving, is entitled to take any interest in the property to which that parent would have been entitled if the child had been born legitimate.[40] There is, however, a presumption that an illegitimate child shall be presumed not to have been survived by his father unless the contrary is shown.[41] Section 9 of the Legitimacy Act 1926 is repealed,[42] since its provisions have become unnecessary. It will be seen that the mutual rights of succession on intestacy conferred by section 14 are limited to children and parents, and do not extend to more remote ancestors or to collaterals. Hence, if the facts of *Brook* v. *Brook*[43] were to recur, the decision would still be the same, assuming of course that the marriage was within the prohibited degrees of English domestic law (*e.g.* a marriage between uncle and niece, or between step-father and step-daughter).

Again, by section 15 of the Family Law Reform Act 1969, any reference in a deed or will executed on or after January 1, 1970, to the children or other relations of any person is to be construed as, or as including, a reference to his illegitimate children or other relations unless the contrary intention appears.[44] Hence, the general rule of construction which was in force before 1970 is now reversed; and the rule of public policy which invalidated gifts to future-born illegitimate children is expressly abolished.[45] Therefore, a gift to A for life, and then to A's children, will include A's illegitimate children, unless the contrary intention appears. However, this provision applies only where the reference is to a person who is to benefit

---

[37] *Hill* v. *Crook* (1873) L.R. 6 H.L. 265, 282–283, *per* Lord Cairns.
[38] *Crook* v. *Hill* (1876) 3 Ch.D. 773; *Re Shaw* [1894] 2 Ch. 573; but see *Re Hyde* [1932] 1 Ch. 95.
[39] s.14(1). See Morris (1969) 19 I.C.L.Q. 328.
[40] s.14(2).
[41] s.14(4).
[42] s.14(7).
[43] (1861) 9 H.L.C. 193; *ante*, p. 161.
[44] s.15(1).
[45] s.15(7).

or to be capable of benefiting under the disposition.[46] Hence, if the facts of *Re Paine*[47] were to recur, the decision would still be the same (assuming of course that the marriage was within the prohibited degrees of English domestic law), because no benefit was given to Ada's children. Moreover, if the facts of *Shaw* v. *Gould*[48] were to recur, the decision would now be different with regard to the movables, but it would be the same with regard to the land, because the reference to "sons lawfully begotten" would no doubt be held to amount to a contrary intention.

So far, we have assumed that the child is claiming to succeed to property under an English deed, or will, or intestacy. What happens if the succession is governed by foreign law? This is the classic case of the incidental question,[49] much discussed by jurists: should the legitimacy of the child be determined by the conflict rules of the forum, or by the conflict rules of the foreign *lex successionis*? There is no English authority on this question. One may hazard the guess that English courts would probably permit the foreign *lex successionis* to determine not only what classes of children were entitled to succeed, but also (if legitimacy was a necessary qualification under the foreign law) whether any individual was or was not legitimate, and what law determined this question.[50]

LEGITIMATION

The law on this subject is needlessly complicated because there are two conflict rules for the recognition of foreign legitimations, a rule of common law and a statutory rule contained in section 3 of the Legitimacy Act 1976.

Recognition of the Status

(a) At common law

Recognition by subsequent marriage. Before 1927 English domestic law was almost alone in the world in refusing to recognise legitimation by subsequent marriage.[51] That doctrine was introduced into Roman law early in the fourth century A.D., in the time of Constantine, the first Christian Emperor. From the civil law it passed into the canon law and thence into the law of most continental European countries and their overseas colonies, and into the law of Scotland. In the nineteenth and early twentieth centuries it was introduced by statute into the law of most American states,[52] of New Zealand and Australia. But until January 1, 1927, English

---

[46] s.15(2).
[47] [1940] Ch. 46; *ante*, pp. 241–242.
[48] (1868) L.R. 3 H.L. 55; *ante*, p. 241.
[49] *Post*, Chap. 32.
[50] See *Baindail* v. *Baindail* [1946] P. 122, 127.
[51] For a comparative survey, see Fitzpatrick (1904) 6 J.Comp.Leg. 22; White (1920) 36 L.Q.R. 255.
[52] One of the pioneering statutes was that of California, where as long ago as 1892 the state Supreme Court described its legitimating statute in the following lyrical terms: "This section takes a wide range; its operation is not confined within state lines; it is as general as language can make it; oceans furnish no obstruction to its wide and beneficient provisions; it is manna to the bastards of the world" (*Blythe* v. *Ayres*, 96 Cal. 572, 31 P. 915 (1892)).

law had long been committed to the view that the status of bastardy is indelible, for when the assembled bishops tried to persuade the House of Lords to accept the doctrine of legitimation by subsequent marriage at the Parliament of Merton in 1235, the barons and earls cried out in Latin "Nolumus mutare leges Angliae."

However, long before 1927, the judges recognised an exception if the father was domiciled both at the time of the child's birth and at the time of the subsequent marriage in a country the law of which recognised legitimation by subsequent marriage.[53] If he was, the child was recognised in England as having been legitimated. This was finally settled in 1881, after a period of hesitation and uncertainty, by the majority decision of the Court of Appeal (Cotton and James L.JJ.; Lush L.J. dissenting) in the leading case of *Re Goodman's Trusts*,[54] reversing Jessel M.R.[55] and overruling *Boyes* v. *Bedale*.[56] So the rule could hardly have been established by a narrower margin. The place of the child's birth,[57] the place of celebration of the marriage,[58] and the domicile of the mother[59] are all irrelevant. All that matters is the domicile of the father at the two critical dates. If the father was domiciled in England at the time of the child's birth[60] or at the time of the subsequent marriage,[61] the child was not recognised as having been legitimated. "The domicile at birth must give a capacity to the child of being made legitimate; but then the domicile at the time of the marriage, which gives the status, must be domicile in a country which attributes to marriage that effect."[62]

The requirement that the father must be domiciled in a country whose law recognises legitimation by subsequent marriage at the time of the child's birth as well as at the time of the subsequent marriage is supported by artificial and unattractive reasoning which has been much criticised.[63] A more liberal rule would be that he must be domiciled in such a country at the time of the marriage only.[64] The requirement that he must also be domiciled in such a country at the time of the child's birth rests (apart from dicta) on two cases only, *Re Wright's Trusts*[65] and *Re Luck's Settlement*.[66] The former was decided at a time when the English courts were still disinclined to allow foreign-legitimated children to succeed to property under English wills; and it is surprising that the majority of the Court of Appeal

---

[53] *Goodman* v. *Goodman* (1862) 3 Giff. 643; *Skottowe* v. *Young* (1871) L.R. 11 Eq. 474; *Re Goodman's Trusts* (1881) 17 Ch.D. 266; *Re Andros* (1883) 24 Ch.D. 637; *Re Grey's Trusts* [1892] 3 Ch. 88; *Re Askew* [1930] 2 Ch. 259; *Re Hurll* [1952] Ch. 722.

[54] (1881) 17 Ch.D. 266.

[55] (1880) 14 Ch.D. 619.

[56] (1863) 1 H. & M. 798.

[57] *Re Wright's Trusts* (1856) 2 K. & J. 595, 610; *Re Grove* (1887) 40 Ch.D. 216, 232.

[58] *Re Wright's Trusts, supra; Re Grove, supra.*

[59] *Re Wright's Trusts, supra; Re Grove, supra,* at p. 238.

[60] *Re Wright's Trusts, supra.*

[61] *Re Grove, supra.*

[62] *Re Grove, supra,* at p. 233.

[63] See *Re Luck's Settlement* [1940] Ch. 864, 909–913, *per* Scott L.J. (dissenting); Dicey and Morris, pp. 476–477; Cheshire and North, pp. 454–455.

[64] This is the rule in the United States: Leflar, s.241.

[65] (1856) 2 K. & J. 595.

[66] [1940] Ch. 864.

did not take the opportunity of overruling it in *Re Luck's Settlement*. Instead, they extended it to a case of legitimation, not by subsequent marriage, but by parental recognition. They held that the child of a father who was domiciled in England at the time of the child's birth, but in California at the time of the parental recognition, was not recognised in England as having been legitimated, and could not take as a "child" under an English marriage settlement and will, although by Californian law the effect of the parental recognition was to render the child legitimate as from the date of his birth. In that case, owing to the rule against perpetuities,[67] it was necessary for the child to prove that his legitimation was retrospective. In such a case there may perhaps be some justification for looking to the law of the father's domicile at the time of the child's birth. There can be no such justification if, as in the normal case, it is not necessary to prove that the legitimation is restrospective. The majority of the Court of Appeal pointed out[68] that legitimation affects the status of the father as well as the status of the child; and they refused to allow a foreign law retrospectively to alter the status of a father who, at the time of the child's birth, was domiciled in England. But this reasoning has subsequently been weakened by the decision of the House of Lords in *Starkowski* v. *Att. Gen.*,[69] where they held that foreign law can retrospectively alter the status of a person domiciled in England.

The decision of the Court of Appeal is also weakened by the vigorous dissenting judgment of Scott L.J., who confessed that "the very idea of attributing to a newly born child, to a *filius nullius*, a sort of latent capacity for legitimation at the hands of the natural father to whom he is denied any legal relation, seems to me an even more absurd legal fiction, and even less convincing, than the mythical contract of marriage supposed by the canonists to have been entered into at the moment of procreation."[70] He could "see no warrant for applying a rule, originating in the special reasons for the doctrine of legitimation by subsequent marriage, and justified by various legal fictions invented to support it, to the simple and straightforward case of a direct command of legitimation by the statute law of the father's domicile."[71]

Legitimation by parental recognition. Re Luck's Settlement is the only reported case in which the English court has had to consider the effect of legitimation otherwise than by subsequent marriage. In that case, counsel for the appellant conceded[72] that if the father had been domiciled in California at the time of the child's birth as well as at the time of the parental recognition, the child would have been recognised in England as having

---

[67] See, for this aspect of the matter, Gray, *Rule against Perpetuities*, pp. 290–292. Owing to the rule, there is some difficulty in accepting the view of Farwell J. at first instance and of Scott L.J. (dissenting) in the Court of Appeal that the child could take under the marriage settlement as well as under the will.

[68] [1940] Ch. 864, 882.

[69] [1954] A.C. 155; *ante*, p. 150. In that case Lord Tucker at pp. 175–176 and Lord Cohen at pp. 180–181 attempted to distinguish *Re Luck's Settlement*, but on very slender grounds.

[70] [1940] Ch. 864, 912.

[71] *Ibid.* at pp. 912–913.

[72] *Ibid.* at pp. 871–872.

been legitimated. The majority of the Court of Appeal made no comment on this concession; but they did cite with approval[73] Dicey's view[74] that in such a case the child would be recognised in England as legitimate. Moreover, section 10(1) of the Legitimacy Act 1976 assumes that the common law rule is not limited to legitimation by subsequent marriage.

Legitimation by foreign statute. The Legitimacy Act 1976, section 2, reenacting section 1(1) of the Legitimacy Act 1926, provides that where the parents of an illegitimate person marry or have married one another, whether before or after January 1, 1927,[75] the marriage shall, if the father was or is at the date of the marriage domiciled in England, render that person, if living, legitimate from January 1, 1927, or from the date of the marriage, whichever last happens. Hence a child is now legitimated by subsequent marriage in English domestic law; but, if the marriage was celebrated before 1927, only from January 1, 1927. If the marriage was celebrated before that date, there is nothing in the section which requires that the father should be domiciled in England, or even alive, on January 1, 1927. Statutes very similar to section 2 of the English Act are in force in other countries, *e.g.* Northern Ireland,[76] the Republic of Ireland,[77] and Australia.[78] What then is the position if the English court is asked to recognise the legitimation under one of these statutes of a person whose father was dead, or no longer domiciled in the country in question, on the date when the statute came into operation, the marriage having taken place earlier? The Legitimacy Acts 1926 and 1976 do not in terms answer this question, and one may therefore be thrown back on the rule of common law. Unfortunately the common law rule for legitimation by subsequent marriage is not well adapted to this situation, which from the point of view of the English court is analogous to the *legitimatio per rescriptum principis* of Roman law rather than to *legitimatio per subsequens matrimonium.*

The English courts have not yet been confronted by a case of this sort, but it has arisen in the Republic of Ireland and also in Australia and New Zealand with reference to children legitimated by the English Act of 1926. The Australian and New Zealand courts apparently recognise the legitimation of the child only if the father was domiciled in England at *three* critical dates, the date of the child's birth, the date of the subsequent marriage, and the coming into operation of the Act on January 1, 1927.[79] On the other hand, the Irish court has recognised the legitimation when the father was domiciled in England at the date of the child's birth and at the date of

---

[73] *Ibid.* at p. 884.
[74] 3rd ed., p. 532.
[75] Technically, s.2 of the 1976 Act only applies to marriages celebrated after its commencement (August 22, 1976): but the rights of children legitimated by s.1 of the 1926 Act are preserved by Sched. 1, para. 1(1) to the 1976 Act.
[76] Legitimacy Act (Northern Ireland) 1928.
[77] Legitimacy Act 1931.
[78] Marriage Act 1961, s.89.
[79] *Re Williams* [1936] V.L.R. 223; *Re Davey* [1937] N.Z.L.R. 56; *Re Pritchard* (1940) 40 S.R.N.S.W. 443; *Re James* [1942] V.L.R. 12; *Thompson* v. *Thompson* (1951) 51 S.R.N.S.W. 102; *In the Estate of Taylor* [1964–65] N.S.W.R. 695; *cf. Re Beatty* [1919] V.L.R. 81 (decided with reference to a New York statute of 1895).

the subsequent marriage, even though he was dead on January 1, 1927.[80] The view of the Irish court seems preferable to that of the Australasian courts, and it is to be hoped that it will be followed in England. For it seems unduly onerous to force the child to prove that his father was domiciled in the country in question at three critical dates; and of course it is an impossible task if the father was dead when the Act came into operation. It seems much better to apply the law of the country where the father was domiciled at the date of the child's birth and at the date of the subsequent marriage, as that law stands at the date of the proceedings in England. This would do much to prevent a person being held legitimate in one country and illegitimate in another. This was in effect the test applied by the Irish court and by the Supreme Court of Victoria in the most recent Australian case on the subject.[81] It may be added that, for the purposes of British citizenship, a person is deemed to have been legitimated by the subsequent marriage of his parents if by the law of the place where his father was domiciled at the time of the marriage the marriage operated immediately *or subsequently* to legitimate him.[82]

(b) Under the Legitimacy Act 1976

As we have seen,[83] section 1(1) of the Legitimacy Act 1926 (now section 2 of the Legitimacy Act 1976) introduced legitimation by subsequent marriage into English domestic law; and section 3 of the Act of 1976 (re-enacting section 8(1) of the Act of 1926) lays down a new conflict rule for recognising foreign legitimations. This section provides that where the parents of an illegitimate person marry or have married one another, whether before or after January 1, 1927, and the father of the illegitimate person was or is, at the time of the marriage, domiciled in a foreign country by the law of which the illegitimate person became legitimated by virtue of such subsequent marriage, that person, if living, shall be recognised in England as having been so legitimated from January 1, 1927, or from the date of the marriage, whichever last happens, notwithstanding that, at the time of his birth, his father was domiciled in a country the law of which did not permit legitimation by subsequent marriage.[84] It has been held in Australia that under section 90 of the Marriage Act 1961 (which was closely modelled on section 8(1) of the English Act of 1926) it is not necessary for the marriage to legitimate the child immediately. Effect will be given to a later change in the law of the foreign country which legitimates the child by virtue of the marriage, even if the father is no longer domiciled in the foreign country at the date of the subsequent change in its law.[85]

---

[80] *Re Hagerbaum* [1933] I.R. 198.

[81] *Heron* v. *National Trustees Executors and Agency Co. of Australasia Ltd.* [1976] V.R. 733, which (unlike the cases cited in n. 79, *supra*) was decided under s.90(1) of the Australian Marriage Act 1961. The cases cited in n. 79, *supra*, were accepted as stating the position at common law.

[82] British Nationality Act 1981, s.47(2).

[83] *Ante*, p. 249.

[84] Technically, s.3 of the 1976 Act (like s.2) only applies to marriages celebrated after its commencement (August 22, 1976); but the rights of children recognised as legitimated by s.8 of the 1926 Act are preserved by Sched. 1, para. 1(1) to the 1976 Act.

[85] *Heron* v. *National Trustees Executors and Agency Co. of Australasia Ltd.* [1976] V.R. 733.

This new statutory rule is a great improvement on the common law rule in that it looks only at the law of the father's domicile at the time of the marriage, and not at the time of the child's birth. The intention was, no doubt, to abolish the old common law rule altogether. But the courts have held that it still continues to exist side by side with the new statutory rule. It may still be necessary to fall back on it, for one of four reasons, of which all but the second are of gradually diminishing importance:

(1) A child is only recognised as having been legitimated under section 3 from January 1, 1927, or from the date of the marriage, whichever is later.

(2) The section only applies to legitimation by subsequent marriage; the common law rule, as we have seen,[86] applies also to other modes of legitimation.

(3) The 1926 Act was not available if the child's father or mother was married to a third person when the child was born.[87] This restriction does not apply to legitimation at common law if there is no similar restriction in the law of the foreign country in question.[88] It was repealed by section 1 of the Legitimacy Act 1959 as from October 29, 1959.

(4) Until January 1, 1976, a child recognised as legitimated under the statutory rule had less extensive rights of succession under English deeds, wills and intestacies than a child recognised as legitimated at common law.

Matrimonial Causes Act 1973, *section* 45(2). This subsection affords a convenient method whereby a person can obtain an authoritative declaration from the High Court or a county court that he has been legitimated by the subsequent marriage of his parents. It provides that any person claiming that he or his parent or any remoter ancestor[89] became or has become a legitimated person may apply by petition to the court for a decree declaring that he or his parent or remoter ancestor became or has become a legitimated person. The jurisdiction of the court under this subsection does not depend in any way on the petitioner's nationality or domicile, nor is it necessary for him to claim any property in England.[90] The jurisdiction is, therefore, theoretically unlimited. The term "legitimated person" means a person legitimated under the Legitimacy Acts 1926 or 1976 and includes a person recognised under section 8 of the Act of 1926 or section 3 of the Act of 1976 as legitimated.[91] Whether it also includes a person recognised as legitimated at common law is doubtful.

The Attorney General must be supplied with a copy of the petition and of supporting affidavits and he will be a respondent on the hearing of the petition.[92] The decree of the court is binding on the Crown and on all other

---

[86] *Ante*, pp. 248–249.
[87] s.1(2).
[88] *Re Askew* [1930] 2 Ch. 259.
[89] This means a direct lineal ancestor and not, *e.g.* a great-uncle: *Knowles* v. *Att. Gen.* [1951] P. 54.
[90] Contrast s.45(1), which deals with petitions for a declaration that a person is legitimate: see *ante*, p. 244.
[91] See Sched. 1, para. 1(2) to the Act of 1976.
[92] s.45(6).

persons, provided they have been given notice of the application or made parties to the proceedings, unless it was obtained by fraud or collusion.[93]

Succession by Legitimated Persons

In 1840, the House of Lords held in *Birtwhistle* v. *Vardill* [94] that a child recognised as legitimated under Scots law could not succeed to real estate in England as heir of his uncle, even though his father was domiciled in Scotland both at the date of his birth and at the date of the subsequent marriage. In 1881, the Court of Appeal held in *Re Goodman's Trusts*[95] that a child recognised as legitimated under Dutch law could succeed to personal property on the intestacy of her aunt, who died domiciled in England. *Birtwhistle* v. *Vardill* was distinguished on the ground that "the English heirship, the descent of English land, required not only that the man should be legitimate, but as it were *porphyro-genitus*, born legitimate within the narrowest pale of English legitimacy. Heirship is an incident of land, depending on the local law, the law of the country, the county, the manor, and even of the particular property itself, the *forma doni*. Kinship is an incident of the person, and is universal."[96] From that time onwards the rule in *Birtwhistle* v. *Vardill* came to look increasingly anomalous and archaic. It was gradually whittled away, first by a decision in 1892 that it only applied to the inheritance of real estate by heirs on intestacy, and not to gifts by deed or will to children[97]; then by the abolition in 1925 of descent to the heir in the case of fee simple estates[98]; and then by section 3(1)(*c*) of the Legitimacy Act 1926, which restricted it to entailed interests created before the date of legitimation. It was finally abolished (in the case of deeds executed or testators or intestates dying on or after January 1, 1976) by section 10(4) of the Legitimacy Act 1976.[99]

Section 3 of the Legitimacy Act 1926 laid down rules of succession for legitimated children which applied equally to children legitimated by section 1 of that Act under English domestic law and children recognised as legitimated by section 8 under foreign law. Under these rules, the children could not succeed to property unless they were legitimated before the deed was executed or before the testator or intestate died.[1] There was no such restriction if the child was recognised as legitimated at common law.[2]

---

[93] s.45(5).
[94] (1826) 5 B. & C. 438 (decision of the Court of King's Bench against the claim to succeed); (1835) 2 Cl. & F. 571 (question argued before all the judges, who advised against the claim; first decision of the House of Lords against the claim; question remitted for further argument before the judges in deference to Lord Brougham's doubts); (1840) 7 Cl. & F. 895 (final decision of the House of Lords against the claim, Lord Brougham still not satisfied but not formally dissenting).
[95] (1881) 17 Ch.D. 266.
[96] At p. 299, *per* James L.J.
[97] *Re Grey's Trusts* [1892] 3 Ch. 88.
[98] Administration of Estates Act 1925, s.45(1).
[99] Re-enacting Children Act 1975, Sched. 1, para. 17, which came into force on that date. There are exceptions in the case of titles of honour and property limited to devolve therewith (Sched. 1, para. 4(2) and (3) to the Act of 1976).
[1] See *Re Hepworth* [1936] Ch. 750; *Re Hoff* [1942] Ch. 298.
[2] See *Re Askew* [1930] 2 Ch. 259; *Re Hurll* [1952] Ch. 722.

Hence foreign-legitimated children might have greater rights of succession under English deeds, wills and intestacies than English-legitimated children had. This anomalous distinction was partially removed by section 15(4) of the Family Law Reform Act 1969, and abolished (in the case of deeds executed or testators or intestates dying on or after January 1, 1976) by section 5 of the Legitimacy Act 1976,[3] which provides that a legitimated person, and any other person,[4] shall be entitled to take any interest in property as if the legitimated person had been born legitimate. A "legitimated person" is defined to mean a person legitimated under section 1 of the Act of 1926 or section 2 of the Act of 1976, a person recognised as legitimated under section 8 of the Act of 1926 or section 3 of the Act of 1976, or a person recognised as legitimated at common law.[5] It follows that if a testator dies on or after January 1, 1976, having by his will given property to A for life and then to A's children, children legitimated before or after the death of the testator will be able to succeed, unless there is a contrary intention.

A person can only be legitimated under section 2 of the Act of 1976, or recognised as legitimated under section 3, if he was living at the date of the subsequent marriage. But, so far as succession is concerned, this requirement is largely neutralised by section 5(6), which provides that if an illegitimate person dies, and after his death his parents marry, and he would, if living at the time of the marriage, have become a legitimated person, the section applies as if he had been legitimated by virtue of the marriage. In other words, he can act as a conduit pipe for the transmission of rights of succession to others.

Although section 5 does not say so in terms, it may be assumed that its provisions are rules of English domestic law and as such only applicable if English law is the *lex successionis*. If the succession is governed by foreign law, the English courts would probably permit the foreign *lex successionis* to determine not only what classes of persons were entitled to succeed, but also (if legitimacy was a necessary qualification under the foreign law) whether any individual had or had not been legitimated, and what law determined this question.[6] But there is no authority on the question.

ADOPTION

Introduction

Adoption may give rise to complicated problems in the conflict of laws, because the laws of different countries differ widely as to the objects which adoption should serve, the methods by which it is effected, the requirements necessary for adoption (especially the age of the adopter and of the adopted person), and the effects of adoption (especially in the matter of succession).

---

[3] Re-enacting Children Act 1975, Sched. 1, para. 12, which came into force on that date.
[4] These words take care of succession *to* a legitimated person.
[5] Legitimacy Act 1976, s.10(1).
[6] See *ante*, p. 246.

It was not until the Adoption of Children Act 1926 that English law made any provision for adoption, and not until the Adoption Act 1950 that an adopted child acquired rights of succession as a child of his adoptive parents and not of his natural parents. Adoption is now governed by the Adoption Act 1958 (as amended by the Adoption Act 1968 and the Children Act 1975) which regulates adoptions both in England and Scotland. There is a consolidating Adoption Act 1976 applying to England only, but it is understood that it will not be brought into force until all the adoption provisions of the Children Act 1975 have come into force, which may not be for some time. But, in case it is brought into force during the currency of this edition of this book, references to it are given in brackets in the footnotes.

In England and Scotland, adoption can only be effected by court order after a judicial inquiry directed mainly to ensuring that it will be for the welfare of the child. In England, such orders can be made by the High Court, a county court or a magistrates' court. In some foreign systems, adoption can be effected by agreement between the parties, sometimes with and sometimes without judicial approval, or even by religious ceremony. In England and Scotland, the child must be a person under the age of eighteen who has not been married.[7] But in many foreign systems the adoption of adults is possible. The effect of an English adoption order is to vest the parental rights and duties relating to a child in the adopters.[8] These parental rights and duties mean all the rights and duties which by law the mother and father have in relation to a legitimate child and his property.[9]

English adoptions

The High Court, a county court or a magistrates' court has jurisdiction to make an adoption order if the applicant (or one of them in the case of a married couple) is domiciled in a part of the United Kingdom or in the Channel Islands or the Isle of Man,[10] and the child is in England when the application is made.[11] If the child is not in Great Britain when the application is made, only the High Court has jurisdiction to make such an order.[12] If the child is in Scotland when the application is made, no English court has jurisdiction to make such an order.[13]

It is surprising that the habitual residence in England of the applicants is not made an alternative to domicile in these jurisdictional provisions, as it is in matrimonial causes.[14] Indeed, a stronger case can be made for habitual residence as a jurisdictional criterion in adoption than in, for example,

---

[7] Adoption Act 1958, s.57, as amended by Children Act 1975, Sched. 3, paras. 21(2), 39(c) (Adoption Act 1976, ss.12(5), 72(1)).
[8] Children Act 1975, s.8(1) (Adoption Act 1976, s.12(1)).
[9] Children Act 1975, s.85(1) (Interpretation Act 1978, Sched. 1).
[10] Children Act 1975, ss.10(2), 11(2) (Adoption Act 1976, ss.14(2), 15(2)).
[11] Children Act 1975, s.100(2) (Adoption Act 1976, s.62(2)).
[12] Children Act 1975, s.100(4) (Adoption Act 1976, s.62(3)).
[13] Children Act 1975, s.100(3) (Adoption (Scotland) Act 1978, s.56(2)).
[14] *Ante*, pp. 190, 208.

divorce. In divorce the main objectives of jurisdictional criteria should be to prevent forum shopping, and to give the decree some chance of being recognised abroad. In adoption the main objective of jurisdictional criteria should be to ensure that the applicants have sufficient connection with the country of the forum to enable the welfare authorities there to determine whether the applicants are suitable persons to adopt the child in question. This is a much more important matter than any question of the recognition of the adoption abroad—a question which arises far less often in relation to adoption orders than it does in relation to divorce decrees. Domicile does not achieve this main objective, because it is so artificial a concept that the applicants could well be domiciled in England, although they never lived there in their lives, or alternatively could well be permanently resident in England, and yet be domiciled abroad. To make domicile the sole jurisdictional criterion, therefore, was a retrograde step.

There is no jurisdictional requirement that the child must be domiciled or even resident in England. This is no doubt because it would render adoptions unduly difficult and expensive if proof of domicile were required in the case of children who are waifs or strays or whose natural parents cannot be traced. Very many adopted children are illegitimate and the domicile of the mother (and hence of the child) may be quite uncertain. There are only two possible justifications for requiring that the child should be domiciled in England. The first is to safeguard the interests of the natural parents. But their interests are sufficiently safeguarded by the requirement that they must agree to the making of the order,[15] unless the court dispenses with their agreement on certain narrowly-defined grounds.[16] The second is that the country of the child's domicile has an interest in his welfare. But the Act provides that the court must be satisfied that the order will be for the welfare of the child.[17]

Yet it has been suggested by some writers[18] that the court should not make an order if the child is domiciled abroad unless satisfied that the adoption will be in accordance with the law of the child's domicile; otherwise, says Cheshire, a limping child will result, i.e. one who is regarded as having been legally adopted in English law, but not by the law of his domicile. The phrase is amusing, but the suggestion seems unsound.[19] There is no justification for bringing back the child's domicile by the back door when the Act deliberately treats it as irrelevant for jurisdictional purposes. Most adoptions take place in county courts and magistrates' courts, and they are not well suited to investigating complicated questions of foreign law and the conflict of laws.

Unfortunately, in Re B.[20] Goff J. preferred Cheshire's view, but it was unnecessary for him to do so and he did it in an extraordinarily confused

---

[15] Children Act 1975, s.12(1) (Adoption Act 1976, s.16(1)).
[16] Children Act 1975, s.12(2) (Adoption Act 1976, s.16(2)).
[17] Children Act 1975, s.3 (Adoption Act 1976, s.6).
[18] Cheshire and North, pp. 459–460; Graveson, pp. 381–382; Anton, pp. 363–365.
[19] See Kennedy (1956) 34 Can. Bar Rev. 507, 520–521; Kahn-Freund, *The Growth of Internationalism in English Private International Law* (1960), pp. 62–66.
[20] [1968] Ch. 204.

way. In that case, applicants domiciled in England applied for an adoption order in respect of a child resident in England who was the legitimate child of an English mother and a Spanish father domiciled in Spain. The parents had been divorced and custody of the child awarded to the mother; so the child was probably domiciled in England as the law then stood.[21] But Goff J., on the assumption that the child might be domiciled in Spain, held that the court had jurisdiction to make the order, but should consider whether its order would be recognised "elsewhere" unless it was clearly for the benefit of the child to be adopted, e.g. in refugee cases. Yet he added that "it is not necessary to prove what the child's domicile actually is, or to go into the adoption laws of the relevant foreign country, for . . . the problem is not one of jurisdiction or of applying the foreign law, but of considering factually whether, having regard to the foreign element, the English order will have general recognition, and if not whether the order would still be for the welfare of the infant." Evidently, this decision does not mean that no adoption order can be made unless it would be in accordance with the law of the child's domicile. It only means that the court should look and see whether its order would be recognised abroad. But even so, it is unusual for English courts to decline to exercise a jurisdiction entrusted to them by Parliament merely because their order might not be recognised abroad.[22]

Convention adoptions

The Adoption Act 1968 was passed primarily to enable the United Kingdom to ratify a Hague Convention on international adoptions which was signed in 1965.[23] The Act, as amended by section 24 of the Children Act 1975 and by the Domestic Proceedings and Magistrates' Courts Act 1978, came into force on October 23, 1978, but at present there are only two other States besides the United Kingdom which have ratified the Convention, namely Austria and Switzerland.[24]

The Act (as amended) extends the jurisdiction of the High Court (but not of county courts or magistrates' courts) to make adoption orders in cases where the applicants are not domiciled in the British Isles, but only under very stringent and complicated conditions. These are as follows[25]:

(1) The child must be a United Kingdom national or a national of a Convention country (i.e. Austria or Switzerland) and must habitually reside in British territory or a Convention country. "United Kingdom national" means a person who is a British citizen, a British Dependent Territories citizen or a British Overseas citizen or such of them as satisfy such con-

---

[21] See Hope v. Hope [1968] N.Ir. 1.
[22] See, e.g. Tursi v. Tursi [1958] P. 54 (divorce).
[23] Cmnd. 2615. The text is also printed in (1965) 14 I.C.L.Q. 558. For comments on the Convention, see Graveson, ibid. pp. 532–538; Lipstein [1965] Camb.L.J. 224; Unger (1965) 28 M.L.R. 463. For comments on the Act, see McClean and Patchett (1970) 19 I.C.L.Q. 1; Blom (1973) 22 I.C.L.Q. 109.
[24] S.I. 1978 No. 1431.
[25] Children Act 1975, s.24 (Adoption Act 1976, s.17).

ditions, if any, as the Secretary of State may specify.[26] "British territory" means the United Kingdom.[27]

(2) The applicant or applicants and the child must not all be United Kingdom nationals living in British territory.

(3) If the application is by a married couple, either (a) each must be a United Kingdom national or a national of a Convention country and both must be habitually resident in Great Britain, or (b) both must be United Kingdom nationals and each must habitually reside in the United Kingdom or in a Convention country.

(4) If the application is by one person, either (a) he must be a United Kingdom national or a national of a Convention country and must be habitually resident in Great Britain, or (b) he must be a United Kingdom national and must habitually reside in the United Kingdom or in a Convention country.

(5) These jurisdictional criteria (i.e. (1) to (4) above) must be satisfied both at the time of the application and when the order is made.

(6) If the applicant is a national of a Convention country, or both applicants are nationals of the same Convention country, the adoption must not be prohibited by a provision in the internal law of that country which has been notified to the United Kingdom Government and specified by order.[28]

(7) If the child is not a United Kingdom national, no adoption order may be made except in accordance with the provisions, if any, of the internal law of the Convention country of which he is a national relating to consents and consultations, other than those by or with the applicant, his or her spouse, or members of his family. The court must also be satisfied that each person who consents to the order in accordance with that internal law does so with full understanding of what is involved.

If the adopter or both adopters or the person adopted is habitually resident in Great Britain, the High Court may annul a Convention adoption (whether English or foreign) on any one of three grounds:

(a) on the ground that it was contrary to a prohibition on adoption which was contained in the internal law of the adopter's nationality and was notified to or by the United Kingdom Government,[29] if under that law the adoption could have been impugned on that ground; or

(b) on the ground that it contravened the provisions relating to consents contained in the internal law of the adopted person's nationality, if under that law the adoption could have been impugned on that ground; or

(c) on any other ground on which the adoption could be impugned under

---

[26] Children Act 1975, s.107(1) (Adoption Act 1976, s.72(1)); British Nationality Act 1981, s.51(3)(a)(ii).

[27] Children Act 1975, s.107(1) (Adoption Act 1976, s.72(1)); S.I. 1978 No. 1432, paras. 5 and 7.

[28] For prohibitions on adoption notified by Austria and Switzerland, see S.I. 1978 No. 1431, para. 3 and Scheds. 1 and 2.

[29] See previous note, and for prohibitions on adoption contained in United Kingdom law and notified to Austria and Switzerland, see S.I. 1978 No. 1431, para. 8 and Sched.

the law for the time being in force in the country in which the adoption was effected.[30]

Recognition of foreign adoptions

Adoptions in the British Isles. There never has been any doubt that adoption orders made in Scotland would be recognised in England without question, if only because the Adoption Act 1958 applied to Scotland as well as to England; and this is now expressly enacted.[31] It is also expressly provided that adoption orders made in Northern Ireland, the Channel Islands and the Isle of Man shall be recognised in England and Scotland.[32]

"Overseas adoptions." As we have seen, the Adoption Act 1968 was passed primarily to enable the United Kingdom to ratify the Hague Convention on Adoptions of 1965. But section 4(3) empowers the Secretary of State to specify as "overseas adoptions" any adoption effected under the law of any country outside Great Britain. The intention was to recognise not only Convention adoptions made in countries which are parties to the Convention, but also adoptions made in countries whose adoption law is broadly similar to our own. In exercise of the power conferred by this subsection, an Order was made in 1973[33] specifying adoptions made in a large number of countries as "overseas adoptions." These countries include most of the Commonwealth (exceptions include India and Bangladesh), all western European countries, Yugoslavia, Greece, Turkey, Israel, South Africa, and the United States. Under this Order, there need be no juristic link of any kind (*e.g.* domicile) between the adopters and the country where the adoption was made. The only reservations are that the adoption must have been effected under statutory law and not under common law or customary law; that the adopted person had not attained the age of eighteen and had not been married; and that recognition must not be contrary to public policy.[34] Subject to this, recognition is automatic.[35]

Other adoptions. The recognition in England of other adoptions (*i.e.* adoptions other than those made in the British Isles and other than "overseas adoptions") still depends on the common law. So many adoptions have been specified as "overseas adoptions" under the Order of 1973 that there is little geographical scope left for the common law to operate in, but it will still apply to adoptions made, *e.g.* in eastern European countries with communist régimes; Middle Eastern countries other than Turkey and Israel; and India, Pakistan, China, Japan and the countries of Central and South America. It will also apply to adoptions effected under the custom-

---

[30] Adoption Act 1968, ss.5(2), 6(1), 7(1)(2)(4) and 11(1), as amended by Domestic Proceedings and Magistrates' Courts Act 1978, s.74(1), adding a new subsection (8A) to s.24 of the Children Act 1975 (Adoption Act 1976, s.53).
[31] Children Act 1975, Sched. 1, paras. 1(2)(*a*) and (*b*), 3 (Adoption Act 1976, ss.38(1)(*c*), 39).
[32] Children Act 1975, Sched. 1, paras. 1(2)(*c*), 3 (Adoption Act 1976, ss.38(1)(*c*), 39), replacing Adoption Act 1964, s.1.
[33] S.I. 1973, No. 19.
[34] *Post*, p. 259.
[35] Children Act 1975, Sched. 1, paras. 1(2)(*d*), 3 (Adoption Act 1976, ss.38(1)(*d*), 39).

ary or common law of countries specified in the 1973 Order, and to the adoption of adults.

What then are the recognition rules of the common law? The majority of the Court of Appeal in *Re Valentine's Settlement*[36] laid it down, in the words of Lord Denning M.R., that at common law "the courts of this country will only recognise an adoption in another country if the adopting parents are domiciled there and the child is ordinarily resident there."[37] Danckwerts L.J. agreed with the Master of the Rolls, except that he was "not sure" whether the ordinary residence of the child was a requirement for recognition. In that case the Court of Appeal refused to recognise two South African adoption orders made in respect of two children who were assumed to be resident and domiciled in South Africa, because the applicants were domiciled in Southern Rhodesia and there was evidence that the Southern Rhodesian courts would not recognise the South African adoptions. There are indications in the judgments that the adoptions would have been recognised without difficulty if they had been recognised by the Southern Rhodesian courts.[38] So perhaps we can say, on the analogy of the rule in *Armitage* v. *Att. Gen.*[39] in divorce, that at common law a foreign adoption will be recognised in England if the adopters were domiciled in the foreign country, or if it would be recognised in the country where the adopters were domiciled.

Public policy. Lord Denning M.R. entered one caveat[40]: the foreign adoption should not be recognised if recognition would be contrary to public policy. It is more than usually important to keep this factor in mind when deciding whether to recognise a foreign adoption, because the laws of some foreign countries differ so widely from English law as to the objects and effects of adoption.[41] Hence, if the adoption was made for some ulterior object other than the welfare of the child, some at least of its effects might have to be denied recognition in England. But the facts would have to be extreme before public policy demanded the total non-recognition of a foreign adoption for all purposes. If, to take an improbable but striking example, the law of a foreign country allowed a bachelor of fifty to adopt a spinster of seventeen, an English court might hesitate to give the custody of the girl to her adoptive parent: but that would be no

---

[36] [1965] Ch. 831, 843, 846. Earlier cases are *Re Wilson* [1954] Ch. 733; *Re Wilby* [1956] P. 174; and *Re Marshall* [1957] Ch. 507.

[37] At that time the residence of the child in England was one of the jurisdictional requirements for adoption. This is no longer so. Hence it seems unlikely that the ordinary residence of the child in the foreign country will continue to be necessary for the recognition of foreign adoptions at common law.

[38] [1965] Ch. 226, 234, *per* Pennycuick J.; p. 855, *per* Salmon L.J.

[39] [1906] P. 135; *ante*, p. 194.

[40] At p. 842. *Cf.* Salmon L.J. at p. 854.

[41] In *Bedinger* v. *Graybill's Executor*, 302 S.W. 2d 594 (1957), the Kentucky Court of Appeals held that a husband could adopt his own wife in order that she might qualify as a "child" under his mother's will. In 1962 a French court allowed the English writer Somerset Maugham, then aged 88, to adopt his secretary, then aged 57, in order to defeat his only daughter's right to a *legitima portio* on her father's death. The adoption order was ultimately rescinded, but only on the ground that as Mr. Maugham was a British subject, the court should have applied English law.

reason for not allowing her to succeed to his property as his "child" on his death. A mere difference between the foreign law and English domestic law should not be sufficient for withholding recognition on this ground. In particular, the fact that the adopted person was over the age of eighteen, or that the adoption was not made by court order,[42] should not prevent recognition. A system of law which is prepared to recognise polygamous marriages[43] and extra-judicial divorces[44] should not be too squeamish about recognising foreign adoptions. The recognition in England of "overseas adoptions" may be refused on the ground of public policy[45]; but of course the recognition of adoptions made elsewhere in the British Isles may not.

Succession by adopted children

Before January 1, 1976, the English law on this topic was both complicated and uncertain. It was complicated because English law was altered more than once since adoption was first introduced in 1926, in order to enlarge the rights of succession of adopted children to their adoptive parents; and on each occasion it was thought necessary to preserve vested interests by transitional provisions in the amending statutes. The law was also uncertain, because the English statutes only dealt with the succession rights of children adopted in the British Isles.[46] The succession rights of children adopted in other foreign countries depended on the common law, and the cases were conflicting.[47]

Schedule 1 to the Children Act 1975, which came into force on January 1, 1976, has enormously simplified and improved the law. It provides that, in the case of deeds executed or testators or intestates dying on or after that date, an adopted child shall be treated in law as if he had been born to the adopter or adopters in wedlock, and as if he were not the child of any other person.[48] This means that he can take property as the child of his adoptive parents under a disposition made before as well as after the date of his adoption. So, if a testator dies on or after January 1, 1976, having by his will given property to A for life and then to A's children, children adopted by A before or after the death of the testator will be entitled to succeed, unless there is a contrary intention. An adopted child is defined to mean one adopted in the British Isles, or under an "overseas adoption,"[49] or one whose adoption is recognised at common law.[50] Thus, the succession rights

---

[42] The Children Act 1975, Sched. 1, para. 1(2)(d)(e) and (4) (Adoption Act 1976, s.38(1)(d)(e) and (2)) assumes that a foreign adoption can be recognised at common law although not made by court order.

[43] *Ante*, pp. 181–186.

[44] *Ante*, pp. 203–206.

[45] Adoption Act 1968, s.6(3)(a), (4) (Adoption Act 1976, s.53(2)(a), (3)).

[46] Adoption Act 1958, ss.16, 17; Adoption Act 1964, s.1(1).

[47] *Re Wilson* [1954] Ch. 733; *Re Wilby* [1956] P. 174; *Re Marshall* [1957] Ch. 507; *Re Valentine's Settlement* [1965] Ch. 831.

[48] Sched. 1, para. 3; and see paras. 5 and 6 (Adoption Act 1976, ss.39(1) and (2), 42, 46, 72(1)).

[49] *Ante*, p. 258.

[50] Children Act 1975, Sched. 1, para. 1(2) (Adoption Act 1976, s.38(1)).

of adopted children have now been assimilated to those of legitimated and legitimate children.

Although Schedule 1 of the Children Act does not say so in terms, it may be assumed that its provisions on succession are rules of English domestic law and as such only applicable if English law is the *lex successionis*. If the succession is governed by foreign law, the English courts would probably refer the whole question to the foreign *lex successionis*, leaving it to that law to determine whether, and to what extent, the child could succeed as a child of his adoptive parents, and what law determined this question.[51] But there is no English authority on this matter.

---

[51] *Ante*, pp. 246, 253.

Part Five

LAW OF OBLIGATIONS

CHAPTER 15

CONTRACTS[1]

THE PROPER LAW OF THE CONTRACT

Introduction

"The problem of ascertaining the *lex causae*" says Cheshire[2] "is more perplexing in the case of contracts than in almost any other topic." Two reasons for this may be suggested. First, contracts are almost infinitely various. It is unlikely that a mechanical choice of law rule which is appropriate for a contract to sell land will be equally appropriate for, *e.g.* a contract of employment or a contract for the carriage of goods by sea. Secondly, the problems that may arise are so numerous, as may easily be seen by looking at the Table of Contents of any book on the domestic law of contract. It is unlikely that a mechanical choice of law rule which is appropriate for essential validity will be equally appropriate for questions of offer and acceptance, capacity of parties, formalities or illegality.

In the English conflict of laws most of these matters are governed by a flexible rule known as the "proper law" of the contract.

> "The proper law of the contract," said Lord Wright in a leading case,[3] "means that law which the English . . . court is to apply in determining the obligations under the contract. English law in deciding these matters has refused to treat as conclusive, rigid or arbitrary criteria such as *lex loci contractus* or *lex loci solutionis*, and has treated the matter as depending on the intention of the parties to be ascertained in each case on a consideration of the terms of the contract, the situation of the parties, and generally on all the surrounding facts. It may be that the parties have in terms in their agreement expressed what law they intend to govern, and in that case prima facie their intention will be effectuated by the court. But in most cases they do not do so. The parties may not have thought of the matter at all. Then the court has to impute an intention, or to determine for the parties

---

[1] The reader should realise that there are more reported cases on this topic than on any other topic in the English conflict of laws except possibly domicile. An adequate analysis of all of them would require a chapter of 100 pages. All that can be done, therefore, is to call attention to general trends without descending to too much detail.

This chapter does not deal with marriage settlement contracts, which are considered in Chap. 25, *post.*

[2] Cheshire and North, p. 196. Statements by American writers are to the same effect: "No topic in the conflict of laws is more confused than that which deals with the law applying to the validity of contracts" (Beale, Vol. 2, p. 1077). "There is no topic in the conflict of laws in regard to which there is greater uncertainty than that of contract" (Lorenzen, p. 261).

[3] *Mount Albert Borough Council* v. *Australasian etc., Assurance Society Ltd.* [1938] A.C. 224, 240.

what is the proper law which, as just and reasonable persons, they ought [to] or would have intended if they had thought about the question when they made the contract."

Before we consider how the English courts determine the proper law of a contract, it may be instructive to consider briefly two other alternatives, both mentioned by Lord Wright in the passage just quoted, which have sometimes been relied on by courts or advocated by writers. These are the law of the place of contracting and the law of the place of performance.

Law of the place of contracting. This law was the one most usually relied upon by English courts until 1865[4] and by the courts of some American states, including New York, until 1954.[5] Its advantages are said to be those of certainty and predictability, both of which are important in commercial transactions. "There can only be one place in which a contract is made, and what that place is can never be subject to serious doubt."[6] But its disadvantages are many. First, the place of contracting may be fraudulently selected in order to give validity to an otherwise invalid contract. Secondly, the place of contracting may be fortuitous and have no real connection with the contract. It is unreasonable to say that a contract made between two Englishmen whereby one agrees to build a house for the other in England must be governed by French law merely because the letter of acceptance was posted in Paris. Thirdly, it may be impossible to determine the place of contracting until the contract is concluded. This can easily happen when the parties are negotiating from different countries, which of course is a common situation in the conflict of laws. For parties do not enter into negotiations with one of them labelled "offeror" and the other "offeree"; the contract is concluded when a firm offer is unconditionally accepted; and again the place of contracting may be quite fortuitous. Fourthly, it may be impossible to determine the place of contracting without arguing in a circle, as when an offer is posted from London and an acceptance from Hamburg, and a telegraphic revocation of the offer reaches the offeree before the letter of acceptance reaches the offeror. By English law, there is a contract made in Germany; by German law, there is no contract, but if there was one, it would be made in England. These considerations reduce the force of the predictability argument almost to vanishing point.

Law of the place of performance. The great advantage of this is that, besides avoiding the difficulties so far considered, it is based on an internal or substantial connection between the contract and its governing law instead of an external and fortuitous one. Whatever else the place of per-

---

[4] The law of the place of contracting was abandoned by the Privy Council in *P. & O. Steam Navigation Co.* v. *Shand* (1865) 3 Moo.P.C.(N.S.) 272 and by the Exchequer Chamber in *Lloyd* v. *Guibert* (1865) L.R. 1 Q.B. 115.

[5] The law of the place of contracting was abandoned by the New York Court of Appeals in *Auten* v. *Auten*, 308 N.Y. 155; 124 N.E. 2d 99 (1954). "Massachusetts is the only American state that has adhered consistently to this rule to the exclusion of all other rules": Leflar, p. 297 n.

[6] Beale, p. 1091. The statement, as will be seen, is demonstrably untrue.

formance may be, it is not fortuitous. Hence "the arguments in its favour are undoubtedly very weighty."[7] But it has formidable difficulties of its own. First, the law of the place of performance furnishes no solution if the contract is bilateral (as most commercial contracts are) and each party has to perform in a different country (as is common in a conflict of laws situation). Secondly, the law of the place of performance furnishes no solution if the place of performance is optional, as when an international loan secured by debentures is repayable at the debenture-holder's option either in New York or London.

Origin and development of the proper law doctrine

The English proper law doctrine can be traced back at least as far as Huber, a seventeenth-century Dutch jurist whose influence on the English conflict of laws has been profound. Having stated that contracts are entirely governed as regards form and substance by the *lex loci contractus*, Huber in effect retracts his statement by warning the reader that "if the parties in contracting have another place in mind," the *lex loci contractus* should not prevail.[8] Unfortunately Huber sought to buttress his argument by citing a misleading text from Justinian's Digest[9]: "*Contraxisse unusquisque in eo loco intelligitur in quo ut solveret se obligavit.*" This fiction has produced a curious misapprehension (echoes of which can still be heard to this day[10]) that any law other than that of the place of contracting can claim application only by masquerading as a *lex loci contractus*.

The first English case to show Huber's influence was *Robinson v. Bland*,[11] where Lord Mansfield said: "The general rule established *ex comitate et jure gentium* is that the place where the contract is made, and not where the action is brought, is to be considered in expounding and enforcing the contract. But this rule admits of an exception where the parties at the time of making the contract had a view to a different kingdom." He quoted Huber's statement and the Digest text cited above. This case is the *fons et origo* of the proper law doctrine in the English conflict of laws.

However, during the next hundred years English judges continued to rely on the law of the place of contracting more frequently than on any other law. But in 1865 the law of the place of contracting was finally abandoned in favour of the proper law. The case which shows the transition most clearly is *P. & O. Steam Navigation Co. v. Shand*.[12] The plaintiff, who had been appointed Chief Justice of Mauritius, took a ticket in Eng-

---

[7] Lorenzen, p. 289.

[8] For translations of and comments on Huber's *De Conflictu Legum*, see Lorenzen, Chap. 6, and Llewelfryn Davies (1937) 18 B.Y.I.L. 49. The statements quoted in the text are Nos. 5 and 10.

[9] D. 44, 7, 21: "Everyone is deemed to have contracted in that place in which he is bound to perform."

[10] In *British Controlled Oilfields Ltd. v. Stagg* [1921] W.N. 319 and again in *Golden Acres Ltd. v. Queensland Estates Ltd.* [1969] St.R.Qd. 378, the contract was executed in one country but contained a clause providing that it should be deemed to have been entered into in another. In each case the court assumed that this clause was intended to select the governing law.

[11] (1760) 1 W.Bl. 257, 258–259.

[12] (1865) 3 Moo. P.C.(N.S.) 272.

land for his passage from Southampton to Alexandria and from Suez to Mauritius on board the defendants' steamships. An exemption clause excluded the defendants' liability for loss of or damage to passengers' luggage. The plaintiff's luggage was lost in Egypt. The Supreme Court of Mauritius held that the contract was governed by French law (which prevailed at Mauritius) and that by that law the defendants were liable in spite of the exemption clause. The Privy Council reversed this decision. The judgment of a weak Board (consisting of Knight-Bruce and Turner L.JJ. and Coleridge J.) begins by laying down the general rule that contracts are governed by the *lex loci contractus*, and then seeks to justify it on a somewhat specious ground:

> "The general rule is, that the law of the country where a contract is made governs as to the nature, the obligation and the interpretation of it. The parties to a contract are either the subjects of the Power there ruling or as temporary residents owe it temporary allegiance: in either case equally they must be understood to submit to the law there prevailing, and to agree to its actions upon their contract."

But then the judgment (which perhaps, like the Book of Genesis, was written by three different hands) goes on to stress the fact that the greater part of the performance was to be on board two English ships "which for this purpose carry their country with them," and that the application of English law must have been intended by both parties. The decision is not a very good advertisement for the *lex loci contractus*. For suppose that the plaintiff was a Frenchman who took his ticket and boarded the ship at a French port; or that the contract was made in Mauritius and the voyage was to be in the reverse direction. In either case the application of the *lex loci contractus* would lead to the opposite result; but surely in both cases the decision should be that English law was applicable.

Formulation of the proper law doctrine

The doctrine of the proper law, emphasising as it does the freedom of the parties to choose the law which should govern their contract, was congenial to nineteenth-century English judges because it was in tune with Benthamite doctrines of freedom of contract. The following are some well-known formulations of the doctrine, derived from leading cases:

> "It is necessary to consider by what general law the parties intended that the transaction should be governed, or rather to what general law it is just to presume that they have submitted themselves" (Willes J. in 1865[13]).
>
> "Their intention will be ascertained by the intention expressed in the contract if any, which will be conclusive" (Lord Atkin in 1937[14]).

---

[13] *Lloyd* v. *Guibert* (1865) L.R. 1 Q.B. 115, 120–121.

[14] *R.* v. *International Trustee for the Protection of Bondholders A/G* [1937] A.C. 500, 529. According to Lord Wright (*Legal Essays and Addresses*, p. 164) Lord Atkin must have meant "prima facie conclusive."

"It is now well settled that by English law . . . the proper law of the contract is the law which the parties intended to apply" (Lord Wright in 1939[15]).

It will be seen from the first of these quotations that, as so often happened, there is a fatal ambiguity lurking in Willes J.'s formulation: did he mean that the proper law is the law intended by these parties, or the law which reasonable men in the position of these parties would presumably have intended? Should the doctrine be formulated subjectively or objectively? This is a question which has long been controversial among English writers.[16] Dicey preferred the subjective formulation; and, largely because of his influence, the subjective formulation was the fashionable one at least until 1939. But the difficulty is that to try to ascertain what would have been the intention of the contracting parties if they had considered the matter is often a fruitless task, since, in cases where there is no express choice, "neither party has given it a thought, and neither has formed an intention upon it; still less can it be said that they have any common intention."[17] Westlake and Cheshire preferred an objective formulation. According to them, the proper law is the law with which the contract has the closest and most real connection. As will be seen from the following quotation, there has been a judicial reaction in favour of this view during the last thirty years, and the pendulum has swung back sharply towards a more objective formulation:

"The proper law of the contract [is] the system of law by reference to which the contract was made or that with which the transaction had its closest and most real connection" (Lord Simonds in 1951[18]).

This formulation was adopted by the House of Lords in *Re United Railways of the Havana and Regla Warehouses Ltd.*[19] in 1961 and since then has been almost invariably used by English judges.[20]

Unfortunately, there is some doubt whether the correct formulation is the law of the country, or the system of law, with which the transaction had its closest and most real connection. Lord Denning in *Re United Railways* adopted the former and Lord Morris the latter. In *Rossano v. Manufacturers Life Insurance Co.*[21] McNair J. found that Egypt was the country, but Ontario law was the system of law, with which the contract had its

---

[15] *Vita Food Products Inc.* v. *Unus Shipping Co.* [1939] A.C. 277, 289–290.
[16] See, *e.g.* Dicey and Morris, pp. 753–758, 769–770; Westlake, s.212; Cheshire and North, pp. 197–202; F. A. Mann (1950) 3 Int. L.Q. 60, 597; Morris (1950) 3 Int.L.Q. 197.
[17] *The Assunzione* [1954] P. 150, 164, *per* Singleton L.J.
[18] *Bonython* v. *Commonwealth of Australia* [1951] A.C. 201, 219. Lord Simonds evidently derived his statement from the judgment of Starke J. in *Goldsborough Mort & Co.* v. *Hall* (1949) 78 C.L.R. 1, 27.
[19] [1961] A.C. 1007, *per* Lord Denning at p. 1068; *per* Lord Morris at p. 1081.
[20] *Rossano* v. *Manufacturers Life Insurance Co.* [1963] 2 Q.B. 352; *Tzortzis* v. *Monark Line A/B* [1968] 1 W.L.R. 406; *Whitworth Street Estates Ltd.* v. *James Miller and Partners Ltd.* [1970] A.C. 583; *Compagnie Tunisienne de Navigation S.A.* v. *Compagnie d'Armement Maritime S.A.* [1971] A.C. 572; *Coast Lines Ltd.* v. *Hudig and Veder Chartering N/V* [1972] 2 Q.B. 34; *Amin Rasheed Shipping Corporation* v. *Kuwait Insurance Co.* [1984] A.C. 50, 61.
[21] *Supra*, at pp. 361, 368–369.

closest and most real connection; and he applied the latter, holding that Lord Denning's statement must have been a slip. In *Whitworth Street Estates Ltd.* v. *James Miller and Partners Ltd.*[22] Lord Denning admitted that this was so. But when that case reached the House of Lords Lord Reid said that "the two tests must be combined"[23] and Lord Hodson said that he did not himself "see that this variation of language is important, although in some contexts one word may be more appropriate than another."[24] In *Amin Rasheed Shipping Corporation* v. *Kuwait Insurance Co.*[25] it is obvious that the House of Lords thought that Kuwait was the country, but English law was the system of law, with which the contract had its closest and most real connection, though they did not say so; and they applied the latter. If we have to choose between the two formulations, it would seem that "system of law" is the better.

Renvoi

The proper law applies either because the parties have chosen it or because it is the law most closely connected with the contract. In the absence of strong evidence to the contrary, the parties must be deemed to have intended to refer to the domestic rules and not to the conflict rules of their chosen law; and the connection with a given legal system is a connection with substantive legal rules and not with conflict rules. Hence it has been laid down by the Court of Appeal that "the principle of renvoi finds no place in the law of contract."[26]

Ascertainment of the proper law

When ascertaining the proper law of a contract, English judges inquire first, whether there was an express selection of the proper law by the parties; secondly, if not, whether there was an implied selection; thirdly, if not, with which system of law did the transaction have its closest and most real connection. There is inevitably some overlap between the second stage and the third. These three stages will now be discussed in turn.

(1) Express selection of the proper law

"When the intention of the parties to a contract, as to the law governing the contract, is expressed in words, this expressed intention in general determines the proper law of the contract."[27] "Parties are entitled to agree

---

[22] [1969] 1 W.L.R. 377, 380.
[23] [1970] A.C. 583, 604. *Cf.* Lord Reid in *Compagnie Tunisienne de Navigation S.A.* v. *Compagnie d'Armement Maritime S.A.* [1971] A.C. 572, 583F ("country or system of law").
[24] [1970] A.C. 583, 606.
[25] [1984] A.C. 50.
[26] *Re United Railways of the Havana and Regla Warehouses Ltd.* [1960] Ch. 52, 96–97, 115, disapproving a statement by Lord Wright in *Vita Food Products Inc.* v. *Unus Shipping Co.* [1939] A.C. 227, 292, which was probably a *lapsus calami*: Falconbridge, p. 404. For renvoi, see *post*, Chap. 30. *Cf. Amin Rasheed Shipping Corporation* v. *Kuwait Insurance Co.* [1984] A.C. 50, 61–62, *per* Lord Diplock.
[27] Dicey and Morris, Rule 145, Sub-Rule 1, p. 753.

what is to be the proper law of their contract. . . . There have been from time to time suggestions that parties ought not to be so entitled, but in my view there is no doubt that they are entitled to make such an agreement, and I see no good reason why, subject it may be to some limitations, they should not be so entitled."[28] If the parties choose the proper law of the contract they relieve the court of the difficult task of ascertaining it when the facts are nicely balanced between two systems of law. To allow them to do so thus injects some certainty into the English proper law doctrine, which has sometimes been criticised on the ground that it may take a lawsuit to determine what law governs. Moreover, by not pleading foreign law, the parties can always make English law applicable to a contract unconnected in any way with English law, because if foreign law is not pleaded English law is applied.[29] A striking illustration of this is afforded by *Suisse Atlantique Société d'Armement Maritime S.A.* v. *N.V. Rotterdamsche Kolen Centralen*,[30] where a contract made between Swiss shipowners and Dutch charterers for the carriage of coal from the United States to ports in Belgium, Holland and Germany was treated as governed by English law, although it had no connection of any kind with English law except that it contained a clause providing for arbitration in London. Presumably neither party pleaded that any other law than English law was applicable.

The leading case on the freedom of the parties to choose the proper law is *Vita Food Products Inc.* v. *Unus Shipping Co.*,[31] which requires close attention. The defendant, a company incorporated in Nova Scotia, agreed in Newfoundland to carry a cargo of herrings from Newfoundland to New York in a Nova Scotian ship and deliver them there to the plaintiff, a New York corporation. Bills of lading were signed in Newfoundland by the agents of the parties. The Newfoundland Carriage of Goods by Sea Act 1932 provided in section 1 that "subject to the provisions of this Act" the Rules set out in the Schedule thereto should have effect in relation to the carriage of goods by sea from any port in Newfoundland to any other port. These Rules (generally known as the Hague Rules) were identical with those scheduled to the United Kingdom Carriage of Goods by Sea Act 1924 and were settled by an international Conference held at Brussels in 1922 and 1923. Section 3 of the Newfoundland Act provided that "every bill of lading issued in Newfoundland which contains or is evidence of any contract to which the Rules apply shall contain an express statement that it is to have effect subject to the provisions of the Rules." Owing to the negligence of the parties in using obsolete forms the bills of lading did not contain the statement required by section 3. Both the Rules and the bills of lading exempted the carrier from liability for damage due to the negli-

---

[28] *Whitworth Street Estates Ltd.* v. *James Miller and Partners Ltd.* [1970] A.C. 583, 603, *per* Lord Reid. The statement was *obiter* because there was no express choice of the proper law in that case.

[29] *Ante*, p. 41.

[30] [1967] 1 A.C. 361.

[31] [1939] A.C. 277. For a detailed comment on this case, see Morris and Cheshire (1940) 56 L.Q.R. 320. The pleadings were made available to the present author by the Clerk to the Privy Council.

gence of the master. The bills also contained a statement that "this contract shall be governed by English law."

During the voyage the ship ran into a gale and owing to the negligence of the master ran aground off the coast of Nova Scotia. The herrings were unloaded and forwarded in a damaged condition to New York. The plaintiffs sued the defendants in Nova Scotia for failure to deliver the cargo in like condition as received on board. They claimed that the defendants operated the ship as a common carrier and so were insurers of the safety of the cargo. The defendants pleaded that the bills of lading, or alternatively the Rules, exempted them from liability. The plaintiffs alleged that the bills of lading were illegal, null and void because of their failure to incorporate the statement required by section 3 of the Act; and that therefore the defendants could not take advantage of any of the exemptions from liability provided by the Rules or by the bills of lading.

The Privy Council rejected the plaintiffs' claim. They held (1) that since section 1 was the dominant section, the plaintiffs' contention that the Rules could not apply unless the terms of section 3 were complied with could not be accepted; (2) that English law was the proper law of the contract; (3) that the failure to comply with section 3 did not make the bills of lading illegal by Newfoundland law; and (4) that even if it did, illegality by the *lex loci contractus* was not fatal. The statement that English law was the proper law was only a dictum, because it was held that the failure to comply with section 3 of the Act did not make the bills of lading illegal under Newfoundland law. Hence the decision would have been the same whatever the proper law of the contract.

Lord Wright said that "where the English rule that intention is the test applies, and where there is an express statement by the parties of their intention to select the law of the contract, it is difficult to see what qualifications are possible, provided the intention expressed is bona fide and legal, and provided there is no reason for avoiding the choice on the ground of public policy."[32] It might have been supposed that an attempt to evade the application of an internationally agreed set of Rules expressly applicable to all outward shipments from Newfoundland was not bona fide and was a reason for avoiding the choice on the ground of public policy.[33] It is difficult to attach a meaning to Lord Wright's statement that the choice must be "legal" since he did not indicate by what law the legality of the choice was to be tested. He proceeded to dispose of the objection that the contract was not connected in any way with English law by stating, first, that "connection with English law is not as a matter of principle essential"; and secondly, that there was a connection with English law because "the underwriters are likely to be English" and "parties may reasonably desire that the familiar principles of English commercial law should apply."[34]

---

[32] At p. 290.
[33] The gap thus revealed in the Hague Rules was closed by article X of the new Hague-Visby Rules scheduled to the Carriage of Goods by Sea Act 1971. See Morris (1979) 95 L.Q.R. 61, and *infra*.
[34] At p. 291.

Neither of these suggested connections with English law seems very convincing.

In *The Hollandia*[35] the House of Lords held that carriers cannot contract out of the amended Hague-Visby Rules scheduled to the Carriage of Goods by Sea Act 1971, whether by a choice of law clause or a choice of jurisdiction clause or otherwise. Lord Diplock said:

> "The Carriage of Goods by Sea Act 1971 deliberately abandoned what may conveniently be termed the 'clause paramount' technique employed in section 3 of the Carriage of Goods by Sea Act 1924, the Newfoundland counterpart of which provided the occasion for wide-ranging dicta in *Vita Food Products Inc.* v. *Unus Shipping Co.* Although the actual decision in that case would have been the same if the relevant Newfoundland statute had been in the terms of the 1971 Act, those dicta have no application to the construction of the latter Act and this has rendered it no longer necessary to embark upon what I have always found to be an unrewarding task of ascertaining precisely what those dicta meant."

The question arises whether the parties are free to select a proper law with which their contract has no connection whatsoever, not even the tenuous ones suggested by Lord Wright in the *Vita Food* case. This problem gives rise to the following dilemma: there is need to prevent the parties from evading the mandatory provisions of the law with which the contract is objectively most closely connected; but there is also need to enable them to submit their contract to a law connected with it through financial, commercial or other links not relevant to the decision of the court and hence not disclosed to it.[36] "In international transactions, particularly on commodity markets where the same shipment of goods may be bought and sold many times before delivery of the actual goods to the last buyer, it is of great commercial convenience that all the contracts relating to such sales should be subject to the same proper law irrespective of the place of shipment or discharge, the residence or nationality of the parties, or the place where the contract was made."[37] On the other hand, the court "will not necessarily regard" an express choice of law "as being the governing consideration where a system of law is chosen which has no real or substantial connection with the contract looked upon as a whole."[38] The reason is that the lack of connection may be evidence of an evasive intent.

There appears to be no reported case in which an English court has

---

[35] [1983] 1 A.C. 565.

[36] Dicey and Morris, p. 755.

[37] *Compagnie Tunisienne de Navigation S.A.* v. *Compagnie d'Armement Maritime S.A.* [1971] A.C. 572, 609F, *per* Lord Diplock.

[38] *Re Helbert Wagg & Co. Ltd.'s Claim* [1956] Ch. 323, 341, *per* Upjohn J. *Cf.* Denning L.J. in *Boissevain* v. *Weil* [1949] 1 K.B. 482, 491 and Lord Denning M.R. in *The Fehmarn* [1958] 1 W.L.R. 159, 162. But contrast Lord Denning M.R. in *Tzortzis* v. *Monark Line A/ B* [1968] 1 W.L.R. 406, 411: "It is clear that, if there is an express clause in a contract providing what the proper law is to be, that is conclusive in the absence of some public policy to the contrary."

refused to give effect to an express choice of the proper law[39]; nor have the qualifications stated by Lord Wright in the *Vita Food* case[40] ever been judicially discussed.

Sometimes the legislature intervenes to limit the effect of an express choice of law where the chosen law is foreign and where, but for the choice, English law would have governed the contract.[41] In such cases the choice of foreign law is valid but nevertheless the mandatory provisions of English law apply. It is less clear what the result would be if the parties choose a law (English or foreign) in order to avoid the mandatory provisions of the system of law with which the contract had its closest and most real connection.

Incorporation of foreign law. A distinction must be drawn between the parties' express selection of the proper law of the contract, and their incorporation of some of the provisions of a foreign law other than the proper law as a term or terms of the contract. It is open to the parties to an English contract (subject to any statutory prohibition to the contrary[42]) to agree that their rights and liabilities shall be determined in accordance with the relevant articles of the French Civil Code. The effect is not to make French law the proper law but rather to incorporate the French articles as contractual terms into an English contract. This is a convenient "shorthand" alternative to setting out the French articles verbatim. It often happens that statutes governing the liability of a sea carrier, such as the English Carriage of Goods by Sea Acts 1924 or 1971 or the American Carriage of Goods by Sea Acts 1893 or 1936, are thus incorporated in a contract governed by a law other than that of which the statute forms part.[43] The statute then operates not as a statute but as a set of contractual terms agreed upon by the parties.

The distinction between incorporation of foreign law and an express choice of the proper law emerges most clearly if there is a change in the law between the time of making the contract and its performance. It is well settled that the proper law is a living law and must be applied as it is when the contract is to be performed and not as it was when the contract was made.[44] Thus legislation passed in the country of the proper law may have the effect of modifying or discharging the contractual obligation, *e.g.* by reducing the rate of interest[45] or declaring a gold value clause invalid.[46] On

[39] The doubts of Langton J. in *The Torni* [1932] P. 27, 41 hardly amount to a decision on the point. They were not shared by the Court of Appeal: [1932] P. 78. The decision of the Court of Appeal was itself dissented from in the *Vita Food* case at pp. 298–300.

[40] *Ante*, p. 272.

[41] See, *e.g.* Unfair Contract Terms Act 1977, s.27(2), *post*, p. 280.

[42] *Post*, pp. 279–280.

[43] For examples, see *Dobell* v. *S.S. Rossmore Co. Ltd.* [1895] 2 Q.B. 408; *Stafford Allen & Sons Ltd.* v. *Pacific Steam Navigation Co.* [1956] 1 W.L.R. 629; *Adamastos Shipping Co. Ltd.* v. *Anglo-Saxon Petroleum Co.* [1959] A.C. 133.

[44] *Re Chesterman's Trusts* [1923] 2 Ch. 466, 478; *Perry* v. *Equitable Life Assurance Society* (1929) 45 T.L.R. 468; *De Béeche* v. *South American Stores Ltd.* [1935] A.C. 148; *Kahler* v. *Midland Bank* [1950] A.C. 24; *Re Helbert Wagg & Co. Ltd.'s Claim* [1956] Ch. 323, 341; *Rossano* v. *Manufacturers Life Insurance Co.* [1963] 2 Q.B. 352, 362.

[45] *Barcelo* v. *Electrolytic Zinc Co. of Australasia Ltd.* (1932) 48 C.L.R. 391.

[46] *R.* v. *International Trustee for the Protection of Bondholders A/G* [1937] A.C. 500.

the other hand, where a foreign statute is incorporated in a contract as a contractual term, it remains part of the contract, although as a statute it may have been amended or repealed.

(2) Implied selection of the proper law

"When the intention of the parties to a contract with regard to the law governing the contract is not expressed in words, their intention is to be inferred from the terms and nature of the contract, and from the general circumstances of the case, and such inferred intention determines the proper law of the contract."[47] In the absence of an express selection "the only certain guide is to be found in applying sound ideas of business, convenience, and sense to the language of the contract itself, with a view to discovering from it the true intention of the parties."[48] In some cases it is possible thus to "discover" an implied common intention of the parties to a contract. If they agree that the courts of a given country shall have exclusive jurisdiction over the contract, and especially if they agree that arbitration shall take place in a given country, this usually permits the inference that the law of that country is the proper law of the contract.[49] This is not an express but an implied choice of law. "The provision in a contract (*e.g.* of sale) for English arbitration imports English law as the law governing the transaction, and those familiar with international business are aware how frequent such a provision is even where the parties are not English and the transactions are carried on completely outside England."[50] However, the principle was stretched to the limit in *Tzortzis* v. *Monark Line A/B*,[51] where a contract made and to be performed in Sweden for the sale of a ship by Swedish sellers to Greek buyers had no connection whatsoever with English law except that it contained a clause providing for arbitration in London. Yet the Court of Appeal held that English law was the proper law of the contract. Salmon L.J. said that the arbitration clause "raises an irresistible inference which overrides all other factors."[52] It is now clear, however, that this is putting the matter much too high. In *Compagnie Tunisienne de Navigation S.A.* v. *Compagnie d'Armement Maritime S.A.*[53] a contract for the carriage of oil by sea from one Tunisian port to another, made in Paris between a Tunisian company and French shipowners, had no connection with any other system of law than French law except for a clause providing for arbitration in London. The House of Lords held that French law was the proper law and that the arbitration clause was merely one of the factors to be taken into account. "It would

---

[47] Dicey and Morris, Rule 145, Sub-Rule 2, p. 761.
[48] *Jacobs* v. *Crédit Lyonnais* (1884) 12 Q.B.D. 589, 601, *per* Bowen L.J.
[49] *Hamlyn* v. *Talisker Distillery* [1894] A.C. 202; *Spurrier* v. *La Cloche* [1902] A.C. 446; *N.V. Kwik Hoo Tong Handel Maatschappij* v. *James Finlay & Co.* [1927] A.C. 604; *Tzortzis* v. *Monark Line A/B* [1968] 1 W.L.R. 406.
[50] *Vita Food Products Inc.* v. *Unus Shipping Co.* [1939] A.C. 277, 290, *per* Lord Wright.
[51] *Supra.*
[52] At p. 413.
[53] [1971] A.C. 572.

be highly anomalous," said Lord Reid,[54] "if our law required the mere fact that arbitration is to take place in England to be decisive as to the proper law of the contract." "An arbitration clause," said Lord Wilberforce,[55] "must be treated as an indication, to be considered together with the rest of the contract and relevant surrounding facts. Always it will be a strong indication. . . . But in some cases it must give way where other indications are clear." It is true that arbitrators are, as often as not, tradesmen and not lawyers, and that as a rule it is better for a lay tribunal not to have to concern itself with questions of foreign law. But it is also true that commercial arbitrators in the City of London, even when they are not lawyers, are so sophisticated and experienced that they are quite capable of ascertaining and applying a foreign law.

It has sometimes been said that the courts will lean in favour of applying a system of law under which the contract would be valid rather than one under which it would be void, on the ground that the parties must have intended their contract to be valid.[56] But the courts have been rightly cautious about making use of this argument.[57] If one accepts the principle that the parties' freedom to choose the proper law is not limited to systems of law which have a visible connection with the contract,[58] one is driven to an especially cautious application of the argument in favour of validity, particularly in relation to standard form contracts exhibiting a gross disparity of bargaining power between the parties.

(3) The closest and most real connection

"When the intention of the parties to a contract with regard to the law governing it is not expressed and cannot be inferred from the circumstances, the contract is governed by the system of law with which the transaction has its closest and most real connection."[59] In the absence of an express or implied selection of the proper law "the court has to impute an intention or to determine for the parties what is the proper law which, as just and reasonable persons, they ought to or would have intended if they had thought about the question when they made the contract."[60] The judge, putting himself in the place of the reasonable man, determines the proper law for the parties. He attempts to ascertain not the actual intention of the contracting parties, because that is non-existent, but "how a just and

[54] At p. 584E.
[55] At p. 600C–D.
[56] P. & O. Steam Navigation Co. v. Shand (1865) 3 Moo.P.C.(N.S.) 272; N.V. Handel Maatschappij J. Smits v. English Exporters (London) Ltd. [1955] 2 Lloyd's Rep. 317; Coast Lines Ltd. v. Hudig and Veder Chartering N.V. [1972] 2 Q.B. 34, 44F, 48C.
[57] British South Africa Co. v. De Beers Consolidated Mines Ltd. [1910] 2 Ch. 502, 513; Sayers v. International Drilling Co. [1971] 1 W.L.R. 1176, 1184F.
[58] Ante, p. 273.
[59] Dicey and Morris, Rule 145, Sub-Rule 3, p. 769.
[60] Mount Albert Borough Council v. Australasian etc. Assurance Society Ltd. [1938] A.C. 224, 240, per Lord Wright. In The Assunzione [1954] P. 150, 175, Singleton L.J. adopted this statement, but with the deliberate and significant omission of the words "or would," thus indicating a shift to a more objective formulation.

reasonable person would have regarded the problem,"[61] what intention "ordinary, reasonable and sensible business men would have been likely to have had if their minds had been directed to the question,"[62] and to the contingencies of which the judge is, but the parties may not have been, aware. In this inquiry "many matters have to be taken into consideration. Of these the principal are the place of contracting, the place of performance, the places of residence or business of the parties respectively, and the nature and subject-matter of the contract."[63]

The Assunzione[64] is an instructive illustration because the facts were so nicely balanced between French and Italian law that the Court of Appeal had to use a very delicate pair of scales in order to determine the proper law. The contract was one for the carriage of wheat from Dunkirk to Venice on board an Italian ship. The charterers were an organisation of French grain merchants. The wheat was shipped under an exchange agreement between the French and Italian Governments, but the Italian shipowners did not know this. The contract was negotiated by correspondence between brokers in France and brokers in Italy. It was formally concluded in Paris in the English language and in an English standard form. Freight and demurrage were payable in Italian currency in Italy. It was unanimously held that Italian law was the proper law of the contract. The decisive factor was that both parties had to perform in Italy.

Whitworth Street Estates Ltd. v. James Miller and Partners Ltd.[65] was another difficult case because the House of Lords was divided 3–2 ("a scarcely discernible majority"[66]). A Scottish company agreed to convert an English company's factory in Scotland into a bonded warehouse. The contract, which was made in Scotland, was in the standard form published by the Royal Institute of British Architects, a body composed of Scottish as well as English members. The architect was English and it was at his suggestion that the R.I.B.A. form was used. That form was "redolent of English law." Although the contract was made and to be performed in Scotland and its subject-matter was land situated in Scotland, a majority of the House of Lords (Lords Hodson, Guest and Dilhorne) held that English law was the proper law. Both the majority and the minority (Lords Reid and Wilberforce) emphasised that, contrary to the view of the Court of Appeal, the conduct of the parties after the making of the contract could not be considered in ascertaining the proper law, unless it amounted to an estoppel or to the making of a fresh contract.[67]

Until quite recently it was supposed that the ascertainment of the proper

---

[61] *The Assunzione, supra*, p. 176, *per* Singleton L.J.
[62] *The Assunzione* [1953] 1 W.L.R. 929, 939, *per* Willmer J.
[63] *Re United Railways of the Havana and Regla Warehouses Ltd.* [1960] Ch. 52, 91.
[64] [1954] P. 150. For comments on this important case, see Kahn-Freund (1954) 17 M.L.R. 255; Cheshire (1955–56) 32 B.Y.I.L. 123; Clarence Smith (1969) 18 I.C.L.Q. 449.
[65] [1970] A.C. 583.
[66] *Amin Rasheed Shipping Corporation* v. *Kuwait Insurance Co.* [1984] A.C. 50, 70, *per* Lord Wilberforce (who had been in the minority in the *Whitworth* case).
[67] At pp. 603, 606, 611, 614–615.

law could be assisted by presumptions in favour of the law of the place of contracting, or the law of the place of performance, or the *lex situs* if the contract related to an immovable, or the law of the ship's flag if the contract was for the carriage of goods by sea.[68] But the modern practice is to weigh the relevant factors without the aid of any presumption. The use of presumptions was deprecated by all three members of the Court of Appeal in *Coast Lines Ltd.* v. *Hudig and Veder Chartering N.V.*[69] It may be doubted whether there is any longer even the faintest of presumptions in favour of the law of the place of contracting.[70] The presumption that a contract relating to land is governed by the *lex situs* is one which seems to be rebutted[71] at least as often as it is applied.[72] Even the presumption in favour of the law of the flag has become virtually non-existent in modern times, at any rate so far as contracts made before the commencement of the voyage are concerned.[73] This is partly because of the rise of flags of convenience and partly because in modern commercial conditions the nationality of the ship is often a matter of indifference, or even unknown, to the cargo owner. It has however been repeatedly held that the law of the flag governs contracts made by the master during the voyage in virtue of his inherent authority.[74] This is convenient, for the master may have to act as agent of necessity for a multitude of cargo-owners whose contracts with the shipowner may be governed by different laws. But the practical importance of this is greatly reduced by the development of wireless and of international banking facilities.

Effect of statutes on contracts

As a general rule, a statute does not normally apply to a contract unless it forms part of the proper law of the contract, or unless (being a statute in force in the forum) it is procedural. This is true, *e.g.* of Stamp Acts,[75] statutes reducing the rate of interest,[76] statutes providing for moratoria[77]

---

[68] See, for instance, *R.* v. *International Trustee for the Protection of Bondholders A/G* [1937] A.C. 500, 529, *per* Lord Atkin; *Mount Albert Borough Council* v. *Australasian etc. Assurance Society Ltd.* [1938] A.C. 224, 240, *per* Lord Wright.

[69] [1972] 2 Q.B. 34, 44, 47, 50. *Cf.* Cheshire and North, p. 210.

[70] *Amin Rasheed Shipping Corporation* v. *Kuwait Insurance Co.* [1984] A.C. 50, 62, *per* Lord Diplock.

[71] *British South Africa Co.* v. *De Beers Consolidated Mines Ltd.* [1910] 2 Ch. 502; reversed on other grounds [1912] A.C. 52; *Re Smith* [1916] 2 Ch. 206; *Re Anchor Line (Henderson Brothers) Ltd.* [1937] Ch. 483; *Whitworth Street Estates Ltd.* v. *James Miller and Partners Ltd.* [1970] A.C. 583.

[72] *Mount Albert Borough Council* v. *Australasian etc. Assurance Society Ltd.* [1938] A.C. 224. See Dicey and Morris, Rule 153.

[73] See Dicey and Morris, pp. 853–854; *Chartered Mercantile Bank of India* v. *Netherlands India Steam Navigation Co.* (1883) 10 Q.B.D. 521; *The Industrie* [1894] P. 58; *The Adriatic* [1931] P. 241; *The Njegos* [1936] P. 90; *The Assunzione* [1954] P. 150; contrast *Coast Lines Ltd.* v. *Hudig and Veder Chartering N.V.* [1972] 2 Q.B. 34, where the law of the flag was the decisive consideration.

[74] *Lloyd* v. *Guibert* (1865) L.R. 1 Q.B. 115; *The Gaetano and Maria* (1882) 7 P.D. 137; *The August* [1891] P. 328.

[75] *e.g. Royal Exchange Assurance* v. *Vega* [1902] 2 K.B. 384.

[76] *Barcelo* v. *Electrolytic Zinc Co. of Australasia Ltd.* (1932) 48 C.L.R. 391; *Mount Albert Borough Council* v. *Australasian etc. Assurance Society Ltd.* [1938] A.C. 224.

[77] *Re Helbert Wagg & Co. Ltd.'s Claim* [1956] Ch. 323.

and statutes abrogating gold clauses.[78] It is equally true whether the statute forms part of English law or (unless the statute is procedural) of foreign law.

A distinction must be drawn between a statute which renders a contract void and one which renders it unenforceable. An English statute of the first type normally applies only to contracts governed by English law. But an English statute of the second type lays down a rule of procedure and is thus applicable in an English court irrespective of the proper law of the contract. The Statute of Frauds 1677 is perhaps the best known example.

Sometimes a statute deals both with the validity and with the enforceability of a contract. Thus, section 18 of the Gaming Act 1845 makes wagering contracts null and void. It also forbids suits being brought to recover money won on wagers. A wagering contract governed by foreign law is not caught by the first limb of the section, but, though valid, it is caught by the second limb.[79] Again, section 1(1) of the Law Reform (Miscellaneous Provisions) Act 1970 provides that an agreement between two persons to marry one another shall not have effect as a contract giving rise to legal rights, and that no action shall lie in England for breach of such an agreement, whatever the law applicable to the agreement. This means that no action can be brought in an English court for breach of promise of marriage, whatever the proper law of the contract.

An English statute may be applicable even if English law is not the proper law of the contract and the statute is not procedural. If the statute is according to its true construction applicable to the transaction in question, then it must be applied regardless of the proper law of the contract. It is what is sometimes called an "overriding" statute. A good example is furnished by the Defence Regulations 1939 which were considered in the leading case of *Boissevain* v. *Weil*.[80] A British subject, involuntarily resident in Monaco during the war, borrowed French francs from a Dutchman also so resident, and promised to repay him in sterling as soon as the law of England would allow her to do so. In borrowing foreign currency she contravened the Defence Regulations 1939 which, according to section 3(1) of the Emergency Powers (Defence) Act 1939, applied to all British subjects wherever resident. The House of Lords held that the contract was illegal and void, irrespective of its proper law.

A further example is furnished by the Employment Protection (Consolidation) Act 1978,[81] which provides that "for the purposes of this Act it is immaterial whether the law which (apart from this Act) governs any person's employment is the law of the United Kingdom, or of a part of the United Kingdom, or not." This does not mean that the Act applies to all contracts of employment in the world, regardless of their connection with the United Kingdom, because another section of the Act lays down that

---

[78] R. v. *International Trustee for the Protection of Bondholders A/G* [1937] A.C. 500.
[79] *Hill* v. *William Hill (Park Lane) Ltd.* [1949] A.C. 530, 579.
[80] [1950] A.C. 327.
[81] s.153(5), re-enacting earlier legislation, on which see F. A. Mann (1966) 82 L.Q.R. 316; Hughes (1967) 83 L.Q.R. 180; Unger (1967) 83 L.Q.R. 427, 428–433; F. A. Mann (1972–73) 46 B.Y.I.L. 117, 136–137.

certain of its provisions do not apply where under his contract of employment the employee ordinarily works outside Great Britain.[82] What it does mean is that the draftsman, instead of enacting (or leaving it to be assumed) that the Act only applies when the proper law of the contract of employment is that of some part of the United Kingdom, has cut across the normal rules of the conflict of laws and laid down his own rules for the application of the Act. His method has two advantages. First, it prevents the parties evading the Act by choosing a foreign law as the proper law of the contract of employment. Secondly, it secures the benefits of the Act to employees who work here for foreign employers and whose contracts of employment might well be governed by foreign law.

An even more important example is provided by the Unfair Contract Terms Act 1977. That Act imposes severe restrictions on the validity of exemption clauses in many kinds of contract, and restates the control of exemption clauses in contracts for the sale or supply of goods that had originally been imposed by the Supply of Goods (Implied Terms) Act 1973.[83] The provisions of the Act are mandatory; the parties cannot contract out of them.[84] To prevent them from doing so indirectly by selecting a foreign law as the proper law, section 27(2) provides that the Act has effect notwithstanding any contract term purporting to apply the law of some country outside the United Kingdom, if (a) the term appears to have been imposed wholly or mainly for the purpose of enabling the party imposing it to evade the application of the Act; or (b) in the making of the contract one of the parties dealt as consumer[85] and was then habitually resident in the United Kingdom and the essential steps necessary for the making of the contract were taken there. Section 27(2)(a) is a novelty in that it introduces for the first time a doctrine of evasion of law into English law.[86]

All these are examples of "overriding" statutes. The opposite of an overriding statute is a "self-denying" statute, one which does not apply even though it would be applicable under the normal rules of the conflict of laws. Examples are extremely rare, but one is furnished by section 27(1) of the Unfair Contract Terms Act 1977. This provides that where the proper law of a contract is the law of any part of the United Kingdom only by choice of the parties (and apart from that choice would be the law of some country outside the United Kingdom), certain provisions of the Act (including the most important ones) do not operate as part of the proper law. The two Law Commissions have explained why it was considered necessary to include section 27(1) in the Act.[87] They point out that the par-

---

[82] s.141, re-enacting earlier legislation, which is also discussed in the articles cited above.

[83] ss.5, 13. For comments on these sections, see F. A. Mann (1974) 90 L.Q.R. 42; Hall (1973) 22 I.C.L.Q. 740. For a comment on s.27 of the 1977 Act, see F. A. Mann (1978) 27 I.C.L.Q. 661. For earlier judicial attempts in Scotland and Australia to grapple with the problem, see *English* v. *Donnelly*, 1958 S.C. 494; *Kay's Leasing Corporation Pty. Ltd.* v. *Fletcher* (1964) 116 C.L.R. 124.

[84] Unless a contract is an "international supply contract" as defined in s.26. That definition follows closely the definition in the Uniform Laws on International Sales Act 1967.

[85] "Dealt as consumer" is widely defined by s.12.

[86] See *ante*, p. 153.

[87] *Second Report on Exemption Clauses*, Law Com. No. 69, Scots Law Com. No. 39, para. 232.

ties to contracts of which the proper law would otherwise be the law of some country other than England or Scotland often choose English law or Scots law as the proper law of their contracts, sometimes by an express term to that effect, more often through the medium of an arbitration clause.[88] The Commissions then point out that the effect of imposing the controls contained in the Act in relation to these contracts might well be to discourage foreign business men from agreeing to arbitrate their disputes in England or Scotland. The suggestion is that this would strike a heavy blow at the City of London as a centre for international arbitration.

We may as well face it: English law is now having to pay a heavy price for its decision to allow contracting parties almost unlimited freedom to choose the proper law. Section 27 of the Unfair Contract Terms Act 1977 is part of that price.

Advantages and disadvantages of the proper law doctrine

The English doctrine of the proper law is one of the outstanding contributions made by English lawyers to the general science of the conflict of laws. The doctrine has many advantages. First, it provides an all-embracing formula into which all types of contract can be fitted. Had it not been invented, it is quite likely that English courts would have had to develop different conflict rules for the validity of each type of contract. Secondly, it provides an all-embracing formula which (exceptions apart) governs all types of question that can arise in connection with a contract. Subject to a number of exceptions[89] the formation and validity of the contract, its interpretation and its discharge are all governed by the same law. It is open to the parties to agree that one aspect of the contract shall be governed by the law of one country (*e.g.* the law of the place of contracting) and another aspect by the law of another country (*e.g.* the law of the place of performance). There is no authority to the effect that "there can be but one proper law in respect of any given contract," but "the courts of this country will not split the contract readily and without good reason."[90] Thirdly, the obligations of both parties are governed by the same law. English law thus avoids some of the difficulties involved in a rigid theory of the *lex loci solutionis* adopted in some foreign countries.

Nevertheless the proper law doctrine has some disadvantages.[91] One is that, if the parties have not chosen the proper law, it may take a lawsuit to determine what law governs; and, if the contract is nicely balanced between one system of law and another, this lawsuit may ultimately be decided by a bare and "scarcely discernible" majority of the House of Lords.[92] To meet this objection, English judges have perhaps overstressed the freedom of the parties to choose the proper law and thus achieve certainty. This has encouraged the idea that the parties can readily escape

---

[88] *Ante*, p. 275.
[89] As to these, see *post*, pp. 284–291.
[90] *Kahler* v. *Midland Bank* [1950] A.C. 24, 42, *per* Lord MacDermott.
[91] Some of them were pointed out by Dixon J. in *McClelland* v. *Trustees Executors and Agency Co. Ltd.* (1936) 55 C.L.R. 483, 491–492.
[92] *e.g. Whitworth Street Estates Ltd.* v. *James Miller and Partners Ltd.* [1970] A.C. 583; *ante*, p. 277.

from the mandatory provisions of the objectively ascertained proper law. This in turn has meant that Parliament, when seeking to protect employees or consumers against the superior bargaining power of employers or suppliers of goods or services, has to guard against the possibility that the parties might seek to escape from the statutory controls by choosing a foreign law as the proper law of the contract. It has done so in tortuous language and by means of dubious techniques which must inevitably breed uncertainty and therefore litigation, and which do not commend themselves to the majority of conflict of laws lawyers.[93] Another disadvantage of the proper law doctrine is the opposite to this: the parties may select a proper law under which their contract (or a term therein) turns out to be invalid. At first sight at any rate it does not seem rational to hold them to a choice which has the result of disappointing their expectations.[94]

PARTICULAR TOPICS

We must now consider whether all the aspects of a contract are governed by its proper law or whether some aspects are governed by a different law. We shall find that while the proper law is always relevant, it is necessary to consider other laws in matters of formal validity, capacity of parties and illegality.

Formation of the contract

The term "formation" is used here to denote such requirements as offer and acceptance, consideration, and reality of consent. The question what law governs formal validity and capacity of parties is reserved for separate discussion.[95]

We begin with consideration because it is the easiest and least controversial. In English domestic law consideration is necessary for the validity of every contract not under seal. Other systems do not have this rule. In *Re Bonacina*[96] the Court of Appeal held that a promise to pay made in Italy by one Italian to another, but unsupported by consideration, constituted a debt provable in English bankruptcy proceedings. Hence an agreement can be a contract if it lacks one of the elements necessary for a valid contract by English domestic law, but not by its proper law.

More difficult problems are raised by cases of offer and acceptance, for the question here is whether an agreement has been concluded; hence it is arguing in a circle to refer the question either to the law of the place of contracting[97] or to the proper law of the contract. But there is no such difficulty in referring it to the putative proper law, *i.e.* the law which would have been the proper law of the contract if it had been concluded.[98] There

---

[93] See *ante*, pp. 279–280, nn. 81, 83.
[94] See Jaffey (1974) 23 I.C.L.Q. 1, and *post*, p. 289.
[95] *Post*, pp. 284–288.
[96] [1912] 2 Ch. 394.
[97] See the hypothetical example stated on p. 266, *ante*.
[98] Dicey and Morris, pp. 776–777; Cheshire and North, pp. 215–219; Wolff, p. 439; Anton, pp. 205–207.

is only one English decision on offer and acceptance in the conflict of laws. In *Albeko Schuhmaschinen* v. *Kamborian Shoe Machine Co. Ltd.*,[99] A in England wrote a letter to B in Switzerland in which A offered to appoint B his agent in Switzerland. B alleged that he posted a letter of acceptance in Switzerland, but that it was lost in the post. By English law, a contract is concluded when the letter of acceptance is posted, even if it is not received.[1] By Swiss law, a contract is concluded when the letter of acceptance is received by the offeror. Salmon J. held that there was no contract because it had not been proved that the letter of acceptance had in fact been posted. He expressed the view that if it had been, Swiss law would govern and there would still be no contract, because if a contract had been concluded, Swiss law would have been its proper law.

Wolff[2] points out that there are situations in which the application of the putative proper law would lead to grave injustice to one at least of the parties, and that in such situations a party must be able to rely on the law of his place of business or residence. Suppose, for instance, that an enterprising Danish yacht builder writes a letter to a well-known English yachtsman offering to build a yacht for him in Denmark. The Englishman puts the letter in his waste paper basket and does not reply to it. By Danish law, silence on the part of the offeree amounts to an acceptance of the offer; by English law it does not.[3] It would surely be wrong to hold the Englishman liable, even though Danish law is the putative proper law.

Offer and acceptance problems can sometimes be complicated by the requirement of consideration. A promise to keep an offer open is binding in Scots law but not in English law if there is no consideration. Suppose that a boilermaker in Scotland offers to manufacture a boiler and instal it in an English company's factory in England, and promises to keep the offer open for a week.[4] Would he be liable if within the week he revoked the offer but the English company accepted it? The question should probably be answered by applying the putative proper law.

There seems no reason in principle why this law should not also govern such matters as mistake or why the proper law should not govern misrepresentation, duress and undue influence. In *Mackender* v. *Feldia*[5]:

> The plaintiffs, Lloyd's underwriters, insured the defendant diamond merchants against the loss of their stock. The contract, which was made in England, contained a clause providing that it was to be governed by Belgian law and subject to the exclusive jurisdiction of the Belgian courts. But for this clause, English law would have been the proper law of the contract. Some diamonds were stolen from one of the defendants at Naples and they presented a claim against the plaintiffs which after inquiry was rejected. The plaintiffs brought an action in England claiming a declaration that the contract was void because

---

[99] (1961) 111 L.J. 519.
[1] *Household Fire Insurance Co.* v. *Grant* (1879) 4 Ex.D. 216.
[2] Wolff, p. 439.
[3] *Felthouse* v. *Bindley* (1862) 11 C.B.(N.S.) 869.
[4] Case put by Anton, pp. 205–206.
[5] [1967] 2 Q.B. 590.

the defendants had made a practice of smuggling diamonds into Italy and had failed to disclose this practice when the contract was made. They applied for leave to serve notice of the writ out of the jurisdiction under what is now Order 11, rule 1(1)(*d*)(i), of the Rules of the Supreme Court on the ground that the contract was made in England.[6] They countered the foreign jurisdiction clause by contending that the defendants' non-disclosure made the contract void and therefore the foreign jurisdiction clause was also void. But the Court of Appeal refused leave on the ground that the non-disclosure did not make the contract void but only voidable and therefore the clause must receive effect. They indicated that it would have been different if the contract had been void for mistake, *e.g. non est factum*.[7] Apparently they would have referred the effect of *non est factum* to English law *qua* the putative proper law.[8]

The solution here suggested, namely that questions of formation should be governed by the putative proper law, has the advantage that it submits the question to the same law as that which governs the essential validity of the contract. It has, however, been suggested[9] that questions of formation should be solved by considering who is suing whom. For instance, in the hypothetical yacht-building case mentioned above, the Englishman should not be bound because he should be able to rely on the law of his residence or place of business. But suppose that the Englishman sues the Danish yacht builder for not building the yacht: should not the builder be bound because by his own law there was a contract? Or suppose that an offer is sent by post from England to an offeree in a continental European country and that the acceptance is lost in the post. By English law there is a contract, but by the foreign law there is not. It is arguable that if the offeree sues the English offeror the latter should be bound, because by the law of his residence or place of business there was a contract; but that if the offeror sues the foreign offeree the latter should not be bound, because by the law of his residence or place of business there was not.

Formal validity

There is very little modern authority on what law governs the formal validity of a contract, no doubt because in modern systems of law formal requirements for the validity of a commercial contract have been reduced to a minimum, and because those which remain are usually regarded by English courts as procedural. There can be no doubt, however, that it is sufficient to comply with the formalities prescribed by the *lex loci contractus*, for *locus regit actum* is the time-honoured maxim. The justification for this is that the parties must be able to rely on local legal advice when making their contract. The question is whether compliance with the local for-

[6] *Ante*, p. 71.
[7] At p. 598, *per* Lord Denning M.R.; at p. 603 *per* Diplock L.J.
[8] It must be admitted that Diplock L.J.'s statement at p. 603 is rather confused, perhaps because he found the concept of the putative proper law "confusing": see at p. 602G. The judgments were delivered immediately at the conclusion of the argument.
[9] Jaffey (1975) 24 I.C.L.Q. 603.

malities is not only sufficient, but necessary; or, to put it differently, whether the maxim *locus regit actum* is in this context obligatory or facultative. Notwithstanding some early dicta to the contrary,[10] it is now generally agreed among English writers that it is sufficient to comply with the formalities prescribed by the proper law.[11] This is in accordance with reason, for why should two Englishmen be compelled to resort to the Swiss notarial form if they happen to be temporarily in Switzerland when contracting for the sale of land situated in England? Moreover, as we have seen,[12] the place of contracting is often uncertain and fortuitous.

It must however be borne in mind that the provisions of section 4 of the Statute of Frauds 1677 and of section 40 of the Law of Property Act 1925, which require written evidence for the enforceability of contracts of guarantee and contracts for the sale or other disposition of an interest in land, respectively, have been held to be procedural, and thus applicable to contracts within their terms which are made abroad and governed by a foreign proper law.[13]

Capacity of parties

There is an extraordinary dearth of English authority on the question of what law governs capacity to make a contract. There is only one decision (dating from 1800) and a few stray and contradictory dicta. But the topic has a theoretical interest and perhaps a practical importance[14] much greater than the sparseness of the case law would seem to suggest. Before the English and some American and Commonwealth cases are examined, let us consider the question on principle.

A person's capacity to contract can be looked at as an emanation of his status and therefore as governed by the law of his domicile. Alternatively, it can be considered as a factor determining the validity of the contract and therefore as governed by its proper law. There is general agreement among writers that in this context the proper law must be objectively ascertained. Any other view would lead to the unacceptable result that a minor or a married woman could confer capacity on himself or herself by agreeing that some more favourable system than the objectively ascertained proper law should govern the contract.[15]

Four hypothetical cases illustrate the difficulty of deciding between the law of the domicile and the proper law of the contract.

[10] *Trimbey* v. *Vignier* (1834) 1 Bing.N.C. 151, concerned with the indorsement of a negotiable instrument; *Alves* v. *Hodgson* (1797) 7 T.R. 241; *Clegg* v. *Levy* (1812) 3 Camp. 166; *Bristow* v. *Sequeville* (1850) 5 Exch. 275 (all concerned with failure to stamp a contract as required by the *lex loci contractus*).

[11] Dicey and Morris, Rule 148; Cheshire and North, pp. 219–220. Their views are indirectly supported by *Van Grutten* v. *Digby* (1862) 31 Beav. 561, a marriage settlement case.

[12] *Ante*, p. 266.

[13] *Leroux* v. *Brown* (1852) 12 C.B. 801; *post*, pp. 456–457.

[14] Its practical importance is likely to be enhanced by s.1 of the Family Law Reform Act 1969, which reduces the age of majority in English law from 21 to 18. The topic receives extended treatment here because of its intrinsic interest, which is perhaps due to the lack of authority.

[15] *Cf. Cooper* v. *Cooper* (1888) 13 App.Cas. 88, 108, where Lord Macnaghten said: "It is difficult to suppose that Mrs. Cooper could confer capacity on herself by contemplating a different country as the place where the contract was to be fulfilled."

(1) A domiciled Ruritanian aged twenty buys goods on credit from a London shop. Could he refuse to pay for them on the ground that by Ruritanian law minority ends at twenty-one and contracts made by minors cannot be enforced against them? Here we have a conflict of policy between Ruritanian law, anxious to protect its domiciliary (or national) from making an improvident bargain; and English law, which we may assume to be the *lex loci contractus*, the putative proper law, and (for what it is worth) the *lex fori*. Most students coming fresh to this topic say that the Ruritanian minor should be held liable because commercial convenience requires this result. In the great majority of cases this answer is surely correct. But if we change the facts and suppose (a) that the Ruritanian minor never left Ruritania, the contract being concluded by correspondence; (b) that the shopkeeper opened negotiations by sending him a catalogue depicting, *e.g.* attractive-looking motor-bicycles or electric guitars; (c) that the letter of acceptance was posted in Ruritania; and (d) that the shop was owned and managed by Ruritanians, then the case for applying English law becomes progressively weaker. But in the normal case, where the contract is made *inter praesentes* in the London shop and the shop is English owned and managed, then the case for applying English law is strong. It would lead to inconvenience and injustice if the validity of an ordinary contract made in England was allowed to depend on the law of one party's foreign domicile with which the other party could not be expected to be familiar. The best reason for applying English law is surely that it is the putative proper law, not that it is the *lex loci contractus* or the *lex fori*.

(2) If we now reverse the facts and suppose that a domiciled Englishman aged twenty buys goods on credit from a shop in Ruritania, the problem is different and requires a different analysis. We may presume that in the normal case Ruritanian law is the *lex loci contractus* and the putative proper law. But there seems to be no real conflict between English and Ruritanian law. Both agree that contracts should be enforced unless there is some vitiating element. But is there such an element? It could be plausibly argued that the customer is not entitled to the protection of English law, because by that law he is of full age, nor of Ruritanian law, because he is not a Ruritanian. If so, the contact should be valid and the Englishman liable. As the American Law Institute's Restatement Second says:

> "If the state of a person's domicile has chosen to give him capacity to contract, or in other words has determined that he is not in need of the protection which a rule of incapacity would bring, there can usually be little reason why the local law of some other state should be applied to give him this protection and to declare the contract invalid to the disappointment of the parties' expectations. This should only be done in an unusual situation . . . for example when the person involved is a resident of the state with the rule of incapacity and when his relationship to the state of his domicile is relatively slight."[16]

---

[16] Comment *b* to s.198, quoted with approval in Dicey and Morris, pp. 780–781.

We have here what the Americans call a false conflict[17]; and if this is recognised, there is no problem.

(3) A domiciled Englishman aged seventeen borrows money in Arcadia from an Arcadian moneylender at an exorbitant rate of interest. By English law the contract is void,[18] but by Arcadian law it is valid because minority ends at seventeen. Here there is a true conflict between the protective policy of English law and the law of Arcadia which emphasises commercial convenience and the desirability of enforcing contracts. Since Arcadian law is the putative proper law it would seem that an English court, if it applied English law in case (1) above, should apply Arcadian law in this case also and hold the contract valid. The argument in favour of the proper law should not be put in terms of public policy. However, there may be a way of escape by means of renvoi if Arcadian law regards capacity to contract as governed by the law of the domicile or nationality. Although, as we have seen,[19] it has been said that renvoi has no place in the law of contract, it may be that an exception is required in the case of capacity.

(4) A domiciled Arcadian aged seventeen who is at an English boarding school is allowed an overdraft by his English bank. The contract is void by English law but valid by the law of Arcadia. Here the conflict is a false one and there is no real problem. For the schoolboy is not entitled to the protection of Arcadian law, because by that law he is of full age, nor of English law, because he is not English. When Parliament reduced the age of majority from twenty-one to eighteen[20] in order to implement the recommendations of the Latey Committee, it did so with English people and no others in mind; for all the evidence and statistics assembled by the Latey Committee were English evidence and English statistics. The desirable result therefore is that the contract should be valid. This result can only be reached by frankly recognising that this is a false conflict. It cannot, consistently with the decisions in (1) and (3) above, be reached by applying the law of the domicile; nor can it be reached by accepting a renvoi from Arcadian law.

We must now abandon theory and see how English and other courts have handled this problem.

Dicta favouring the *lex domicilii* can be quoted,[21] but they were all delivered in cases concerning capacity to marry or to make a marriage settlement, and they have been much criticised. Dicta can also be quoted

---

[17] For false conflicts, see *post*, pp. 526–530.

[18] Infants Relief Act 1874, s.1.

[19] *Ante*, p. 270.

[20] Family Law Reform Act 1969, s.1. In Scotland, the law was altered by s.1 of the Age of Majority (Scotland) Act 1969, and in Northern Ireland by the Age of Majority Act (N.I) 1969.

[21] *Sottomayor* v. *De Barros* (*No.* 1) (1877) 3 P.D. 1, 5 (criticised in *Sottomayor* v. *De Barros* (*No.* 2) (1879) 5 P.D. 94, 100, and in *Ogden* v. *Ogden* [1908] P. 46, 73); *Re Cooke's Trusts* (1887) 56 L.J.Ch. 637, 639; *Cooper* v. *Cooper* (1888) 13 App.Cas. 88, 99, 100, 108.

in favour of the *lex loci contractus*,[22] and so can one Scottish case[23] where a contract made in Scotland by a minor domiciled in Ireland was held valid. In a Canadian case[24] a married woman domiciled in Saskatchewan was held not liable on a contract made in Florida because by Florida law married women were incapable of making contracts of the kind in question. But surely she was not entitled to the protection of the law of Florida because she was not domiciled there. The conflict was a false one and there should have been no problem. In a later Canadian case[25] a husband and wife, domiciled in Quebec but resident for many years in Ontario, made a separation agreement in Ontario. When sued in Ontario for arrears of maintenance due under the agreement, the husband's executor pleaded that by the law of their domicile the spouses had no capacity to make such a contract. The court rejected this defence on the ground that capacity to contract is governed by the proper law of the contract. The court said that had the parties been resident as well as domiciled in Quebec, and had made the contract during a short visit to Ontario, "it would be against common sense to decide the parties' capacity by Ontario law." This dictum is perhaps more significant than the decision itself.

The leading American case is *Milliken* v. *Pratt*,[26] where a married woman domiciled in Massachusetts was held liable on a contract made in Maine because it was made there. But the decision was assisted by the fact that the contractual incapacity of married women under Massachusetts law was removed by statute after the date of the contract but before the hearing. There is one decision of the Supreme Court of the United States which favours the law of the domicile.[27]

In view of what has been said, the law which an English court would apply to the question is obviously anybody's guess. The best solution, it is suggested, is to say that if a person has capacity either by the proper law of the contract or by the law of his domicile and residence, then the contract is valid, so far as capacity is concerned.

Illegality

In order to find out what law determines whether a contract or a contrac-

---

[22] *Male* v. *Roberts* (1800) 3 Esp. 163 (the nearest English case to a decision on the matter); *Simonin* v. *Mallac* (1860) 2 Sw. & Tr. 67; *Baindail* v. *Baindail* [1946] P. 122, 128 (both cases of marriage). In *Republica de Guatemala* v. *Nunez* [1927] 1 K.B. 669, 689–690, 700–701, Scrutton and Lawrence L.JJ. refused to decide between the *lex domicilii* and the *lex loci contractus*, because they coincided.

[23] *McFeetridge* v. *Stewarts and Lloyds Ltd.*, 1913 S.C. 773. See especially at p. 789, *per* Lord Salvesen.

[24] *Bondholders Securities Corporation* v. *Manville* [1933] 4 D.L.R. 699.

[25] *Charron* v. *Montreal Trust Co.* (1958) 15 D.L.R. (2d) 240.

[26] (1878) 125 Mass. 374. In a celebrated article on this case (reprinted as Chap. 2 of his book), Currie demonstrated with the aid of tables that the application of the *lex loci contractus* would produce anomalous results in 10 out of 14 possible variations of the law-fact pattern. See *post*, p. 516.

[27] *Union Trust Co.* v. *Grosman* (1918) 245 U.S. 412. The judgment was delivered by Holmes J. For an analysis of the American cases, see Clarence Smith (1952) 1 I.C.L.Q. 446, 458–465. He concludes that in the United States "the balance is far more even than antagonists of the domicile would have us think." The law of the domicile is advocated by Cook, Chap. 16.

tual term is illegal we have to look at other systems of law than the proper law of the contract, namely the *lex fori,* the *lex loci contractus* and the *lex loci solutionis.* Four propositions must be examined; only the fourth is open to any real doubt.

(1) A contract which is illegal by its proper law cannot be enforced in England.[28] It has been objected that it is not rational to apply an invalidating rule of the proper law if the proper law was expressly or impliedly selected by the parties, because the parties, if they were in good faith, must have intended their contract to be valid.[29] The answer is that not only English courts[30] but also courts in other countries[31] do in fact apply invalidating rules of the proper law if they were intended to apply to the contract in question, however irrational this may seem. The irrationality (if any) is part of the price we have to pay for allowing the parties such a wide freedom to choose the governing law.

(2) A contract which is illegal under an English statute which is intended to apply to the contract,[32] or which is contrary to the public policy of English law, cannot be enforced in England, even if it is valid by the proper law. But the modern tendency is to confine the doctrine of public policy in conflict of laws cases within narrow limits.[33]

(3) Is illegality by the *lex loci contractus* fatal to the enforcement of a contract in England? In *Re Missouri Steamship Co.*,[34] Lord Halsbury said that if the *lex loci contractus* prohibits the making of a contract, the contract is void all the world over. But this statement was only a dictum, because the question at issue was the validity of an exemption clause; the clause was illegal by the law of the place of contracting (Massachusetts law) but valid by the proper law of the contract (English law), and the Court of Appeal upheld it. Lord Halsbury's dictum was quoted with approval in *The Torni*,[35] but again the statement was only a dictum because the law of the place of contracting and the proper law coincided. These dicta were disapproved by the Privy Council in *Vita Food Products Inc.* v. *Unus Shipping Co.*[36] There can be no doubt that on this point at any rate *The Torni* is wrong and the *Vita Food* case was right. Illegality by the *lex loci contractus* ought not to be fatal, because that law is so often uncertain and fortuitous. It is generally inadvisable, in modern conditions of commerce, rigidly to apply the *lex loci contractus* to any problem affecting the existence, validity or interpretation of a contract.

(4) Numerous dicta in the Court of Appeal and the House of Lords can be cited for the proposition that a contract which is illegal by the *lex loci*

---

[28] *Kahler* v. *Midland Bank* [1950] A.C. 24; *Zivnostenska Banka* v. *Frankman* [1950] A.C. 57.
[29] Jaffey (1974) 23 I.C.L.Q. 1.
[30] *e.g. Royal Exchange Assurance* v. *Vega* [1902] 2 K.B. 384; *R.* v. *International Trustee for the Protection of Bondholders A/G* [1937] A.C. 500; *Re Helbert Wagg & Co. Ltd.'s Claim* [1956] Ch. 323 (three cases discussed by Jaffey at pp. 5–7 of his article).
[31] See *International Encyclopaedia of Comparative Law*, Vol. III, Chap. 24, para. 80.
[32] *Boissevain* v. *Weil* [1950] A.C. 327 (exchange control legislation); *ante,* p. 279.
[33] *Ante,* pp. 42–44.
[34] (1889) 42 Ch.D. 321, 336.
[35] [1932] P. 78, 88.
[36] [1939] A.C. 277, 296–300.

solutionis cannot be enforced in England.[37] The judges have frequently approved Dicey's Exception 1 to Rule 149, which runs as follows:

> A contract (whether lawful by its proper law or not) is, in general, invalid in so far as the performance of it is unlawful by the law of the country where the contract is to be performed (*lex loci solutionis*).

In *R. v. International Trustee*[38] Lord Wright said that the principle "is too clearly established now to require any further discussion." But the only modern English authority for it is the decision of the Court of Appeal in *Ralli Brothers* v. *Compania Naviera Sota y Aznar*.[39] In that case, an English contract for the carriage of jute by sea from Calcutta to Barcelona provided for the payment of freight on delivery of the cargo at Barcelona at the rate of £50 a ton. After the date of the contract, but before the arrival of the ship, a Spanish decree fixed the maximum freight on jute at £10 a ton and made it illegal to pay more. The shipowners' action to recover the difference between £10 and £50 a ton was dismissed.

It has been convincingly argued by learned writers[40] that the principle of this case is not a rule of the conflict of laws at all but merely a rule of the domestic English law of contracts, and that it would not apply if the proper law were that of a third country, *e.g.* France. That is to say, whether an English court would enforce a French contract for the payment in Spain of freight beyond the maximum permitted by Spanish law would be determined not by Spanish law, the *lex loci solutionis*, but by French law, the proper law of the contract. There is no direct authority on the point. In two companion cases in the House of Lords Lord Reid stated the two opposing views without showing any sign that he was aware of the difference between them. In *Kahler* v. *Midland Bank*[41] he said: "The law of England will not require an act to be done *in performance of an English contract* if such act . . . would be unlawful by the law of the country in which the act is done." But in *Zivnostenska Banka* v. *Frankman*[42] he said: "It is now settled law that, *whatever be the proper law of the contract*, an English court will not require a party to do an act in performance of a contract which would be an offence under the law in force at the place where the act has to be done." However, it is only for the former and narrower formulation that any authority exists.

The principle of the *Ralli* case does not apply if the *lex loci solutionis* merely gives the defendant an excuse for non-performance without making

---

[37] *Ralli Brothers* v. *Compania Naviera Sota y Aznar* [1920] 2 K.B. 287, 291, 295, 300; *Foster* v. *Driscoll* [1929] 1 K.B. 470, 520; *R.* v. *International Trustee for the Protection of Bondholders A/G* [1937] A.C. 500, 519; *Kleinwort* v. *Ungarische Baumwolle Industrie A/G* [1939] 2 K.B. 678, 694, 697, 700; *cf. De Béeche* v. *South American Stores Ltd.* [1935] A.C. 148, 156.
[38] *Supra*, at p. 519.
[39] [1920] 2 K.B. 287.
[40] F. A. Mann (1937) 18 B.Y.I.L. 97, 107–113; Falconbridge, pp. 387, 391–394; Cheshire and North, pp. 227–229; Rabel, Vol. 2, pp. 535–539.
[41] [1950] A.C. 24, 48 (italics added).
[42] [1950] A.C. 57, 59 (italics added).

it illegal for him to perform in the agreed manner.[43] Nor does the principle apply if the illegality is imposed by the law of the defendant's residence or place of business and not by the law of the place of performance. Thus in *Kleinwort* v. *Ungarische Baumwolle Industrie A/G.*[44] Hungarian exchange control legislation was held to afford no defence to debtors resident in Hungary who had promised to pay in London under a contract governed by English law.

Essential validity

The essential validity of the contract or of any particular contractual term, *e.g.* an exemption clause[45] or an arbitration clause,[46] is governed by the proper law. That law will determine, *e.g.* whether a carrier is liable for loss of or damage to goods,[47] whether a seller of goods is liable for defects in their quality,[48] whether the master of a ship is justified in selling the cargo at a port of distress,[49] whether an agent has exceeded his authority,[50] whether the defendant has an excuse for non-performance,[51] whether a provision in a contract for a mortgage is void as a clog on the equity of redemption[52]; and many other questions of a similar kind. In matters of essential validity, the proper law is omnipotent.

Substance of the obligation and mode of performance

Once a valid contract has been created the performance of which is not illegal, it is necessary to consider what is the extent of the parties' obligation. This is called the substance of the obligation and is a matter for the proper law of the contract, which of course may or may not coincide with the law of the place of performance. At first sight it may look plausible to say that all matters concerning performance should be governed by the law of the place of performance as such and not by the proper law.[53] But the difficulty is that any such principle as this is wide enough to cover every question that could arise in the course of performing a valid contract. Its adoption would restrict the scope of the proper law almost entirely to matters of formation. Although English law came perilously close to adopting

---

[43] *Jacobs* v. *Crédit Lyonnais* (1884) 12 Q.B.D. 589; *R.* v. *International Trustee for the Protection of Bondholders A/G* [1937] A.C. 500 (the decision of the Court of Appeal).

[44] [1939] 2 K.B. 678; *cf. Trinidad Shipping Co.* v. *Alston* [1920] A.C. 888.

[45] *P. & O. Steam Navigation Co.* v. *Shand* (1865) 3 Moo.P.C.(N.S) 272; *Re Missouri Steamship Co.* (1889) 42 Ch.D. 321; *Jones* v. *Oceanic Steam Navigation Co.* [1924] 2 K.B. 730; *Sayers* v. *International Drilling Co.* [1971] 1 W.L.R. 1176.

[46] *Hamlyn* v. *Talisker Distillery* [1894] A.C. 202; *Spurrier* v. *La Cloche* [1902] A.C. 446. In both these cases the arbitration clause was void under the *lex fori*, yet it was held valid.

[47] *P. & O. Steam Navigation Co.* v. *Shand, supra.*

[48] *Benaim* v. *Debono* [1924] A.C. 514.

[49] *The August* [1891] P. 328; *The Industrie* [1894] P. 58.

[50] *Maspons* v. *Mildred* (1882) 9 Q.B.D. 530; affirmed on other grounds (1883) 8 App.Cas. 874; *Chatenay* v. *Brazilian Submarine Telegraph Co.* [1891] 1 Q.B. 79.

[51] *Jacobs* v. *Crédit Lyonnais* (1884) 12 Q.B.D. 589.

[52] *British South Africa Co.* v. *De Beers Consolidated Mines Ltd.* [1910] 2 Ch. 502; reversed on other grounds [1912] A.C. 52.

[53] See, to this effect, Dicey, 5th ed., Rule 161, Sub-Rule 2, Second Presumption; American Law Institute's First *Restatement of the Conflict of Laws*, s. 358.

such a principle because of a misleading dictum by Lord Wright in 1934,[54] it is now clear that it has been abandoned.

In 1884 the Court of Appeal decided that excuses for non-performance are a matter for the proper law. In the leading case of *Jacobs* v. *Crédit Lyonnais*,[55] French sellers contracted to sell esparto to London buyers. The contract, which was made in London, provided that the esparto was to be shipped by instalments from Algiers and paid for in London. After less than half the quantity had been delivered, an insurrection broke out in Algiers and the French sellers refused to deliver any more. When sued for damages for non-delivery, their defence was that by French law they were excused by *force majeure*. But it was held that the proper law was English and that by English law they were not excused, since it is a rule of English domestic law that a seller of goods is not excused if his source of supply dries up.[56]

If excuses for non-performance are a matter for the proper law and not for the law of the place of performance as such, it surely follows that the sufficiency of performance is also a matter for the proper law. The court in *Jacobs* v. *Crédit Lyonnais*[57] said that the law of the place of performance might well regulate the "method and manner" of performance: but this must no doubt be confined to matters of detail, matters which do not affect the substance of the obligation. If, for instance, under an English contract a seller undertakes to deliver goods in Paris "during usual business hours," it will presumably be for French law to say what business hours are usual; but English law will determine whether performance is excused by frustration or to what extent the seller is liable for defects in the goods delivered. If, by an English contract, an English seller agrees to sell goods in Lisbon to an American buyer for export to East Germany, Portuguese law will say whether an export licence is required and whether the goods have to be cleared through the customs, but English law will determine whether the seller or the buyer is under a duty to obtain the licence, and if no licence is obtained, which party has broken the contract or whether the contract has been frustrated.[58] If a New York contract made between an Australian and a Canadian provides for the payment of dollars in London, New York law will determine whether this means American or Australian or Canadian dollars (money of account), *i.e.* the extent of the debtor's indebtedness, but English law will determine whether payment may or must be made in dollar bills or can be made in pound notes (money of payment), *i.e.* how the debtor's obligation is to be performed.

---

[54] *Adelaide Electric Supply Co. Ltd.* v. *Prudential Assurance Co. Ltd.* [1934] A.C. 122, 151: "Whatever is the proper law of the contract regarded as a whole, the law of the place of performance should be applied in respect of any particular obligation which is performable in a particular country other than the country of the proper law of the contract." The chequered career of Lord Wright's dictum is traced by Morris (1953) 6 Vanderbilt L. Rev. 505.

[55] (1884) 12 Q.B.D. 589. The headnote is misleading in treating the question as one of illegality.

[56] See, *e.g. Blackburn Bobbin Co. Ltd.* v. *Allen* [1918] 2 K.B. 467.

[57] *Supra*, at p. 601.

[58] *Pound & Co. Ltd.* v. *Hardy & Co. Inc.* [1956] A.C. 588.

Two authoritative decisions of the Privy Council illustrate clearly the rule that the proper law of the contract governs the substance of the obligation. In *Mount Albert Borough Council* v. *Australasian etc. Assurance Society Ltd.*[59]:

> In 1926 a New Zealand borough corporation borrowed £130,000 from an insurance company incorporated in Victoria and carrying on business in Australia and New Zealand. To secure the loan the borough corporation issued debentures charged on the borough rates, and therefore on New Zealand land. The proper law of the contract was New Zealand law. Interest on the debentures at the rate of $5\frac{2}{3}$ per cent. was payable in Victoria. In 1931, during the Great Depression, a Victorian statute reduced the rate of interest on all mortgages to 5 per cent. It was held that this statute did not apply to the debentures, although Victoria was the place of performance, because New Zealand law was the proper law of the contract.[60]

Again, in *Bonython* v. *Commonwealth of Australia*[61]:

> In 1895 the Government of Queensland issued debentures to secure a loan of £2 million of which rather more than half was raised in England and the rest in Australia. The debentures entitled the holders to repayment in "pounds sterling" in 1945 (together with interest in the meantime) either in Brisbane, Sydney, Melbourne or London at the holder's option. In 1931 the Australian pound was devalued in relation to the English pound by 25 per cent. The plaintiff debenture-holder exercised his option for repayment in London and claimed to be entitled to be paid the face value of his stock in English currency. The Privy Council rejected his claim. "It has been urged," said Lord Simonds,[62] "that if London is chosen as the place of payment, then English law as the *lex loci solutionis* governs the contract and determines the measure of the obligation. But this contention cannot be accepted. The mode of performance of the obligation may, and probably will, be determined by English law; the substance of the obligation must be determined by the proper law of the contract," *i.e.* the law of Queensland.

Lord Simonds also pointed out that "the same substantial obligation was imposed on the Queensland Government whatever the place chosen for payment, the choice being given to the debenture-holder purely as a matter of convenience."

Thus, Lord Wright's heretical doctrine[63] that the law of the place of performance governs any obligation to be performed in a country other than

[59] [1938] A.C. 224.
[60] If the Victorian statute had made it illegal for the debtor to pay interest at more than 5 per cent. instead of merely affording him a good defence when sued for interest at a higher rate, it would have been necessary to consider whether the principle of *Ralli Brothers* v. *Compania Naviera Sota y Aznar* [1920] 2 K.B. 287 (*ante*, p. 290) was applicable.
[61] [1951] A.C. 201; discussed by F. A. Mann (1952) 68 L.Q.R. 195.
[62] At p. 219.
[63] See *ante*, p. 292, note 54.

that of the proper law has been finally eliminated from English law. This is
as it should be, for the cases show that chaos results if the law of the place
of performance is allowed to encroach on the sphere of the proper law.

Privity and assignment

In English domestic law the general rule is that (exceptions apart) a contract cannot confer rights on third persons who are not parties to the contract.[64] In Scotland, in many continental European countries and in most
American states, an opposite rule prevails. It is therefore surprising that
there should be such a dearth of English authority on what law governs this
question. One early case suggests that, as might be expected, it is governed
by the proper law of the contract.[65]

For reasons that are not entirely clear, English books on the conflict of
laws discuss the question what law governs the assignment of contractual
debts not in connection with the law of contract but in connection with the
law of property. This is too strong a tide to swim against; accordingly, the
question is reserved for discussion in a later chapter of this book.[66]

Interpretation

It is important to distinguish between the interpretation or construction
of the contract, and its legal effect once its meaning has been deduced from
the words used by the parties and the relevant surrounding circumstances.
The first question is basically a question of fact, namely, what did the parties mean? The second question is a question of law, namely, what effect
can be given to the contract as thus interpreted? It is best regarded as an
aspect of essential validity. A Scottish judge once warned against confusing
"two questions which are perfectly different and must be kept distinct—the
question of the construction of the contract and the question of its legal
effect once its meaning has been ascertained."[67] And in a leading English
case Lindley L.J. said[68]: "The expression 'construction' as applied to a
document, at all events as used by English lawyers, includes two things:
first, the meaning of the words; and secondly, their legal effect or the effect
which is to be given to them. The meaning of the words I take to be a question of fact in all cases, whether we are dealing with a poem or a legal document. The effect of the words is a question of law."[69]

The interpretation of a contract is determined in accordance with the
proper law of the contract. There is no reason in principle why the parties
should not be free to select the law which should govern the interpretation
of the words they have used. Although this is basically a question of fact,

---

[64] *Tweddle* v. *Atkinson* (1861) 1 B. & S. 393; *Dunlop* v. *Selfridge* [1915] A.C. 847; *Beswick* v.
Beswick [1968] A.C. 58.
[65] *Scott* v. *Pilkington* (1862) 2 B. & S. 11.
[66] *Post*, Chap. 20.
[67] *Robertson* v. *Brandes, Schonwald & Co.* (1906) 8 F. 815, 819, *per* Lord Kinnear.
[68] *Chatenay* v. *Brazilian Submarine Telegraph Co.* [1891] 1 Q.B. 79, 85.
[69] In *Alcock* v. *Smith* [1892] 1 Ch. 238, 256, Romer J. suggested that the word "interpretation" in s.72(2) of the Bills of Exchange Act 1882 was wide enough to cover legal effect.
But other judges have shown some reluctance to accept this proposition. See *post*, p. 368,
n. 24.

a question of law may arise if they use a technical expression which has different meanings in different legal systems. To construe a contract in accordance with its proper law means to apply the rules of construction which form part of that law. If the proper law attaches no specific meaning to the words used, the intention of the parties must be ascertained in accordance with any established principle of construction which forms part of the proper law. Thus in one case[70] a life insurance policy issued in England by a Scottish insurance company contained a warranty against suicide, but with a qualification that this should "not affect the interest of bona fide onerous holders." English law was the proper law of the contract. The trial judge held that while the contract as a whole had to be construed in accordance with English law, yet since the expression "bona fide onerous holder" was unknown to English law, evidence of its technical meaning in Scots law was admissible. However, the Court of Appeal held that the words could be given a meaning under English law, so that evidence of their meaning in Scots law was inadmissible.

The proper law will decide how far trade usages must be deemed to be incorporated in the contract, and how far words used in a contract can be interpreted in the light of preceding or subsequent negotiations between the parties.[71] To exclude those parts of the foreign law of contract which in English domestic law are classified as part of the law of evidence would be tantamount to distorting the foreign law.

The cases on gold clauses afford a striking illustration of construction in accordance with the proper law. Such clauses are sometimes introduced into international contracts of loan in order to protect the creditor from a depreciation of the currency in which the loan is expressed. The proper law will determine whether a gold clause is (a) a gold coin clause, *i.e.* a clause requiring the payment of gold coins (in which case it is likely to become ineffective just when the creditor needs its protection most, because if there is a serious depreciation of the currency, legislation is likely to be passed making it illegal to acquire or transfer gold coins); or (b) a gold value clause, *i.e.* a clause requiring the debtor to pay an amount of paper money equivalent in value to the price of gold coins[72]; or (c) a merely descriptive repetition of the unit of currency which is legal tender[73] (in which case the gold clause is ineffective); or (d) a clause indicating that the contract is for the sale of bullion or of coins, *i.e.* a sale of goods and not a loan of money.

Discharge

As a general rule the discharge of a contract depends upon the proper

[70] *Rowett Leaky & Co.* v. *Scottish Provident Institution* [1927] 1 Ch. 55.
[71] *St. Pierre* v. *South American Stores Ltd.* [1937] 1 All E.R. 206, 209; [1937] 3 All E.R. 349; contrast *Korner* v. *Witkowitzer* [1950] 2 K.B. 128, 162–163; see *post*, p. 456.
[72] See *Feist* v. *Société Intercommunale Belge d'Electricité* [1934] A.C. 161; *International Trustee for the Protection of Bondholders A/G* v. *R.* [1936] 3 All E.R. 407, reversed [1937] A.C. 500, but not on this point.
[73] See *St. Pierre* v. *South American Stores Ltd.* [1937] 3 All E.R. 349; *Treseder-Griffin* v. *Co-operative Insurance Co. Ltd.* [1956] 2 Q.B. 127; *Campos* v. *Kentucky and Indiana Railroad Co.* [1962] 2 Lloyd's Rep. 459.

law of the contract.[74] Thus, a discharge in accordance with the proper law of the contract is valid and effective in England[75]; conversely, a discharge not in accordance with the proper law but in accordance with some other law, *e.g.* the *lex loci solutionis* or the *lex situs* of a debt, is not valid or effective in England.[76] This principle applies to discharge by performance,[77] accord and satisfaction,[78] frustration,[79] bankruptcy[80] or subsequent legislation.[81] "The power of legislation to affect a contract by modifying or annulling some term thereof is a question of discharge of the contract which, in general, is governed by the proper law."[82] A moratorium, for instance, suspending liability on a debt enures for the benefit of the debtor if the legislation was enacted in the country of the proper law,[83] but not otherwise.[84] Similarly, the discharge of the debtor by novation, *i.e.* the substitution of another debtor, involves two elements. The first is the discharge of the original debtor which is governed by the proper law of the contract.[85] The second is the assumption by the new debtor of liability for the debt and is governed by the system of law with which the substitution of the new debtor is most closely connected.[86]

It is true that in some cases concerned with the winding up of dissolved foreign corporations the courts have sometimes treated the *lex situs* of the debt as governing its discharge.[87] But these cases "were cases of so special a character as to afford little guidance in the elucidation and application of principles of private international law in general."[88]

A discharge by bankruptcy is an exception to the general principle stated above if the bankruptcy takes effect under a Bankruptcy Act of the United Kingdom Parliament. Thus, an order of discharge under an English, Scottish or Northern Irish bankruptcy discharges the debtor from liability for

---

[74] Dicey and Morris, Rule 152.
[75] *Ralli* v. *Dennistoun* (1851) 6 Exch. 483; *Perry* v. *Equitable Life Assurance Co.* (1929) 45 T.L.R. 468; *R.* v. *International Trustee for the Protection of Bondholders A/G* [1937] A.C. 500; *Re Helbert Wagg & Co. Ltd.'s Claim* [1956] Ch. 323.
[76] *Jacobs* v. *Crédit Lyonnais* (1884) 12 Q.B.D. 589; *Gibbs* v. *Société Industrielle des Métaux* (1890) 25 Q.B.D. 399; *Mount Albert Borough Council* v. *Australasian etc. Assurance Society Ltd.* [1938] A.C. 224; *National Bank of Greece and Athens S.A.* v. *Metliss* [1958] A.C. 509; *Adams* v. *National Bank of Greece S.A.* [1961] A.C. 255; *Re United Railways of Havana and Regla Warehouses Ltd.* [1961] A.C. 1007.
[77] *Ante*, p. 292.
[78] *Ralli* v. *Dennistoun, supra.*
[79] *Jacobs* v. *Crédit Lyonnais, supra.*
[80] *Gibbs* v. *Société Industrielle des Métaux, supra.*
[81] *Perry* v. *Equitable Life Assurance Co., supra*; *R.* v. *International Trustee for the Protection of Bondholders A/G, supra*; *Mount Albert Borough Council* v. *Australasian etc. Assurance Society Ltd., supra.*
[82] *Re Helbert Wagg & Co. Ltd.'s Claim* [1956] Ch. 323, 340, *per* Upjohn J.
[83] *Re Helbert Wagg & Co. Ltd.'s Claim, supra.*
[84] *National Bank of Greece and Athens S.A.* v. *Metliss* [1958] A.C. 509; *Adams* v. *National Bank of Greece S.A.* [1961] A.C. 255.
[85] *Re United Railways of the Havana and Regla Warehouses Ltd.* [1960] Ch. 52; affirmed [1961] A.C. 1007.
[86] *Re United Railways, supra*, at p. 91.
[87] *Re Russian Bank for Foreign Trade* [1933] Ch. 745; *Re Banque des Marchands de Moscou (No. 1), Royal Exchange Assurance* v. *The Liquidator* [1952] 1 All E.R. 1269; *Re Banque des Marchands de Moscou (No. 2)* [1954] 1 W.L.R. 1108.
[88] *Re United Railways, supra*, at p. 90.

all debts provable in bankruptcy, irrespective of the proper law of the contract giving rise to the debt.[89]

Agency

Under this heading two entirely different questions may arise, which it is important to keep distinct. The first concerns the mutual rights and liabilities of the principal and agent. The second concerns the mutual rights and liabilities of the principal or the agent and the third party. The first question is governed by the proper law of the contract between the principal and the agent. The second is governed by the proper law of the contract between the agent and the third party.

Questions between principal and agent. The mutual rights and liabilities of the principal and agent are governed by the proper law of the contract between them, which is more often than not the law of the country where the relation of principal and agent is created.[90] This is usually the law of the country where the principal carries on business,[91] but it may be the law of the country where the agent carries on business if the work is to be done there.[92] Thus a contract between a solicitor or advocate and a foreign client will presumably be governed by the law of the country where the solicitor or advocate is entitled to practise[93]; and a contract with an estate agent by the law of the country where the land to be purchased or sold is situated.[94] The proper law of the contract between the principal and agent will determine such matters as the agent's right to salary or commission, his liability to be dismissed from his employment, and the extent of the agent's actual authority *as between him and his principal.*

Questions between principal and third party. The mutual rights and liabilities of the principal and third party are governed by the proper law of the contract concluded between the agent and the third party.[95] "If I, residing in England, send down my agent to Scotland, and he makes contracts for me there, it is the same as if I myself went there and made them."[96] Hence if a principal in one country authorises an agent to act for him in a specified or unspecified number of countries, the agent has authority to act in each country according to the laws thereof. The extent of the agent's actual authority is determined by the proper law of the contract between principal and agent; but the extent of his ostensible authority is determined by the

---

[89] *Post*, pp. 437–438, 441.
[90] Dicey and Morris, Rule 167.
[91] *Arnott v. Redfern* (1825) 2 C. & P. 88; *Re Anglo-Austrian Bank* [1920] 1 Ch. 69; *Mauroux v. Pereira* [1972] 1 W.L.R. 962.
[92] Of course this will not be a decisive consideration if, as in *Mauroux v. Pereira, supra,* the agent is intended to act in more countries than one, *e.g.* the United Kingdom or the British Isles.
[93] *R. v. Doutre* (1884) 9 App.Cas. 745; *Re Maugham* (1885) 2 T.L.R. 115.
[94] *Dudley Brothers v. Barnet,* 1937 S.C. 632, 640–641; *Ross v. McMullen* (1971) 21 D.L.R. (3d) 228.
[95] Dicey and Morris, Rule 168.
[96] *Pattison v. Mills* (1828) 1 Dow & Cl. 342, 363, *per* Lord Lyndhurst.

proper law of the contract which he makes with a third party.[97] That law
will determine whether the agent has created privity of contract between
the principal and the third party, *i.e.* whether an undisclosed principal can
sue or be sued on the contract[98]; whether the agent's authority is revocable[99] and whether it has been revoked, *e.g.* by the principal's death,
bankruptcy or insanity, or whether it has expired by lapse of time.[1]

It has never been decided whether a principal is bound by a law under
which the agent acts but had no actual authority to act. If, for example, a
principal in New York instructs an agent to buy goods for him in Europe
but not in England, would he be bound, in accordance with English principles of authority by "holding out," if the agent purported to buy goods
for the principal in England? It is submitted that he would be so bound. On
the other hand, the principal can hardly be bound (or entitled) by virtue of
a law which became the proper law of the contract with the third party only
because the agent, in excess of his actual authority, agreed to its selection
as the proper law of the contract. An agent can hardly confer upon himself
the power to make contracts binding on his principal, any more than a contracting party can confer capacity on himself by agreeing to the selection of
a favourable proper law.[2]

The proper law of the contract between the agent and the third party no
doubt determines whether the agent is liable for breach of warranty of
authority. But there is no decision on the point.

THE EEC CONTRACTS CONVENTION

Introduction

A Convention on the law applicable to Contractual Obligations[3] was
concluded in Rome in 1980 between the then nine Member States of the
EEC. It has been signed by all of them, but not yet by Greece. No State
has ratified the Convention and it will not come into force until seven
States have done so. It has not yet been decided whether to give the European Court jurisdiction to interpret the Convention. Until this question is
settled, ratifications are unlikely.

Scope

The Convention is world-wide in effect[4]: it will apply to all contract cases
having a foreign element, whether or not they have any connection with

---

[97] *Chatenay* v. *Brazilian Submarine Telegraph Co.* [1891] 1 Q.B. 79.
[98] *Maspons* v. *Mildred* (1882) 9 Q.B.D. 530; affirmed *sub nom. Mildred* v. *Maspons* (1883) 8
App.Cas. 874; *Girvin Roper & Co.* v. *Monteith* (1895) 23 R. 129.
[99] *Sinfra A/G* v. *Sinfra Ltd.* [1939] 2 All E.R. 675; contrast *Ruby Steamship Corporation Ltd.*
v. *Commercial Union Assurance Co.* (1933) 150 L.T. 38, which is out of line with other
authority and is criticised by Dicey and Morris, pp. 913–914; Cheshire and North, p. 238,
n.; Falconbridge, Chap. 18.
[1] *Employers' Liability Assurance Corporation* v. *Sedgwick Collins & Co. Ltd.* [1927] A.C.
95, 109; *First Russian Insurance Co.* v. *London and Lancashire Insurance Co. Ltd.* [1928]
Ch. 922, 938–940.
[2] *Ante*, p. 285.
[3] For the text of the Convention, the Official Report, and a commentary, see North (ed.)
Contract Conflicts (1982). The more important articles are also printed in Morris and
North, *Cases and Materials on Private International Law* (1984), pp. 459–465.
[4] Art. 2.

the EEC. But some matters are excluded from its scope by article 1, *e.g.* negotiable instruments, arbitration agreements and agreements on the choice of court, and contracts of insurance covering risks situated within the EEC. Moreover, article 21 provides that the Convention does not prejudice the application of international conventions to which a Contracting State is or becomes a party, *e.g.* the conventions on carriage by sea, air or road.

Freedom of choice

Article 3 provides that the parties are free to choose the governing law. The choice need not be express but it must be demonstrated with reasonable certainty.

Applicable law in the absence of choice

Article 4 provides that in the absence of choice, the contract is governed by the law of the country with which it is most closely connected. This is rebuttably presumed to be the country where the party who is to effect the performance which is characteristic of the contract has his habitual residence or, in the case of a corporation, its central administration. This doctrine of "characteristic performance," which is derived from Swiss law, will of course be a novelty in English law. The Official Report suggests that the payment of money is not the characteristic performance of a contract for the supply of goods or services; instead it is the provision of the goods or the services.

Mandatory rules

These are defined in article 3(3) as "rules which cannot be derogated from by contract." Such rules continue to apply notwithstanding the parties' choice of a different law. This applies generally[5] and especially to consumer contracts[6] and contracts of employment.[7] Article 7(2) provides that the forum may apply its mandatory rules whatever may be the governing law. This will preserve the effect of, *e.g.* section 27(2) of the Unfair Contract Terms Act 1977.[8] Article 7(1) goes much further and permits the court to give effect to the mandatory rules of some third country with which the situation has a close connection. However, the British Government reserved its right under article 22(1)(*a*) not to apply the provisions of article 7(1).

Material validity

Article 8 provides that the existence and validity of the contract or of any term therein shall be determined by the law which would govern the contract if the contract or term were valid, *i.e.* the putative proper law. However, a party may rely on the law of his habitual residence to establish that

[5] Art. 3(3).
[6] Art. 5(2).
[7] Art. 6(1).
[8] See *ante*, p. 280.

he did not consent if it would not be reasonable to determine the effect of his conduct in accordance with the putative proper law.[9]

Formal validity

Article 9 provides that a contract concluded between persons in the same country is formally valid if it satisfies the formal requirements of the proper law or of the law of the country where it was concluded; and that if the parties are in different countries the contract is formally valid if it satisfies the formal requirements of the proper law or of the law of one of those countries.

Capacity

The Convention makes no provision for capacity except to the limited extent of article 11. This provides that if the parties are in the same country, a natural person can only invoke his incapacity under some other law (*e.g.* that of his domicile or nationality) if the other party was or ought to have been aware of it.

Conclusion

The Convention will make fewer changes in English law than might have been expected. But, as might also have been expected, it has had a mixed reception from expert opinion in this country. Dr. North, who participated in its drafting, is enthusiastic.[10] Two of his contributors, who did not, are far more sceptical.[11] And Dr. F. A. Mann is highly critical.[12]

---

[9] See *ante*, p. 283.
[10] *Contract Conflicts*, p. 23.
[11] Morse at p. 172; Collins at p. 215.
[12] Book Review of *Contract Conflicts* (1983) 32 I.C.L.Q. 265.

CHAPTER 16

TORTS

INTRODUCTION

FOR centuries the law of torts was a neglected topic in the conflict of laws. Story did not refer to it at all. The last edition of Westlake, published in 1925, contains only seven pages devoted to torts other than collisions at sea. The sixth edition of Dicey, published in 1949, contained only nine pages on torts compared with 175 pages on contracts. All this is now changed. The literature on torts in the conflict of laws has now become almost unmanageable. Almost as many articles and notes are written each year on torts as on all the rest of the conflict of laws put together. Not only are centuries of neglect suddenly being made good, but also (especially in the United States) the problem of torts has moved into the centre of the discussion of methodological issues in the conflict of laws, or (in simpler language) the discussion of why courts apply foreign law, and on what basis do they choose it. It is as though someone has at last released the safety valve, with the result that a vast mass of words suddenly issues from the academic power-house in a cloud of escaping steam.[1]

The reason for this new-found interest is not far to seek. Just as the law of contract responded to the pressures of international trade in the nine-teenth century, so in the twentieth century the law of torts has responded to the pressures of the technological revolution as applied to the manufac-ture and distribution of products and to the means of transport and com-munications. Most of these pressures operate regardless of national or other frontiers. Dangerous drugs can cause babies to be born without arms or legs thousands of miles from the laboratory where the drugs were made. Unfair competition is no longer confined to a single country. Every year English motor-cars visit the continent of Europe in their thousands; acci-dents occur; people are injured or killed. English television aerials receive programmes from continental Europe, and even (with the aid of satellites in space) from America and Australia; private reputations sometimes suffer. For all these reasons, the conflict of laws can no longer rest content with solutions designed for nineteenth-century conditions.

Unfortunately, in stark contrast to the burgeoning of the literature, the English case law is (for reasons which will appear) extremely sparse; less

---

[1] See Dicey and Morris, Chap. 31; Cheshire and North, Chap. 10; Anton, Chap. 8; Falcon-bridge, pp. 14–19, Chaps. 44–46; Lorenzen, Chap. 13; Cook, Chap. 13; Currie, Chaps. 3, 7, 14: Cavers, Chaps. 1, 2, 6; Hancock, *Torts in the Conflict of Laws* (1942); Strömholm, *Torts in the Conflict of Laws* (1960); Kahn-Freund (1968) *Recueil des Cours*, II, 5 (a pro-found and penetrating study from the point of view of comparative law); Morse, *Torts in Private International Law* (1978).

than a dozen cases of any significance have been reported in the last
hundred years.

THE THEORIES

Before this case law is examined, some of the theories must first be considered. These are first, that the governing law should be the *lex fori*;
secondly, that it should be the *lex loci delicti*; and thirdly, that it should be
the proper law of the tort.

The lex fori

The theory that tort liability should be governed by the *lex fori* is of German origin. It was advocated by Savigny in 1849[2] and his advocacy has pro-
foundly influenced the development of English law. It still has at least one
supporter in the United States.[3] But outside the Commonwealth it has
been abandoned nearly everywhere as impractical and unjust. The principal arguments in its favour are, first, that liability for tort is closely akin to
liability for crime, where no one doubts that foreign law is inapplicable;
and secondly, that liability for tort is closely connected with the fundamental public policy of the forum and therefore must be governed by its law.
Neither of these reasons seems very convincing today. The law of torts has
long since been emancipated from the criminal law and furthers very different objectives. "The general purpose of the law of torts," said Holmes J.,[4]
"is to secure a man indemnity against certain forms of harm, not because
they are wrong, but because they are harms." The law of torts, like the law
of contract, serves the purpose of adjusting economic and other interests.
It is increasingly an instrument of distributive rather than of retributive justice. Nor is it any easier to maintain that the law of torts is more closely
connected with the fundamental public policy of the forum than is the law
of contract. Of course it may sometimes be necessary to deny a foreign tort
claim on the ground that its enforcement would be contrary to the public
policy of the forum. But it does not follow that it is necessary to do so
merely because there is a difference between the foreign law and the *lex
fori*. As Cardozo J. said in what was once a leading American case on torts
in the conflict of laws: "We are not so provincial as to say that every solution of a problem is wrong because we deal with it otherwise at home."[5]

Another argument against the application of the *lex fori* is this. Since the
jurisdictional rules of the English courts in actions *in personam* are
extremely liberal, the plaintiff may sometimes have a choice of forum in
which to sue. Hence, to apply the *lex fori* is an encouragement to forum
shopping—the deliberate choice of a suitable forum in order to attract the
application of a system of law favourable to the plaintiff's claim.[6]

---

[2] *System des heutigen roemische Rechts* (1849), Vol. 8, pp. 275 *et seq.*
[3] Ehrenzweig, *Treatise on the Conflict of Laws* (1962), pp. 541 *et seq.*; Ehrenzweig (1968) 17
I.C.L.Q. 1.
[4] *The Common Law* (1881), p. 144.
[5] *Loucks* v. *Standard Oil Co. of New York*, 224 N.Y. 99; 120 N.E. 198, 201 (1918).
[6] The problem of forum shopping is discussed *post*, pp. 317–318.

The lex loci delicti

The application of the *lex loci delicti* is the prevailing doctrine on the continent of Europe today and was the prevailing doctrine in the United States until yesterday. It can be justified by much more cogent arguments than those which support the *lex fori*. The first of these is the argument from territorial sovereignty. It has seemed natural to many lawyers to argue that the law of the place where events occur is the only law which can attribute legal consequences to them. In England, Willes J. paid lip service to this argument when he said that " the civil liability arising out of a wrong derives its birth from the law of the place, and its character is determined by that law."[7] In the United States, Holmes J. on several occasions emphasised that the *lex loci delicti* was the only possible law which could claim to govern liability for tort. "The theory of the foreign suit," he said,[8] "is that, although the act complained of was subject to no law having force in the forum, it gave rise to an obligation, an *obligatio*, which, like other obligations, follows the person and may be enforced wherever the person may be found. But as the only source of this obligation is the law of the place of the act, it follows that that law determines not merely the existence of the obligation, but equally determines its extent." This "*obligatio*" theory or "vested rights" doctrine was espoused by Professor Beale and formed the keystone of the American Law Institute's First Restatement of the Conflict of Laws (1934), not only in torts but also in contracts. As we shall see, it has been completely abandoned in the Second Restatement.

Another argument in favour of the *lex loci delicti* is that its application usually accords with the legitimate expectations of the parties. The law of torts attaches certain liabilities to certain kinds of conduct and to the creation of certain social risks. Those engaging in activities which may involve liability should be able to calculate the risks they are incurring, and to insure against them. Everyone should be entitled to adjust his conduct to the law of the country in which he acts. The ancient adage "when in Rome do as the Romans do" becomes, in modern life, "when in Rome see that your insurance policy covers the risks against which Romans insure."[9]

However, there are situations in which strong arguments can be advanced against a mechanical application of the *lex loci delicti* to each and every issue arising out of each and every kind of tort. First, the *locus delicti* is, in modern conditions, often as fortuitous as the *locus contractus* is apt to be. This is particularly true in transport accidents. An aircraft may disintegrate in flight, or may be forced off its course by bad weather and crash in a country in which neither the passenger nor the airline contemplated that the journey would end. A motor accident may occur in Switzerland between an English and a French motor-car—it might just as well have

[7] *Phillips* v. *Eyre* (1870) L.R. 6 Q.B. 1, 28.
[8] *Slater* v. *Mexican National Ry.* (1904) 194 U.S. 120, 126. *Cf.* Holmes J. in *Western Union Telegraph Co.* v. *Brown* (1914) 234 U.S. 542, 547. *Cf.* Cardozo J. in *Loucks* v. *Standard Oil Co. of New York*, 224 N.Y. 99; 120 N.E. 198, 200 (1918): "A tort committed in one state creates a right of action that may be sued upon in another unless public policy forbids."
[9] Kahn-Freund (1968) *Recueil des Cours*, II, 44.

occurred in Italy or France. Secondly, the *locus delicti* may be ambiguous, as where the defendant's acts take place in one country, and the ensuing harm to the plaintiff is inflicted in another. Thirdly, and most important of all, the application of the *lex loci delicti* regardless of the domicile and residence of the tortfeasor and his victim, and regardless of the type of issue and the type of tort involved, may lead to results which shock one's common sense. If, for instance, a Scotsman employed by a Scottish firm, negligently driving his employer's lorry, causes the death of another Scotsman employed by the same firm who is a passenger in the lorry, so committing a tort under both English and Scots law, there is hardly a strong case for applying English law to the widow's claim for compensation, just because the accident happened at Shap in England, a mere forty miles south of the border.[10]

The proper law of the tort

Considerations of this kind led the present writer to suggest, thirty-five years ago, that tort liability should be governed by the proper law of the tort.[11] The gist of this theory is that, while in many, perhaps most, situations there would be no need to look beyond the place of wrong, we ought to have a conflict rule broad enough and flexible enough to take care of the exceptional situations as well as the more normal ones: otherwise the results will begin to offend our common sense. It was suggested that a proper law approach, intelligently applied, would furnish a much-needed flexibility and enable different issues to be segregated and thus facilitate a more adequate analysis of the social factors involved. (In view of subsequent developments in the United States,[12] it may be pointed out that one of the issues which it was suggested should not necessarily be governed by the *lex loci delicti* was the liability of the driver of a motor-car to a gratuitous passenger, if the lift was given and the parties were domiciled in another country.) It was also suggested that a proper law approach would facilitate a more rational solution of the problems which arise when acts are done in one country and harm ensues in another. The analogy from contract was invoked: "English courts have reached results which, on the whole, seem commercially convenient and sound by applying the proper law doctrine to the question whether the defendant is liable for breach of contract. Why should we not reach results which are socially convenient and sound by applying the proper law doctrine to the question whether the defendant is liable for tort?"[13] For there are as many different kinds of torts as there are different kinds of contracts, and as many different issues in tort cases as there are in contract cases. Hence it seems unlikely that a single mechanical formula will produce satisfactory results when applied to all kinds of torts and to all kinds of issues.

[10] These are the facts in *M'Elroy* v. *M'Allister*, 1949 S.C. 110; *post*, p. 311.
[11] (1949) 12 M.L.R. 248, commenting on *M'Elroy* v. *M'Allister, supra*; and (in more detail) (1951) 64 Harv.L.Rev. 881. See also Nygh (1977) 26 I.C.L.Q. 932.
[12] *Post*, pp. 325–328.
[13] (1951) 64 Harv.L.Rev. 881, 883.

This thesis has now been adopted by the American Law Institute's Restatement Second of the Conflict of Laws. The leading section on torts provides that "the rights and liabilities of the parties with respect to an issue in tort are determined by the local law of the state which, as to that issue, has the most significant relationship to the occurrence and the parties."[14] The factors to be taken into account in determining this most significant relationship are listed as follows: the place where the injury occurred; the place where the conduct causing the injury occurred; the domicile, nationality, place of incorporation and place of business of the parties; and the place where the relationship, if any, between the parties is centred.

On the other hand, the proper law doctrine has been criticised by some because it sacrifices the advantages of certainty, predictability and uniformity of result which are claimed to follow from the application of the *lex loci delicti*. It is also said that the analogy from contract is not useful because the parties to a contract can avoid uncertainty by choosing the proper law.[15] It must be conceded that predictability of result is important because it facilitates the lawyer's task of advising his client and negotiating a settlement. Yet surely it is not such an important factor in the law of torts as it is in the law of contract or the law of property. In the non-intentional torts at any rate, liability is always unexpected, and people rarely give advance thought to the legal consequences of their actions. Motor-car accidents are seldom planned. In any event, continued adherence to a bad rule is a high price to pay for predictability of result.

THE MODERN ENGLISH LAW

Introduction: Phillips v. Eyre

Ever since Lord Mansfield's decision in *Mostyn* v. *Fabrigas*,[16] it has been settled law that English courts have jurisdiction to hear actions based on torts committed abroad. The only exception was that they had no jurisdiction to hear actions for trespass or other torts to foreign land. This exception was abolished in 1982.[17]

What law do they apply? The answer is contained in a celebrated dictum by Willes J. in *Phillips* v. *Eyre*[18]:

"As a general rule, in order to found a suit in England for a wrong alleged to have been committed abroad, two conditions must be ful-

---

[14] s.145. Almost identical is the draft Foreign Torts Act prepared by the Conference of Commissioners on Uniformity of Legislation in Canada, quoted in Hancock (1968) 46 Can. Bar Rev. 226, 248–250, and in Morris, *Cases in Private International Law*, 4th ed., p. 315. Hancock (1968) 18 U. of Tor.L.J. 331, 334–340 shows how the draft statute might be expected to apply in some typical situations.

[15] *Boys* v. *Chaplin* [1971] A.C. 356, *per* Lord Hodson at pp. 377–378; *per* Lord Wilberforce at p. 391D–E. *Cf. per* Lord Upjohn in the C.A.: [1968] 2 Q.B. 1, 32.

[16] (1774) 1 Cowp. 161.

[17] Civil Jurisdiction and Judgments Act 1982, s.30. See *post*, Chap. 18.

[18] (1870) L.R. 6 Q.B. 1, 28–29. This famous formula was approved in the Court of Appeal (*The Mary Moxham* (1876) 1 P.D. 107, 115), in the House of Lords (*Carr* v. *Fracis Times & Co.* [1902] A.C. 176, 182) and in the Privy Council (*Walpole* v. *Canadian Northern Ry.* [1923] A.C. 113, 119; *McMillan* v. *Canadian Northern Ry.* [1923] A.C. 120, 124).

filled. First, the wrong must be of such a character that it would have been actionable if committed in England. . . . Secondly, the act must not have been justifiable by the law of the place where it was done."

Three points should be noted at the outset about this famous formula. First, Willes J. admitted the possibility of exceptions to his general rule. Secondly, in the first part of the formula he says the *wrong* must be *actionable* in England, whereas in the second part he says the *act* must not have been *justifiable* by the law of the place where it was done. Thirdly, the residence, domicile and nationality of the parties are all apparently irrelevant.[19]

The first branch of the rule

The only authority cited by Willes J. for his first requirement of actionability in England was *The Halley*.[20] In that case a Norwegian barque was damaged in a collision with a British steamship in Belgian territorial waters. To an action in England by the owners of the barque, the owners of the British ship pleaded that the collision was caused by the negligence of the pilot whom they were compelled by Belgian law to have on board. This was no defence by Belgian law, but it was a defence at that time by English law.[21] The Privy Council, reversing the decision of Sir Robert Phillimore in the High Court of Admiralty, held that the defence succeeded. The decision would not have been important outside the somewhat narrow issue presented by the facts, had it not been for a sweeping dictum by Selwyn L.J. at the end of his judgment[22]:

> "It is, in their Lordships' opinion, alike contrary to principle and to authority to hold that an English Court of Justice will enforce a foreign municipal law, and will give a remedy in the shape of damages in respect of an act which, according to its own principles, imposes no liability on the person from whom damages are claimed."

This wide statement, which is not even limited to tort, simply is not true. Thus, for example, damages can be given for breach of a foreign contract which is not supported by consideration.[23] Nowhere in the English conflict of laws, except in tort, does the plaintiff have to surmount the double hurdle and show that his claim is valid not only by the appropriate foreign law, but also by English domestic law.[24] But in tort this double hurdle means

---

[19] However, in *Scott* v. *Seymour* (1862) 1 H. & C. 219, 235, Wightman J. said that if one British subject assaulted another in Naples, an action for damages would lie in England, even if by Neapolitan law no damages were recoverable. Willes J. at p. 236 expressed his general concurrence with Wightman J.'s judgment. Lord Hodson in *Boys* v. *Chaplin* [1971] A.C. 356, 377 D, derived "some assistance" from Wightman J.'s dictum.

[20] (1868) L.R. 2 P.C. 193. The historical background to this case is sketched by Hancock (1968) 18 U. of Tor.L.J. 331, 341–346.

[21] The law was altered by the Pilotage Act 1913, s.15, now s.35 of the Pilotage Act 1983.

[22] At p. 204.

[23] *Re Bonacina* [1912] 2 Ch. 394; *ante*, p. 282.

[24] e.g. *Re Bozzelli's Settlement* [1902] 1 Ch. 751; *Cheni* v. *Cheni* [1965] P. 85; *Mohamed* v. *Knott* [1969] 1 Q.B. 1; *ante*, pp. 165, 165 n. (marriage); *Re Lewal's Settlement* [1918] 2 Ch. 391; *post*, p. 404 (wills); *Cammell* v. *Sewell* (1860) 5 H. & N. 728; *De Nicols* v. *Curlier* [1900] A.C. 21; *post*, pp. 353, 413–414 (proprietary rights).

that the plaintiff gets the worst of both worlds, and that only the defendant, not the plaintiff, stands to gain by pleading foreign law. This is one reason why there are so few reported cases in England on torts in the conflict of laws.

Academic lawyers have severely criticised the first rule in *Phillips* v. *Eyre* on the ground that it closes the doors of the court to every action in tort not recognised by English domestic law, and requires the application of that law even though the case has no connection with England except that the defendant took refuge there after the tort was committed. Lorenzen says that "the illiberal attitude manifested by the English courts does not obtain elsewhere except in China and Japan."[25] Hancock says "one would look far to find a more striking example of 'mechanical jurisprudence,' blind adherence to a verbal formula without any regard for policies or consequences."[26] Kahn-Freund says "it is difficult to think of any principle more inimical to international harmony than this."[27]

In spite of these criticisms, and although *The Halley* has never been followed in England,[28] it has been followed by the Supreme Court of Canada[29] and by the High Court of Australia,[30] and it has now been unanimously approved by the House of Lords in *Boys* v. *Chaplin*.[31] But it must be stressed that this approval was *obiter* because, as we shall see, not only was the defendant's wrongful act actionable by English domestic law, but also English domestic law was applied to the exclusion of foreign law. Hence there was no occasion to consider what the position would have been if the wrong had not been actionable in English law. Yet the House of Lords, impervious to academic criticisms, went out of their way unanimously to approve *The Halley*. (It was the only point on which they were unanimous.) The only criticism came from Lord Wilberforce, who admitted that the rule "bears a parochial appearance; that it rests on no secure doctrinal principle; that outside the world of the English-speaking common law it is hardly to be found."[32] Yet he justified it on the extraordinary ground that "to adopt the *lex loci delicti* as the substantive rule would require proof of a foreign law"[33]—a ground which strikes at the whole basis of the conflict of laws. For if we are going to be daunted by the diffi-

---

[25] Lorenzen, p. 376. This chapter first appeared as an article in (1931) 47 L.Q.R. 483.

[26] *Torts in the Conflict of Laws*, p. 89. *Cf.* Hancock (1968) 46 Can. Bar Rev. 226; Robertson (1940) 4 M.L.R. 27; Cheshire and North, pp. 266–268; Anton, p. 239; Dicey and Morris, pp. 931–932; Morse, pp. 50–55.

[27] (1974) *Recueil des Cours*, III, 147, 287.

[28] On the other hand, the only judge in the United Kingdom who has ever ventured to question *The Halley* appears to be Lord Keith in *M'Elroy* v. *M'Allister*, 1949 S.C. 110, 132–133.

[29] *O'Connor* v. *Wray* [1930] 2 D.L.R. 899. But, as Hancock points out (46 Can. Bar Rev. 226, 246–247), the result can be defended because the defendant was domiciled in the Quebec forum.

[30] *Anderson* v. *Eric Anderson Radio and T.V. Pty. Ltd.* (1965) 114 C.L.R. 20. Here again the result can be defended because the plaintiff resided and the defendant was incorporated and carried on business in the N.S.W. forum.

[31] [1971] A.C. 356, *per* Lord Hodson at p. 374 E–G, *per* Lord Guest at p. 381 E, *per* Lord Donovan at p. 383 D, *per* Lord Wilberforce at pp. 385 B–387 A, 387 F–388 C, *per* Lord Pearson at pp. 396 E–397 C, 400 G–401 A, 406 A.

[32] At p. 387 F.

[33] At p. 387 H.

culty of proving foreign law, then the whole of the conflict of laws should be scrapped. Lord Pearson justified the rule on the ground "that it has a high degree of certainty and that it enables an English court to give judgment according to its own ideas of justice."[34] Neither of these reasons can withstand a moment's scrutiny, for each of them "represents a total negation of any system of conflict of laws and shows a predilection for the sole application of English law, whatever the tort and wherever committed."[35] And indeed, if certainty and the promotion of English ideas of justice are to be the only goals, why not scrap the second rule in *Phillips* v. *Eyre* and dispense with any reference to foreign law whatsoever?

In a well-meaning attempt to rescue English law from the trammels of the first rule in *Phillips* v. *Eyre*, suggestions have sometimes been made that Willes J. merely meant that the wrong must be *triable* in England.[36] In other words, he was laying down a rule of jurisdiction, not a rule for the choice of law; and all that he meant to assert was a threshold jurisdictional requirement similar to the former rule that English courts did not hear actions for trespass to foreign land. But these suggestions cannot be accepted. For Willes J. did not say that the wrong must be actionable in English law; he said it must be of such a character that it would have been actionable if committed in England—a very different proposition. Moreover, he would hardly have cited *The Halley* as his sole authority for this proposition if he had intended to lay down a rule of jurisdiction, since no question of jurisdiction was involved in that case. In *Boys* v. *Chaplin* Lord Wilberforce was quite explicit that the first rule is a rule for the choice of law and not a jurisdictional rule.[37]

The second branch of the rule

Phillips v. *Eyre*[38] was an action for assault and false imprisonment alleged to have been committed in Jamaica by the defendant, who was governor of the island. He pleaded that the acts complained of were done by him in the course of suppressing a rebellion which had broken out in Jamaica, and that his acts were subsequently declared lawful by an Act of Indemnity passed by the island legislature. The Court of Exchequer Chamber, in a judgment delivered by Willes J., held that the defendant was not liable. After disposing of a number of constitutional objections to the validity of the Act of Indemnity, Willes J. considered the final objection that since the local legislature had no power to pass a law having extra-

---

[34] At p. 400 H.
[35] McGregor (1970) 33 M.L.R. 1, 5.
[36] See, *e.g.* Yntema (1949) 27 Can. Bar Rev. 116, 118; Spence (1949) 27 Can. Bar Rev. 661, 666; Yntema (1951) 4 Int.L.Q. 1, 8–9; Nygh, p. 258; North (1967) 16 I.C.L.Q. 379, 386–391; *cf.* Cheshire and North, pp. 271–273; *Anderson* v. *Eric Anderson Radio and T.V. Pty. Ltd.* (1965) 114 C.L.R. 20, 41–42, *per* Windeyer J.
[37] [1971] A.C. 356, 385 E–387 A; *cf.* Morse, pp. 46–47. It is true that in *Boys* v. *Chaplin* there are some equivocal remarks by Lord Hodson at p. 375 E and Lord Donovan at p. 383 H which might be taken to imply that in their opinion the first rule is a rule of jurisdiction, as was clearly the opinion of Diplock L.J. (dissenting) in the C.A.: [1968] 2 Q.B. 1, 38.
[38] (1870) L.R. 6 Q.B. 1.

territorial effect, the Act of Indemnity could not take away the plaintiff's right of action in England. He said[39]:

> "This objection is founded upon a misconception of the true character of a civil or legal obligation and the corresponding right of action. The obligation is the principal to which a right of action in whatever court is only an accessory, and such accessory, according to the maxim of the law, follows the principal, and must stand or fall therewith. . . . The civil liability arising out of a wrong derives its birth from the law of the place, and its character is determined by that law."

That would have been enough to dispose of the case; but then Willes J. went on to announce his famous formula which has been quoted above. For the second branch of the rule he cited some old cases in which the defendant had acted either in exercise of governmental authority abroad or in the service of or with the authority of a foreign government.

It was natural for Willes J. to use the phrase "not justifiable," for not only did these words echo a statement of Lord Mansfield in *Mostyn* v. *Fabrigas*[40] that "whatever is a justification in the place where the thing is done ought to be a justification where the cause is tried," but also in the case before him, and in the cases which he cited, the words were apt to describe the subsequent legalisation of the defendant's acts by governmental authority.

But difficulties arose when Willes J.'s formula was mechanically applied to situations which it did not fit. In *The Mary Moxham*[41] an action was brought in England against the owner of a British ship for damaging the plaintiff's pier in Spain. By English law the owner was vicariously liable for the negligence of his servants, the master and crew of the ship; by Spanish law he was not. The Court of Appeal held the owner not liable because his act was "justifiable" by Spanish law. But since the shipowner had done no act in Spain, and since the ship's master was liable for his own acts by Spanish law, it is hard to see how by any stretch of the imagination the act of either person could have been called "justifiable" by the *lex loci delicti*. The true *ratio* surely was that Spanish law imposed no civil liability on the defendant.

However, in *Machado* v. *Fontes*[42] the Court of Appeal consisting of Lopes and Rigby L.JJ. held in an interlocutory appeal that an act was "not justifiable" by the *lex loci delicti* if that law imposed criminal but not tortious liability on the defendant. The action was for damages for a libel published in Brazil. The defendant took out a summons for leave to amend his defence by pleading that by Brazilian law the publication of the libel (a) could not be the ground of legal proceedings in which damages could be claimed, or alternatively (b) could not be the ground of legal proceedings in which the plaintiff could recover general damages for injury to his credit,

---

[39] At p. 28.
[40] (1774) 1 Cowp. 161, 175. Lord Mansfield's statement in turn echoed that of Lord Nottingham in *Blad's Case* (1673) 3 Swans. 603.
[41] (1876) 1 P.D. 107.
[42] [1897] 2 Q.B. 231.

character or feelings. The Court of Appeal refused to allow the amendment on the ground that the plea did not state that the publication was not criminal by Brazilian law. Lopes L.J. equated "not justifiable" with "wrongful" and "justifiable" with "innocent." Rigby L.J. equated "justifiable" with "authorised, or innocent or excusable." He said[43]: "It is not really a matter of any importance what the nature of the remedy for a wrong in a foreign country may be."

The decision on (a) above was so startling that until quite recently attention was concentrated upon it to the exclusion of (b). But, as we shall see, it was the decision on (b) that required consideration in *Boys* v. *Chaplin*.

Machado v. *Fontes* has been mildly criticised by the Privy Council,[44] severely criticised by the High Court of Australia,[45] not followed in Scotland,[46] and castigated by most academic writers who have discussed it.[47] It was, however, followed by the Supreme Court of Canada in *McLean* v. *Pettigrew*[48] in circumstances sufficiently remarkable to deserve attention here. The plaintiff and defendant were both domiciled and resident in Quebec. In that province the defendant gave a lift to the plaintiff in his car and the plaintiff was injured in Ontario by reason of the defendant's negligent driving. By the law of Quebec the defendant was liable to pay damages to the plaintiff. But Ontario had a statute which provided that "the owner or driver of a motor-vehicle, other than a vehicle óperated in the business of carrying passengers for compensation, is not liable for any loss or damage resulting from bodily injury to, or the death of, any person being carried in the motor-vehicle."[49] Hence the defendant was under no civil liability to the plaintiff by the *lex loci delicti*. But the Supreme Court of Canada, on appeal from the courts in Quebec, held the defendant liable because, in the opinion of the court, he was guilty of a traffic offence by the law of Ontario, even though he had been prosecuted for it in Ontario and acquitted!

The result of the case (but not the reasoning) can be defended, because the object of the Ontario statute was to prevent claims by ungrateful guests against their benevolent hosts and to prevent insurers being defrauded by collusive claims.[50] If we ask, what guests? what hosts? and what insurers? the answer obviously is Ontario guests, Ontario hosts and Ontario insurers. Therefore the plaintiff and defendant and the defendant's insurer

---

[43] At p. 235.

[44] *Canadian Pacific Ry.* v. *Parent* [1917] A.C. 195, 205, *per* Lord Haldane.

[45] *Koop* v. *Bebb* (1951) 84 C.L.R. 629, 643; *cf. Varawa* v. *Howard Smith Co. Ltd.* (*No.* 2) [1910] V.L.R. 509, 526–530, *per* Cussen J.

[46] *Naftalin* v. *L.M.S.*, 1933 S.C. 259; *M'Elroy* v. *M'Allister*, 1949 S.C. 110; *MacKinnon* v. *Iberia Shipping Co.*, 1955 S.C. 20.

[47] Dicey and Morris, pp. 939–940; Cheshire and North, p. 269; Hancock, *Torts in the Conflict of Laws*, pp. 15–18, 121–122; Robertson (1940) 4 M.L.R. 27, 34–43; Falconbridge Chap. 44; Hancock (1944) 22 Can. Bar Rev. 843, 853–855; (1945) 23 Can. Bar Rev. 348; Morse, pp. 56–61. Its only academic defenders appear to be Lorenzen, Chap. 13; Gutteridge (1936) 6 Camb.L.J. 16, 20; and Clarence Smith (1956) 5 I.C.L.Q. 466.

[48] [1945] 2 D.L.R. 65.

[49] This notorious statute was repealed by Highway Traffic Act Amendment Act 1977, s.16(1).

[50] The objects of the Ontario statute are discussed by Linden (1962) 40 Can. Bar Rev. 284; Trautman (1967) 67 Col. L.Rev. 465; Baade (1973) 1 Hofstra L.Rev. 150.

were outside the policy range of the statute, because they were all domiciled and resident in Quebec. From this point of view, the situation would have been very different if the parties had all been domiciled and resident in Ontario and the lift had been given there.[51]

In *M'Elroy* v. *M'Allister*[52] the Court of Session refused to follow *Machado* v. *Fontes*. The case is a classic because it shows so clearly how a rigid application of Willes J.'s formula can lead to gross injustice. The pursuer's husband was killed on an English road in Cumbria. At the time of the accident he was a passenger in a lorry owned by his employers and driven by their servant the defender. All parties concerned were natives of and resident in Glasgow. If the accident had happened in Scotland, the pursuer would have been entitled to substantial damages for *solatium*. If the action had been brought in England, she would have been entitled to substantial damages under the Fatal Accidents Acts and also for loss of the deceased's expectation of life under the Law Reform (Miscellaneous Provisions) Act 1934. But it was held, by a special court of seven judges, that she could only recover £40 in respect of funeral expenses, that being the only point at which Scots and English law coincided. The claim for *solatium* failed because it was a substantive and independent right of action and not a mere item in a claim for damages, and was not recognised by English law, the *lex loci delicti*. The implication of this is that in Scotland "not justifiable" means actionable and that *Machado* v. *Fontes* would not be followed. The claim under the Fatal Accidents Acts failed because the action was begun more than twelve months after the accident, contrary to section 3 of the Act of 1846. The court regarded this statute of limitation as substantive and not procedural.[53] The claim under the Law Reform (Miscellaneous Provisions) Act 1934 failed because in Scots law all rights of action for personal injuries due to negligence die with the injured person, and therefore the wrong was not actionable by the *lex fori*. Lord Keith dissented on both the last two points; and it is difficult to disagree with his view that "the present case is a typical case where insistence on the double rule enunciated by Willes J. may work injustice."[54]

It will be seen that there was no difference between English and Scots law on whether the driver was negligent, *i.e.* guilty of a tort. The only question was whether the widow could recover substantial or paltry damages; and because of the differences between English and Scots law and of the double-barrelled rule in *Phillips* v. *Eyre,* she recovered only paltry damages, although under either system she could have recovered a substantial sum. Was it not fortuitous that the accident happened forty miles south of the border and not in Scotland? It was surely far more significant that the parties were residents of Glasgow, that the fatal trip began in Scot-

---

[51] *Cf. Lieff* v. *Palmer* (1937) 63 Que.K.B. 278, and comments thereon by Hancock (1968) 46 Can. Bar Rev. 226, 241–243. In this case the Quebec court refused to apply the *Phillips* v. *Eyre* formula because it realised that the result would be contrary to common sense.

[52] 1949 S.C. 110.

[53] As to this, see *post*, p. 454.

[54] 1949 S.C. 110, 132. It was in a note on this case in (1949) 12 M.L.R. 248 that the present writer first formulated his theory of the proper law of the tort.

land, and that the pursuer's husband was a passenger in the lorry and not, *e.g.* a pedestrian on the highway. The parties were thus socially insulated from their geographical environment in England. It would have been more sensible for the Court of Session to have disregarded English law entirely, and to have applied Scots law as the proper law of the tort.

Boys v. Chaplin

Machado v. *Fontes* has now been overruled by a majority of the House of Lords in *Boys* v. *Chaplin*.[55] In that case the House of Lords at last had an opportunity to review the whole question of liability for torts in the conflict of laws. But the chance to restate the law in practical modern terms was lost, because though there was no dissent there were many conflicting opinions. The plaintiff and defendant were both normally resident in England but temporarily stationed in Malta in the British armed services. While both were off duty, the plaintiff, riding as a pillion passenger on a motor scooter, was seriously injured in a collision with a motor car negligently driven by the defendant. By the law of Malta, he could only recover special damages for his expenses and proved loss of earnings, which in the circumstances amounted to no more than £53. By English law, he could recover general damages for pain and suffering, *i.e.* a further £2,250. Milmo J., following *Machado* v. *Fontes* as he was bound to do, held that it was immaterial that no general damages could be awarded under the *lex loci delicti,* and awarded the plaintiff a total of £2,303. The Court of Appeal by a majority affirmed his judgment, but for different reasons. Lord Denning M.R. applied English law as the proper law of the tort since both parties were English.[56] Lord Upjohn applied English law on the grounds (a) that in his opinion *Machado* v. *Fontes* was rightly decided, and (b) that all questions relating to the remedy were a matter for the *lex fori*.[57] Diplock L.J. dissented and would have applied Maltese law as the *lex loci delicti*.[58] Both Lord Denning and Diplock L.J. agreed that *Machado* v. *Fontes* was wrongly decided and should be overruled.[59]

The House of Lords dismissed the defendant's appeal. Lords Hodson and Wilberforce, though critical of the proper law of the tort approach, eventually applied it and held that English law must govern for this reason. They both cited the Restatement Second with approval.[60] Lords Guest and

---

[55] [1971] A.C. 356. For comments on this case, see McGregor (1970) 33 M.L.R. 1; Karsten (1970) 19 I.C.L.Q. 35 (a shorter but most perceptive comment); North and Webb (1970) 19 I.C.L.Q. 24; Graveson (1969) 85 L.Q.R. 505; Reese (1970) 18 Am.Jo.Comp.L. 189; Carter (1970) 44 B.Y.I.L. 222; Morse, pp. 278–299.

[56] [1968] 2 Q.B. 1, 20, 24–26.

[57] At pp. 31, 32–33.

[58] At pp. 41–45. He conceded that there might have been a plausible argument for applying the proper law of the tort if there had been a special relationship between plaintiff and defendant, *e.g.* that of carrier and passenger or host driver and gratuitous passenger.

[59] At pp. 23–24, 35–37, 43. The power of the C.A. to overrule a decision of its own in an interlocutory appeal ("to be disposed of in an hour or two by two lords justices only") was asserted because nothing said in *Young* v. *Bristol Aeroplane Co. Ltd.* [1944] K.B. 718 was intended to refer to interlocutory appeals.

[60] [1971] A.C. 356 at pp. 379 G—380 C, 389 D—392 D. But Lord Hodson at p. 378 B thought the doctrine was an American doctrine; and Lord Wilberforce at p. 390 A attributed its origin to Westlake!

Donovan held that all questions of the remedy were a matter for English law as the *lex fori*.[61] Lords Donovan and Pearson held that English law must apply because *Machado* v. *Fontes* was rightly decided and actionability by the *lex loci delicti* was not necessary.[62]

At this point a significant and disquieting feature of their Lordships' speeches must be noticed. Only three justifications for applying English law were canvassed, (1) that it was the proper law of the tort, (2) that all questions of the remedy were a matter for English law *qua lex fori*, and (3) that *Machado* v. *Fontes* was rightly decided and that actionability by the *lex loci delicti* was not necessary. Yet there was no clear majority for any of these views, for (1) Lords Guest and Donovan expressly and Lord Pearson perhaps rejected the proper law of the tort doctrine[63]; (2) Lords Hodson and Pearson clearly and Lord Wilberforce apparently thought that the question of heads of damage (as opposed to assessment or quantification of damages) was a question of substance, not governed by the *lex fori*[64]; and (3) Lords Hodson and Wilberforce expressly and Lord Guest implicitly held that *Machado* v. *Fontes* was wrongly decided and should be overruled.[65] What then is the *ratio decidendi*?[66] It is submitted that there are only two possible answers to this question. The first is that there is none: but this is a counsel of despair. The second is that we can pick and choose which *ratio* we prefer. The author's preference of course is for the proper law of the tort, not only because he invented it, but also because both the other possible *rationes* seem retrograde, and likely to produce unacceptable results. If, for example, the plaintiff had suffered no economic loss, but only pain and suffering, there would have been a cause of action according to English law, but not according to Maltese law. How could such a question possibly be labelled procedural?[67] Or if the parties had both been Maltese, the proper law of the tort would clearly have been the law of Malta, and only Maltese damages should have been recoverable. Yet the procedural *ratio* and the *Machado* v. *Fontes ratio* would both result in the award of English damages.

Two learned commentators on *Boys* v. *Chaplin* think that it sounds the

---

[61] At pp. 381 G–383 C, 383 H. Lord Donovan's judgment is less than a page long.

[62] At pp. 383 D, 398 C–F, 399–400, 406 A. This was Lord Donovan's second *ratio*. It must be admitted that it is difficult to extract any clear *ratio decidendi* from Lord Pearson's judgment. See further *post*, p. 314.

[63] At pp. 381 C–D, 383 G–H, 405 G–H. But as to Lord Pearson's views, see *post*, p. 314. Lord Donovan appeared to think that the application of the proper law of the tort would be a breach of the Act of Union with Scotland. Lord Upjohn in the C.A. appeared to think that every air crash in the U.S.A. involves 50 aircraft, one registered in each state ([1968] 2 Q.B. 1, 32).

[64] At pp. 379 D–F, 392 F–393 B, 394 E–395 B. On this question, see *post*, pp. 460–461.

[65] At pp. 377 C, 381 E–F, 388 D. Lord Guest did not expressly overrule *Machado* v. *Fontes*; but, in reliance on the Scottish cases which refused to follow it (*ante*, p. 310, n. 46), he required double actionability by the *lex fori* and the *lex loci delicti*.

[66] As to this, see McGregor (1970) 33 M.L.R. 1, 14–15; Karsten (1970) 19 I.C.L.Q. 35, 37–38; Morse, pp. 281–283. For the difficulty in extracting the *ratio decidendi* of the decision of a plural tribunal whose members are agreed in the result but not in their reasons for it, see Cross, *Precedent in English Law*, 3rd ed., pp. 96–102; Honoré (1955) 71 L.Q.R. 196.

[67] See Lord Pearson at p. 394 F–G.

death-knell of the proper law of the tort. "It is now beyond controversy" they say[68] "that these notions can have no place in English legal thinking." But is this really so? Even if we have to count heads and weigh degrees of emphasis, Lords Hodson and Wilberforce were in favour of it and Lords Guest and Donovan against it. What did Lord Pearson say? He canvassed three possible amendments to the traditional English rule, of which the third was "that a flexible rule, which has been referred to as 'the proper law of the tort,' should be substituted."[69] He then cited some of the American cases and concluded[70]:

> "The new American flexible rule or flexible approach, with its full degree of flexibility, seems—at present at any rate, when the doctrine is of recent origin and further developments may be expected—to be lacking in certainty and likely to create or prolong litigation. Nevertheless, it may help the English courts to deal with the danger of 'forum shopping' which is inherent in the English rule."

This diffident language hardly closes the door on the proper law of the tort doctrine, nor does it justify the dogmatic comment quoted above. Moreover, in the last sentence of his judgment, Lord Pearson said that "if the general rule is that the alleged wrongful act must be actionable by the law of the place where it was committed . . . and by the law of the forum, an exception will be required to enable a plaintiff in a case such as the present case to succeed in his claim for adequate damages." This suggests that if his *Machado* v. *Fontes ratio* turned out to be a minority one (as it did), Lord Pearson was prepared to range himself alongside Lords Hodson and Wilberforce in order to do justice.

It is not contended here that the House of Lords has suddenly adopted the theory of the proper law of the tort in its entirety. All that is contended is that the first step has been taken in the direction of injecting some flexibility into the rules in *Phillips* v. *Eyre.* And as the French say, *ce n'est que le premier pas qui coûte.*

Summary of the present law

As a result of *Boys* v. *Chaplin,* the present English law can be restated as follows.

(1) An action in England on a tort committed abroad will fail unless the conduct complained of is actionable as a tort by English domestic law. This regrettably follows from their Lordships' unanimous approval of *The Halley*. Thus, whatever the foreign law may say, no action will lie in England for unfair competition as such, or invasion of privacy as such, or damages for adultery, or for the enticement, seduction or harbouring of a spouse or child, or for damages for loss of expectation of life, or for the

[68] North and Webb (1970) 19 I.C.L.Q. 24, 25. *Cf.* Cheshire and North, pp. 264–266.
[69] [1971] A.C. 356, 401 E.
[70] At p. 405 G–H.

deprivation of the services of a wife, child or servant,[71] for none of these is a tort in English domestic law.

(2) As a general rule, the action will also fail if there is no civil liability under the *lex loci delicti* as between the actual parties to the litigation. Civil liability of course excludes criminal liability; but there is no requirement that the defendant's conduct must be tortious by the *lex loci delicti*; it is sufficient if by that law the defendant's liability to pay damages is contractual, quasi-contractual, quasi-delictual, proprietary or *sui generis*.[72]

(3) But as an exception to the general rule, a particular issue may be governed by the law of the country which, with respect to that issue, has the most significant relationship with the occurrence and the parties.[73] For Lord Hodson stressed that the rule in *Phillips* v. *Eyre* must be given a flexible interpretation because Willes J. himself said that the rule was only applicable "as a general rule."[74] Lord Wilberforce stressed the need to segregate the relevant issue and to consider whether, in relation to that issue, the general rule ought to be applied or whether, "on clear and satisfactory grounds," it should be departed from.[75] In *Boys* v. *Chaplin* such grounds existed because both parties were normally resident in England and only temporarily present in Malta. If both parties, or only the defendant, had been Maltese, the decision would have been different.[76] Or if the issue had been whether the defendant was absolutely liable or liable only for negligence, the case for applying Maltese law would have been much stronger.

Is the exception to the general rule limited to cases where it would result in the application of English law, the *lex fori*? It is not in terms so limited; and as we shall see, the American decisions on which is is largely based do not always result in the application of the law of the forum. If, for example, the parties in *Boys* v. *Chaplin* had been Italian, there seems no reason why Italian law should not have been applied.

Is the exception to the general rule limited to cases where the tort was committed abroad? Nothing that was said in *Boys* v. *Chaplin* has any reference to torts committed in England. In the past, English law and no other has been applied to such torts, no matter how tenuous was the connection between the parties and England. Thus, in one case,[77] one official of the Czechoslovak Government (then in exile in England during the war)

---

[71] Liability to pay damages for adultery and liability in tort for the enticement, seduction or harbouring of a spouse or child were abolished by ss.4 and 5 of the Law Reform (Miscellaneous Provisions) Act 1970. Actions for damages for loss of expectation of life or for the deprivation of the services of a wife, child or servant were abolished by ss. 1 and 2 of the Administration of Justice Act 1982.

[72] In *Boys* v. *Chaplin*, Lord Hodson at p. 377 B and Lord Wilberforce at p. 389 D, F both require "civil liability" (not tortious liability) by the *lex loci delicti*. The term would not include the duty of an employer to pay compensation awarded by a Board for an industrial accident: *Walpole* v. *Canadian Northern Ry.* [1923] A.C. 113; *McMillan* v. *Canadian Northern Ry.* [1923] A.C. 120.

[73] *Per* Lord Hodson at p. 380 B–C; *per* Lord Wilberforce at pp. 390 G–392 F.

[74] At pp. 377 D, 378 D, 380 B.

[75] At pp. 391 E–392 A.

[76] *Per* Lord Hodson at p. 379 F–G; *per* Lord Wilberforce at pp. 389 F, 392 B.

[77] *Szalatnay-Stacho* v. *Fink* [1947] K.B. 1.

claimed that another official of that Government had libelled him in a report published in England to the Czechoslovak President. The Court of Appeal held that English law was applicable. Yet here was a case which cried out for the application of Czech law on the ground that the parties were politically and psychologically insulated from their geographical environment, just as the parties in *M'Elroy* v. *M'Allister*[78] were socially insulated from their geographical environment. It is much to be hoped that the exception recognised in *Boys* v. *Chaplin* will be given a liberal interpretation so as to permit its application to torts committed in England in appropriate circumstances. If, for example, the accident in *Boys* v. *Chaplin* had happened in England, and both parties had been Maltese, then damages for pain and suffering should not have been recoverable.

When will the *lex loci delicti* be displaced in favour of the *lex fori*, as it was in *Boys* v. *Chaplin*, or in favour of some other law?[79] Until the scope of the decision has been elucidated by judicial decisions (a process which is bound to take time, because there are so few English tort cases in which foreign law is pleaded) it is impossible to be dogmatic on this question. But it may be suggested that the case for displacement is strong if the parties are physically and socially insulated from their geographical environment, as when the tort is committed in a ship in territorial waters,[80] in an aircraft in flight, or in a sparsely inhabited country.[81] The same is true if the parties are politically and psychologically insulated from their geographical environment, as when they are members of a foreign government in exile in England[82] or (perhaps) of an identifiable colony of political refugees. The case for displacement is also stronger when there is some pre-tort relationship between the parties, centred in some country other than the *locus delicti*, than when there is not.[83] If the parties are linked by some contractual relationship, *e.g.* that of carrier and paying passenger, or by some noncontractual relationship, *e.g.* that of host driver and gratuitous passenger,[84] or of common employment with the same employer,[85] or by some domestic relationship, *e.g.* that of husband and wife[86] or parent and child, then the case of displacement is stronger than if they meet for the first time as strangers at the scene of the accident. Yet even in this case, as *Boys* v. *Chaplin* shows, the *lex loci* can be displaced in appropriate circumstances. Much depends of course on the kind of tort which is complained of. If one

---

[78] 1949 S.C. 100; *ante*, p. 311.

[79] For a close analysis of situations and issues in which the *lex loci delicti* might be displaced, see Kahn-Freund (1968) *Recueil des Cours*, II, 63–128; McGregor (1970) 33 M.L.R. 1, 15–21.

[80] As in *MacKinnon* v. *Iberia Shipping Co.*, 1955 S.C. 20.

[81] As in *Walton* v. *Arabian American Oil Co.*, 233 F. 2d 541 (1956) (Saudi Arabia), discussed by Currie, Chap. 1.

[82] As in *Szalatnay-Stacho* v. *Fink* [1947] K.B. 1, *supra*.

[83] This was conceded by Diplock L.J. in *Boys* v. *Chaplin* [1968] 2 Q.B. 1, 44 E–F.

[84] As in *McLean* v. *Pettigrew* [1945] 2 D.L.R. 65, *ante*, p. 310, and *Babcock* v. *Jackson*, 12 N.Y. 2d 473, 191 N.E. 2d 279 (1963), *post*, p. 325.

[85] As in *M'Elroy* v. *M'Allister*, 1949 S.C. 110, *ante*, p. 311.

[86] In *Corcoran* v. *Corcoran* [1974] V.R. 164, where the question was whether a wife could sue her husband in tort, the *lex loci delicti* was displaced in favour of the *lex fori*, which was also the law of the parties' domicile. *Cf. Warren* v. *Warren* [1972] Qd.R. 386, and contrast *Schmidt* v. *Government Insurance Office of N.S.W.* [1973] 1 N.S.W.L.R. 59.

member of a foreign government in exile in England libels another in a report to the President of the Republic, the case for displacement of English law is obviously stronger than if he negligently knocks him down while driving his car in London. Much depends, too, on the type of issue before the court. The case for displacement is perhaps weakest when the issue is that of the quality of the act or standards of conduct, *e.g.* whether the defendant is strictly liable or liable only for negligence or gross negligence. It is perhaps strongest when the issue is peripheral to the law of torts or belongs to another branch of law, as in some of the peripheral situations about to be discussed.[87]

Forum shopping

A few words must be said about the problem of forum shopping with which most of their Lordships in *Boys* v. *Chaplin* expressed concern.[88] Forum shopping occurs when the plaintiff brings his action not in the natural forum but in what is for him a more favourable one. If the law of Brazil gives no civil remedy for libel, it seems shocking that a plaintiff should be allowed to recover damages in England for a libel published in Brazil. But in fact it is only shocking if two assumptions are made: (a) that the parties are Brazilian; and (b) that the plaintiff had a choice between suing in Brazil and suing in England. In *Boys* v. *Chaplin* Lord Donovan made the first of these assumptions,[89] but without any supporting evidence except the foreign names of the parties. In the Court of Appeal Lord Denning made the second of these assumptions,[90] but without any supporting evidence at all. For all we know, the plaintiff may have been compelled to sue in England, because the defendant may not have been amenable to the jurisdiction of the Brazilian courts.

Similarly, if the law of Ontario imposes no liability on a host driver for negligent injury to his guest passenger, it seems shocking that a plaintiff injured there by his host's negligence should be able to recover damages in Quebec. But in fact it is only shocking if the parties were domiciled and resident in Ontario and the plaintiff had a choice of forum. If the parties were domiciled and resident in Ontario, and therefore within the policy range of the Ontario statute, it is doubly shocking that the plaintiff should choose to sue in Quebec and not in Ontario, because he may have been acting in collusion with the defendant, and in fraud of the defendant's insurance company.[91]

Again, if the law of Malta allows no damages to be recovered for pain and suffering, it seems shocking that a plaintiff injured there should be able to recover such damages in England. But in fact it is only shocking if the parties are Maltese and the plaintiff had a choice of forum. Again he may have chosen to sue in England in collusion with the defendant and in fraud

---

[87] *Post*, pp. 318–322.
[88] [1971] A.C. 356, *per* Lord Hodson at pp. 378 C, 380 A ("bare-faced"), *per* Lord Donovan at p. 383 F ("blatant"), *per* Lord Wilberforce at p. 389 A, *per* Lord Pearson at pp. 400 A–B, 401 B, 406.
[89] At p. 383 F.
[90] [1968] 2 Q.B. 1, 22.
[91] As in *Lieff* v. *Palmer* (1937) 63 Que.K.B. 278, *ante*, p. 311, n. 51.

of the defendant's insurance company. If on the other hand the parties are both English, as they were in *Boys* v. *Chaplin*, it is not shocking that the plaintiff should recover general damages in England, because England is the natural forum and may well be the only possible forum.

Hence it appears that a mechanical application of the rule in *Phillips* v. *Eyre* cannot prevent forum shopping unless the court is willing to inquire whether the plaintiff had a choice of forum, whether the defendant was insured and whether the plaintiff and defendant were acting in collusion to defraud the defendant's insurance company. A court trying a tort case does not usually ask itself such questions. On the other hand forum shopping can be prevented by the application of a flexible or proper law doctrine, because only in this way is any regard paid to the domicile and residence of the parties.[92]

Peripheral situations

There are some situations in which some law other than the law governing the tort may have to be applied to what looks at first sight like an issue in a tort claim. Some examples will now be given; they are of course not intended to be exhaustive. The law governing the tort may be a combination of the *lex fori* and the *lex loci delicti* (*e.g.* where the tort is committed abroad and the general rule applies), or a combination of the *lex fori* and the proper law of the tort (*e.g.* where the tort is committed abroad and the exception applies), or English law (*e.g.* where the tort is committed abroad but the exception applies and English law is the proper law, or where the tort is committed in England and no other law is the proper law of the tort). In the paragraphs that follow, to avoid repetition, all these laws are compendiously described as the *lex delicti*.

(1) The plaintiff may be able to by-pass the *lex delicti* by framing his claim in contract instead of in tort.[93] In English domestic law "it is trite law that a single act of negligence may give rise to a claim either in tort or for breach of a term express or implied in a contract."[94] Thus a railway passenger who has paid for his ticket and is injured in a railway accident can sue the British Railways Board either in contract or in tort[95]; and a workman who is injured in an accident at work has alternative claims in contract or tort against his employer.[96] However, the Scottish courts seem to treat the railway passenger's claim as exclusively delictual, at any rate if he is killed in the accident and his relatives are claiming *solatium*. So if a Scotsman takes a return ticket from Glasgow to London, and on the return journey is killed while the train is still in England, his relatives cannot recover *solatium* according to Scots law because their claim is delictual and *solatium* is unknown to English law, the *lex loci delicti*.[97] It would seem to fol-

---

[92] See, further, McGregor (1970) 33 M.L.R. 1, 7–8.

[93] See Dicey and Morris, pp. 934–935; Collins (1967) 16 I.C.L.Q. 103, 109–111, 142; Kahn-Freund (1968) *Recueil des Cours*, II, 129–141.

[94] *Lister* v. *Romford Ice and Cold Storage Co. Ltd.* [1957] A.C. 555, 573, *per* Lord Simonds.

[95] *Taylor* v. *M.S. & L. Ry.* [1895] 1 Q.B. 134; *Kelly* v. *Metropolitan Ry.* [1895] 1 Q.B. 944.

[96] *Matthews* v. *Kuwait Bechtel Corporation* [1959] 2 Q.B. 57.

[97] *Naftalin* v. *L.M.S. Ry.*, 1933 S.C. 259, not following *Horn* v. *North British Ry.* (1878) 5 R. 1055.

low that if an Englishman takes a return ticket from London to Glasgow and is killed in Scotland, his relatives could recover *solatium* in a Scottish court, because Scotland is the *lex loci delicti*. It would seem that more sensible results would be arrived at by characterising the claim as contractual and applying Scots law in the first case and English law in the second and not the other way round.[98] The whole problem would cease to exist if the claim in tort was governed by its proper law and if that law was the same as the proper law of the contract, which is likely to be the case.

(2) A different and more difficult situation arises when the law of contract and the law of tort lead, not to similar, but to opposite results. This can happen when the terms of a contract are used as a defence to a claim in tort.[99] A simple illustration is afforded by an English case[1] in which some Greek sailors were discharged from their Greek ship in an English port and refused to leave the ship. When the Greek shipowners sued them for trespass it was relevant to consider whether under the terms of their Greek contract of employment they had a right to stay on board. Again, an action in detinue against a bank for failing to redeliver the plaintiff's securities in England may be defeated by the terms of a foreign contract between the parties,[2] or even by those of a foreign contract between the plaintiff and a third party.[3]

Exemption clauses in a contract, *e.g.* a contract of carriage or a contract of employment, raise more difficult questions. It would seem that the validity and scope of the exemption clause (*e.g.* whether it is available as a defence to strangers to the contract) should be governed by the proper law of the contract of which it forms part; but that whether the clause is available as a defence to an action in tort should be governed by the *lex delicti*.

In *Canadian Pacific Railway* v. *Parent*,[4] a stockman was employed to bring cattle by rail from Winnipeg in Manitoba to Montreal in Quebec. He travelled on a pass at less than the full fare and signed a form exempting the railway company from liability for his injury or death. He was killed in Ontario owing to the negligence of the railway company's servants. His widow brought an action for damages in Quebec. By the law of Quebec she was entitled to recover notwithstanding the exemption clause; but under the Manitoba and the Ontario Fatal Accidents Acts she was not, because the deceased himself could not have recovered if he had been injured and not killed. The Privy Council, reversing the Canadian courts, held that the widow could not recover because the act was "justifiable" by the law of Ontario, the *lex loci delicti*. This decision seems correct in principle even if the proper law of the contract of carriage was the law of Quebec (*e.g.* because the stockman was domiciled in Quebec and the company had its

---

[98] Kahn-Freund (1968) *Recueil des Cours*, II, 135.
[99] See Dicey and Morris, pp. 927–928, 962–964; Collins (1967) 16 I.C.L.Q. 103, 112–116; Kahn-Freund (1968) *Recueil des Cours*, II, 141–149; Collins (1972) 21 I.C.L.Q. 320; North (1977) 26 I.C.L.Q. 914.
[1] *Galaxias S.S. Co.* v. *Panagos Christofis* (1948) 81 Ll.L.R. 499.
[2] *Zivnostenska Banka* v. *Frankman* [1950] A.C. 57.
[3] *Kahler* v. *Midland Bank* [1950] A.C. 24.
[4] [1917] A.C. 195.

head office in Montreal). The validity of the exemption clause would have been a matter for Quebec law as the proper law of the contract; but its availability as a defence to an action in tort would be a matter for the *lex delicti*.

In *Sayers* v. *International Drilling Co.*,[5] an English workman employed by a Dutch company on an oil rig in Nigerian territorial waters was unable to recover damages from his employer for injuries caused by the negligence of a fellow-employee, because an exemption clause in his contract of employment was valid by the Dutch proper law of the contract, though it was void by English domestic law under section 1(3) of the Law Reform (Personal Injuries) Act 1948. This decision has been much criticised.[6] The Court of Session adopted a far better approach in *Brodin* v. *A/R Seljan*,[7] where on similar facts (except that the delict occurred in Scotland) it was held that an exemption clause in a foreign contract of employment afforded no defence to the action. The *Sayers* case was distinguished on the ground that the delict occurred in the country of the forum; but there are dicta suggesting that even if it did not, the Act would be binding on and would have to be applied by the Scottish courts.

Once again it must be pointed 'out that these very difficult questions would be avoided if the claim in tort was governed by the proper law of the tort, and the proper law of the tort was the same as the proper law of the contract. In the *Sayers* case, the Lords Justices contented themselves with inquiring what was the proper law of the contract. But Lord Denning M.R. preferred to say that the claim was one in tort which raised a contractual defence. "We cannot apply two systems of law, one for the claim in tort, and the other for the defence in contract. We must apply one system of law by which to decide both claim and defence."[8] He decided the case by applying the proper law of the issue, which he held to be Dutch law.

In English domestic law, under the Unfair Contract Terms Act 1977, a person cannot exclude or restrict his liability for death or personal injury resulting from negligence by means of any contract term or notice; and in the case of any other loss or damage, he cannot so exclude or restrict his liability for negligence except in so far as the term or notice satisfies the requirement of reasonableness.[9] This provision has effect notwithstanding any contract term which purports to apply the law of some country outside the United Kingdom, if (a) the term appears to have been imposed to enable the party imposing it to evade the operation of the Act, or (b) in the making of the contract one of the parties dealt as consumer, and he was then habitually resident in the United Kingdom, and the essential steps necessary for the making of the contract were taken there.[10] So, if the facts of *Sayers* v. *International Drilling Co.* were to recur, and the contract of

---

[5] [1971] 1 W.L.R. 1176.
[6] Raymond Smith (1972) 21 I.C.L.Q. 164; Collins, *ibid.* 320; North (1977) 26 I.C.L.Q. 914, 923–925; Cheshire and North, pp. 282–284; Morse, pp. 188–194.
[7] 1973 S.L.T. 198. See Thomson (1974) 23 I.C.L.Q. 458.
[8] [1971] 1 W.L.R. 1176, 1181.
[9] s.2. The meaning of the requirement of reasonableness is spelt out in s.11.
[10] s.27(2). "Dealt as consumer" is widely defined in s.12.

employment contained an express term that Dutch law should be the proper law, the result would now be different, because in making the contract the plaintiff "dealt as consumer" within the meaning of the Act, he was habitually resident in England, and the contract was made there. But, if the proper law of the contract was Dutch law without any express term to that effect, the result would be the same.

(3) If the plaintiff claims damages (or an injunction) for interference with a contractual, proprietary or domestic right, it would seem on principle that whether the right exists should be governed by the proper law of the contract, the *lex situs* of the thing, or the law of the plaintiff's domicile respectively, and that whether there is a remedy for its violation should be governed by the *lex delicti*.[11] Thus, it would surely be a defence to an action for inducement in England of a breach of contract to show that by its proper law the contract was void; but it should not be a defence to show that, by the proper law of the contract, inducement of breach of contract gave rise to no civil liability. On the other hand, it would be a defence to an action for inducement abroad of an English contract to show that inducement of breach of contract gave rise to no civil liability by the *lex loci delicti*.

If the plaintiff claims damages for conversion of a chattel, there is clear English authority for the proposition that, even though the demand and refusal takes place in England, the plaintiff will fail if he was deprived of the ownership of the chattel under a foreign *lex situs*. Thus in *Cammell* v. *Sewell*,[12] timber belonging to an Englishman was shipped to England from a Russian port. The ship was wrecked off the coast of Norway and the master sold the timber to a Norwegian in circumstances that conferred a good title on him by Norwegian but not by English law. The Norwegian brought the timber to England but refused to deliver it to the Englishman on demand. The plaintiff's action of trover was dismissed on the ground that the defendant's Norwegian title prevailed.

The Supreme Court of Canada has held that a husband could not recover damages for the loss of the *consortium* of his wife where the right to *consortium* had been abolished by the law of the spouses' domicile, though it was still in existence according to the *lex delicti*.[13] A lower federal court in the United States has reached an opposite result on similar facts.[14] The Canadian case appears to be more in accordance with principle. For rights of this kind are based on status and their existence should be governed by the law governing the status.

(4) The question whether a cause of action in tort survives against the estate of a deceased tortfeasor or in favour of the estate of a deceased victim appears to be a question of administration or succession, governed by the law of the tortfeasor's or victim's domicile as the case may be, and not

---

[11] See Dicey and Morris, pp. 952–954; Kahn-Freund (1968) *Recueil des Cours*, II, 118–121; Morris (1951) 64 Harv.L.Rev. 881, 886–887.

[12] (1860) 5 H. & N. 728.

[13] *Lister* v. *McAnulty* [1944] 3 D.L.R. 673, discussed by Hancock (1944) 22 Can. Bar Rev. 843.

[14] *Gordon* v. *Parker*, 83 Fed.Supp. 40 (1949) (claim for enticing a wife).

a question of tort governed by the *lex delicti*.[15] There is no English authority on either question. In a leading American case[16] the Supreme Court of California applied the law of the tortfeasor's domicile (which was also the law of the forum) to the former question, and in *M'Elroy* v. *M'Allister*[17] the Court of Session applied the law of the victim's domicile to the latter question: but they applied it *qua lex fori* rather than *qua lex domicilii*.

The locus delicti

A problem of some difficulty may be raised by the question: where is the *locus delicti*? It is perfectly simple to answer it in a case where all the events, except the bringing of the action, occur within one country. It is not so simple when the defendant's act takes place in one country, and the ensuing harm is inflicted on the plaintiff in another. For instance, if the defendant broadcasts a statement defamatory of the plaintiff from an English radio station, and the broadcast is heard in several other countries; or if the defendant negligently manufactures poisoned chocolates in country A which are bought in country B and consumed in country C, with the result that the consumer dies in country D, then the problem becomes more difficult. It has assumed major dimensions in the United States, since it frequently required an answer under the *lex loci delicti* rule at one time applied by the American courts. The First Restatement answered it by laying down the rule of thumb that "the place of wrong is in the state where the last act necessary to make an actor liable for an alleged tort takes place."[18] But this view has not been followed by all American cases by any means,[19] and has been cogently criticised by writers.[20] The Second Restatement contains no rule on the point but simply lists the place where the injury occurred and the place where the conduct causing the injury occurred as among the factors to be taken into account in determining the law of the state which has the most significant relationship to the occurrence and the parties.[21] As we have seen,[22] one of the advantages claimed for the proper law of the tort doctrine is that it would facilitate a more rational approach to the problem here discussed than the First Restatement's mechanical "last event" rule.

In England, Australia and Canada the problem has been considered mainly in connection with applications for leave to serve the writ out of the jurisdiction on the ground that the alleged tort was committed within the

---

[15] See Dicey and Morris, pp. 955–956, 959–960; Webb and Brownlie (1965) 14 I.C.L.Q. 1; Kahn-Freund (1968) *Recueil des Cours*, II, 110–113.
[16] *Grant* v. *McAuliffe*, 41 Cal. 2d 859; 264 P. 2d 944 (1953); discussed by Currie, Chap. 3.
[17] 1949 S.C. 110; *ante*, p. 311.
[18] s.377.
[19] For interesting examples, see *Schmidt* v. *Driscoll Hotel Inc.*, 249 Minn. 376; 82 N.W. 2d 365 (1957); *Gaither* v. *Myers*, 404 F. 2d 216 (D.C. 1967).
[20] Rheinstein (1944) 19 Tulane L.Rev. 4, 165; Cook, Chap. 13; Morris (1951) 64 Harv.L.Rev. 881, 887–892; Webb and North (1965) 14 I.C.L.Q. 1314.
[21] s.145; *ante*, p. 305.
[22] *Ante*, p. 304.

jurisdiction.[23] The value of these decisions as precedents on the question of choice of law is very limited. This is because the granting of leave is a matter of discretion, and when the court refuses leave it may do so on the ground that the tort was not committed in England or on the alternative ground that the case is not a proper one for the exercise of the court's discretion. The handful of English, Australian and Canadian cases do not tell a consistent story and are not always easy to reconcile. All that can be said with confidence is that not all torts are governed by the same rule. It seems that the tort of negligent manufacture or distribution of products is committed where the negligent act is done, and not where the harm is suffered[24]; but the Privy Council[25] and the Supreme Court of Canada[26] have each taken a different view, and it may be that the older cases require reconsideration in the light of these decisions. Thus the correct test has been said to be, look at the sequence of events and ask: where in substance did this cause of action arise?[27] On the other hand, the torts of libel and slander are committed where the defamatory statements are published and not where they are posted or uttered.[28] But leave to serve the writ out of the jurisdiction has been refused where a fraudulent misrepresentation was made abroad and acted on in England, because "one must look at the substance of the tort complained of," and "the substantial wrongdoing" was committed where the statement was made.[29] More recently, however, the Court of Appeal has taken the view that where false or negligent misrepresentations are made by telex or telephone by a person in a foreign country to a person in England, the tort is committed here.[30] A bare majority of the Supreme Court of Canada has held that the tort of negligently or intentionally polluting a stream is committed where the pollutant was poured in and not where the damage was suffered.[31] But the European Court of Justice has held (in a jurisdictional context) that the tort is committed in either place and that the plaintiff can choose between them.[32]

Torts at sea

In considering what law governs torts committed at sea, it is necessary to distinguish between (1) torts committed in foreign territorial or national waters, and (2) torts committed on the high seas.

---

[23] Under what used to be R.S.C., Ord. 11, r. 1(1)(*h*). The rule has since been relettered and amended: R.S.C. Ord. 11, r.1(1)(*f*), *ante*, p. 75. The problem does not arise under the new rule.

[24] *George Monro Ltd.* v. *American Cyanamid Corporation* [1944] K.B. 432; followed in *Abbott-Smith* v. *University of Toronto* (1964) 45 D.L.R. (2d) 672.

[25] *Distillers Co. Ltd.* v. *Thompson* [1971] A.C. 458.

[26] *Moran* v. *Pyle National (Canada) Ltd.* (1973) 43 D.L.R. (3d) 239.

[27] *Castree* v. *E. R. Squibb Ltd.* [1980] 1 W.L.R. 1248; *Multinational Gas Co.* v. *Multinational Gas Services Ltd.* [1983] Ch. 258, 267, 272, 284.

[28] *Bata* v. *Bata* [1948] W.N. 366; *Jenner* v. *Sun Oil Co.* [1952] 2 D.L.R. 526; *Gorton* v. *Australian Broadcasting Commission* (1973) 22 F.L.R. 181.

[29] *Cordova Land Co. Ltd.* v. *Victor Brothers Inc.* [1966] 1 W.L.R. 793.

[30] *Diamond* v. *Bank of London and Montreal* [1979] Q.B. 333. Cf. *Original Blouse Co. Ltd.* v. *Bruck Mills Ltd.* (1963) 42 D.L.R. (2d) 174.

[31] *Interprovincial Co-operatives Ltd.* v. *The Queen* (1975) 53 D.L.R. (3d) 321. This is one of the very few Commonwealth cases which did not arise in a jurisdictional context.

[32] *Handelskwekerij G.J. Bier B.V.* v. *Mines de Potasse D'Alsace S.A.* [1978] Q.B. 708.

(1) *Torts in foreign territorial waters.* Foreign territorial or national waters are regarded as part of the territory of the foreign country. Hence an action in England in respect of a tort committed in foreign territorial or national waters will succeed only if the act is actionable as a tort in England and (as a general rule) actionable by the law of the foreign country in question.[33] The law of the ship's flag is irrelevant.[34] Different considerations may perhaps apply if the tort is committed on board a ship or structure and is entirely unconnected with the littoral State. In *MacKinnon* v. *Iberia Shipping Co.*[35] the plaintiff, an engineer employed in a ship registered in Scotland, claimed damages against the owners for injuries received through the negligence of a fellow-employee while the ship was at anchor just within the territorial waters of the Republic of San Domingo. The Court of Session held that he could only recover if the act was actionable by the law of the Republic as well as by Scots law. The court rejected a distinction sometimes made in American decisions between cases where the acts affect the littoral State or its subjects and cases where everything takes place within the ship itself. But in *Sayers* v. *International Drilling Co.*[36] the plaintiff was injured by the negligence of a fellow-employee while working on an oil rig in Nigerian territorial waters. The case turned on the validity of an exemption clause in his contract of employment, the proper law of which was Dutch. But the Court of Appeal was clearly of opinion that Nigerian law was irrelevant.

(2) *Torts on the high seas.* If an action is brought in England on a tort committed in a ship on the high seas, and only one ship is involved in the case and no question arises as to damage done to submarine cables or other maritime installations, the law to be applied is that of the country to which the ship belongs. That is to say, the act must be actionable as a tort in England and (as a general rule) actionable under the law of the State to which the ship belongs, and if that State consists of two or more countries, the law of the place where the ship is registered.[37]

Collisions on the high seas are governed "not indeed by the common law of England, but by the maritime law, which is part of the common law of England as administered in this country."[38] This dictum appears to postulate the existence of an internationally-recognised "general maritime law"; but, as Willes J. had demonstrated,[39] there is no such law. Since it would obviously be impossible to apply the laws of two or more ships involved in a collision together with English law, there really is no alternative to applying English law to collisions on the high seas. This has sometimes led to results which seem at first sight surprising. In *The Esso Malaysia*[40] a Pana-

[33] *The Arum* [1921] P. 12; *The Waziristan* [1953] 1 W.L.R. 1446.
[34] *The Mary Moxham* (1876) 1 P.D. 107.
[35] 1955 S.C. 20.
[36] [1971] 1 W.L.R. 1176; *ante*, p. 320.
[37] *Canadian National S.S. Co.* v. *Watson* [1939] 1 D.L.R. 273.
[38] *Chartered Mercantile Bank of India* v. *Netherlands India Steam Navigation Co.* (1883) 10 Q.B.D. 521, 537.
[39] *Lloyd* v. *Guibert* (1865) L.R. 1 Q.B. 115, 123–125.
[40] [1975] Q.B. 198.

manian ship negligently collided with a Russian trawler in the western Atlantic, and the Russian sailors on board the trawler were drowned. It was held that their personal representatives could maintain an action in England under the Fatal Accidents Acts against the owners of the Panamanian ship.

THE AMERICAN REVOLUTION

In the United States, chiefly under the influence of Holmes J.,[41] the courts at one time applied the *lex loci delicti* to all questions of liability in tort. In doing so, they emancipated themselves from the stifling influence of *The Halley*[42] and the first rule in *Phillips* v. *Eyre*.[43] However, increasing dissatisfaction was felt with a mechanical rule according to which each and every issue in each and every kind of tort had to be referred to the *lex loci delicti*, regardless of the residence, the domicile and the social environment of the parties. Numerous devices were used to escape from the application of that law, *e.g.* by characterising the issue as contractual,[44] or procedural,[45] or as a problem in domestic relations,[46] or in the administration of estates,[47] or by refusing to apply the *lex loci delicti* on the ground that it was in conflict with the public policy of the forum.[48]

In 1963 the opportunity arose of getting rid of the *lex loci delicti* rule altogether: and the New York Court of Appeals seized the opportunity with both hands. In the famous case of *Babcock* v. *Jackson*,[49] perhaps the most important case in the conflict of laws ever decided by an American court, the factual setting was truly ideal for demonstrating the unjust and anomalous results which flow from the application of that rule. Mr. and Mrs. Jackson were domiciled in New York state and resident in Rochester, a town near the Canadian border. They invited their friend Miss Babcock, also so domiciled and resident, to accompany them in their car on a weekend trip to Canada. The car was licensed, garaged and insured in New York state. During the trip Miss Babcock was seriously injured in Ontario by the negligent driving of Mr. Jackson. She sued him for damages in New

---

[41] *Ante*, p. 303, n. 8.
[42] (1868) L.R. 2 P.C. 193.
[43] (1870) L.R. 6 Q.B. 1.
[44] Well-known examples are *Dyke* v. *Erie R.R. Co.*, 45 N.Y. 113 (1871); *Levy* v. *Daniels U-Drive Auto Renting Co.*, 108 Conn. 333, 143 Atl. 163 (1928).
[45] *Grant* v. *McAuliffe*, 41 Cal. 2d 859, 264 P. 2d 944 (1953) (survival of action against tortfeasor's estate); *Kilberg* v. *Northeast Airlines Inc.*, 9 N.Y. 2d 34, 172 N.E. 2d 526 (1961), on which see Currie, pp. 690–710 (measure of damages for wrongful death). These were two very bold creative decisions in which the judges shook off the fetters of the *lex loci delicti*.
[46] *Haumschild* v. *Continental Casualty Co.*, 7 Wis. 2d 130, 95 N.W. 2d 814 (1959) (whether wife can sue husband in tort).
[47] *Grant* v. *McAuliffe, supra* (a second, and preferable, *ratio decidendi*).
[48] *Kilberg* v. *Northeast Airlines Inc., supra*. The decision would now be based on the ground that, though the aircraft crashed in Massachusetts, New York law was the proper law of the tort because the plaintiff was resident and the flight began there.
[49] 12 N.Y. 2d 473, 240 N.Y.S. 2d 743, 191 N.E. 2d 279 (1963); reported in England in [1963] 2 Lloyd's Rep. 286. For a symposium of comment, see (1963) 63 Col.L.Rev. 1212. Two judges out of seven dissented.

York. By the law of New York she could recover; but Ontario had a statute (the same one which was considered in *McLean* v. *Pettigrew*[50]) which prevented a gratuitous passenger in a motor-vehicle from recovering damages from his host driver. The New York Court of Appeals nevertheless allowed recovery.

"The question presented is simply drawn," said Fuld J.[51] "Shall the law of the place of the tort *invariably* govern the availability of relief for the tort or shall the applicable choice of law rule also reflect a consideration of other factors which are relevant to the purposes served by the enforcement or denial of the remedy?"

Despite the advantages of certainty, ease of application and predictability which the traditional *lex loci delicti* rule afforded, he concluded that[52]

"Justice, fairness and 'the best practical result' may best be achieved by giving controlling effect to the law of the jurisdiction which, because of its relationship or contact with the occurrence or the parties, has the greatest concern with the specific issue raised in the litigation."

Three lines of reasoning contributed to this decision. The first was that the "centre of gravity" or "grouping of contacts" doctrine which had recently been adopted by the court in cases of contract[53] was equally applicable in cases of tort. The second was that the Ontario statute, on its true construction, did not apply to the case, because its object was to prevent the fraudulent assertion of claims by passengers, in collusion with the drivers, against Ontario insurance companies[54]; but no such company was involved. The third was that New York had far more concern with the outcome of the litigation than Ontario had, for the parties were all New Yorkers and the place of the accident was fortuitous.[55] Fuld J. pointed out that Ontario's concern was quite different from what it would have been if the issue had been whether or not the defendant was driving negligently.

Any breach with tradition as dramatic as this is bound for a time to produce some uncertainty. Any revolutionary new doctrine is sure to develop teething troubles until its rationale and scope have been clarified by judicial decisions. This is especially true if the new doctrine won the day in the teeth of powerful dissent. Such has been the subsequent history of

---

[50] [1945] 2 D.L.R. 65; *ante*, p. 310. The Ontario statute was repealed by Highway Traffic Act Amendment Act 1977, s.16(1).

[51] 12 N.Y. 2d 473, 477, 240 N.Y.S. 2d 743, 746, 191 N.E. 2d 279, 280–281; [1963] 2 Lloyd's Rep. 286, 287.

[52] 12 N.Y. 2d 473, 481, 240 N.Y.S. 2d 743, 749, 191 N.E. 2d 279, 283; [1963] 2 Lloyd's Rep. 286, 289.

[53] *Auten* v. *Auten*, 308 N.Y. 155, 124 N.E. 2d 99 (1954); *ante*, p. 266, n. 5.

[54] It is perhaps the Achilles' heel of the opinion that it dealt so casually with the object of the Ontario statute. For a fuller analysis, see the articles cited in n. 50, p. 310, *ante*.

[55] All three of these techniques for deciding tort cases had been suggested by the present writer in (1951) 64 Harv.L.Rev. 881. The court cited that article with approval. The third technique is the most prominent one in the subsequent case law.

Babcock v. *Jackson* in the New York courts. In *Dym* v. *Gordon*,[56] the New York Court of Appeals reached an opposite result because, although the parties were New Yorkers, they had met casually in Colorado (where the lift was given and the accident happened) while attending a summer school at the University there. Colorado had a guest statute relieving the host from liability unless he was guilty of wilful and wanton negligence; and the court applied Colorado law. However, *Dym* v. *Gordon* was virtually overruled in *Macey* v. *Rozbicki*[57] and expressly overruled in *Tooker* v. *Lopez*.[58] In both these cases the parties were New Yorkers. In *Macey* v. *Rozbicki* the defendant had invited her sister to spend ten days with her at her country cottage in Ontario, and during that time gave her a lift to church in her car; the sister was injured but the court applied New York law and allowed her to recover damages. In *Tooker* v. *Lopez* two New York girls were classmates at the University of Michigan; the lift was given there and the accident happened there; though Michigan had a guest statute which barred recovery unless the driver was guilty of wilful misconduct or gross negligence, the court allowed recovery.

A more difficult question arises when the host and guest are resident in different states with different laws. In this situation the New York Court of Appeals applied the law of Ontario where the plaintiff resided and the accident happened, in preference to that of New York where the defendant resided, with the result that the plaintiff failed to recover.[59] This is a classic example of what Currie called "the unprovided for case," where New York has no "interest" in having its compensatory law applied because the plaintiff is not a New Yorker, and Ontario has no "interest" in having its protective law applied because the defendant is not an Ontarian, and therefore neither country "cares what happens."[60]

Another difficult question arises in the converse situation to that in *Babcock* v. *Jackson*, namely, where the parties reside and the lift is given in Ontario, and the accident happens in New York. It might have been expected that the Ontario guest statute would be applied; but the intermediate appellate court in New York has, on three occasions, applied the law

---

[56] 16 N.Y. 2d 120, 209 N.E. 2d 792 (1965). Three judges (including Fuld J.) out of seven dissented. For an analysis of the decision, see Cavers, pp. 293–312, who approves of the decision, as does Kahn-Freund (1968) *Recueil des Cours*, II, 71. The present writer ventures to disagree.

[57] 18 N.Y. 2d 289, 221 N.E. 2d 380 (1966). One judge out of seven dissented.

[58] 24 N.Y. 2d 569, 249 N.E. 2d 394 (1969). Three judges out of seven dissented.

[59] *Neumeier* v. *Kuehner*, 31 N.Y. 2d 121, 286 N.E. 2d 454 (1972). One judge out of seven dissented. For a symposium of comment, see (1973) 1 Hofstra L.Rev. 91, also Trautman (1976) 1 Vt.L.Rev. 1. An opposite result has been reached on similar facts in Rhode Island: *Labree* v. *Major*, 111 R.I. 657, 306 A. 2d 808 (1973). *Cf. Cipolla* v. *Shaposka*, 439 Pa. 563, 267 A. 2d 854 (1970); for a symposium of comment, see (1971) 9 Duquesne L.Rev. 347.

[60] See Currie, pp. 152–156. For Currie's views on choice of law generally, see *post*, pp. 516–518.

of New York and allowed recovery.[61] This result is extremely controversial. It has been defended on the ground that, though Ontario had an
interest in the application of its law, so also had New York: for (1) New
York was concerned to impose liability on drivers who violated its standards of careful driving; (2) New York had a humanitarian concern to see
that persons injured on its highways were adequately compensated; and (3)
New York was concerned that New York doctors and hospital services who
cared for the injured victim should be promptly and adequately compensated.[62]

No American writer on the conflict of laws now defends the automatic
application of the *lex loci delicti*. Nearly all American courts which have
considered the matter now prefer a more flexible approach in which the
various policy factors are considered and some other law may be applied,
though not necessarily on the same grounds. This new flexible approach
has been adopted by the highest courts in at least twenty-six states.[63] It
usually (but not invariably[64]) leads to the application of the law of the
forum; but this is simply because the plaintiff naturally sues in the courts of
the defendant's residence, so that that state's law is often the proper law. It
usually (but not invariably[65]) results in judgment for the plaintiff, whereas
application of the *lex loci delicti* would lead to the opposite result.

One of the best known and most interesting of the cases is *Reich* v. *Purcell*,[66] which involved a head-on collision between two motor-cars in
Missouri. The negligent defendant was on his way from his home in California to a holiday in Illinois. The other car was occupied by a family (two
members of which were killed) on their way from Ohio to California where
they intended to live. The estates of the two deceased were being administered in Ohio. Neither California nor Ohio imposed any limit on the
damages recoverable, but Missouri imposed a limit of $25,000. The
Supreme Court of California applied the law of Ohio; and Traynor C.J.

---

[61] *Kell* v. *Henderson*, 270 N.Y.S. 2d 552 (1966); *Rye* v. *Colter*, 333 N.Y.S. 2d 96 (1972); *Bray*
v. *Cox*, *ibid.* 783 (1972); *contra*, *Arbuthnot* v. *Allbright*, 316 N.Y.S. 2d 391 (1970). For
comments on *Kell* v. *Henderson*, see Rosenberg (1967) 67 Col.L.Rev. 459; Trautman, *ibid.*
465. A similar result to that in *Kell* v. *Henderson* was reached by the Supreme Court of
Wisconsin in *Conklin* v. *Horner*, 38 Wis. 2d 468, 157 N.W. 2d 579 (1968), and by the
Supreme Court of Minnesota in *Milkovich* v. *Saari*, 295 Minn. 155, 213 N.W. 2d 408
(1973).

[62] This argument has frequently been advanced by American courts and writers; but, in the
absence of evidence that there were such medical creditors and that the injured party
would be unable to pay them unless he recovered damages, it seems rather far-fetched. See
Reese (1963) 63 Col.L.Rev. 1212, 1256; Cavers, p. 179, n. 62. If the victim is killed and the
action is brought on behalf of his dependants under a Fatal Accidents Act, the argument
cannot apply because no creditors, medical or otherwise, have any interest in the damages
recovered.

[63] The number grows each year. Only in ten states have the courts refused to follow *Babcock*
v. *Jackson*. See Weintraub (1977) 41 Law and Contemp. Prob. 146, n. 1.

[64] *e.g. Long* v. *Pan-American World Airways*, 16 N.Y. 2d 337; 231 N.E. 2d 796 (1965); *Reich*
v. *Purcell*, 63 Cal. 2d 31; 432 P. 2d 727 (1967); *Cipolla* v. *Shaposka*, 439 Pa., 563, 267 A. 2d
854 (1970); *Neumeier* v. *Keuhner*, 31 N.Y. 2d 121, 286 N.E. 2d 454 (1972); *Offshore Rental
Co.* v. *Continental Oil Co.*, 22 Cal. 3d 157, 583 P. 2d 721 (1978).

[65] *e.g. Cipolla* v. *Shaposka, supra*; *Neumeier* v. *Kuehner, supra*.

[66] 63 Cal. 2d 31, 432 P. 2d 727 (1967). For a symposium of comment, see (1968) 15 U.C.L.A.
L.Rev. 551.

said that "limitations of damages for wrongful death have little or nothing to do with conduct. They are concerned not with how people should behave but how survivors should be compensated."

Thus, the displacement of the *lex loci delicti* by some other law is becoming a commonplace in the United States, though not always for the same reasons. But it must be admitted that this has led to a great deal of uncertainty, especially in New York. A distinguished American writer has remarked that the "struggle" of the New York courts with *Babcock* v. *Jackson* and its progeny "has been awesome to behold—dissents, shifting doctrine, results not easily reconcilable. In short, a law professor's delight but a practitioner's and judge's nightmare."[67] In *Tooker* v. *Lopez*[68] and again in *Neumeier* v. *Kuehner*[69] Fuld C.J. (the author of the opinion in *Babcock*) attempted to inject some certainty into the law by formulating three "guidelines" for dealing with the host driver and guest passenger situation. But these guidelines have been much criticised by American writers on the grounds that they are premature, not warranted by the previous decisions, and almost as mechanical as the doctrine of the *lex loci delicti* which was discarded in *Babcock*.[70] A cynic might be tempted to say that in *Babcock* the court created a monster and that Fuld C.J.'s guidelines are their attempt to control it. Perhaps the House of Lords in *Boys* v. *Chaplin*[71] were right after all in stigmatising the new flexible approach as productive of uncertainty. But surely Lord Wilberfore went too far when he said that "if one lesson emerges from the United States decisions it is that case to case decisions do not add up to a system of justice."[72] For if that is true, then we might as well scrap not only the conflict of laws but also the common law itself.

---

[67] Weintraub (1977) 41 Law and Contemp.Prob. 146, 148.
[68] 24 N.Y. 2d 569, 249 N.E. 2d 394 (1969); *ante*, p. 327.
[69] 31 N.Y. 2d 121, 286 N.E. 2d 454 (1972); *ante*, p. 327.
[70] Sedler (1973) 1 Hofstra L.Rev. 125, 130–137; Trautman (1976) 1 Vt.L.Rev. 1, 3, 9–22; Weintraub (1977) 41 Law and Contemp.Prob. 146, 148–153; contrast Reese (1971) 71 Col. L.Rev. 548, 562–564, who approves of the guide-lines.
[71] [1971] A.C. 356, 377 H, 381 D, 383 G, 391 C, 405 B, H.
[72] At pp. 391–392.

Part Six

LAW OF PROPERTY

CHAPTER 17

THE DISTINCTION BETWEEN MOVABLES AND IMMOVABLES

IN English domestic law, the leading distinction between proprietary interests in things is the historical and technical distinction between realty and personalty. In the English conflict of laws, however, the leading distinction between things is the more universal and natural distinction between movables and immovables.[1] This distinction is capable of application to other systems of law in which the English distinction between realty and personalty is unknown. "In order to arrive at a common basis on which to determine questions between the inhabitants of two countries living under different systems of jurisprudence, our courts recognise and act on a division otherwise unknown to our law into movable and immovable."[2]

The judge who uttered this dictum suggested[3] that our courts should only adopt the distinction between movables and immovables when the conflict is between English law and the law of some country (*e.g.* France or Scotland) which does not recognise the distinction between realty and personalty, and not when the conflict is between English law and the law of some country (*e.g.* Ontario or New York) which does recognise it. The suggestion looks plausible, but is believed to be unsound, because it would mean that England would have to have one conflict rule for the common law jurisdictions of the Commonwealth and the United States, and another conflict rule for the rest of the world.[4] At any rate it has not been followed.[5]

The importance of the distinction between movables and immovables is most apparent in the field of succession, because succession to movables is governed (in general) by the law of the deceased's domicile, whereas succession to immovables is governed (in general) by the *lex situs* of the land.[6]

Different systems of law may characterise things as movable or immovable in different ways. In all systems, some physically movable things are so closely connected with the land that they are characterised as immovables for legal purposes. Thus, in English domestic law the title deeds to land and the keys of a house are characterised as real estate and therefore

---

[1] *Freke* v. *Carbery* (1873) L.R. 16 Eq. 461; *Duncan* v. *Lawson* (1889) 41 Ch.D. 394; *Re Hoyles* [1911] 1 Ch. 179; *Macdonald* v. *Macdonald,* 1932 S.C.(H.L.) 79. See, generally, Cheshire and North, Chap. 15; Dicey and Morris, Chap. 19; Falconbridge, Chap. 21; Cook, Chap. 12; Robertson, pp. 190–212; Clarence Smith (1963) 26 M.L.R. 16.
[2] *Re Hoyles* [1911] 1 Ch. 179, 185, *per* Farwell L.J.
[3] *Ibid.*
[4] See Robertson, p. 201.
[5] *Macdonald* v. *Macdonald,* 1932 S.C.(H.L.) 79; *Re Cutcliffe* [1940] Ch. 565; but see *Haque* v. *Haque* (*No.* 2) (1965) 114 C.L.R. 98, 109–110, *per* Barwick C.J.
[6] *Post,* Chap. 24

as immovable. In Scots law, heritable bonds[7] are characterised as part of the heritage, at least for some purposes,[8] and therefore as immovable: and this has been recognised by English courts.[9] When slavery existed in Jamaica, slaves on an estate were considered to be appurtenant to the land, and have been held by our courts to pass under a devise of land in Jamaica.[10]

There may, therefore, be a conflict between the *lex fori* and the *lex situs* as to whether a particular thing is movable or immovable. In such a situation, it is well settled that the *lex situs* determines the characterisation.[11]

Leasehold interests in land in England are interests in immovables for the purposes of the conflict of laws,[12] and it is quite immaterial that English domestic law regards them as personal estate. The same is true of a mortgagee's interest in land in England, including his right to repayment of the debt.[13] But in Australia and New Zealand it is equally well settled that a mortgagee's interest in land is an interest in a movable, on the theory that the debt is the principal thing and the security only an accessory.[14]

The equitable doctrine of conversion, under which a trust for sale of land notionally converts the interests of the beneficiaries from real estate to personal estate, raises more intricate problems. In the United States, some courts have used the doctrine as a means of escape from the general rule that all questions relating to immovables are governed by the *lex situs*, and have held that a trust for sale converts the land into personalty and so into a movable.[15] In England, the courts have usually resisted this temptation and have adopted a more logical (though more inexorable) line of reasoning. The leading case is *Re Berchtold*,[16] where a domiciled Hungarian died intestate, having been entitled to an interest in English freehold land which was subject to a trust for sale but had not yet been sold. His next-of-kin by Hungarian law claimed his interest in this land on the ground that it was converted into personalty. But it was held that his interest was an interest in an immovable, that therefore English domestic law applied (including its doctrine of conversion), and that his next-of-kin by English law were entitled. Russell J. said[17]:

> "But this equitable doctrine only arises and comes into play where the question for consideration arises as between real estate and per-

---

[7] A heritable bond is a bond for a sum of money, to which is joined, for the creditor's further security, a conveyance of land or of heritage, to be held by the creditor in security of the debt.

[8] See Meston, *The Succession (Scotland) Act 1964*, 2nd ed., pp. 46, 122–123.

[9] *Jerningham* v. *Herbert* (1829) 4 Russ. 388, 395; *Re Fitzgerald* [1904] 1 Ch. 573, 588.

[10] *Ex p. Rucker* (1834) 3 Dea. & Ch. 704.

[11] *Re Hoyles* [1911] 1 Ch. 179; *Re Berchtold* [1923] 1 Ch. 192, 199; *Macdonald* v. *Macdonald*, 1932 S.C.(H.L.) 79, 84; *Re Cutcliffe* [1940] Ch. 565, 571.

[12] *Freke* v. *Carbery* (1873) L.R. 16 Eq. 461; *Duncan* v. *Lawson* (1889) 41 Ch.D. 394; *Pepin* v. *Bruyere* [1900] 2 Ch. 504.

[13] *Re Hoyles* [1911] 1 Ch. 179.

[14] *Re O'Neill* [1922] N.Z.L.R. 468; *Re Young* [1942] V.L.R. 4; *Re Williams* [1945] V.L.R. 213; *Haque* v. *Haque* (*No. 2*) (1965) 114 C.L.R. 98, 133, 146.

[15] See Hancock (1965) 17 Stan.L.Rev. 1095.

[16] [1923] 1 Ch. 192.

[17] At p. 206.

sonal estate. It has no relation to the question whether property is movable or immovable. The doctrine of conversion is that real estate is treated as personal estate, or personal estate is treated as real estate; not that immovables are turned into movables, or movables into immovables."

However, section 75(5) of the Settled Land Act 1925[18] contains a statutory enactment of the doctrine of conversion which, unlike the judge-made doctrine, is expressed in terms of land and money and not in terms of real estate and personal estate: and different reasoning has been applied to it in a conflict of laws context. The Act provides that the tenant for life of settled land may sell the settled land or any part of it, and that if the purchaser pays the price to at least two trustees or a trust corporation (in which case it becomes "capital money"), he gets a good title to the fee simple. Section 75(5) then provides that capital money arising under the Act while remaining uninvested or unapplied, and securities on which an investment of any such capital money is made, shall for all purposes of disposition, transmission and devolution be treated as land. In *Re Cutcliffe*,[19] a man died intestate in 1897 domiciled in Ontario. He was entitled to a contingent reversionary interest in stock situated in England which represented the reinvestment of the proceeds of sale of English freehold settled land. His next-of-kin by the law of Ontario claimed his interest in the stock on the ground that it was an interest in a movable. But it was held, quite correctly, that under the terms of the English statute the stock must be treated as land and therefore as an immovable, with the result that the intestate's English heir at law was entitled to it.

The distinction between the two cases is that in the *Berchtold* case the judge-made doctrine of conversion which had to be considered said that realty was to be treated as personalty, and was therefore inapplicable on the conflicts plane; whereas in the *Cutcliffe* case the statute which had to be considered said that money was to be treated as land, and was therefore applicable on the conflicts plane.[20] An Australian court has reached a similar conclusion on the construction of the English statute.[21]

In *Re Piercy*[22] an English court was unable to resist the temptation to apply the equitable doctrine of conversion in order to avoid a result which it evidently regarded as inconvenient or absurd. A testator domiciled in England who owned land in Sardinia devised all his real and personal property to trustees upon trust for sale and conversion and to hold the proceeds upon trust for his children for their respective lives with remainders to their issue. The law of Italy provided that any condition imposed on an heir or legatee, no matter how expressed, that he was to retain the property and hand it over to a third party was a trust substitution and was forbidden. There was some doubt whether the trustees or the children were the "heirs

[18] Re-enacting Settled Land Act 1882, s. 22(5).
[19] [1940] Ch. 565.
[20] Contrast Falconbridge, p. 589, refuted in Dicey and Morris, pp. 526–527.
[21] *Re Crook* (1936) 36 S.R.N.S.W. 186.
[22] [1895] 1 Ch. 83.

or legatees" within the meaning of this rule of Italian law; but North J. assumed that the children were. He held that the rents and profits until sale must devolve on the children in accordance with Italian law, but that as the Italian law did not prohibit a sale of the land, it was the duty of the trustees to sell it and remit the proceeds to England, and that the proceeds were not subject to Italian law. There was no evidence that the Italian law of the *situs* regarded the land as notionally converted into money, and the decision has been criticised on this ground.[23] But it has been approved in the House of Lords[24]; and however suspect the reasoning, the conclusion seems entirely proper.

Difficult problems arise if things which are physically movable are moved from a jurisdiction which regards them as legally immovable into a jurisdiction which regards them as legally movable. Logically, the new *lex situs* should determine their character. In *Re Midleton's Settlement*,[25] the proceeds of sale of Irish settled land were reinvested in English securities. Notwithstanding section 22(5) of the Settled Land Act 1882, which was still in force in Ireland, though in England it had been repealed and replaced by section 75(5) of the Settled Land Act 1925, it was held that for purposes of taxation the securities were situated in England. It is a legitimate inference from this decision that, had it been necessary to determine for purposes of the conflict of laws whether they were movable or immovable, they would have been held to be movable. The Irish Settled Land Act 1882 would not apply because the securities were in England. The English Settled Land Act 1925 would not apply either because the capital money did not arise "under this Act."

---

[23] Cheshire and North, pp. 508–509; Beale, pp. 958–959.
[24] *Philipson-Stow* v. *I.R.C.* [1961] A.C. 727, 744–745, *per* Lord Simonds.
[25] [1947] Ch. 583; affirmed *sub nom. Midleton* v. *Cottesloe* [1949] A.C. 418.

CHAPTER 18

IMMOVABLES

JURISDICTION

The Moçambique rule

As a general rule, English courts have no jurisdiction to entertain an action for the determination of the title to, or the right to possession of, any immovable situated outside England.[1] The origins of this rule have been traced to the ancient common law practice whereby juries were chosen from persons acquainted with the facts of a case, who therefore decided questions of fact from their own knowledge and not from the evidence of witnesses. In order that the right jury might be empanelled it was necessary to lay the venue exactly. The consequence was that English courts had no jurisdiction to entertain actions where the facts occurred abroad. This led to such inconvenience that the rule was evaded by the fiction of *videlicet, i.e.* by the untraversable allegation that a foreign place was situated in, *e.g.* the parish of St. Marylebone.[2] Unfortunately this relaxation only applied to transitory actions, that is, actions where the facts might have occurred anywhere (*e.g.* actions for breach of contract). It did not apply to local actions, that is, actions where the facts could only have occurred in a particular place (*e.g.* actions relating to foreign land).

This technical and somewhat arbitrary distinction between transitory and local actions did not appeal to Lord Mansfield, who on two occasions entertained actions for trespass to land in Nova Scotia and Labrador, on the ground that there were no local courts in those then uncivilised places and that therefore the plaintiff would otherwise have been without a remedy.[3] Unfortunately Lord Mansfield's liberal view was overruled in *Doulson* v. *Matthews*,[4] where Buller J. said:

> "It is now too late for us to inquire whether it were wise or politic to make a distinction between transitory and local actions: it is sufficient for the courts that the law has settled the distinction, and that an action *quare clausum fregit* is local."

The Judicature Act 1873 and Rules of Court made thereunder abolished local venues, and accordingly it was arguable that there was no longer any reason why English courts should not decide questions of title to foreign

---

[1] *British South Africa Co.* v. *Companhia de Moçambique* [1893] A.C. 602.
[2] Holdsworth, *History of English Law,* Vol. 5, pp. 140–142.
[3] Cited in *Mostyn* v. *Fabrigas* (1774) 1 Cowp. 161.
[4] (1792) 4 T.R. 503, 504.

land, or at least grant damages for trespass thereto.[5] But in the leading case
of *British South Africa Co.* v. *Companhia de Moçambique*[6] the House of
Lords decided that "the grounds upon which the courts have hitherto
refused to exercise jurisdiction in actions of trespass to lands situated
abroad were substantial and not technical, and that the rules of procedure
under the Judicature Acts have not conferred a jurisdiction which did not
exist before." Unfortunately neither Lord Herschell nor Lord Halsbury,
who delivered speeches in that case, vouchsafed a hint as to what these
"substantial" grounds were.

The facts of the case were as follows:

> The plaintiff, a Portuguese chartered company, alleged that it was
> in possession of large tracts of lands in southern Africa, and that the
> defendant, an English chartered company, by its agents wrongfully
> broke and entered and took possession of the lands and ejected the
> plaintiff company therefrom. The plaintiff claimed (1) a declaration
> that it was lawfully in possession of the lands; (2) an injunction
> restraining the defendant from asserting any title to the lands; (3)
> £250,000 damages for trespass. The defendant pleaded that because
> the lands were outside the jurisdiction the statement of claim disclosed
> no cause of action. The question of law was ordered to be heard
> before a Divisional Court of the Queen's Bench Division, which gave
> judgment for the defendant and dismissed the action. In the Court of
> Appeal the plaintiff formally abandoned claims (1) and (2), and that
> court by a majority declared that the High Court had jurisdiction. The
> House of Lords unanimously restored the judgment of the Divisional
> Court.

Section 30 of the Civil Jurisdiction and Judgments Act 1982 provides that
English courts have jurisdiction to entertain proceedings for trespass to or
other torts affecting foreign land, unless the proceedings are principally
concerned with a question of title to, or the right to possession of, the land.
This section reverses the much-criticised decision of the House of Lords in
Hesperides Hotels Ltd. v. *Aegean Turkish Holidays Ltd.*,[7] where the
House refused to limit the *Moçambique* rule to cases where title or the
right to possession was in issue, conceding only that it does not prevent an
action for damages for trespass to the contents of a building situated
abroad.

Under article 16(1) of the Brussels Convention set out in the First Schedule to the 1982 Act, the courts of the Contracting State in which the property is situated have exclusive jurisdiction regardless of domicile in
proceedings which have as their object rights *in rem* in or tenancies of
immovable property.[8]

---

[5] See *Whitaker* v. *Forbes* (1875) 1 C.P.D. 51; *The Tolten* [1946] P. 135, 141–142, *per* Scott
L.J.; contrast pp. 163–164, *per* Somervell L.J.; pp. 168–169, *per* Cohen L.J.
[6] [1892] 2 Q.B. 358; [1893] A.C. 602.
[7] [1979] A.C. 508.
[8] See *ante*, p. 85. Sched. 4, art. 16(1) applies the same rule as between the different parts of
the United Kingdom.

If the *Moçambique* rule is one of policy, as the House of Lords insisted that it was, the better opinion would seem to be that it cannot be waived by any agreement between the parties.[9]

The common law rule is subject to two not very well defined exceptions, both of which are derived from the practice of Courts of Equity.[10] These will now be considered.

First exception: contracts and equities

If the court has jurisdiction *in personam* over a defendant, either because he is in England when the writ is served on him, or because he submits to the jurisdiction, or because the court grants leave to serve notice of the writ out of the jurisdiction under Order 11, r. 1(1), of the Rules of the Supreme Court,[11] the court has jurisdiction to entertain an action against him in respect of a contract or an equity affecting foreign land. "Courts of Equity have from the time of Lord Hardwicke's decision in *Penn* v. *Baltimore*[12] exercised jurisdiction *in personam* in relation to foreign land against persons locally within the jurisdiction of the English court in cases of contract, fraud and trust."[13] This exception can be traced back to *Arglasse* v. *Muschamp*[14] (1682), but the leading case is *Penn* v. *Baltimore*[15] (1750), where the facts (slightly simplified) were as follows:

> Penn was the owner of the then province of Pennsylvania. Lord Baltimore was the owner of the then province of Maryland. They made a contract to settle the boundaries between the two provinces. Lord Hardwicke decreed specific performance of the contract.

The obligations which the courts will thus enforce are not easily brought under one head. "They all depend," said Parker J.,[16] "upon the existence between the parties to the suit of some personal obligation arising out of contract or implied contract, fiduciary relationship or fraud, or other conduct which, in the view of the Court of Equity in this country, would be unconscionable, and do not depend for their existence on the law of the locus of the immovable property." The jurisdiction is substantially confined to cases in which there is either a contract or an equity between the parties. Examples of contracts are an action by a lessor to recover rent due

---

[9] *The Tolten* [1946] P. 135, 166; Cheshire and North, p. 502, n. 5; Dicey and Morris, p. 540. Contrast *The Mary Moxham* (1876) 1 P.D. 107, 109 and *Re Duke of Wellington* [1948] Ch. 118, where waiver seems to have been allowed: but the latter case would now fall under the second exception to the rule, and the former would raise no jurisdictional problem in view of s.30 of the Civil Jurisdiction and Judgments Act 1982.

[10] In *The Tolten, supra,* the Court of Appeal created a third exception and allowed an action *in rem* against a ship to enforce a maritime lien on the ship for damage done to a wharf in Nigeria. Since this was an exception to the second branch of the *Moçambique* rule which has now been abolished, it need not be further considered.

[11] See *ante,* Chap. 6.

[12] (1750) 1 Ves.Sen. 444.

[13] *Companhia de Moçambique* v. *British South Africa Co.* [1892] 2 Q.B. 358, 364, *per* Wright J.; *cf. Ewing* v. *Orr-Ewing* (1883) 9 App.Cas. 34, 40, *per* Lord Selborne.

[14] (1682) 1 Vern. 75.

[15] (1750) 1 Ves.Sen. 444.

[16] *Deschamps* v. *Miller* [1908] 1 Ch. 856, 863.

under a lease of foreign land,[17] or an action by a vendor or purchaser of foreign land for specific performance of a contract of sale.[18] Examples of equities are actions to redeem[19] or foreclose[20] a mortgage on foreign land, or to prevent a creditor from purchasing foreign land at an undervalue by making unfair use of local procedure,[21] or actions to reclaim gifts made under undue influence,[22] or for a declaration that the defendant holds foreign land as trustee.[23]

The decided cases have emphasised the following general points:

(a) The jurisdiction cannot be exercised if the *lex situs* would prohibit the enforcement of the decree. "If, indeed," said Lord Cottenham,[24] "the law of the country where the land is situate should not permit, or not enable, the defendant to do what the court might otherwise think it right to decree, it would be useless and unjust to direct him to do the act." But this rule must be taken *cum grano salis*. For in the case in which Lord Cottenham was speaking, a mortgagee by deposit of title deeds was held entitled to priority over the mortgagor's unsecured creditors, although by the *lex situs* of the land the deposit gave him no lien or equitable mortgage over the land at all.

(b) The jurisdiction cannot be exercised against strangers to the equity unless they have become personally affected thereby. But it is difficult to determine what degree of privity prevents a defendant from being a stranger to the equity. If A agrees to sell foreign land to B, and instead conveys it to C who has notice of the contract, C is a stranger to the equity and the jurisdiction cannot be invoked against him.[25] But if a company creates an equitable charge on foreign land in favour of debenture-holders, and sells the land to a purchaser "subject to the mortgage lien or charge now subsisting," and the purchaser expressly undertakes to pay the debentures and interest thereon, the court has jurisdiction to entertain an action by the debenture-holders against the purchaser to enforce their security.[26] The distinction between buying land with notice of a contract and buying land subject to a charge seems to be a tenuous one, not easily reconcilable with equitable doctrines of constructive notice.

(c) The jurisdiction cannot be exercised if the court cannot effectively supervise the execution of its decree. For this reason the court will not order a sale of foreign land at the instance of a mortgagee.[27] But it will order the foreclosure of a mortgage,[28] decree specific performance of a

---

[17] *St. Pierre* v. *South American Stores Ltd.* [1936] 1 K.B. 382.
[18] *Richard West and Partners Ltd.* v. *Dick* [1969] 2 Ch. 424; *Ward* v. *Coffin* (1972) 27 D.L.R. (3d) 58.
[19] *Beckford* v. *Kemble* (1822) 1 S. & St. 7.
[20] *Toller* v. *Carteret* (1705) 2 Vern. 494; *Paget* v. *Ede* (1874) L.R. 18 Eq. 118.
[21] *Cranstown* v. *Johnston* (1800) 5 Ves. 277.
[22] *Razelos* v. *Razelos* (*No. 2*) [1970] 1 W.L.R. 392.
[23] *Cook Industries Inc.* v. *Galliher* [1979] Ch. 439.
[24] *Re Courtney, ex p. Pollard* (1840) Mont. & Ch. 239, 250.
[25] *Norris* v. *Chambres* (1861) 29 Beav. 246; 3 D.F. & J. 583.
[26] *Mercantile Investment Co.* v. *River Plate Co.* [1892] 2 Ch. 303.
[27] *Grey* v. *Manitoba Ry. Co.* [1897] A.C. 254.
[28] *Paget* v. *Ede* (1874) L.R. 18 Eq. 118, criticised by Falconbridge, pp. 618–620.

contract to sell foreign land,[29] and make an order for the inspection of foreign land.[30]

(d) The jurisdiction cannot be exercised unless there is some personal equity running from the plaintiff to the defendant. "There must be some personal element, something more than a mere naked question of title to foreign land."[31] Thus in *Re Hawthorne,*[32] by reason of an intestacy the title to a house in Dresden was in dispute between A and B. B sold the house and received part of the purchase-money. A brought an action against B to make him account for the purchase-money, but it was held that the court had no jurisdiction. And in *Deschamps* v. *Miller,*[33] a husband and wife, domiciled in France, married there. Their marriage contract provided that the marriage should be governed by the *régime dotal* with community of after-acquired property under French law. The husband acquired land in India, where he went through a bigamous ceremony of marriage with Q, and settled the land on trusts for the benefit of Q and her children. After the deaths of the husband and wife the plaintiff, their only son, brought an action against the trustees of the settlement claiming his share of the land in India under French law. It was held that the court had no jurisdiction.

The equitable jurisdiction is anomalous and, as Lord Esher said,[34] "seems to be open to the strong objection that the court is doing indirectly what it dare not do directly." In the early cases in which the jurisdiction was invoked, the land was situated within British territory, and the exercise of jurisdiction could perhaps be justified on the ground that, if there were any courts in the countries then being colonised by Englishmen, the decisions of those courts could not command the same respect as those of the courts in England. In modern times, however, the jurisdiction is much less easy to justify, especially when the land is situated in a country which is politically as well as legally foreign. A modern judge could hardly say, as Shadwell V.-C. once said,[35] "I consider that in the contemplation of the Court of Chancery every foreign court is an inferior court."

There is no English authority on the converse question, whether the decree of a foreign court purporting to operate *in personam* on the parties to some contract or equity affecting English land will be enforced in England. But there is some Canadian authority. In *Duke* v. *Andler*[36]:

> A agreed with B in California to sell to B land in British Columbia. A and B were both residents of California. A conveyed the land to B in accordance with British Columbian law. A then brought an action against B in California to set aside the conveyance because of B's fraud. The Californian court ordered B to reconvey the land to A. On B's refusal to do so, the clerk of the court purported to reconvey the

---

[29] *Richard West and Partners Ltd.* v. *Dick* [1969] 2 Ch. 424; *Ward* v. *Coffin* (1972) 27 D.L.R. (3d) 58.

[30] *Cook Industries Inc.* v. *Galliher* [1979] Ch. 439.

[31] Cheshire, 4th ed., p. 576.

[32] (1883) 23 Ch.D. 743.

[33] [1908] 1 Ch. 856.

[34] *Companhia de Moçambique* v. *British South Africa Co.* [1892] 2 Q.B. 358, 404–405.

[35] *Bent* v. *Young* (1838) 9 Sim. 180, 191.

[36] [1932] 4 D.L.R. 529. See D. M. Gordon (1933) 49 L.Q.R. 547.

land in B's name. A sued B in British Columbia for a declaration that A was the owner of the land. The Supreme Court of Canada held that A was not entitled to the declaration.

Second exception: estates and trusts

If the court has jurisdiction to administer a trust[37] or the estate of a deceased person, and the property includes movables or immovables situated in England and immovables situated abroad, the court has jurisdiction to determine questions of title to the foreign immovables for the purposes of the administration. This formulation of the exception is that of Dicey and Morris,[38] because it has never been precisely formulated by English judges, though it has been approved by the Court of Session.[39] But the existence of the exception can scarcely be doubted. The principal authority on which it rests is the well-known case of *Nelson* v. *Bridport*[40]:

> The King of the Two Sicilies granted land in Sicily to Admiral Nelson for himself and the heirs of his body, with power to appoint a successor. By his will, which dealt also with property in England, the Admiral devised the land to trustees in trust for his brother William for life with remainders over. After the Admiral's death, and in the lifetime of William, a law was passed in Sicily abolishing entails and making the persons lawfully in possession of such estates the absolute owners thereof. Taking advantage of this law, brother William devised the land to his daughter Lady Bridport. The remainderman under the Admiral's will claimed to be entitled to the land. The court assumed jurisdiction.

Here, it will be noticed, there was no contract, no fiduciary relationship and no equity between the parties: for all that appears from the report, they were complete strangers to each other. There was nothing but a mere naked question of title to foreign land, and therefore the case could not possibly have fallen under the first exception discussed above.

This second exception is also supported by a number of other cases.[41] These cases cannot be explained on the ground that the jurisdictional objection was waived, because as we have seen[42] the better opinion is that the *Moçambique* rule cannot be waived; and in any case it is difficult to see how waiver could be allowed in cases where the interests of minors or of unborn persons are involved. They may perhaps be justified on the ground that the court can make its adjudication effective indirectly through its control of the trustees or of the other assets situated in England. It may be that

---

[37] It may be that this should now be confined to trusts arising under wills or intestacies, since these are excluded from the Brussels Convention, whereas *inter vivos* trusts might fall within art. 16(1), *ante*, p. 338.

[38] Rule 77, Exception 2, p. 545.

[39] *Jubert* v. *Church Commissioners for England*, 1952 S.C. 160, 162.

[40] (1846) 8 Beav. 547.

[41] *Hope* v. *Carnegie* (1866) L.R. 1 Ch.App. 320; *Ewing* v. *Orr-Ewing* (1883) 9 App.Cas. 34; *Re Piercy* [1895] 1 Ch. 83; *Re Moses* [1908] 2 Ch. 235; *Re Stirling* [1908] 2 Ch. 344; *Re Pearse's Settlement* [1909] 1 Ch. 304; *Re Hoyles* [1911] 1 Ch. 179; *Re Ross* [1930] 1 Ch. 377; *Re Duke of Wellington* [1948] Ch. 118.

[42] *Ante*, p. 339, n. 9.

Lord Herschell had these cases in mind when in the *Moçambique* case[43] he said:

> "It is quite true that in the exercise of the undoubted jurisdiction of the courts it may become necessary incidentally to investigate and determine the title to foreign lands; but it does not seem to me to follow that because such a question may incidentally arise and fall to be adjudicated upon, the courts possess, or that it is expedient that they should exercise, jurisdiction to try an action founded on a disputed claim of title to foreign lands."

CHOICE OF LAW

Introduction

One of the most deeply-rooted principles of the English and American conflict of laws is that all questions relating to immovables are governed by the *lex situs*. At first sight this proposition seems an almost self-evident one, for *ex hypothesi* the land can never be moved, and can only be dealt within a manner permitted by the *lex situs*. Although the rule has to some extent been eroded by statute and judicial decision, it still retains a remarkable vitality. Two reasons may be suggested for this. First, it was vigorously advocated by Story in his influential treatise. Story was extremely dogmatic on this topic:

> "The consent of the tribunals, acting under the common law, both in England and America, is, if possible, still more uniform on the subject. All the authorities recognise the principle in its fullest import, that real estate is exclusively subject to the laws of the government, within whose territory it is situate."[44] "The common law has wisely adhered to the doctrine, that the title to real property can pass only in the manner, and by the forms, and to the extent, allowed by the local law. It has thus cut off innumerable disputes, and given simplicity, as well as uniformity, to its operations."[45]

Secondly, the rule was eagerly seized upon as an excuse for English courts to apply English law to English land.[46] Any rule of the conflict of laws which led almost invariably to the application of English domestic law was bound to be attractive to English judges. The reason why it leads so often to the application of English domestic law is, of course, the *Moçambique* rule which, as we have seen,[47] says that English courts have, in general, no jurisdiction to determine questions of title to foreign land.

In the United States, some very extravagant language has sometimes been used to explain and justify the *situs* rule. According to Judge Redfield, the author of a treatise on wills, the very dignity, independence and security of the State are at stake in the descent of real property:

[43] [1893] A.C. 602, 626.
[44] Story, s.428.
[45] s.444.
[46] Westlake, p. 9.
[47] *Ante,* p. 338.

"The descent of real estate, as well as the devise of it, is governed exclusively by the law of the place where the property is situated. It would not comport with the dignity, the independence, or the security of any independent state or nation, that these incidents should be liable to be affected, in any manner, by the legislation, or the decisions of the courts, of any state or nation besides itself."[48]

In similar vein the Connecticut Supreme Court of Errors and Appeals once observed that

"succession to the real estate of a deceased person . . . has always been regarded as a matter of grave political consequence. . . . Owner-ship of land controls its occupancy, and largely determines the char-acter of the population."[49]

However, in the last forty-five years the *situs* rule has been subjected to devastating academic criticism[50] on the ground that it is much too broad, hopelessly undiscriminating, and careless of the important policies of dom-estic law. Admittedly it achieves certainty, uniformity and symmetry in the law, and is easy and simple to apply: but as we shall see[51] it can lead to extremely harsh and inconvenient results. The first of the critics was Cook, who in an influential article[52] pointed out that when a court sitting at the *situs* of the land is confronted by a document (*e.g.* a deed or will) executed abroad by a person domiciled abroad, the real question is, should the court apply to such a document the same rule of decision that it would apply to a purely domestic document. He argued cogently that in matters of form, capacity and matrimonial property it should not, but that in matters of essential validity it should.

Cook's analysis was carried several stages further by Professor Hancock, who in an important series of articles[53] argued that, apart from questions of the marketability or use of land, the *situs-forum* should not necessarily apply the domestic law of the *situs* but should consider whether that law, properly interpreted and understood, was intended to apply to foreign-executed documents or to persons domiciled abroad. Nobody can doubt that in Hancock's two exceptional cases (as he frequently stressed) a court sitting at the *situs* of the land must for obvious reasons of policy apply its own law to questions of marketability or use. For instance, no English court could allow a testator domiciled abroad to create an unbarrable entail in English land, or future interests which infringed the rule against perpetuities, or to devise it on charitable trusts which infringed English housing or town planning legislation.

It remains to be seen whether the arguments of Cook and Hancock will

---

[48] *Redfield on Wills*, 4th ed. (1876), Vol. I, p. 404.
[49] *Clarke's Appeal*, 70 Conn. 195, 210–211, 39 Atl. 155, 159 (1898).
[50] Cook, Chap. 10; Hancock (1964) 16 Stanford L.Rev. 561; (1965) 17 Stanford L.Rev. 1095; (1966) 18 Stanford L.Rev. 1299; (1967) 20 Stanford L.Rev. 1; Weintraub (1966) 52 Cornell L.Q. 1; Morris (1969) 85 L.Q.R. 339.
[51] See *post,* pp. 348, 391–392.
[52] See note 50 above.
[53] See note 50 above.

persuade English judges to reconsider their traditional reliance on the *situs* rule as an all-embracing formula by which, in the absence of statute or judicial precedent to the contrary, all questions relating to land must be governed. But it may be pointed out that, long before they wrote, it was held that a foreign marriage contract or settlement (even if it was not express but was imposed or implied by foreign law) could affect the devolution of land in England[54]; that wills of immovables are, as a general rule, interpreted by reference to the law of the testator's domicile[55]; that now by statute a will of immovables must be treated as properly executed if its execution conformed to the law of the country where it was executed, or where the testator was domiciled or habitually resident, or of which he was a national.[56] Moreover, as we have seen,[57] the proper law of a contract affecting land is not necessarily the *lex situs*. This last example is particularly instructive because in many situations the distinction between contract and conveyance is apt to be tenuous. This is because in English domestic law a specifically enforceable contract for the sale of land operates as an equitable conveyance of the land to the purchaser. The vendor becomes a trustee for the purchaser, though he has a lien on the land for the purchase price. Hence, although a conveyance of land in England executed abroad by a person domiciled abroad might not be valid as a conveyance unless it complied with English formalities, it might be valid as a contract to convey, of which specific performance might be given, if there was a note or memorandum in writing or some act of part performance sufficient to satisfy section 40 of the Law of Property Act 1925.

Nearly all writers on the conflict of laws agree that, in the rare cases where an English court is dealing with a question of title to land situated abroad, it should apply whatever system of domestic law the *lex situs* would apply[58]: and there are cases in which this has been done.[59] In other words, this situation is one in which it is justifiable to apply the doctrine of renvoi in order to achieve uniformity with the *lex situs*.[60] Uniformity with the *lex situs* is important because in the last resort the land can only be dealt with in a manner permitted by that law. Consequently, any decision by a non-*situs* court which ignored what the courts of the *situs* had decided or would decide might well be a *brutum fulmen*.

With these preliminary observations in mind we now proceed to consider how English courts have dealt with questions concerning immovables in the conflict of laws. Our discussion will be brief because the effect of grants of administration on immovables, succession to immovables, marriage and bankruptcy are reserved for separate discussion in later chapters.[61]

---

[54] *Re De Nicols (No. 2)* [1900] 2 Ch. 410; *post,* p. 414.
[55] *Post,* p. 399.
[56] Wills Act 1963, s.1; *post,* p. 393.
[57] *Ante,* p. 278.
[58] Falconbridge, pp. 141, 217–220; Dicey and Morris, pp. 74–75, 548–549; Cheshire and North, pp. 75, 504; Cook, pp. 264, 279–280; Lorenzen, p. 78; Hancock (1965) 17 Stanford L.Rev. 1095, 1096, n. 4.
[59] *Re Ross* [1930] 1 Ch. 377; *Re Duke of Wellington* [1947] Ch. 506.
[60] See *post,* p. 476.
[61] Chaps. 23, 24, 25, 27.

Formal validity

There appears to be only one reported English case in which the formal validity of a deed affecting land has been considered. In *Adams* v. *Clutterbuck*,[62] a domiciled Englishman conveyed to a purchaser domiciled in England a right of shooting over land in Scotland. The conveyance was made in England by an instrument in writing but not under seal. The law of England required such conveyances to be under seal, but the law of Scotland did not. It was held that the conveyance was valid. Perhaps we may conclude from this that if the facts had been reversed, *i.e.* if a domiciled Scotsman had conveyed shooting rights over land in England to another domiciled Scotsman by an instrument in writing but not under seal executed in Scotland, the conveyance would have been held void.[63] But, as we have seen,[64] it might be valid as a contract to convey.

On the other hand, a contract relating to land need not necessarily comply with the formalities of the *lex situs*. It will be formally valid if it complies with those of the proper law or, probably, of the *lex loci contractus*. Thus in *Re Smith*,[65] a man domiciled in England executed a deed in England by which he charged all his share and interest in land in Dominica in favour of his sisters in consideration of a loan, and covenanted to execute a legal mortgage in their favour. He died without having done so. It was held that although equitable mortgages were unknown to the law of Dominica (*lex situs*), the English contract created a valid equitable mortgage over the land.

Essential validity

Although the cases all concern wills, there can be no doubt that the essential validity of a deed affecting land in England is governed by English law. That law will determine what estates can legally be created,[66] what are the incidents of those estates,[67] whether gifts to charities are valid,[68] and whether the interests given infringe the rule against perpetuities or accumulations.[69]

On the other hand, the essential validity of a contract affecting land is governed by its proper law and not necessarily by the *lex situs*. The leading case is *British South Africa Company* v. *De Beers Consolidated Mines Ltd.*[70] By a contract made in England and governed by English law a South African company agreed to grant a loan to an English company on the security of a floating charge to be created by debentures issued by the borrower. The contract further provided that the borrower would grant the

---

[62] (1883) 10 Q.B.D. 403.

[63] This is supported by cases on the formal validity of wills before the Wills Act 1963, in which it was held that a will devising land in England was void unless it complied with the formalities of English domestic law, even if it was formally valid by the law of the testator's domicile: *Coppin* v. *Coppin* (1725) 2 P.Wms. 291; *Pepin* v. *Bruyere* [1900] 2 Ch. 504.

[64] *Ante*, p. 345.

[65] [1916] 2 Ch. 206.

[66] *Nelson* v. *Bridport* (1846) 8 Beav. 547.

[67] *Re Miller* [1914] 1 Ch. 511. **b**

[68] *Duncan* v. *Lawson* (1889) 41 Ch.D. 394; *Re Hoyles* [1911] 1 Ch. 179.

[69] *Freke* v. *Carbery* (1873) L.R. 16 Eq. 461.

[70] [1910] 2 Ch. 502; reversed on a point of English domestic law, [1912] A.C. 52.

lender an exclusive licence to work all the diamondiferous mines owned by the borrower in Northern and Southern Rhodesia. The Court of Appeal held that the question whether this provision was void as a clog on the equity of redemption must be decided in accordance with English law as the proper law of the contract and not Southern Rhodesian law as one of the two *leges situs*. Cozens-Hardy M.R. said[71]:

> "In my opinion an English contract to give a mortgage on foreign land, although the mortgage has to be perfected according to the *lex situs,* is a contract to give a mortgage which—*inter partes*—is to be treated as an English mortgage, and subject to such rights of redemption and such equities as the law of England regards as necessarily incident to a mortgage."

Again, in *Re Anchor Line (Henderson Brothers) Ltd.*[72] it was held that an English company with a head office in Glasgow could create a valid floating charge over land in Scotland in favour of a Scottish bank, although floating charges were at that time unknown to the law of Scotland.[73]

Capacity

As usual, capacity raises more difficult problems. There is much to be said for the view that capacity to transfer land should be governed, not by the *lex situs,* but by the law of the transferor's domicile. On the other hand, the claims of the *lex situs* cannot be entirely ignored. It is necessary to distinguish between capacities and incapacities, and between cases where the court is sitting at the *situs* of the land and cases where it is not.

There appears to be no reported case in which the English court has had to consider the question of capacity to transfer land in England when the transferor was domiciled abroad. In the American case of *Proctor* v. *Frost,*[74] a married woman domiciled in Massachusetts in that state became surety for her husband and gave a mortgage on her New Hampshire land as security. The mortgagee brought a bill in equity in New Hampshire to foreclose the mortgage. The lady-mortgagor's defence was that by a New Hampshire statute a married woman could not become surety for her husband. The Supreme Judicial Court of New Hampshire rejected this defence on the ground that "the primary purpose of the statute was not to regulate the transfer of New Hampshire real estate, but to protect married women in New Hampshire from the consequences of their efforts, presumably ill-advised, to reinforce the credit of embarrassed husbands." This unorthodox decision seems sound and sensible; but the reasoning is not entirely satisfactory because it emphasises the place where the mortgage was executed and not where the mortgagor was domiciled. The lady-mortgagor was surely outside the scope of the New Hampshire statute, not

[71] [1910] 2 Ch. 502, 515.
[72] [1937] Ch. 483.
[73] The decision was criticised by Lord Keith in *Carse* v. *Coppen*, 1951 S.C. 233, 248 for failure to give effect to s.327(2) of the Companies Act 1948. Companies can now create floating charges in Scots law under the Companies (Floating Charges) (Scotland) Act 1961.
[74] 89 N.H. 304, 197 Atl. 813 (1938).

because she executed the mortgage in Massachusetts, but because she was domiciled there.[75] If the laws of the two states had been reversed and the mortgagor was incapable of making the mortgage by the law of her domicile (Massachusetts), but capable by the *lex situs* (New Hampshire), there would have been something to be said for applying the *lex situs* and holding the mortgage valid, at any rate if the mortgagee was domiciled and resident in New Hampshire. For New Hampshire mortgagees ought not to be deprived of their security because of some lurking incapacity in the law of the mortgagor's domicile.

The question what law governs capacity to transfer land situated abroad came before the Court of Appeal in *Bank of Africa* v. *Cohen*,[76] where the *lex situs* was applied. The reasoning is, however, most unsatisfactory. A married woman, domiciled and resident with her husband in England, executed a deed in England whereby she agreed to mortgage land in Johannesburg to an English bank as security for past and future advances made and to be made by the bank to her husband. The bank sued for specific performance of the deed. The lady-mortgagor's defence was that by South African law a married woman was incapable of becoming surety for her husband unless (a) she obtained a pecuniary benefit from the contract, or (b) she was engaged in trade, or (c) she clearly and specifically renounced the benefits of certain statutory provisions of South African law. None of these exceptions applied, but the trial judge found as a fact that she knew quite well what she was doing. It was held that her capacity to make the contract was governed by South African law and the contract was therefore void.

This decision seems harsh and unjust. The bank was left without security for advances made on the strength of the lady-mortgagor's promise; and she was allowed to break her promise with impunity although she knew quite well what she was doing. The court made no attempt to ascertain the policy of the South African law, nor whether a South African court would have applied South African domestic law to this very case. Had it done so, it might well have discovered that the South African law laid down a policy not for South African land but for South African married women, and that the defendant was outside the scope of that law because she was domiciled in England. Moreover, the court was dealing not with a mortgage but with a contract to make a mortgage. If, as seems likely, the proper law of the contract was English law, what was there to prevent the court from making a decree of specific performance? From this point of view the case is difficult to reconcile with *British South Africa Co.* v. *De Beers Consolidated Mines Ltd.*,[77] *Re Anchor Line* (*Henderson Brothers*) *Ltd.*,[78] and *Re Smith*.[79] For the court made no attempt to determine the proper law of the

---

[75] The reasoning is criticised on this ground by Cook, p. 275, n. 48, and Hancock (1967) 20 Stanford L.Rev. 1, 31, though both writers approve the result.

[76] [1909] 2 Ch. 129; criticised by Dicey and Morris, pp. 550–551; Cheshire and North, pp. 506–507, 510; Falconbridge, p. 629.

[77] [1910] 2 Ch. 502; *ante,* pp. 346–347.

[78] [1937] Ch. 483; *ante,* p. 347.

[79] [1916] 2 Ch. 206; *ante,* p. 346.

contract, but baldly asserted that the defendant's capacity was governed by the *lex situs,* and mechanically applied its domestic law.

Capacity to take (as opposed to transfer) land in England is governed by English domestic law. Perhaps the most striking illustration of this principle is the former rule, abolished in 1870,[80] that an alien could not own land in England. A more modern, but still obsolete, illustration is afforded by *Att. Gen.* v. *Parsons,*[81] where the House of Lords held that a company incorporated in the Republic of Ireland could not hold land in England without a licence in mortmain from the Crown.

[80] Naturalisation Act 1870, s.2.
[81] [1956] A.C. 421.

CHAPTER 19

THE TRANSFER OF TANGIBLE MOVABLES

In this chapter we are concerned with the question what law governs the validity of particular transfers of tangible movables and its effect on the proprietary interests of the parties thereto and those claiming under them.[1] By a particular transfer is meant, *e.g.* a transfer by way of sale, gift, pledge, hire-purchase or conditional sale. We are not concerned with general transfers made on occasions like marriage, bankruptcy or death; these are considered elsewhere.[2] Nor are we concerned with the contractual as opposed to the proprietary effects of a transfer.

THE THEORIES

The English authorities on this question are scanty and (with two exceptions[3]) inconclusive. There are some more satisfactory and more comprehensive Canadian authorities. Before the cases are examined, we shall consider three possible laws which have been advocated by writers. These are the law of the domicile, the proper law of the transfer, and the *lex situs*.

The law of the domicile

The early continental writers laid down the maxims "*mobilia sequuntur personam*" (movables follow the person) and "*mobilia ossibus inhaerent*" (movables inhere in the bones) and applied them to the transfer of chattels. These maxims mean that chattels wherever situated are deemed to follow the law of the owner's domicile. This is a useful rule for general transfers and is applicable today, broadly speaking, to general transfers made on marriage or on death, where it is clearly desirable that all the chattels comprised in a marriage settlement or will should devolve in the same way. But it does not follow that the same rule should be applied to particular transfers of individual chattels. It may have been true in medieval times that articles of personal estate were few and were usually situated in the owner's domicile. It is entirely untrue in modern commerce. Accordingly, although strong dicta favouring the law of the domicile can be found in some early cases,[4] the test of domicile has been abandoned by modern writers and judges, and need not be taken seriously today.

---

[1] See Cheshire and North, pp. 520–536; Lalive, *The Transfer of Chattels in the Conflict of Laws* (1955); Zaphiriou, *The Transfer of Chattels in Private International Law* (1955); Dicey and Morris, pp. 555–569; Chesterman (1973) 22 I.C.L.Q. 213.
[2] *Post*, Chaps. 24, 25, 27.
[3] *Cammell* v. *Sewell* (1860) 5 H. & N. 728; *Winkworth* v. *Christie* [1980] Ch. 496.
[4] *Sill* v. *Worswick* (1791) 1 H.Bl. 665, 690; *Re Ewin* (1830) 1 Cr. & J. 151, 156.

The proper law of the transfer

This has strong claims to be considered when a transfer is made in one country of chattels situated in several countries, or of chattels in the course of transit from one country to another. Moreover, a transfer may be invalid as a transfer but valid as an executory agreement to transfer. And a dictum of Kay L.J. in *Alcock* v. *Smith*[5] supports, not perhaps the proper law of the transfer, but the law of the country in which the transfer takes place (*lex loci actus*):

> "As to personal chattels, it is settled that the validity of a transfer depends not upon the law of the domicile of the owner but upon the law of the country in which the transfer takes place."

But *Alcock* v. *Smith* was concerned with a bill of exchange, where the *lex loci actus* must necessarily coincide with the *lex situs*, since a bill of exchange can only be drawn, accepted or negotiated by writing words on the bill itself, or (in the case of negotiation) by delivery. Moreover, the examples given by Kay L.J. make it clear that he was thinking of cases where the *lex loci actus* and the *lex situs* coincide.

The claims of the proper law of the transfer are less obvious when there are two independent transfers, each governed by the law of a different country, *e.g.* where the title to goods is in dispute between an unpaid seller and a pledgee from the purchaser.[6] Moreover, a problem may arise although there has been no transfer at all. For instance, A finds B's ring in Scotland, takes it to England, and possesses it there for a period sufficient to extinguish B's title under the English, but not the Scottish, Statute of Limitations.

The lex situs

This has the great advantage of certainty, because, except where goods are in transit from one country to another, the *lex situs* is likely to be more easily ascertainable than either the proper law of the transfer or the law of the owner's domicile. Moreover, if the goods remain in a foreign country at all material times, any decision by an English court which ignored the *lex situs* might be a *brutum fulmen,* since in the last resort only persons appointed by the courts of the *situs* can lawfully deal with the goods. There can be no doubt that English and American courts prefer the *lex situs* to any other law. "I do not think," said Maugham J.,[7] "that anyone can doubt that, with regard to the transfer of goods, the law applicable must be the *lex situs*. Business could not be carried on if that were not so." "The rule which looks to the law of the *situs*," said an American judge,[8] "has the merit of adopting the jurisdiction which has the actual control of the goods

---

[5] [1892] 1 Ch. 238, 267.
[6] See, *e.g. Inglis* v. *Robertson* [1898] A.C. 616.
[7] *Re Anziani* [1930] 1 Ch. 407, 420.
[8] *Lees* v. *Harding, Whitman & Co.* (1905) 68 N.J.Eq. 622, 629; 60 A. 352, 355, *per* Swayze J.

and the merit of certainty." "There is little doubt," said Devlin J.,[9] "that it is the *lex situs* which, as a general rule, governs the transfer of movables when effected contractually." "The proper law governing the transfer of corporeal movable property," said Diplock L.J.,[10] "is the *lex situs.*"

STATEMENT OF THE MODERN LAW

Where the situs remains constant

In simple cases where the *situs* of the chattel remains constant at all material times, it is reasonably well settled that the *lex situs* governs the validity and effect of the transfer.[11] Of course, the transfer may be invalid as an executed conveyance; if so, and if the transaction was contractual, the proper law of the transfer may say that the transferor must make the transferee owner. To that extent the proper law of the transfer cannot be ignored. But we are here concerned not with the law of contract but with the law of property. It is no use saying that the seller is contractually bound to deliver the goods to the buyer if, *e.g.* he has fraudulently delivered the goods to a third party, or if he has become insolvent. And, of course, the transfer may be by way of a gift, so that the transferor is under no contractual obligation at all. In the intriguing case of *Cochrane* v. *Moore*[12]:

> A by oral words of gift spoken in England purported to give one undivided fourth part of a racehorse situated in France to B. A and B were presumably domiciled and resident in England. It was held that the gift was void, since there was neither delivery nor a deed, one or other of which is necessary for the validity of a gift in English law. French law was not pleaded. If it had been, and if by French law the oral words constituted a valid gift without any delivery, the decision should have been otherwise.

The *lex situs* also determines the validity of a *donatio mortis causa,* since such transactions are thought to have a closer affinity to gifts *inter vivos* than to gifts by will.[13]

The paramount controlling influence of the *lex situs* is also well illustrated by the cases on the effect of foreign confiscatory decrees on proprietary rights in particular chattels. For, as will be seen in a later chapter,[14] such decrees have no effect in England on property situated outside the jurisdiction of the country making the decree, but do receive effect on property within that jurisdiction, even if it is later brought to England.

---

[9] *Bank voor Handel en Scheepvart N.V.* v. *Slatford* [1953] 1 Q.B. 248, 257.

[10] *Hardwick Game Farm* v. *Suffolk Agricultural Poultry Producers Association* [1966] 1 W.L.R. 287, 330; affirmed by the House of Lords [1969] 2 A.C. 31.

[11] *Inglis* v. *Usherwood* (1801) 1 East 515; *City Bank* v. *Barrow* (1880) 5 App.Cas. 664; *Inglis* v. *Robertson* [1898] A.C. 616.

[12] (1890) 25 Q.B.D. 57.

[13] *Re Korvine's Trusts* [1921] 1 Ch. 343. Contrast *Re Craven's Estate* [1937] Ch. 423, better reported in 53 T.L.R. 694, where the matter was treated (wrongly, it would seem) as one of administration; see Falconbridge, Chap. 33.

[14] *Post,* Chap. 22.

Where the situs changes

Much more complicated problems arise if the *situs* of the goods does not remain constant at all material times, so that a choice has to be made between two or more *leges situs*. For example, a thief steals my watch in Scotland and sells it in market overt in England; or a car is delivered to a hirer in England under a hire-purchase contract, taken by him to France, and sold there to a purchaser in circumstances which give him a good title under the general doctrine of French law *"en fait de meubles, la possession vaut titre."*[15]

It is convenient to begin discussion of these problems by considering the leading English case of *Cammell* v. *Sewell*[16]:

> A, a domiciled Englishman, bought some timber in Russia and shipped it to England in a Prussian ship. The ship was wrecked off the coast of Norway. B, the master of the ship, sold the timber in Norway to C in circumstances which gave C a good title by the law of Norway, but not by English law. C brought the timber to England. It was held that C's title conferred by the *lex situs* prevailed over that of A.

Cammell v. *Sewell* was followed in *Winkworth* v. *Christie*[17] where works of art were stolen from the plaintiff's house in England, taken to Italy without his knowledge or consent, and there sold to the second defendant, an Italian, who sent them to the first defendant in England to be auctioned. By Italian law the second defendant had a good title. It was held that Italian law governed.

Cammell v. *Sewell* is usually cited for the proposition that the English owner's title, validly acquired in Russia where he bought the timber, was lost by what happened in Norway. But it also decides that the Norwegian buyer's title, validly acquired in Norway, was not lost when he brought the timber to England. This second aspect of the case is just as important as the first; and it leads to the following distinction[18]:

> A title to a tangible movable acquired or reserved under the *lex situs* will be recognised as valid in England if the movable is removed from the country where it was situated when such title was acquired, unless and until such title is displaced by a new title acquired in accordance with the law of the country to which it is removed.

For the sake of clarity, let us call the country of the first *situs* X, and the country of the second *situs* Y. The law can be stated in four propositions.

(a) A title to goods acquired in X will be recognised in England if the goods are subsequently removed to Y, until some new title validly acquired in Y overrides the title acquired in X. If no such new title is acquired in Y after the removal of the goods to Y, the fact that the title acquired by the law of X would not have been acquired by the law of Y is immaterial, for

[15] French Civil Code, art. 2279.
[16] (1860) 5 H. & N. 728.
[17] [1980] Ch. 496.
[18] See Dicey and Morris, Rule 80.

the goods were in X at the material time. This is the result of the decision in *Cammell* v. *Sewell*.[19] "If, according to [Norwegian] law, the property passed by the sale in Norway to Clausen as an innocent purchaser, we do not think that the subsequent bringing of the property to England can alter the position of the parties."

(b) If a new title is acquired under the law of Y after the removal of the goods to Y, which has the effect of overriding prior titles, the title previously acquired under the law of X is displaced. It was for this reason that A's Russian title was displaced by C's Norwegian title in *Cammell* v. *Sewell*, since the sale by the master of the ship had by Norwegian law the effect of overriding prior titles. It was for this reason that A's English title was displaced by C's Italian title in *Winkworth* v. *Christie,* since the sale by the thief had by Italian law the effect of overriding prior titles. Other instances of transactions which override prior titles in English domestic law are sales in market overt, levying distress for rent, the acquisition of a repairer's lien, sales by a mercantile agent under statutes like section 2 of the Factors Act 1889, and sales by a buyer in possession with the consent of the seller under statutes like section 25 of the Sale of Goods Act 1979.[20] It makes no difference that the goods were removed to Y without the owner's consent. "We do not think that goods which were wrecked here would on that account be less liable to our laws as to market overt or as to the landlord's right of distress, merely because the owner did not foresee that they would come to England."[21]

(c) The difficult intermediate case is where A has acquired or reserved a title to goods in X, and B, the person in possession of the goods, takes them to Y, where they are sold by B to a purchaser, the sale not being one which overrides prior titles, or attached by B's creditors, not being creditors claiming a paramount lien. By the law of X, the owner's title prevails over that of the purchaser or creditors; by the law of Y, it does not. But the reason why it does not is quite different from what it was in paragraph (b) above. Here the purchaser or creditors are not saying to A "Our title prevails over yours because the sale to or attachment by us overrides all prior titles by the law of Y." They are saying "Our title prevails over yours because your title, validly acquired or reserved by the law of X, was not validly acquired or reserved by the law of Y."

In this situation, most of the English, American and Canadian cases uphold the title of the owner A against that of purchasers from or creditors of B.[22] The reason is simple: since the goods were in X when A's title was

[19] (1860) 5 H. & N. 728, 742–743; *cf. Todd* v. *Armour* (1882) 9 R. 901.

[20] *Cammell* v. *Sewell, supra,* at p. 744; *Alcock* v. *Smith* [1892] 1 Ch. 238, 267; *Embiricos* v. *Anglo-Austrian Bank* [1905] 1 K.B. 677; *Mehta* v. *Sutton* (1913) 108 L.T. 214; *Traders Finance Corporation* v. *Dawson Implements Ltd.* (1959) 15 D.L.R. (2d) 515; *Century Credit Corporation* v. *Richard* (1962) 34 D.L.R. (2d) 291; *Price Mobile Home Centres Inc.* v. *National Trailer Convoy of Canada* (1974) 44 D.L.R. (3d) 443; *Re Fuhrmann and Miller* (1977) 78 D.L.R. (3d) 284; *Maden* v. *Long* [1983] 1 W.W.R. 649.

[21] *Cammell* v. *Sewell, supra,* at p. 745.

[22] *Simpson* v. *Fogo* (1863) 1 H. & M. 195; *Goetschius* v. *Brightman* (1927) 245 N.Y. 186; 156 N.E. 660; *Industrial Acceptance Corporation* v. *La Flamme* [1950] 2 D.L.R. 822; *Rennie Car Sales* v. *Union Acceptance Corporation* [1955] 4 D.L.R. 822.

reserved, the law of X should govern that reservation of title. Very often the law of Y differs from the law of X in that it requires hire-purchase or conditional sales contracts to be registered in Y. There is an observable tendency for courts, even courts in Y, to hold that the statutory registration requirements of the law of Y are confined to domestic transactions,[23] or can be satisfied if A registers soon after he becomes aware that the chattel has been removed to Y, even though this may not be until after it has been sold there to a purchaser.[24] Thus in a leading American case[25]:

> A & Co., a Californian corporation, sold a motor car in California to B, a Californian resident, on hire-purchase terms. It was agreed that title should remain with A until the price was fully paid and that until then B would not remove the car out of California. Before the price was fully paid, B took the car to New York without A's knowledge or consent and sold it there to C, a bona fide purchaser. By the law of California, A's title was superior to any title derived from B on resale, even to an innocent purchaser for value. By the law of New York, all such reservations of title were void against subsequent purchasers in good faith unless the contract was registered in New York. The contract never was so registered. The New York Court of Appeals held that A & Co.'s title was good against C.

It follows from what has been said that the question whether A loses his title when his goods are removed to Y and dealt with there depends entirely on the reason why the law of Y would say that his title is lost.[26] It may do so, generally speaking, for one of two reasons: either because it says that an event which has occurred in Y has the effect of overriding prior titles, or because it does not recognise that the transaction whereby A acquired or reserved his title in X had this effect by the law of Y. In the former case, the law of Y governs, and A's title is lost, because the law of Y (*lex situs*) determines the effect of the transaction in Y when the goods were in Y, and the law of X is irrelevant to that transaction. In the latter case, the law of X governs, and A retains his title, because the law of X (*lex situs*) determines the effect of the transaction in X when the goods were in X, and the law of Y is irrelevant to that transaction. This conclusion is the necessary consequence of the proposition advanced in paragraph (a) above. If A acquires a valid title to goods in X, we have seen that his title is upheld if the goods are removed to Y, even though he would not have acquired a good title by the law of Y. Thus, if B removes A's goods to Y, A's title is still good. If B now sells the goods in Y to C, there is no reason why B should be capable of passing a better title than he has himself, unless the law of Y attributes this special effect to the sale there.

---

[23] See, *e.g. Goetschius v. Brightman, supra.*
[24] *Rennie Car Sales v. Union Acceptance Corporation, supra; McAloney v. McInnes and General Motors Acceptance Corporation* (1956) 2 D.L.R. (2d) 666. See Davis (1964) 13 I.C.L.Q. 53.
[25] *Goetschius v. Brightman, supra.*
[26] See Morris (1945) 22 B.Y.I.L. 232, 238–246.

The distinction here submitted was drawn very clearly in a Canadian case[27]:

> A & Co. sold a motor car in Quebec to B, a resident of Quebec, under a conditional sales contract which provided that the car should remain the property of A & Co. until the price was fully paid. Before the price was fully paid, B took the car to Ontario without the knowledge or consent of A & Co. and sold it there to C, a resident of Ontario, who had no knowledge of A & Co.'s rights in the car. The law of Ontario required conditional sales contracts to be registered; the law of Quebec did not. The Ontario Court of Appeal held that A & Co.'s title would have prevailed against C, but for the fact that B was a person who had agreed to buy goods and was in possession of them with the consent of the seller and could therefore pass a good title to C under section 25(2) of the Ontario Sale of Goods Act.

In the course of his judgment, Kelly J.A. said:

> "If the laws of Ontario were to seek to invalidate [A & Co.'s] title by refusing to recognise that the transaction which took place in Quebec had the effect of continuing the title in [A & Co.], this attempt of Ontario law to invalidate a transaction taking place in Quebec would be bad because the validity of a Quebec transaction must be determined by the laws of Quebec, the *lex situs*. . . . However, if the laws of Ontario provide that a later transaction which takes place wholly within Ontario has the effect of overriding prior titles, then since Ontario does not seek to give its laws any extra-territorial effect the laws of Ontario prevail and the title created under the laws of Ontario displaces the title reserved in the Quebec transaction."

(d) In the situations so far discussed, it has been assumed that the law of Y affords greater protection to purchasers and creditors than the law of X. The reverse side of the usual picture is presented when chattels are taken into Y and dealt with there in circumstances which deprive the owner of his title by the law of X, but not by the law of Y. Two apparently conflicting American cases, both decided in New Jersey, illustrate the problem well. In *Marvin Safe Co.* v. *Norton*[28]:

> A sold an iron safe to B in Pennsylvania on the terms that A was to remain owner until the price was fully paid. Before the price was fully paid B took the safe to New Jersey and sold it there to C, who bought without notice of A's rights. By the law of Pennsylvania A's reservation of title was valid against B but void as against subsequent creditors of or purchasers from B. By the law of New Jersey A's reservation

---

[27] *Century Credit Corporation* v. *Richard* (1962) 34 D.L.R. (2d) 291, 293–294. Cf. *Traders Finance Corporation* v. *Dawson Implements Ltd.* (1959) 15 D.L.R. (2d) 515. Contrast *Industrial Acceptance Corporation* v. *La Flamme* [1950] 2 D.L.R. 822, approved in *Century Credit Corporation* v. *Richard, supra,* but distinguished on the ground that the court overlooked s. 25(2) of the Ontario Sale of Goods Act.

[28] (1886) 48 N.J.L. 410; 7 A. 418. Cf. *Cline* v. *Russell* (1908) 2 Alta.L.R. 79; *Rennie Car Sales* v. *Union Acceptance Corporation* [1955] 4 D.L.R. 822; *McAloney* v. *McInnes and General Motors Acceptance Corporation* (1956) 2 D.L.R. (2d) 666.

of title was good as against third parties. It was held that the law of New Jersey applied and that A's reservation of title was valid as against C.

An opposite result was reached on similar facts in *Dougherty & Co.* v. *Krimke*[29]:

> A, a jeweller, delivered a diamond in New York to B, a broker, for the purposes of sale, but on the terms that no title was to pass to B. B took the diamond to New Jersey and pledged it there to C. Under the New York Factors Act, a factor entrusted with the possession of a chattel for the purposes of sale was deemed to be the true owner thereof so far as to give validity to any contract of sale made by him. By the law of New Jersey A's reservation of title was good as against third parties. It was held that the law of New York governed and that C's title prevailed over A's.

These two decisions can be reconciled by assuming that in the *Marvin* case the court must have held that the Pennsylvania law only applied to subsequent creditors or purchasers in Pennsylvania, while in the *Dougherty* case the court must have held that the New York Factors Act was wide enough to cover subsequent purchasers anywhere. It would seem that in most situations the wider construction is the more sensible, since A must surely know that when he delivers the chattel to B in X, B has power by the law of X to deprive him of his title. A's reservation of title is therefore potentially ineffective, since B could pass a good title in X. What possible difference can it make if he does so in Y?[30]

---

[29] (1929) 105 N.J.L. 470; 144 A. 617. *Cf. Hannah* v. *Pearlman* [1954] 1 D.L.R. 282, criticised in 32 Can. Bar Rev. 900.
[30] See Morris (1945) 22 B.Y.I.L. 232, 246–247.

CHAPTER 20

THE ASSIGNMENT OF INTANGIBLE MOVABLES

THE THEORIES

IN this chapter we are concerned with the question what law governs the validity and effect of an assignment of an intangible movable, *e.g.* a simple contract debt or a share in a trust fund. Three possible laws have been advocated by writers, namely, the law of the creditor's domicile, the *lex situs* of the debt, and the proper law of the debt.

The law of the creditor's domicile

This was advocated by older writers on the conflict of laws.[1] It is a relic of the outworn maxim *mobilia sequuntur personam*[2] and is not adopted by modern writers, though echoes of it are still to be found in some modern cases.[3] Domicile is of great importance in family law, but has little significance in commercial transactions, except perhaps as an element to be considered in determining the proper law of a transaction.

The lex situs

It was at one time supposed that a chose in action has no locality.[4] But this doctrine, deduced as it was from the maxim *mobilia sequuntur personam*, is exploded, and it is now recognised that an artificial *situs* may have to be ascribed to intangible movables for many purposes.[5] The governing principle is that a simple contract debt is deemed to be situated where it is properly recoverable,[6] that is, where the debtor resides and presumably has assets to satisfy the debt.

Westlake[7] and Dicey[8] thought that the *lex situs* of the debt governs the validity of its assignment. But this view involves the difficulty that the debt may be situated in more countries than one if the debtor has more than one residence; and it has been pronounced erroneous in two cases, one of them a decision of the Court of Appeal,[9] at any rate so far as the validity of voluntary assignments is concerned.

---

[1] Story, *Conflict of Laws,* s.362; Phillimore, *Commentaries on Private International Law,* Vol. 4, p. 544.
[2] *Ante,* p. 350.
[3] See, *e.g. Republica de Guatemala* v. *Nunez* [1927] 1 K.B. 669, 686, 689, 690, 700.
[4] *Lee* v. *Abdy* (1886) 17 Q.B.D. 309, 312, *per* Day J.
[5] See, for a full discussion, Dicey and Morris, pp. 528–537; *post,* p. 375.
[6] *New York Life Insurance Co.* v. *Public Trustee* [1924] 2 Ch. 101.
[7] s.152.
[8] 5th ed., Rule 153.
[9] *Republica de Guatemala* v. *Nunez* [1927] 1 K.B. 669; *Re Anziani* [1930] 1 Ch. 407.

The proper law of the debt

Some modern writers[10] think that the proper law of the debt should be the test. Like the *lex situs*, this test would have the great advantage that only one law would apply to all aspects of the problem. But the difficulty is that in most cases the proper law of the debt coincides with the law of its artificial *situs*, and therefore this test, like the *lex situs*, is inconsistent with the most recent authorities[11] on the validity of the assignment.

THE MODERN LAW

The key to the problem lies, it is thought, in distinguishing between (1) questions of assignability, governed by the proper law of the debt; (2) questions of the intrinsic validity of the assignment, governed by the proper law of the assignment; (3) questions of priorities, governed by the proper law of the debt; and (4) questions of garnishment, governed by the *lex situs* of the debt.[12] All the cases appear to be consistent with this view.

Assignability

In some systems of law some kinds of debts cannot be assigned at all, for obvious reasons of social policy: *e.g.* policies of life insurance, future wages, pensions, maintenance payable to a wife or child. The question whether the debt is assignable is governed exclusively by the proper law of the debt and not by the proper law of the assignment. If the debt is assignable by its proper law, it can be assigned anywhere; if the debt is not assignable by its proper law, it cannot be assigned anywhere, regardless of the proper law of the assignment. The positive and negative aspects of the rule are neatly illustrated by two contrasting American cases:

> A policy of life insurance made in Wisconsin and valid by its law was assigned in Minnesota. By the law of Wisconsin, policies of life insurance were assignable; by the law of Minnesota they belonged to the beneficiary alone. The assignment was held valid.[13]
>
> A was employed in Indiana. As security for a loan he assigned to B in Illinois all the wages earned or to be earned by him under his contract of employment. Assignments of future wages were allowed by the law of Illinois, but prohibited by the law of Indiana. The assignment was held invalid.[14]

Two English cases provide support for the rule suggested above. In *Re Fry*[15]:

---

[10] Cheshire and North, pp. 539–541; Wolff, ss.512, 516; Falconbridge, pp. 494–498.

[11] See note 9, *supra*.

[12] This is now accepted by Cheshire and North, pp. 541–549.

[13] *Northwestern Mutual Life Insurance Co.* v. *Adams* (1914) 155 Wis. 335; 144 N.W. 1108.

[14] *Coleman* v. *American Sheet and Tinplate Co.* (1936) 285 Ill.App. 542; 2 N.E. 2d 349. The positive and negative aspects of the rule are also illustrated by two contrasting Scottish cases, *Grant's Trustees* v. *Ritchie's Executors* (1886) 13 R. 646, and *Pender* v. *Commercial Bank of Scotland*, 1940 S.L.T. 306.

[15] [1946] Ch. 312.

A, who was domiciled in Florida and resident in New Jersey, owned shares in an English company. In 1940 A in New Jersey executed transfers of the shares to his son as a gift, and sent the transfers to England to be registered. By the English Defence Regulations 1939, the company could not register the transfers without the consent of the Treasury. A in New Jersey signed the forms necessary for obtaining that consent and returned them to England, but he died before consent was obtained. It was held that the transfers were incomplete and invalid and that the shares formed part of A's residuary estate.

Again, in *Campbell Connelly & Co. Ltd.* v. *Noble*[16]:

A was the composer of a popular tune and the owner of the American copyright therein. American law gave two periods of copyright, namely, 28 years from the date of publication and a renewal period for a further 28 years if the composer was still living at the end of the first period. Before the first period expired A, by a contract governed by English law, purported to assign the copyright to B. It was held that American law must determine whether the renewal copyright could be assigned before the renewal period began.

The proper law of the debt also determines the conditions under which the debt can be assigned, so far as they concern the debtor. The original liability of the debtor ought not to be increased by an assignment of the debt governed by a different law. So the proper law of the debt determines whether the assignee takes subject to equities and whether notice of the assignment must be given to the debtor.[17]

In English domestic law, an equitable assignee of a legal chose in action who cannot bring his case within section 136 of the Law of Property Act 1925 must join the assignor as a party to the action. Though the English authorities are old and inconclusive,[18] it is thought that this rule is one of substance, governed by the proper law of the debt, and not of procedure, governed by the *lex fori*, and that it would not necessarily apply when the debt is governed by a foreign proper law. If by that law the effect of an assignment of part of the debt is to expose the debtor to more actions than one, he cannot complain if he is sued more than once in England.

Intrinsic validity of the assignment

It is convenient to begin discussion of this question by considering the leading case of *Republica de Guatemala* v. *Nunez*[19]:

In 1906 the President of Guatemala deposited £20,000 in a London

---

[16] [1963] 1 W.L.R. 252.

[17] *Kelly* v. *Selwyn* [1905] 2 Ch. 117.

[18] See *Innes* v. *Dunlop* (1800) 8 T.R. 595; *O'Callaghan* v. *Thomond* (1810) 3 Taunt. 82; *Wolff* v. *Oxholm* (1817) 6 M. & S. 92; *Jeffery* v. *M'Taggart* (1817) 6 M. & S. 126. In *Regas Ltd.* v. *Plotkins* (1961) 29 D.L.R. (2d) 282, the Supreme Court of Canada held the rule to be procedural; but in that case the proper law of the debt and the *lex fori* coincided. See *post*, pp. 464–465.

[19] [1927] 1 K.B. 669. The judgment of Greer J. at first instance is reported in (1926) 95 L.J.K.B. 955.

bank. In 1919 in Guatemala he assigned this sum to his illegitimate son Nunez, a minor domiciled and resident in Guatemala. In 1920 he was deposed and imprisoned by his political opponents. In 1921, while in prison in Guatemala, he was forced to assign the sum to the Republic of Guatemala. By English law the assignment to Nunez was valid. But by Guatemalan law an assignment of a debt exceeding 100 dollars, if made without consideration, was void unless made on stamped paper before a notary; these formalities were not complied with. Further, a minor could not accept a voluntary assignment unless a tutor had been appointed by a judge on his behalf; this was not done.

The Republic claimed the sum from the London bank, which, having notice of Nunez' claim, interpleaded. Greer J. and the Court of Appeal held that the assignment to the Republic was void for duress, and that the assignment to Nunez was governed by Guatemalan law and was also void, with the result that the fund went to the ex-President's creditors.

Unfortunately the judges gave different reasons for their decision that the assignment to Nunez was governed by Guatemalan law. Greer J.'s reason was that it was made in Guatemala. Bankes L.J.'s reason was that the assignor and assignee were domiciled in Guatemala. Scrutton and Lawrence L.JJ. distinguished between (a) invalidity on the ground of Nunez' lack of capacity and (b) formal invalidity. With regard to (a), both judges held that capacity is governed either by the law of the domicile or by the *lex loci*, and since they coincided, there was no need to decide between them. With regard to (b), Scrutton L.J., rejecting Dicey's Rule 153, held that the formal validity of the assignment was governed, not by the *lex situs* of the debt, but by the law of the place where the assignment was made; but Lawrence L.J. (dissenting on this point) held that it was governed by English law *qua* the *lex situs* of the debt.

The judgments of Scrutton and Lawrence L.JJ. suggest that we must distinguish between formal validity, capacity, and essential validity.

Formal validity. This is governed by the law of the place where the assignment was made.[20] But no doubt an assignment, like a contract,[21] which complied with the formalities prescribed by its proper law would also be held formally valid.

Capacity. The judgments of Scrutton and Lawrence L.JJ. in the *Guatemala* case hold that capacity to take under an assignment (and no doubt the same is true of capacity to make an assignment) is governed either by the law of the domicile or by the *lex loci*. So do the judgments of Day and Wills JJ. in *Lee* v. *Abdy*[22]:

H, domiciled in Cape Province, insured his life with an English

---

[20] *Republica de Guatemala* v. *Nunez* [1927] 1 K.B. 669.
[21] *Ante,* pp. 284–285.
[22] (1886) 17 Q.B.D. 309.

insurance company and assigned the policy to his wife in Cape Province. The assignment was valid by English law but void by the law of the Cape as a gift between husband and wife. It was held that Cape law governed and that the assignment was void.

However, there can be no doubt that in the *Guatemala* case Guatemalan law was the proper law of the assignment to Nunez, and that in *Lee* v. *Abdy* the law of the Cape was the proper law of the assignment to the wife. It is submitted that the proper law of the assignment is a far better test of capacity than either the law of the domicile or the *lex loci*.

Essential validity. This is governed by the proper law of the assignment.[23] The term "essential validity" no doubt includes that vexed question in English domestic law, namely, whether consideration is necessary to the validity of an assignment.

Priorities

Questions of priorities arise if there are two or more competing assignments, each intrinsically valid by its proper law, of a debt which is capable of assignment under its proper law. In the *Guatemala* case[24] Bankes L.J. said that the dispute there was one of priorities. But this remark must have been made *per incuriam*, since each of the assignments was, for different reasons, invalid, and therefore no question of priorities arose.

It is obvious that questions of priorities cannot be governed either by the law of the place where an assignment is made or by the proper law of the assignment, because the competing assignments may have been made in different countries or may be governed by different proper laws, and there is no reason why one law should govern rather than the other. It appears that the only possible laws which can govern priorities are the proper law of the debt, the *lex situs* of the debt, and the *lex fori*; and it is submitted that the first of these laws is the most appropriate. There are two relevant English cases. In *Le Feuvre* v. *Sullivan*[25]:

> A, domiciled in Jersey, effected a policy of insurance on his life with an English insurance company. In 1833 A in England deposited the policy with B as security for a loan. In 1834 A falsely told the company that he had lost the policy and asked for a duplicate. The company issued a duplicate to A without inquiry. In 1835 A assigned the duplicate policy to his wife in Jersey in consideration of a loan by her. The Privy Council, reversing the Jersey court, held that the priorities were governed by English law and not by Jersey law.

The ratio was clearly the proper law of the policy, for the Privy Council said that the policy was "in every sense an English instrument forming or evidencing an English contract." It was obviously not the *lex fori*, Jersey law.

---

[23] *Re Anziani* [1930] 1 Ch. 407. The judgment refers to the *lex loci actus*; but there can be no doubt that it was also the proper law.

[24] [1927] 1 K.B. 669, 684.

[25] (1855) 10 Moo.P.C. 1.

In *Kelly* v. *Selwyn*[26]:

> Under the will of a testator domiciled in England, A, who was domiciled in New York, was entitled to a share in an English trust fund. In 1891 A assigned his interest to his wife in New York. No notice of this assignment was given to the English trustees, notice not being necessary by New York law. In 1894 A assigned his interest to B in England as security for a loan; and B forthwith gave notice to the trustees. It was held that B had priority in accordance with English law.

In this case there is more doubt about the *ratio decidendi* because the proper law of the debt, the *lex situs* of the debt and the *lex fori* all coincided. Warrington J. said[27]:

> "The ground on which I decide it is that, the fund here being an English trust fund and this being the court which the testator may have contemplated as the court which would have administered the trust fund, the order in which the parties are to be held entitled to the trust fund must be regulated by the law of the court which is administering that fund."

It is submitted that the true ratio was the proper law of the debt. In the *Guatemala* case,[28] Scrutton L.J. said that the ground of the decision was that priorities are governed by the *lex fori*; but this, as we have seen, is not compatible with *Le Feuvre* v. *Sullivan*. It is true that the *lex fori* governs priorities in bankruptcy, in the administration of insolvent estates, and as between competing claims against a ship in Admiralty law.[29] But the objection to elevating this to the status of a general rule is that it would allow the *lex fori* to regulate a question of substance, which is contrary to principle and unacceptable unless there is no convenient alternative.

Garnishment

To garnish a debt does not mean to put vegetables round it. It is a process whereby a judgment creditor A is allowed to attach a debt owed to his judgment debtor B by a third party C (called the garnishee). A similar process (called arrestment in Scotland) is allowed by the laws of other countries. In a purely domestic case, where the judgment debtor and the garnishee are both subject to the jurisdiction of the court, the garnishee is of course effectively discharged from further liability once he has paid the judgment creditor. But if the judgment debtor is not subject to the jurisdiction of the English court, there may be a real risk that the garnishee will be compelled to pay the debt to the principal debtor a second time in a foreign country. In such circumstances the English rule is that garnishment proceedings will be allowed if the debt is properly recoverable, that is situ-

[26] [1905] 2 Ch. 117.
[27] At p. 122.
[28] [1927] 1 K.B. 669, 693.
[29] *Post,* pp. 387, 437, 465–466.

ated, in England, but not otherwise. Thus a debt due from an English bank to a foreign debtor can be garnished,[30] but a debt due from the foreign branch of an English or foreign bank to a foreign debtor cannot be garnished.[31] The leading case is *Swiss Bank Corporation* v. *Boehmische Bank*[32]:

> A sued B, a Czech bank carrying on business in Prague, in the High Court and recovered judgment for £29,000. B submitted to the jurisdiction. A obtained a garnishee order nisi attaching a debt owed to B by C, an English bank. C opposed the order on the ground that it might have to pay B a second time in Prague. The order was made absolute, because the debt was properly recoverable in England.

The making of a garnishment order is discretionary and it will be refused if there is a risk that the garnishee will be compelled to pay again abroad. But the risk must be a real one, not a mere speculative or theoretical hazard.[33]

There is surprisingly little English authority on the converse question, namely, when will effect be given by English courts to a foreign garnishment order. Clearly, if no effect at all is given, there will be a risk that the garnishee will be compelled to pay his debt twice over. Here again it seems that the test is whether the debt is situated, that is properly recoverable, in the foreign country where the order was made.[34]

If the foreign garnishment proceedings are recognised in England, the *lex situs* of the debt determines their effect. Thus, if the effect of the foreign garnishment or attachment is by the *lex situs* of the debt to give the attaching creditor priority over earlier or later assignees of the same debt, it will have that effect in England.[35]

---

[30] *Swiss Bank Corporation* v. *Boehmische Bank* [1923] 1 K.B. 673.

[31] *Martin* v. *Nadel* [1906] 2 K.B. 26; *Richardson* v. *Richardson* [1927] P. 228; contrast *Brooks Associates Inc.* v. *Basu* [1983] Q.B. 220 (National Savings Bank).

[32] *Supra.*

[33] *Employers' Liability Assurance Corporation* v. *Sedgwick, Collins & Co.* [1927] A.C. 95, 112; contrast *Sea Insurance Co.* v. *Rossia Insurance Co.* (1924) 20 Ll.L.R. 308.

[34] *Gould* v. *Webb* (1855) 4 E. & B. 933; *Rossano* v. *Manufacturers' Life Insurance Co. Ltd.* [1963] 2 Q.B. 352, 374–383. In this case there were other reasons for non-recognition: (1) the creditor's claim was for taxes and thus recognition would have indirectly enforced a foreign revenue law (see *ante*, p. 50); (2) the garnishment proceedings were administrative and not judicial; (3) the debtor was not subject to the jurisdiction of the foreign court.

[35] *Re Queensland Mercantile Agency Co.* [1891] 1 Ch. 536; affirmed on other grounds [1892] 1 Ch. 219; *Re Maudslay, Sons & Field* [1900] 1 Ch. 602.

CHAPTER 21

NEGOTIABLE INSTRUMENTS[1]

Introduction

THE principal characteristics of a negotiable instrument are that the title to it passes by indorsement and delivery, if it is payable to order, or by mere delivery, if it is payable to bearer; and that, under favourable circumstances, a holder can pass a better title than he has himself to a bona fide holder for value (called a holder in due course). In English law, the most important, but not the only, negotiable instruments are bills of exchange, cheques and promissory notes, the law relating to which is codified in the Bills of Exchange Act 1882.

A bill of exchange is an unconditional order in writing, addressed by one person to another, signed by the person giving it, requiring the person to whom it is addressed to pay on demand or at a fixed or determinable future time a sum certain in money to or to the order of a specified person, or to bearer.[2] The person who draws the bill is called the drawer. The person to whom it is addressed is called the drawee or acceptor. The person in whose favour it is drawn is called the payee. A bill is negotiated when it is transferred from one person (*e.g.* the payee) to another, either by delivery, if the bill is payable to bearer, or by indorsement and delivery, if it is payable to order. Indorsement is effected by the indorser writing on the bill "Pay X" and signing it. The liability of the acceptor is equivalent to that of a principal debtor and the liability of the drawer and of each subsequent indorser is equivalent to that of a surety.

A cheque is a bill of exchange drawn on a banker payable on demand.[3] A promissory note is an unconditional promise in writing made by one person to another signed by the maker, engaging to pay, on demand or at a fixed or determinable future time, a sum certain in money, to or to the order of a specified person, or to bearer.[4] The maker of a note corresponds with the acceptor of a bill, and the first indorser of a note corresponds with the drawer of an accepted bill payable to drawer's order.[5] Generally speaking, the provisions of the Act relating to bills apply also to cheques[6] and notes.[7]

---

[1] See Dicey and Morris, pp. 877–903; Cheshire and North, pp. 251–257, 549–555; Falconbridge, Chap. 14; Anton, Chap. 19. Negotiable instruments belong partly to the law of contract and partly to the law of property, but it has been thought convenient to deal with them in a single chapter.
[2] Bills of Exchange Act 1882, s.3(1).
[3] s.73.
[4] s.83(1).
[5] s.89(2).
[6] s.73.
[7] s.89(1).

Bills, cheques and notes from their very nature are likely to give rise to a conflict of laws. A bill may be drawn in one country, accepted in another, be payable in a third, and indorsed in a fourth. The Act contains a section, section 72, which is expressed to contain "rules where laws conflict." It is noteworthy as the only attempt so far made to codify part of the English conflict of laws. But its provisions are open to serious criticism in that they are ambiguous and at times unintelligible, and they do not deal with all matters that can arise but only with formal validity, interpretation, the duties of the holder, and the due date of payment. The section does not deal in terms with such matters as capacity, essential validity or illegality, or with the proprietary as opposed to the contractual aspects of bills and notes.

It is important to realise that a bill of exchange does not contain a single contract but a series of promises to pay made by the acceptor, the drawer and each subsequent indorser, all of which are contained in the same instrument. Section 72 clearly treats each of these contracts as a separate one for the purposes of the conflict of laws and thus adopts what has been called the "several laws" doctrine as opposed to the "single law" doctrine which at one time found favour with English courts in cases decided before the Act.[8]

From the proprietary point of view a bill of exchange is regarded by English law as a chattel—a chose in possession, not a chose in action. Thus, an action for conversion can be brought in respect of a bill; and, as we shall see, to the extent that the transfer of a bill is not regulated by section 72, it is regulated by the law relating to the transfer of tangible movables, not by the law relating to the assignment of debts.

Negotiability

An instrument for securing the payment of money may acquire the characteristics of a negotiable instrument either by Act of Parliament, or by the custom of the mercantile world in England,[9] but not otherwise. Thus in *Goodwin* v. *Robarts,*[10] scrip issued by the Russian Government, containing a promise on full payment to issue a bond in respect of a loan, was treated as negotiable, because it was negotiable by the custom of merchants in England. On the other hand, in *Picker* v. *London and County Banking Co.*[11] bonds issued by the Prussian Government were not treated as negotiable in England, though they were negotiable by the law of Prussia.

---

[8] *De la Chaumette* v. *Bank of England* (1831) 2 B. & Ad. 385; *Trimbey* v. *Vignier* (1834) 1 Bing.N.C. 151; *Lebel* v. *Tucker* (1867) L.R. 3 Q.B. 77. The shift to the "several laws" doctrine was effected by *Bradlaugh* v. *De Rin* (1868) L.R. 3 C.P. 538; reversed (1870) L.R. 5 C.P. 473, but only on a question of French law. See also *Re Marseilles Extension Ry.* (1885) 30 Ch.D. 598, decided after the Act, but in relation to bills drawn and indorsed before the Act.

[9] *Goodwin* v. *Robarts* (1875) L.R. 10 Ex. 337; (1876) 1 App.Cas. 476; *Bechuanaland Exploration Co.* v. *London Trading Bank* [1898] 2 Q.B. 658; *Edelstein* v. *Schuler* [1902] 2 K.B. 144.

[10] *Supra.*

[11] (1887) 18 Q.B.D. 515.

Capacity

The Bills of Exchange Act provides[12] that capacity to incur liability as a party to a bill is co-extensive with capacity to contract; and section 72, as we have seen,[13] contains no special provisions about capacity in the conflict of laws. The case law is extremely sparse, but it would appear that capacity to incur liability as a party to a bill is governed by the *lex loci contractus*.[14] The Geneva Convention of 1930 on the Conflict of Laws in Connection with Bills of Exchange refers the question of capacity to the *lex patriae,* and this has prevented the United Kingdom from adopting that Convention.

Form

Section 72(1) of the Bills of Exchange Act provides as follows:

> Where a bill drawn in one country is negotiated, accepted or payable in another, the rights, duties and liabilities of the parties are determined as follows:
>
> (1) The validity of a bill as regards requisites in form is determined by the law of the place of issue, and the validity as regards requisites in form of the supervening contracts, such as acceptance, or indorsement, or acceptance suprà protest, is determined by the law of the place where such contract was made.

As we have seen,[15] a contract is formally valid if it complies with the requirements of either the law of the place of contracting or the proper law. But a bill of exchange must comply with the formal requirements of the law of the place of contracting. The "place of issue" means the place where the instrument, being complete in form, is first delivered to a holder,[16] not necessarily the place where it is signed. It is not as clear as it should be what exactly is a "requisite in form," but it has been held to include the question whether a bill is conditional or unconditional[17] and the question whether the chain of indorsements is broken if a person signs in his own name as agent for the payee without adding the words "per pro" to indicate that he is signing as agent.[18]

The general rule stated in section 72(1) is subject to two exceptions or provisos:

> (a) Where a bill is issued out of the United Kingdom it is not invalid by reason only that it is not stamped in accordance with the law of the place of issue.
>
> (b) Where a bill, issued out of the United Kingdom, conforms, as

---

[12] s.22(1).

[13] *Ante,* p. 366.

[14] The clearest case is *Bondholders Securities Corporation* v. *Manville* [1933] 4 D.L.R. 699. Cf. *Re Soltykoff* [1891] 1 Q.B. 413. For capacity to contract generally, see *ante,* pp. 285–288.

[15] *Ante,* pp. 284–285.

[16] Bills of Exchange Act 1882, s.21(1). See *Nova (Jersey) Knit Ltd.* v. *Kamngarn Spinnerei G.m.b.H.* [1977] 1 W.L.R. 713, 718H (H.L.).

[17] *Guaranty Trust Co. of New York* v. *Hannay* [1918] 1 K.B. 43, 53; [1918] 2 K.B. 623, 634, 670.

[18] *Koechlin* v. *Kestenbaum* [1927] 1 K.B. 889.

regards requisites in form, to the law of the United Kingdom, it may, for the purpose of enforcing payment thereof, be treated as valid as between all persons who negotiate, hold, or become parties to it in the United Kingdom.

The general rule is that if a foreign stamp law merely renders an unstamped contract inadmissible in evidence, it does not apply to an action in an English court because it is procedural[19]; but that, if it renders an unstamped contract void, it bars an action on the contract in England.[20] But proviso (a) means that a foreign stamp law can be disregarded in either event.

The object of proviso (b) presumably is to make bills issued abroad more easily negotiable in the United Kingdom. Under this proviso, the bill may only be treated as valid "for the purpose of enforcing payment thereof," and not, *e.g.* in an action for a declaration.[21]

Interpretation and legal effect

Section 72(2) of the Bills of Exchange Act provides as follows:

> The interpretation of the drawing, indorsement, acceptance, or acceptance suprà protest of a bill is determined by the law of the place where such contract is made.

The scope of "interpretation" in section 72(2) is even more doubtful than that of "requisites in form" in section 72(1). It probably includes such questions as whether a bill drawn payable "to X" without the addition of the words "to order" is negotiable or not,[22] and whether the acceptance is general or qualified.[23] It has been said that "interpretation" means not only the construction or meaning of the words used by the parties but also their legal effect, *i.e.* the obligations of the parties as deduced from such interpretation.[24] But this seems an unwarrantable extension of the meaning of the word. On the other hand, if section 72(2) does not cover legal effect, the section is silent on essential validity. This perhaps is not of much moment, because in a formal contract like one contained in a bill of exchange the question of essential validity is apt to merge in that of formal validity, and that is already covered by section 72(1).

The general rule stated in section 72(2) is subject to one exception or proviso:

> Where an inland bill is indorsed in a foreign country the indorse-

---

[19] *Bristow* v. *Sequeville* (1850) 5 Exch. 275.

[20] *Alves* v. *Hodgson* (1797) 7 T.R. 241; *Clegg* v. *Levy* (1812) 3 Camp. 166.

[21] *Guaranty Trust Co. of New York* v. *Hannay* [1918] 1 K.B. 43; but see the remarks of Scrutton L.J. in the C.A. [1918] 2 K.B. 623, 670.

[22] Falconbridge, p. 328; Dicey and Morris, pp. 889–890.

[23] *Bank Polski* v. *Mulder* [1942] 1 K.B. 497.

[24] *Alcock* v. *Smith* [1892] 1 Ch. 238, 256, *per* Romer J. This dictum was not adopted by the C.A.; and Walton J. in *Embiricos* v. *Anglo-Austrian Bank* [1904] 2 K.B. 870, 875, evidently had doubts about it. See also *per* Scrutton L.J. in *Guaranty Trust Co. of New York* v. *Hannay* [1918] 2 K.B. 623, 670; Chalmers, *Bills of Exchange Act,* 13th ed., p. 241.

ment shall as regards the payer be interpreted according to the law of the United Kingdom.

This proviso states the effect of the pre-1882 case of *Lebel* v. *Tucker*.[25] An inland bill is one which is or on the face of it purports to be (a) drawn and payable within the British Islands, or (b) drawn within the British Islands upon some person resident therein. Any other bill is a foreign bill.[26] The British Islands mean the United Kingdom, the Channel Islands and the Isle of Man.[27] The "payer" means the acceptor[28]; hence the proviso does not apply if the contest is between two indorsees and the liability of the acceptor is not in issue.[29]

Illegality

The Gaming Act 1710 provided that all notes, bills or other securities where the whole or any part of the consideration was money won by gaming, or money lent for gaming, should be void. The Gaming Act 1835 provides that all such notes and bills should not be void but should be deemed to be given for an illegal consideration. In *Moulis* v. *Owen*,[30] the defendant gave the plaintiff in Algiers a cheque drawn by him on an English bank, partly for payment of money lent by the plaintiff to the defendant for gaming in Algiers, and partly for money won from the defendant at gaming. The consideration for the cheque was not illegal by French law, but the Court of Appeal by a majority held that English law as the *lex loci solutionis* applied and that therefore the action on the cheque failed. The judgments contain no reference to section 72 of the Bills of Exchange Act.

Transfer

The law which determines whether property in a bill or a note passes to the transferee is the *lex loci actus,* the law of the place where the transfer is made, which in the case of a negotiable instrument must necessarily coincide with the *lex situs*. There is no doubt about the principle, but it is far from clear whether it rests upon (1) section 72(1) of the Bills of Exchange Act, or (2) upon section 72(2), or upon the general principles of the conflict of laws relating to (3) the assignment of debts,[31] or (4) to the transfer of chattels.[32] Of these four possibilities there is little to be said for (1), because the questions involved cannot by any stretch of imagination be classified as questions of form, or for (3), because, as we have seen,[33] negotiable instruments are regarded as tangible and not as intangible movables. The choice therefore lies between (2) and (4). In the three cases decided since the Act the judges have on the whole preferred to rely on general

[25] (1867) L.R. 3 Q.B. 77.
[26] Bills of Exchange Act 1882, s.4.
[27] s.2. The Republic of Ireland is not included: S.R. & O. (1923) No. 405, s.2.
[28] *Alcock* v. *Smith* [1892] 1 Ch. 238, 257, 262.
[29] *Alcock* v. *Smith, supra.*
[30] [1907] 1 K.B. 746.
[31] *Ante,* Chap. 20.
[32] *Ante,* Chap. 19.
[33] *Ante,* p. 366.

principles applicable to tangible movables and have had recourse to section 72 only in a very hesitating manner.

In *Alcock* v. *Smith*[34]:

> A bill of exchange was drawn, accepted and payable in England and was indorsed in Norway in blank to an agent for the plaintiffs. Thenceforward it was a bill payable to bearer and needed no further indorsement. It was seized from the plaintiffs' agent to satisfy a judgment that had been given against them in Norway, and after an interval sold by public auction to X and later sold by X to the defendant, a Swedish bank, who bought it in good faith. At the time of the judicial sale the bill was overdue and by English law, but not by the law of Norway or Sweden, could only be transferred subject to equities.[35]

In an action in England by the plaintiffs against the defendant it was held that Norwegian law governed and that the title of the defendant must prevail. Romer J. at first instance and Lindley L.J. in the Court of Appeal referred to section 72(2) of the Act, but based their judgments more on general principles. Lopes and Kay L.JJ. did not even mention the section. It is difficult to see how it could have been relevant, for at the critical time the bill was payable to bearer and the disputed transfers were not effected by indorsement. There was therefore no subject-matter on which the section could operate.

In *Embiricos* v. *Anglo-Austrian Bank*[36]:

> A Roumanian bank drew a cheque in Roumania on a London bank, payable to the plaintiffs L. & M. Embiricos or order. The plaintiffs indorsed the cheque to G. Embiricos & Co., an English firm, and posted it to them in London. The cheque was stolen from the envelope by a clerk of the plaintiffs, who forged the signature of G. Embiricos & Co. and cashed the cheque at a Vienna bank, which acted in good faith. The Vienna bank sent it to the defendants in London for collection. By Austrian law the Vienna bank got a good title to the cheque even though the indorsement was forged; by English law they did not.[37]

It was held that Austrian law governed and that the title of the defendants must prevail. Section 72(2) was relied on but faintly by the defendants' counsel and by Walton J., Vaughan Williams L.J. and Romer L.J., who based their judgments on general principles and on *Alcock* v. *Smith*.[38] Only Stirling L.J. in a very short judgment was prepared to attach more

---

[34] [1892] 1 Ch. 238.
[35] Bills of Exchange Act 1882, s.36(2). But it is difficult to see the logic of the plaintiffs' position, because even if, as they alleged, the bill was not negotiable and had to be treated as an ordinary chattel, the title would have passed by the judicial sale in Norway: *Cammell* v. *Sewell* (1860) 5 H. & N. 728; *ante*, p. 353.
[36] [1904] 2 K.B. 870; [1905] 1 K.B. 677.
[37] Bills of Exchange Act 1882, s.24.
[38] [1892] 1 Ch. 238.

weight to the subsection than his brethren. Here again it is difficult to see the relevance of section 72(2), because the simple words "Pay G. Embiricos & Co." hardly needed interpretation. Their meaning was the same whether they were written by G. Embiricos or by a thief. English and Austrian law differed not on the interpretation of the words, but on the effect of the forged indorsement.

In *Koechlin* v. *Kestenbaum*[39] it was held that the chain of indorsements was not broken when an indorsement was made in France, not by the payee, but by his son acting under his authority. The indorsement was valid by French law but not by English law because the son did not add the words "per pro" to indicate that he was signing as agent. The Court of Appeal were clearly right in regarding the validity of the French indorsement as governed by French law because of the provisions of section 72(1). Hence the principle that questions of transfer are governed by the general principles of the conflict of laws relating to tangible chattels does not apply when the validity of the transfer depends on the formal validity of the indorsement, since that question is governed by section 72(1) of the Act. Sargant L.J.[40] seemed to think that the decision in *Embiricos* v. *Anglo-Austrian Bank*[41] was based on section 72(2), whereas as we have seen it clearly was not.

The question whether the *lex loci actus* governs the transfer of a bill by virtue of section 72(2) or by virtue of the general principles of the conflict of laws relating to the transfer of chattels is not devoid of practical importance. For in *Alcock* v. *Smith* the bill was an inland bill, and if section 72(2) governed the question, and if the action had been brought against the acceptor, the decision must have gone the other way because the case would have fallen within the proviso to the subsection. From a practical point of view it seems better to avoid the somewhat artificial distinction between inland bills and foreign bills, and to prevent the question of transfer being governed by different laws in accordance with whether the action is brought against the acceptor or a transferee. It is therefore submitted that the simplest and most satisfactory solution is to regard the question as governed not by section 72(2) but by the general principles of the conflict of laws relating to chattels, except where, as in *Koechlin* v. *Kestenbaum*, the transferee's title depends on the formal validity of an indorsement, in which case it is governed by section 72(1). As Falconbridge says,[42] "the matter is primarily one of the transfer of the property in an obligation to pay money which is in effect merged in a tangible document." Hence the matter is in general unaffected by section 72 of the Act, which deals with the law of contract, not the law of property.

Duties of the holder

Where a bill is dishonoured, either by non-acceptance or by non-pay-

---

[39] [1927] 1 K.B. 889.
[40] At p. 899.
[41] [1904] 2 K.B. 870; [1905] 1 K.B. 677.
[42] Falconbridge, p. 342; *cf.* Dicey and Morris, p. 897.

ment, the holder immediately gets a right of recourse against the drawer and the indorsers, but in order to enforce this right he is, as a general rule, required by English law to give notice of dishonour to the drawer and to each indorser,[43] and, in the case of a foreign bill, cause it to be protested before a notary public.[44] The object of protesting it is to provide authentic proof of due presentation and dishonour which will be accepted as sufficient by any tribunal at home or abroad.

Section 72(3) of the Bills of Exchange Act provides as follows:

> The duties of the holder with respect to presentment for acceptance or payment and the necessity for or sufficiency of a protest or notice of dishonour, or otherwise, are determined by the law of the place where the act is done or the bill is dishonoured.

The language of this subsection is obscure. It should probably be construed *reddendo singula singulis*, so that "act is done" refers to presentment for acceptance or payment, and "bill is dishonoured" refers to the necessity for or sufficiency of a protest or notice of dishonour.

It is not clear whether the law of the place where the act is done determines whether the holder has to present the bill at all or merely how he has to do so. In the former case the words "act is done" would have to be read "act is done or to be done." But there is judicial authority for the view that the existence or non-existence of the duty to present is not within the terms of the subsection.[45] On the other hand, the necessity for and sufficiency of a notice of dishonour are determined by the law of the place where the bill is dishonoured.[46]

Due date of a bill

The due date of a bill is determined by the *lex loci solutionis*. The Bills of Exchange Act, section 72(5), provides as follows:

> Where a bill is drawn in one country and is payable in another, the due date thereof is determined according to the law of the place where it is payable.

This is a concession to the "single law" principle: the due date of a bill or note is determined by the law of the place of payment as regards all parties who become liable thereon. Thus, if a moratorium is declared in the place of payment, postponing the maturity of all current bills, *e.g.* because of war, effect will be given to it in England.[47]

Measure of damages

Section 57(1) of the Bills of Exchange Act provides that where a bill is

---

[43] Bills of Exchange Act 1882, s.48.
[44] s.51(2).
[45] *Bank Polski* v. *Mulder* [1941] 2 K.B. 266, affirmed on other grounds [1942] 1 K.B. 497; *Cornelius* v. *Banque Franco-Serbe* [1942] 1 K.B. 29, 32, better reported [1941] 2 All E.R. 728, 732.
[46] *Rothschild* v. *Currie* (1841) 1 Q.B. 43; *Hirschfeld* v. *Smith* (1866) L.R. 1 C.P. 340; *Horne* v. *Rouquette* (1878) 3 Q.B.D. 514.
[47] *Rouquette* v. *Overmann* (1875) L.R. 10 Q.B. 525; *Re Francke and Rasch* [1918] 1 Ch. 470.

dishonoured, the measure of damages is (a) the amount of the bill; (b) interest thereon from the time of presentment for payment if the bill is payable on demand, and from the maturity of the bill in any other case; and (c) the expenses of noting or, when protest is necessary, the expenses of protest.[48] But this list is not exhaustive. A foreign drawer of a bill drawn abroad and accepted and dishonoured in England can recover from the acceptor not only the above damages but also the "re-exchange" which, under the foreign law, he is obliged to pay to an indorsee.[49]

---

[48] ss.57(2) and 72(4) of the Act were repealed by s.4 and also by s.32(4) of and Sched. 5, Part I, to the Administration of Justice Act 1977, in consequence of the decision in *Miliangos* v. *George Frank* (*Textiles*) *Ltd.* [1976] A.C. 443 (*post,* p. 462).
[49] *Re Gillespie, Ex p. Robarts* (1886) 18 Q.B.D. 286.

CHAPTER 22

GOVERNMENTAL SEIZURE OF PROPERTY

A FACT of twentieth-century life which is becoming increasingly familiar is the tendency of governments to seize private property on various pretexts and in the supposed interests of the State, often with inadequate compensation payable to the owners, and sometimes with no compensation payable at all. Difficult questions in the conflict of laws are presented if such decrees purport to have extra-territorial effect, or if the property affected by the decree is later brought to England.[1] It has been said that such decrees may take one of three forms[2]:

First, requisition, which is the seizure of property in the public interest for a limited period, usually until the end of some emergency such as war and in return for compensation.

Secondly, nationalisation, which is the permanent absorption of private property into public ownership in pursuance of some political or economic objective, and in return for compensation.

Thirdly, confiscation, which is the permanent seizure of private property without payment of compensation.

The law on this subject tends to become confused with two important principles which are discussed elsewhere in this book. These are, first, the principle that English courts will not enforce directly or indirectly a foreign penal law[3]; and, secondly, the principle that English courts have in general no jurisdiction to entertain an action which affects a foreign sovereign's interest in property.[4]

The principle on which English courts proceed when deciding whether to recognise foreign governmental decrees purporting to seize private property is comparatively simple to state, but often difficult to apply. The principle is that the decree will be recognised as having deprived the owner of his property if the property was within the territory of the foreign State at the time of the decree,[5] but not otherwise.[6] The application of the principle

---

[1] See Dicey and Morris, Chap. 21; Cheshire and North, pp. 137–145; Adriansee, *Confiscation in Private International Law* (1956).

[2] Cheshire and North, p. 137.

[3] *Ante,* pp. 48–49.

[4] *Ante,* pp. 59–60.

[5] *Luther* v. *Sagor* [1921] 3 K.B. 532; *Princess Paley Olga* v. *Weisz* [1929] 1 K.B. 718; *Re Banque des Marchands de Moscou* [1952] 1 All E.R. 1269; *Jabbour* v. *Custodian of Israeli Absentee Property* [1954] 1 W.L.R. 139; *Re Helbert Wagg & Co. Ltd.'s Claim* [1956] Ch. 323, 344–349.

[6] *Lecouturier* v. *Rey* [1910] A.C. 262; *The Jupiter* (*No. 3*) [1927] P. 122, 250; *Re Russian Bank for Foreign Trade* [1933] Ch. 745, 766–767; *Government of the Republic of Spain* v. *National Bank of Scotland,* 1939 S.C. 413; *Frankfurther* v. *W. L. Exner Ltd.* [1947] Ch. 629; *Novello & Co. Ltd.* v. *Hinrichsen Edition Ltd.* [1951] Ch. 595; *Bank voor Handel en Scheepvart N.V.* v. *Slatford* [1953] 1 Q.B. 248; *Att. Gen of New Zealand* v. *Ortiz* [1984] A.C. 1; affmd. on other grounds *ibid.* p. 41.

in any particular case involves answering three questions. First, what was the legal situation of the property at the time of the decree? Secondly, did the decree purport to affect property situate at that place? Thirdly, is the decree a part of the law of that place which the English courts can recognise? These three questions will now be discussed in turn.

The situation of property. Artificial rules have to be adopted in order to ascribe a *situs* to intangible things or choses in action. The general principle is that choses in action are situated where they are properly recoverable. Thus a simple contract debt is situated where the debtor resides and can be sued and presumably keeps his assets.[7] This is so even if the contract provides for payment at another place.[8] But if the debtor resides in more countries than one, and the creditor either expressly or impliedly stipulates for payment at one of them, then the debt will be situated there.[9] If there is no such stipulation, the debt is situated at that place of residence where it would be paid in the ordinary course of business.[10] Shares in a company are situated where, as between the shareholder and the company, they can be effectively dealt with according to the law under which the company was incorporated. Thus if shares are transferable only upon a register they will be situated at the place where the appropriate register is kept.[11] Where they are transferable upon more than one register they will be situated at the register where they would be dealt with in the ordinary course of his affairs by the registered owner.[12]

Tangible things are, as a general rule, situate where they physically are. But ships and aircraft may be an exception. There are dicta indicating (though somewhat faintly) that a ship on the high seas is deemed to be situate at her port of registry.[13] But this only applies to ships on the high seas. When a ship is in territorial or national waters, the artificial *situs* is displaced by the actual *situs,* and the ship is treated like any other chattel.[14] Hence a foreign governmental decree requisitioning a ship registered in the foreign State will not be recognised if, at the time of the decree, the ship is in an English port.[15] What has been said about ships may also be true of aircraft. An aircraft in flight over the high seas or over a no-man's land like the North Pole or the Antarctic might well be situate in its country of registration.[16]

The interpretation of the decree. Whether the decree purports to affect the property in question can only be answered by interpreting the decree.

---

[7] *New York Life Insurance Co.* v. *Public Trustee* [1924] 2 Ch. 101; see, generally, Dicey and Morris, pp. 528–537.
[8] *Re Helbert Wagg & Co. Ltd.'s Claim* [1956] Ch. 323, 342–344.
[9] *Jabbour* v. *Custodian of Israeli Absentee Property* [1954] 1 W.L.R. 139.
[10] *Ibid.*
[11] *Brassard* v. *Smith* [1925] A.C. 371; *R.* v. *Williams* [1942] A.C. 541.
[12] *R.* v. *Williams, supra; Treasurer of Ontario* v. *Aberdein* [1947] A.C. 24; *Standard Chartered Bank Ltd.* v. *I.R.C.* [1978] 1 W.L.R. 1160.
[13] *The Jupiter* [1924] P. 236, 239; *The Cristina* [1938] A.C. 485, 509.
[14] *Trustees Executors and Agency Co. Ltd.* v. *I.R.C.* [1973] Ch. 254.
[15] *Government of the Republic of Spain* v. *National Bank of Scotland,* 1939 S.C. 413; *Laane* v. *Estonian State Cargo and Passenger Line* [1949] 2 D.L.R. 641.
[16] See Dicey and Morris, p. 537.

There is an observable tendency for English courts to hold whenever possible that the decree did not purport to have extra-territorial effect,[17] since this will often provide an easy answer to the dispute between the parties.

The recognition of the government. English courts have never recognised a law or act of a foreign government unless it is a law or act either of a government recognised by Her Majesty's Government in the United Kingdom, or of a subordinate body set up by such a government to act on its behalf. Forcible seizure of property by a revolutionary mob will not be recognised, unless it is subsequently adopted by the revolutionary government.[18] In one case,[19] where the acts and decrees of the East German Government were in issue, the Foreign Office certified that "Her Majesty's Government have not granted any recognition *de jure* or *de facto* to (a) the 'German Democratic Republic' or (b) its 'Government,' " but that they had recognised the State and Government of the Union of Soviet Socialist Republics as *de jure* entitled to exercise governing authority in respect of East Germany. The House of Lords recognised the acts and decrees of the East German Government as "acts done by a subordinate body which the U.S.S.R. set up to act on its behalf."

De facto recognition is sufficient[20]; and the doctrine of retroactivity may make it immaterial that recognition was not granted until after the decree was made.[21] Where there are two governments claiming to represent the same State, one of which is recognised by Her Majesty's Government *de facto* and the other *de jure*, then the competence of each is limited to the area under its effective control.[22] The Foreign Office certificate is conclusive; but its interpretation is sometimes a matter of some difficulty.

If the foreign government is recognised, and the decree purports to affect the property in question, and the property was within the territory controlled by the foreign government at the time of the decree, English courts have (with one exception) consistently held that the owner's rights in the property are destroyed or otherwise affected by the decree.[23] There are two leading cases. In *Luther* v. *Sagor*[24]:

> A & Co., a Russian company, had a factory or mill in Russia where in 1919 they had a large stock of manufactured boards. The Soviet Government promulgated a decree vesting the property of all sawmills and woodworking establishments in the State. In reliance on this

---

[17] *e.g. Lecouturier* v. *Rey* [1910] A.C. 262; *The Jupiter (No. 3)* [1927] P. 122, 145; *Re Russian Bank for Foreign Trade* [1933] Ch. 745. 767.

[18] *Princess Paley Olga* v. *Weisz* [1929] 1 K.B. 718.

[19] *Carl Zeiss Stiftung* v. *Rayner & Keeler Ltd. (No. 2)* [1967] 1 A.C. 853. *Cf. Hesperides Hotels Ltd.* v. *Aegean Turkish Holidays Ltd.* [1978] Q.B. 205, 216–218; affirmed on other grounds [1979] A.C. 508.

[20] *Luther* v. *Sagor* [1921] 3 K.B. 532.

[21] See *Luther* v. *Sagor, supra; Gdynia Ameryka Linie* v. *Boguslawski* [1953] A.C. 11; *Civil Air Transport Inc.* v. *Central Air Transport Corporation* [1953] A.C. 70.

[22] *Banco de Bilbao* v. *Sancha* [1938] 2 K.B. 176; *The Arantzazu Mendi* [1939] A.C. 256; see also *Bank of Ethiopia* v. *National Bank of Egypt* [1937] Ch. 513; *Gdynia Ameryka Linie* v. *Boguslawski, supra; Civil Air Transport Inc.* v. *Central Air Transport Corporation, supra.*

[23] See cases cited in note 5, *supra.*

[24] [1921] 3 K.B. 532.

decree State officials seized A & Co.'s timber and sold it to B, an American firm carrying on business in London. B imported the timber into England. A & Co. claimed a declaration that the timber was their property. Roche J. granted the declaration, on the ground that His Majesty's Government had not recognised the Soviet Government as the government of a sovereign State. B appealed. Before the hearing of the appeal the Foreign Office informed B's solicitors that His Majesty's Government recognised the Soviet Government as the *de facto* government of Russia. The Court of Appeal gave judgment for B.

The facts in *Princess Paley Olga* v. *Weisz*[25] were even more striking:

A owned pictures which she kept in her palace in Russia. In 1918 a mob of revolutionaries, whose act was subsequently adopted by the Soviet Government, took forcible possession of the palace and its contents. In 1919 A escaped to England without a passport. Meanwhile the palace was maintained by the Soviet Government as a State museum. In 1921 a Soviet decree confiscated the movable property of all Russian citizens who fled from Russia. In 1923 another Soviet decree confiscated all works of art in State museums. In 1928 the Soviet Government sold some of the pictures to B, who brought them to England. It was held that A could not recover them from B, because the decrees of 1921 and 1923 vested the property in the Government, and so did its adoption of the forcible seizure by the revolutionary mob.

Thus, if the property was situate within the territory controlled by the foreign government at the time of the decree, the decree will be recognised, even if the property is later brought to England. Moreover, although English case authority is lacking, it would seem that the decree could be used not only as a shield but also as a sword. If, for example, the Princess when she escaped to England brought some of her pictures with her, it would seem that Weisz could have recovered them from her by action in England. But if the foreign government itself or its nominee sues to recover the property seized, the action will fail on the ground that English courts do not enforce foreign public laws.[26]

The solitary exception referred to above is *The Rose Mary*,[27] a decision of the Supreme Court of Aden:

Under a concession of 1933 the Persian Government granted to A & Co., an English company, the exclusive right to extract oil from a defined territory in Persia. In 1951 the Iranian Government purported to nationalise and expropriate the property vested in A & Co. under the concession of 1933 with only the vaguest promises of compensa-

---

[25] [1929] 1 K.B. 718.
[26] *Att. Gen. of New Zealand* v. *Ortiz ibid.* affmd. on other grounds [1984] A.C. 1 p. 41.
[27] [1953] 1 W.L.R. 246.

tion. The Government sold 700 tons of oil to B & Co., an Italian company, which shipped it to Italy. While on passage to Italy the ship carrying the oil put into Aden. Campbell J. held that A & Co. could recover the oil from B & Co. because, by expropriating the property of a foreign national without compensation, the Iranian Government were in breach of international law, which was part of the law of Aden.

Campbell J. distinguished *Luther* v. *Sagor*[28] and *Princess Paley Olga* v. *Weisz*[29] on the ground that the Russian decrees in those cases purported to affect the property of Russian nationals and hence were not a breach of international law. This distinction was rejected (it is submitted correctly) by Upjohn J. in *Re Helbert Wagg & Co. Ltd.'s Claim,*[30] where he pointed out that the actual decision in *The Rose Mary* could be justified on the ground that the Iranian decree was penal, because it was directed against the property of a single company.

Conversely, English courts have (again with one exception) held that the owner's rights in the property are not affected by the decree if the property was outside the territory controlled by the foreign government at the time of the decree.[31] However, it must be remembered that if the foreign government is in possession or control of the property, the owner cannot as a general rule recover it by legal process in England, because his action would normally be stayed if the foreign government pleaded sovereign immunity.[32]

The solitary exception referred to above is *Lorentzen* v. *Lydden & Co. Ltd.*[33]

> On the eve of its departure from Norway in May 1940, the Norwegian Government made a decree requisitioning (in return for compensation) all ships registered in Norway and situated outside German-occupied Norway, and empowered a curator to take over ships under construction and to collect claims by the owners and enforce them by action. The curator brought an action against B & Co., an English company, for damages for breach of an English contract to charter a ship. (The ship itself had been sunk in April 1940.) Atkinson J. gave extra-territorial effect to this decree and allowed the curator's claim to succeed.

His principal reason for doing so was that, England and Norway being engaged together in a desperate war for their existence, public policy required that effect should be given to the decree. But in *Bank voor Handel en Scheepvart N.V.* v. *Slatford*[34] Devlin J. (it is submitted correctly), after an exhaustive review of the authorities, refused to give effect to a

---

[28] [1921] 3 K.B. 532.
[29] [1929] 1 K.B. 718.
[30] [1956] Ch. 323, 344–349.
[31] See cases cited in note 6, *supra.*
[32] *Ante,* pp. 55–56.
[33] [1942] 2 K.B. 202.
[34] [1953] 1 Q.B. 248.

decree of the Netherlands Government in exile in England which purported to transfer to the State the property in England and elsewhere of
persons resident in enemy-occupied Holland. He followed the Scottish
case of *Government of the Republic of Spain* v. *National Bank of Scotland*[35]
in preference to *Lorentzen* v. *Lydden & Co.* With reference to Atkinson
J.'s public policy argument, Devlin J. pertinently observed:

> "This reasoning at once gives rise to three comments. The first is
> that it amounts to the formulation of a new head of public policy, and
> that is not a matter to be lightly undertaken. The second is that it is
> using public policy, not in accordance with precedent, as a restriction
> upon acts which are thought to be harmful to the community, but in a
> novel way as a positive force to give to an act validity which it would
> otherwise lack. The third is that it appears to cast on the court the duty
> of considering to some extent the political merits of the decree
> itself."[36]

The last sentence quoted above raises the question whether the English
court is entitled or bound to examine the political merits of the decree,
with a view to giving greater effect to decrees which it approves than to
those which it disapproves. The difficulties and dangers inherent in a task
which seems more appropriate to the executive than to the judiciary are
obvious enough. But there are two rules of English law which are sometimes invoked in this connection. One is the rule that English courts will
not enforce a foreign penal law.[37] The other is the rule that they will not
give effect to any result of a foreign status which is penal.[38] The word
"penal" is not used in the same sense in these two rules. In the first it
means criminal. In the second it means discriminatory, or contrary to public policy. But the language of the courts does not always make this distinction clear.

Some governmental decrees expropriating private property are
obviously penal in both these senses. Others equally obviously are not. At
one end of the scale is the decree of the Spanish Republican Government
in 1931 declaring the ex-King of Spain guilty of high treason and an outlaw
and declaring that all his poperty, rights and grounds of action should be
seized for its own benefit by the Spanish State.[39] At the other end of the
scale are the decrees of allied Governments in war-time temporarily
requisitioning property against compensation in order to prevent it falling

---

[35] 1939 S.C. 413, 433.
[36] [1953] 1 Q.B. at pp. 263–264. At pp. 266–267 Devlin J. said: "I need hardly say that it is
only after much thought that I have rejected the guidance given by the decision of Atkinson
J. in *Lorentzen* v. *Lydden & Co.*; and I have done so only because upon reflection I think
that it cannot be made to conform with the authorities which regulate the use of public
policy. In this respect I may say that I have had from the Solicitor-General the benefit of a
much fuller and more able presentation of the relevant considerations than Atkinson J. had
in the unsuccessful argument before him." The reader will find that that argument was presented by Mr. Devlin as he then was. A nicer example of judicial modesty would be hard to
find.
[37] See *ante,* pp. 48–49.
[38] See *ante,* pp. 44–46.
[39] *Banco de Vizcaya* v. *Don Alfonso de Borbon y Austria* [1935] 1 K.B. 140.

into enemy hands.[40] It is impossible to define precisely what decrees are likely to be treated as penal, but it seems that one which is directed against the property of a particular individual[41] or a particular company[42] or a particular family[43] or of persons of a particular race[44] or a particular alien nationality[45] may be so treated. The importance of the matter lies in this, that if the decree is penal, it probably will not be recognised as divesting the owner of his property, even if it was situated within the territory controlled by the foreign government at the time of the decree, if it is in England at the time of the action.[46]

The question arises whether a decree should be treated as penal because no compensation, or inadequate compensation, is payable to the owner under the decree. In one case,[47] Scott L.J. considered that a decree providing for only 25 per cent. compensation was obviously penal. In two later cases,[48] Nazi decrees directed against Jewish businesses were treated as penal not so much because the owners of the businesses were Jews as because the decrees were confiscatory and no compensation was payable. On the other hand, in *Luther* v. *Sagor*[49] and *Princess Paley Olga* v. *Weisz*[50] the decrees were not treated as penal although no compensation at all was payable. The better view would seem to be that the question whether compensation is payable is irrelevant.[51] This is certainly the more convenient view, for it would be a thankless task for a court to have to decide what amount of compensation is adequate, and whether a promise to pay compensation at some time in the future is worth more than the paper it is written on. On the other hand, by treating the recognition of the foreign government by Her Majesty's Government in the United Kingdom as the sole test to be considered on the political plane, English courts have

---

[40] *Lorentzen* v. *Lydden & Co. Ltd.* [1942] 2 K.B. 202; *Bank voor Handel en Scheepvart N.V.* v. *Slatford* [1953] 1 Q.B. 248.

[41] *Banco de Vizcaya* v. *Don Alfonso de Borbon y Austria, supra.*

[42] *The Rose Mary* [1953] 1 W. L.R. 246, as explained in *Re Helbert Wagg & Co. Ltd.'s Claim* [1956] Ch. 323, 346.

[43] See the decree confiscating property of the House of Romanoff mentioned in *Princess Paley Olga* v. *Weisz* [1929] 1 K.B. 718, 722. The plaintiff's property was not caught by this decree because her marriage to the Grand Duke Paul was morganatic.

[44] *Frankfurther* v. *W. L. Exner Ltd.* [1947] Ch. 629; *Novello & Co. Ltd.* v. *Hinrichsen Edition Ltd.* [1951] Ch. 595.

[45] *Wolff* v. *Oxholm* (1817) 6 M. & S. 92; *Re Fried Krupp A/G* [1917] 2 Ch. 188; *Re Helbert Wagg & Co. Ltd.'s Claim* [1956] Ch. 323, 345–346. See also *Oppenheimer* v. *Cattermole* [1976] A.C. 249, 265, 278, 283.

[46] *Folliott* v. *Ogden* (1789) 1 H.Bl. 123; *The Rose Mary* [1953] 1 W.L.R. 246, as explained in *Re Helbert Wagg & Co. Ltd.'s Claim* [1956] Ch. 323, 346; Dicey and Morris, p. 587, Illustration 9. However, in *Frankfurther* v. *W.L. Exner Ltd., supra*, at pp. 636–637, and *Novello & Co. Ltd.* v. *Hinrichsen Edition Ltd., supra*, at p. 604, it was said that though the decrees were penal, they would be recognised as valid and effective so far as property in Germany was concerned.

[47] *A/S Tallina Laevauhisus* v. *Estonian State S.S. Line* (1947) 80 Ll.L.R. 99, 111. *Cf. Laane* v. *Estonian State Cargo and Passenger Line* [1949] 2 D.L.R. 641.

[48] *Frankfurther* v. *W. L. Exner Ltd., supra; Novello & Co. Ltd.* v. *Hinrichsen Edition Ltd, supra.*

[49] [1921] 3 K.B. 532.

[50] [1929] 1 K.B. 718.

[51] See especially the judgments of Devlin J. in *Bank voor Handel en Scheepvart N.V.* v. *Slatford* [1953] 1 Q.B. 248, 258, 260–263, and of Upjohn J. in *Re Helbert Wagg & Co. Ltd.'s Claim* [1956] Ch. 323, 349.

undoubtedly been forced to give decisions which seem on the face of them unjust. For the decision to recognise a foreign government *de facto* or *de jure* is often taken on grounds of political expediency, without regard to the effect which recognition will have on private rights of property.

CHAPTER 23

ADMINISTRATION OF ESTATES

INTRODUCTION

ENGLISH law and the systems based on it differ widely from modern civil law systems in their attitude to the administration of the estates of deceased persons. In English law the general principle is that no one is entitled to deal with the property of a deceased person unless he has obtained the authority of the court.[1] If the deceased made a will appointing an executor who is willing to act, the necessary authority is acquired by the executor obtaining a grant of probate of the will, either in common form from a probate registry or (if the validity of the will is contested) in solemn form, *i.e.* after probate proceedings. If the deceased died intestate, the necessary authority is acquired by some person (*e.g.* one of the next-of-kin, or a creditor) obtaining a grant of letters of administration. Where there is a will but no executor the grant is made with the will annexed. The executors or administrators (generically called the personal representatives) succeed to the property of the deceased, and are bound to clear the estate of debts, duties and expenses, and then to distribute the surplus among the persons entitled under the deceased's will or intestacy. This chapter is concerned with the first of these duties, the payment of debts etc.; the next chapter deals with the beneficial distribution of the net surplus of the estate.

On the Continent, the general rule is that the property of a deceased person passes directly to his heirs or universal legatee; personal representatives in the English sense need not be appointed; and when personal representatives are appointed, their duties are usually of a supervisory nature, quite different from those of English personal representatives.[2] But, whatever the foreign law may say, no property in England can pass directly to a foreign heir or universal legatee. In order to have the right to deal with the property in England, he must obtain an English grant.

ENGLISH GRANTS OF REPRESENTATION

Jurisdiction to make a grant

Before 1858 grants of representation were made exclusively by the ecclesiastical courts. Their jurisdiction depended upon the presence of movable property (called *bona notabilia*) within the diocese. In 1857 this

---

[1] *New York Breweries Co. Ltd.* v. *Att. Gen.* [1899] A.C. 62. There are statutory exceptions, *e.g.* the proceeds of a policy of life insurance effected by the deceased can be recovered without a grant: Revenue Act 1884. s.11, as amended by Revenue Act 1889, s.19; *Haas* v. *Atlas Assurance Co. Ltd.* [1913] 2 K.B. 209. See also Administration of Estates (Small Payments) Act 1965.
[2] See, *e.g. Re Achillopoulos* [1928] Ch. 433.

jurisdiction was transferred to the Court of Probate and is now vested in the High Court.[3] Until 1932 the High Court could only make a grant if there was property of the deceased situated in England. This restriction could be very inconvenient. When a person died domiciled in England leaving property in a continental European country, the foreign court would sometimes refuse to make a grant of representation until a grant had been obtained in England. If the deceased left no property in England the result was an impasse.[4] The Administration of Justice Act 1932[5] therefore provided that the court should have jurisdiction to make a grant in respect of any deceased person, even if he left no property in England. But if there is no property of the deceased in England and he died domiciled abroad, the court is very reluctant to make a grant.[6]

Separate wills

Testators sometimes make separate wills disposing of their property in England and abroad. If one instrument confirms the other, they both together constitute the last will of the testator, and an executor seeking a grant of representation must take probate of both. But if the wills are independent of each other, the court had until 1932 no jurisdiction to make a grant in respect of the will which disposed only of property situated abroad.[7] The present practice is to admit only the English will to probate unless there is some reason for making a grant of probate in respect of the foreign will as well.[8]

Person to whom the grant will be made

Where a person dies domiciled in a foreign country, the court will make a grant in the first instance to the person entrusted with the administration of the estate by the court of the deceased's domicile.[9] If there is no such person, e.g. because no application for a grant has yet been made in the country of the domicile or because its courts do not appoint personal representatives in the English sense, the grant will be made to the person entitled to administer the estate by the law of the domicile.[10] But the making of such a grant is discretionary, and the court may make a grant to such other person as it thinks fit, either because there is no one who qualifies

---

[3] Non-contentious or common form probate business is assigned to the Family Division, and all other probate business to the Chancery Division: Supreme Court Act 1981, Sched. 1, paras. 1, 3.

[4] *In the Goods of Tucker* (1864) 3 Sw. & Tr. 585.

[5] s. 2(1). This Act is repealed by Supreme Court Act 1981, Sched. 7, but in substance kept alive by s.25(1).

[6] *Aldrich* v. *Att. Gen* [1968] P. 281, 295.

[7] *In the Goods of Coode* (1867) L.R. 1 P. & D. 449; *In the Goods of Smart* (1884) 9 P.D. 64; *In the Goods of Tamplin* [1894] P. 39.

[8] *Re Wayland* [1951] 2 All E.R. 1041.

[9] Non-Contentious Probate Rules 1954, r. 29(*a*), as amended by Non-Contentious Probate (Amendment) Rules 1967, r. 2(10) and by Non-Contentious Probate (Amendment) Rules 1982.

[10] Non-Contentious Probate Rules 1954, r. 29(*b*).

under the foregoing rules or because there are special circumstances which appear to require it.[11]

If the deceased left a formally valid will which names an executor as such in English or Welsh, or which describes (in any language) the duties of a named person in terms which according to English law are sufficient to constitute him an executor according to the tenor, probate may be granted to that person.[12] If the law of the domicile restricts the powers of the representative to a fixed period from the death of the deceased, such restriction will be disregarded in England.[13]

A grant under the foregoing rules may be made either to the foreign personal representative himself, or to an attorney whom he has authorised to apply for a grant on his behalf. In either case the English administration is said to be "ancillary" to the "principal" administration in the domicile.

In making a grant to the foreign personal representative the court is not concerned with the ground on which he was appointed.[14] Thus the court has followed a grant made by the court of the domicile after an order presuming the death of the deceased and vesting his estate in the personal representative, although an order presuming death would not by itself have had any legal effect in England.[15] But the foreign personal representative must be a person to whom a grant can properly be made in English law. Thus the court will not make a grant to a foreign personal representative who is a minor.[16] And if there is a minority or a life interest arises under a will or intestacy the court must normally[17] make a grant to not less than two individuals or a trust corporation, and will therefore not make a grant to a single individual even if he is entitled to administer the estate by the law of the domicile.[18]

The practice of making a grant to the foreign personal representative by the law of the domicile has been based on two grounds. The first is the convenience of having the whole administration carried on by the same person irrespective of the situation of the deceased's assets. The second is the general rule that succession to movables is governed by the law of the deceased's domicile.[19] But the latter argument is weakened by two considerations. The first is that under the Wills Act 1963 a will may be formally

---

[11] *Ibid.* r. 29(c); *In the Goods of Kaufman* [1952] P. 325; see also *Practice Direction* [1953] 1 W.L.R. 1237. And see *Bath* v. *British and Malayan Trustees Ltd.* [1969] 2 N.S.W.R. 114, where the court made a grant to a residuary legatee and not to the domiciliary administrator, because the latter would have been obliged to remit the assets to the country of the domicile in order to pay death duties.

[12] Non-Contentious Probate Rules 1954, r. 29, proviso (*a*).

[13] *In the Estate of Goenaga* [1949] P. 367, a case difficult to reconcile with *Laneuville* v. *Anderson* (1860) 2 Sw. & Tr. 24; see Morris (1950) 3 Int.L.Q. 243; Lipstein (1949) 26 B.Y.I.L. 498.

[14] *In the Goods of Earl* (1867) L.R. 1 P. & D. 450; *Miller* v. *James* (1872) L.R. 3 P. & D. 4; *In the Estate of Humphries* [1934] P. 78.

[15] *In the Goods of Spenceley* [1892] P. 255; *In the Goods of Schulhof* [1948] P. 66; *In the Goods of Dowds* [1948] P. 256; contrast *In the Goods of Wolf* [1948] P. 66.

[16] *In the Goods of H.R.H. the Duchesse d'Orleans* (1859) 1 Sw. & Tr. 253.

[17] See Supreme Court Act 1981, s.114(2), under which the court has a discretionary power to make a grant to one individual if it thinks fit.

[18] Non-Contentious Probate Rules 1954, r. 29(*d*).

[19] *Post,* Chap. 24.

valid under English rules of the conflict of laws although it is formally invalid by the law of the deceased's domicile.[20] The second is that since the Land Transfer Act 1897, a grant to a personal representative vests in him real as well as personal property; and the general rule is that succession to immovables is governed, not by the law of the deceased's domicile, but by the *lex situs*.[21] For this reason the High Court of Australia has refused a grant to a foreign personal representative where the local estate consisted of immovables as well as movables.[22] But the English practice is in general still to make a grant to the foreign personal representative,[23] except that where the English estate consists wholly of immovables a grant limited thereto may be made to the person who would have been entitled if the deceased had died domiciled in England.[24]

Under the Consular Conventions Act 1949, the court may make a grant to a consular officer of a foreign State to which the Act has been extended by Order in Council, if a national of that State is entitled to a grant of probate or administration in respect of property in England, is not resident in England, and has not by an attorney applied to the court for a grant.

Effect in England of Scottish, Northern Irish and Commonwealth grants

Scottish and Northern Irish grants. Before 1972, a Scottish confirmation of an executor of a person who died domiciled in Scotland, or a Northern Irish grant in respect of the estate of a person who died domiciled in Northern Ireland, could be resealed in England and thereafter had the same effect as an English grant. The need for resealing was abolished by section 1 of the Administration of Estates Act 1971, which provides that where a person dies domiciled in Scotland or Northern Ireland, a Scottish confirmation or Northern Irish grant will, without being resealed, be treated as if it had originally been made by the English High Court. There are of course reciprocal provisions for the direct recognition of English grants in Scotland and Northern Ireland,[25] of Northern Irish grants in Scotland[26] and of Scottish confirmations in Northern Ireland.[27]

Commonwealth grants. Under the Colonial Probates Act 1892, a grant of representation made in a country to which the Act has been applied by Order in Council may be sealed with the seal of the probate registry and will thereafter have the same effect as an English grant. The Act cannot be applied to a country unless Her Majesty is satisfied that the local legislature has made adequate provision for the recognition of United Kingdom grants. But it has been applied to almost the whole Commonwealth,[28] and

---

[20] *Post,* p. 393. See *Re Manifold* [1962] Ch. 1 (decided under the Wills Act 1861).
[21] *Post,* Chap. 24.
[22] *Lewis* v. *Balshaw* (1935) 54 C.L.R. 188.
[23] *In the Goods of Meatyard* [1903] P. 125. *Cf. In the Estate of von Brentano* [1911] P. 172.
[24] Non-Contentious Probate Rules 1954, r. 29, proviso (*b*).
[25] ss.2(1), 3(1).
[26] s.3(1).
[27] s.2(2).
[28] See the Colonial Probates Act Application Order 1965, S.I. No. 1530, and S.I. 1976 No. 579 (New Hebrides).

it continues to apply to South Africa although it has left the Commonwealth.[29] The Act does not require that the deceased should have been domiciled in the country where the grant was made, but the probate registry has a discretion whether or not to reseal. Unless there are special reasons, a grant not made by the court of the domicile will not be resealed unless it was made to a person who would have been entitled to an original grant in England, *e.g.* as an executor named in a will written in English or Welsh, or as the person entitled to administer the estate by the law of the domicile.[30]

EFFECT OF AN ENGLISH GRANT

An English grant vests in the personal representatives all property of the deceased, movable or immovable, which at the time of his death is locally situated in England[31]; and also, probably, any movables of the deceased which after his death are brought to England.[32] But, although there is no authority on the point, it would be consistent with principle to recognise the title of a third party who under the *lex situs* had obtained a good title to such movables before they were brought to England.[33] Even if the deceased died domiciled in England, an English grant does not of its own force vest in the personal representatives any property which is and remains outside England.[34] At most it gives the personal representative a "generally recognised claim" to be appointed as such by the courts of the country where the movables are situated.[35]

An English personal representative may legitimately take such steps as are open to him to recover property of the deceased wherever situated. Whether he is under a duty to recover assets situated outside England is less clear. Usually he will be unable to recover such assets unless he first obtains a grant of representation from the foreign court. If he attempts to deal with foreign assets without a grant he may find himself liable as an executor *de son tort* under the foreign law. In practice, therefore, an English personal representative will be concerned with foreign assets only if the deceased died domiciled in England, since only in such case has the English personal representative a "generally recognised claim" to a grant from the foreign court.[36] If there are sufficient assets in England to pay the debts and duties, an English personal representative is not obliged to collect a specifically bequeathed chattel situated abroad. He may simply assent to its vesting in the legatee and leave the latter to bear the expense of bringing it home[37] or paying any foreign duty which it may have attracted.[38]

---

[29] South Africa Act 1962, s.2 and Sched. 2.
[30] Non-Contentious Probate Rules 1954, r. 41(3).
[31] Administration of Estates Act 1925, s.1.
[32] *Whyte* v. *Rose* (1842) 3 Q.B. 493, 506, *per* Parke B.; *In the Goods of Coode* (1867) L.R. 1 P. & D. 449, *per* Sir J. P. Wilde P.
[33] Dicey and Morris, p. 597; see *ante*, Chap. 19.
[34] *Blackwood* v. *R.* (1882) 8 App.Cas. 82, 92.
[35] *Ibid.*
[36] *Blackwood* v. *R., supra.*
[37] *Re Fitzpatrick* [1952] Ch. 86.
[38] *Re Scott* [1915] 1 Ch. 592.

A personal representative will be liable to account for assets under an English grant only if he received them in his character as English personal representative. If he also has a grant from a foreign court he is not accountable in England *qua* personal representative for assets recovered in this capacity.[39]

An order for the judicial administration of the estate will not ordinarily be confined to English assets,[40] although the court may of course be unable to exercise effective control over assets situated elsewhere.[41] If the English personal representative also holds assets in his capacity as a foreign personal representative, the administration order cannot affect his duty to administer those assets according to the foreign law. But once the foreign assets have been duly administered, the court may compel the personal representative to carry out the trusts of the testator's will upon which the surplus is held. The court's power to enforce trusts exists whenever the trustee is personally subject to the jurisdiction, irrespective of where the assets are situated or whether they are movable or immovable.[42]

CHOICE OF LAW

The administration of a deceased person's estate is governed wholly by the law of the country in which the personal representative obtained his grant.[43] Every question as to the admissibility of debts and as to the priority in which debts are to be paid is governed by the *lex fori*. Foreign creditors rank equally with English creditors, whether the English administration is principal or ancillary.[44] The only difference is that the English ancillary administrator need not advertise for foreign claims.[45]

Administration does not include the distribution of surplus assets to beneficiaries under the deceased's will or intestacy. That is a matter of succession and is governed, broadly speaking, by the law of the deceased's domicile so far as movables are concerned.[46] If the deceased died domiciled abroad, the English administration is, as previously explained, ancillary to that which takes place in the country of the domicile. Normally the English ancillary personal representative will hand over the surplus to the principal representative appointed by the courts of the domicile.[47] But the court has a discretionary power to restrain him from doing so. Thus in *Re Lorillard*[48] assets in the hands of an English representative would, if sent

---

[39] Dicey and Morris, p. 599.
[40] *Stirling-Maxwell* v. *Cartwright* (1879) 11 Ch.D. 522; *Ewing* v. *Orr-Ewing* (1883) 9 App. Cas. 34.
[41] *Ewing* v. *Orr-Ewing* (1885) 10 App.Cas. 453.
[42] *Ewing* v. *Orr-Ewing* (1883) 9 App.Cas. 34.
[43] *Preston* v. *Melville* (1841) 8 Cl. & F. 1.
[44] *Re Kloebe* (1884) 28 Ch.D. 175.
[45] *Re. Achillopoulos* [1928] Ch. 433, 445.
[46] *Post*, Chap. 24.
[47] *Re Achillopoulos, supra; In the Estate of Weiss* [1962] P. 136.
[48] [1922] 2 Ch. 638; criticised by Cheshire and North, pp. 593–594; approved by Lord Simonds in *Government of India* v. *Taylor* [1955] A.C. 491, 509; followed in *Jones* v. *Borland*, 1969 (4) S.A. 29, and *Permanent Trustee Co. (Canberra) Ltd.* v. *Finlayson* (1968) 122 C.L.R. 338, 342–343, 346.

to the domiciliary representative, have gone to pay debts which by English domestic law were statute-barred. In *Re Manifold*[49] the domiciliary executor would have had to distribute the assets in accordance with a will which by the English rules of the conflict of laws had been revoked. In both these cases the court exercised its discretionary power and ordered the English representative not to hand over the assets but to distribute them himself to the persons entitled by English law.

The courts have occasionally had to decide whether particular rules of English domestic law relate to administration or to succession. The order of priority for payment of creditors is a matter of administration, but the rules for deciding whether debts or legacies are payable out of realty or personalty, property specifically bequeathed or residue, are concerned with the adjustment of beneficial interests and are therefore a matter of succession.[50] The power to postpone the sale of assets[51] and the power to pay maintenance out of the estate to infant beneficiaries[52] have both been held to be matters of administration.

FOREIGN PERSONAL REPRESENTATIVES

The general rule is that a foreign personal representative of the deceased who wishes to represent him in England must obtain an English grant and cannot sue in his character of foreign representative.[53] No person will be recognised in England as personal representative of the deceased unless and until he has obtained an English grant. If anyone else intermeddles with the assets of the deceased he incurs all the liabilities but none of the privileges of such a representative.[54] This rule contrasts curiously with the fact that a foreign trustee in bankruptcy has his title recognised as a matter of course, but it has been justified as the most effective means of protecting English creditors. This reasoning does not apply if the foreign personal representative is suing, not on behalf of the deceased's estate, but on behalf of his dependants under the Fatal Accidents Act 1976, because in that case no creditor, English or foreign, has any right to the damages recovered. But even in this case it seems that a foreign personal representative cannot sue in England unless he gets an English grant.[55]

However, a foreign personal representative who has obtained a judgment against a debtor of the estate in the foreign country can enforce the judgment in England in his personal capacity without taking out an English grant.[56]

A question which has been much discussed by writers, but on which

[49] [1962] Ch. 1.
[50] *Re Hewit* [1891] 3 Ch. 568; *Re Voet* [1949] N.Z.L.R. 742.
[51] *Re Wilks* [1935] Ch. 645.
[52] *Re Kehr* [1952] Ch. 26.
[53] *Carter and Crost's Case* (1585) Godb. 33; *Tourton* v. *Flower* (1735) 3 P.Wms. 369; *New York Breweries Co. Ltd.* v. *Att. Gen* [1899] A.C. 62; *Finnegan* v. *Cementation Co. Ltd.* [1953] 1 Q.B. 688. For statutory exceptions, see *ante*, p. 382, n. 1.
[54] *New York Breweries Co. Ltd.* v. *Att. Gen.*, *supra*.
[55] *Finnegan* v. *Cementation Co. Ltd.*, *supra*. It is otherwise in Ontario (*Byrn* v. *Paterson S.S. Co.* [1936] 3 D.L.R. 111) and in the United States (Restatement, s.180).
[56] *Vanquelin* v. *Bouard* (1863) 15 C.B. (N.S.) 341; *Re Macnichol* (1874) L.R. 19 Eq. 81.

there is no direct authority, is whether payment of a debt to a foreign personal representative gives the debtor a good discharge and bars a subsequent action in England by the English personal representative.[57] The effect of such a payment should in principle depend on the *lex situs* of the debt, that is, in general where the debtor ordinarily resides.[58] If the deceased died domiciled, *e.g.* in New York and a debtor resident in New York pays the debt to the New York representative, such payment should be a discharge from the debt in England against any claim by the English personal representative. The same result should follow if the debtor is resident in New York but the deceased died domiciled in England. If, on the othe hand, a debtor resident in England, indebted to a deceased person who died domiciled in England, voluntarily pays the debt to the New York representative, the payment should not discharge the debtor. The same result should follow if the debtor is resident in England but the deceased died domiciled in New York. For in both cases the debtor is under no compulsion to pay the New York representative, who cannot as such sue for the debt in England; but the debtor, because he is resident in England, is liable at any moment to be sued by the English personal representative. The question whether payment to the foreign personal representative under compulsion, *e.g.* in satisfaction of a judgment, discharges the debtor is equally unsettled, though the argument that it should do so is of course much stronger.

Just as a foreign personal representative without an English grant cannot sue in England, so he cannot be made liable in England for property held or acts done by him in his capacity of foreign representative.[59] The only way in which he can be made to account for assets which he has brought to England is by an action for judicial administration of the estate.[60] The English personal representative must be a party to such an action.[61]

The foreign personal representative may also be liable in England if he personally places himself in a position where he incurs liabilities as a debtor or trustee, *e.g.* by entering into a contract in England in respect of the estate, or by making an improper investment.[62] Moreover, if he intermeddles with English assets, he will make himself liable as an executor *de son tort*.[63]

---

[57] See Story, ss.514–515a; Westlake, s.98; Cheshire and North, pp. 595–596; Dicey and Morris, pp. 604–605.

[58] For the *situs* of debts, see *ante*, p. 375.

[59] *Jauncy* v. *Sealey* (1686) 1 Vern. 397; *Beavan* v. *Hastings* (1856) 2 K. & J. 724; *Flood* v. *Patterson* (1861) 29 Beav. 295; *Re McSweeney* [1919] 1 Ir.R. 16; *Electronic Industries Imports Ltd.* v. *Public Curator of Queensland* [1960] V.R. 10; *Boyd* v. *Leslie* [1964] V.R. 728.

[60] *Tyler* v. *Bell* (1837) 2 My. & Cr. 89; *Bond* v. *Graham* (1842) 1 Hare 482.

[61] *Ibid.*

[62] *Harvey* v. *Dougherty* (1887) 56 L.T. 322.

[63] *New York Breweries Co. Ltd.* v. *Att. Gen.* [1899] A.C. 62.

CHAPTER 24

SUCCESSION

WHEN the estate of a deceased person has been fully administered, that is to say when all debts, duties and expenses have been paid, the question arises by what law the beneficial distribution of his net estate is to be governed. As a general rule, succession to immovables is governed by the *lex situs,* and succession to movables by the law of the deceased's last domicile. Few qualifications need to be made to these propositions so far as intestate succession is concerned. But in succession under wills it may sometimes be necessary to look at the law of the testator's domicile at the date when the will was executed; and other laws are made relevant by statute if the question is one of formal validity. If the will exercises a power of appointment, it may be necessary to have regard to the law governing the creation of the power, either because the donee is considered to be disposing of the property of the donor, or because powers of appointment are unknown to the law of the donee's domicile.

We need to consider, therefore, first intestate succession, secondly wills, and thirdly the exercise of powers by will. Under the second and third heads we shall consider separately (1) capacity, (2) formal validity, (3) material or essential validity, (4) construction, and (5) revocation.

If any of these questions has been decided by the courts of the country of the deceased's last domicile in the case of movables[1] or of the *situs* in the case of immovables, English courts will follow that decision.

INTESTATE SUCCESSION

It has been settled law for over 200 years that intestate succession to movables is governed by the law of the deceased's last domicile.[2] But this rule applies only to succession in the strict sense of that term. It does not apply to the right of the Crown or of a foreign government to take ownerless property as *bona vacantia* or under a *jus regale.* The title to movables so claimed is governed by the *lex situs* and not by the law of the deceased's last domicile. Thus if a person dies intestate and without next-of-kin domiciled in a foreign country, and the foreign State claims his movables in England as ownerless property, the Crown's claim to the movables as *bona vacantia* will be preferred.[3] In such a case the foreign State claims not by way of succession but because there is no succession. It is otherwise, how-

---

[1] *Enohin* v. *Wylie* (1862) 10 H.L.C. 1; *Doglioni* v. *Crispin* (1866) L.R. 1 H.L. 301; *Re Trufort* (1887) 36 Ch.D. 600.
[2] *Pipon* v. *Pipon* (1744) Amb. 799; *Somerville* v. *Somerville* (1801) 5 Ves. 750.
[3] *Re Barnett's Trusts* [1902] 1 Ch. 847; *Re Musurus* [1936] 1 All E.R. 1666.

ever, if the foreign State claims as *ultimus heres* under the foreign law and not under a *jus regale*. In such a case there is a true claim of succession which is governed by the law of the domicile, and the claim of the foreign State will be preferred to that of the Crown.[4]

According to the traditional rule of the English conflict of laws, intestate succession to immovables is governed by the *lex situs*[5]; but there is far less direct authority for this rule than is sometimes supposed.[6] The rule made some sense before 1926 when there were two systems of intestate succession in English domestic law, one for realty and the other for personalty. It makes no sense today when England and all other countries in the world have adopted one system of intestate succession for all kinds of property. Moreover, outside the common law world the *lex situs* rule for intestate succession to land has been abandoned almost everywhere except in Austria, Belgium and France. The author has elsewhere[7] developed reasons for thinking that the *situs* rule has outlived its usefulness in England and should be abandoned in favour of the law of the intestate's domicile.

The retention of the *situs* rule frequently frustrates the intention of Parliament. For when Parliament passes a modern statute on intestate succession, it seeks to give effect to what the average intestate would have wished to do with his property, if he had made a will. What average intestate? Surely the obvious answer is, English intestates if the statute applies to England, and Scottish intestates if the statute applies to Scotland.

Even within the United Kingdom there are striking differences between the English, Scottish and Northern Irish laws of intestate succession, particularly with regard to the rights of the surviving spouse. Thus in England[8] and Northern Ireland[9] the surviving spouse is now entitled to a statutory legacy of £40,000 if the intestate left issue or £85,000 if he did not. A single example will serve to show the anomalies that can arise if intestate succession to land is governed by the *lex situs*. Suppose that a man dies intestate domiciled in Northern Ireland leaving a widow and no issue and leaving movables in Northern Ireland worth £85,000 and land in England worth the same amount. Would the widow be entitled to two statutory lega-

---

[4] *Re Maldonado's Estate* [1954] P. 223. This is an extreme example of characterisation in accordance with the *lex causae* (*post,* p. 484) and as such has been much criticised, see Gower (1954) 17 M.L.R. 167; Cohn (1954) 17 M.L.R. 381; Lipstein [1954] Camb.L.J. 22; Anton, p. 517. The decision does seem to treat the form of the foreign law as more important than its substance.

[5] Dicey and Morris, Rule 98; Cheshire and North, p. 511; Anton, pp. 511–514.

[6] The existence of the rule was assumed in *Balfour* v. *Scott* (1793) 6 Bro.P.C. 550; *Brodie* v. *Barry* (1813) 2 V. & B. 127, 131; *Dundas* v. *Dundas* (1830) 2 Dow & Cl. 349; *Freke* v. *Carbery* (1873) L.R. 16 Eq. 461; *Duncan* v. *Lawson* (1889) 41 Ch.D. 394; *Re Berchtold* [1923] 1 Ch. 192; and *Re Cutcliffe* [1940] Ch. 565.

[7] Morris (1969) 85 L.Q.R. 339.

[8] Administration of Estates Act 1925, s.46(1)(*i*) para. (3), as amended by Intestates' Estates Act 1952, s.1, Family Provision Act 1966, s.1(1)(*b*), and S.I. 1981 No. 255.

[9] Administration of Estates Act (N.I.) 1955, s.7, as amended by Family Provision Act (N.I.) 1969, s.1(*c*), and S.R. & O. 1981 No. 124.

cies under the English and Northern Irish legislation, thereby leaving nothing for the next-of-kin (perhaps the mother of the intestate)?[10]

WILLS

Capacity

The law of the testator's domicile determines whether he has personal capacity to make a will of movables.[11] "Personal capacity" is here used to denote such questions as whether a minor or a married woman or a person suffering from bodily or mental illness[12] can make a valid will. It does not include what are sometimes called questions of proprietary capacity, for example, whether a testator can leave property away from his wife and children. Such questions are best regarded as questions of material or essential validity and will be dealt with later under that heading.[13]

There is no difficulty in applying the principle stated above if the testator's domicile is the same at the date of his death as it was when he made his will. But if his domicile changes between these two dates, and the two laws differ, it is necessary to choose between them. It is submitted that, on principle, the law of his domicile at the date of the will should govern.[14] Hence, if the testator makes his will at the age of eighteen while domiciled in a country where minority ends at twenty-one and minors cannot make wills, and dies domiciled in England, the will would be void. Conversely, if the testator makes his will at the age of eighteen while domiciled in England, and dies domiciled in a country where minority ends at twenty-one and minors cannot make wills, the will should be valid. It may be noted that by English domestic law (and presumably by the domestic laws of other countries) a testator must have personal capacity to make a will at the date when the will is made, and it is neither necessary nor sufficient that he should be capable of making a will at the date of his death.

There is no English authority on what law governs capacity to make a will of immovables. Probably the *lex situs* would be held to govern.[15]

So far as capacity to take movables under a will is concerned, it has been held that a legacy can be paid to a legatee if he is of age to receive it by the law of his domicile or by the law of the testator's domicile, whichever first happens.[16]

---

[10] *Cf. Re Rea* [1902] 1 Ir.R. 451, where it was held that the widow was entitled to a double portion under the Irish and Victorian Intestates Estates Acts 1890 and 1896. See also *Re Ralston* [1906] V.L.R. 689. These two cases are discussed by Morris (1969) 85 L.Q.R. 339, 348–352.

[11] *In bonis Maraver* (1828) 1 Hagg.Ecc. 498; *In bonis Gutteriez* (1869) 38 L.J.P. & M. 48; *In the Estate of Fuld (No.* 3) [1968] P. 675, 696.

[12] *In the Estate of Fuld (No.* 3), *supra.*

[13] *Post,* p. 396.

[14] Most writers adopt this view: Story, s.465; Savigny, s.377; Dicey and Morris, p. 615; Cheshire and North, p. 600; Wolff, s.557; F. A. Mann (1954) 31 B.Y.I.L. 217, 230–231. *Re Lewal's Settlement* [1918] 2 Ch. 391 supports the statement in the text; but that was a case on the exercise of a power of appointment by will.

[15] See *Bank of Africa* v. *Cohen* [1909] 2 Ch. 129, *ante,* p. 348; a case on capacity to transfer land *inter vivos.*

[16] *Re Hellman's Will* (1866) L.R. 2 Eq. 363.

Formal validity

At common law, a will of immovables had to comply with the formalities prescribed by the *lex situs*,[17] and a will of movables had to comply with the formalities prescribed by the law of the testator's last domicile.[18] This latter rule led to much inconvenience and hardship when, for example, the testator changed his domicile after executing his will, or became mortally ill while travelling in a country other than that of his domicile. So the courts tried to inject some flexibility into the rigid rule of common law by admitting to probate wills which complied with the formalities prescribed by either the domestic law of the testator's last domicile, or the domestic law of any system of law referred to by the conflict rules of that law.[19] This, as a matter of history, is how the doctrine of renvoi obtained a foothold in English law, obviously as an escape device.[20] The Wills Act 1861 (Lord Kingsdown's Act) allowed other forms as alternatives; but it was confined to the wills of British subjects (though extended to wills of personal estate and thus to some kinds of immovables); and it was notoriously badly drafted. After plaguing law students and courts for just over a century it was repealed and replaced by the Wills Act 1963, which gives effect to the Fourth Report of the Private International Law Committee[21] and to an international Convention on the Formal Validity of Wills made at The Hague in 1961.[22]

Section 1 of the Act provides that a will shall be treated as properly executed if its execution conformed to the internal law in force in the territory where it was executed, or in the territory where, at the time of its execution or of the testator's death, he was domiciled or had his habitual residence, or in a State of which, at either of those times, he was a national. This section applies to wills of movables and to wills of land; and section 2(1)(*b*) additionally provides that a will of immovables shall be treated as properly executed if its execution conformed to the internal law in force in the territory where the property was situated.

Under section 1, if a testator is domiciled in one country, habitually resident in a second, and a national of a third, and changes all three between the time of execution of the will and the time of his death, he has a choice of no less than six systems of law available to him, or seven if he makes his will in a different country. This should be enough to save most wills from formal invalidity so far as the conflict of laws is concerned. There is no requirement in the Act that all the testamentary instruments executed by a testator must conform to the same system of law. Hence, a will and six codicils could each derive its formal validity from a different system.

The reference to the law of the testator's nationality is an even greater innovation than the reference to the law of his habitual residence. If the

---

[17] *Coppin* v. *Coppin* (1725) 2 P.Wms. 291; *Pepin* v. *Bruyere* [1900] 2 Ch. 504.
[18] The leading case is *Bremer* v. *Freeman* (1857) 10 Moo.P.C. 306.
[19] *Collier* v. *Rivaz* (1841) 2 Curt. 855; *In bonis Lacroix* (1877) 2 P.D. 94.
[20] *Post*, p. 471.
[21] Cmnd. 491 (1958).
[22] Cmnd. 1729 (1961). For comments on the Act, see Kahn-Freund (1964) 27 M.L.R. 55; Morris (1964) 13 I.C.L.Q. 684.

testator is a national of a composite State comprising many countries, like the Commonwealth or the United States of America, or is, *e.g.* a British citizen, there is an obvious difficulty in ascertaining his nationality for the purposes of the Act. Section 6(2) attempts to solve this problem. It provides as follows: (*a*) if there is in force throughout the State in question a rule indicating which of its systems of internal law can properly be applied in the case in question, that rule shall be followed; but (*b*) if there is no such rule, the system shall be that with which the testator was most closely connected at the relevant time.[23] It is not easy to imagine circumstances in which the provisions of section 6(2)(*a*) will be applicable, or to assign a precise meaning to the provisions of section 6(2)(*b*). One has to think of a testator who is, *e.g.* a British citizen or a citizen of the United States of America and who is domiciled and habitually resident elsewhere and who makes his will elsewhere, the will being formally invalid by the law of the place where it was made and of the testator's domicile and habitual residence, so that it is necessary to invoke the law of his nationality in order to admit it to probate. Section 6(2)(*a*) can rarely help in circumstances like these, because it is doubtful if there is a composite State in the world which has a uniform conflicts rule, but different rules of domestic law, for the formal validity of wills. Certainly the United Kingdom has not, nor has the United States. And as for section 6(2)(*b*), how can we determine whether our hypothetical testator is "most closely connected" with, *e.g.* England or Scotland or New York or California, when *ex hypothesi* he is domiciled and habitually resident outside the United Kingdom or the United States? The only possible answer seems to be, look and see where he keeps the bulk of his property. This answer will not help if, as is likely in the circumstances here envisaged, he keeps it in the country where he is domiciled or habitually resident, and not in the State of which he is a national. It might have been more sensible to make the formalities of the *lex situs* available for wills of movables, as they are for wills of immovables.[24] At best it can be said that the alternative of the law of the nationality, though it will not work for British or American citizens, will do no obvious harm in relation to them, and will be beneficial in relation to citizens of most other countries.

The law of the country where the will was executed is given an extended meaning in the case of wills made on board a vessel or aircraft "of any description." In addition to the law of the place where the vessel or aircraft happens to be (including, no doubt, the country in whose territorial waters the vessel is sailing or the country over which the aircraft is flying), section 2(1)(*a*) of the Act allows as an alternative the internal law in force in the territory with which, having regard to its registration (if any) and other relevant circumstances, the vessel or aircraft may be taken to have been most closely connected. This will normally be the law of the flag or, in the case of ships wearing flags like the Red Ensign or the Stars and Stripes, the law

---

[23] "The relevant time" is defined (very obscurely) as the time of the testator's death where the matter is to be determined by reference to circumstances prevailing at his death, and the time of execution of the will in any other case.

[24] s.2(1)(*b*); *ante,* p. 393.

in force at the port of registration. The cautious drafting is presumably designed to allow of exceptions in the case of flags of convenience. There is no requirement that the vessel or aircraft should be in motion when the will is made. Hence a will formally valid by French law would be admissible to probate if executed on board a French ship alongside in an English port, or on board a French aircraft on the runway at London Airport.

Section 6(3) of the Act provides that regard shall be had to the formal requirements of a particular law at the time of execution, but that this shall not prevent account being taken of an alteration of the law affecting wills executed at that time if the alteration enables the will to be treated as properly executed. Thus, retrospective alterations in the law are relevant if they validate a will, but irrelevant if they invalidate it. This subsection is not in terms confined to alterations in the law made before the death of the testator; and there is no reason to read into it words which are not there.[25]

It will be seen that the Act refers throughout to the "internal law" of the various systems which it allows. Thus, any reference to another system from the conflicts rules of the systems of law authorised by the Act is excluded. But the Act does not abolish, either expressly or by implication, the doctrine of renvoi in relation to the formal validity of wills, nor the rule of common law that the formal validity of a will of movables is governed by the law of the testator's last domicile. Hence, if a British citizen with an English domicile of origin and an Italian domicile of choice makes a will of movables which is formally valid by English domestic law but formally invalid by Italian domestic law, and it is proved that the Italian courts would regard the will as formally valid, it could be admitted to probate in England by way of renvoi from Italian law instead of under sections 1 and 6(2) of the Act.[26]

Under some foreign systems of law, certain classes of testators can only make wills in a special form. Thus, in Dutch law Dutch nationals cannot make wills, even outside Holland, except in the "authentic form" prescribed by Dutch law[27]; and in German law testators over sixteen and under eighteen years of age can make wills only in notarial form.[28] It has long been controversial among continental jurists whether such provisions relate to form or to capacity.[29] Section 3 of the Act settles this question by providing that where a law in force outside the United Kingdom falls to be applied (whether in pursuance of the Act or not), any requirement of that law whereby special formalities are to be observed by testators answering a particular description, or witnesses to the execution of the will are to possess certain qualifications, shall be treated as a formal requirement, notwithstanding any rule of that law to the contrary. Thus, if a Dutch national, domiciled and habitually resident in England, makes an unattested holo-

---

[25] If this is right, the subsection renders *Lynch* v. *Provisional Government of Paraguay* (1871) L.R. 2 P. & M. 268 obsolete. See *post,* pp. 497–498.
[26] For renvoi, see *post,* Chap. 30.
[27] Dutch Civil Code, art. 992.
[28] German Civil Code, paras. 2229, 2231, 2247.
[29] See Robertson, pp. 235–238; Lorenzen, pp.129–130; Falconbridge, pp. 90–94; Beckett (1934) 15 B.Y.I.L. 46, 73, n.1; Wolff, p. 589.

graph will in England, formally invalid by English domestic law and not in the authentic form required for Dutch nationals by article 992 of the Dutch Civil Code, the will would not be admitted to probate in England. The only law which can make the will formally valid is Dutch law, the law of the testator's nationality; and under section 3 of the Act the requirement of article 992 must be treated as a formal requirement, whatever Dutch law may say. Again, if a German national, domiciled and habitually resident in Germany and aged seventeen, makes a will in Germany in holograph form, the will would not be admitted to probate in England because not made in notarial form as required by German law. If, however, the will had been made in France and was formally valid by French law, it would be admitted to probate. For the testator had capacity by the law of his domicile; and the will was formally valid by the law of the country where it was executed.

Material or essential validity

The material or essential validity of a will of movables, or of any particular gift of movables contained therein, is governed by the law of the testator's domicile at the time of his death.[30] The term material or essential validity includes such questions as whether the testator must leave a certain proportion of his estate to his children or widow,[31] whether gifts to attesting witnesses are valid,[32] whether gifts to charities are valid, and whether a gift infringes the rule against perpetuities or accumulations.[33]

If the will bequeathes movables on trusts which are void for remoteness under the rule against perpetuities in force in the country of the testator's last domicile, but the movables are situated and the trust is to be administered in another country by whose law it is valid, it has been suggested[34] that the law of the place of administration should govern and that the trust should be valid. There is some English and Commonwealth authority[35] which supports this suggestion, and it seems reasonable in principle. The same rule should no doubt be applied also to the rule against accumulations and to the question whether gifts to charities are valid. Thus, if a testator domiciled in the Republic of Ireland gives movables in England to English trustees on trust for such of A's children as should attain the age of twenty-five, the gift should be valid under the "wait and see" provisions of section 3 or the age-reducing provisions of section 4 of the English Perpetuities and Accumulations Act 1964, and not void as it would be under the common law rule against perpetuities in force in the Republic. Conversely, if a testator domiciled in Northern Ireland gives movables in Eng-

---

[30] *Whicker* v. *Hume* (1858) 7 H.L.C. 124.
[31] *Thornton* v. *Curling* (1824) 8 Sim. 310; *Campbell* v. *Beaufoy* (1859) Johns. 320; *Re Groos* [1915] 1 Ch. 572; *Re Annesley* [1926] Ch. 692; *Re Ross* [1930] 1 Ch. 377; *Re Adams* [1967] I.R. 424.
[32] *Re Priest* [1944] Ch. 58; see now Wills Act 1968.
[33] *Cf. Freke* v. *Carbery* (1871) L.R. 16 Eq. 461.
[34] Cheshire and North, pp. 607–609; Dicey and Morris, p. 623.
[35] *Fordyce* v. *Bridges* (1848) 2 Ph. 497; *Re Mitchner* [1922] St.R.Qd. 252; *cf. Jewish National Fund* v. *Royal Trustee Co.* (1965) 53 D.L.R. (2d) 577.

land on trusts for accumulation extending beyond any of the statutory periods for which accumulations are permitted by English law, the gift should be invalid, although there is no statutory rule against accumulations in Ireland.

Under the law of England and of some other countries, a beneficiary under a will is sometimes required to elect between taking a benefit under the will and taking a benefit outside the will. Thus, if a testator gives property to A, and gives property belonging to A to B, A will not be allowed to receive the property given to him by the will unless he allows B to receive the property of A which the testator has given to B. The English doctrine may once have depended on the actual or presumed intention of the testator, but it has long since hardened into a fixed rule of equity. "The doctrine of election does not depend on any supposed intention of the testator, but is based on a general principle of equity."[36] "The doctrine of election has nothing to do with intention, and consequently, nothing to do with construction of the testator's will."[37] Consequently, the general rule is that the question whether a legatee of movables must elect between benefits under and outside the will is governed by the law of the testator's domicile at the time of his death.[38]

The doctrine of election has frequently been applied in cases where the testator devises land away from his heir and gives him other benefits under a will which for some reason, *e.g.* want of capacity, defect of form or material invalidity, is inoperative to pass the land to the devisee. In such circumstances a somewhat illogical distinction has been drawn between the English heir of land in England and the foreign heir of foreign land. The English heir was not put to his election because of the "strange tenderness" which courts of equity showed to the heir-at-law.[39] But the foreign heir is bound to elect when the testator gives him immovable property situated in England,[40] or when the testator, being domiciled in England, gives him movables.[41] But the doctrine does not apply unless it is clear from the face of the will that the testator intended to dispose of property that did not belong to him. If he uses general words like "all my real estate wherever situated," the heir is not bound to elect.[42]

The material or essential validity of a gift by will of immovables is governed by the *lex situs*. That law will determine what estates can legally be created,[43] what are the incidents of those estates,[44] whether the interests given infringe the rule against perpetuities or accumulations,[45] whether

---

[36] *Jarman on Wills,* 8th ed., p. 546.
[37] *Re Mengel* [1962] Ch. 791, 800, *per* Buckley J.
[38] Dicey and Morris, Rule 105; *Re Ogilvie* [1918] 1 Ch. 492, 498, *per* Younger J.; *Re Mengel, supra,* not following *Re Allen's Estate* [1945] 2 All E.R. 264 (a much criticised decision).
[39] *Hearle* v. *Greenbank* (1749) 1 Ves.Sen. 298; *Re De Virte* [1915] 1 Ch. 920.
[40] *Dundas* v. *Dundas* (1830) 2 Dow & Cl. 349 (a Scottish case); *Dewar* v. *Maitland* (1866) L.R. 2 Eq. 834; *Orrell* v. *Orrell* (1871) L.R. 6 Ch.App. 302.
[41] *Brodie* v. *Barry* (1813) 2 V. & B. 127; *Re Ogilvie* [1918] 1 Ch. 492.
[42] *Trotter* v. *Trotter* (1828) 4 Bli.(N.S.) 502; *Maxwell* v. *Maxwell* (1852) 2 D.M. & G. 705.
[43] *Nelson* v. *Bridport* (1846) 8 Beav. 547.
[44] *Re Miller* [1914] 1 Ch. 511.
[45] *Freke* v. *Carbery* (1873) L.R. 16 Eq. 461.

gifts to charities are valid,[46] and whether the testator is bound to leave a certain proportion of his estate to his children or widow.[47]

Closely analogous to the question whether the testator is bound to leave a certain proportion of his estate to his wife or children (as he is bound to do under the laws of Scotland, France and many continental European countries) is the question whether the court can make an order for the payment of part of the income of his estate to his dependants (as it can in England under the Inheritance (Provision for Family and Dependants) Act 1975). In England the statute itself limits the court's power to cases where the testator died domiciled in England, whether the property is movable or immovable.[48]

Construction

The construction of a will of movables is governed by the law intended by the testator. In the absence of indications to the contrary, this is presumed to be the law of his domicile at the time when the will was made[49]; but this is only a rebuttable presumption.[50] A change of domicile between the time when the will was made and the time of the testator's death does not affect the construction of the will. "If a question arises as to the interpretation of the will" said Lord Denning[51] "and it should appear that the testator has changed his domicile between making his will and his death, his will may fall to be construed according to the law of his domicile at the time he made it." This is reinforced by section 4 of the Wills Act 1963, which (re-enacting a very ill-drafted section of the Wills Act 1861) provides that the construction of a will shall not be altered by reason of any change in the testator's domicile after the execution of the will.

The term "construction" includes not only the meaning of words and phrases used by the testator, but also the way in which the law fills up gaps in his dispositions when he has failed to foresee and provide against certain events (e.g. that one of several named residuary legatees might predecease him). This of course is not construction in the sense that it has reference to the intentions of the actual testator, for ex hypothesi he never directed his mind to the events which have happened; but it is construction in the sense that the law supposes that the average testator would wish the gap to be filled in a particular way.

A good instance of construction in accordance with the law of the testator's domicile is afforded by Re Cunnington,[52] where a British subject domiciled in France made a will in the English language and form in which he gave his residue on trust for division betwen ten named legatees, most

---

[46] Duncan v. Lawson (1889) 41 Ch.D. 394; Re Hoyles [1911] 1 Ch. 179.

[47] Re Hernando (1884) 27 Ch.D. 284; Re Ross [1930] 1 Ch. 377.

[48] Inheritance (Provision for Family and Dependants) Act 1975, s.1(1).

[49] Anstruther v. Chalmer (1826) 2 Sim. 1; Re Fergusson [1902] 1 Ch. 483; Re Cunnington [1924] 1 Ch. 68.

[50] Bradford v. Young (1885) 29 Ch.D. 617; Re Price [1900] 1 Ch. 442, 452, 453; Re Adams [1967] I.R. 424.

[51] Philipson-Stow v. I.R.C. [1961] A.C. 727, 761.

[52] [1924] 1 Ch. 68.

of whom resided in England. Two of these legatees predeceased him. It
was held that their shares were divisible among the survivors in accordance
with French law, and did not lapse to the next-of-kin as they would have
done by English domestic law. Again, if a testator domiciled in one of the
United States were to give legacies expressed in dollars to legatees resident
in Canada and Australia, there can be little doubt that the amount of the
legacies would be calculated in American dollars.[53]

If a testator domiciled in England gives movables to the "heirs" or
"next-of-kin" of a person who died domiciled in a foreign country, should
the heirs or next-of-kin be ascertained in accordance with English law or
the law of the foreign country? The English courts have adopted the former solution,[54] and the Scottish courts the latter.[55] The view of the Scottish
courts seems preferable. For surely the question is not who would have
been A's next-of-kin if he had died domiciled in England? but rather who
are A's next-of-kin having regard to the fact that he died domiciled
abroad?[56]

There is no reason to suppose that a different general rule applies to the
construction of wills of immovables. Indeed, Lord Denning was dealing
with a will of immovables when he made the statement which was quoted
above. But the use of technical language of the *lex situs* may indicate an
intention that its law should govern the construction of the will.[57] Difficult
problems arise when the testator devises land in two different countries
and aims at producing identical results by the use of the technical language
of one system of law only. The court, when interpreting the will in accordance with the law of the testator's domicile, will endeavour to see that the
dispositions will operate in the country where the land is situated to the
fullest extent that they can operate under the *lex situs*.[58] But if the *lex situs*
makes it illegal or impossible to give effect to the terms of the will as construed by the law of the testator's domicile, then the *lex situs* will prevail.[59]

These propositions can be illustrated by two contrasting cases. In *Studd*
v. *Cook*[60]:

> By a will in English form a testator domiciled in England devised
> lands in England and Scotland to the use of A for life and then to the
> use of A's first and other sons successively in tail male. By English law,
> the effect was to confer a life interest upon A with remainder in tail to
> his sons. But by Scots law the effect was to confer a fee simple upon A,
> because A's sons were unborn when the testator died and he did not
> say "only" after "for life." The House of Lords held that English law
> governed and that A took a life interest in the land in Scotland.

[53] *Saunders* v. *Drake* (1742) 2 Atk. 465; Dicey and Morris, pp. 629–630.
[54] *Re Fergusson's Will* [1902] 1 Ch. 483.
[55] *Mitchell's Trustee* v. *Rule* (1908) 16 S.L.T. 189; *Smith's Trustee* v. *Macpherson,* 1926 S.C. 983.
[56] *Smith's Trustee* v. *Macpherson, supra,* at pp. 991–992, *per* Lord Sands.
[57] *Bradford* v. *Young* (1885) 29 Ch.D. 617, 623.
[58] *Studd* v. *Cook* (1883) 8 App.Cas. 577, 591, *per* Lord Selborne.
[59] *Re Miller* [1914] 1 Ch. 511; *Philipson-Stow* v. *I.R.C.* [1961] A.C. 727, 761.
[60] *Supra.*

On the other hand, in *Re Miller*[61]:

> By a will in Scottish form a testator domiciled in Scotland devised lands in England and Scotland to trustees for behoof of A and the heirs male of his body, whom failing for B and the heirs male of his body. By Scots law, the effect was that A could dispose by will of the Scottish land. But by English law the effect was to create a strict entail of the English land which A could not, as the law then stood, dispose of by will. It was held that English law governed the testator's disposition of the English land and that A could not devise it.

It is not difficult to reconcile these cases. In *Studd* v. *Cook*, the omission of the word "only" raised a pure question of construction which was governed by the law of the testator's domicile. As construed by that law, the will could take effect in Scotland, because life estates are of course known to Scots law. In *Re Miller,* the effect of the will by Scots law was to create an estate then unknown to English law, an estate tail devisable by will, and therefore the *lex situs* had to prevail. "The question really is not so much what is the construction of the will, but what is the estate conferred by the disposition in question after I have arrived at its true construction."[62]

Questions of construction must be distinguished not only from questions of material or essential validity but also from questions of status. Thus, if a testator domiciled in England gives movables to the children of X, who is domiciled in Germany, English law will determine whether illegitimate or step-children are included, and at what time the class of children is to be ascertained, for these are questions of construction; but once these questions have been answered, there may arise a question of status, *e.g.* whether a particular child is legitimate or has been legitimated, and this may well be governed by German law in accordance with principles discussed elsewhere.[63]

Revocation

The question what law determines whether a will has been revoked is one of considerable nicety. A will may be revoked either (a) by a later will or codicil; or (b) by some other testamentary mode of revocation, *e.g.* in English domestic law by burning, tearing or destroying; or (c) by a change of circumstances, *e.g.* in English domestic law by the subsequent marriage of the testator, or in some other systems by his subsequent divorce or by the birth of children. Each of these modes requires separate discussion.

Revocation by later will or codicil. A later will or codicil may revoke an earlier will either expressly or by implication. It may do so expressly, as when the testator says "I hereby revoke all testamentary dispositions heretofore made by me." In such a case the question whether the second instru-

---

[61] *Supra.*
[62] *Re Miller, supra,* at p. 518, *per* Warrington J.
[63] *Ante,* Chap. 14.

ment revokes the first depends on the intrinsic validity of the second will, especially with regard to the capacity of the testator and the formal validity of the will.[64] Both these matters have already been discussed.[65] It may be added that under section 2(1)(c) of the Wills Act 1963 a later will, in so far as it revokes an earlier will or any provision therein, will be treated as properly executed if its execution conformed to any law by reference to which the revoked will would be so treated. Hence, if the testator is domiciled in one country, habitually resident in a second, and a national of a third, and changes all three between the execution of the earlier and the later will, and again between the execution of the later will and the time of his death, there may be a choice of nine systems of law for the formal validity of the revoking (as opposed to the disposing) provisions of the later will, or eleven if the wills are made in different countries.

However, if one will deals only with property in a foreign country and is made in foreign form, and the other deals only with property in England, the later will does not necessarily revoke the earlier one even if it contains a revocation clause.[66]

If the later will does not contain an express revocation clause, it may nevertheless revoke the first will by implication, *e.g.* if it is described as a "last" will (though this is not sufficient by English domestic law), or if its provisions cannot stand with those of the earlier will, as when the earlier will gives property to A and the later will gives the same property to B. In such cases the question is one of construction and is governed prima facie by the law of the testator's domicile at the time of making the later will.

Other testamentary modes of revocation. The question whether a will is revoked by burning, tearing or destroying or the like is no doubt governed by the *lex situs* in the case of immovables[67] or by the law of the testator's domicile in the case of movables. If his domicile is the same at all material times there is no difficulty. But if his domicile changes between the date of the alleged act of revocation and the date of his death, and the two laws differ, it is necessary to determine which law governs. They may differ, *e.g.* because in English law the will must be destroyed in the presence of the testator,[68] but in other systems (*e.g.* Italian law[69]) this is not necessary. If a testator domiciled in Italy writes to his solicitor instructing him to destroy his will, and by Italian law this amounts to an effective revocation, it is thought that the will would be revoked even if the testator died domiciled in England. For the will is effectively revoked by the law of the testator's domicile; it ceases to exist as a will just as though it had never been made, so that there is no will upon which English domestic law can operate. The converse case is perhaps more difficult. *E.g.* a testator domiciled in Eng-

---

[64] *Cottrell* v. *Cottrell* (1872) L.R. 2 P. & M. 397; *Re Manifold* [1962] Ch. 1.
[65] *Ante*, pp. 392–396.
[66] *Re Wayland* [1951] 2 All E.R. 1041; *Re Yahuda's Estate* [1956] P. 388.
[67] See *Re Estate of Barrie*, 240 Iowa 431, 35 N.W. 2d 658 (1949); criticised by Hancock (1967) 20 Stanford L.Rev. 1–11.
[68] Wills Act 1837, s.20.
[69] See *Velasco* v. *Coney* [1934] P. 143.

land writes to his solicitor instructing him to destroy his will, and dies domiciled in Italy. Here again it is thought that the law of the testator's domicile at the date of the alleged act of revocation would govern, with the result that the will would not be revoked. For at the time when the act was done there was no revocation in law, and at the time when the act might have amounted to revocation in law the act did not in fact occur. There is however no English authority on either of these questions.[70]

Revocation by subsequent marriage. In English domestic law a marriage *ipso facto* revokes any previous will made by either party to the marriage.[71] In the laws of most other countries (including Scotland) it does not. It is well settled that the question whether a will is revoked by subsequent marriage is governed by the law of the testator's domicile at the time of the marriage. Thus in the leading case of *Re Martin*,[72] a lady domiciled in France made a will, married a domiciled Englishman (thereby acquiring an English domicile by operation of law as the law then stood), and died domiciled in France: it was held that her will was revoked. Conversely, in *In the Estate of Groos*[73] a lady domiciled in Holland made a will, married a domiciled Dutchman, and died domiciled in England: it was held that her will was not revoked.

In *Re Martin*,[74] Vaughan Williams L.J. said that the rule that marriage revokes a will is part of English matrimonial law and not part of English testamentary law. It seems to follow from this that the law of the testator's domicile at the time of the marriage should determine whether the will is revoked not only in the case of movables but also in the case of immovables, notwithstanding an earlier decision to the contrary in which the question was referred to the *lex situs*.[75] On this ground, courts in Canada and Australia have refused to follow the earlier English decision.[76]

Of course, a subsequent marriage will not revoke a will if the marriage is void under English rules of the conflict of laws, *e.g.* because the parties are within the prohibited degrees of consanguinity or affinity.[77] But it will revoke a will if the marriage is voidable.[78]

EXERCISE OF POWER BY WILL

Introduction

In English law a person can by an instrument such as a settlement or will

---

[70] See Dicey and Morris, p. 638; Cheshire and North, pp. 612–613; F. A. Mann (1954) 31 B.Y.I.L. 216, 231.

[71] Wills Act 1837, s.18, as substituted by Administration of Justice Act 1982, s.18, where some exceptions are stated.

[72] [1900] P. 211.

[73] [1904] P. 269. *Cf. In bonis Reid* (1866) L.R. 1 P. & M. 74; *Westerman* v. *Schwab*, 1905 S.C. 132.

[74] *Supra*, at p. 240.

[75] *Re Caithness* (1890) 7 T.L.R. 354; see Dicey and Morris, pp. 639–640.

[76] *Davies* v. *Davies* (1915) 24 D.L.R. 737; *In the Estate of Micallaf* [1977] 2 N.S.W.L.R. 929.

[77] *Mette* v. *Mette* (1859) 1 Sw. & Tr. 416.

[78] *Re Roberts* [1978] 1 W.L.R. 653; *Will of Swan* (1871) 2 V.R. (I.E. & M.) 47.

give to another person power to appoint by will[79] the person or persons who shall succeed to the property after the death of the person to whom the power is given. The person who creates the power is called the donor. The person to whom the power is given is called the donee, or appointor. The person in whose favour the power is exercised is called the appointee. The instrument by which the power was created is called the instrument of creation. The instrument by which the power is exercised is called the instrument of appointment. If the donee can appoint to anyone he likes, including himself, the power is called a general power. If he can only appoint among a specified class of persons, *e.g.* his own issue (called the objects of the power), the power is called a special power. In both types of power the donee when he makes an appointment is dealing in strictness not with his own property but with the property of the donor. In the case of special powers, this is true in substance as well as in theory, because the donee can only appoint to an object of the power. In the case of general powers exercisable by deed or will, this is only true in theory, because the donee could by a stroke of the pen make himself the owner of the property.

The donor of the power, the donee and the appointee may each be domiciled in a different country. The question therefore arises, what law governs the validity of a will exercising a power? At first sight it might be thought that the validity of such a will would be governed by the same law as the validity of any other will. But for two reasons this is not always so. In the first place, powers of appointment are unknown to the laws of many continental European countries.[80] Hence, if the donee dies domiciled *e.g.* in France or Germany, French or German law cannot answer the question whether, or to what extent, his will is a valid exercise of the power; and therefore one is thrown back on the law governing the instrument of creation (which in most of the reported cases is English law). A further reason for referring to the law governing the instrument of creation is that the donee exercising a power is dealing not with his own property but with the property of the donor; he is to be regarded not as a testator making his own will, but as a mandatory or agent filling up blanks in the deed or will of the donor. This is true in theory of general powers, and true in substance as well as theory of special powers. There is therefore more justification for looking to the law governing the instrument of creation when the power is special than there is when the power is general. However, the distinction between general and special powers has not always been treated as decisive or material; and the principles about to be discussed are applicable to both types of power unless the contrary is stated.

As with ordinary wills, we need to consider separately (1) capacity, (2) formalities, (3) construction, (4) material or essential validity, and (5) revocation. Nearly all the English cases are concerned with wills of movables.

---

[79] Powers of appointment may, of course be exercisable by deed as well as by will, but we are here concerned only with the question of testamentary exercise.

[80] They are, however, known to countries like Scotland and South Africa whose law has been influenced by English law, but which are not common law countries.

Capacity

A testator has capacity to exercise by will a power of appointment over movables if he has testamentary capacity by the law of his domicile at the time of making his will, though not by the law governing the instrument creating the power. Thus in *Re Lewal's Settlement*,[81] an English marriage settlement was executed prior to the marriage of a domiciled English girl aged nineteen and a domiciled Frenchman. The settlement conferred a general power of appointment on the wife. Immediately after the marriage the wife, now domiciled in France, made a will in which she said "J'institue mon mari pour mon légataire universel" ("I institute my husband my universal legatee"). She died ten years later, domiciled in France. By English law she had no capacity to exercise the power, because she was under twenty-one; but by French law persons over sixteen and under twenty-one years of age can dispose by will of one-half of the property they could have disposed of if of full age. It was held that one-half of the property subject to the power passed to the husband, and that the other half went as in default of appointment.

There is no authority as to what the position is in the converse situation, *i.e.* the donee has capacity by the law governing the instrument of creation, but not by the law of his domicile. Cheshire's view[82] is that the donee would in that event have capacity to exercise a special, but not a general, power; and this seems reasonable in principle.

Formal validity

A will made in exercise of a power of appointment will be treated as properly executed if its execution conformed to any system of law applicable under sections 1 and 2 of the Wills Act 1963,[83] that is to say the internal law in force in the country where it was executed, or in the country where, at the time of its execution or of the testator's death, he was domiciled or had his habitual residence, or in a State of which, at either of those times, he was a national, or (in the case of immovables) the internal law of the *situs*.

Alternatively, under section 2(1)(*d*) of the same Act, a will exercising a power will be treated as properly executed if its execution conformed to the law governing the essential validity of the power, that is, the law governing the instrument of creation. This subsection confirms a line of English cases[84] which decided that a will exercising a power of appointment over movables conferred by an English instrument was well executed if its execution conformed to English domestic law, though not to the law

---

[81] [1918] 2 Ch. 391. But the decision was assisted by the fact that the settlement said that the power could be exercised by a will executed in such a manner as to be valid by the law of the donee's domicile.

[82] Cheshire and North, p. 615.

[83] *Ante*, p. 393.

[84] *Tatnall* v. *Hankey* (1838) 2 Moo.P.C. 342; *In bonis Alexander* (1860) 29 L.J.P. & M. 93; *In bonis Hallyburton* (1866) L.R. 1 P. & M. 90; *In bonis Huber* [1896] P. 209; *Murphy* v. *Deichler* [1909] A.C. 446. In Allen, *Law in the Making,* 7th ed., pp. 323–325, these cases are cited as a good illustration of the maxim "*communis error facit jus.*"

of the donee's domicile. Neither the cases nor the statute confirming them draws any distinction between general and special powers; the principle is therefore illogical, but it does make for useful liberality.

Sometimes the donor of the power requires it to be exercised with formalities additional to, or different from, those imposed by the general law, *e.g.* three witnesses instead of two. Section 10 of the Wills Act 1837 provides that such additional or other formalities are not to be required; but this is a rule of English domestic law, not necessarily applicable if the donee dies domiciled abroad. Before 1964 the question whether it was so applicable led to some troublesome distinctions and to some complicated law. But now the matter has been set at rest by section 2(2) of the Wills Act 1963, which provides that a will so far as it exercises a power of appointment shall not be treated as improperly executed by reason only that its execution was not in accordance with any formal requirements contained in the instrument creating the power.

Construction

The rules laid down in the preceding section indicate when a will is capable of exercising a power as a matter of form: they do not indicate when a will does exercise a power as a matter of construction. This question arises when the donee uses general words like "I give all my property to X": do these words exercise a power? On this question, different systems of domestic law have different rules. For instance, in Scotland, no specific reference to the power appears to be necessary. In South Africa, there must be such a reference, either express or implied. In England, a distinction is drawn between general and special powers: there must be a specific intention shown to exercise a special power, but a general power is exercised by a general devise or bequest unless a contrary intention appears by the will.[85] In many continental European countries, there is no answer to this question, for the whole doctrine of powers of appointment is unknown.

As one would expect, the general rule is that the question whether the will was intended to exercise the power, since it is a question of construction, must be determined (in the absence of indications to the contrary) by the law of the donee's domicile at the time when the will was made. Thus, where a special power was created by an English instrument, and alleged to be exercised by the will of a testator domiciled in Scotland, it was held that Scots law determined whether the words used by the testator were sufficient to exercise the power.[86] And where a general power was created by a Scottish instrument, and alleged to be exercised by the will of a testator domiciled in South Africa, it was held in Scotland that South African law determined whether the words used were sufficient to exercise the power.[87]

---

[85] Wills Act 1837, s.27.
[86] *Re McMorran* [1958] Ch. 624.
[87] *Durie's Trustees* v. *Osborne*, 1960 S.C. 444.

On the other hand, the effect of a line of English cases[88] is that if there are indications in the will that the testator intended it to be construed in accordance with the law governing the instrument creating the power, or if powers of appointment are unknown to the law of the testator's domicile, the law governing the instrument of creation will determine whether the power was exercised. If this is English law, then under section 27 of the Wills Act 1837 a general devise or bequest will amount to an exercise of a general (but not a special) power, unless a contrary intention appears by the will. In all these cases, the doctrine of powers was unknown to the law of the donee's domicile. In the first of them, there were indications in the will (albeit somewhat faint) that the donee intended her will to be construed in accordance with English law. In all the other cases, there were no such indications. In some of the cases,[89] the will was formally valid by English domestic law; in others, it was not. These latter cases thus present the curious anomaly that sections 9 and 10 of the Wills Act 1837 (which deal with formalities) were held to be inapplicable to the will, but section 27 of the same statute was held to be applicable. However, in spite of some early dissent, the doctrine of these cases, anomalous and exceptional though it may be, is now well established.

Material or essential validity

Even if the donee of a power to appoint movables has testamentary capacity, the requisite formalities have been complied with, and the will exercises the power as a matter of construction, the appointment may still fail if it contravenes some rule of the law of the donee's domicile, e.g. the rule found in many civil law countries that a testator must leave a fixed portion of his estate (*legitima portio*) to his children or other relatives. Do such rules apply to property subject to a power of appointment created by an English instrument? If the power is special, they do not[90]; and this is logical, because the donee is not dealing with his own property but is regarded as an agent carrying out the wishes of the donor. If the power is general, a distinction must be drawn between (a) cases where the donee makes an appointment and keeps the appointed property separate from his own property (a very rare case), and (b) cases where the donee deals with the appointed property and his own property as one mass so as to take the appointed property out of the instrument creating the power for all purposes (a much more common case). In English domestic law, this distinction determines whether the property goes as in default of appointment or as part of the donee's estate if an appointment fails, e.g. because the appointee predeceases the appointor, or witnesses his will, or because the

[88] *Re Price* [1900] 1 Ch. 442; *Re Baker's Settlement* [1908] W.N. 161; *Re Simpson* [1916] 1 Ch. 502, 510; *Re Wilkinson's Settlement* [1917] 1 Ch. 620, 627; *Re Lewal's Settlement* [1918] 2 Ch. 391; *Re Strong* (1925) 95 L.J.Ch. 22; *Re Waite's Settlement* [1958] Ch. 100. These cases establish the doctrine as against the contrary view in *Re D'Este's Settlement* [1903] 1 Ch. 898; *Re Scholefield* [1905] 2 Ch. 408, compromised on appeal [1907] 1 Ch. 664.
[89] *Re Baker's Settlement, supra; Re Waite's Settlement, supra.*
[90] *Pouey* v. *Hordern* [1900] 1 Ch. 492.

trusts declared do not exhaust the fund, or infringe the rule against perpetuities.[91] In the English conflict of laws, if the donee dies domiciled in a country where the rule is that he must leave a *legitima portio* to his children or other relatives, the rule does not apply in case (a) above,[92] but does apply in case (b) above.[93] This also is logical, because in case (a) the donee can be regarded, like the donee of a special power, as the agent of the donor: he could have made the property his own, but he has not chosen to do so. In case (b) on the other hand he is in substance dealing with his own property.

The question naturally arises, what law determines whether a power is general or special? Some powers are difficult to classify from this point of view,[94] and the line between general and special powers may be drawn in different places by different systems of law, or even by the same system for different purposes. Thus in English domestic law, for the purposes of the rule against perpetuities, a power to appoint by will (but not by deed) to such persons as the donee thinks fit is treated as special so far as the validity of the power is concerned, but as general so far as the validity of the appointment is concerned[95]; but in the United States it is treated as special for both purposes.[96] In principle it would seem that the law governing the instrument of creation should determine whether the power is general or special for the purposes of the conflict of laws; and there is American authority which supports this view.[97]

If the donee of a power of appointment over land in England dies domiciled in a country by whose law he must leave a fixed portion of his property to his children or other relatives, he can nevertheless make an appointment to other persons.[98] In other words, the material or essential validity of an appointment of immovables is governed by the *lex situs*.

Revocation

The exercise by will of a power of appointment over movables will be held to have been effectively revoked if the will was revoked in a manner sufficient by the law of the donee's domicile,[99] or by a later will which is properly executed in accordance with section 1[1] or 2(1)(c)[2] of the Wills Act

[91] See *Farwell on Powers*, 3rd ed., pp. 268–277; *Jarman on Wills*, 8th ed., pp. 816–818; *Theobald on Wills*, 14th ed., pp. 316–317.
[92] *Re Mégret* [1901] 1 Ch. 547; and perhaps *Re Lewal's Settlement* [1918] 2 Ch. 391 (but the question was not fully discussed).
[93] *Re Pryce* [1911] 2 Ch. 286; *Re Khan's Settlement* [1966] Ch. 567; *Re Fenston's Settlement* [1971] 1 W.L.R. 1640, 1647. The contrary decision of Danckwerts J. in *Re Waite's Settlement* [1958] Ch. 100 has been much criticised, see, *e.g.* Dicey and Morris, pp. 650–651; Morris (1957) 73 L.Q.R. 459; was not followed in *Re Khan's Settlement, supra*; and is, it is submitted, manifestly wrong.
[94] See Morris and Leach, *The Rule against Perpetuities*, 2nd ed., pp. 135–138.
[95] Perpetuities and Accumulations Act 1964, s.7.
[96] Gray, *Rule against Perpetuities*, 4th ed., Appendix L; Morris and Leach, p. 137.
[97] *Re Bauer's Trust*, 14 N.Y. 2d 272; 200 N.E. 2d 207 (1964). But three out of seven judges dissented; and the result of the case cannot be regarded with equanimity.
[98] *Re Hernando* (1884) 27 Ch.D. 284.
[99] *Velasco v. Coney* [1934] P. 143.
[1] *Ante*, p. 392.
[2] *Ante*, p. 401.

1963. As we have seen,[3] a will exercising a power of appointment will be treated as properly executed if its execution conformed to the law governing the essential validity of the power. But this does not apply to a will which merely revokes a testamentary appointment without substituting any other appointment. Such a will does not "exercise a power of appointment" within the meaning of section 2(1)(*d*) of the Act. But if the second will is executed in accordance with the law governing the essential validity of the power it does revoke the appointment under section 2(1)(*c*).

It will be remembered that the question whether a will is revoked by the subsequent marriage of the testator depends upon the law of the testator's domicile at the date of the marriage.[4] However, in English domestic law a will exercising a power of appointment is not revoked by the subsequent marriage of the testator unless the appointed property would pass to the donee's personal representatives in default of appointment.[5]

---

[3] *Ante*, p. 404.
[4] *Ante*, p. 402.
[5] Wills Act 1837, s.18, as substituted by Administration of Justice Act 1982, s.18.

CHAPTER 25

THE EFFECT OF MARRIAGE ON PROPERTY

INTRODUCTION

SINCE the Married Women's Property Act 1882, marriage as such has no effect on the property of the spouses in English law. They remain separately entitled to the property owned by them at the time of the marriage or acquired afterwards, unless they choose to regulate their rights therein by a marriage contract or settlement. The position is very different in many continental European countries, in South Africa, and in eight of the United States,[1] where a species of community of property prevails. In these countries marriage has the effect of vesting the property owned by either spouse at the time of the marriage or acquired during its subsistence in both of them jointly. There are many different systems of community property,[2] but for present purposes they may be divided into three main types: full community, community of gains (acquests), and community of chattels and gains. In full community, which exists in South Africa, the community extends to all movables and to immovables acquired during the marriage. In community of gains, which applies in some of the United States and, in a very attenuated form, in France since 1965, the community is confined to property acquired during the marriage otherwise than by gift or inheritance. The mixed form, the community of gains and chattels, comprises all chattels whether owned at the time of the marriage or acquired during its subsistence, but only such land as the spouses acquired during the marriage through work or thrift and not land either of them had at the time of the marriage or acquired during its subsistence through inheritance or gift. This is the classical form of community under the original French Civil Code of 1804 and still applies in Belgium. "Deferred community" or "participation," which exists in the Scandinavian countries, Holland, Germany, Quebec and elsewhere, is a system of separation of property: no assets are held as joint assets during the marriage, but when the marriage is dissolved, either by death or divorce, each spouse is entitled to a half share of most of the property of both spouses.

Nearly all systems of community property allow the spouses to contract out of the system if they so desire; and in most systems, the failure of the spouses to do so means that they become subject to the standard com-

---

[1] Arizona, California, Idaho, Louisiana, Nevada, New Mexico, Texas, Washington.
[2] See Wolff, s.334; Friedmann, *Matrimonial Property Law* (1955); Amos and Walton, *Introduction to French Law*, 3rd ed., Chap. 12; Cohn, *Manual of German Law*, 2nd ed., Vol. I, ss.515–522.

munity régime provided by law. The effect of this is often that the spouses adopt the standard régime by a kind of tacit consent.[3]

In the conflict of laws, the effect of marriage on the property of the spouses differs in accordance with whether there is or is not a marriage contract or settlement between them.[4] Most of the English cases are concerned with the former situation, and English authority on the latter is sparse.

WHERE THERE IS NO MARRIAGE CONTRACT OR SETTLEMENT

"It is not necessary to cite authorities to show that it is now settled that, according to international law as understood and administered in England, the effect of marriage on the movable property of spouses depends (in the absence of any contract) on the domicile of the husband in the English sense."[5]

Dicey and Morris say that where there is no marriage contract or settlement, and where there is no subsequent change of domicile by the parties to the marriage, the governing law so far as movables are concerned is the law of the matrimonial domicile; and that (in the absence of special circumstances) this means the husband's domicile at the time of the marriage.[6] Before 1956 there was a difference of opinion between Dicey and Cheshire as to what the matrimonial domicile means in this connection. Cheshire's view,[7] which is consistent with his theory on the law governing capacity to marry,[8] was that it meant the intended matrimonial home, *i.e.* the domicile which the husband and wife intended to acquire and did acquire within a reasonable time after the marriage. If, for instance, a man domiciled in England married a woman domiciled in South Africa, and the husband and wife flew to South Africa immediately after the ceremony, intending to make it their matrimonial home, Cheshire would say that South Africa, not England, was their matrimonial domicile, and that South African law should determine the effect of their marriage on their movable property. But, as Dicey pointed out,[9] there is no conclusive English authority in favour of this view, and there are practical difficulties in its application. What if the husband and wife do not fly to South Africa until a month—or a year—after the ceremony? Where is the line to be drawn? Are the rights of the spouses to remain in suspense until they actually acquire a new domicile in pursuance of their pre-matrimonial intention? Dicey concluded that the safer rule to adopt was that the matrimonial domicile means the husband's domicile at the time of the marriage, except perhaps in a clear case where the domicile is changed very shortly after the marriage.

---

[3] Anton, p. 455.
[4] The validity of this distinction is denied by Goldberg (1970) 19 I.C.L.Q. 557.
[5] *Re Martin* [1900] P. 211, 233, *per* Lindley M.R.
[6] Rule 115.
[7] Cheshire and North, pp. 573–574.
[8] *Ante*, p. 159.
[9] Dicey and Morris, pp. 668–669.

In 1956, in *Re Egerton's Trusts*,[10] Roxburgh J. considered the rival views and preferred that of Dicey. Since the change of domicile in that case did not take place until two years after the marriage, the learned judge's remarks about the effect of an immediate change of domicile were (as he pointed out) *obiter*. Nevertheless he made it clear that the law of the intended matrimonial domicile can only apply in very special circumstances, *e.g.* where the change of domicile follows immediately on the marriage and the spouses are at that time without means.[11]

In 1950, the Appellate Division of the Supreme Court of South Africa had reached a similar decision, after an elaborate argument in which counsel cited cases from all over the world and the opinions of jurists from the sixteenth century onwards. In that case[12] the change of domicile took place four months after the marriage.

It may therefore be taken that the law of the husband's domicile at the time of the marriage governs its effect on the movable property of the spouses. But now that a married woman is capable of having a domicile different from that of her husband, it may perhaps be easier for the court to select a law other than that of the husband's domicile to govern this matter.

What happens if the domicile changes during the marriage? It is a disputed question whether such a change of domicile alters the governing law. The prevailing doctrine on the Continent of Europe and in South Africa is the doctrine of immutability, according to which the rights of the spouses "are regulated once and for all by the law of the domicile of marriage."[13] In the United States, on the other hand, the prevailing doctrine is the doctrine of mutability, according to which the rights of the spouses to after-acquired movables are regulated by the law of the domicile at the time of acquisition.[14]

English law is not yet committed either to the doctrine of mutability or to the doctrine of immutability. In *Lashley* v. *Hog*,[15] the House of Lords held (on appeal from the Court of Session) that a change of domicile from England to Scotland carried with it the application of Scots law. On the other hand, in *De Nicols* v. *Curlier*[16] the House of Lords held that, on a change of domicile from France to England, the French system of community of goods continued to apply to movables acquired by the husband and wife after they had become domiciled in England. The House of Lords evidently regarded *Lashley* v. *Hog* as an embarrassing rather than a helpful decision. They distinguished it on two grounds: (1) in *De Nicols* v. *Curlier* the effect of marriage without an express contract was assumed to be that an implied contract was imposed on the parties by French law, whereas there was no such contract in *Lashley* v. *Hog*[17]; (2) in *Lashley* v. *Hog* the

---

[10] [1956] Ch. 593.
[11] At pp. 604–605.
[12] *Estate Frankel* v. *The Master*, 1950 (1) S.A. 220.
[13] *Brown* v. *Brown*, 1921 A.D. 478, 482.
[14] Restatement, s.258.
[15] (1804) 4 Paton 581; analysed by Goldberg (1970) 19 I.C.L.Q. 557, 580–584.
[16] [1900] A.C. 21.
[17] *Ibid. per* Lord Macnaghten at pp. 34, 36; *per* Lord Shand at p. 37; *per* Lord Brampton at p. 44.

question was not one of matrimonial property law at all but of the law of succession.[18] If the first ground of distinction is the one to be preferred, it means that *De Nicols* v. *Curlier* belongs exclusively to the next section of this chapter, and that we are left with *Lashley* v. *Hog* as our only authority on mutability versus immutability. The first ground of distinction was adopted by the majority of their Lordships, but some eminent writers have preferred the second.[19] It is therefore an open question whether an English court will apply the doctrine of mutability or immutability in the event of a change of domicile, and in the absence of a contract express or implied.

The doctrine of immutability does not work well if the spouses are forced to change their domicile by political or economic pressure. It does not seem reasonable that refugees from central or eastern Europe, who have acquired a domicile of choice in England or elsewhere after their marriage, should continue to be governed for the rest of their lives by the law of their matrimonial domicile—the one country in the world which they will probably never revisit. Moreover, the doctrine of immutability may give rise to difficult questions of characterisation, and may require the court to draw delicate distinctions between questions of matrimonial property law and questions of the law of succession. If, for example, a husband and wife were married while domiciled in France and were subject to the French system of community, and the husband died intestate domiciled in England, French law would (if the doctrine of immutability were applied) determine how much of the common movable property of the spouses belonged to the husband at the time of his death, but English law would determine what proportion of the husband's movables passed to the wife by reason of his intestacy.[20] The result might be to give the wife a much larger share than she would have got if either French law alone or English law alone had governed the property rights of the spouses from the time of the marriage. Under English law, she would have acquired no rights in her husband's movables by reason of the marriage, but only by reason of his death intestate; under French law she would have had no rights on his death intestate except to her share of the community property. In the converse case of a change of domicile from England to France, she might get nothing.[21] This is because by French law community of gains is constituted by a marriage under French law, and not by married people coming to France and settling there. It must begin from the day of the marriage.[22]

The compromise solution submitted in Dicey and Morris is a limited form of the doctrine of mutability which is formulated as follows[23]:

> Where there is no marriage contract or settlement, and where there is a subsequent change of domicile, the rights of husband and wife to

---

[18] *Ibid. per* Lord Halsbury at p. 29; *per* Lord Morris at p. 36.
[19] Westlake, p. 74; Foote, *Private International Law,* 5th ed., p. 355; Falconbridge, p. 106; Cheshire and North, pp. 577–578; *cf.* F. A. Mann (1954) 31 B.Y.I.L. 217, 224–226.
[20] See *Beaudoin* v. *Trudel* [1937] 1 D.L.R. 216.
[21] See Lipstein, *Recueil des Cours* (1972) I, 209; Kahn-Freund, *Recueil des Cours* (1974), III, 377–380.
[22] *De Nicols* v. *Curlier* [1900] A.C. 21, 33; *cf. Re Egerton's Trusts* [1956] Ch. 593, 600.
[23] Rule 116.

each other's movables, both *inter vivos* and in respect of succession, are governed by the law of the new domicile, except in so far as vested rights have been acquired under the law of the former domicile.

What this means in effect is that movables acquired after a change of domicile will be subject to the law of the domicile at the time of acquisition, since (in the absence of a contract) there can be no vested right in hypothetical future acquisitions. It does not mean that if two spouses marry while domiciled in a country like England, where spouses remain separate as to property, and later change their domicile to a country like France, where a marriage without a contract creates community of gains, they thereby become subject to the community system.

There is very little authority on the effect of marriage on the immovable property of the spouses in the absence of a contract express or implied. It seems that the *lex situs* governs. In *Welch* v. *Tennent*[24] a husband and wife were married in 1877 (*i.e.* before the Married Women's Property Act 1882). They were domiciled in Scotland. The wife owned land in England which she sold with her husband's concurrence, and the proceeds of sale were paid to him. The parties then separated and the wife took proceedings in the Scottish courts asking for a declaration that the proceeds of sale were not subject to her husband's *jus mariti*. The House of Lords, reversing the Scottish courts which had applied Scots law, held that English law applied and that the proceeds of sale belonged to the husband.

WHERE THERE IS A MARRIAGE CONTRACT OR SETTLEMENT

If there is a marriage contract or settlement, the terms of the contract (assuming it to be valid) govern the rights of the husband and wife to all property within its terms which are then owned or subsequently acquired, notwithstanding any subsequent change of domicile. Whether any particular property, *e.g.* after-acquired property, is within its terms is a question of construction of the contract, governed by its proper law.

The rule applies even if the contract is implied by law. Thus in the leading case of *De Nicols* v. *Curlier*[25]:

> H & W, French citizens domiciled in France, married there without an antenuptial contract. There was evidence that by French law the effect was the same as if they had made an express contract incorporating the system of community of goods. At the time of the marriage they had no means whatever, but nine years later they emigrated to England with joint savings of £400, and acquired an English domicile. They set up a small restaurant called the Cafe Royal in Regent Street, London, which prospered exceedingly. H died having by his will given all his real and personal estate on trust for sale and to hold the proceeds on trust for W for life, and then for his daughter and her husband and children. He left about £600,000 worth of property in England and about £100,000 worth of wine in France.

[24] [1891] A.C. 639.
[25] [1898] 1 Ch. 403; [1898] 2 Ch. 60; [1900] A.C. 21.

Dissatisfied with the provision made for her by H's will, W claimed that despite the change of domicile and the provisions of the will she was entitled to one-half of H's property under the system of community of goods. It was arranged that the argument should be confined in the first instance to the effect of the change of domicile on the testator's movables only. The House of Lords, reversing the Court of Appeal and restoring the judgment of Kekewich J., held that W was so entitled.

When the summons came on for further argument as to the effect of the change of domicile on the testator's immovables in England, Kekewich J. held in *Re De Nicols (No. 2)*[26] that the wife was also entitled to one-half of the immovables. He was pressed with section 4 of the Statute of Frauds 1677, which provided that no action should be brought on an oral contract for the sale or other disposition of an interest in land. But he followed (and perhaps extended) earlier cases deciding that the section did not apply to a partnership.

This unorthodox decision is supported by an earlier one of Stirling J. in *Chiwell v. Carlyon,*[27] where the facts were similar except that the parties were domiciled at the time of their marriage in South Africa. The husband acquired land in Cornwall. The question was whether this land was subject to the South African system of community. Stirling J. sent a case for the opinion of the Supreme Court of Cape Colony under the British Law Ascertainment Act 1859. In other words, he decided that the rights of the spouses in the English land were governed by South African law. The South African court gave an opinion that by South African law the English land was held in community, whether or not the spouses had acquired an English domicile. Stirling J. then gave judgment in accordance with this opinion.

In *Re De Nicols (No. 2)* and *Chiwell v. Carlyon* it was clear that the French and South African systems of community included land situated outside France and South Africa respectively. In *Callwood v. Callwood,*[28] there was no evidence that under the law of the Danish West Indian island where the parties were domiciled the Danish system of community extended to land situated outside the island. Consequently it was held that when the husband acquired land in the British Virgin Islands, it was not subject to community.

The essential validity, interpretation and effect of the marriage contract or settlement are governed by its proper law. The search for the proper law of a marriage contract or settlement is generically similar to the search for the proper law of an ordinary commercial contract.[29] But owing to the nature of the subject-matter the weight to be given to the various factors is different. In the absence of an express selection of the proper law by the parties, the most important single factor is undoubtedly the matrimonial

[26] [1900] 2 Ch. 410.
[27] (1897) 14 S.C. 61. The case is unreported in England.
[28] [1960] A.C. 659; criticised by Unger (1967) 83 L.Q.R. 427, 440–441.
[29] See *ante,* Chap. 15.

domicile, though perhaps it is putting the matter too strongly to say that there is a presumption in favour of this law. The matrimonial domicile means the husband's domicile at the time of the marriage, and not the domicile which the spouses intend to acquire and do acquire immediately after the marriage.[30]

Other factors which may have to be considered, and which frequently point to some other law, are: the fact that the settled property belonged to the wife or her family, and that her domicile before or after the marriage was different from the husband's[31]; the language and legal style of the settlement[32]; the fact that its provisions are invalid by the law of the matrimonial domicile[33]; the place of management of the trust[34]; the place of residence of the trustees[35]; the place of investment of the securities.[36] Since the last two factors may change, the relevant time for giving effect to them is the date of the settlement.[37]

The case of *Duke of Marlborough* v. *Att. Gen.*[38] illustrates the application of the law of the matrimonial domicile:

> H, the ninth Duke of Marlborough, who was domiciled in England, married W, the daughter of a wealthy New Yorker. A marriage settlement in English language and form was made whereby W's father settled $2\frac{1}{2}$ million dollars and covenanted that his executors would settle a further $2\frac{1}{2}$ million dollars after his death. The settlement comprised no English property at all. (Evidently it is an expensive business to marry an English Duke.) The settled property was and remained invested in American securities. One trustee was English and the other American. The settlement contained ancillary clauses which were meaningless (but not invalid) by New York law. The question was whether English estate duty was payable on the death of H. The Court of Appeal held that the proper law of the settlement was English law and that estate duty was payable.

The case of *Re Bankes*,[39] which is typical of many others, illustrates the application of some other law:

> H, domiciled in Italy, married W, domiciled in England. A marriage settlement in English language and form was made whereby property belonging to W, which was invested in English securities, was vested in English trustees. By Italian law the settlement was invalid (a)

---

[30] *Ante*, pp. 410–411.

[31] *Van Grutten* v. *Digby* (1862) 31 Beav. 561; *Re Mégret* [1901] 1 Ch. 547; *Re Bankes* [1902] 2 Ch. 333; *Re Fitzgerald* [1904] 1 Ch. 573; *Re Mackenzie* [1911] 1 Ch. 578.

[32] *Re Mégret, supra; Re Bankes, supra; Re Fitzgerald, supra; Re Mackenzie, supra; Re Hewitt's Settlement* [1915] 1 Ch. 228.

[33] *Re Bankes, supra; Re Fitzgerald, supra.*

[34] *Re Cloncurry's Estate* [1932] I.R. 687.

[35] *Van Grutten* v. *Digby, supra; Re Mégret, supra; Re Cloncurry's Estate, supra.*

[36] *Ibid.*

[37] *Re Hewitt's Settlement, supra; Duke of Marlborough* v. *Att. Gen.* [1945] Ch. 78.

[38] *Supra;* criticised by Morris (1945) 61 L.Q.R. 223.

[39] [1902] 2 Ch. 333.

because it was not executed before a notary (a question of form) and (b) because it altered Italian rules of succession (a question of essential validity). It was held that the proper law of the settlement was English law, and that it was valid.

There can be no doubt that the parties are free to choose the proper law by an express clause in the settlement, at any rate if the transaction has a substantial connection with the selected law.[40] "As a general rule the law of the matrimonial domicile is applicable to a contract in consideration of marriage. But this is not an absolute rule. It yields to an express stipulation that some other law shall apply."[41]

There is very little authority on the essential validity and interpretation of a marriage settlement comprising immovables. In *Re Pearse's Settlement*,[42] an English marriage settlement contained a covenant by the wife to settle her after-acquired property. She acquired land in Jersey. By the law of Jersey no trusts of land were permitted and all transfers thereof had to be for value. It was held that the land in Jersey was not caught by the covenant.

A marriage settlement will be formally valid if it complies with the formalities prescribed by either the law of the place where it was executed[43] or the proper law.[44]

The question what law governs capacity to make a marriage settlement is rather more difficult. On principle, capacity should be governed by the proper law of the settlement. That is the law which governs capacity to make a commercial contract,[45] and there seems no reason why a different principle should apply here. It is sometimes said, however, that capacity to make a marriage settlement is governed, not by the proper law (which as we have seen is usually but not necessarily the law of the matrimonial domicile), but by the law of the domicile of the party alleged to be incapable. According to this view, the capacity of an English girl under eighteen years of age to make an antenuptial settlement prior to her marriage with a domiciled foreigner would be governed by English law. The three cases usually cited for this proposition are *Re Cooke's Trusts*[46], *Cooper* v. *Cooper*[47] and *Viditz* v. *O'Hagan*.[48] It is submitted that properly considered these cases lay down no such proposition but, on the contrary, decide that capacity is governed by the proper law.[49]

In *Re Cooke's Trusts* a domiciled English girl aged under twenty-one made a notarial contract in French form prior to her marriage with a domiciled Frenchman. She died domiciled in New South Wales having by her

---

[40] *Montgomery* v. *Zarifi*, 1918 S.C.(H.L.) 128.
[41] *Re Fitzgerald* [1904] 1 Ch. 573, 587.
[42] [1909] 1 Ch. 304.
[43] *Guépratte* v. *Young* (1851) 4 De G. & Sm. 217.
[44] *Van Grutten* v. *Digby* (1862) 31 Beav. 561; *Viditz* v. *O'Hagan* [1899] 2 Ch. 569; *Re Bankes* [1902] 2 Ch. 333.
[45] *Ante*, pp. 285–288.
[46] (1887) 56 L.T. 737.
[47] (1888) 13 App.Cas. 88.
[48] [1900] 2 Ch. 87.
[49] See Morris (1938) 54 L.Q.R. 78.

will given all her property to X. Her children attacked her will on the ground that the contract gave them vested rights in her property. Stirling J. rejected their claim on the ground that her capacity to make the contract was governed by English law as the law of her antenuptial domicile and that by English law the contract was "void." But the value of this case as an authority is impaired by the erroneous assumption made by the court as to English domestic law. In English domestic law (and the law of Ireland is the same), marriage settlements made by minors are not void but voidable in the sense that they are binding on the minor unless the minor repudiates them within a reasonable time after attaining the age of majority.

In *Cooper* v. *Cooper*,[50] a domiciled Irish girl aged under twenty-one married a domiciled Scotsman in Dublin. By an antenuptial contract made in Scottish form the husband covenanted to pay her a small annuity if she survived him and the wife accepted this in full satisfaction of her rights as a Scottish widow. Thirty-six years later the husband died domiciled in Scotland and the wife claimed to repudiate the contract. The House of Lords held that she was entitled to do so. It is true that Lord Halsbury and Lord Macnaghten gave as their reason for this conclusion that the wife was an infant by Irish law when she made the contract. But it is impossible to accept these statements at their face value. For Lord Halsbury said that by Irish law an infant's marriage settlement contracts are "void,"[51] and Lord Macnaghten said that Mrs. Cooper's contract was "voidable" in the sense that it was binding on her until she repudiated it, which she had elected to do.[52] Yet in *Edwards* v. *Carter*[53] (which was not a case on the conflict of laws) the House of Lords held that a minor's marriage settlement contract was neither void, nor voidable whenever the minor chose to repudiate it, but voidable only within a reasonable time after the minor had attained his majority. The House of Lords further held that it was too late for the minor to repudiate when he attained the age of twenty-six, yet Mrs. Cooper was allowed to repudiate at the age of fifty-four. It is plain that there is a direct inconsistency between *Cooper* v. *Cooper* and *Edwards* v. *Carter* which cannot be reconciled unless we assume that Scots law as the law of the matrimonial domicile as well as Irish law as the law of the wife's antenuptial domicile exerted an influence on the decision in the former case. The true position would appear to be that by Irish law the contract was voidable for a short time only, but by Scots law it was voidable for ever, because any ratification by Mrs. Cooper would have been revocable as a donation between husband and wife[54]: and therefore she never had capacity to make a binding contract.

In *Viditz* v. *O'Hagan*[55] the Court of Appeal expressly adopted this view of *Cooper* v. *Cooper*. A domiciled Irish girl aged under twenty-one married a domiciled Austrian. She made an antenuptial settlement in English

---

[50] (1888) 13 App.Cas. 88.
[51] At p. 99.
[52] At pp. 107–108.
[53] [1893] A.C. 360.
[54] See *per* Lord Watson at p. 106.
[55] [1900] 2 Ch. 87.

form, settling her property on the usual trusts of an English marriage settlement. Twenty-nine years later the husband and wife, still domiciled in Austria, purported to revoke the settlement by a notarial act made in Austria in Austrian form. By Austrian law such revocation was valid notwithstanding the birth of children. It was held that the revocation was valid, because the wife never possessed capacity to make an irrevocable settlement either before or after her marriage. Two passages from Lord Lindley's judgment are instructive. Speaking of the case before him, he said[56]:

> "By the Austrian law she was unable to ratify or confirm this contract; she could always repudiate it, but could never ratify it, *i.e.* deprive herself of the right to repudiate it. *This was the case in Cooper* v. *Cooper, but it was not so in Edwards* v. *Carter.*"

And speaking of *Cooper* v. *Cooper* he said[57]:

> "In that case a lady did succeed in repudiating a marriage settlement made when she was an infant after the lapse of much more than a reasonable time, *if you shut out of consideration the change of her domicile between the execution of the settlement and the repudiation.*"

The clear inference from the concluding words in this passage is that in Lord Lindley's view the House of Lords in *Cooper* v. *Cooper* did not shut out of consideration the law of Scotland. If so, *Cooper* v. *Cooper* is no authority for the proposition that capacity to make a marriage settlement is governed by the law of the domicile of the party alleged to be incapable. It is therefore submitted that such capacity is governed by the proper law of the contract, which means, in this connection, the system of law with which the contract is most closely connected, and not the law intended by the parties. As Lord Macnaghten said in *Cooper* v. *Cooper,*[58] "it is difficult to suppose that Mrs. Cooper could confer capacity on herself by contemplating a different country as the place where the contract was to be fulfilled."

Of course, the significance of the problem here discussed is much reduced by the lowering of the age of majority in English law from twenty-one to eighteen.[59]

---

[56] At p. 96 (italics added).
[57] At p. 98 (italics added).
[58] (1888) 13 App.Cas. 88, 108.
[59] Family Law Reform Act 1969, s.1(1).

CHAPTER 26

TRUSTS

INTRODUCTION

THE trust is perhaps the most distinctive contribution made by English law to the science of general jurisprudence. Nothing like it is known in most (but not all) continental European countries, though the institution has been adopted by the laws of some civil law countries influenced by English law, *e.g.* Scotland and South Africa. It is therefore surprising that there should be such a dearth of English and Commonwealth authority on what law governs the validity and administration of trusts in the conflict of laws. There are cases on trusts of land and trusts of movables created by will or by marriage settlement, but hardly any cases on trusts created by other instruments *inter vivos*. It is even more surprising that the literature should be equally sparse.[1] By contrast, the American case law is voluminous, and the Restatement (Second) devotes 122 pages to a discussion of the topic. In these circumstances, anything like an attempt at systematic exposition would be premature. All that can be done is to call attention to some of the matters that have been the subject-matter of express decision in this complex field.

The Restatement and the few writers who have discussed the subject draw a number of distinctions which have been adopted in the arrangement of this chapter. First there is the distinction between trusts of movables and trusts of land. Secondly there is the distinction between the validity and the administration of the trust. The former comprises such questions as whether the trust is formally valid, whether the settlor or testator had capacity to create the trust, whether the trust can be revoked, and whether the trust is essentially valid. Administration comprises such questions as the powers and duties of the trustees; their liability for breach of trust; their right to indemnity from the beneficiaries or to contribution from their co-trustees; their right to remuneration; the question what is income and what is capital; the question what are proper trustee investments; the question who can appoint a new trustee, and what persons may be so appointed; and the power of the court to frame a scheme for a charitable trust, or to direct an application of charitable trust funds *cy-près*. There are three matters which do not properly belong either to validity or to administration and which will therefore be given separate treatment. These are the

---

[1] See Dicey and Morris, Chap. 25; Nygh, pp. 436–443; Cavers (1930) 44 Harv.L.Rev. 161; Hoar (1948) 26 Can. Bar Rev. 1415; Latham (1953) *Current Legal Problems* 176; Delany (1961) 10 I.C.L.Q. 385. For the Scots law, see Anton, Chap. 22. For the American law, see Land, *Trusts in the Conflict of Laws* (1940); Restatement, ss.267–282.

construction of the trust instrument; the right of the beneficiaries to alienate their interests; and the power of the court to vary the terms of the trust.

It must be said at the outset that very many of these questions, especially those which have been described as questions of administration, are not covered by English authority.

Perhaps the most salient feature of a trust which requires to be borne in mind when considering what law should govern these questions is that it may last for a very long time. It is therefore quite different from an out-and-out conveyance of a chattel, *e.g.* on sale. Even if the rule against perpetuities imposes restrictions on remoteness of vesting, it is common for a private trust to last for thirty or fifty years, and theoretically possible for it to last for a century[2]; and a charitable trust may last for ever. Hence to hold a private trust invalid may disappoint expectations and have disastrous consequences for the family concerned; and the invalidation of a charitable trust may have even more unfortunate consequences. Therefore, in cases involving a conflict of laws, there is an observable tendency for courts to choose a law which will sustain the validity of a trust, if they can reasonably do so.

TRUSTS OF MOVABLES

The validity of testamentary trusts

A distinction must be drawn between questions relating to the validity of the will as a testamentary disposition and questions relating to the validity of the trust provisions contained therein. If the will is formally invalid[3] or has been revoked[4] or if the testator had no capacity to make a will,[5] of course it follows that any trust contained therein will fail. If the will is admitted to probate as the formally valid and unrevoked will of a capable testator, the essential validity of any particular gift of movables contained therein is, as we have seen,[6] governed by the law of the testator's last domicile. As a general rule, there is no need to distinguish between ordinary legacies and legacies on trust. But there is no reason why the will of a testator domiciled in England should not set up a trust to be governed by some foreign law, or conversely why the will of a testator domiciled in a foreign country should not set up an English trust[7]; and if it does, the validity of the trust will normally be governed by its proper law, usually the law of the place of administration. The place of administration is likely to be the place where the trustees reside or carry on business, especially if the trustee is a trust corporation. But these cases are exceptional: there is a presumption that the validity of a testamentary trust is governed by the law

---

[2] In *Cadell* v. *Palmer* (1833) 1 Cl. & F. 372, one of the leading English cases on the rule against perpetuities, the testator died in 1818, and the trust was finally wound up by Astbury J. in 1918.

[3] As to this, see *ante,* pp. 393–396.

[4] As to this, see *ante,* pp. 400–402.

[5] As to this, see *ante,* p. 392.

[6] *Ante,* pp. 396–397.

[7] For examples, see *Att. Gen.* v. *Campbell* (1872) L.R. 5 H.L. 524; *Mayor of Canterbury* v. *Wyburn* [1895] A.C. 89.

of the testator's domicile at the date of his death.[8] As we have seen,[9] there is some authority for saying that the law of the place of administration, and not the law of the testator's domicile, determines whether the trusts infringe the rule against perpetuities. The same should no doubt apply also to the rule against accumulations and to the question whether and to what extent gifts to charities are valid.

There is no English authority for the proposition that a testator can select the law which is to govern the validity of the trust. In some American states there are statutes which enable him to do this; and some American courts have reached the same result without the aid of any statute.[10]

The validity of trusts inter vivos

It is obviously desirable that a trust should be treated as a unit and that the trusts of all the movables contained therein should be governed by a single law. This is just as true in the case of a trust created *inter vivos* as it is in the case of a trust created by will. Hence the *lex situs* of the movables included in the trust is an inappropriate law to govern its validity, because they may be situated in different countries. Moreover, the movables included in a trust are usually intangible, *e.g.* stock, shares and bonds; and the *situs* of an intangible movable is to some extent a fiction.[11] The place where the trust is executed is also inappropriate, because it is not sufficiently related to the substance of the transaction; it may be fortuitous or, worse still, carefully contrived to take advantage of a favourable law. The domicile of the settlor is more significant, especially if the trust is created by a marriage settlement; but even when it is, the domicile of the settlor is not the only consideration which the courts take into account.[12] The domicile of the beneficiaries is much less significant, because they may not all be domiciled in the same country, and because, at the time when the trust is created, the most important beneficiaries (those who will ultimately become entitled to the capital) may not yet be born. The place of administration of the trust is a very significant factor, perhaps more so in questions relating to administration than in questions relating to validity. The legal style of the trust instrument is also significant; the fact that it is expressed in the technical terms of one country and not in those of another may serve to warn those dealing with the beneficiaries that it was intended to be governed by the law of the former country.

In English law, the validity of an *inter vivos* trust is governed by its proper law, that is, the system of law with which it has its closest and most real connection.[13] The leading English case on the proper law of a trust not created by a marriage settlement is *Iveagh* v. *I.R.C.*[14] A settlor domiciled and resident in Ireland made a voluntary settlement in 1907 for the benefit

---

[8] *Re Lord Cable* [1977] 1 W.L.R. 7, 20.
[9] *Ante,* pp. 396–397.
[10] See Restatement, Reporter's Note to s.269.
[11] See *ante*, p. 375.
[12] See *ante*, pp. 414–416.
[13] Dicey and Morris, Rule 120; *Iveagh* v. *I.R.C.* [1954] Ch. 365.
[14] [1954] Ch. 365.

of his son, also domiciled and resident in Ireland, and the son's wife and children. At the date of the settlement the trust property consisted of bearer bonds and of shares in an English company carrying on business in Ireland. All the securities were kept in England; the settlement was prepared by the settlor's English solicitors, and it was executed in England. The day to day management of the trust was in Ireland. At the date of the settlement there was no significant difference between English and Irish law; but by 1949, when the son died, Ireland had become a separate country and fiscal differences had emerged between English and Irish law. It was held that, for purposes of estate duty, the proper law of the settlement was Irish law. The decisive factors were the domicile of the settlor and of his son.

Although there is no English decision in point, it is probable that the settlor could select the proper law, at any rate if his chosen law had some substantial connection with the trust.[15] There is plenty of American authority to this effect.[16]

It is well settled that, once the trust has been created, the proper law continues to govern its validity and cannot be changed, *e.g.* by a change in the place of investment of the trust property,[17] or in the place of residence of the trustees,[18] or in the domicile of the beneficiaries.[19] The only ways in which the proper law can be changed are (a) by an agreement by the beneficiaries to change it and thus in effect make a new settlement,[20] or (b) by the court sanctioning such a change under the powers conferred by the Variation of Trusts Act 1958, or a similar enactment in a foreign country.[21]

Although, as we have seen, it is desirable that a trust should be treated as a unit and governed by one law irrespective of the *situs* of the movables contained therein, it does not follow that all questions of validity are governed by the same law. For instance, the trust will be formally valid if it complies with either the proper law[22] or the law of the place of execution.[23] The cases on capacity to create the trust all relate to trusts created by a marriage settlement, and as we have seen[24] they are open to more than one interpretation. But it is at least a possible interpretation that capacity is governed by the proper law. The question whether the settlor can revoke the trust is also governed by the proper law[25]; and so is the question of essential validity. In this connection there are two interesting cases from Australia which may be briefly examined.

---

[15] See *ante*, p. 416.
[16] See Restatement, Reporter's Note to s.270.
[17] *Re Fitzgerald* [1904] 1 Ch. 573, 588; *Duke of Marlborough* v. *Att. Gen.* [1945] Ch. 78, 85.
[18] *Re Hewitt's Settlement* [1915] 1 Ch. 228, 233–234; *Duke of Marlborough* v. *Att. Gen., supra.*
[19] *Re Hewitt's Settlement, supra.*
[20] *Duke of Marlborough* v. *Att. Gen., supra.*
[21] *Post*, p. 427.
[22] *Van Grutten* v. *Digby* (1862) 31 Beav. 561; *Viditz* v. *O'Hagan* [1899] 2 Ch. 569; *Re Bankes* [1902] 2 Ch. 333.
[23] *Guépratte* v. *Young* (1851) 4 De G. & Sm. 217.
[24] *Ante*, pp. 416–418.
[25] *Viditz* v. *O'Hagan* [1900] 2 Ch. 87; *Fattorini* v. *Johannesburg Board of Executors and Trust Co. Ltd.*, 1948 (4) S.A. 806.

In *Lindsay* v. *Miller*,[26] the parties to a voluntary settlement were the settlor, domiciled in Scotland but resident in England, and three trustees, resident in China, Western Australia and Victoria. The settlement was in Scottish form and contained limitations which were valid by Scots law but probably too remote under the rule against perpetuities in force in England and Victoria. The settlement was executed by the settlor and by two of the trustees in Scotland and by the third trustee in Victoria. The trust was to be administered in Victoria. The trust property was situated entirely in Australia and mainly in Victoria. The Supreme Court of Victoria held that the proper law was that of Victoria. The decisive factor was the place of administration of the trust. This was held to outweigh the settlor's Scottish domicile, the Scottish style of the drafting and the Scottish place of execution.

In *Augustus* v. *Permanent Trustee Co.* (*Canberra*) *Ltd.*,[27] a settlor domiciled and resident in New South Wales made a voluntary settlement for the benefit of his children and grandchildren born and to be born. At the date of the settlement those of the beneficiaries who were in existence were also domiciled and resident in New South Wales. The settlement was drafted and engrossed in Sydney and sent to Canberra for execution there by the settlor and by a trust corporation incorporated and carrying on business in the Australian Capital Territory. The trust property was a cheque for £42,000 drawn on a Canberra bank. One of the objects of the settlement was to avoid New South Wales death duties, which no doubt explains the care which was taken to centre the trust in Canberra. Unfortunately some of the limitations contained in the settlement postponed the vesting of property in unborn persons until they attained the age of twenty-five. These limitations were too remote under the common law rule against perpetuities in force in the Australian Capital Territory. But they would have been cured by a New South Wales statute of 1919 (the model for the now repealed section 163 of the English Law of Property Act 1925), which would have reduced the age of vesting to twenty-one. A clause in the settlement provided that the rights and liabilities of the trustee and of the beneficiaries as between themselves and as against the trustee should be regulated by the laws of New South Wales. The High Court of Australia held that the proper law was that of New South Wales and that the limitations were valid.

Construction

On principle, the law governing the construction of a trust is the law intended by the testator or settlor, and this is presumed to be the law of the testator's domicile at the date of making his will in the case of a testamentary trust,[28] and the proper law of the trust in the case of an *inter vivos* trust.[29]

---

[26] [1949] V.L.R. 13. *Cf. Permanent Executors and Trustees Association of Australia Ltd.* v. *Roberts* [1970] V.R. 732.
[27] (1971) 124 C.L.R. 245.
[28] *Philipson-Stow* v. *I.R.C.* [1961] A.C. 727, 761; Wills Act 1963, s.4; *ante*, p. 398.
[29] Dicey and Morris, Rule 120.

Restraints on alienation of beneficial interests

The questions whether a beneficiary can alienate his interest in a trust and whether his interest can be reached by his creditors are governed by the proper law of the trust or, in the case of a testamentary trust, presumably by the law of the testator's last domicile. Thus in *Re Fitzgerald*,[30] a marriage settlement was made in Scottish form on the marriage of a domiciled Scotswoman to a domiciled Englishman. Under the settlement, the husband was given an "alimentary" life interest in property belonging to the wife. The settlement provided that his interest should not be assignable nor liable to arrestment or any other legal diligence at the instance of his creditors. Such an interest was valid by Scots law but invalid by English law. The husband mortgaged his life interest to an English creditor in England. It was held that Scots law governed and that the mortgage was void. This was no doubt hard on the English mortgagee; but surely the Scottish form of the settlement should have put him on inquiry.

Again, in an Australian case[31] an English marriage settlement was made on the marriage of a domiciled Englishwoman to a domiciled Italian. Thirty years later, the question arose in Victoria whether the wife's life interest was subject to a restraint upon anticipation. Such restraints had been retrospectively abolished in English law and abolished, though not retrospectively, in Victorian law. It was held that English law governed and that the life interest was not subject to the restraint.

Administration

There is very little English authority on the matters which, as previously suggested, relate to the administration rather than to the validity of the trust. Indeed English courts have not always adverted to the distinction.

As a general rule, the administration of a trust is governed by the law of the place of administration.[32] This is likely to be the place where the trustees reside or carry on business, especially if the trustee is a trust corporation. Of course, if the law of the place of administration does not recognise trusts, this rule would offer no guidance. In that case one would be thrown back on the law governing the validity of the trust.

There is no legal bar to the appointment of trustees resident abroad as trustees of an English trust. But such an appointment is improper except in exceptional circumstances, *e.g.* where all the beneficiaries have become resident in the foreign country concerned.[33] On the other hand, there is no power to appoint the English Public Trustee as trustee of a foreign trust, even though all the beneficiaries are domiciled and resident in England, the trust property is situated in England, and the trustees who wish to retire from the trust are all resident in England.[34]

The statutory power to postpone the sale of assets is a matter of adminis-

---

[30] [1904] 1 Ch. 573.

[31] *Trustees Executors and Agency Co. Ltd.* v. *Margottini* [1960] V.R. 417.

[32] Dicey and Morris, Rule 121.

[33] *Meinertzhagen* v. *Davis* (1844) 1 Coll.N.C. 335; *Re Smith's Trusts* (1872) 20 W.R. 695; *Re Liddiard* (1880) 14 Ch.D. 310; *Re Whitehead's Trusts* [1971] 1 W.L.R. 833.

[34] *Re Hewitt's Settlement* [1915] 1 Ch. 228.

tration, governed by English law as the place of administration and not by the law of the deceased's domicile.[35] The same is true of the statutory powers of maintenance and advancement.[36]

The English courts will not administer a foreign charity under the supervision of the court, nor will they settle a scheme for such a charity.[37] They may, however, authorise an application to the appropriate foreign court to frame such a scheme.[38] But if the foreign objects of an English charitable trust fail, the court will direct an application of the trust funds *cy-près*.[39]

TRUSTS OF IMMOVABLES

What law governs the validity of a trust of immovables? Traditionally, all questions relating to immovables are governed by the *lex situs*; but as we have seen,[40] the *situs* rule has come under attack from writers during the last forty-five years on the ground that it is much too broad, hopelessly undiscriminating, and careless of the important policies of domestic law. So far as the validity of trusts is concerned, there may be something to be said for applying the *lex situs* if the trust property comprises only immovables situated in one country and no movables. But if it comprises immovables situated in different countries, or both immovables and movables, a strong counter-argument can be made on the ground that it is desirable that the trust should be treated as a unit and that the trusts of all the property contained therein should be governed by a single law, *i.e.* the proper law of the trust. And, if we look at the matter functionally rather than conceptually, should it really make all that difference to the governing law whether the trust income reaches the trustees' desk in the form of dividend warrants paid by companies twice a year or in the form of quarterly cheques for rent paid by tenants of land? Particularly since shares in a property-owning company are regarded as movables? Of course it must be admitted that for obvious reasons of policy, questions of the marketability or use of land must be governed by the *lex situs*. For instance, no English court could allow a settlor or testator to create an unbarrable entail in English land, or future interests which infringed the rule against perpetuities, or charitable trusts which fell foul of English housing or town planning legislation. But apart from obvious cases such as these, the argument for applying the *lex situs* to the validity of a trust of land does not seem compelling.

In *Re Fitzgerald*,[41] the Court of Appeal held that a marriage settlement in Scottish form made by a lady domiciled in Scotland before her marriage to a domiciled Englishman was governed by Scots law. Most of the prop-

---

[35] *Re Wilks* [1935] Ch. 645.
[36] *Re Kehr* [1952] Ch. 26.
[37] *Provost of Edinburgh* v. *Aubrey* (1754) Ambler 256; *Att. Gen* v. *Lepine* (1818) 2 Swanst. 181; *Emery* v. *Hill* (1826) 1 Russ. 112; *New* v. *Bonaker* (1867) L.R. 4 Eq. 655.
[38] *Re Fraser* (1883) 22 Ch.D. 827; *Re Marr's Will Trusts* [1936] Ch. 671.
[39] *Re Colonial Bishoprics Fund* [1935] Ch. 148.
[40] *Ante,* p. 344.
[41] [1904] 1 Ch. 573, 588.

erty settled (to the amount of £13,200) was invested in Scottish heritable bonds, *i.e.* in immovables; the only movable was a sum of £500 in cash. One reason given by Cozens-Hardy L.J. for holding that Scots law was the proper law was the following:

> "It can scarcely be denied that the *lex loci*—*i.e.* the law of Scotland—must apply to the extent of the £13,200. There was £500 cash belonging to the lady which was paid over to the trustees for investment. It seems to me that this sum cannot fairly be treated as intended to be subject to a different law from that which is applicable to the bulk of the property."

But if the trust property had consisted of £13,200 worth of movables and a cottage in England worth £500, the same reasoning inverted would have led to the conclusion that the land in England was subject to the same law as the movables, *i.e.* to Scots law.

However, the English courts have always applied the *lex situs* to the essential validity of trusts of immovables. That law determines what estates can be created[42]; what are the incidents of those estates[43]; whether gifts to charities are valid[44]; and whether the trusts infringe the rules against perpetuities or accumulations.[45] And, of course, if the foreign *lex situs* does not recognise trusts of land, the trust will fail.[46] There may, however, be a means of escape from this unpalatable conclusion if the settlement or will contains a trust for sale and the equitable doctrine of conversion can be invoked.[47] If the property consists of land in England, the *lex situs* means English domestic law; if it consists of land situated abroad, it means whatever system of domestic law the *lex situs* would apply.[48]

On the other hand, trusts of immovables are construed in accordance with the law intended by the testator or settlor, and not necessarily in accordance with the *lex situs*.[49] A foreign marriage contract or settlement (even if not express but imposed or implied by foreign law) can affect the devolution of land in England.[50] And by statute, a will of immovables must be treated as properly executed if its execution conformed to the domestic law of the country where it was executed, or where the testator was domiciled or habitually resident, or of which he was a national,[51] as well as if it conformed to the domestic law of the *situs*.[52]

There is no doubt that English courts have jurisdiction to administer a trust even if part of the trust property consists of foreign land.[53] And, although English authority is scanty, it does not seem reasonable that the

---

[42] *Nelson* v. *Bridport* (1846) 8 Beav. 547.
[43] *Re Miller* [1914] 1 Ch. 511.
[44] *Duncan* v. *Lawson* (1889) 41 Ch.D. 394; *Re Hoyles* [1911] 1 Ch. 179.
[45] *Freke* v. *Carbery* (1873) L.R. 16 Eq. 461.
[46] *Re Pearse's Settlement* [1909] 1 Ch. 304.
[47] *Re Piercy* [1895] 1 Ch. 83; *ante*, pp. 335–336.
[48] *Re Ross* [1930] 1 Ch. 377; *Re Duke of Wellington* [1947] Ch. 506.
[49] *Studd* v. *Cook* (1883) 8 App.Cas. 577; *Philipson-Stow* v. *I.R.C.* [1961] A.C. 727, 761.
[50] *Re De Nicols* (*No.* 2) [1900] 2 Ch. 410; *ante*, p. 414.
[51] Wills Act 1963, s.1.
[52] s.2(1)(*b*); *ante*, p. 393.
[53] *Hope* v. *Carnegie* (1866) L.R. 1 Ch.App. 320; *Ewing* v. *Orr-Ewing* (1883) 9 App.Cas. 34.

lex situs should govern questions which we have suggested relate to administration rather than to validity. The English court has sometimes authorised the trustees of an English trust to apply to the Court of Session for leave to sell land in Scotland which formed part of the trust property.[54]

THE VARIATION OF TRUSTS

Under section 24 of the Matrimonial Causes Act 1973 (replacing and extending earlier legislation), the court has power, after granting a decree of divorce, nullity of marriage or judicial separation, to vary any ante-nuptial or post-nuptial settlement made on the parties to the marriage. This power is exercisable although the settlement is governed by some foreign law and the property is situated abroad.[55] But it will not be exercised if the order of the court will not be effective in the foreign country.[56] It is perfectly understandable that the statutory power should not be confined to English settlements, because the order is ancillary to the main decree, and as we have seen[57] the court has jurisdiction to make any ancillary order whenever it has jurisdiction in the main suit.

Under section 1(1) of the Variation of Trusts Act 1958, the court has power to approve any arrangement varying or revoking all or any of the trusts on which the property is held under any will, settlement or other disposition. The situation under this Act is quite different from what it is under the Act of 1973. The order made by the court is not ancillary to anything. It might therefore have been expected that the court would only make an order if the proper law of the trust is English law. But unfortunately in *Re Ker's Settlement*[58] Ungoed-Thomas J., following the divorce cases referred to above, held that the jurisdiction is unlimited and that the court can vary a settlement even if it is governed by foreign law—in that case, Northern Irish law. He disposed of an argument to the contrary based on section 2(2) of the Act (which provides that it does not extend to Scotland or Northern Ireland) by observing that the subsection merely means that the Northern Irish court has no power to make such an order. In *Re Paget's Settlement*[59] Cross J., while accepting that he had jurisdiction to vary a settlement assumed to be governed by the law of New York, said:

"Where there are substantial foreign elements in the case, the court must consider carefully whether it is proper for it to exercise the jurisdiction. If, for example, the court were asked to vary a settlement which was plainly a Scottish settlement, it might well hesitate to exercise its jurisdiction to vary the trusts, simply because some of, or even

---

[54] See *Re Forrest* (1910) 54 S.J. 737; *Re Georges* (1921) 65 S.J. 311; and the Scottish cases *Carruthers' Trustees* (1896) 24 R. 238; *Allan's Trustees* (1897) 24 R. 718; *Harris' Trustees*, 1919 S.C. 432; *Campbell-Wyndham-Long's Trustees*, 1951 S.C. 685.
[55] *Nunneley* v. *Nunneley* (1890) 15 P.D. 186; *Forsyth* v. *Forsyth* [1891] P. 363.
[56] *Tallack* v. *Tallack* [1927] P. 211; *Goff* v. *Goff* [1934] P. 107.
[57] *Ante*, pp. 220–221.
[58] [1963] Ch. 553; criticised by F. A. Mann (1964) 80 L.Q.R. 29.
[59] [1965] 1 W.L.R. 1046, 1050.

all, the trustees and beneficiaries were in this country. It may well be that the judge would say that the Court of Session was the appropriate tribunal to deal with the case."[60]

In *Re Seale's Marriage Settlement*,[61] it was held that the court has power under the Variation of Trusts Act 1958 to approve an arrangement revoking the trusts of an English settlement, substituting the trusts of a foreign settlement and appointing a foreign trustee. In that case the husband and wife and their children had all emigrated to Canada many years before the application was made to the court. But in *Re Weston's Settlements*,[62] the Court of Appeal refused to approve a similar arrangement where the settlor and his two sons (on whom the settlements in question had been made) emigrated from England to Jersey a bare three months before the application was made. Although the parties' evidence that they intended to remain permanently in Jersey was uncontradicted, the court obviously disbelieved it: the application was "an essay in tax avoidance naked and unashamed."

In that case it appeared that there was no Trustee Act in force in Jersey and that the courts there had never made an order executing the trusts of a settlement, though there was also evidence that they would probably do so if required. But the inexperience of the Jersey courts in matters of trusts does not prevent the English court from approving a revocation of an English settlement and the substitution of a Jersey settlement in a proper case. Thus in *Re Windeatt*[63] the court made such an order. It distinguished *Re Weston's Settlements* on the ground that the life tenant had been living in Jersey for nineteen years before the application was made, that she was probably domiciled there, and that her children were born there.

The powers of the court to vary trusts under the Matrimonial Causes Act 1973 and the Variation of Trusts Act 1958 extend to trusts of immovables as well as to trusts of movables, and this is why they have been considered in a separate section of this chapter.

---

[60] *i.e.* under the Trusts (Scotland) Act 1961.
[61] [1961] Ch. 574.
[62] [1969] 1 Ch. 223.
[63] [1969] 1 W.L.R. 692.

Part Seven

BANKRUPTCY AND CORPORATIONS

CHAPTER 27

BANKRUPTCY

BANKRUPTCY is a topic which raises complicated questions in the conflict of laws.[1] These questions affect the jurisdiction of courts, the law of property and the law of contract, since the effect of an adjudication in bankruptcy may be to vest in the trustee in bankruptcy property of the debtor situated in foreign countries, and the effect of an order of discharge may be to terminate the debtor's liabilities under contracts governed by foreign law. The law is not in a satisfactory state, because modern cases are few and far between, and because the Bankruptcy Act 1914 contains some provisions based on constitutional assumptions as to the powers of the Imperial Parliament which are no longer valid after the Statute of Westminster 1931.

ENGLISH BANKRUPTCIES

Jurisdiction of the English court

Two conditions must be satisfied before an English court can exercise bankruptcy jurisdiction over a person. First, he must have committed an "act of bankruptcy" as defined by section 1(1) of the Bankruptcy Act 1914. Secondly, he must be a "debtor" as defined by section 1(2) thereof.

It is unnecessary to enumerate the eight acts any one of which constitutes an act of bankruptcy under section 1(1), but it must be noticed that four of them may take place in a foreign country. These are as follows:

(a) If in England or elsewhere the debtor makes a conveyance of his property to a trustee for the benefit of his creditors generally.

(b) If in England or elsewhere he makes a fraudulent conveyance of his property.

(c) If in England or elsewhere he makes a conveyance that is void as a fraudulent preference.

(d) If with intent to defeat or delay his creditors he departs out of England, or being out of England remains out of England.

With regard to the first of these four acts, however, it was held by the House of Lords in 1901 that a conveyance of property situated in England, made abroad by a person domiciled in a foreign country and intended to operate according to the law of that country and not according to English law, was not an available act of bankruptcy.[2] But this decision was given

---

[1] See Dicey and Morris, Chap. 26; Cheshire and North, pp. 557–572; Blom-Cooper, *Bankruptcy in Private International Law* (1954). There is a draft EEC Convention on Bankruptcy which has been under negotiation in the EEC for over 15 years. For comments on the Convention see Muir Hunter (1972) 21 I.C.L.Q. 682; (1976) 25 I.C.L.Q. 310; Report of the Advisory Committee on the EEC Bankruptcy Convention (1976) Cmnd. 6602. It seems unlikely that the Convention will be finally agreed in the near future.

[2] *Cooke* v. *Charles A. Vogeler Co.* [1901] A.C. 102, following *Ex p. Crispin* (1873) L.R. 8 Ch.App. 374, 380.

at a time before the present definition of "debtor" was enacted in section
1(2) of the Act; and though it was followed by the Court of Appeal in
1936,[3] it may be that it is now an obsolete restriction on the jurisdiction of
the court.[4]

The definition of "debtor" was considerably widened by section 1(2) of
the Bankruptcy Act 1914. Before 1914 it was held that only British subjects
or foreigners residing in England could be adjudicated bankrupt here.[5]
The result was that a foreigner resident abroad who carried on business in
England through an agent was immune from the jurisdiction.[6] This was
altered by section 1(2) of the Act, which defines a debtor as any person,
whether a British subject or not, who at the time when the act of bankruptcy was committed

(a) was personally present in England; or

(b) ordinarily resided or had a place of residence in England; or

(c) was carrying on business in England, personally or by means of an
agent or manager; or

(d) was a member of a firm or partnership which carried on business in
England.

The House of Lords has held that a person still carries on business in England even though he gives up the business and goes abroad, if he leaves
unpaid trading debts behind him.[7]

The court has jurisdiction to adjudicate bankrupt on his own petition any
person who is a debtor within the meaning of section 1(2) above, since the
presentation of such a petition is itself an act of bankruptcy.[8] But in the
case of creditors' petitions there is a further restriction on the jurisdiction.
For section 4(1)(d) of the Act provides:

> A creditor may not present a bankruptcy petition against a debtor
> unless the debtor is domiciled in England, or within a year before the
> date of the presentation of the petition has ordinarily resided,[9] or had
> a dwelling-house or place of business, in England, or (except in the
> case of a person domiciled in Scotland or Northern Ireland or a firm or
> partnership having its principal place of business in Scotland or North-
> ern Ireland) has carried on business[9] in England, personally or by
> means of an agent or manager, or (except as aforesaid) is or within the
> said period has been a member of a firm or partnership of persons
> which has carried on business in England by means of a partner or
> partners or an agent or manager.

[3] *Re Debtors (No. 836 of* 1935) [1936] Ch. 622.
[4] *Theophile* v. *S.-G.* [1950] A.C. 186, 199; Dicey and Morris, pp. 693–694.
[5] *Ex p. Crispin* (1873) L.R. 8 Ch.App. 374, 380; *Ex p. Blain* (1879) 12 Ch.D. 522; *Re Pear-son* [1892] 2 Q.B. 263.
[6] *Ex p. Blain, supra; Cooke* v. *Charles A. Vogeler Co.* [1901] A.C. 102.
[7] *Theophile* v. *S.-G.* [1950] A.C. 186; *Re Bird* [1962] 1 W.L.R. 686; see Lipstein (1949) 12 M.L.R. 454.
[8] Bankruptcy Act 1914, s.1(1)(f).
[9] As to when a debtor ordinarily resides or carries on business in England, see *Re Brauch* [1978] Ch. 316 and cases there cited.

The most important practical effect of this enactment is that a creditor may not present a bankruptcy petition against a debtor merely because the debtor, not being domiciled or resident in England, committed an act of bankruptcy during a temporary visit to England.

If the above conditions are satisfied, the jurisdiction of the English court is not excluded by the fact that the debtor has already been adjudged bankrupt by a foreign court.[10] Thus, English law does not recognise the principle of "unity of bankruptcy," according to which all creditors must have recourse to the courts of the debtor's domicile, or of his principal place of business, and no other court has jurisdiction to adjudicate him bankrupt.[11] But the fact that the debtor has been adjudged bankrupt abroad is a reason for the court in its discretion not to exercise jurisdiction,[12] though little weight will be given to this factor if the foreign adjudication was obtained by the debtor on his own petition.[13] If, as a result of the foreign adjudication or otherwise, there are no assets in England, that is a strong reason for the court to refuse to exercise its jurisdiction.[14]

Effect of English bankruptcy as an assignment of property

Under sections 18 and 53 of the Bankruptcy Act 1914, the effect of an adjudication in bankruptcy is that the property of the bankrupt vests in his trustee; and under section 167 property includes "every description of property, whether real or personal and whether situate in England or elsewhere." Thus, the principle is that an English adjudication in bankruptcy purports to have a universal effect as an assignment. English law, while not admitting the doctrine of the unity of bankruptcy, does admit the doctrine of universality, at least so far as English bankruptcies are concerned. But, by including immovables situated abroad among the property of the bankrupt, the Act attributes a wider effect to an English bankruptcy than English courts would, apart from statute, give to a foreign bankruptcy.[15]

Of course, no Act of Parliament can of its own force and effect transfer property situated in a politically foreign country such as France or Germany from the bankrupt to the trustee. Hence the question whether property situated in such a country does or does not pass to the English trustee in bankruptcy must depend in the last resort on the *lex situs*. So, although English law says that all the property of the bankrupt vests in his trustee, it may be difficult for the trustee to make his title effective, so far as property in a politically foreign country is concerned, as against, *e.g.* a judgment creditor levying execution there, or a trustee in a later local bankruptcy.

---

[10] *Ex p. McCulloch* (1880) 14 Ch.D. 716; *Re Artola Hermanos* (1890) 24 Q.B.D. 640; *Re A Debtor (No. 199 of 1922)* [1922] 2 Ch. 470; *Re A Debtor (No. 737 of 1928)* [1929] 1 Ch. 362, 370.

[11] *Re Artola Hermanos, supra,* at pp. 648–649.

[12] *Ex p. McCulloch, supra,* at pp. 719, 723; *Ex p. Robinson* (1883) 22 Ch.D. 816, 818; but see *Re Artola Hermanos, supra,* at p. 647.

[13] *Ex p. McCulloch, supra; Re A Debtor (No. 199 of 1922)* [1922] 2 Ch. 470.

[14] *Ex p. Robinson, supra; Re A Debtor, supra,* at p. 473. As to what property of a debtor is deemed by English law to pass to his trustee under a foreign bankruptcy, see *post*, pp. 438–440.

[15] See *post*, p. 440.

If, however, the property is situated in Scotland or Northern Ireland, there is no difficulty, because section 121 of the Act provides that any order made by a bankruptcy court in England, Scotland or Northern[16] Ireland shall be enforced in the courts having jurisdiction in bankruptcy in the other two countries as if the order had been made by the court which is required to enforce it.

If the property is situated in an independent country of the Commonwealth or in the Republic of Ireland, there is a difficulty today which did not exist in 1914. The Imperial Parliament of those days could legislate for all countries of the Empire, and sometimes did so. The sections of the Act relating to the vesting of the bankrupt's property in his trustee (and also those relating to the discharge of his debts[17]) purport to have a universal effect. In the past the view of English judges has been that these sections are binding on and form part of the law of all countries of the Empire as well as the United Kingdom.[18] This may still be true in constitutional theory so far as the law of the United Kingdom is concerned, even in the case of independent countries of the Commonwealth which have assumed republican forms of government, for it is commonly enacted that the existing law of the United Kingdom shall continue to apply in relation to them as if they had not become republics.[19] But of course any independent country of the Commonwealth has power to repeal any enactment of the Parliament at Westminster so far as the same is part of its law.[20] Even in the absence of such a repeal, it may be doubted whether some of the independent countries of the Commonwealth would admit that the "Imperial" Act of 1914 still formed part of their law. In particular, it seems unlikely that the courts of any independent country inside or outside the Commonwealth would allow the bankrupt's property situated there to be made available as a fund out of which United Kingdom taxes could be paid.[21] However, the Federal Court of Australia, acting in aid of a New Zealand court, allowed the debtor's assets in New South Wales to be used to pay New Zealand taxes.[22]

Provisions in aid of the assignment. Although it may be difficult for English law to prevail against the *lex situs* in causing the bankrupt's property situated outside the United Kingdom to vest in his trustee, there are certain provisions of the Bankruptcy Act 1914 which sometimes diminish this difficulty.

---

[16] The restriction to Northern Ireland follows from s.2 of the Irish Free State (Consequential Adaptation of Enactments) Order 1923 (S.R. & O. No. 405).

[17] *Post*, pp. 387–388.

[18] See *Gill* v. *Barron* (1868) L.R. 2 P.C. 157, 175–176; *Ellis* v. *M'Henry* (1871) L.R. 6 C.P. 228 (discharge); *Callender, Sykes & Co.* v. *Colonial Secretary of Lagos* [1891] A.C. 460, 465–467; *New Zealand Loan and Mercantile Agency Co.* v. *Morrison* [1898] A.C. 349, 358 (vesting of property).

[19] See, *e.g.* India (Consequential Provision) Act 1949, s.1.

[20] Statute of Westminster 1931, s.2.

[21] *Cf. Government of India* v. *Taylor* [1955] A.C. 491; *Peter Buchanan Ltd.* v. *McVey* [1954] I.R. 89; *Re Gibbons, ex p. Walter* (1960) 26 Irish Jurist 60.

[22] *Re Ayres, ex p. Evans* (1982) 39 A.L.R. 129.

(a) Under section 53(4), the certificate of appointment of a trustee is deemed to be a conveyance or assignment of property for all purposes of any law in force in "any part of the British dominions." This enactment seeks to overcome the difficulty that in many such countries, land and shares can only be transferred by entry on the register.[23]

(b) Under section 122, the courts having jurisdiction in bankruptcy in England, Scotland and Ireland[24] and every British court elsewhere having jurisdiction in bankruptcy or insolvency must act in aid of and be ancillary to each other in all bankruptcy matters. So far as English law is concerned, the expression "British court" has been widely construed. Thus, during the mandate, it was held that a bankruptcy court in Palestine was a British court.[25] Not surprisingly, the Royal Court of Jersey is a British court.[26] On the other hand, during the illegal regime the High Court of Rhodesia was held not to be a British court.[27] But two factors reduce the efficacy of section 122 as an aid to the English trustee in obtaining possession of the bankrupt's property situated in the Commonwealth outside the United Kingdom or in the Republic of Ireland. First, all courts (and the English courts are no exception[28]) whose aid is sought under this section reserve to themselves a discretion and decide for themselves what form of aid to give.[29] Secondly, the Commonwealth court whose aid is sought may not admit that it is a "British" court within the meaning of the section. Even before the Statute of Westminster 1931, courts in Victoria and Saskatchewan were bold enough to wonder whether they were not Australian and Canadian courts respectively rather than British ones; though it is true that each court ultimately admitted that it was British.[30]

(c) Under section 22(2), the debtor may be ordered to execute such powers of attorney, conveyances, deeds and instruments as may reasonably be required by the trustee, and must aid in the realisation of his property. No doubt this subsection can only be invoked if the debtor is personally present in England, as he usually but not necessarily is. But, unlike sections 53(4) and 122, it may assist the trustee to obtain possession of property situated in a politically foreign country as well as in one forming part of the Commonwealth.

What property passes to the trustee. Under section 37 of the Bankruptcy Act 1914, the title of the trustee in bankruptcy relates back to the first act of bankruptcy committed within three months before the date of the petition on which the debtor was adjudicated bankrupt. The effect of this provision is, broadly speaking, to set aside all transactions which take place

---

[23] See *Callender, Sykes & Co.* v. *Colonial Secretary of Lagos* [1891] A.C. 460.
[24] In s.122 (unlike s.121, *supra*), "Ireland" includes the Republic of Ireland: Irish Free State (Consequential Adaptation of Enactments) Order 1923, s.2 and Sched. (S.R. & O. No. 405); Ireland Act 1949, s.3(1)(*a*)(iii).
[25] *Re Maundy Gregory* (1934) 103 L.J.Ch. 267.
[26] *Re A Debtor* [1981] Ch. 384.
[27] *Re James* [1977] Ch. 41.
[28] *Re Osborn* (1931–1932) 15 B. & C.R. 189.
[29] See, *e.g. Re Gibbons, ex p. Walter* (1960) 26 Irish Jurist 60.
[30] *Re Mann, Stogdale and Henry* (1887) 13 V.L.R. 590, 595; *Re Graham* (*No.* 1) [1928] 4 D.L.R. 375; (*No.* 2) [1929] 3 D.L.R. 353.

after this first act of bankruptcy. But this doctrine of relation back does not extend to property situated outside England.[31]

In so far as an English bankruptcy operates as an assignment of property situated abroad, the property passes to the trustee subject to any charges which are recognised as affecting it by the *lex situs*.[32]

Apart from the doctrine of relation back, only the property of the bankrupt vests in the trustee. Property which once belonged to the bankrupt, but is now vested in the trustee in a foreign bankruptcy, is not the property of the bankrupt, and does not vest in the English trustee in bankruptcy.[33]

Restraining creditors from suing abroad. The courts will, in certain circumstances, restrain a creditor from taking proceedings abroad to recover a debt due from the bankrupt, in order to maintain an equal distribution of the assets among the creditors generally. They will grant an injunction to restrain a creditor resident in England from suing abroad[34]; but they will not restrain a creditor resident abroad from suing abroad,[35] unless he had claimed to prove his debt in the English bankruptcy.[36]

Compelling creditors to refund property obtained abroad. The courts also have power, in certain circumstances, to force creditors who satisfy their claims against the bankrupt abroad, whether by judicial proceedings or otherwise, to bring these assets into hotchpot for the benefit of the creditors generally.

It is clearly established that a creditor who receives abroad any part of the bankrupt's property will not be allowed to prove under the English bankruptcy unless he brings the part so acquired into the common fund.[37]

But what is the position if the creditor who so recovers property from the bankrupt abroad does not seek to prove in the English bankruptcy? In three cases decided between 1791 and 1795 it was held that a creditor resident in England who recovered a debt due from the bankrupt in a foreign country could be compelled to hand over the sum to the English trustee.[38] The judgments stress the fact that the creditor resided in England, and recovered the debt by legal process with full knowledge of the bankruptcy. Recent authorities are entirely lacking. Hence there has been much speculation as to precisely when the diligent creditor can be compelled to disgorge the fruits of his diligence. No doubt it depends on whether the creditor was subject to the English bankruptcy jurisdiction at the time when he recovered the property. But when exactly is he subject to the Eng-

[31] *Galbraith* v. *Grimshaw* [1910] A.C. 508, 510, 513; *cf. Geddes* v. *Mowat* (1825) 1 Gl. & J. 414, 422.
[32] *Re Somes, ex p. De Lemos* (1896) 3 Mans. 131; *Re Sykes* (1932) 101 L.J.Ch. 298.
[33] *Ante*, p. 433.
[34] *Re Distin, ex p. Ormiston* (1871) 24 L.T. 197.
[35] *Re Chapman* (1873) L.R. 15 Eq. 75.
[36] *Re Tait* (1872) L.R. 13 Eq. 311. For the analogous rules in the winding up of companies, see *post*, p. 449.
[37] *Ex p. Wilson, Re Douglas* (1872) L.R. 7 Ch.App. 490; *Banco de Portugal* v. *Waddell* (1880) 5 App.Cas. 161.
[38] *Sill* v. *Worswick* (1791) 1 H.Bl. 665; *Hunter* v. *Potts* (1791) 4 T.R. 182; *Phillips* v. *Hunter* (1795) 2 H.Bl. 402.

lish bankruptcy jurisdiction? Cheshire[39] says that the creditor can be ordered to refund if at the time when he recovers the property he satisfies in his own person the same jurisdictional requirements as section 4(1)(d) of the Bankruptcy Act 1914 requires of the debtor in the case of a creditor's petition.[40] But there is no authority for transferring the jurisdictional requirements of section 4(1)(d) from debtors to creditors. That enactment is not related in any way to the need for protecting the creditors generally from the activities of an individual creditor. A better view, it is submitted, is that the jurisdiction to compel a creditor to refund property recovered abroad is the same as the jurisdiction to restrain creditors from suing the bankrupt abroad.[41] In other words, the creditor can be ordered to refund if, at the time when he recovered the property, he was resident in England, and not otherwise.

Choice of law

In an English bankruptcy, a creditor, whether an alien or a British subject, can prove in accordance with the ordinary rules of English bankruptcy law for any debt which is due to him from the bankrupt, no matter whether the debt is governed by English law or by foreign law. Of course, it may be necessary to refer to foreign law in order to discover whether a debt governed by a foreign proper law is valid by that law. But subject to this, a foreigner proving for a foreign debt stands in the same position as an English creditor proving for an English debt.[42] The distribution of the assets among the creditors; the priorities among the creditors *inter se*[43]; the rules of double proof in the case of partnerships[44]; set-off and limitation of actions: these are all determined in accordance with English law *qua lex fori*.

Effect of English bankruptcy as a discharge of debts

The general rule of the English conflict of laws is that the discharge of a contract or debt depends upon the proper law of the contract.[45] Thus, a discharge in accordance with the proper law of the contract or debt is a valid discharge in England, and a discharge not in accordance with the proper law of the contract or debt is not a valid discharge in England. But an order of discharge under an English bankruptcy is an exception to the second limb of this proposition. An order of discharge under an English bankruptcy releases the debtor from all debts provable in bankruptcy[46]; and these debts, as we have just seen, are not limited to those which are governed by English law. Hence a discharge from any debt or liability

---

[39] Cheshire and North, pp. 566–567.
[40] See *ante*, p. 432.
[41] See *ante*, p. 436.
[42] *Ex p. Holthausen* (1874) L.R. 9 Ch.App. 722; *Re Wiskemann* (1923) 92 L.J.Ch. 349.
[43] *Ex p. Melbourn* (1870) L.R. 6 Ch.App. 64; *Thurburn* v. *Steward* (1871) L.R. 3 P.C. 478.
[44] *Re Doetsch* [1896] 2 Ch. 836.
[45] *Ante*, pp. 295–296.
[46] Bankruptcy Act 1914, s.28(2).

under an English bankruptcy operates irrespective of the proper law of the contract or debt.[47] Its effect is universal.

FOREIGN BANKRUPTCIES

Jurisdiction of foreign courts

Courts in Scotland and Northern Ireland. Section 121 of the Bankruptcy Act 1914 provides that any order made by a bankruptcy court in England, Scotland or Northern[48] Ireland shall be enforced in the courts having jurisdiction in bankruptcy in the other two countries as if the order had been made by the court which is required to enforce it. The effect of this enactment appears to be that the courts in England cannot question the jurisdiction of the courts in Scotland or Northern Ireland to make a bankruptcy order, and vice versa. At any rate, the view taken in the Scottish courts is that they cannot question the bankruptcy jurisdiction of the English courts,[49] though English authority for the converse proposition is lacking.

Courts in other foreign countries. It is uncertain when English courts will recognise the jurisdiction of courts outside the United Kingdom to adjudicate a debtor bankrupt, because they have had few opportunities of considering the matter. It was at one time supposed that English courts would recognise the bankruptcy jurisdiction of foreign courts only if the debtor was domiciled in the foreign country.[50] But it has since become clear that they will also do so if the debtor submitted to the jurisdiction of the foreign court, whether by presenting the petition himself,[51] or by appealing against the adjudication,[52] or by appearing in the proceedings at some stage either personally or by his counsel or solicitor.[53] It is probable that English courts would recognise the bankruptcy jurisdiction of the courts of a foreign country in which the debtor carried on business.[54] It seems unlikely that the mere presence of assets in the foreign country would be regarded as a sufficient ground for jurisdiction.[55]

Effect in England of foreign bankruptcy as an assignment of property

Bankruptcy in Scotland or Northern Ireland. So far as the law of the United Kingdom is concerned, a Scottish or Northern Irish bankruptcy

---

[47] *Gill* v. *Barron* (1868) L.R. 2 P.C. 157, 175–176; *Ellis* v. *M'Henry* (1871) L.R. 6 C.P. 228, 235–236.

[48] The restriction to Northern Ireland follows, as we have seen, from s.2 of the Irish Free State (Consequential Adaptation of Enactments) Order 1923 (S.R. & O. No. 405).

[49] *Wilkie* v. *Cathcart* (1870) 9 M. 168, 171; *Salaman* v. *Tod*, 1911 S.C. 1214, 1220, 1222.

[50] *Re Blithman* (1866) L.R. 2 Eq. 23; *cf. Re Hayward* [1897] 1 Ch. 905.

[51] *Re Davidson's Settlement* (1873) L.R. 15 Eq. 383; *Re Lawson's Trusts* [1896] 1 Ch. 175; *Re Burke* (1919) 54 L.J. 430.

[52] *Bergerem* v. *Marsh* (1921) 6 B. & C.R. 195.

[53] *Re Anderson* [1911] 1 K.B. 896, 900, 902; *Re Craig* (1917) 86 L.J.Ch. 62. See Raeburn (1949) 26 B.Y.I.L. 177, 195 *et seq.*

[54] There is some Scottish authority to this effect: *Obers* v. *Paton's Trustee* (1897) 24 R. 719, 732, 733; *Home's Trustees* v. *Home's Trustees*, 1926 S.L.T. 214.

[55] See *Re Artola Hermanos* (1890) 24 Q.B.D. 640, 649.

passes the bankrupt's movable or immovable property wherever situated to his trustee or assignee.[56] The property in England will pass to the Scottish trustee or Northern Irish assignee subject to any charges which are recognised by English law; and neither the English doctrine of relation back nor its Scottish or Northern Irish equivalents will apply to property in England. Thus in *Galbraith* v. *Grimshaw*,[57] the House of Lords held that a Scottish trustee in bankruptcy was not entitled to a judgment debt due to the bankrupt which was situate in England and which the English judgment creditor was in process of garnishing when the judgment debtor was adjudicated bankrupt. The title of the trustee would have prevailed if garnishee proceedings had taken place in Scotland[58] or if the bankruptcy proceedings had taken place in England.[59] Yet the House of Lords held that neither the English doctrine of relation back nor its Scottish equivalent applied and that the trustee therefore fell between two stools.

Galbraith v. *Grimshaw* was decided under the Bankruptcy Act 1883 and the Bankruptcy (Scotland) Act 1856, both of which are now repealed. It is possible that some extra words introduced into section 97(3) of the Bankruptcy (Scotland) Act 1913, which replaces section 102(3) of the Act of 1856, may lead to a different result in the case of real estate in England, if the Scottish act and warrant of confirmation in favour of the trustee is registered in the English bankruptcy court.[60]

Bankruptcy in other foreign countries. English courts recognise that bankruptcy, or any proceeding in the nature of bankruptcy, in any country outside the United Kingdom whose courts are recognised by English law as having jurisdiction over a debtor operates as an assignment to the foreign trustee, assignee, curator or syndic in bankruptcy of all the debtor's movables situate in England, if that is its effect under the foreign law.[61] The property in England will pass to the foreign trustee subject to any charges recognised by English law, even if these charges would be postponed under the foreign law to the claim of the creditors, and even if under an English bankruptcy the charges would be defeated by the title of the trustee in bankruptcy. In the old case of *Solomons* v. *Ross*,[62] it was held that a Dutch curator appointed by the Chamber of Desolate Estates in Amsterdam was entitled to a debt due to the bankrupt which was situate in England and which an English creditor had begun to attach shortly before the adjudication in bankruptcy. But in *Galbraith* v. *Grimshaw*[63] the

---

[56] Irish Bankrupt and Insolvent Act 1857, ss.267, 268; Bankruptcy (Scotland) Act 1913, s.97. As to the scope of s.97, see Anton, p.439.

[57] [1910] A.C. 508; *cf. Singer* v. *Fry* (1915) 84 L.J.K.B. 2025.

[58] Bankruptcy (Scotland) Act 1856, s.108; now Bankruptcy (Scotland) Act 1913, s.104.

[59] Bankruptcy Act 1883, s.45; now Bankruptcy Act 1914, s.40.

[60] See Dicey and Morris, p. 715.

[61] *Solomons* v. *Ross* (1764) 1 H.Bl. 131, n.; also reported in Wallis & Lyne's Irish Chancery Reports (1839) 59, n.; *Jollet* v. *Deponthieu* (1769) 1 H.Bl. 132, n.; *Alivon* v. *Furnival* (1834) 1 Cr. M. & R. 277; *Re Blithman* (1866) L.R. 2 Eq. 23; *Re Davidson's Settlement* (1873) L.R. 15 Eq. 383; *Re Lawson's Trusts* [1896] 1 Ch. 175; *Re Anderson* [1911] 1 K.B. 896; *Re Craig* (1917) 86 L.J.Ch. 62; *Bergerem* v. *Marsh* (1921) 6 B. & C.R. 195.

[62] *Supra*; discussed by Nadelmann (1946) 9 M.L.R. 154.

[63] [1910] A.C. 508, 511, *supra. Cf. Levasseur* v. *Mason & Barry Ltd.* [1891] 2 Q.B. 73.

House of Lords refused to follow this decision; and Lord Loreburn said that the test was: "Could the bankrupt have assigned to the trustee, at the date when the trustee's title accrued, the debt or assets in question situated in England?" The rule in *Galbraith* v. *Grimshaw* may now be subject to an exception as regards real estate situated in England in a Scottish bankruptcy[64]; but it is of general application as between attaching creditors and trustees in bankruptcy appointed outside the United Kingdom. But, of course, the title of the foreign trustee would prevail if the foreign adjudication in bankruptcy preceded the attachment or garnishment of the debt.[65]

A foreign bankruptcy in any country outside the United Kingdom does not operate as an assignment of the bankrupt's immovables situated in England.[66] It has, however, twice been held that a bankruptcy taking place in a country of the Commonwealth outside the United Kingdom may work a forfeiture of the bankrupt's life interest in English land under a clause in a will providing for forfeiture on bankruptcy.[67] It has since been held that, on the application by the trustee in a bankruptcy taking place in the Isle of Man, the English court has jurisdiction under section 122 of the Bankruptcy Act 1914 to appoint a receiver of the rents and profits of English land, with authority to sell it and retain the proceeds of sale as trustee for the benefit of the creditors, but without prejudice to the rights of prior incumbrancers.[68] And it has also been held that the court has jurisdiction, without the aid of section 122, to make a similar order on the application of the trustee in bankruptcy appointed by the court of a politically foreign country.[69]

If a debtor is adjudicated bankrupt in more countries than one, the question arises whether property of his which comes into existence, or is discovered, between the dates of the two adjudications in bankruptcy passes to the trustee in the earlier or the later bankruptcy. The answer appears to be that it passes to the trustee in the earlier bankruptcy,[70] notwithstanding section 39 of the Bankruptcy Act 1914, which provides that where there are successive bankruptcies, any property acquired by the bankrupt since he was last adjudged bankrupt shall vest in the trustee in the subsequent bankruptcy. This section does not apply if the first bankruptcy took place in England and the second in a foreign country, or vice versa.

If the English and the foreign bankruptcies are practically simultaneous, the court has jurisdiction to sanction an agreement between the English and the foreign trustee in bankruptcy for pooling all the assets and distributing them rateably among the creditors in England and the creditors in the foreign country.[71]

---

[64] *Ante*, p. 439.
[65] *Galbraith* v. *Grimshaw* [1910] A.C. 508, 510.
[66] *Waite* v. *Bingley* (1882) 21 Ch.D. 674, 682; *Re Levy's Trusts* (1885) 30 Ch.D. 119, 123.
[67] *Re Aylwin's Trusts* (1873) L.R. 16 Eq. 585; *Re Levy's Trusts, supra*.
[68] *Re Osborn* (1931–1932) 15 B. & C.R. 189. For s.122, see *ante*, p. 435.
[69] *Re Kooperman* (1928) 13 B. & C.R. 49.
[70] *Re Anderson* [1911] 1 K.B. 896; *Re Temple* [1947] Ch. 345.
[71] *Re Macfadyen & Co.* [1908] 1 K.B. 675.

Effect in England of foreign bankruptcy as a discharge of debts

Bankruptcy in Scotland or Northern Ireland. A discharge from any debt or liability under a Scottish[72] or Northern Irish[73] bankruptcy, like a discharge under an English bankruptcy,[74] is a discharge therefrom in England, irrespective of the proper law of the contract. This is because the Bankruptcy (Scotland) Act 1913 and the principal Northern Irish Bankruptcy Act, *i.e.* the Irish Bankrupt and Insolvent Act 1857, are enactments of the United Kingdom Parliament which are binding on the English courts.

It was held in *Re Nelson*[75] that a composition with creditors under the Irish Bankruptcy Acts does not operate as a discharge in England from a debt due to a non-assenting English creditor, because the relevant sections[76] were not, on their true construction, intended to operate outside Ireland. It has never been decided whether a composition with creditors under the Bankruptcy (Scotland) Act 1913 operates as a discharge in England.

Bankruptcy in other foreign countries. A discharge from any debt or liability under the bankruptcy law of any foreign country outside the United Kingdom is a discharge therefrom in England if, and only if, it is a discharge under the proper law of the contract. In considering whether such a discharge is a defence to an action in England to recover the debt, English courts have not regarded the foreign discharge as an order of a foreign court, and therefore have not considered whether the foreign court had jurisdiction over the bankrupt, nor whether its order purported to have extra-territorial effect. Instead, they have concentrated their attention on whether the discharge operated under the proper law of the contract. A discharge of a debt under the bankruptcy law of the foreign country whose law governs the contract is a valid discharge in England.[77] Conversely, a discharge of a debt under the bankruptcy law of any other foreign country outside the United Kingdom is not a valid discharge in England.[78] Hence it follows that a discharge under an English, Scottish or Northern Irish bankruptcy is a discharge from a debt governed by the law of, *e.g.* Victoria or France; but a discharge under an Australian or French bankruptcy is not a valid discharge in England, unless it is a discharge under the proper law of the contract.

Another curious result follows from concentrating attention on the proper law of the contract. If the bankruptcy takes place in a country other than that of the proper law, the discharge is not recognised in England, and

---

[72] *Sidaway* v. *Hay* (1824) 3 B. & C. 12.
[73] *Ferguson* v. *Spencer* (1840) 1 M. & G. 987; *Simpson* v. *Mirabita* (1869) L.R. 4 Q.B. 257.
[74] *Ante*, pp. 437–438.
[75] [1918] 1 K.B. 459.
[76] Irish Bankrupt and Insolvent Act 1857, ss.346, 347; Bankruptcy (Ireland) Amendment Act 1872, s.64.
[77] *Potter* v. *Brown* (1804) 5 East 124; *Gardiner* v. *Houghton* (1862) 2 B. & S. 743; *Ellis* v. *M'Henry* (1871) L.R. 6 C.P. 228, 234.
[78] *Smith* v. *Buchanan* (1800) 1 East 6; *Phillips* v. *Allan* (1828) 8 B. & C. 477; *Bartley* v. *Hodges* (1861) 1 B. & S. 375; *Ellis* v. *M'Henry, supra,* at p. 234; *Gibbs* v. *Société Industrielle des Métaux* (1890) 25 Q.B.D. 399.

the debtor remains liable on the debt. But (assuming that the foreign court had jurisdiction over the debtor[79]) English law recognises that his assets have passed to the foreign trustee in bankruptcy.[80] Hence English law says, almost in the same breath, that the debtor remains liable on the debt in England, and yet has no assets with which to satisfy it. A possible way of escape from this impasse would exist if the proper law of the contract recognised the discharge in bankruptcy as valid, and English law also recognised it as valid by way of renvoi from the proper law.[81]

---

[79] *Ante*, p. 438.
[80] *Ante*, pp. 438–440.
[81] Dicey and Morris, p. 722.

Chapter 28

CORPORATIONS

STATUS

THREE questions arise here: will English law recognise the existence of a foreign corporation, its amalgamation with another foreign corporation, and its dissolution?

Existence

English law recognises the existence of a corporation duly created in a foreign country and will allow it to sue and be sued in England in its corporate capacity. The law of the place of incorporation determines the person or persons who are entitled to act on behalf of the corporation.[1] Companies incorporated outside England or Scotland which established a place of business in Great Britain are (as "overseas companies") subject to certain obligations under Part X of the Companies Act 1948. For purposes of the conflict of laws the most important of these obligations is the duty to file with the Registrar of Companies the name and address of a person resident in Great Britain who is authorised to accept service of process on behalf of the company.[2] As we have seen,[3] this provides an effective mode for the service of process on foreign companies.

Amalgamation

If a foreign corporation is amalgamated with another foreign corporation under the law of the place of incorporation, the new entity will be recognised in England. If that law provides for the new corporation to succeed to the assets and liabilities of its predecessors, it will be recognised in England as having done so. But the law of the place of incorporation cannot discharge the new company from the liabilities of the old unless it happens to be the proper law of the contract giving rise to those liabilities.

Authority for the above statements is to be found in two remarkable cases decided by the House of Lords in 1958 and 1961. In *National Bank of Greece and Athens S.A.* v. *Metliss*[4]:

> The National Mortgage Bank of Greece issued 7 per cent. sterling bonds in 1927. Principal was repayable in 1957. The bonds were guaranteed by the National Bank of Greece. English law was the proper law of the bonds and of the guarantee. No interest was paid

---

[1] *Bank of Ethiopia* v. *National Bank of Egypt* [1937] Ch. 513; *Banco de Bilbao* v. *Sancha* [1938] 2 K.B. 176; *Carl Zeiss Stiftung* v. *Rayner and Keeler Ltd. (No. 2)* [1967] 1 A.C. 853.
[2] Companies Act 1948, ss.407(1)(*c*), 412.
[3] *Ante*, p. 66.
[4] [1958] A.C. 509.

from 1941 onwards and in 1949 the Greek Government declared a moratorium on the bonds. This would have afforded both banks a good defence if they had been sued in Greece, but not if they had been sued in England. In 1953 the National Bank of Greece and the Bank of Athens were amalgamated into the National Bank of Greece and Athens under a Greek Law No. 2292 of 1953 which provided that the new bank should become the universal successor to the rights and obligations of the old ones. Unlike the National Mortgage Bank of Greece and the National Bank of Greece, the Bank of Athens and therefore the new bank owned assets in England. A bondholder brought an action against it as guarantor of the bonds claiming $14\frac{1}{2}$ years of interest. On July 12, 1956, Sellers J. gave judgment in his favour for six years' arrears of interest (the rest was statute-barred). This judgment was affirmed by the Court of Appeal and the House of Lords.

The sequel to this case was *Adams* v. *National Bank of Greece S.A.*[5]:

On July 16, 1956, four days after the date of Sellers J.'s judgment in the previous case, the Greek Government retrospectively amended Law No. 2292 of 1953 by excepting obligations under bonds payable in gold or foreign currency from the obligations taken over by the new bank. It was held by the House of Lords, reversing the Court of Appeal, that a bondholder could nevertheless recover arrears of interest from the new bank.

Dissolution

Similarly, English law will recognise that a foreign corporation has been dissolved under the law of the place of incorporation, for "the will of the sovereign authority which created it can also destroy it."[6] The consequences of this have been worked out in a long series of cases on the effect of Soviet Russian decrees purporting to dissolve banking and insurance companies during the Bolshevik revolution. At first it was held that the Soviet decrees declaring banking and insurance to be state monopolies did not have the effect of dissolving the Russian companies engaged in those activities, but merely of winding them up, and they were allowed to sue and be sued in England.[7] But from 1932 onwards it has been consistently held, in the light of more precise evidence as to the effect of the decrees in Soviet law, that the Russian banks were in fact dissolved in or about December 1917 or January 1918.[8] This has brought a number of problems in its train.[9]

Any foreign corporation may establish a branch in England, and many of

---

[5] [1961] A.C. 255. Both cases are discussed by Grodecki (1961) 24 M.L.R. 701.
[6] *Lazard Brothers* v. *Midland Bank* [1933] A.C. 289, 297, *per* Lord Wright.
[7] *Russian Commercial and Industrial Bank* v. *Comptoire d'Escompte de Mulhouse* [1925] A.C. 112; *Banque Internationale de Commerce de Petrograd* v. *Goukassow* [1925] A.C. 150; *Employers' Liability Insurance Corporation Ltd.* v. *Sedgwick, Collins & Co. Ltd.* [1927] A.C. 95.
[8] *Russian and English Bank* v. *Baring Brothers Ltd.* [1932] 1 Ch. 435; *Lazard Brothers* v. *Midland Bank* [1933] A.C. 289.
[9] See M. Mann (1955) 18 M.L.R. 8.

the Russian banks did so. Others carried on mercantile business in England through agents. All these had assets and liabilities in England when they were dissolved. Difficulties arose when the English branch of a dissolved Russian bank continued to transact banking business in England in ignorance of the dissolution or of its precise legal effect. For one consequence of the dissolution is that all the English assets of a dissolved foreign corporation vest in the Crown as *bona vacantia*,[10] even though the decree of dissolution purports to vest them in the foreign State. This is because a foreign governmental decree purporting to confiscate private property has no effect on property in England.[11] Another consequence of the dissolution is that neither the dissolved foreign corporation nor its unincorporated English branch can sue[12] or be sued[13] in the English Courts. Hence the English branch of a dissolved foreign corporation and those who meddle in its affairs are in an unenviable position. It has been graphically described as "a submerged wreck floating on the ocean of commerce," with "neither compass nor officers nor crew: no one who would direct its movements."[14] But, as we shall see, the position has been largely rectified by a bold interpretation of the winding-up provisions of the Companies Acts 1929 and 1948.

WINDING UP

Jurisdiction of the English courts

The English courts have jurisdiction to wind up any company registered in England,[15] even though it was formed solely to carry on business abroad. They have no jurisdiction to wind up a company registered in Scotland[16] or (with one possible exception[17]) in Northern Ireland.[18]

The courts also have jurisdiction to wind up an unregistered company, the definition of which includes a company incorporated outside the United Kingdom,[19]

(a) if the company is (*i.e.* has been[20]) dissolved, or has ceased to carry on business, or is carrying on business only for the purpose of winding up its affairs; or

---

[10] *Russian and English Bank* v. *Baring Brothers Ltd.* [1936] A.C. 405, 444; *Re Banque Industrielle de Moscou* [1952] Ch. 919; *Re Banque des Marchands de Moscou* [1952] 1 All E.R. 1269, 1277; *Re Azoff-Don Commercial Bank* [1954] Ch. 315.

[11] *Re Russian Bank for Foreign Trade* [1933] Ch. 745, 766–767; *Re Banque des Marchands de Moscou, Royal Exchange* v. *The Liquidator* [1952] 1 All E.R. 1269; *Re Banque des Marchands de Moscou (No. 2)* [1954] 1 W.L.R. 1108; *ante*, Chap. 22.

[12] *Russian and English Bank* v. *Baring Brothers Ltd.* [1932] 1 Ch. 435.

[13] *Lazard Brothers* v. *Midland Bank* [1933] A.C. 289.

[14] *Re Russian Bank for Foreign Trade* [1933] Ch. 745, 764, *per* Maugham J.

[15] Companies Act 1948, s.218(1).

[16] *Ibid.* s.220(1).

[17] A company registered in Northern Ireland which has carried on business in Great Britain and has ceased to carry on business in Great Britain could be wound up under s.400 of the Act, but not under s.399: see Dicey and Morris, p. 737; *post*, p. 446.

[18] Companies Act 1948, s.461(1).

[19] *Ibid.* s.398. See *Re Matheson Brothers Ltd.* (1884) 27 Ch.D. 225; *Re Commercial Bank of South Australia* (1886) 33 Ch.D. 174.

[20] *Re Family Endowment Society* (1870) L.R. 5 Ch.App. 118.

(b) if the company is unable to pay its debts; or

(c) if the court is of the opinion that it is just and equitable that the company should be wound up.[21]

But there is no jurisdiction to wind up an unregistered company which has a principal place of business in Scotland or Northern Ireland but no principal place of business in England.[22]

It was at one time supposed that there was no jurisdiction to wind up an unregistered company unless it had a place of business in England.[23] But now it is clear that there is jurisdiction if there are assets in England and there are persons who would benefit from the winding-up order.[24] The assets can be assets of any description: a claim against the company which would vest in the claimant under the Third Parties (Rights against Insurers) Act 1930 in the event of a winding-up order being made has been held to be sufficient.[25] Even if there are no assets in England and the company has no place of business here, it may be wound up if that would benefit creditors, *e.g.* if they are employees of the company unfairly dismissed who might be entitled to payments from the Department of Employment out of its redundancy fund under section 122 of the Employment Protection (Consolidation) Act 1978, if the company is ordered to be wound up.[26]

It is under the first of the above heads (namely, that the company is dissolved) that the dissolved Russian banks have been wound up in England.[27] The difficulty that the bank has no assets because they have already vested in the Crown as *bona vacantia* has been surmounted by treating the Crown's title as defeasible and as defeated by the making of a winding-up order.[28]

In the Companies Act 1928 there appeared for the first time what is now section 400 of the Companies Act 1948,[29] which provides that

"where a company incorporated outside Great Britain which has been carrying on business in Great Britain ceases to carry on business in Great Britain, it may be wound up as an unregistered company, notwithstanding that it has been dissolved or otherwise ceased to exist as a company under or by virtue of the laws of the country under which it was incorporated."

---

[21] Companies Act 1948, s.399(5), re-enacting Companies Act 1929, s.338(1)(*d*) and earlier legislation.

[22] Companies Act 1948, s.399(2) and (3).

[23] *Re Lloyd Generale Italiano* (1885) 29 Ch.D. 219.

[24] *Banque des Marchands de Moscou* v. *Kindersley* [1951] Ch. 112; *Re Azoff-Don Commercial Bank* [1954] Ch. 315.

[25] *Re Compania Merabello San Nicholas S.A.* [1973] Ch. 75; *Re Allobrogia S.S. Corporation* [1978] 3 All E.R. 423.

[26] *Re Eloc Electro-Optieck B.V.* [1982] Ch. 43.

[27] *Re Russian and English Bank* [1932] 1 Ch. 663; *Re Russian Bank for Foreign Trade* [1933] Ch. 745; *Banque des Marchands de Moscou* v. *Kindersley, supra; Re Azoff-Don Commercial Bank, supra.*

[28] *Russian and English Bank* v. *Baring Brothers Ltd.* [1936] A.C. 405, 426–427, *per* Lord Atkin; *Re Banque Industrielle de Moscou* [1952] Ch. 919; *Re Azoff-Don Commercial Bank, supra.*

[29] Re-enacting Companies Act 1929, s.338(2).

This section was presumably designed to enable the dissolved Russian companies to be wound up in England. But it has remained a dead letter, because it has been held not to be retrospective, and therefore not applicable to companies dissolved before 1929.[30] Although this view has been challenged,[31] it has never been overruled, and the Russian banks have, as we have seen, been wound up under another section of the Act.

Effect of an English winding-up order

The effect of an English winding-up order on the property of the company is quite different from that of an adjudication in bankruptcy on the property of the debtor.[32] For one thing, the Companies Acts do not extend to the Commonwealth overseas.[33] For another, there is no question of the whole of the company's property wherever situated vesting automatically in the liquidator.[34] Instead the making of a winding-up order terminates the company's beneficial interest in its property and impresses it with a trust for its application for the benefit of the company's creditors and (if there is a surplus) shareholders.[35] In particular, the liquidator must take into his custody or under his control all the property and things in action to which the company is or appears to be entitled.[36] However, the court may provide in the order that the liquidator is not to get in assets situated outside England, or settle a list of foreign creditors, without first obtaining a direction from the court.[37]

Recovery of debts due to the company. Section 245(1) of the Companies Act 1948[38] provides that "the liquidator in a winding up by the court shall have power, with the sanction either of the court or of the committee of inspection, to bring any action in the name of the company and on behalf of the company." In *Russian and English Bank* v. *Baring Brothers Ltd.*[39] it was held by a bare majority of the House of Lords, reversing both the courts below, that under this section the liquidator could bring an action to recover the assets of a dissolved Russian bank, even though it had been dissolved under Russian law, and even though an action by the bank claiming precisely similar relief, but brought before the winding-up order, had been stayed.[40] Lord Atkin said[41]:

> "The legislature has provided that a dissolved foreign corporation may be wound up in accordance with the provisions of the Companies Act.

---

[30] *Re Russian and English Bank* [1932] 1 Ch. 663.
[31] *Russian and English Bank* v. *Baring Brothers Ltd.* [1936] A.C. 405, *per* Lord Blanesburgh at p. 416; *per* Lord Atkin at pp. 424–425.
[32] See *ante*, pp. 433–436.
[33] *New Zealand Loan and Mercantile Agency Co. Ltd.* v. *Morrison* [1898] A.C. 349, 357.
[34] *Ibid.* at p. 358.
[35] *Re Oriental Inland Steam Co.* (1874) L.R. 9 Ch.App. 557, 559, 560; *Ayerst* v. *C. & K. (Construction) Ltd.* [1976] A.C. 167.
[36] Companies Act 1948, s.243(1).
[37] *Re Hibernian Merchants Ltd.* [1958] Ch. 76.
[38] Re-enacting Companies Act 1929, s.191(1).
[39] [1936] A.C. 405.
[40] *Russian and English Bank* v. *Baring Brothers Ltd.* [1932] 1 Ch. 435.
[41] [1936] A.C. 405, 427–428.

The provisions of the Companies Act as to winding up are only applicable to corporations which are in existence. Are we to say that the legislative enactment is completely futile; or is there another solution? My Lords, I think that we are entitled to imply, indeed I think it is a necessary implication, that the dissolved foreign company is to be wound up as though it had not been dissolved, and therefore continued in existence."

Thus the dissolved foreign corporation is wound up as though it had not been dissolved: it is revivified by the English winding-up order. This does not mean that English law calls a new corporation into existence on the ashes of the old. It means that English law only recognises the dissolution of a foreign corporation until a subsequent winding-up order is made in England. Thus the remarkable result follows that a corporation owing its existence to foreign law can be dissolved under foreign law, with the result that all its English assets pass to the Crown as *bona vacantia*: yet on the making of a winding-up order it rises from the grave, perhaps twenty or thirty years later, and can sue to recover property which for all that time has been at least notionally the property of the Crown. Yet any other conclusion would have meant that the English winding-up order was a hollow farce.

Payment of creditors of the company. It is now well settled that pre-dissolution assets may be got in, pre-dissolution debtors sued and pre-dissolution creditors paid. But what if the corporation's English branch or agents carried on business during the interregnum between its dissolution under foreign law and the making of a winding up order? Is the effect of such an order to revivify the corporation retrospectively, or only with effect from its date? At a later stage of his speech in *Russian and English Bank* v. *Baring Brothers Ltd.*[42] Lord Atkin said: "Nor is it any easier to confine the distribution to assets existing at the date of the dissolution among creditors in existence at the same date." In reliance on this observation, Wynn Parry J. held[43] that the English branch of a dissolved Russian bank could operate a banking account during the interregnum between the dissolution of the bank under Russian law and the making of a winding-up order. But his attention was not called to an earlier inconsistent decision of Vaisey J. where he held[44] that an agent employed by the corporation during the interregnum could not prove for his commission in the subsequent winding up. Vaisey J. said:

"These metaphysical conceptions seem to me to be extremely difficult, and when there is a hypothesis on a hypothesis, such as one has when it is said that the non-existent bank was nonetheless deemed to be employing a non-appointed agent to conduct its non-existent

[42] [1936] A.C. 405, 429.
[43] *Re Russian Commercial and Industrial Bank* [1955] Ch. 148.
[44] *Re Banque des Marchands de Moscou, Wilenkin* v. *The Liquidator* [1952] 1 All E.R. 1269, 1277. See M. Mann (1952) 15 M.L.R. 479; (1955) 4 I.C.L.Q. 226.

affairs, one gets into a maze of metaphysics from which there is really no logical escape."

But though logic may be affronted, the view of Lord Atkin and of Wynn Parry J. seems much more realistic.

Foreign creditors are entitled to be paid *pari passu* with English creditors, because the liquidation is a liquidation of the company and not merely of its English affairs.[45] But since the winding-up order can only affect English assets and not foreign assets, there is a danger that English creditors may be prejudiced if all creditors, foreign as well as English, are entitled to share equally in the assets. This danger was to some extent mitigated by the decision of Maugham J. in *Re Russian Bank for Foreign Trade*,[46] where he held that a creditor could not prove for his debt if it was situated in Russia or governed by Russian law, because in that event it was extinguished by the confiscatory Russian decrees. Yet creditors so excluded have nearly always been English creditors. Neither the Soviet State nor any Soviet citizen has ever laid claim to the assets of a dissolved Russian company in an English winding up.

Restraining creditors from suing abroad. The Companies Act 1948 provides that when a winding-up order has been made no action or proceeding against the company is to be continued or commenced without the leave of the court.[47] This provision restrains proceedings in courts throughout the United Kingdom,[48] but it does not apply to proceedings in courts outside the United Kingdom.[49] However, a creditor who is subject to the jurisdiction of the court may be restrained from continuing or commencing proceedings against a company outside the United Kingdom by an exercise of the court's inherent but discretionary power to restrain foreign proceedings.[50] The justification for exercising the power is that the creditor is thereby prevented from obtaining more than his fair share of the assets.

Compelling creditors to refund property obtained abroad. The Act also provides that any attachment, sequestration, distress or execution put in force against the estate or effects of the company after the commencement of the winding up shall be void.[51] There are also elaborate provisions invalidating execution against the estate or effects of the company in Scotland.[52] The Act does not make provision for the invalidity of executions

---

[45] *Re Azoff-Don Commercial Bank* [1954] Ch. 315.
[46] [1933] Ch. 745, 766–767; followed in *Re Banque des Marchands de Moscou, Royal Exchange Assurance* v. *The Liquidator* [1952] 1 All E.R. 1269; *Re Banque des Marchands de Moscou (No. 2)* [1954] 1 W.L.R. 1108.
[47] s.231. For the position between presentation of the petition and the making of the order see s.226, and *Re Dynamics Corporation of America* [1973] 1 W.L.R. 63.
[48] *Re International Pulp and Paper Co. Ltd.* (1876) 3 Ch.D. 594; *Re Hermann Loog Ltd.* (1887) 36 Ch.D. 502; *Re Thurso New Gas Co. Ltd.* (1889) 42 Ch.D. 486; *Martin* v. *Port of Manchester Insurance Co.* 1934 S.C. 143; *Boyd* v. *Lee Guinness Ltd.* [1963] N.Ir. 49.
[49] *Re Vocalion (Foreign) Ltd.* [1932] 2 Ch. 196.
[50] *Re North Carolina Estate Co.* (1889) 5 T.L.R. 328; *Re Central Sugar Factories of Brazil* [1894] 1 Ch. 369; *Re Vocalion (Foreign) Ltd., supra.*
[51] s.228(1).
[52] s.327(2).

elsewhere. However, an unsecured creditor who levies execution on effects situated outside Great Britain after the commencement of the winding up may, if he is subject to the jurisdiction of the court, be compelled to surrender the fruits of his execution for the general benefit of the creditors.[53] At any rate this is so if the creditor seeks to prove in the liquidation for other sums due to him from the company.[54] But in the converse situation, an English judgment creditor has been allowed to levy execution on the assets of a foreign company, notwithstanding that a winding-up order was made in the country of incorporation after the date of the judgment and that the execution was void under the foreign law.[55]

Distribution of surplus assets. If a foreign company is being wound up in England and also in its country of incorporation, and there are surplus assets in the hands of the English liquidator after the creditors have been paid, he would normally hand them over to the foreign liquidator, because the English liquidation is regarded as ancillary to that which takes place in the country of incorporation.[56] However, this course is impracticable if, as in the Russian bank cases, there is no liquidation taking place in the country of incorporation and no machinery there for the payment of creditors or disposal of the assets. In such a case it has been held by Roxburgh J.[57] that the surplus assets are divisible among the former shareholders in such proportions as their shares bear to the total issued capital of the bank at the date of dissolution, and do not pass to the Crown as *bona vacantia*. His Lordship considered that the reasoning of Wynn Parry J. in *Re Azoff-Don Commercial Bank*[58] postponing the title of the Crown to the claims of creditors was equally applicable to the claims of beneficiaries. His conclusion was based on the uncontradicted evidence of a single expert witness who asserted that under Soviet law any surplus assets not caught by the Soviet confiscatory decrees would belong to the shareholders. When confronted with clause 2 of the Soviet Decree of January 26, 1918, which provided that "all bank shares are declared null and void and payment of dividends is unconditionally stopped," the witness replied that the Decree did not mean what it said, because in September 1917 Lenin had made a speech saying: "Do not be afraid of our project of nationalising the banks. No one will suffer the slightest injury. Anyone who had shares will after the nationalisation retain his money again in shares as before. Everyone who had a deposit will retain his deposit." The witness was positive that in Russia "you have to construe statutes in the light of speeches made by politicians, otherwise you get lost." Similar evidence by the same witness as to the effect of the same Decree had been rejected with incredulity by another judge twenty-five years earlier.[59]

---

[53] *Re Oriental Inland Steam Co.* (1874) L.R. 9 Ch.App. 557.
[54] *Ibid.*; see also *Re Vocalion (Foreign) Ltd.* [1932] 2 Ch. 196, 210.
[55] *Re Suidair International Airways Ltd.*[1951] Ch. 165.
[56] *Re Commercial Bank of South Australia* (1886) 33 Ch.D. 174, 178; *Re Vocalion (Foreign) Ltd.* [1932] 2 Ch. 196, 207.
[57] *Re Banque des Marchands de Moscou* [1958] Ch. 182. See M. Mann (1958) 21 M.L.R. 95.
[58] [1954] Ch. 315; *ante*, p. 446, n. 28.
[59] *Re Russian Bank for Foreign Trade* [1933] Ch. 745, 759–760, *per* Maugham J.

Part Eight

LAW OF PROCEDURE

CHAPTER 29

SUBSTANCE AND PROCEDURE

INTRODUCTION

THE rule that all matters of procedure are governed exclusively by the *lex fori* is one which is found in all systems of the conflict of laws. In English law this means that an English court will apply to a case containing foreign elements any rule of English law which, in its view, is procedural, and will refuse to apply any rule of foreign law which, in its view, is procedural. The reason for the rule is that it would be quite impracticable to have different kinds of process for cases containing foreign elements and purely domestic cases.

The principle is well established but the line between substance and procedure is a difficult one to draw. It is of course a question of characterisation; and we shall see how controversial that doctrine is.[1] At one time it was possible to say that "English lawyers give the widest possible extension to the meaning of the term 'procedure.' "[2] But in the last fifty years it has become clear, at any rate to academic writers, that a mechanical application of the procedural rules of the *lex fori* may well defeat the whole object of the conflict of laws and destroy rights which are still in existence in a foreign country or, conversely, allow claims which no longer exist in the land of their birth to be enforceable in England. The tendency of English courts to characterise the English Statute of Frauds and foreign statutes of limitation as procedural is particularly objectionable.[3]

It is essential that the line between substance (governed by the *lex causae*[4]) and procedure (governed by the *lex fori*) should be drawn with some regard for the reason for drawing it. Cook[5] suggested as a practical test: "How far can the court of the forum go in applying the rules taken from the foreign system of law without unduly hindering or inconveniencing itself?" Cook also pointed out that the line between substance and procedure may have to be drawn in one place for the purposes of the conflict of laws and in another place for other purposes, *e.g.* for the purpose of the rule that statutes affecting procedure are, but statutes affecting substance are not, presumed to have retrospective effect. This is not to say that the distinction may not be drawn in the same place for many purposes: it is merely to deny that it must necessarily be drawn in the same place for all purposes. The primary object of the rule that procedural matters are governed by the *lex*

---

[1] *Post,* Chap. 31.
[2] Dicey, 1st ed. (1896), p. 712.
[3] See *post,* pp. 454, 456–457; Lorenzen, pp. 134–135.
[4] A convenient shorthand expression denoting the applicable foreign law.
[5] Cook, p. 166.

fori is to obviate the inconvenience of conducting the trial of a case containing foreign elements in a manner with which the court is unfamiliar. If,
therefore, it is possible to apply a foreign rule, or to refrain from applying
an English rule, without causing any such inconvenience, those rules
should not necessarily be characterised as procedural for the purposes of
the conflict of laws.

STATUTES OF LIMITATION[6]

Traditionally, statutes of limitation are of two kinds: those which merely
bar the plaintiff's remedy, and those which extinguish his right. For the
purposes of the conflict of laws, statutes of the former kind are procedural,
while statutes of the latter kind are substantive. Most English statutes of
limitation are procedural. But sections 3 and 17 of the Limitation Act 1980
are probably substantive, since they extinguish the title of the former
owner.

Sometimes a statute creates an entirely new right of action unknown to
the common law and at the same time imposes a shorter period of limitation than that applicable under the general law. The Fatal Accidents Act
1846 (now replaced by the Fatal Accidents Act 1976) is a good example:
under section 3 the limitation period was twelve months, and is now three
years.[7] There is American and Scottish authority for the proposition that
such special statutes of limitation are not procedural but substantive.[8]

The rule that foreign statutes of limitation are characterised as procedural if they merely bar the remedy[9] is open to a number of criticisms.
(1) The distinction between right and remedy is an unreal one, for "a right
for which the legal remedy is barred is not much of a right."[10] (2) The rule
may bar a claim which is still alive in the country where it arose, *e.g.* if the
English period of limitation is shorter than the foreign one.[11] (3) Conversely, the rule may work hardship on a debtor in the opposite situation if,
in reliance on the foreign law, he has destroyed his receipts. (4) The rule
may encourage forum-shopping. (5) It would be no more difficult for an
English court to apply a foreign statute of limitations than any other rule of
foreign law. Not to do so in a situation where the foreign statute of limitations, unlike most other foreign rules of procedure, would determine the
outcome of the litigation seems perverse.

The Law Commission has recommended[12] that all foreign periods of
limitation, whether characterised as substantive or procedural by the
foreign law, should be characterised as substantive for the purposes of the

[6] See Lorenzen, Chap. 12; Falconbridge, Chap. 12; Ailes (1932) 31 Mich.L.Rev. 474.
[7] Limitation Act 1980, s.12(2).
[8] *The Harrisburg,* 119 U.S. 199 (1886); *Davis* v. *Mills,* 194 U.S. 451 (1904); *M'Elroy* v. *M'Allister,* 1949 S.C. 110, 125–128, 137.
[9] *Huber* v. *Steiner* (1835) 2 Bing.N.C. 202; *Harris* v. *Quine* (1869) L.R. 4 Q.B. 653; *Alliance
Bank of Simla* v. *Carey* (1880) 5 C.P.D. 429; *S.A. de Prayon* v. *Koppel* (1933) 77 S.J. 800.
[10] Leflar, p. 253.
[11] *British Linen Co.* v. *Drummond* (1830) 10 B. & C. 903.
[12] Law Com. No. 114 (1982).

English rules of the conflict of laws. The Foreign Limitation Periods Act 1984 gives effect to this recommendation.

EVIDENCE

"The law of evidence" said Lord Brougham[13] "is the *lex fori* which governs the courts. Whether a witness is competent or not; whether a certain matter requires to be proved by writing or not; whether certain evidence proves a certain fact or not; that is to be determined by the law of the country where the question arises, and where the court sits to enforce it." On the other hand, "it is not everything that appears in a treatise on the law of evidence that is to be classified internationally as adjective law, but only provisions of a technical or procedural character—for instance, rules as to the admissibility of hearsay evidence or what matters may be noticed judicially."[14] Thus, the *lex causae* generally determines what are the facts in issue[15]; and it may do so by providing that no evidence need, or may, be given as to certain matters, for instance as to compliance, or failure to comply, with certain formalities of a marriage ceremony. Such provisions are substantive.[16] On the other hand the *lex fori* determines how the facts in issue must be proved.

The following problems in the law of evidence call for special consideration.

Admissibility

Questions as to the admissibility of evidence are decided in accordance with the *lex fori*.[17] Thus a document may be received in evidence by the English court although it is inadmissible by the *lex causae*.[18] Conversely, copies of foreign documents are generally inadmissible in England although they may be admissible by the *lex causae*.[19] But this rule is now subject to a statutory exception. Under the Evidence (Foreign, Dominion and Colonial Documents) Act 1933,[20] the Crown has power to make Orders in Council providing that official and properly authenticated copies of foreign public registers shall be admissible in the United Kingdom to prove the contents of such registers.

A distinction has been drawn between extrinsic evidence adduced to interpret a written document, *e.g.* a contract, and extrinsic evidence adduced to add to, vary or contradict its terms. The admissibility of the former is a question of interpretation, governed by the proper law of the con-

---

[13] *Bain* v. *Whitehaven and Furness Ry.* (1850) 3 H.L.C. 1, 19.
[14] *Mahadervan* v. *Mahadervan* [1964] P. 233, 243, *per* Simon P.
[15] *The Gaetano and Maria* (1882) 7 P.D. 137.
[16] *Mahadervan* v. *Mahadervan, supra.*
[17] *Yates* v. *Thompson* (1835) 3 Cl. & F. 544; *Bain* v. *Whitehaven and Furness Ry.* (1850) 3 H.L.C. 1.
[18] *Bristow* v. *Sequeville* (1850) 5 Exch. 275.
[19] *Brown* v. *Thornton* (1837) 6 Ad. & El. 185.
[20] As amended by s.5 of the Oaths and Evidence (Overseas Authorities and Countries) Act 1963, which abolished the requirement of reciprocity.

tract.[21] The admissibility of the latter is a question of evidence, governed by the *lex fori*.[22] Thus in *St. Pierre* v. *South American Stores Ltd.*[23] a question arose as to the meaning of the covenant to pay rent contained in a lease of land in Chile and governed by Chilean law. It was held that evidence of negotiations prior to the contract and of subsequent writings was admissible, although it was inadmissible by English law. On the other hand, in *Korner* v. *Witkowitzer*[24] the plaintiff sued to recover arrears of pension due under a contract governed by Czech law. In order to obtain leave to serve notice of the writ out of the jurisdiction he had to prove that the contract was broken in England. It was held by Denning L.J. that evidence of an oral agreement whereby the plaintiff was to receive his pension in the country in which he might be living when it accrued was inadmissible, since this would be to vary the terms of the written agreement.

Requirement of written evidence

Section 4 of the Statute of Frauds 1677 provided that "no action shall be brought" on a number of contracts unless the agreement, or some note or memorandum thereof, was in writing. The original section 4 now applies only to contracts of guarantee,[25] but that part of it dealing with contracts for the sale or other disposition of an interest in land has been re-enacted by section 40 of the Law of Property Act 1925. In the famous (or notorious) case of *Leroux* v. *Brown*[26] it was held that section 4 contained a rule of procedure and therefore prevented the enforcement in England of an oral contract governed by French law which could have been sued upon in France. The decision has been much criticised by writers[27] on the ground that no serious procedural inconvenience would be caused by admitting oral evidence of a contract within section 4; indeed the court is bound to admit such evidence if the contract is not relied upon for the purpose of enforcement but as a defence. To characterise the section as procedural merely because it says "no action shall be brought" is to regard the form of the section as more important than its substance. To characterise it as procedural for the purposes of the conflict of laws merely because it had previously been characterised as procedural for some purposes of English domestic law is to lose sight of the purpose of the characterisation. The decision has been judicially doubted[28] and, though it has twice been approved *obiter* in the House of Lords,[29] it appears never to have been fol-

---

[21] *St. Pierre* v. *South American Stores Ltd.* [1937] 1 All E.R. 206, 209; affirmed C.A. [1937] 3 All E.R. 349.

[22] *Korner* v. *Witkowitzer* [1950] 2 K.B. 128, 162–163; affirmed *sub nom. Vitkovice* v. *Korner* [1951] A.C. 869.

[23] *Supra.*

[24] *Supra.*

[25] Law Reform (Enforcement of Contracts) Act 1954, s.1.

[26] (1852) 12 C.B. 801.

[27] Cheshire and North, pp. 48–49, 692–693; Lorenzen, pp. 339–345; Falconbridge, pp. 98–102; Robertson, p. 255; Cook, pp. 229–231; Beckett (1934) 15 B.Y.I.L. 46, 69–71.

[28] *Williams* v. *Wheeler* (1860) 8 C.B.(N.S.) 299, 316; *Gibson* v. *Holland* (1865) L.R. 1 C.P. 1, 8, *per* Willes J.

[29] *Maddison* v. *Alderson* (1883) 8 App.Cas. 467, 474, *per* Lord Selborne; *Morris* v. *Baron* [1918] A.C. 1, 15, *per* Lord Haldane.

lowed in England in a conflict of laws case. Indeed, the court once refused
to apply the section to a French contract relating to English land[30]; but its
reasons were somewhat specious.

Very different from the approach of the Court of Common Pleas in
Leroux v. *Brown* was that of the Supreme Court of California in *Bernkrant*
v. *Fowler.*[31] There the court refused to apply the Californian Statute of
Frauds to an oral Nevada contract on the ground that, having regard to
"the scope of the statute in the light of applicable principles of the conflict
of laws," it did not apply to foreign contracts. The court reached its conclusion without once mentioning the distinction between substance and procedure.

Difficult problems arise when both the *lex causae* and the *lex fori* contain provisions analogous to the Statute of Frauds which differ from each
other in the stringency of their requirements and in their nature.
Although questions of this kind have not yet arisen in England, it is
thought that the following rules would apply. If the provisions of the *lex
causae* and of the *lex fori* are both procedural, it should be sufficient and
necessary to comply with the *lex fori*. If the provision of the *lex causae* is
substantive while that of the *lex fori* is procedural, it should be necessary
to comply with the *lex causae,* and *Leroux* v. *Brown* would make it
necessary to comply also with the *lex fori*. If the provisions of the *lex causae* and of the *lex fori* are both substantive, it should be sufficient and
necessary to comply with the *lex causae*. If the provision of the *lex causae*
is procedural while that of the *lex fori* is substantive, logic might suggest
that neither should apply; and indeed a lower New York court once
reached this result.[32] But it is to be hoped that an English court would
decide differently.

Witnesses

Whether a witness is competent[33] or compellable appears to be a question for the *lex fori*. Of course, if the question depends, as it often does, on
the witness' matrimonial status, the question of status must be referred to
the appropriate *lex causae* before the English rule of evidence can be
applied.

Taking of evidence on commission

Under the Evidence (Proceedings in Other Jurisdictions) Act 1975 (re-
enacting earlier statutes) evidence may be taken on commission in England
at the request of a foreign court. The Act sets out a comprehensive code

---

[30] *Re De Nicols* (*No.* 2) [1900] 2 Ch. 410; *ante*, p. 414.
[31] 55 Cal. 2d 588, 360 P. 2d 906 (1961). For a comment on this case, see Cavers in *Perspectives
of Law* (ed. Pound, Griswold and Sutherland), pp. 38–68.
[32] *Marie* v. *Garrison* (1883) 13 Abb.N.C. 210; criticised by Lorenzen, p. 338, n. 59; Cook, pp.
225–228.
[33] *Bain* v. *Whitehaven and Furness Ry.* (1850) 3 H.L.C. 1, 19.

for the taking of evidence in England on behalf of courts in other parts of the United Kingdom and abroad.[34]

Burden of proof

It seems that in English law questions relating to the burden of proof are matters for the *lex fori*.[35] Yet there is much to be said for treating them as substantive, for the outcome of a case can depend on where the burden of proof lies. As Lorenzen says,[36] "the statement that courts should enforce foreign substantive rights but not foreign procedural laws has no justifiable basis if the so-called procedural law would normally affect the outcome of the litigation." There is American authority that the question whether the burden of proving or disproving contributory negligence lies on the defendant or the plaintiff is a question of substance governed by the *lex causae*.[37] Of course, difficult problems can arise if the *lex fori's* rule about the burden of proof is substantive, while that of the *lex causae* is procedural, or vice versa. For in the former situation there would logically be no applicable rule as to the burden of proof, and in the latter situation there might be conflicting rules. But writers have suggested various ways of escape from this dilemma.[38]

Presumptions

Presumptions are of three kinds: presumptions of fact, and irrebuttable and rebuttable presumptions of law. Presumptions of fact arise when, on proof of certain basic facts, the trier of fact may, but need not, find the existence of a presumed fact. Presumptions of fact have, strictly speaking, no legal effect at all, and need not be considered here. Irrebuttable presumptions of law arise when, on proof of the basic facts, the trier of fact must find the presumed fact in any event. An example is the presumption of survivorship contained in section 184 of the Law of Property Act 1925. It is now generally agreed that, even for the purposes of domestic law, irrebuttable presumptions of law are rules of substance,[39] and this is also true for the purposes of the conflict of laws.[40] Rebuttable presumptions of law arise when, on proof of the basic facts, the trier of fact must find the presumed fact unless the contrary is proved. For the purposes of the conflict of laws such presumptions must be divided into those which only apply in certain contexts, and those which apply in all types of case. Examples of the first type are the presumptions of resulting trust, advancement, satisfaction

---

[34] The Act implements a Hague Convention on the Taking of Evidence Abroad of 1968 (Cmnd. 3991), as to which, see (1969) 18 I.C.L.Q. 618, 646–651. See *Re Westinghouse Uranium Contract Litigation M.D.L. Docket* 235 (*Nos. 1 and* 2) [1978] A.C. 547. See also Protection of Trading Interests Act 1980, s.4.
[35] *The Roberta* (1937) 58 Ll.L.Rep. 159, 177; *In the Estate of Fuld* (*No. 3*) [1968] P. 675, 696–697. The law in Scotland is the same: Anton, p. 545, citing *Mackenzie* v. *Hall* (1854) 17 D. 164.
[36] Lorenzen, p. 134.
[37] *Fitzpatrick* v. *International Ry.*, 252 N.Y. 127; 169 N.E. 112 (1929).
[38] Beckett (1934) 15 B.Y.I.L. 46, 76–77; Cook, pp. 220 *et seq.*; Falconbridge, pp. 292–295; Dicey and Morris, p. 41.
[39] Cross, *Evidence*, 5th ed., p. 124.
[40] *Re Cohn* [1945] Ch. 5.

and ademption, and the presumptions contained in section 2 of the Perpetuities and Accumulations Act 1964 to the effect that a female under the age of twelve or over the age of fifty-five cannot have a child. All these are thought to be so closely connected with the existence of substantive rights that they ought to be characterised as rules of substance. If a trust is governed by a foreign law in which the common law rule against perpetuities is in operation, it is surely inconceivable that an English court would apply to it the statutory presumptions of fertility and infertility contained in section 2 of the Act, any more than it would apply the "wait and see" provisions of section 3 or the age-reducing or class-splitting provisions of section 4.

Examples of the second type of rebuttable presumptions are the presumptions of marriage, legitimacy[41] and death. It is uncertain whether these presumptions are rules of substance or rules of procedure. In cases involving presumptions of marriage the courts have applied the *lex causae* whenever that law was proved[42]; and the most recent dictum on the subject treats such a presumption as a rule of substance.[43]

MODE OF TRIAL AND NATURE OF THE REMEDY

All questions as to the mode of trial are questions of procedure for the *lex fori*. It stands to reason that that law must alone determine such questions as how process is to be served, whether the action should be an action at common law or a suit in equity, whether it should be tried before a judge and jury or before a judge alone, and whether in a superior or in an inferior court, and what rights of appeal exist.

The nature of the plaintiff's remedy is also a matter of procedure to be determined by the *lex fori*. Thus if the plaintiff is by the *lex causae* entitled only to damages but is by English law entitled to specific relief, *e.g.* specific performance or an injunction, that type of remedy is available in England.[44] Conversely, an English court will not grant specific relief where to do so is contrary to the principles of English law.[45]

Although an action in England will not fail merely because the claim is unknown to English law, it will fail if English law has no appropriate remedy for giving effect to the plaintiff's alleged foreign right. Thus in *Phrantzes* v. *Argenti*[46]:

A Greek daughter who had just been married claimed that by Greek law her father was under an obligation to provide her with a dowry. Her claim failed, not because it was unknown to English law,

---

[41] Now much weakened by s.26 of the Family Law Reform Act 1969.
[42] *Hill* v. *Hibbit* (1871) 25 L.T. 183; *De Thoren* v. *Att.-Gen.* (1876) 1 App.Cas. 686; *Re Shephard* [1904] 1 Ch. 456.
[43] *Mahadervan* v. *Mahadervan* [1964] P. 233, 242.
[44] *Baschet* v. *London Illustrated Standard* [1900] 1 Ch. 73; *Boys* v. *Chaplin* [1971] A.C. 356, 394D, *per* Lord Pearson.
[45] Consider *Warner Brothers Pictures* v. *Nelson* [1937] 1 K.B. 209, where however foreign law was not pleaded. Of course it goes without saying that the statements in the text are confined to judicial remedies. The buyer's right to reject defective goods, for example, is obviously a question of substance, governed by the *lex causae*.
[46] [1960] 2 Q.B. 19.

but because by Greek law the amount of the dowry was within the discretion of the court and varied in accordance with the wealth and social position of the father and the number of his children, and with the behaviour of the daughter. The English court therefore had no remedy for giving effect to the Greek claim.

DAMAGES

It now seems clear that the law relating to damages is partly procedural and partly substantive.[47] A distinction must be drawn between remoteness of damage, which is a question of substance governed by the *lex causae,* and measure or quantification of damages, which is a question of procedure governed by the *lex fori.*[48] The former includes the question in respect of what items of loss the plaintiff can recover compensation. The latter includes the question how the monetary compensation which the defendant must pay is to be assessed.

In *D'Almaida Araujo Lda.* v. *Sir Frederick Becker & Co. Ltd.*[49] the plaintiffs, a Portuguese company, contracted to sell palm-oil to the defendants, an English company. The proper law of the contract was Portuguese law. The defendants broke the contract and in consequence the plaintiffs had to pay an indemnity of £3,500 to a third party from whom they had previously agreed to buy the palm-oil. By English domestic law this sum was irrecoverable because its loss was not reasonably foreseeable. By Portuguese law it was recoverable. Pilcher J. following the decision of the Supreme Court of Canada in *Livesley* v. *Horst*[50] and adopting the distinction drawn by Cheshire[51] between remoteness of damage and measure of damages, held that this was a question of remoteness of damage, governed by Portuguese law.

The rule that questions of remoteness or heads of damage are substantive applies to actions in tort as well as to actions in contract. In *Boys* v. *Chaplin*[52] the plaintiff was injured in a road accident in Malta as a result of the defendant's negligence. Both parties were British servicemen ordinarily resident in England and stationed temporarily in Malta. By Maltese law the plaintiff could only recover damages for financial loss directly suffered, expenses and loss of wages—in this case, £53. By English law he could also recover damages for pain and suffering—in this case, a further £2,250. As we have already seen,[53] the House of Lords held unanimously that English law was applicable, though for a bewildering variety of reasons. Here we are only concerned with what was said about damages. A majority of their

---

[47] Dicey and Morris, p. 1178; *Boys* v. *Chaplin* [1971] A.C. 356, 379D, *per* Lord Hodson.
[48] This distinction was recognised by four of their Lordships in *Boys* v. *Chaplin, supra, per* Lord Hodson at p. 379D, *per* Lord Guest at pp. 381H–382A, *per* Lord Wilberforce at p. 393A–B, *per* Lord Pearson at p. 395A–B.
[49] [1953] 2 Q.B. 329.
[50] [1925] 1 D.L.R. 159; approved in *Boys* v. *Chaplin, supra, per* Lord Hodson at p. 379.
[51] Cheshire, 4th ed., pp. 659–660; see now Cheshire and North, pp. 708–709.
[52] [1971] A.C. 356.
[53] *Ante,* pp. 312–313.

Lordships held that the question whether damages were recoverable for pain and suffering was a question of substance.[54]

The rule that remoteness or heads of damage is governed by the *lex causae* is supported by a number of Scottish cases in which it was held that no claim for *solatium* could be maintained in Scotland in respect of injuries inflicted in a country by whose law no such claim was recognised.[55]

The rule that the measure or quantification of damages is a question of procedure for the *lex fori* may be illustrated by the fact that in an English court damages must be assessed once and for all. An English court has no power to order periodical payments by way of damages, nor to increase an award of damages if the plaintiff's injuries become aggravated after judgment has been given. These rules would undoubtedly be applied even though different rules might exist in the *lex causae*.[56]

JUDGMENTS IN FOREIGN CURRENCY

Prior to 1975 it had been regarded as settled law for nearly 400 years that an English court could not give judgment for the payment of an amount expressed in foreign currency. The reason was that the sheriff could not be expected to know the value of foreign currency and thus could not enforce any money judgment by execution unless it was expressed in pounds sterling. The rule was re-asserted by the Court of Appeal in 1898 in *Manners* v. *Pearson*[57] and by a unanimous House of Lords in 1961 in *Re United Railways of the Havana and Regla Warehouses*.[58] In that case Lord Denning began his discussion of the problem with the emphatic statement:

"If there is one thing clear in our law, it is that the claim must be made in sterling and the judgment given in sterling. We do not give judgments in dollars any more than the United States courts give judgments in sterling."[59]

It followed from this rule that the amount of the claim in foreign currency had to be converted into sterling on or before the date of the judgment; and it was settled by a number of decisions of the Court of Appeal and the House of Lords that the date for conversion was the date when the cause of action arose, whether the claim was for damages for breach of contract[60] or for tort[61] or was for a liquidated debt.[62]

This rule was an unjust rule, because it made an anomalous and

[54] *Per* Lord Hodson at p. 379D, Lord Wilberforce at p. 393A–B, and Lord Pearson at pp. 394B–395B. The dissentients were Lord Guest at p. 382G and Lord Donovan at p. 383H.
[55] *Kendrick* v. *Burnett* (1897) 25 R. 82; *Naftalin* v. *L.M.S. Ry.*, 1933 S.C. 259; *M'Elroy* v. *M'Allister*, 1949 S.C. 110; *MacKinnon* v. *Iberia Shipping Co.*, 1955 S.C. 20.
[56] *Kohnke* v. *Karger* [1951] 2 K.B. 670; *Boys* v. *Chaplin, supra, per* Lord Pearson at p. 394C–D.
[57] [1898] 1 Ch. 581.
[58] [1961] A.C. 1007.
[59] At pp. 1068–1069.
[60] *Di Ferdinando* v. *Simon, Smits & Co.* [1920] 3 K.B. 409.
[61] *S.S. Celia* v. *S.S. Volturno* [1921] 2 A.C. 544 (Lord Carson dissenting).
[62] *Re United Railways* [1961] A.C. 1007.

unnecessary exception to the principle of nominalism, which "of all the principles which govern the treatment of money obligations in this country . . . is the most fundamental."[63] If a debt is expressed in foreign currency, both parties expect to measure their rights and obligations in terms of that currency and no other. The creditor should bear the risk of a depreciation of that currency after the date of maturity of the debt; the debtor should bear the risk of its appreciation. Yet if the creditor can (or must) bring his action in England, *e.g.* because the debtor is resident there or is not resident anywhere else, it might be just the other way round, because the debt had to be converted into sterling at the rate of exchange prevailing on the date when it became payable. Hence, if the foreign currency depreciated in terms of sterling after that date, the creditor recovered more than the debtor promised to pay, while if it appreciated, he recovered less.

Yet most English judges remained impervious to the injustice of the rule until sterling depreciated in terms of the foreign currency instead of the other way round, as in the earlier cases. Lord Denning M.R. was the first to realise this injustice, and gave effect to his views in a series of trenchant judgments,[64] even though this meant eating the emphatic words he had uttered in the *United Railways* case, and even though it involved a head-on clash with the House of Lords.

In 1975 the House of Lords in *Miliangos* v. *George Frank (Textiles) Ltd.*[65] discarded the rule, overruled its own previous decision in *Re United Railways,* and held that judgment could be given for an amount expressed in foreign currency or the sterling equivalent at the date when the court authorises enforcement of the judgment in terms of sterling. The action was by a Swiss seller against an English buyer for the price of goods sold. The price was quoted in Swiss francs and Swiss law was the proper law of the contract. The sterling equivalent of the price was £42,000 in 1971 when payment was due and (owing to the depreciation of the pound) £60,000 in 1974 at the date of the hearing. The House of Lords held that the Swiss seller was entitled to the larger sum.

As a precedent, the decision in the *Miliangos* case was expressly confined to claims for a liquidated debt expressed in foreign currency in cases where the proper law of the contract was that of a foreign country and where the money of account and payment was that of that country or possibly of some third country outside the United Kingdom. The House of Lords declined to review the whole field of the law regarding foreign currency obligations, leaving it open to future discussion whether the same rule should apply to claims for damages for breach of contract or for tort. But a spate of cases rapidly clarified the scope of the decision. It is now clear that the court can give judgment for payment of an amount in foreign

---

[63] Dicey and Morris, p. 984.

[64] *The Teh Hu* [1970] P. 106 (a dissenting judgment); *Jugoslavenska Oceanska Plovidba* v. *Castle Investment Co.* [1974] Q.B. 292; *Schorsch Meier G.m.b.H.* v. *Hennin* [1975] Q.B. 416; *Miliangos* v. *George Frank (Textiles) Ltd.* [1975] Q.B. 487.

[65] [1976] A.C. 443 (Lord Simon of Glaisdale dissenting). See *Practice Direction* [1976] 1 W.L.R. 83, as amended by *Practice Direction* [1977] 1 W.L.R. 187.

currency as damages for breach of contract[66] or for tort.[67] It can also do so on making an award under section 1(3) of the Law Reform (Frustrated Contracts) Act 1943 for the restoration of a valuable benefit to the plaintiff.[68] It has also been held that the principle of *Miliangos* applies even though the proper law of the contract is English law.[69] This is clearly in accordance with principle, because the rule is a rule of the English law of procedure, and therefore the proper law of the contract or (in a tort case) the *lex loci delicti* should be irrelevant. But there must of course be some foreign element. In the case of a liquidated debt, it is presumably sufficient if the debt was expressed in foreign currency. In the case of damages for breach of contract or for tort, the test adopted by the House of Lords is that damages can be awarded in a foreign currency if that was the currency in which the loss was effectively felt or borne by the person suffering it, having regard to the currency in which he generally operates or with which he has the closest connection.[70] In the case of restitution for unjust enrichment, the award will be made in the currency in which the defendant's benefit can be most fairly and appropriately valued.[71]

In *Miliangos* the House of Lords adopted the formula that had been devised by Lord Denning M.R. in an earlier case[72] for the date of conversion into sterling and put it as late as possible, namely, the date when the court authorises enforcement of the judgment in terms of sterling. "This date gets nearest to securing the creditor exactly what he bargained for."[73] In the case of an insolvent company in compulsory liquidation, the date is the date of the winding-up order, so that all creditors can be treated alike[74]; in the case of claims against a deceased person's estate, the date is the date of the administration order.[75] Sometimes a statute (usually one implementing an international convention) fixes a different date,[76] and then that date has to be followed.

If a debt is payable in foreign currency, very difficult questions arise as to the rate of interest payable by way of damages for withholding payment of the debt. To give judgment for the creditor in an amount expressed in

---

[66] *Jean Kraut A/B* v. *Albany Fabrics Ltd.* [1977] Q.B. 182; *Services Europe Atlantique Sud* v. *Stockholm Rederiaktiebolag Svea* [1979] A.C. 685.

[67] *The Despina R* [1979] A.C. 685.

[68] *B.P. Exploration Co. (Libya) Ltd.* v. *Hunt (No. 2)* [1979] 1 W.L.R. 783, 840–841.

[69] *Barclays Bank International Ltd.* v. *Levin Brothers (Bradford) Ltd.* [1977] Q.B. 270; *Federal Commerce and Navigation Co. Ltd.* v. *Tradax Export S.A.* [1977] Q.B. 324, 341–342, 349, 354, reversed on other grounds [1978] A.C. 1; *Services Europe Atlantique Sud* v. *Stockholm Rederiaktiebolag Svea, supra.*

[70] *The Despina R, supra; Services Europe Atlantique Sud* v. *Stockholm Rederiaktiebolag Svea, supra.*

[71] *B.P. Exploration Co. (Libya) Ltd.* v. *Hunt (No. 2), supra.*

[72] *Schorsch Meier G.m.b.H.* v. *Hennin* [1975] Q.B. 416, 425.

[73] [1976] A.C. 443, 469, *per* Lord Wilberforce.

[74] *Re Dynamics Corporation of America* [1976] 1 W.L.R. 757. The same is true in a creditors' voluntary liquidation. The date is the date of the winding up resolution: *Re Lines Bros. Ltd.* [1983] Ch. 1.

[75] *Re Hawkins* [1972] Ch. 714.

[76] *e.g.* Carriage by Air Act 1961, Sched. 1, art. 22(5); Carriage of Goods by Road Act 1965, Sched., art. 27(2); Maintenance Orders (Reciprocal Enforcement) Act 1972, s.16(2) and (5); Civil Jurisdiction and Judgments Act 1982, s.8.

foreign currency, and also to award him interest at the English sterling rate, might well be to overcompensate him if the foreign currency is a stronger currency than sterling and less liable to inflation.[77] It seems that the proper law of the contract giving rise to the debt determines whether the creditor is entitled to interest as damages for non-payment and also determines the rate of such interest.[78] This does not mean that, if English law is the proper law, the applicable rate will be the domestic English rate. What it does mean is that if the debtor delays payment and so keeps the creditor out of his money, and the creditor reasonably reimburses himself by borrowing money in his own country and currency, the debtor should be ordered to compensate the creditor by an award of interest at the rate at which a loan in that currency was normally obtainable in that country. The currency of the creditor may or may not coincide with the currency in which the debt is expressed. If it does not, the rate of interest appropriate to the latter currency is surely irrelevant; it has nothing to do with the rate at which the creditor had to borrow money, and therefore nothing to do with the loss he had sustained. This consideration was overlooked by Bristow J. in *Miliangos* v. *George Frank (Textiles) Ltd. (No.* 2)[79] when he said: "If you opt for a judgment in foreign currency, for better or worse you commit yourself to whatever rate of interest obtains in the context of that currency." In *Helmsing Schiffahrts G.m.b.H.* v. *Malta Drydocks Corporation*[80] Kerr J. rejected this "rule of thumb" which, as he pointed out, might lead to a just result in a case like *Miliangos* where the currency of the creditor coincided with the currency of the contract, but would not do so in a case like the one before him where the two currencies did not coincide.

PARTIES

An equitable assignee of a chose in action, *i.e.* one who cannot bring his case within section 136 of the Law of Property Act 1925, cannot sue the debtor alone. He must join the assignor as co-plaintiff if he is willing or as co-defendant if he is not. Is this rule of English domestic law a rule of substance or a rule of procedure? If it is a rule of substance it would not necessarily apply if the debt was governed by a foreign proper law. The English cases are old and conflicting. But those which support the view that the rule is procedural can be explained on other grounds,[81] while those which treat the rule as substantive[82] can be supported on the ground that

---

[77] See Bowles and Phillips (1976) 39 M.L.R. 196.

[78] Dicey and Morris, Rule 166; *Helmsing Schiffahrts G.m.b.H.* v. *Malta Drydocks Corporation* [1977] 2 Lloyd's Rep. 444, 449–450, *per* Kerr J.; but see *Miliangos* v. *George Frank (Textiles) Ltd. (No.* 2) [1977] Q.B. 489, 496–497, where Bristow J. preferred the view expressed in older editions of Dicey that the *lex fori* determines the rate.

[79] *Supra,* at p. 495.

[80] *Supra,* at p. 449.

[81] In *Wolff* v. *Oxholm* (1817) 6 M. & S. 92 English law was both the *lex fori* and the *lex causae.* In *Jeffery* v. *M'Taggart* (1817) 6 M. & S. 126 and again in *Barber* v. *Mexican Land Co.* (1899) 16 T.L.R. 127 the *lex causae* was not intended to have extraterritorial effect. In *Regas Ltd.* v. *Plotkins* (1961) 29 D.L.R. (2d) 282 the *lex fori* was also the proper law of the debt.

[82] *Innes* v. *Dunlop* (1800) 8 T.R. 595; *O'Callaghan* v. *Thomond* (1810) 3 Taunt. 82.

since its principal object is to protect the debtor, it is hard to see why he should have such protection in England if he does not enjoy it under the *lex causae*.

A similar question is whether the person sued is the proper defendant to the action. In some foreign systems of law a defendant cannot be sued unless and until some other person has been sued first. For instance, in some foreign systems a creditor cannot sue an individual partner until he has first sued the firm and its assets have been exhausted, or cannot sue a surety until he has first sued the principal debtor. Such rules are in sharp contrast to the rule of English law that any partner may be sued alone for the whole of the partnership debts, or that a surety may be sued without joining the principal debtor. The question is whether such a rule of foreign law is substantive or procedural. If the *lex causae* regards the defendant as under no liability whatever unless other persons are sued first, the rule is substantive and must be applied in English proceedings.[83] If on the other hand the *lex causae* regards the defendant as liable, but makes his liability conditional on other persons being sued first, then the rule is procedural and is ignored in English proceedings.[84] Thus in an action brought against the executors of a deceased partner in a Spanish firm, it was pleaded that by Spanish law creditors could not sue the executors of a deceased partner until they had had recourse to and exhausted the property of the firm. The plea was held bad.[85]

PRIORITIES

It is sometimes said that all questions of priorities are questions of procedure and governed by the *lex fori*. But this rule really applies only to the claims of creditors in bankruptcy and winding up of companies and in the administration of insolvent estates[86] and to claims in Admiralty against a ship. In the last of these cases, the question whether a creditor has a maritime lien against the ship must in an English court be decided in accordance with English law.[87] No difficulty arises in applying this principle to cases where the foreign transaction which is alleged to give rise to the lien is of a type with which English law is familiar.[88] But where the foreign transaction is one with which English law is not familiar, regard must be had to its proper law in order to see what rights arise out of the transaction under that law; the court then decides whether those rights amount to what, according to English notions, is a maritime lien. Having determined the

---

[83] *General Steam Navigation Co.* v. *Guillou* (1843) 11 M. & W. 877; *The Mary Moxham* (1876) 1 P.D. 107.
[84] *General Steam Navigation Co.* v. *Guillou, supra*; *Bullock* v. *Caird* (1875) L.R. 10 Q.B. 276; *Re Doetsch* [1896] 2 Ch. 836; *Subbotovsky* v. *Waung* [1968] 3 N.S.W.R. 261, affirmed on other grounds *ibid.* at p. 499. This rule is criticised by Wolff, p. 240; Rabel, Vol. II, pp. 118–119; Anton, p. 544.
[85] *Re Doetsch, supra*.
[86] *Pardo* v. *Bingham* (1868) L.R. 6 Eq. 485; *Ex p. Melbourn* (1870) L.R. 6 Ch.App. 64; *Re Kloebe* (1884) 28 Ch.D. 175; *ante*, pp. 387, 437, 449.
[87] *The Milford* (1858) Swa. 362, approved in *The Tagus* [1903] P. 44; *The Jonathan Goodhue* (1859) Swa. 524.
[88] *The Tagus, supra*; *The Zigurds* [1932] P. 113.

nature of the foreign claim, the *lex fori* determines its rank. Thus in *The Colorado*[89] claims against a French ship were made by A, the holder of a French *hypothèque,* and B, an English necessaries man. By French law, necessaries men had priority over holders of *hypothèques.* By English law, necessaries men were postponed to creditors with maritime liens. The court examined French law to determine what rights were created by a *hypothèque,* and English law to determine whether those rights amounted to a maritime lien. Since the conclusion was that a *hypothèque* did confer rights amounting to a maritime lien, it followed that A had priority over B. But in *The Halcyon Isle*[90] it was held by a bare majority in the Privy Council that English mortgagees of a British ship had priority over foreign ship-repairers, even though the foreign law gave the ship-repairers a maritime lien which would have given them priority over the mortgagees. *The Colorado* was explained away on the ground that the French *hypothèque* did not confer rights amounting to a maritime lien but merely conferred rights equivalent to those of a mortgagee. *Todd Shipyards Corporation* v. *Altema Compania Maritima S.A.* was disapproved as based on a misunderstanding of *The Colorado.*

But the rule that priorities are governed by the *lex fori* is by no means a universal one. As we have seen,[91] it does not apply to the priority of competing assignments of a debt, which is governed by the proper law of the debt. It is possible, too, that the priority of claims against foreign land is governed by the *lex situs.*[92] In all the cases in which English law has been applied to decide questions of priorities, the contest has been between claims governed by different laws. In such cases the ground for applying the *lex fori* is not that the procedural convenience of the forum demands this course, but simply that there is no good reason for applying one rather than the other of two conflicting *leges causae.* It is therefore submitted that the priority of competing claims all of which are governed by the same law ought to be determined according to that law.

EXECUTION

The execution of judgments is necessarily governed by the *lex fori.* This principle applies to such matters as whether the judgment may be satisfied out of land or goods; whether debts in the hands of third parties can be attached by garnishment; and whether the judgment debtor can be imprisoned if he does not pay.[93]

[89] [1923] P. 102; followed in *Todd Shipyards Corporation* v. *Altema Compania Maritima S.A.* (1972) 32 D.L.R. (3d) 571 (Sup. Court of Can.).
[90] [1981] A.C. 221.
[91] *Ante,* pp. 362–363.
[92] *Norton* v. *Florence Land Co.* (1877) 7 Ch.D. 332.
[93] *De la Vega* v. *Vianna* (1830) 1 B. & Ad. 284.

Part Nine

GENERAL CONSIDERATIONS

CHAPTER 30

RENVOI

Nature of the problem

THE problem of renvoi[1] arises whenever a rule of the conflict of laws refers to the "law" of a foreign country, but the conflict rule of the foreign country would have referred the question to the "law" of the first country or to the "law" of some third country. Suppose, for instance, that a British citizen dies intestate domiciled in Italy, leaving movables in England; and that by the English conflict rule, succession to movables is governed by the law of the domicile (Italian law), but by the Italian conflict rule succession to movables is governed by the law of the nationality (English law). Which law, English or Italian, will regulate the distribution of the English movables? This is a relatively simple case of remission from Italian law (the *lex causae*) to English law (the *lex fori*). Had the intestate been a German instead of a British citizen we should have had a more complicated case of transmission from Italian to German law. It will be as well to focus attention on cases of remission at the outset.[2] In such situations, three solutions are possible.

The internal law solution. The English court might apply the purely domestic rule of Italian law applicable to Italians, disregarding the fact that the intestate was a British citizen, which is irrelevant anyway in the English conflict of laws. This method requires proof of Italian domestic law, but not of its choice of law rules. It has been recommended (*obiter*) by two English judges on the ground that it is "simple and rational,"[3] but rejected in another case after a comprehensive review of the authorities.[4]

Partial or single renvoi theory. The English court might accept the reference back from Italian law and apply English domestic law, disregarding the fact that the intestate was domiciled in Italy. This process is technically known as "accepting the renvoi."[5] This method requires proof of the

---

[1] There is an immense literature on this subject, and the following is only a selection: Cheshire and North, pp. 58–76; Wolff, ss.178–195; Falconbridge, Chaps. 6–10; Cook, Chap. 9; Lorenzen, Chaps. 2, 3, 5; Dicey and Morris, Chap. 5; Morris (1937) 18 B.Y.I.L. 32; Griswold (1938) 51 Harv.L.Rev. 1165; Inglis (1958) 74 L.Q.R. 493; Kahn-Freund (1974) *Recueil des Cours*, III, 431–437.

[2] Transmission is briefly considered *post*, p. 477.

[3] *Re Annesley* [1926] Ch. 692, 708–709, *per* Russell J.; *Re Askew* [1930] 2 Ch. 259, 278, *per* Maugham J.

[4] *Re Ross* [1930] 1 Ch. 377, 402. The review was so comprehensive that four months elapsed between the hearing and delivery of the judgment.

[5] This expression must be distinguished from accepting the doctrine of the renvoi, which the forum may do without necessarily accepting the first reference back. The former expression means stopping the game of ping-pong with the return of the service. The latter means continuing the game until the other player gets tired of it.

Italian conflict rules relating to succession, but not of the Italian rules about renvoi. It has been adopted by some continental courts in a number of celebrated cases[6] and is sometimes required by continental legislatures,[7] but it is not the current doctrine of the English courts.

Total or double renvoi. The English court might decide the case in the same way as it would be decided by the Italian court. If the Italian court would refer to English "law" and would interpret that reference to mean English domestic law, then the English court would apply English domestic law. If on the other hand the Italian court would refer to English "law" and interpret that reference to mean English conflict of laws and would "accept the renvoi" from English law and apply Italian domestic law, then the English court would apply Italian domestic law. This method requires proof not only of the Italian conflict rules relating to succession but also of the Italian rules about renvoi.

How this theory works in practice can best be seen by comparing two leading cases. In *Re Annesley*[8]:

> T, a British subject of English domicile of origin, died domiciled in France in the English sense, but not in the French sense because she had not obtained authority to establish her domicile in France as required by Article 13 of the Civil Code (since repealed). She left a will which purported to dispose of all her property. By French law, T could only dispose of one-third of her property because she left two children surviving her. Evidence was given that a French court would refer to English law as T's national law and would accept the renvoi back to French law. French domestic law was applied and T's will was only effective to dispose of one-third of her property.

In *Re Ross*,[9] on the other hand:

> T, a British subject domiciled in Italy, died leaving movables in England and Italy and immovables in Italy. She left two wills, one in English and the other in Italian. By her English will she gave her property in England to her niece X. By her Italian will she gave her property in Italy to her grand-nephew Y, subject to a life interest to his mother X. She left nothing to her only son Z. Z claimed that by Italian law he was entitled to one-half of T's property as his *legitima portio*. By the English conflict rules, the validity of T's will was governed by Italian law as the law of her domicile in respect of movables and by Italian law as the *lex situs* in respect of immovables. Evidence was given that an Italian court would refer to English law as T's national law in respect of both movables and immovables, and would not

---

[6] *e.g. L'Affaire Forgo* (Clunet, 1883, p. 64); *L'Affaire Soulié* (Clunet, 1910, p. 888). As to these, see Falconbridge, pp. 147–149.

[7] *e.g.* Article 27 of the Introductory Law of the German Civil Code. Contrast article 30 of the Introduction to the Italian Civil Code, which rejects renvoi.

[8] [1926] Ch. 692.

[9] [1930] 1 Ch. 377.

accept the renvoi back to Italian law. English domestic law was applied and Z's claim was rejected.

Origin and development

The doctrine of renvoi obtained a foothold in English law in 1841 through the medium of cases on the formal validity of wills. In that context, three factors favoured its recognition: first, the rigid English conflict rule which at that time insisted on compliance with one form and one form only for wills, that of the testator's last domicile[10]; secondly, a more flexible conflict rule in neighbouring European countries (where people of English origin were likely to settle), which allowed compliance with the forms prescribed by either the testator's personal law or the law of the place where the will was made; and thirdly, a judicial bias in favour of upholding wills which admittedly expressed the last wishes of the testator and were defective only in point of form. The fountain-head of authority is *Collier* v. *Rivaz*,[11] where the court had to consider the formal validity of a will and six codicils made by a British subject who died domiciled in Belgium in the English sense, but in England in the Belgian sense because he had not obtained the authority of the Belgian Government to establish his domicile in Belgium as required by Article 13 of the Code Napoleon. The will and two of the codicils were made in local Belgian form and were admitted to probate in England without argument. Four of the codicils were opposed because they were not made in local Belgian form, though they were made in English form. Upon proof that by Belgian law the validity of wills made by foreigners not legally domiciled in Belgium was governed by "the laws of their own country," Sir H. Jenner admitted these codicils to probate, remarking that "the court sitting here to determine it, must consider itself sitting in Belgium under the peculiar circumstances of this case." He did not consider the possibility that a Belgian court might have accepted the renvoi from English law and applied Belgian domestic law.

So the doctrine of renvoi was invoked, obviously as an escape device, in order to get round the rigidity of the English conflict rule. The fact that the will and the two codicils made in Belgian form were admitted to probate as well as the four codicils made in English form means that the English conflict rule was interpreted as a rule of alternative reference either to the domestic rules or to the conflict rules of Belgian law. A rule of alternative reference, while practicable for the formal validity of wills, is impracticable for the essential (or intrinsic) validity of wills or for intestacy. In such cases the court must choose between the domestic rules and the conflict rules of the foreign law. It cannot apply both, for it must decide whether or not the testator had disposing power, whether or not he died intestate, and if so who are his next-of-kin. It is one thing to uphold a will if it complies with the formalities prescribed by either the domestic rules or the conflict rules

---

[10] The law has since been amended, first by the Wills Act 1861, and now by the Wills Act 1963. See *ante*, p. 393.
[11] (1841) 2 Curt. 855.

of the foreign law. It is quite another thing to allow the next-of-kin entitled under the domestic rules of the foreign law to share the property with the next-of-kin entitled under its conflict rules.

Collier v. *Rivaz* was disapproved in *Bremer* v. *Freeman*,[12] where on almost identical facts the Privy Council refused to admit to probate the will of a British subject who died domiciled in France in the English sense, but in England in the French sense because she had not complied with Article 13, on the ground that it was made in English but not in French form.

The decision in *Bremer* v. *Freeman* led to the passing of Lord Kingsdown's Act 1861 which in certain circumstances enabled testators who were British subjects and who were disposing of personal estate to choose between the forms prescribed by no less than four systems of law. This extreme indulgence might have been supposed to destroy the argument in favour of interpreting the reference to foreign law as an alternative reference either to its domestic rules or to its conflict rules; and it seems likely that Parliament intended to refer only to the former. However, in *In the Goods of Lacroix*[13] a British subject made two wills in France, one in French form and one in English form, and both were admitted to probate, the latter on the ground that it was made in accordance with the conflict rules of the law of the place where it was made (*lex loci actus*). As in *Collier* v. *Rivaz*, it was necessary to refer to the domestic rules as well as the conflict rules of the foreign law in order to admit both wills to probate.

Down to 1926, the few decisions and dicta which recognised the renvoi doctrine were all consistent with a theory of partial or single renvoi. That is to say, the English court first referred to the conflict rules of the foreign law and then applied the domestic rules either of English law or of the law of a third country,[14] without considering the possibility that the foreign court might accept the renvoi from English law and apply its own domestic law. In *Re Annesley*,[15] Russell J. introduced the doctrine of double or total renvoi (but without citing any authority or giving any reasons for doing so) and applied French domestic law as the law of the domicile on the ground that a French court would have done so by way of renvoi from English law. He expressed his personal preference for reaching this result by a more direct route, that is, by the application of French domestic law in the first instance without any renvoi at all[16]; but this part of his judgment has not been followed.[17] This theory of double renvoi is of course quite different from the theory of single or partial renvoi because, by inquiring how the foreign court would decide the case, it envisages the possibility that the foreign court might "accept the renvoi" and apply its own domestic law, as happened in *Re Annesley*.

---

[12] (1857) 10 Moo.P.C. 306, 374; followed in *Hamilton* v. *Dallas* (1875) 1 Ch.D. 257 (partial intestacy).

[13] (1877) 2 P.D. 94.

[14] As in *Re Trufort* (1887) 36 Ch.D. 600, and *Re Johnson* [1903] 1 Ch. 821, a much criticised decision.

[15] [1926] Ch. 692; *ante*, p. 470.

[16] At pp. 708–709.

[17] *Re Ross* [1930] 1 Ch. 377, 402. See however *Re Askew* [1930] 2 Ch. 259, 278.

Confusion between the two theories was, however, introduced by an *obiter dictum* of the Privy Council in *Kotia* v. *Nahas*,[18] where it was said:

"In the English courts, phrases which refer to the national law of a *propositus* are to be construed, not as referring to the law which the courts of that country would apply in the case of its own national domiciled in its own country with regard (where the situation of the property is relevant) to property in its own country, but to the law which the courts of that country would apply to the particular case of the *propositus*, having regard to what in their view is his domicile (if they consider that to be relevant) and having regard to the situation of the property in question (if they consider that to be relevant)."

This statement was no more than a dictum, because the Privy Council was considering a clause in a Palestine Ordinance which expressly provided for partial renvoi. The Privy Council was sitting on appeal from a Palestine court and was considering a rule of the Palestine conflict of laws which was expressed in statutory form and had no counterpart in the English conflict of laws, and therefore anything said about the English conflict of laws was necessarily *obiter*. Moreover, the dictum cannot be considered accurate, because it confuses two different theories, the theory of partial renvoi and the theory of total renvoi, which differ not only in their starting point but also in their result. They differ in their starting point because the former theory does not inquire how the foreign court would decide the case nor consider the possibility that the foreign court might "accept the renvoi" from the law of the forum. They differ in their result because, if the foreign law refers to the law of the forum, that law is invariably applied under the former theory but is not invariably applied under the latter.

Nevertheless, the dictum of the Privy Council was the principal authority relied upon for the application of the renvoi doctrine in *Re Duke of Wellington*.[19] This case is not an impressive authority in favour of the doctrine, because neither the judge nor the reporter indicated any difference between the domestic rules of English law and the foreign law, nor why it was necessary to choose between them. The testator, who was a British subject domiciled in England, made a Spanish will giving land and movables in Spain to the person who should fulfil two stated qualifications, and made an English will giving all the rest of his property on trust for the person who should fulfil one of the qualifications. At his death there was no person who fulfilled both qualifications, and questions arose as to the devolution of the property in Spain. It appeared that Spanish law, as the *lex situs* of the land, referred questions of succession to the national law of the testator and would not accept the renvoi back to Spanish law. Wynn Parry J. therefore applied English domestic law and held that the gift in the Spanish will failed for uncertainty and that the Spanish property fell into the residue disposed of by the English will. However, it was nowhere

---

[18] [1941] A.C. 403, 413.
[19] [1947] Ch. 506; affirmed on other grounds, [1948] Ch. 118; discussed by Morris (1948) 64 L.Q.R. 264; Jennings (1948) 64 L.Q.R. 321; F. A. Mann (1948) 11 M.L.R. 232; Falconbridge, pp. 229–232.

stated that the construction of the Spanish will would have been different in Spanish domestic law; and, indeed, if the construction of the Spanish will was the only point at issue, it would seem that English domestic law should have been applied without any reference to Spanish law, because the testator was domiciled in England.[20] One of the counsel engaged in the case has furnished the information that by Spanish domestic law the testator could in the circumstances only dispose of half of his property and that the other half passed to his mother as heiress. It may be that this is the explanation of the decision; but it must be admitted that there is no trace of this to be found in the report. Whatever may have been the reason for referring to Spanish law, it is clear that the judge, although he relied mainly on a dictum enunciating a theory of single renvoi, was in fact adopting a theory of double renvoi. Otherwise, there would have been no occasion to inquire whether Spanish law would "accept the renvoi" from English law—an inquiry which occupied much space in the judgment.

Lord Kingsdown's Act 1861 was repealed and replaced by the Wills Act 1963 which allows an even wider choice of law for the formal validity of wills. The Act refers throughout to the internal law of the legal systems which it authorises, thus apparently excluding any renvoi. But it does not in terms abolish the old rule of common law that a will is formally valid if it complies with the formalities prescribed by the law of the testator's last domicile: and it may be that a renvoi from this law may still be possible.[21]

General conclusion from the cases

The history of the renvoi doctrine in English law is the history of a chapter of accidents. The doctrine originated as a device for mitigating the rigidity of the English conflict rule for the formal validity of wills. The passing of Lord Kingsdown's Act in 1861 rendered this mitigation no longer necessary, at any rate in cases where the testator was a British subject. But the doctrine was applied in cases falling within that Act, and was extended far beyond its original context to cases of intrinsic validity of wills and to cases of intestacy. In 1926 the theory underlying the doctrine underwent a significant change, but no authorities were cited nor reasons given for making the change.[22] Two of the cases which have been relied upon as establishing the doctrine have been subsequently overruled or dissented from.[23] In three other cases, the decision would have been the same if the court had referred to the domestic rules of the foreign law in the first instance.[24] And in three cases,[25] none of the parties was concerned to argue that the foreign law meant foreign domestic law.

[20] See *ante*, p. 399.
[21] See *ante*, p. 395.
[22] *Re Annesley* [1926] Ch. 692.
[23] *Collier* v. *Rivaz* (1841) 2 Curt. 855, see *ante* pp. 471–472; *Re Johnson* [1903] 1 Ch. 821, see *Re Annesley* [1926] Ch. 692, 705; *Re Askew* [1930] 2 Ch. 259, 272.
[24] *Re Annesley* [1926] Ch. 692; *Re Askew* [1930] 2 Ch. 259; *In the Estate of Fuld* (*No.* 3) [1968] P. 675.
[25] *Re Johnson* [1903] 1 Ch. 821; *Re O'Keefe* [1940] Ch. 124; *Re Duke of Wellington* [1947] Ch. 506. In *Re O'Keefe*, the originating summons did not even suggest the possibility that Italian domestic law was applicable.

Scope of the doctrine

The English renvoi doctrine has been applied to the formal[26] and intrinsic[27] validity of wills and to cases of intestate succession.[28] It has been applied when the reference has been to the law of the domicile,[29] the law of the place where a will was made (*lex loci actus*),[30] and the law of the place where an immovable was situated (*lex situs*).[31] Outside the field of succession, it seems to have been applied only to legitimation by subsequent marriage.[32] (The rule that a foreign decree of divorce or nullity will be recognised in England if it would be recognised by the courts of the parties' domicile[33] relates to jurisdiction of courts and not to choice of law and therefore has nothing to do with renvoi.) There are indications that it might be applied to the formal validity of marriage[34] and to capacity to marry.[35] It no longer applies to the formal validity of wills in cases falling within the Wills Act 1963. The Court of Appeal has held unanimously that "the principle of renvoi finds no place in the field of contract."[36]

Even in the sphere in which the doctrine has been most frequently applied, namely succession to movables and immovables, it must be stressed that for every case which supports the doctrine there are hundreds of cases in which the domestic rules of the foreign law have been applied as a matter of course without any reference to its conflict rules, though it must be admitted that most of these can be explained on the ground that no one was concerned to argue that the reference to foreign law included its rules of the conflict of laws. There is, therefore, no justification for generalising the few English cases on renvoi into a general rule that a reference to foreign "law" always means the conflict rules of the foreign law, and no justification for the statement that "the English courts have generally, *if not invariably*, meant by 'the law of the country of domicile' the whole law of that country."[37]

Much of the discussion of the renvoi doctrine has proceeded on the basis that the choice lies in all cases between its absolute acceptance and its absolute rejection. The truth would appear to be that in some situations

---

[26] *Collier* v. *Rivaz* (1841) 2 Curt. 855; *In the Goods of Lacroix* (1877) 2 P.D. 94; *In the Estate of Fuld* (*No.* 3) [1968] P. 675.
[27] *Re Trufort* (1887) 36 Ch.D. 600; *Re Annesley* [1926] Ch. 692; *Re Ross* [1930] 1 Ch. 377; and (perhaps) *Re Duke of Wellington* [1947] Ch. 506.
[28] *Re Johnson* [1903] 1 Ch. 821; *Re O'Keefe* [1940] Ch. 124.
[29] *Collier* v. *Rivaz, supra*; *Re Trufort, supra*; *Re Johnson, supra*; *Re Annesley, supra*; *Re Ross, supra*; *Re Askew* [1930] 2 Ch. 259; *Re O'Keefe, supra*; *In the Estate of Fuld* (*No.* 3), *supra*.
[30] *In the Goods of Lacroix, supra*.
[31] *Re Ross, supra*; *Re Duke of Wellington, supra*.
[32] *Re Askew, supra*.
[33] *Armitage* v. *Att.-Gen* [1906] P. 135; *Abate* v. *Abate* [1961] P. 29; *ante*, pp. 194, 212.
[34] *Taczanowska* v. *Taczanowski* [1957] P. 301, 305, 318; *ante*, p. 151.
[35] *R.* v. *Brentwood Marriage Registrar* [1968] 2 Q.B. 956; *ante*, p. 168.
[36] *Re United Railways of the Havana and Regla Warehouses Ltd.* [1960] Ch. 52, 96–97, 115; *cf. Amin Rasheed Shipping Corporation* v. *Kuwait Insurance Co.* [1984] A.C. 50, 61–62, *per* Lord Diplock; art. 15 of the EEC Contracts Convention, *ante*, p. 298. Dicta to the contrary in *Vita Food Products Inc.* v. *Unus Shipping Co.* [1939] A.C. 277, 292 and *Ocean Steamships Co.* v. *Queensland State Wheat Board* [1941] 1 K.B. 402 must now be taken to have been overruled. See *ante*, p. 270.
[37] *Re Ross* [1930] 1 Ch. 377, 390, *per* Luxmoore J. (italics added).

the doctrine is convenient and promotes justice, and that in other situations the doctrine is inconvenient and ought to be rejected. In some situations the doctrine may be a useful means of arriving at a result which is desired for its own sake; but often this is because the English conflict rule is defective. For instance if the court wishes to sustain a marriage which is alleged to be formally invalid, or to promote uniformity of distribution in a case of succession to movables where the deceased left movables in more countries than one, or to avoid conflicts with the *lex situs* in a case of title to land or conflicts with the law of the domicile in a case involving personal status, then the doctrine of renvoi may sometimes afford a useful (though troublesome) device for achieving the desired result. On the other hand, in all but exceptional cases the theoretical and practical difficulties involved in applying the doctrine[38] outweigh any supposed advantages it may possess. The doctrine should not, therefore, be invoked unless it is plain that the object of the English conflict rule in referring to a foreign law will on balance be better served by construing the reference to mean the conflict rules of that law.

From the above point of view, the following situations present a relatively strong case for the application of the doctrine:

Title to land situated abroad.[39] If the question before the English court is whether a person has acquired a title to land situated abroad, the court (so far as it has jurisdiction to deal with the matter at all[40]) will apply the *lex situs*, the law of the place where the land is situated. One of the reasons for applying the *lex situs* is that any adjudication which was contrary to what the *lex situs* had decided or would decide would in most cases be a *brutum fulmen*, since in the last resort the land can only be dealt with in a manner permitted by the *lex situs*. This reason requires that the *lex situs* should be interpreted to mean the law which the *lex situs* would apply. Suppose, for instance, that a British citizen domiciled in England dies intestate leaving land in Spain; and that by Spanish domestic law X is entitled to the land, but that Spanish courts would apply English domestic law according to which Y is entitled. It would be manifestly useless for an English court to decide that X was entitled to the land, because he could never recover it from Y in Spain.[41] However, the Wills Act 1963 excludes renvoi even in the case of immovables so far as the formal validity of wills is concerned.

Title to movables situated abroad.[42] A similar argument suggests that when the English court applies the *lex situs* to determine the title to movables situated abroad, it should interpret the *lex situs* broadly so as to include whatever the courts of the *situs* have decided or would decide. The

---

[38] *Post*, pp. 478–480.

[39] See Falconbridge, pp. 141, 217–220; Cheshire and North, pp. 75, 504; Cook, pp. 264, 279–280; Lorenzen, p. 78; *ante*, p. 345.

[40] English courts do not normally try questions of title to foreign land: see *ante*, p. 337.

[41] For this reason it is thought that the decision in *Re Ross* [1930] 1 Ch. 377 (*ante*, p. 470) was correct so far as the immovables were concerned, subject to what is said later (p. 479) about the difficulty arising from the reference by the foreign law to the national law of a British citizen.

[42] Falconbridge, p. 142; Cheshire and North, p. 75.

argument is not so strong as in the case of land, because the movables may be taken out of the jurisdiction of the foreign court.

Formal validity of marriage. Factors similar to those which originally favoured the application of the renvoi doctrine as a device for sustaining the formal validity of wills[43] also favour its application as a device for sustaining the formal validity of a marriage celebrated abroad. These factors are, first, a rigid rule of the English conflict of laws which normally requires compliance with the *lex loci celebrationis*[44]; secondly, a more flexible rule in neighbouring European countries (where English people are likely to get married) which allows compliance with either the *lex loci* or the personal law of the parties; and thirdly, a strong judicial bias in favour of the validity of marriage. There is, however, no English case which actually sustains the validity of a marriage on the ground that it was formally valid by the law which the *lex loci celebrationis* would apply. But it is a legitimate inference from *Taczanowska* v. *Taczanowski*[45] that such a marriage would be upheld. This does not mean that a marriage would be held formally invalid for failure to comply with the formalities prescribed by whatever system of domestic law would have been referred to by the conflict rules of the *lex loci celebrationis*. It merely means that a marriage may be formally valid if the parties comply with the formalities prescribed by either the domestic rules of the *lex loci celebrationis* or whatever system of domestic law the *lex loci celebrationis* would apply. Thus, the reference to the *lex loci celebrationis* in the case of formalities of marriage is an alternative reference to either its conflict rules or its domestic rules, just as it was in the case of formalities of wills.

Certain cases of transmission.[46] Where the foreign law referred to by the English court would refer to a second foreign law, and the second foreign law would agree that it was applicable, the case for applying the second foreign law is strong. Thus, if a German national domiciled in Italy died leaving movables in England, and Italian and German law both agreed that German domestic law was applicable because the *propositus* was a German national, the English court should accept the situation and apply German domestic law. For the practical advantages of deciding the case the way the Italian and German courts would decide it (especially if the *propositus* left movables in Italy and Germany as well as in England) seem to outweigh the theoretical disadvantages of this mild form of transmission. If, on the other hand, the second foreign law would not agree that it was applicable, then there seems no reason why it should be applied. Thus, if a Danish national domiciled in Italy died leaving movables in England, and Italian law would apply the law of the nationality, and Danish law would apply the law of the domicile, neither law recognising any renvoi from the other,

---

[43] *Ante*, p. 471.
[44] *Ante*, p. 150.
[45] [1957] P. 301, 305, 318.
[46] Griswold (1938) 51 Harv.L.Rev. 1165, 1190; Lorenzen, pp. 76–77; *cf. Re Trufort* (1887) 36 Ch.D. 600; *R.* v. *Brentwood Marriage Registrar* [1968] 2 Q.B. 956.

then the English court should apply Italian domestic law, thus ignoring ren-voi altogether.[47]

Difficulties in the application of the doctrine

It remains to discuss certain difficulties in the application of the English renvoi doctrine, some of which perhaps have not been adequately considered by English courts. These are as follows.

Unpredictability of result. The doctrine makes everything depend on "the doubtful and conflicting evidence of foreign experts."[48] Moreover, it is peculiar to this theory of renvoi that it requires proof, not only of the foreign choice of law rules, but of the foreign rules about renvoi—and there are few matters of foreign law about which it is more difficult to obtain reliable information. In continental countries, decided cases, at least of courts of first instance, are not binding as authorities to be followed, and doctrine changes from decade to decade. Consequently, we find Wynn Parry J. saying in *Re Duke of Wellington*[49]:

> "It would be difficult to imagine a harder task than that which faces me, namely, of expounding for the first time either in this country or in Spain the relevant law of Spain as it would be expounded by the Supreme Court of Spain, which up to the present time has made no pronouncement on the subject, and having to base that exposition on evidence which satisfies me that on this subject there exists a profound cleavage of legal opinion in Spain and two conflicting decisions of courts of inferior jurisdiction."

The English cases show that the effect of acquiring a domicile in a foreign country may sometimes be to make the foreign domestic law applicable,[50] sometimes English domestic law,[51] sometimes the law of the domicile of origin,[52] and sometimes the law of yet a fourth country.[53] There is no certainty that different results will not be reached in any future case in which the same foreign laws are involved, because foreign law is a question of fact and has to be proved by evidence in each case.[54] Moreover, if the evidence of foreign law is misleading or inadequate, the English court may reach a result which is unreal or unjust to the point of absurdity. Thus, in *Re O'Keefe*[55] the intestate had lived in Italy for the last forty-seven years of her life and was clearly domiciled there. Yet the effect of the English ren-

---

[47] Wolff, p. 203.

[48] *Re Askew* [1930] 2 Ch. 259, 278, *per* Maugham J. *Cf.* Lorenzen, p. 127.

[49] [1947] Ch. 506, 515.

[50] *Re Annesley* [1926] Ch. 692; *Re Askew* [1930] 2 Ch. 259.

[51] *Re Ross* [1930] 1 Ch. 377.

[52] *Re Johnson* [1903] 1 Ch. 821; *Re O'Keefe* [1940] Ch. 124.

[53] *Re Trufort* (1887) 36 Ch.D. 600; *R.* v. *Brentwood Marriage Registrar* [1968] 2 Q.B. 956.

[54] *Ante*, p. 37. In *Simmons* v. *Simmons* (1917) 17 S.R.N.S.W. 419, the N.S.W. court concluded, on expert evidence, that French law does not accept the renvoi, but an opposite conclusion was reached on expert evidence in *Re Annesley* [1926] Ch. 692.

[55] [1940] Ch. 124; a much criticised decision. The short unreserved judgment has given rise to "a flood of writings in all corners of the world, but particularly in Italy": Nadelmann (1969) 17 Am.J.Comp.L. 418, 444.

voi doctrine was that her movables were distributed not in accordance with the Italian domestic law with which she might be expected to be most familiar, and in reliance on which she may have refrained from making a will, but in accordance with the domestic law of Eire, a political unit which only came into existence during her long sojourn in Italy, of which she was not a citizen, and which she had never visited in her life except for a "short tour" with her father sixty years before her death. The only possible justification for such a result is that it may have enabled the movables in England to devolve in the same way as the movables in Italy. But of course in many cases uniformity of distribution is unattainable so long as some systems of law refer to the national law and others to the law of the domicile. For instance, uniformity of distribution would be impossible on any theory if an Italian national died intestate domiciled in England, for the English and Italian courts would each distribute the movables subject to its control in accordance with its own domestic law.

The national law of a British citizen.[56] The most frequent occasion for applying the renvoi doctrine has been the conflict between English law, which refers succession to movables to the law of the domicile, and the laws of some continental countries, which refer to the law of the nationality. If the *propositus* is a British citizen or an American citizen, the foreign court's reference to his national law is meaningless, for there is no such thing as a "British" or "American" or even a "Canadian" or "Australian" law of succession, nor is there any such thing as "English" nationality. If the English court decides for itself how the foreign court might be expected to interpret its reference to the national law of a British citizen, as has been done in some cases, it is not necessarily deciding the case as the foreign court would decide it. Thus in *Re Johnson*[57] and *Re O'Keefe*[58] it was assumed, without any evidence of foreign law, that the national law of a British subject meant the law of his domicile of origin. If, on the other hand, the English court allows the foreign expert witness to assume that the national law of a British citizen is English law, as has been done in other cases, it is basing its decision on a manifestly false premise. Thus in *Re Ross*[59] the evidence was that "the Italian courts would determine the case on the footing that the English law applicable is that part of the law which would be applicable to an English national (*sic*) domiciled in England." In *Re Askew*,[60] the expert witness stated: "I am informed and believe that John Bertram Askew was an Englishman (*sic*). Therefore English law would be applied by the German court." Of course it can be argued that if the English court seeks to discover what decision the foreign court would reach, the grounds on which the foreign court would arrive at its decision are irrelevant. But there is reason to believe that at least the Italian courts do not now interpret the national law of a British citizen to

---

[56] See Falconbridge, pp. 199–216. *Cf.* Cook, pp. 239–244.
[57] [1903] 1 Ch. 821.
[58] [1940] Ch. 124, 129: "Italian lawyers cannot say what is the meaning of the law of the nationality when there is more than one system of law of the nationality."
[59] [1930] 1 Ch. 377, 404.
[60] [1930] 2 Ch. 259, 276.

mean either English law or the law of his domicile of origin, but on the contrary interpret it to mean Italian law if he is domiciled in Italy.[61] If this is so, it means that for this reason also the cases of *Re Ross* and *Re O'Keefe* are no longer reliable guides.

Circulus inextricabilis. As we have seen,[62] the effect of applying the doctrine of double renvoi is to make the decision turn on whether the foreign court rejects the renvoi doctrine altogether or adopts a doctrine of single or partial renvoi. But if the foreign court also adopts the doctrine of double renvoi, then logically no solution is possible at all unless either the English or the foreign court abandons its theory, for otherwise a perpetual *circulus inextricabilis* would be constituted.[63] So far, this difficulty has not yet arisen, because English courts have not yet had occasion to apply their renvoi doctrine to the law of a country which adopts the same doctrine. Yet the possibility remains, and the *circulus inextricabilis* cannot surely be dismissed as "a (perhaps) amusing quibble."[64] "With all respect to what Maugham J. said in *Re Askew*," said the Private International Law Committee,[65] "the English judges and the foreign judges would then continue to bow to each other like the officers at Fontenoy." It is hardly an argument for the doctrine of double renvoi that it will only work if the other country rejects it.

Conclusion

As a purely practical matter it would seem that a court should not undertake the onerous task of trying to ascertain how a foreign court would decide the question, unless the situation is an exceptional one and the advantages of doing so clearly outweigh the disadvantages. In most situations, the balance of convenience surely lies in interpreting the reference to foreign law to mean its domestic rules. Although the doctrine of renvoi was favoured by Westlake[66] and Dicey,[67] the great majority of writers, both English and foreign, are opposed to it. Lorenzen says[68]: "Notwithstanding the great authority of Westlake and Dicey, it may reasonably be hoped that, when the doctrine with all its consequences is squarely presented to the higher English courts, they will not hesitate to reject the decisions of the courts that have lent colour to renvoi in the English law." There is no case which prevents the Court of Appeal (still less the House of Lords) from reviewing the whole problem, and it is submitted that such a review is long overdue.

---

[61] See Falconbridge, pp. 207–210, and literature there cited.
[62] *Ante*, p. 470.
[63] Even writers who approve of the double renvoi doctrine admit that it may produce a *circulus inextricabilis*: Wolff, p. 201; Griswold (1938) 51 Harv.L.Rev. 1165, 1192–1193.
[64] *Re Askew* [1930] 2 Ch. 259, 267, *per* Maugham J.
[65] First Report (1954) Cmd. 9068, para. 23(3).
[66] Chap. 2.
[67] 3rd ed., Appendix I.
[68] Lorenzen, p. 53. The sentence was first published in 1910, but the learned author left it unchanged in 1947.

CHAPTER 31

CHARACTERISATION[1]

THE problem of characterisation[2] has been regarded by many continental and some English and American writers as a fundamental problem in the conflict of laws. It was "discovered" independently and almost simultaneously by the German jurist Kahn[3] and the French jurist Bartin[4] at the end of the nineteenth century, and was introduced to American lawyers by Lorenzen in 1920[5] and to English lawyers by Beckett in 1934.[6]

Nature of the problem

The conflict of laws exists because there are different systems of domestic law. But systems of the conflict of laws also differ. Yet all systems have at least one thing in common. They are expressed in terms of juridical concepts or categories and localising elements or connecting factors.[7] This may be seen by considering some typical rules of the English conflict of laws: "succession to immovables is governed by the law of the *situs*"; "the formal validity of a marriage is governed by the law of the place of celebration"; "capacity to marry is governed by the law of each party's antenuptial domicile." In these examples, succession to immovables, formal validity of marriage and capacity to marry are the categories, while *situs*, place of celebration, and domicile are the connecting factors. In the majority of cases it is obvious that the facts must be subsumed under a particular legal category, that a particular conflict rule is available, and the connecting factor indicated by that conflict rule is unambiguous. But sometimes it is not obvious, because there may be a conflict between the conflict rule of the forum and the conflict rules of the foreign country or countries in which some of the significant facts occurred. The problem then becomes one of the correct analysis of legal concepts or rules of law.

Such conflicts of conflict rules are of at least three kinds. In the first

---

[1] There is a vast literature on this subject and the following is only a selection: Lorenzen, Chaps. 4 and 5; Beckett (1934) 15 B.Y.I.L. 46; Robertson, *Characterisation in the Conflict of Laws* (1940); Falconbridge, Chaps. 3–5; Dicey and Morris, Chap. 2; Cheshire and North, pp. 42–54; Wolff, ss.138–157; Cook, Chap. 8; Rabel, Vol. I, pp. 47–72; Anton, pp.43–55; Lederman (1951) 29 Can. Bar Rev. 3, 168; Inglis (1958) 74 L.Q.R. 493, 503–516; Kahn-Freund (1974) *Recueil des Cours*, III, 369–382.
[2] "Qualification" is the term used by continental writers. "Classification" is used by some English writers. But both these terms have other connotations.
[3] (1891) 30 *Jhering's Jahrbücher* 1.
[4] (1897) Clunet 225, 466, 720.
[5] (1920) 20 Col.L.Rev. 247; reprinted in Lorenzen, Chap. 4.
[6] (1934) 15 B.Y.I.L. 46.
[7] This expression (first suggested by Falconbridge) seems the best English equivalent to the French and German technical terms "point de rattachement" and "Anknüpfungspunkt."

place, there may be a patent conflict, that is, the conflict rules may differ on their faces, as when a British citizen dies intestate domiciled in Italy, and the English conflict rule says that succession to movables is governed by the law of the domicile, but the Italian conflict rule says that succession to movables is governed by the law of the nationality. This type of conflict raises the problem of renvoi.[8] Secondly, the conflict rules may be apparently the same in that they employ the same connecting factor, but in reality different because they interpret the connecting factor in different senses. For instance, the conflict rule of the forum and of the foreign country may be apparently the same in that they both say that succession to movables is governed by the law of the domicile, but domicile may mean one thing in one country and another thing in the other. It is a disputed question whether this type of conflict raises a question of renvoi, or a question of characterisation, or is *sui generis*; but it seems better to regard it as a separate problem.[9] Thirdly, there may be a latent conflict of another kind, that is, the forum and the foreign country may have the same conflict rule and may interpret the connecting factor in the same sense, but may yet reach different results because they characterise the question differently. For instance, the forum may regard the question as one of succession, while the foreign law may regard the same question as one of matrimonial property. This is the problem of characterisation.

It was Bartin's thesis that even if the countries of the world agreed upon uniform conflict rules, cases involving the same facts would still be decided differently in different countries, quite apart from such factors as public policy and differences in procedure, because they might characterise the question differently.

Some illustrations derived from English and Scottish cases will show the precise nature of the problem.

(1) A man takes a ticket in London for a railway journey from London to Glasgow. He is injured in an accident in Scotland. Is his cause of action for breach of contract, in which case English law will govern as the proper law of the contract, or for tort, in which case a combination of English and Scots law will apply? By which law, English or Scottish, is this question to be answered?[10]

(2) A Frenchman under the age of twenty-one marries an Englishwoman in England without obtaining the consent of his parents as required by French law. The French and English conflict rules agree that the formalities of marriage are governed by the law of the place of celebration (English law), and also that the husband must have capacity to marry by his personal law (French law).[11] But is the French rule about parental consents a rule relating to formalities (in which case it will not apply to a marriage in England), or is it a rule relating to capacity to marry (in which case it

---

[8] *Ante*, Chap. 30.
[9] See *ante*, p. 10.
[10] See *Horn* v. *North British Ry.* (1878) 5 R. 1055; *Naftalin* v. *L.M.S. Ry.*, 1933 S.C. 259.
[11] The fact that the personal law means the law of the nationality in France and the law of the domicile in England is immaterial if we assume that the husband was French by nationality and French by domicile.

will apply to the marriage of a Frenchman)?[12] The problem is to know by which law, French or English, the characterisation of the French rule about parental consent is to be governed.

(3) An action is brought in England on a promissory note made in France and governed by French law after the expiry of the period fixed by the French (but not by the English) statute of limitations. By the English and French rules of the conflict of laws, questions of substance are governed by the *lex causae* (French law), but questions of procedure are governed by the *lex fori* (English law). By English law, the statutes of limitation are procedural, by French law they are substantive.[13] The problem is to know by which law, French or English, the characterisation of the French statute of limitation is to be governed.

What exactly is it that we characterise? In illustration (1) above, the answer is the nature of the cause of action; in illustrations (2) and (3), the relevant rule of French law. It is not parental consents to marriage or the statutes of limitation in the abstract. If it were, we should have to characterise foreign requirements of parental consent, or foreign statutes of limitation, in the same way that we characterise English requirements of parental consent or English statutes of limitation. Though English courts have shown a tendency to do just this,[14] the results have been widely criticised.[15]

Various solutions

Various solutions of the problem of characterisation have been suggested by writers. None of them is entirely satisfactory. The principal suggestions are as follows.

Lex fori. The great majority of continental writers follow Kahn and Bartin in thinking that, with certain exceptions,[16] characterisation should be governed by the *lex fori*. The forum should characterise rules of its own domestic law in accordance with that law, and should characterise rules of foreign law in accordance with their nearest equivalents in its own domestic law. This is in substance what was done in *Ogden* v. *Ogden* and *Huber* v. *Steiner*, illustrations (2) and (3) above. The main argument in favour of this view is that if the foreign law is allowed to determine in what situations it is to be applied, the law of the forum would lose all control over the application of its own conflict rules, and would no longer be master in its own home. The main objections to this view are as follows. In the first place,

---

[12] *Ogden* v. *Ogden* [1908] P. 46.

[13] *Huber* v. *Steiner* (1835) 2 Bing.N.C. 202. See now Foreign Limitation Periods Act 1984, under which all foreign statutes of limitation are characterised as procedural, irrespective of their characterisation under the foreign law.

[14] See, *e.g., Simonin* v. *Mallac* (1860) 2 Sw. & Tr. 67; *Ogden* v. *Ogden* [1908] P. 46 (parental consents to marriage); *Huber* v. *Steiner, supra*; *S.A. de Prayon* v. *Koppel* (1933) 77 S.J. 800 (statutes of limitation).

[15] *Ante*, pp. 153, 454.

[16] One of Bartin's exceptions was the characterisation of interests in property as interests in movables or immovables, which he said must be determined by the *lex situs*.

to argue by analogy from a rule of domestic law to a rule of foreign law is to indulge in mechanical jurisprudence of a particularly objectionable kind, and may result in the forum seriously distorting the foreign law, applying it in cases where it would not be applicable and vice versa, so that the law applied to the case is neither the law of the forum nor the foreign law nor the law of any country whatever. In the second place, this view breaks down altogether if there is no close analogy to the foreign rule of law or institution in the domestic law of the forum.

Lex causae. A few continental writers[17] think that characterisation should be governed by the *lex causae, i.e.* the appropriate foreign law. According to Wolff,[18] "every legal rule takes its characterisation from the legal system *to which it belongs.*" This view was in substance adopted in *Re Maldonado*,[19] where the Court of Appeal had to decide whether the Spanish Government's claim to the movables in England of a Spanish intestate who died without next-of-kin was a right of succession (in which case the Spanish Government was entitled to the movables) or a *jus regale* (in which case the Crown was entitled to them). The court held that this question must be decided in accordance with Spanish law, with the result that the Spanish Government was entitled. The argument in favour of this view is that to say that the foreign law governs, and then not apply its characterisation, is tantamount to not applying it at all. But this view is open to even more serious objections than the first one. In the first place, it is arguing in a circle to say that the foreign law governs the process of characterisation before the process of characterisation has led to the selection of the foreign law. Secondly, if there are two potentially applicable foreign laws, why should the forum adopt the characterisation of one rather than the other?

Analytical jurisprudence and comparative law. Other writers[20] think that the process of characterisation should be performed in accordance with the principles of analytical jurisprudence and comparative law. This view has its attractions, because judicial technique in conflicts cases should be more internationalist and less insular than in domestic cases. But the objections to this view are that there are very few principles of analytical jurisprudence and comparative law of universal application; and that while the study of comparative law is capable of revealing differences between domestic laws, it is hardly capable of resolving them. For instance, comparative law may reveal that parental consents to marriage are sometimes regarded as affecting formalities and sometimes as affecting capacity to marry, or that statutes of limitation are sometimes treated as procedural and sometimes as substantive: but how can comparative law determine how these matters should be characterised in a particular case? Moreover, the method proposed seems quite inconsistent with the pragmatic spirit and traditions of the common law. There is no reported case in which this method has been adopted by an English court.

[17] *e.g.* Despagnet (1898) Clunet 253; Wolff, ss.138–157.
[18] At p. 154 (Wolff's italics).
[19] [1954] P. 223; *ante*, pp. 390–391.
[20] *e.g.* Rabel, Vol. I, pp. 54–56; Beckett (1934) 15 B.Y.I.L. 46, 58–60.

Primary and secondary characterisation. According to another view,[21] the problem can be solved by distinguishing between primary characterisation, a matter for the *lex fori*, and secondary characterisation, a matter for the *lex causae*. The difference between them is that primary characterisation precedes, and secondary characterisation follows, the selection of the proper law. This theory has been effectively criticised,[22] and has long been abandoned by its principal exponent.[23] Perhaps the chief objection to it is that its advocates are not even approximately agreed on what for them is the crucial point, namely, where to draw the line between primary and secondary characterisation. It seems that the same situation can be made to appear as a case of primary or secondary characterisation by simply formulating it differently without any change of substance.[24] There is no reported case in which this theory has been adopted by an English court.

Falconbridge's via media. Falconbridge,[25] following Raape,[26] sought for a *via media* between the two extremes of characterisation by the *lex fori* and characterisation by the *lex causae*. He suggested that the forum should engage in a process of provisional or tentative characterisation before finally selecting the *lex causae*, and should consider the provisions of any potentially applicable laws in their context. If, for example, the court is considering the validity of a marriage celebrated in one country between parties domiciled in another, it should proceed as follows. First it should examine the provisions of the *lex loci celebrationis* in their context in that law in order to ascertain whether they relate to formalities and may therefore affect the formal validity of the marriage, disregarding provisions of that law which relate to capacity to marry. Next it should examine the provisions of the law of the parties' domicile in their context in that law in order to ascertain whether they relate to capacity to marry, disregarding provisions of that law which relate to formalities. Only if the marriage is valid as to form by the *lex loci celebrationis* and valid as to capacity by the law of the parties' domicile should it be pronounced valid.

There is one case in which this method, or something very like it, has been adopted by an English court. In *Re Cohn*,[27] one of the very few cases in which the court seems to have been aware of the existence of the problem, the facts were as follows:

> A mother and daughter, both domiciled in Germany but resident in England, were killed in an air raid on London by the same high explosive bomb. The daughter was entitled to movables under her mother's will if, but only if, she survived her mother. By the English conflict

[21] Robertson, *Characterisation in the Conflict of Laws* (1940); Cheshire, 3rd ed., pp. 63–85.
[22] See Nussbaum, Book Review of Robertson (1940) 40 Col.L.Rev. 1467–1468; Lorenzen, pp. 128–135; Falconbridge, 1st ed., pp. 98–108, 161–164; Dicey, 6th ed., pp. 68–70.
[23] Cheshire, 4th ed., pp. 46–60; Cheshire and North, pp. 42–54.
[24] Compare, as to parental consents to marriage, Robertson, pp. 239–245 (secondary); Cheshire, 2nd ed., pp. 34–36 (primary); Cheshire, 3rd ed., pp. 80–83 (secondary); as to the Statute of Frauds and the Statutes of Limitation, Robertson, pp. 248–259 (secondary); Cormack (1941) 14 So.Calif.L.Rev. 221, 233 (primary).
[25] pp. 58–62.
[26] *Recueil des Cours* (1934), IV, 477 *et seq.*
[27] [1945] Ch. 5; discussed by Morris (1945) 61 L.Q.R. 340.

rules, succession to movables is governed by the law of the domicile, but questions of procedure are governed by the *lex fori*. By section 184 of the Law of Property Act 1925, the presumption was that the elder died first; but by article 20 of the German Civil Code the presumption was that the deaths were simultaneous.

Uthwatt J. first decided, as a matter of first impression, that the English presumption was substantive, not procedural, and therefore did not apply. He next decided that the German presumption was also substantive and not procedural, and therefore did apply. He reached this conclusion for himself by examining the terms of article 20 in its context in the German Civil Code, uninfluenced by the characterisation placed upon it by the German courts or by the characterisation which he had already placed upon section 184. If he had decided that section 184 was substantive and article 20 procedural, or vice versa, he would have been faced with a more difficult problem, to the solution of which (it is submitted) Falconbridge's theory of characterisation contributes little guidance. If section 184 had been characterised as substantive and article 20 as procedural, then no presumption would have been applicable, with the result that those interested in the daughter's estate would not have been entitled to the mother's movables, because they would have been unable to prove that the daughter survived her mother. If on the other hand section 184 had been characterised as procedural and article 20 as substantive, the court would have been faced with conflicting presumptions and would have had to choose between them. Conflicting presumptions are not, of course, unknown in English domestic law.[28]

Examples of characterisation in English law

English law is relatively rich in cases raising questions of characterisation,[29] but poor in judicial discussion of the problem. It is well settled that the *lex situs* determines whether proprietary interests in things are interests in movables or immovables.[30] But apart from this, it cannot be said that English courts have adopted any consistent theory of characterisation. Their decisions have ranged between the two extremes of characterisation in accordance with the *lex fori*, of which *Ogden* v. *Ogden*[31] is perhaps the most celebrated (or notorious) example, and characterisation in accord-

---

[28] *R.* v. *Willshere* (1881) 6 Q.B.D. 366.

[29] In addition to the cases discussed in the text, see *Leroux* v. *Brown* (1852) 12 C.B. 801 (Statute of Frauds 1677, s.4: substance or procedure); *Re Martin* [1900] P. 211, 240 (Wills Act 1837, s.18: testamentary or matrimonial law); *Re Wilks* [1935] Ch. 645 (Administration of Estates Act 1925, s.33(1): administration or succession); *Re Priest* [1944] Ch. 58 (Wills Act 1837, s.15: formal or essential validity of wills); *Apt* v. *Apt* [1948] P. 83 (proxy marriages: formal validity or capacity to marry); *Re Kehr* [1952] Ch. 26 (Trustee Act 1925, ss.31 and 32: administration or succession); *In the Estate of Fuld (No. 3)* [1968] P. 675, 696–697 (onus of proof of testamentary capacity: substance or procedure). For other examples, see Robertson, pp. 164–188, 245–279; Falconbridge, pp. 73–123; Beckett (1934) 15 B.Y.I.L. 46, 66–81.

[30] *Ante*, p. 334.

[31] [1908] P. 46; *cf. Huber* v. *Steiner* (1835) 2 Bing.N.C. 202.

ance with the *lex causae*, exemplified by *Re Maldonado*.[32] Of course the approach adopted by the court is influenced by considerations of policy, not always articulate in the judgments. In *Ogden* v. *Ogden*, for example, the result of characterising the French rule about parental consents in accordance with English law was to uphold the validity of a marriage celebrated in England and valid by English law, one party to which was English. As we have seen,[33] this result can be defended on grounds of policy; but there was other reasoning by which it could have been (and was) arrived at. In *Re Maldonado*, there may have been strong reasons of policy for deciding that the intestate's movables in England belonged to the Spanish Government and not to the Crown, but it is not easy to see what they could have been.

Illusory problems and false conflicts

Sometimes a conflict of characterisations produces the appearance of a problem when no problem exists in reality. In the following examples, F stands for the forum, and X for a foreign country.

(1) A lends his car to B in country F. B, negligently driving the car, injures C in country X. By the laws of F and X, a person who lends his car to another is vicariously liable for the bailee's negligence. By the law of F, its rule does not apply to negligent driving outside F; by the law of X, its rule does not apply to bailments made outside X. The result of applying both these rules is that C's action for damages against A will not succeed.[34]

(2) An action is brought in F for breach of a contract governed by the law of X after the relevant periods of limitation fixed by the laws of F and X have both expired. By the law of F, the statutes of limitation are substantive; by the law of X, they are procedural. The result of applying both these characterisations is that the action will succeed, although neither statute is complied with.[35]

(3) An action is brought in F for breach of an oral contract to sell land in X which is governed by the law of X. Both F and X have a statute, modelled on the English Statute of Frauds, which requires contracts for the sale of an interest in land to be in writing. By the law of F, the statute is substantive; by the law of X, it is procedural. The result of applying both these characterisations is that the action will succeed, although neither statute is complied with.[36]

These results are in varying degrees absurd, but they can be avoided if the court in F recognises that no real difference exists between its own domestic law and that of X, and applies its own domestic law accordingly.

[32] [1954] P. 223; *ante*, p. 484.
[33] *Ante*, p. 166.
[34] Suggested by *Scheer* v. *Rockne Motors Corporation* (1934) 68 F. 2d 942, discussed by Cavers (1950) 63 Harv.L.Rev. 822; Morris (1951) 64 Harv.L.Rev. 891.
[35] See the notorious decision of the German Supreme Court (1882) 7 RGZ 21. More recent German decisions have refused to follow this precedent.
[36] See *Marie* v. *Garrison* (1883) 13 Abb.N.C. 210, a decision of a New York court to this effect.

This method of solving the difficulty seems especially suitable for adoption by English courts, which require foreign law to be proved as a fact and apply English law if such proof is not forthcoming.[37]

Conclusion

The reader who has read thus far may be disconcerted to discover that this chapter poses problems but does not offer solutions. The author begs indulgence. If he could recommend a solution of the problem here discussed with any degree of confidence, he would certainly do so. It remains to add that, in the opinion of some writers, the problem of characterisation has no practical significance and its importance has been exaggerated. It is true that conflicts of characterisation have arisen in relatively few cases, and that the process of characterisation is frequently simple and even obvious. But in some cases it is difficult, and these are the cases which have been most discussed and the results in which have been received with least enthusiasm. Hence the problem of characterisation does seem to have practical importance as well as academic interest; and some knowledge of its nature is essential for any serious student of the conflict of laws.

---

[37] *Ante*, pp. 37, 41.

CHAPTER 32

THE INCIDENTAL QUESTION

A PROBLEM similar to that of Renvoi and Characterisation was discovered or invented by the German jurist Wengler in 1934.[1] It is called the incidental question,[2] and it arises in this way. Suppose that an English court is considering a main question which has foreign elements, in the course of which other subsidiary questions, also having foreign elements, incidentally arise. Suppose that by the appropriate rule of the English conflict of laws, the main question is governed by the law of a foreign country. Should the subsidiary questions be governed by the English conflict rule appropriate to such questions, or should they be governed by the appropriate conflict rules of the foreign law which governs the main question? An illustration will make this clearer. Suppose that a testator domiciled in France gives movables in England to his "wife." The main question here is the succession to the movables, governed by French law, the law of the testator's domicile. The incidental question is the validity of the marriage, which may in turn depend on the validity of some previous divorce. Should these questions be referred to the English or the French rules of the conflict of laws relating to the validity of marriages and the recognition of divorces?

In order that a true incidental question may squarely be presented, three conditions must be fulfilled. First, the main question must by the English conflict rule be governed by the law of some foreign country. Secondly, a subsidiary question involving foreign elements must arise which is capable of arising in its own right or in other contexts and for which there is a separate conflict rule. Thirdly, the English conflict rule for the determination of the subsidiary question must lead to a different result from the corresponding conflict rule of the country whose law governs the main question. Such cases are rare. Thus, in a case of succession to movables, the first condition would not be satisfied if the deceased died domiciled in England. The third condition would not be satisfied if a testator domiciled abroad gave a legacy to his legitimate children, but the English and the foreign conflict rule agreed that the children were or were not legitimate.[3]

Decisions, or even dicta, involving the incidental question in English, Commonwealth or American case law are extremely rare.

---

[1] Wengler, "Die Vorfrage im Kollisionenrecht" (1934) 8 *Rabel's Zeitschrift*, 148–251; Robertson, Chap. 6; Wolff, ss.196–200; Dicey and Morris, Chap. 3; Cheshire and North, pp. 54–57; Gotlieb (1955) 33 Can. Bar Rev. 523–555; Wengler (1966) 55 Rev. Crit. 165–215; Hartley (1967) 16 I.C.L.Q. 680–691; Gotlieb (1977) 26 I.C.L.Q. 734.
[2] This term is used by Wolff and is considered the most suitable English expression. The French and German terms are "question préalable" and "Vorfrage."
[3] *Cf. Doglioni* v. *Crispin* (1866) L.R. 1 H.L. 301.

In *Schwebel* v. *Ungar*,[4] a husband and wife, both Jews, were domiciled in Hungary. They decided to emigrate to Israel. While en route to Israel they were divorced by a Jewish ghet (or extra-judicial divorce) in Italy. This divorce was not recognised by the law of Hungary (where they were still domiciled) but was recognised by the law of Israel. The parties then acquired a domicile in Israel, and the wife while so domiciled went through a ceremony of marriage in Toronto with a second husband, who subsequently petitioned the Ontario court for a decree of nullity on the ground that the ceremony was bigamous. The main question here was the wife's capacity to remarry, which by the conflict rule of Ontario was governed by the law of Israel. The incidental question was the validity of the divorce. This was not recognised as valid by the conflict rule of Ontario but was recognised as valid by the conflict rule of Israel. The Supreme Court of Canada, affirming the decision of the Ontario Court of Appeal, held that the remarriage was valid, because by the law of her antenuptial domicile the wife had the status of a single woman. Thus, the incidental question was determined by the conflict rule of Israeli law, the law governing the main question, and not by the conflict rule of the forum.

In *R.* v. *Brentwood Marriage Registrar*,[5] an Italian husband married a Swiss wife and later obtained a divorce from her in Switzerland, where they were both domiciled. After the divorce the wife remarried. The husband wanted to marry in England a Spanish national domiciled in Switzerland. But the Registrar refused to marry them because in his view there was an impediment. By Swiss law, capacity to marry is governed by the law of the nationality; and Italian law did not recognise the divorces of Italian nationals. The main question here was the husband's capacity to remarry, which by the English conflict rule was governed by Swiss law, the law of his domicile. The incidental question was the validity of the divorce. This was recognised as valid by the English conflict rule; but was not recognised as entitling the husband to remarry by the Swiss conflict rule. The Divisional Court upheld the Registrar's objections to the remarriage. Thus the incidental question was determined by the conflict rule of Swiss law, the law governing the main question, and not by the conflict rule of the forum.

The actual decision in *R.* v. *Brentwood Marriage Registrar* would now be different because section 7 of the Recognition of Divorces and Legal Separations Act 1971, as amended by section 15(2) of the Domicile and Matrimonial Proceedings Act 1973, provides that where a foreign divorce is entitled to recognition under the Act, neither spouse shall be precluded from remarrying in the United Kingdom on the ground that the divorce would not be recognised in any other country. This section reduces the possibility of difficult incidental questions arising in the context of capacity to marry after a foreign divorce. But its scope is limited: it only applies to remarriages after a foreign decree of divorce (not nullity), it only applies

---

[4] (1963) 42 D.L.R. (2d) 622; (1964) 48 D.L.R. (2d) 644; discussed by Lysyk (1965) 43 Can. Bar Rev. 363; approved by Simon P. in *Padolecchia* v. *Padolecchia* [1968] P. 314, 339. The facts of *Schwebel* v. *Ungar* are misstated by Gotlieb in (1977) 26 I.C.L.Q. 734, 775, 793.
[5] [1968] 2 Q.B. 956.

to remarriages in the United Kingdom, and to remarriages after a foreign (not English) decree of divorce. Now that domicile has ceased to be the sole or even the main ground for divorce jurisdiction or for the recognition of foreign divorces,[6] but capacity to marry is still governed by the law of the parties' domicile,[7] it seems likely that such problems will become more numerous and more acute. They will be obviated if the Law Commission's provisional proposals on capacity to marry after a decree of divorce or nullity are implemented.[8]

In *Baindail* v. *Baindail*,[9] Lord Greene M.R., in the course of a discussion of the extent to which polygamous marriages might be recognised in England, said:

> "If a Hindu domiciled in India died intestate in England leaving personal property in this country, the succession to the personal property would be governed by the law of his domicile; and in applying the law of his domicile effect would have to be given to the rights of any children of the Hindu marriage and of his Hindu widow."

Thus, this dictum recognises that the incidental questions of the validity of the marriage and the legitimacy of the children would be governed by Indian law (the *lex successionis*) and not necessarily by the English conflict rule.

In *Haque* v. *Haque*,[10] a succession case on appeal from Western Australia, the High Court of Australia applied the conflicts rule of the *lex successionis* (Indian law) and not that of the *lex fori* to determine the formal validity of a marriage celebrated in Western Australia.

In an American case,[11] the court applied the conflict rule of the place of wrong and not its own conflict rule in order to determine whether the plaintiff was the widow of a deceased workman within the meaning of an Employers' Liability Act.

Thus the weight of English, Canadian, Australian and American authority (so far as it goes) seems to indicate that the incidental question is usually determined by the conflict rule of the foreign law governing the main question and not by the conflict rule of the forum.

The writers who have discussed the incidental question are about equally divided in opinion between those who think it should be determined by the conflict rule of the foreign law and those who think it should be determined by the conflict rule of the forum.[12] They usually discuss the classic case of the testator domiciled in France who gives movables in England to his "wife." The writers who take the first view mentioned above emphasise that the question is not the abstract question, was the claimant the wife of the deceased? but rather, was she his wife according to the law of his domicile at the time of his death and as such entitled to succeed to his movables

---

[6] *Ante*, pp. 190, 197–201.
[7] *Ante*, pp. 159–170.
[8] See *ante*, p. 169.
[9] [1946] P. 122, 127.
[10] (1962) 108 C.L.R. 230.
[11] *Meisenhelder* v. *Chicago and N.W. Ry.*, 170 Minn. 317, 213 N.W. 32 (1927).
[12] See the analysis in Gotlieb (1977) 26 I.C.L.Q. 734, 751–760.

under his will? Those who take the second view emphasise that since *ex hypothesi* the incidental question is capable of arising in its own right or in other contexts than the one before the court, and has conflict rules of its own available for its determination, the court (if it applied the foreign conflict rule) might have to give a decision contrary to its own conceptions of justice, and different from what it would have decided if the question had been presented to it in some other form. Thus, if the husband had petitioned for nullity on the ground of consanguinity, the court would have applied its own conflict rules and might have dismissed the petition and held the marriage valid. But if the wife claimed to succeed to the husband's movables on his death, the court, if it applied the conflict rule of the *lex successionis*, might have to hold that she was not entitled to succeed because the marriage was invalid.

The first view harmonises well with the tendency of English courts to decide questions of succession to movables in the same way as the courts of the deceased's domicile would decide them, so as to promote uniformity of distribution.[13] But this international harmony has to be purchased at the price of internal dissonance: and sometimes the price may seem too high. Suppose, for instance, that a Spanish national domiciled in England obtains a divorce from his wife in the English court. The divorce is, of course, valid in England, but it is not valid in Spain. After the divorce the husband, while still domiciled in England, marries a second wife. He dies intestate domiciled in Spain leaving movables in England. By the English conflict rule the succession to these movables is governed by Spanish law as the law of the intestate's domicile (main question); and by Spanish law the intestate's wife is entitled to a share: but which wife is entitled, the first or the second or neither (incidental question)? By Spanish law, the first wife is entitled, because she was never validly divorced and therefore the husband's remarriage was invalid. But the English court might well be reluctant to deny the validity of its own divorce decree,[14] and if it was the second wife should be entitled.[15]

Such cases show that the problem of the incidental question is not capable of a mechanical solution and that each case may depend on the particular factors involved. As one writer puts it, "there is really no problem of the incidental question, but as many problems as there are cases in which incidental questions may arise."[16] Like the problem of characterisation, the incidental question is seldom discussed by courts, but it does seem to involve a fundamental problem which is necessarily present in certain types of case.

---

[13] See *ante*, pp. 470, 475.

[14] However, in *Breen* v. *Breen* [1964] P. 144 (*ante*, p. 168) it seems that Karminski J. was prepared to do just that. The case did not involve an incidental question. Gotlieb (1977) 26 I.C.L.Q. 734, 779 n. 268 cites cases where continental courts have denied the validity of their own divorce decrees and refused to recognise a remarriage after such a divorce.

[15] Writers have suggested varying answers to this difficult problem. Wolff (1st ed, p. 211) thought that neither wife should succeed, but later (2nd ed., p. 210) thought that the second wife should do so. Gotlieb (1977) 26 I.C.L.Q. 734, 796–797 favours the first wife's claim.

[16] Gotlieb, *supra*, at p. 798.

CHAPTER 33

THE TIME FACTOR

THE conflict of laws deals primarily with the application of laws in space. Yet as in other branches of law, so in the conflict of laws, problems of time cannot be altogether ignored. There is a considerable continental literature on the time factor in the conflict of laws, and a growing awareness of the problem by English-speaking writers,[1] though as might be expected the courts have dealt with it in a somewhat empirical fashion.

Three different types of problem have been identified by writers. The time factor may become significant if there is a change in the content of the conflict rule of the forum (called *le conflit transitoire* by French writers), or in the content of the connecting factor[2] (which the French call *le conflit mobile*), or, most important of all, in the content of the *lex causae*, that is, the foreign law to which the connecting factor refers. These will now be discussed in turn.

Changes in the conflict rule of the forum

A change in the conflict rule of the forum probably does not differ from a change in any other rule of law and its effect must therefore be ascertained in accordance with the familiar English rules of statutory interpretation and of judicial precedent. It is unnecessary to discuss these rules in detail in a book like this, but attention may be briefly called to the different ways in which such changes may occur and to some problems which are peculiar to the conflict of laws.

In English law such changes may occur in three ways: a statute may alter an earlier rule of judge-made law; a statute may alter an earlier statutory rule; or a judicial decision may reverse an earlier judicial rule or declare a new one. Section 72 of the Bills of Exchange Act 1882[3] is an example of the first type, and the Wills Act 1963[4] is an example of the second. That Act laid down a new conflict rule (or rules) for the formal validity of wills in substitution for those contained in the Wills Act 1861; and section 7 contains precise rules laying down which wills will continue to be governed by the earlier statute, and which by the later one. Of course it is usual for a modern statute to state precisely when it comes into force and to what

---

[1] See F. A. Mann (1954) 31 B.Y.I.L. 217; Grodecki (1959) 35 B.Y.I.L. 58; Spiro (1960) 9 I.C.L.Q. 357; Rabel, Vol. 4, pp. 503–519; Dicey and Morris, Chap. 4; Grodecki, *International Encyclopaedia of Comparative Law*, Vol. III, Chap. 8 (1975); Pryles (1980) Monash U.L.Rev. 225.

[2] For the meaning of this expression, see *ante*, p. 9.

[3] See *ante*, p. 366. In *Re Marseilles Extension Railway and Land Co.* (1885) 30 Ch.D. 598 the court in 1885 applied the pre-1882 rules of common law to a bill of exchange drawn, accepted and indorsed before the Act came into force.

[4] *Ante*, p. 393.

extent, if any, it is retrospective. If it does not do so, one is thrown back on the general principles of statutory construction, according to which there is a strong but rebuttable presumption that a statute is not intended to have retrospective effect unless it is procedural or declaratory.[5]

One curious example may be noted of a statutory provision which was evidently intended to lay down a new conflict rule in substitution for an earlier judge-made rule, but which, because it did not expressly abolish the earlier rule, was held by the courts to leave the old rule subsisting side by side with the new. This is section 8(1) of the Legitimacy Act 1926 (now repealed and replaced by section 3 of the Legitimacy Act 1976). At common law, the question whether an illegitimate child was legitimated by the subsequent marriage of his parents was held to depend on the law of his father's domicile at the date of the child's birth and at the date of the subsequent marriage.[6] Section 8(1) of the Legitimacy Act 1926 provided that where the parents of an illegitimate person marry or have married one another, whether before or after the commencement of the Act, and the father was or is, at the time of the marriage, domiciled in a foreign country by the law of which the illegitimate person became legitimated by virtue of such subsequent marriage, that person, if living, should be recognised as having been legitimated from the commencement of the Act or from the date of the marriage, whichever last happened, notwithstanding that his father was not at the time of the birth of such person domiciled in a country in which legitimation by subsequent marriage was permitted by law. One may surmise that the framers of this subsection intended to abolish the rule of common law and to make the father's domicile at the date of the child's birth irrelevant in future. But they did not use express language to this effect, and so our courts have held that the old rule of common law still exists and can still be resorted to by a litigant if it suits him to do so, as in some situations it does.[7]

Judge-made law is retrospective in operation, whereas statute law is usually prospective. Some very strange consequences sometimes follow from a retrospective alteration in a conflict rule of the forum by judicial or legislative action, especially in the field of family relations. Thus, the English conflict rule for the recognition of foreign divorces was radically altered by judicial action in 1953[8] and again in 1967,[9] and by legislative action in 1971.[10] In *Hornett* v. *Hornett*,[11] a man domiciled in England married in 1919 a woman domiciled before her marriage in France. They lived together in France and England until 1924, when the wife obtained a divorce in France. The husband heard about this divorce in 1925. He then resumed cohabitation with his wife in England until 1936, when they

[5] Maxwell, *Interpretation of Statutes*, 12th ed., pp. 215–227.
[6] See *ante*, pp. 247–248.
[7] See, *e.g. Re Askew* [1930] 2 Ch. 259; *Re Hurll* [1952] Ch. 722; and *ante*, p. 251.
[8] *Travers* v. *Holley* [1953] P. 246; *ante*, p. 194.
[9] *Indyka* v. *Indyka* [1969] 1 A.C. 33; *ante*, p. 194.
[10] Recognition of Divorces and Legal Separations Act 1971; *ante*, pp. 196–200. The provisions of the Act for recognising divorces obtained in foreign countries outside the British Isles are retrospective: s.10(4).
[11] [1971] P. 255; discussed by Karsten (1971) 34 M.L.R. 450.

parted. No children were born of this cohabitation. In 1969 the husband petitioned for a declaration that the divorce would be recognised in England. Although it could not have been recognised before 1967, the divorce was recognised under the new judge-made rule declared by the House of Lords in that year.[9]

If we alter the facts a little, the consequences of this retrospective alteration of the conflict rule are startling:

(1) If children had been born of the resumed cohabitation between the parties after the divorce, they would have been legitimate when born, but bastardised by the subsequent recognition of the decree.

(2) If the husband had gone through a ceremony of marriage with another woman in 1945, and his second marriage had been annulled for bigamy in 1950, and his second wife had then remarried, would the result of recognising the divorce in 1971 be to invalidate the nullity decree and also the second wife's second marriage?

(3) If the husband had died intestate in 1940, and a share in his property had been distributed to his French wife as his surviving spouse, would she have had to return it when the new conflict rule declared by the House of Lords in 1967 validated her French divorce?[12]

Changes in the connecting factor

From the temporal point of view the connecting factor in a rule of the conflict of laws may be either constant or variable. It may be of such a character that it necessarily refers to a particular moment of time and no other, or it may be liable to change so that further definition is required. For instance, a conflict rule which referred the question of an illegitimate child's legitimation to the law of his father's domicile would be meaningless unless it defined the moment of time at which the father's domicile was relevant. This is achieved by section 3 of the Legitimacy Act 1976, which defines this moment as the time of the father's marriage.

Examples of constant connecting factors in the English conflict of laws include the *situs* of an immovable, the place where a marriage is celebrated, a will executed, or a tort committed, and the domicile of a corporation.[13] Examples of varying connecting factors include the *situs* of a movable, the flag of a ship, and the nationality, domicile or residence of an individual.

The question whether one should refer, *e.g.* to the law of the father's domicile at the time of the child's birth or at the time of the subsequent marriage in order to discover whether a child has been legitimated by subsequent marriage is simply a question of formulating the most convenient and just conflict rule, and the time factor, though it cannot be disregarded, is not the dominant consideration.[14] It does not seem to differ in principle

---

[12] See the powerful arguments adduced by Latey J. in the court of first instance and by Russell L.J. (dissenting) in the Court of Appeal in *Indyka* v. *Indyka* [1967] P.233, 244–245, 262–263.

[13] A corporation, unlike an individual, cannot change its domicile. See *ante,* p. 31.

[14] For this reason, it has been doubted whether it is appropriate to treat a change in the connecting factor as a problem of time in the conflict of laws. See Grodecki (1959) 35 B.Y.I.L. 58.

from the question whether one should refer to the law of the father's or of
the mother's domicile. The question is discussed elsewhere in this book as
and when it arises, and here it is only necessary to give the reader a brief
reminder of the type of problem which requires solution. Should the law of
the husband's domicile at the time of the marriage or at the time of each
subsequent acquisition determine the rights of husband and wife to movable property acquired after the date of their marriage?[15] Is capacity to
make a will[16] and is the construction of wills[17] governed by the law of the
testator's domicile at the time of making the will or at the time of his
death? Is revocation of wills governed by the law of the testator's domicile
at the time of his death or at the time of the alleged act of revocation?[18] Is
the monogamous or polygamous character of a marriage determined once
and for all at its inception, or may it change by reason of subsequent
events, *e.g.*, a change in the parties' domicile?[19] If chattels are taken from
one country to another by someone not the owner and disposed of there to
a third party, does the first or the second *lex situs* determine whether the
owner loses his title?[20] Since a decision on any of these questions has no
relevance to any of the others, it is obviously impossible to formulate a
general principle.

Changes in the lex causae

Changes in the *lex causae* present much the most important and difficult
problems of time in the conflict of laws, especially when the change purports to have retrospective effect. The overwhelming weight of opinion
among writers is that the forum should apply the *lex causae* in its entirety,
including its transitional rules. This is certainly the prevailing practice of
courts on the continent of Europe. It is probably the prevailing practice of
the English courts, although there is one case, *Lynch* v. *Provisional
Government of Paraguay*,[21] which is often cited for the contrary proposition. Much confusion has resulted from ambiguous formulations of the
conflict rule, and these in turn have suffered from a failure to distinguish
between constant and variable connecting factors. If, for example, the
forum's conflict rule says that succession to immovables is governed by the
lex situs, the connecting factor is constant, no further definition is required,
and it is natural and proper for courts to apply the *lex situs* as it exists from
time to time. But if the forum's conflict rule says that succession to movables is governed by the law of the deceased's domicile, the connecting factor is variable, further definition is required to make the rule more precise,
and so the words "at the time of his death" are added in order to define the
time at which his domicile is relevant. The effect is to exclude reference

[15] *Ante*, pp. 411–413.
[16] *Ante*, p. 392.
[17] *Ante*, p. 398.
[18] *Ante*, pp. 401–402.
[19] *Ante*, pp. 178–179.
[20] *Ante*, pp. 353–357.
[21] (1871) L.R. 2 P. & D. 268.

to any earlier domicile, but courts have sometimes assumed that the effect is also to exclude retrospective changes in the law of the domicile made after the death of the deceased. This assumption seems unnecessary and improper, for the two questions are really quite distinct.

Although it must be emphasised that the problem is always basically the same, namely, should the forum apply or disregard subsequent changes in the *lex causae,* it will be convenient to deal with it under the following heads arranged according to subject-matter: succession to immovables; succession to movables; torts; discharge of contracts; legitimation; matrimonial property; validity of marriage. In conclusion, something will be said on the extent to which public policy may occasionally induce the forum to refuse recognition to foreign retrospective laws.

Succession to immovables. In *Nelson* v. *Bridport,*[22] the King of the Two Sicilies granted land in Sicily to Admiral Nelson for himself and the heirs of his body, with power to appoint a successor. By his will the Admiral devised the land to trustees in trust for his brother William for life with remainders over. After the Admiral's death, and in the lifetime of William, a law was passed in Sicily abolishing entails and making the persons lawfully in possession of such estates the absolute owners thereof. Taking advantage of this law, brother William devised the land to his daughter, from whom it was claimed by the remainderman under the Admiral's will. In giving judgment for the defendant, Lord Langdale M.R. took it for granted that he had to apply the law of Sicily as it existed from time to time and not as it was at the time of the original grant or at the time of the Admiral's death.

Succession to movables. However, an opposite result was reached in *Lynch* v. *Provisional Government of Paraguay.*[23] A testator who had been dictator of Paraguay died domiciled there having by his will left movable property in England to his mistress, the plaintiff. Two months after his death, but before probate of the will had been granted in England, there was a revolution in Paraguay, and the new Government passed a decree declaring all the testator's property wherever situate to be the property of the State and depriving his will of any validity in England or elsewhere. This decree purported to relate back to the time of the testator's death. The plaintiff applied for a grant of probate as universal legatee under the will. Her application was opposed by the new Government. The Government's opposition was bound to fail, because the decree was penal[24] and because property in England could not be confiscated by a foreign Government.[25] But Lord Penzance, in granting probate to the plaintiff, preferred to rest his judgment on the ground that English law adopts the law of the domicile "as it stands at the time of the death" and does not undertake to

---

[22] (1846) 8 Beav. 547.
[23] (1871) L.R. 2 P. & D. 268.
[24] See *Banco de Viscaya* v. *Don Alfonso de Borbon y Austria* [1935] 1 K.B. 140, and *ante,* p. 49.
[25] See *ante,* p. 378.

give effect to subsequent retrospective changes in that law. In support of
this proposition he quoted Story's formulation that succession to movables
is governed by the law of the domicile "at the time of the death," without
appearing to realise that the last six words were intended to qualify "domicile" and not "law," and that Story was never considering the effect of subsequent retrospective changes in the law.

Lord Penzance's manifest inclination to uphold the will on the peculiar
facts of the case is understandable, but his wide formulation has been much
criticised by writers[26] on the ground that it failed to give effect to the transitional law of the *lex causae,* and appeared to do so irrespective of the content of that law. If, for example, the will had been defective in point of
form, *e.g.* because the law of Paraguay required all wills to be witnessed by
a notary public, and after the testator's death it was discovered that a witness, though practising as a notary, was not qualified to do so, and the will
had been validated by retrospective legislation in Paraguay, it is hard to
suppose that Lord Penzance would have thought it "inconvenient and
unjust" to give effect to that legislation.

The decision was followed without much discussion in the curious case of
Re Aganoor's Trusts.[27] In that case, a testatrix died in 1868 domiciled in
Padua having by her will given a settled legacy to A for life and if he died
without children to B for life and then to B's children living at B's death.
This was valid by the Austrian law in force in Padua in 1868; but on September 1, 1871, the Italian Civil Code came into force and forbade trust
substitutions, dividing the ownership between the persons in possession on
that date and the first persons entitled in remainder who were born or conceived before then. B died in 1891 leaving children. A died in 1894 without
children. It was held that the settled legacy was valid and that the change in
the law in force in Padua made after the death of the testatrix would be
ignored. This result is diametrically opposite to that which was reached in
Nelson v. *Bridport.*[28]

If it is true that in succession to movables no account is to be taken of
subsequent changes in the *lex causae* made after the death of the testator,
that proposition is subject to an important qualification so far as the formal
validity of wills is concerned. For section 6(3) of the Wills Act 1963 provides that retrospective alterations in the *lex causae* made after the
execution of the will are relevant in so far as they validate but irrelevant in
so far as they invalidate the will. This enactment is not in terms confined to
alterations in the law made before the death of the testator, and there
seems no reason to read into it words which are not there.

Torts. In *Phillips* v. *Eyre,*[29] an action for assault and false imprisonment
was brought in England against the ex-Governor of Jamaica. The acts com-

---

[26] See F. A. Mann (1954) 31 B.Y.I.L. 217, 234; Grodecki (1959) 35 B.Y.I.L. 58, 67–69,
   where various interpretations of the decision are discussed.
[27] (1895) 64 L.J.Ch. 521; criticised by F. A. Mann (1954) 31 B.Y.I.L. 217, 234; Grodecki
   (1959) 35 B.Y.I.L. 58, 69–70.
[28] (1846) 8 Beav. 547; *ante,* p. 497.
[29] (1870) L.R. 6 Q.B. 1.

plained of took place in Jamaica while the defendant was engaged in suppressing a rebellion which had broken out in the island. The acts were illegal by the law of Jamaica as it stood at the time of the tort; but the defendant pleaded that they had been subsequently legalised by an Act of Indemnity passed in Jamaica with retrospective effect. The Court of Exchequer Chamber gave effect to this defence. It follows from this decision that even in 1870 English law had no objection to foreign retrospective legislation as such; and what was true in 1870 must be even more true today when retrospective legislation has become a more familiar phenomenon in English domestic law. It must be admitted, however, that the circumstances in *Phillips* v. *Eyre* were rather special, in that the *lex causae* was that of a British colony, there was no difference between the *lex fori* and the *lex causae* except in regard to the Act of Indemnity, and that Act was of a kind familiar to English domestic law. Still, it remains true that the Court of Exchequer Chamber adopted a wholly different approach from that of Lord Penzance in *Lynch's* case.

Discharge of contracts. The discharge of contracts affects the substance of the obligation and therefore normally depends upon the proper law of the contract.[30] It is well settled by numerous decisions that in this connection the proper law of the contract means that law as it exists from time to time and that, therefore, legislation enacted in the country of the proper law after the date of the contract may have the effect of discharging or modifying the contractual obligation of the parties.[31] A striking example is the case of *R.* v. *International Trustee for the Protection of Bondholders A/G*.[32] In February 1917, the darkest month of the First World War, the British Government floated a 250 million dollar loan on the New York money market. The capital was repayable at holder's option either in New York in gold coin of the United States or in London in sterling at a specified rate of exchange. In 1933 a Joint Resolution of Congress provided that all gold coin and gold value clauses attached to obligations expressed in dollars were against public policy and that all dollar obligations whenever incurred could be discharged upon payment, dollar for dollar, in any coin or currency which was legal tender at the time of payment. The bondholders sought to enforce the gold clause according to its terms. But the House of Lords held that the proper law of the contract was the law of New York and that therefore the gold clause had been abrogated by the Joint Resolution, with the result that the loan could be repaid in New York in depreciated paper dollars.

In *Adams* v. *National Bank of Greece*[33] the House of Lords refused to apply a Greek law which purported retrospectively to exonerate a Greek

---

[30] *Ante*, pp. 295–296.
[31] See, *e.g. Re Chesterman's Trusts* [1923] 2 Ch. 466, 478; *Perry* v. *Equitable Life Assurance Society* (1929) 45 T.L.R. 468; *De Béeche* v. *South American Stores Ltd.* [1935] A.C. 148; *Kahler* v. *Midland Bank Ltd.* [1950] A.C. 24; *Re Helbert Wagg & Co. Ltd.'s Claim* [1956] Ch. 323, 341–342.
[32] [1937] A.C. 500.
[33] [1961] A.C. 255.

bank from liability under an English contract of guarantee. The House was not unanimous in its reasons for reaching this conclusion[34]; but the main reason seems to have been that since the proper law of the contract was English, no Greek law could discharge one party's obligation thereunder.[35] In other words, Greek law was not the *lex causae*. The case is noteworthy in the present context because all five members of the House of Lords went out of their way to approve the principle of *Lynch's* case.[36] But only Lord Tucker based his judgment squarely on that decision, and Lord Reid was not satisfied that it should be applied to a case like the one before him. This is surely the better view.

Legitimation. As we have seen,[37] section 2 of the Legitimacy Act 1976, re-enacting section 1(1) of the Legitimacy Act 1926, provides that where the parents of an illegitimate person marry or have married one another, whether before or after January 1, 1927, the marriage shall, if the father was or is at the date of the marriage domiciled in England, render that person, if living, legitimate from January 1, 1927, or from the date of the marriage, whichever last happens. If the marriage was celebrated before that date, there is nothing in the section which requires that the father should be domiciled in England, or even alive, on January 1, 1927. Similar statutes are in force in other countries, *e.g.* Northern Ireland, the Republic of Ireland, and Australia. What then is the position if the English court is asked to recognise the legitimation under one of these foreign statutes of a person whose father was dead, or no longer domiciled in the country in question, on the date when the statute came into operation? The English courts have not yet been confronted by a case of this sort, but it has arisen in the Republic of Ireland and in Australia and New Zealand with reference to the English Act of 1926. Applying the common law rule whereby legitimation by subsequent marriage is recognised if the father was domiciled in the foreign country at the date of the child's birth and at the date of the marriage, the Australian and New Zealand courts refused to recognise the legitimation unless the father was also domiciled in England on January 1, 1927.[38] The Irish court on the other hand recognised the legitimation if the father was domiciled in England at the date of the child's birth and at the date of the marriage, even if he was dead on January 1, 1927.[39]

The position is quite different under foreign statutes like section 3 of the Legitimacy Act 1976, re-enacting section 8(1) of the Legitimacy Act 1926. In such a case the legitimation is recognised if the father was domiciled in England at the date of the marriage.[40] In other words, the courts apply the

---

[34] See, for a detailed analysis of the judgments, Grodecki (1961) 24 M.L.R. 701, 706–714.

[35] See in particular the judgment of Lord Reid and that of Diplock J. in the court of first instance: [1958] 2 Q.B. 59.

[36] [1961] A.C. 255, 275–276, 282, 284, 285, 287.

[37] *Ante,* pp. 193–194.

[38] See the cases cited on p. 249, n. 79.

[39] *Re Hagerbaum* [1933] I.R. 198.

[40] *Heron* v. *National Trustees Executors and Agency Co. of Australasia Ltd.* [1976] V.R. 733; *ante,* p. 250.

law of the father's domicile at that date, as that law stands at the date of the proceedings.

Matrimonial property. In *Sperling* v. *Sperling*,[41] a husband and wife, domiciled in East Germany, married there in 1954. The marriage was not subject to any community property régime. They emigrated to South Africa in 1957 and acquired a domicile in the Transvaal. In 1965 the East German law was altered with retrospective effect so as to provide for community of acquisitions after marriage. The Appellate Division of the Supreme Court of South Africa held that this retrospective law must receive effect in South Africa. The reference to East German law as the law of the matrimonial domicile meant the whole of its law, including its transitional law, and public policy did not forbid its application.

Validity of marriage. In *Starkowski* v. *Att.-Gen.*,[42] H 1 and W, both Roman Catholics domiciled in Poland, went through a ceremony of marriage in Austria in May 1945 in a Roman Catholic church. They lived together until 1947, when they separated, having acquired a domicile of choice in England. In 1950 W went through a ceremony of marriage in England with H 2, a Pole domiciled in England. In May 1945 a purely religious marriage without civil ceremony was void by Austrian law. But in June 1945 a law was passed in Austria retrospectively validating such marriages if they were duly registered. By some oversight, the marriage between H 1 and W was not registered until 1949, by which time they had acquired a domicile in England and separated.[43] The House of Lords held that the Austrian ceremony was valid and the English ceremony was bigamous and void. Lord Reid stated the question to be decided as follows: "Are we to take the law of that place (*sc.* the place of celebration) as it was when the marriage was celebrated, or are we to inquire what the law of that place now is with regard to the formal validity of that marriage?"—a question which he answered by saying "There is no compelling reason why the reference should not be to that law as it is when the problem arises for decision."[44] Lord Cohen[45] distinguished *Lynch's* case somewhat faintly on the ground that it involved a remotely different subject-matter. Lord Tucker[46] agreed with Barnard J. in the court of first instance[47] that *Lynch's* case would have been of more assistance if the second ceremony had preceded the registration of the first. But these distinctions seem illusory because, as is shown by Lord Reid's formulation quoted above, the problem was basically the same. The House of Lords adopted a different

---

[41] 1975 (2) S.A. 707. To the same effect is *Topolski* v. *The Queen* (1978) 90 D.L.R. (3d) 66.

[42] [1954] A.C. 155.

[43] Dr. F. A. Mann thinks that the breakdown of the marriage before the registration of the Austrian ceremony should have led the House of Lords to an opposite conclusion: (1954) 31 B.Y.I.L. 217, 243–245. But this seems unacceptable for the reasons given by Grodecki (1959) 35 B.Y.I.L. 58, 75–76.

[44] [1954] A.C. 155, 170, 172.

[45] At p. 180.

[46] At p. 175.

[47] [1952] P. 135, 144.

approach from that of Lord Penzance in *Lynch's* case, and surely a preferable one.

Public policy. The prevailing practice of the English courts thus seems to
be to apply the *lex causae* as it exists from time to time and to give effect if
need be to retrospective changes therein. But the consequences of giving
effect to retrospective changes in the law are sometimes so extraordinary
that public policy must occasionally impose qualifications and exceptions.
There is an almost complete lack of English authority on this question. The
discussion that follows is therefore highly speculative. It will throw the
problem into the clearest possible relief if we consider some variations on
the facts of the *Starkowski* case and consider what decision an English
court might be expected to reach.

(1) If the Austrian marriage had been originally valid but had later been
retrospectively invalidated by Austrian legislation, it would seem that, on
grounds of policy, the marriage should be held valid in England.

(2) If either party had obtained an English nullity decree annulling the
Austrian marriage for informality before it was registered, it would seem
that the foreign retrospective legislation should not be allowed to invalidate the English nullity decree.[48]

(3) What would the position have been if the English ceremony had preceded and not followed the registration of the Austrian ceremony? The
majority of the House of Lords expressly left this question open in the *Starkowski* case.[49] It is thought that the English ceremony should have been
held valid. A similar point was decided by the British Columbia Court of
Appeal in *Ambrose* v. *Ambrose*.[50] A wife obtained an interlocutory judgment for divorce from her first husband in California, where they were
domiciled, on November 25, 1930. This judgment could become final, and
so entitle either party to remarry, at the expiration of one year, either on
the application of either party or on the court's own motion. It was not in
fact made final until 1939. Meanwhile in 1935 the wife went through a ceremony of marriage in the State of Washington with her second husband,
who was domiciled in British Columbia. They lived together in British Columbia until 1956, when they separated. The wife then took advantage of a
Californian statute passed in 1955 and obtained an order from the Californian court in 1958 which retrospectively back-dated the divorce to
November 25, 1931, the earliest date on which final judgment could have
been obtained. The second husband then petitioned for nullity in British
Columbia on the ground that the second ceremony was bigamous. The
court granted a decree. It distinguished *Starkowski* v. *Att.-Gen.* on two
grounds. First, the defect in that case was formal and could be corrected by
the *lex loci celebrationis,* which remained constant throughout; whereas the
defect in the *Ambrose* case related to capacity to marry, a matter which

---

[48] See *Von Lorang* v. *Administrator of Austrian Property* [1927] A.C. 641, 651, *per* Lord Haldane.
[49] [1954] A.C. 155, 168, 176, 182.
[50] (1961) 25 D.L.R. (2d) 1; criticised by Castel (1961) 39 Can. Bar Rev. 604, by Hartley
(1967) 16 I.C.L.Q. 680, 699–703, and by Grodecki, *International Encyclopaedia of Comparative Law,* Vol. III, Chap. 8, para. 34(1).

was governed by the law of the wife's antenuptial domicile: but she ceased to be domiciled in California in 1939, and was therefore domiciled in British Columbia, and not in California, when she obtained her order from the Californian court in 1958.[51] Secondly, in *Starkowski* v. *Att.-Gen.* the retrospective validation of the Austrian ceremony preceded the English ceremony, whereas in the *Ambrose* case the Washington ceremony preceded the retrospective validation of the Californian divorce.

---

[51] In Canadian law, the domicile of a married woman is the same as that of her husband, but a woman whose marriage is void acquires the domicile of the man if she lives with him in the country of his domicile. Therefore W remained domiciled in California until her divorce from H 1 was made final in 1939, whereupon she became domiciled in British Columbia because she had been living there with H 2 since 1935 on the footing that she was married to him.

CHAPTER 34

THEORIES AND METHODS

INTRODUCTION

DURING the last fifty or sixty years there has been a spate of writing in the United States, some of it very vivid and some of it very sophisticated, on theories and methods in the conflict of laws. Nothing like it has been seen in any other country or in any other period of the centuries-long history of our subject. So far, this writing has had but a slight impact on the views of English writers and the attitude of English courts to conflicts problems. But in this rapidly shrinking world we can no longer afford to neglect the American contributions entirely. Hence no apology is needed for devoting this last chapter to an appraisal of this writing, even in a book intended mainly for English law students. Our discussion will have to be brief and thus may run the risk of oversimplifying and distorting the American theories. An adequate discussion of them would require a book twice the size of this one. Still, it is hoped that enough may be said to interest the reader in what is going on on the other side of the Atlantic.

Nearly all the theoretical American writing is concerned with choice of law and not with jurisdiction of courts or with the recognition of foreign judgments. This is no doubt because, from a theoretical standpoint, choice of law is much the most difficult part of the subject. In this chapter we distinguish between theories and methods. The theories (not all of which are of American origin) seek to explain how it is that foreign law is applied in the forum despite the division of the world into independent sovereign States. The methods offer new techniques for solving choice of law problems. Some of the more revolutionary ones would dispense with traditional choice of law rules altogether.

The theories to be discussed are first, the comity theory (associated with Story), secondly, the theory of vested rights (Dicey and Beale) and thirdly, the local law theory (Cook).[1] The methods to be discussed are first, that which prefers rule-selecting rules to jurisdiction-selecting rules (Cavers), secondly, governmental interest analysis (Currie), thirdly, the Californian doctrine of comparative impairment, fourthly, principles of preference (Cavers) and fifthly, the use of choice-influencing factors (the Restatement Second and Leflar).[2] Although we distinguish between theories and methods, there is an undoubted link between the two, since Cavers and Currie were demonstrably influenced by Cook.

---

[1] See, for these three theories, Cheatham (1945) 58 Harv.L.Rev. 361.
[2] See, for an assessment of these and other modern American theories, Westmoreland (1975) 40 Mo.L.Rev. 407; Leflar, ss.90–96.

THEORIES

Introduction

We begin with Ulrich Huber (1636–1694), who was successively a professor of law and a judge in Friesland. He wrote the shortest treatise ever written on the conflict of laws[3] (only five quarto pages), but his influence on its development in England and the United States has been greater than that of any other foreign jurist.

Huber laid down three maxims "for solving the difficulty of this particularly intricate subject." They are as follows[4]:

"(1) The laws of each state have force within the limits of that government, and bind all subject to it, but not beyond.

(2) All persons within the limits of a government, whether they live there permanently or temporarily, are deemed to be subjects thereof.

(3) Sovereigns will so act by way of comity that rights acquired within the limits of a government retain their force everywhere so far as they do not cause prejudice to the power or rights of such government or of its subjects."

In his first two maxims Huber states, more clearly than anyone before him, that all laws are territorial and can have no force and effect beyond the limits of the country where they were enacted, but bind all persons within that country, whether native-born subjects or foreigners. It was this insistence on the territorial nature of law that made Huber's doctrines so congenial to English and American judges. Then in his third maxim Huber offers, almost casually, two explanations of the apparent paradox that, despite the doctrine of territorial sovereignty, foreign law is applied beyond the territory of its enacting sovereign. His first explanation is that this is done simply by the tacit consent of the second sovereign. His second explanation is that what is enforced and applied is not foreign law as such but the rights to which it gives rise. The third maxim also contains the seeds of the doctrine of public policy, discussed in an earlier chapter.[5]

We turn to the two theories to which Huber's explanations gave rise: first, the doctrine of comity; and secondly, the doctrine of vested rights.

The doctrine of comity[6]

Joseph Story (1779–1845) was simultaneously a justice of the Supreme Court of the United States and Professor of Law at the Harvard Law School. His *Commentaries on the Conflict of Laws*, published in 1834, have been described as "the most remarkable and outstanding work on the conflict of laws which had appeared since the thirteenth century in any country

---

[3] *De Conflictu Legum* (1689). For translation and comment, see Lorenzen, Chap. 6; Llewelfryn Davies (1937) 18 B.Y.I.L. 49. Perhaps it is not fanciful to suggest that Huber's practical illustrations, which are such a feature of his work, were used as a model by Dicey and by the American Law Institute's Restatements.

[4] s.2.

[5] *Ante*, Chap. 4.

[6] See Lorenzen, pp. 138–139, 158–160, 199–201; Cheatham (1945) 58 Harv.L.Rev. 361, 373–378; Anton, pp. 21–24; Yntema (1966) 65 Mich.L.Rev. 1.

and in any language."[7] His influence on English and American legal thinking has been immense. Story took over Huber's doctrine of comity and made it the basis of his system. "The true foundation on which the subject rests," he said,[8] "is that the rules which are to govern are those which arise from mutual interest and utility; from the sense of the inconveniences which would arise from a contrary doctrine; and from a sort of moral necessity to do justice in order that justice may be done to us in return."

Lorenzen says[9]: "Most continental writers have been severely critical of Story's theory of comity. As used by the Dutch writers the term 'comity' had a political connotation, which appears to leave the application of foreign law to the discretion of the courts, instead of basing it upon a duty to do justice." In England, it was rejected by Dicey on the following grounds[10]:

> "If the assertion that the recognition or enforcement of foreign law depends upon comity means only that the law of no country can have effect as law beyond the territory of the sovereign by whom it was imposed, unless by permission of the State where it is allowed to operate, the statement expresses, though obscurely, a real and important fact. If, on the other hand, the assertion that the recognition or enforcement of foreign laws depends upon comity is meant to imply that . . . when English judges apply French law, they do so out of courtesy to the French Republic, then the term 'comity' is used to cover a view which, if really held by any serious thinker, affords a singular specimen of confusion of thought produced by laxity of language. The application of foreign law is not a matter of caprice or option; it does not arise from the desire of the sovereign of England, or of any other sovereign, to show courtesy to other States."

We no longer believe that the theory of comity is an adequate explanation of how or why foreign law is applied, still less that it furnishes any guide as to which foreign law should be applied. Still, we must admit that the theory has performed a useful function in freeing our subject from parochialism, and making our judges more internationalist in outlook and more tolerant of foreign law than otherwise they might have been. This perhaps explains the frequency with which "comity" is invoked in English judgments, even to this day. Thus, in *Igra* v. *Igra*[11] Pearce J., in deciding to recognise a German divorce that had been obtained during the war at the instance of the Gestapo on what he suspected were racial grounds, observed that "the interests of comity are not served if one country is too eager to criticise the standards of another country or too reluctant to recognise decrees that are valid by the law of the domicile."

---

[7] Lorenzen, pp. 193–194. But for a ruthless attack on Story's postulates, which were an extension of those of Huber, see Cook, Chap. 2.

[8] Story, s.35.

[9] Lorenzen, p. 199.

[10] Dicey, 3rd ed., p. 10.

[11] [1951] P. 404, 412; *cf. Travers* v. *Holley* [1953] P. 246, 257. And see *Re E.* [1967] Ch. 287, 301 D, where Cross J., having refused to follow an American custody order in respect of a child, sent a copy of his judgment to the judge from whom he was differing.

The theory of vested rights[12]

As we have seen, the theory of vested rights, like the theory of comity, can be traced back to Huber. Its principal English exponent was Dicey, who observed that[13] "the courts never in strictness enforce foreign law; when they are said to do so, they enforce not foreign laws, but rights acquired under foreign laws." And he laid down the following maxim as his General Principle No. 1[14]:

> "Any right which has been duly acquired under the law of any civilised country is recognised and, in general, enforced by English courts, and no right which has been duly acquired is enforced or, in general, recognised by English courts."

He said that this maxim "lies at the foundation of the rules for determining the extra-territorial operation of law"; that the principle was "universally recognised"; and that "the recognition of rights acquired under foreign laws is a leading principle of modern civilisation."[15] But in spite of these dogmatic statements, Dicey never attempted to explain or even to criticise those doctrines of the English courts which were quite inconsistent with his theory, *e.g.* the doctrine that the validity of a contract depends, not on the *lex loci contractus*, but on its proper law; or the doctrine that liability for torts committed abroad depends on English domestic law, subject only to the requirement that the act must have been "not justifiable" by the *lex loci delicti*. It is obvious that when the Court of Appeal in *Machado* v. *Fontes*[16] allowed the plaintiff to recover damages for a libel published in Brazil, although by Brazilian law no damages were recoverable, it was not enforcing a Brazilian right, for there was none, but a right created by English law.

In the United States the theory of vested rights was championed by some of the most distinguished judges who ever sat on the Bench, including Holmes and Cardozo JJ. In *Slater* v. *Mexican National Railway*[17] Holmes J. said:

> "But when such a liability" (in tort) "is enforced in a jurisdiction foreign to the place of the wrongful act, obviously that does not mean that the act in any degree is subject to the *lex fori*, with regard to either its quality or its consequences. On the other hand, it equally little means that the law of the place of the act is operative outside its own territory. The theory of the foreign suit is, that although the act complained of was subject to no law having force in the forum, it gave rise to an obligation, an *obligatio*, which, like other obligations, follows the person and may be enforced wherever the person may be found."

---

[12] See Dicey, 3rd ed., pp. 11, 23–33; Beale, Vol. 3, pp. 1967–1975; Cheatham (1945) 58 Harv.L.Rev. 361, 379–385; Cheshire and North, pp. 25–27; Carswell (1959) 8 I.C.L.Q. 268; Anton, pp. 27–30; Nygh, pp. 12–13.

[13] Dicey, 3rd ed., p. 11. *Cf. Re Askew* [1930] 2 Ch. 259, 267, *per* Maugham J.

[14] pp. 23–24.

[15] pp. 24–25.

[16] [1897] 2 Q.B. 231.

[17] (1904) 194 U.S. 120, 126.

In *Loucks* v. *Standard Oil Co. of New York*[18] Cardozo J. said:

> "A foreign statute is not law in this state, but it gives rise to an obligation which, if transitory, 'follows the person and may be enforced wherever the person may be found'. . . . The plaintiff owns something, and we help him to get it. We do this unless some sound reason of public policy makes it unwise for us to lend our aid."

Even more remarkable was Holmes J.'s statement in *Mutual Life Insurance Co.* v. *Leibing* that "the Constitution and the first principles of legal thinking allow the law of the place where a contract is made to determine the validity and consequences of the act."[19]

It was left to Professor J. H. Beale of Harvard, the Reporter of the American Law Institute's first Restatement of the Conflict of Laws, to elevate the vested rights theory into a dogma and make it the theoretical basis of his system. Obsession with this theory led Beale to make some surprisingly dogmatic statements. "The question whether a contract is valid," he said,[20] "can on general principles be determined by no other law than that which applies to the acts [of the parties], that is, by the law of the place of contracting. . . . If . . . the law of the place where the agreement is made annexes no legal obligation to it, *there is no other law which has power to do so.*" And again: "It is impossible for a plaintiff to recover in tort unless he has been given by some law a cause of action in tort; *and this cause of action can be given only by the law of the place where the tort was committed.* That is the place where the injurious event occurs, and its law is the law *therefore* which applies to it."[21]

The vested rights theory has been effectively destroyed by Arminjon[22] in France and by Cook[23] and Lorenzen[24] in the United States. Cook was trained as a physical scientist and he was something of a philosopher as well as a lawyer. Probably no more incisive mind than his has ever been applied to the problems of the conflict of laws. Certainly it is true that he "discredited the vested rights theory as thoroughly as the intellect of one man can ever discredit the intellectual product of another."[25] The following are among the objections to the theory:

(1) The theory affords no guidance when the cause of action arose in a place having no law that civilised countries would regard as adequate, *e.g.* the high seas.

(2) It sometimes happens that when the applicable law has been deter-

---

[18] 224 N.Y. 99; 120 N.E. 198, 201 (1918).

[19] (1922) 259 U.S. 209, 214. But neither the Constitution nor the first principles of legal thinking prevented him from applying the law of the domicile to the question of capacity to contract in *Union Trust Co.* v. *Grosman* (1918) 245 U.S. 412.

[20] Beale, Vol. 2, p. 1091 (italics added).

[21] *Ibid.*, p. 1288 (italics added).

[22] (1933) *Recueil des Cours*, II, 5–105.

[23] (1924) 33 Yale L.J. 457; reprinted in Cook, Chap. 1. See also Chaps. 13 and 14.

[24] (1924) 33 Yale L.J. 736; reprinted in Lorenzen, Chap. 1. See also pp. 104–111.

[25] Currie, p. 6, *Cf.* Cavers, Book Review of Cook (1943) 56 Harv.L.Rev. 1170, 1172: "the author's technique has enabled him to destroy the intellectual foundations of the system to the erection of which Professor Beale devoted a lifetime."

mined, its rule is found to be contrary to the public policy of the forum and the plaintiff's alleged rights under the foreign law are therefore not enforced.

(3) The same thing may happen when the plaintiff's rights are derived from a foreign law which the forum labels "procedural" or when they cannot be enforced in the forum because of some procedural rule of the forum. Thus, in the *Slater* case[26] itself, the plaintiff failed to recover in Texas for a wrongful death in Mexico because the Texas forum had no machinery for awarding periodical payments under the law of Mexico instead of a lump sum by way of damages.

(4) As Savigny noted long ago, the theory "leads into a complete circle; for we can only know what are vested rights if we know beforehand by what local law we are to decide as to their complete acquisition."[27]

(5) The theory assumes that for every situation in the conflict of laws there is one and only one "jurisdiction" which has power to determine what legal consequences should follow in the given situation. It therefore led to the formulation of broad mechanical rules which had to be applied in order to select the relevant "jurisdiction," regardless of the content of its law and regardless of the social and economic considerations involved. As Fuld J. said in *Babcock* v. *Jackson*[28]:

> "Although espoused by such great figures as Holmes J. and Professor Beale, the vested rights doctrine has long since been discredited because it fails to take account of underlying policy considerations in evaluating the significance to be ascribed to the circumstance that an act had a foreign *situs* in determining the rights and liabilities which arise out of that act. 'The vice of the vested rights theory,' it has been aptly stated, 'is that it affects to decide concrete cases upon generalities which do not state the practical considerations involved.'[29] More particularly, as applied to torts, the theory ignores the interest which jurisdictions other than that where the tort occurred may have in the resolution of particular issues."

(6) The theory derived whatever plausibility it had from simple cases where all the facts occurred in one country but the action was brought in another. If the facts are distributed between two foreign countries, or between one foreign country and the forum, the case presents a problem in the conflict of laws not only for the forum but also for the foreign country or countries and indeed for any court in the world. Hence it is impossible to tell what rights have been acquired under the foreign law unless the forum inquires how the foreign court would decide this very

---

[26] (1904) 194 U.S. 120.

[27] Savigny, p. 147. Yntema (1953) 2 Am.Jo.Comp. Law 297, 313 states that Dicey "does not appear to have considered Savigny's objection that the principle" (*sc.* of vested rights) "is circular." This is wrong, because Dicey quoted Savigny's statement (3rd ed., p. 33), though his attempt to refute it is unconvincing.

[28] 12 N.Y. 2d 473, 478, 191 N.E. 2d 279, 281 (1963); *ante*, pp. 325–326.

[29] Yntema (1928) 37 Yale L.J. 468, 482–483.

case. This introduces the problem of the renvoi, which according to the first Restatement[30] (but not according to Dicey[31]) is ordinarily to be rejected. Dicey, it would seem, "stuck to the logic of the vested rights theory to the bitter end."[32]

This was Cook's great contribution to the discussion. In his original article,[33] published in 1924, which was never adequately answered and not at all by Professor Beale, he discussed the famous case of *Milliken* v. *Pratt*,[34] which we shall meet again later in this chapter. A married woman, domiciled in Massachusetts, in that state signed and gave to her husband an offer addressed to the plaintiff in Maine, offering to guarantee payment by her husband for goods to be sold to him by the plaintiff. The husband posted the letter to the plaintiff in Maine, and the plaintiff accepted the offer there by sending the goods from that state. By the "law" of Massachusetts, a married woman had no capacity to make a contract of guarantee; by the "law" of Maine she had. The Massachusetts court held that the law of Maine governed because the contract was made there, and therefore the lady was liable. Cook pointed out that for the Maine court as well as for the Massachusetts court this case presented a problem in the conflict of laws; and that the Massachusetts court could not have enforced a Maine-created right unless it undertook to discover how a Maine court would have decided this very case, which (since it contented itself with ascertaining the domestic law of Maine) it did not.

We may as well admit it: the vested rights theory is dead. In the sixth edition of Dicey, published in 1949, the editors sought to bring his General Principle No. 1 into line with current thinking by rewording it as follows (the italics show the alteration from Dicey's wording):

> "Any right which has been acquired under the law of any civilised country *which is applicable according to the English rules of the conflict of laws* is recognised and, in general, enforced by English courts, and no right which has not been acquired *in virtue of an English rule of the conflict of laws* is enforced or, in general, recognised by English courts."

This reformulation was considered only partially successful, and so General Principle No. 1 was omitted altogether from the eighth edition, published in 1967, on the ground that "Dicey's views on vested rights no longer command acceptance."[35] In the United States, the Restatement Second has abandoned the vested rights theory and all its consequences. No longer is it said that the validity of a contract and the question of liability for torts are governed by the law of the place where the contract was made or the tort committed. Instead, the Restatement lays down that both

---

[30] ss.7, 8.
[31] 3rd ed., Appendix 1.
[32] Cook, p. 371.
[33] (1924) 33 Yale L.J. 457; reprinted in Cook, Chap. 1. *Cf.* the discussion at pp. 328–337, 370–375.
[34] (1878) 125 Mass. 374.
[35] Dicey and Morris, 8th ed., p. 8, n. 17.

these questions are determined by "the local law of the state which has the most significant relationship to the occurrence and the parties."[36]

The local law theory[37]

Cook's positive contribution to doctrine in the conflict of laws is usually known as the local law theory. His method, congenial to an English lawyer, was not to start with preconceived ideas about the nature of law, but to proceed inductively by a method of scientific empiricism, stressing what the courts have done rather than what the judges have said. Noting the inescapable fact that in a case like *Milliken* v. *Pratt*[38] the court enforced a Massachusetts-created right and not a Maine-created right, and feeling the need to reconcile the application of foreign law with the doctrine of territorial sovereignty, Cook concluded that the forum always enforced rights created by its own law. In his own words[39]:

> "The forum, when confronted by a case involving foreign elements, always applies its own law to the case, but in doing so adopts and enforces as its own law a rule of decision identical, or at least highly similar though not identical, in scope with a rule of decision found in the system of law in force in another state or country with which some or all of the foreign elements are connected, the rule so selected being in many groups of cases, and subject to the exceptions to be noted later, the rule of decision which the given foreign state or country would apply, not to this very group of facts now before the court of the forum, but to a *similar but purely domestic group of facts involving for the foreign court no foreign element.* . . . The forum thus enforces not a foreign right but a right created by its own law."

Cook derived this local law theory from Judge Learned Hand's judgment in *Guinness* v. *Miller*[40]; but Cavers in a thoughtful article[41] pointed out significant differences between the Hand theory and the Cook theory.

Cook admitted that to those accustomed to the more orthodox way of putting the matter, his view might seem to be "needlessly complex." But he retorted that "to the holders of the traditional view that the earth was flat and that the sun went round the earth, the assertion that the earth was round and that it went round the sun seemed needlessly complex, but it won its way because it worked better and, all things considered, really was the simpler view."[42]

Cook's theory was at first enthusiastically received in England, but enthusiasm since has waned.[43] The theory seems sterile because there

---

[36] Restatement Second, s.145 (torts); s.188 (contracts). This is subject (in contracts) to a choice of law by the parties: ss.186, 187.
[37] See Cook, Chap. 1; Cheatham (1945) 58 Harv.L.Rev. 361, 385–391; Cheshire and North, pp. 27–29; Anton, pp. 30–33; Nygh, pp. 13–14.
[38] (1878) 125 Mass. 374; *ante*, p. 510.
[39] Cook, pp. 20–21 (italics in the original).
[40] (1923) 291 Fed. 769.
[41] (1950) 63 Harv.L.Rev. 822.
[42] Cook, p. 33.
[43] *Cf.* Cheshire, 3rd ed. (1947) pp. 50–53, with Cheshire and North, p. 29. *Cf.* Anton, pp. 30–33.

really is no need to reconcile the application of foreign law with the do
trine of territorial sovereignty, as Cook no less than the protagonists of th
vested rights theory assumed.[44] For the law of England includes not onl
the domestic law of England but also its rules of the conflict of laws, whic
are just as much part of English law as the law of contract or the law c
torts. Hence, it is no abdication of English sovereignty to apply foreign la
in English courts if English rules of the conflict of laws lay down tha
foreign law is applicable. To say that in such a case the English court is nc
applying foreign law but enforcing rights acquired under foreign la
(vested rights theory) or modelling its rule of decision on that of the foreig
law (local law theory), is really to play with words.

There can be no doubt of Cook's achievement in destroying the veste
rights theory. He was aware of criticisms that his achievement was destruc
tive rather than constructive. For in the Preface to his book he said tha
"until the intellectual garden is freed of the rank weeds in question usefu
vegetables cannot grow and flourish. The removal of the weeds is thus a
constructive in effect as the planting and cultivation of the useful vege
tables." On this, a distinguished American commentator has remarked[45]
"It is regrettable that Cook did not take account of the incisive criticisms t
which the theory of sovereignty, on grounds of fact as well as principle, ha
been subjected by political and juristic thinkers. Given his destructiv
intent to eliminate the weeds of current dogma from the garden of conflict
law, it would have enabled him to reduce them all—the garden, the prin
ciple of sovereignty and his own analysis included—to ashes from which
phoenix might in time arise."

METHODS

Jurisdiction-selecting rules or rule-selecting rules?

As we have seen,[46] typical rules of the conflict of laws state that suc
cession to immovables is governed by the *lex situs*; the formal validity c
marriage is governed by the *lex loci celebrationis*; capacity to marry is gov
erned by the law of each party's antenuptial domicile. All such rules selec
a particular country (or jurisdiction) whose law will govern the matter i
question, irrespective of the content of that law. They do not select a par
ticular rule of law. Theoretically at least, the court does not need to know
what the content of the foreign law is until after it has been selected.[47]

In 1933, Professor Cavers of Harvard published an important article[48] i
which he deplored the "jurisdiction-selecting" technique (as he called it) c
the traditional conflict of laws system. He pointed out that to apply the la

---

[44] See Cook, p. 51 at n. 9, where he accepted Story's version of Huber's first two axioms.
[45] Yntema (1953) 2 Am.Jo.Comp. Law 297, 315.
[46] *Ante*, p. 481.
[47] There are cases in which neither the judge nor the reporter tells us what difference ther
was between the two systems of law between which a choice had to be made. Instances are
Chatenay v. *Brazilian Submarine Telegraph Co.* [1891] 1 Q.B. 79; *Re Duke of Wellingto*
[1947] Ch. 506; *The Assunzione* [1954] P. 150; *Tzortzis* v. *Monark Line A/B* [1968]
W.L.R. 406.
[48] (1933) 47 Harv.L.Rev. 173.

of a particular jurisdiction without regard to the content of that law was bound to lead to injustice in the particular case and to generate false problems. "The court is not idly choosing a law; it is determining a controversy. How can it choose wisely without considering how that choice will affect that controversy?"[49] The court's duty is to reach a result which is a just one in the particular case and so it should not close its eyes to the content of the two conflicting rules of law.

As an illustration of what he had in mind, Professor Cavers posed a hypothetical case based on *Milliken* v. *Pratt*,[50] but with the laws of the two states reversed. Suppose that a married woman domiciled in Massachusetts makes a contract in Maine, and that by the law of Massachusetts she has capacity to make such a contract, but that by the law of Maine she has not. Does it make sense to say that the law of the place of contracting governs and therefore the contract is void? Surely not: for the Maine law was intended to protect married women domiciled or resident in Maine, not married women domiciled or resident in Massachusetts. The problem is therefore a false one.

For thirty years Professor Cavers' thesis, which was ostensibly directed to the academic world and not to the courts, either went unheeded or was widely misunderstood. But now there are increasing signs in the United States that his thesis appeals to the judges who no doubt were at law school in 1933 when the original article was written. Two examples will be given. In *Babcock* v. *Jackson*,[51] the New York Court of Appeals held that a New York passenger in a New York motor-car could recover damages from her New York host for injuries sustained in Ontario due to his negligent driving, despite an Ontario statute which denied a gratuitous passenger any right of recovery. The problem was a false one, because there was no convincing reason why the law of Ontario should have been applied. The judgment of Fuld J., which reflected a major break-through in American conflicts thinking, was cast mainly in rule-selecting terms and not in jurisdiction-selecting terms. But Fuld C.J. did not remain consistently faithful to Professor Cavers' thesis. In *Tooker* v. *Lopez*[52] and again in *Neumeier* v. *Kuehner*[53] he formulated three guide-lines or rules designed to assist the courts in solving these host-guest problems. The first of his three rules runs as follows: "When the guest-passenger and the host-driver are domiciled in the same state and the car is there registered, the law of that state should control and determine the standard of care which the host owes to his guest." That rule would have meant judgment for the plaintiff in the *Babcock* v. *Jackson* situation. But in the converse situation, *e.g.* where an Ontario guest sues an Ontario host for injuries sustained in New York, it would have meant judgment for the defendant. Yet in that situation, as we have seen,[54] the lower New York courts and the Supreme Courts of Wis-

---

[49] At p. 189.
[50] (1878) 125 Mass. 374; *ante*, p. 510.
[51] 12 N.Y. 2d 473, 191 N.E. 2d 279 (1963); *ante*, pp. 325–326.
[52] 24 N.Y. 2d 569, 585, 249 N.E. 2d 394, 404 (1969); *ante*, pp. 327, 329.
[53] 31 N.Y. 2d 121, 128, 286 N.E. 2d 454, 457–458 (1972); *ante*, pp. 327, 329.
[54] *Ante*, p. 328, n. 61.

consin and Minnesota have held that *Babcock* does not control and that the *lex loci delicti* imposing liability can be applied.

Again, in *Buckeye* v. *Buckeye*[55] the Supreme Court of Wisconsin held in 1931 that a wife could not recover damages from her husband for a tort committed in Illinois, because by the law of Illinois a wife could not sue her husband in tort, even though she could by the law of Wisconsin where they were domiciled. In *Haumschild* v. *Continental Casualty Co.*,[56] the same court held in 1959, overruling *Buckeye* v. *Buckeye*, that the law of the domicile governed this question, and not the *lex loci delicti*, so that a Wisconsin wife could recover damages from her Wisconsin husband for a tort committed in California, despite the contrary rule of the *lex loci delicti*. The court thus substituted one jurisdiction-selecting rule for another; and it overruled not only *Buckeye* v. *Buckeye* but also *Forbes* v. *Forbes*,[57] where it had been held that an Illinois wife could recover damages from her husband for a tort committed in Wisconsin. The court showed little recognition that the case it was overruling was different from the case it was deciding. This part of the judgment has been much criticised.[58] But in 1968 the court abandoned this position and held that an Illinois wife could recover damages from her Illinois husband for a tort committed in Wisconsin.[59] It stigmatised the jurisdiction-selecting rule of the *Haumschild* case as just as "mechanical" as the *lex loci delicti* rule of *Buckeye* v. *Buckeye*.

At first sight Professor Cavers' thesis seems an attractive one. Yet on closer inspection certain doubts arise. They are as follows:

(1) As he admitted in his original article,[60] the thesis may not be workable in international conflicts as opposed to interstate conflicts within the United States, because in the former situation "the application of mechanical rules of law may be regarded as necessary to save the alien litigant from xenophobia. Discretion is a safe tool only in the hands of the disinterested. Such disinterestedness may more readily be credited to courts within the bounds of a federal union."

(2) If the courts are invited to choose between two competing rules of law without being given any guidance as to the principles which should influence their choice, there is a danger that they will choose what they consider to be "the better rule." There is an observable tendency for some American courts to do just this in the fluid situation in torts which has followed the decision in *Babcock* v. *Jackson*. This tendency is deplored by most American commentators (including Cavers[61]). It is fair to say that in his book, *The Choice of Law Process*, published in 1965, Professor Cavers

---

[55] 203 Wis. 248, 234 N.W. 342 (1931).

[56] 7 Wis. 2d 130, 95 N.W. 2d 814 (1959).

[57] 226 Wis. 477, 277 N.W. 112 (1938).

[58] Hancock (1962) 29 U. of Chi.L.Rev. 237, 266–268; Cavers (1963) 63 Col.L.Rev. 1219, 1222.

[59] *Zelinger* v. *State Sand and Gravel Co.*, 38 Wis. 2d 98; 156 N.W. 2d 466, 468 (1968). An opposite result was reached on similar facts in *Johnson* v. *Johnson*, 107 N.H. 30; 216 A. 2d 781 (1966). See Leflar, s.109.

[60] (1933) 47 Harv.L.Rev. 173, 203.

[61] See, *e.g.* Currie, pp. 104–106, 153–154; Cavers, pp. 85–86; Baade (1967) 46 Tex.L.Rev. 141. 151–156; Westmoreland (1975) 40 Mo.L.Rev. 407, 461–462; contrast Leflar, s.107. See *post*, p. 526.

devoted several pages[62] to rebutting the charge that he had advocated "justice in the individual case" as the only aim; and the central theme of that book is the advocacy of certain "principles of preference" as guides to the courts' decision. These will be discussed later in this Chapter.[63]

(3) To expect the courts to discard the accumulated experience of centuries and to abandon the traditional system of the conflict of laws altogether is asking a good deal. Professor Cavers envisaged that in course of time a new body of rules would emerge from the decisions of the courts if his thesis were adopted.[64] In his most recent writings he sees no objection to a jurisdiction-selecting rule if it is the product of two decisions choosing on policy grounds between competing rules in cases in which the law-fact patterns are reversed, provided the way in which it was put together is kept in mind.[65] Thus, if the New York Court of Appeals had decided that an Ontario guest could not recover damages from an Ontario host for injuries sustained in New York, Professor Cavers would see no objection to a jurisdiction-selecting rule referring the issue of a host's liability to his guest passenger to the law of the place where their relationship was centred. And if the Supreme Court of Wisconsin had decided that an Illinois wife could not recover damages from her Illinois husband for injuries sustained in Wisconsin, he would see no objection to a jurisdiction-selecting rule referring the issue of interspousal immunity to the law of the spouses' domicile.

This concession by Professor Cavers is a very important one, because it may well be that many of the traditional rules of the conflict of laws are the product of just such a synthesis as he describes. Take, for example, the rule that the formal validity of a marriage is governed by the *lex loci celebrationis*. As it stands, this rule is a somewhat arid statement. In order to give it colour and texture we need to split it up into its component parts, distinguishing between cases where the *lex loci* holds the marriage valid and cases where it holds the marriage void. We may also have to distinguish between cases where the marriage is celebrated in England and cases where it is celebrated abroad. We then find that our simple arid rule can be expanded into four propositions. (a) A marriage celebrated in England in accordance with the formalities prescribed by English domestic law is valid. (b) A marriage celebrated in England not in accordance with the formalities prescribed by English domestic law is void. (c) A marriage celebrated abroad in accordance with the formalities prescribed by the *lex loci celebrationis* is valid. (d) A marriage celebrated abroad not in accordance with the formalities prescribed by the *lex loci celebrationis* is void. But—and this is the point of the present discussion—proposition (d) was found to be too harsh, and so a number of exceptions to it have been created on policy grounds, some by statute and some by the courts.[66] So if we make the distinctions noted above, and bear in mind the exceptions to prop-

---

[62] pp. 75–87.
[63] *Post*, pp. 521–523.
[64] (1933) 47 Harv.L.Rev. 173, 193 *et seq.*
[65] (1963) 63 Col.L.Rev. 1219, 1225–1226; Cavers, p. 9, n. 24.
[66] *Ante*, pp. 153–158.

osition (d), our simple arid rule for the formal validity of marriage assumes a much less mechanical air. And after all, the rule is derived from the ancient maxim *locus regit actum*; and debate has been proceeding in Europe for centuries as to whether, in various contexts, that maxim should be regarded as facultative or obligatory.

It does not seem necessary to abandon the whole existing system of the conflict of laws, with its apparatus of concepts and rules, as long as it yields acceptable results. It economises thought to be able to apply a conflict rule instead of having to think out each problem afresh each time it arises. But the great value of Cavers' contribution is that it does enable the "false conflict" to be identified and avoided. This is a matter which will be considered in more detail later in this chapter.[67]

Governmental interest analysis

An even more revolutionary opponent of the traditional system than Cavers was Professor Brainerd Currie. In his opinion, "we would be better off without choice of law rules."[68] In a series of challenging articles, he inveighed again and again against "the system"; and he had some very hostile things to say about it. In his opinion it is "conceptualistic," "irrational," "mindless," "ruthless," "wretched," "spurious," "futile," "arbitrary," "hypnotic," "mystical," "intoxicating"; it is "an apparatus," "a machine," "a field of sophism, mystery and frustration"; "it has not worked and cannot be made to work."

Currie began his attack on "the system" by an analysis in depth of *Milliken v. Pratt*.[69] Noting that the policies of the two states concerned were in conflict, he identified the policy of Massachusetts law as designed to protect Massachusetts married women, and the policy of Maine law as designed to protect the security of transactions by giving effect to the reasonable expectations of the parties. He then demonstrated with the aid of a number of ingenious Tables that the application of the law of the place of contracting generated more false problems than there were real ones, and then solved the false problems, more often than not, in an obviously unacceptable way, by defeating the interests of both the states concerned, or by defeating the interests of one without advancing the interests of the other. He did not draw from this the conclusion which Cook had drawn,[70] namely, that the law of the domicile would be a better solution of the problem than the law of the place of contracting. He admitted that the application of this law would eliminate the false problems. But he rejected it on the grounds that "domicile is an intolerably elusive factor in commercial transactions"[71]; and that the application of the law of the domicile "would be commercially inconvenient and would consistently prefer the 'obsolete' to the 'progressive' policy."[72]

---

[67] *Post*, pp. 526–530.
[68] Currie, p. 183.
[69] (1878) 125 Mass. 374; *ante*, p. 510. The article now appears as Chap. 2 of his book.
[70] Cook. Chap. 16.
[71] Currie, p. 103.
[72] Currie, p. 180.

Instead, he proposed a radical new method for solving conflicts problems which would dispense with traditional conflict rules altogether. The latest statement of his thesis is as follows[73]:

"(1) When a court is asked to apply the law of a foreign state different from the law of the forum, it should inquire into the policies expressed in the respective laws, and into the circumstances in which it is reasonable for the respective states to assert an interest in the application of those policies. In making these determinations the court should employ the ordinary processes of construction and interpretation.

(2) If the court finds that one state has an interest in the application of its policy in the circumstances of the case and the other has none, it should apply the law of the only interested state.[74]

(3) If the court finds an apparent conflict between the interests of the two states it should reconsider.[75] A more moderate and restrained interpretation of the policy or interest of one state or the other may avoid conflict.[76]

(4) If, upon reconsideration, the court finds that a conflict between the legitimate interests of the two states is unavoidable, it should apply the law of the forum.[77]

(5) If the forum is disinterested, but an unavoidable conflict exists between the laws of two other states, and the court cannot with justice decline to adjudicate the case, it should apply the law of the forum—until someone comes along with a better idea."

Currie claimed that acceptance of his "governmental interest" analysis would dispense not only with traditional conflict rules but also with such doctrines as renvoi, characterisation and public policy, which he regarded as devices required to make "the system" work.

Before we attempt to evaluate this revolutionary thesis, a few words of explanation are required. First, Currie did not invent the method of "governmental interest" analysis. He derived it from a line of American Supreme Court cases on workmen's compensation[78] in which the court held that either the state of employment or the state of injury could constitutionally apply its law to an industrial accident, provided it had sufficient "governmental interest" to do so. As Stone J. said in the leading case,[79] "the conflict is to be resolved . . . by appraising the governmental interests

---

[73] (1963) 63 Col.L.Rev. 1233, 1242–1243. Other succinct statements of his thesis appear in Currie, pp. 183–184, 188–189; Reese and Rosenberg, *Cases on Conflict of Laws*, 6th ed., pp. 523–524.

[74] This, says Currie, is what the court did in *Babcock* v. *Jackson*, 12 N.Y. 2d 473, 191 N.E. 2d 279 (1963).

[75] This proposition formed no part of Currie's earlier statements of his position. It was added later.

[76] This, says Currie, is what the court did in *Bernkrant* v. *Fowler*, 55 Cal. 2d 588, 360 P. 2d 906 (1961); *ante*, p. 457.

[77] This, says Currie, is what the court did in *Kilberg* v. *Northeast Airlines*, 9 N.Y. 2d 34, 172 N.E. 2d 526 (1961).

[78] Currie, pp. 613–614.

[79] *Alaska Packers Association* v. *Industrial Accident Commission* (1935) 294 U.S. 532, 547. This and the other cases in the series are discussed in Currie, pp. 201–214. The significance of Stone J.'s analysis for conflict of laws cases had already been pointed out by Freund (1946) 59 Harv.L.Rev. 1210, 1211–1225.

of each jurisdiction, and turning the scale of decision according to their weight."

Secondly, if the forum and the foreign state concerned each has an interest in the application of its law, Currie was adamant that the law of the forum must be applied, even though the foreign state has the greater interest. He refused to concede that the forum was entitled to weigh the interests of the two states. His reason was that "assessment of the respective values of the competing legitimate interests of two sovereign states, in order to determine which is to prevail, is a political function of a very high order. This is a function that should not be committed to courts in a democracy. It is a function that the courts cannot perform effectively, for they lack the necessary resources."[80]

Thirdly, as he himself admitted, Currie's method afforded no intellectually satisfying solution of "the intractable problem of the disinterested third state." *i.e.* cases where the forum has no interest in the outcome, but two foreign states have conflicting interests. He discussed this problem several times in his book,[81] and later devoted a special article to it.[82] In that article he minimised the practical importance of the problem by noting that actual cases involving it are extremely rare. He suggested that if possible the forum should avoid the problem by declining jurisdiction on *forum non conveniens* grounds; or, if that proved impossible, by construing it away by finding that the interest of one of the two foreign states did not really exist.[83] Lacking either of these solutions, the forum should either apply the law which it thinks Congress would apply if it legislated on the question, or should apply the law of the forum. He said "If I were a judge I think I should prefer application of the law of the forum as the bolder technique. But then, I am a pretty old-fashioned fellow."[84] His contempt for traditional rules of the conflict of laws was such that he would not apply them even in this situation.

Old-fashioned or not, Currie's avowed object was to reduce the conflict of laws garden to ashes.[85] His ideas have been widely but not universally accepted in the United States, not only by academics but also by courts; but European writers are somewhat more sceptical.[86] The following are among the difficulties which acceptance of his theory would present to an English court:

---

[80] Currie, p. 182.
[81] Currie, pp. 62–64, 120–121, 606–609, 720–721.
[82] Currie (1963) 28 *Law and Contemporary Problems* 754.
[83] This is what the court did in *Reich* v. *Purcell*, 63 Cal. 2d 31; 432 P. 2d 727 (1967); *ante*, pp. 328–329.
[84] 28 *Law and Contemporary Problems* 754, 780.
[85] Currie, p. 185.
[86] For a selection of comments on Currie's theory, see Hill (1960) 27 U. of Chi.L.Rev. 463 (for Currie's reply, see Chap. 12); Ehrenzweig, *Conflict of Laws*, pp. 348–351; (for Currie's reply, see (1964) Duke L.J. 424, 435–436); Leflar, s.92; Kegel (1964) *Recueil des Cours*, II, 95, 180–207; Reese (1964) *Recueil des Cours*, I, 315, 329–333; Reese (1965) 16 U. of Tor.L.J. 228; Chief Justice Traynor (1965) Duke L.J. 426; Cavers, pp. 72–75, 96–102; Baade (1967) 46 Tex.L.Rev. 141–151; Kahn-Freund (1968) *Recueil des Cours*, II, 5, 56–61; (1974) *Recueil des Cours*, III, 147, 413–415; von Mehren (1975) 60 Cornell L.Rev. 927, 935–941; Westmoreland (1975) 40 Mo.L.Rev. 407, 421–423, 455–459; Anton, pp. 38–39; Nygh, pp. 15–16; Fawcett (1982) 31 I.C.L.Q. 189.

(1) The conflict of laws deals mainly with private law and is concerned with the interests of private persons and not with the interests of governments. It may be doubted whether governments really are interested in having their law applied in a conflict of laws situation, unless indeed the government of a country is a party to the action: and even then it may suit its purpose to argue that the foreign law and not its own should be applied. For instance, in *R.* v. *International Trustee for the Protection of Bondholders A/G*,[87] the British Government successfully argued that an international loan which it had raised on the New York money market in 1917 was governed by New York and not by English law, so that a gold clause contained therein was illegal and void under the Joint Resolution of Congress of 1933.

As we have seen, Currie derived his theory from the judgments of Stone J. in the Supreme Court of the United States. The questions with which that court is concerned are as often as not political rather than legal questions. It is therefore natural that the court should view the problems with which it is confronted as demanding an exercise of statecraft. But it does not follow that this is an acceptable attitude for a state court in a federal system, or for any court in a non-federal system.

(2) Over one-third of Currie's book is devoted to a discussion of how his method is affected by the American Constitution, and in particular by the full faith and credit, due process of law, privileges and immunities and equal protection of the laws clauses.[88] To a considerable extent these clauses help to place a curb on the exaggerated pursuit of self-interest by individual states which his theory might seem to encourage. It is evident that he was thinking exclusively in terms of an American forum and almost exclusively in terms of conflicts between the laws of two American states. Transplanted to a different environment, it is difficult to see how his theory would work in the absence of constitutional checks and balances.

(3) It may be doubted whether Currie's refusal to concede that the forum is entitled to weigh its interests in the balance against those of the foreign state concerned is really consistent with his later and more refined view that, if the forum is confronted by an apparent conflict, it may be able to avoid the conflict by a "moderate and restrained interpretation" of its policy or that of the foreign state. For what is this but weighing in disguise?[89]

(4) If the forum has an interest in the application of its law that cannot be construed away by a "moderate and restrained interpretation of its policy," Currie's method requires that the law of the forum should be applied, even if some other state has a much greater interest, and even if the result is to disappoint the reasonable expectations of the parties. Thus the interest of the forum prevails over all other considerations. And, as he

---

[87] [1937] A.C. 500; *ante*, p. 499.

[88] Currie, Chaps. 5, 6, 10, 11. It may be noted that aliens as well as American citizens are within the protection of the due process and equal protection clauses.

[89] Currie's answer to this criticism is to be found in Currie, pp. 604–606, and in (1963) 28 *Law and Contemporary Problems*, 754, 756–761. At least to the present author, it does not seem convincing.

freely admitted, his method sacrifices the goal of uniformity of result irrespective of the forum in which the action is brought, which has always been regarded as one of the most important objectives of the conflict of laws. For if there is a true conflict, and each state applies its own law as Currie's method requires, then the result will depend on the plaintiff's choice of forum. For this reason his method has been criticised as unduly orientated in favour of the *lex fori* and in favour of plaintiffs.

(5) Currie's method requires that the "interest" of the forum and of the foreign state should be easily identifiable by counsel and court. This requirement is only fulfilled in the simplest of cases. It may have been fulfilled in *Babcock* v. *Jackson*[90]; but even in that case, as we have already noted,[91] the casual way in which the court dealt with the object of the Ontario statute was perhaps the Achilles heel of the opinion. In one of his articles,[92] it took Currie nearly forty pages to identify the policy behind a North Carolina statute of 1933 which prohibited actions on the personal covenant by certain kinds of mortgagee after foreclosure proceedings. It is unrealistic to suppose that the purposes behind substantive rules of law are so clear, so unambiguous and so singular that we can hope to discover them in the course of a trial with some degree of certainty and without risk of error. This is true of the substantive rules of the forum, and even more true of the substantive rules of foreign law. For a rule of law is often the outcome of conflicting social, economic, political and legal pressures. It is an amalgam of conflicting interests. It does not express unequivocally a single "governmental interest" to the exclusion of all others. If it is an ancient rule of law, its original purpose may be lost in the mists of antiquity; and its continuance may simply be due to inertia or to lack of Parliamentary time to abolish it. Hence, what Currie said about the weighing of interests applies equally to the determination of policies: "it is a function that the courts cannot perform effectively, for they lack the necessary resources."[93]

(6) To expect the courts to abandon choice of law rules, and proceed on a case by case basis through governmental interest analysis, seems futile. Because of the doctrine of precedent, cases decided on the basis of governmental interest are bound to yield choice of law rules. These rules may differ from the traditional ones, but they are still rules, and as such binding on the courts in future cases. Hence, as has been well said, "trying to throw away choice of law rules is like trying to throw away a boomerang."[94]

However, in spite of these criticisms, it must freely be admitted that Currie, like Cavers, did perform a useful service in enabling us to identify and avoid false problems. These will be discussed in more detail later in this chapter.[95]

---

[90] 12 N.Y. 2d 473, 191 N.E. 2d 279 (1963).
[91] *Ante*, p. 326, n. 54.
[92] Reprinted as Chap. 8.
[93] Currie, p. 182, quoted *ante*, p. 518.
[94] Rosenberg (1967) 67 Col.L.Rev. 459, 464. *Cf.* Cavers, p. 74.
[95] *Post*, pp. 526–530.

Comparative impairment

The Californian courts have adopted a variant on Currie's method which deserves separate treatment here. We have seen that if the forum and the foreign state each has an interest in the application of its law, Currie was adamant that the law of the forum must be applied, even if the foreign state has the greater interest. But the Californian courts have adopted a theory which involves the weighing of interests. A striking example is afforded by *Bernhard* v. *Harrah's Club*.[96] In that case the Supreme Court of California held that a Nevada tavern keeper was vicariously liable under a Californian statute for serving too much liquor to a drunken guest, who negligently injured the plaintiff in California while driving back to her home in that state, even though Nevada law imposed no such liability. The court found that California's interest in protecting its residents would be very seriously impaired if the defendant was held not liable, while Nevada's interest in protecting its tavern keepers would not be so seriously impaired if the defendant was held liable, at least if (as in the instant case) it had actively solicited Californian custom by advertising there. If Nevada had been the forum it seems most unlikely that its courts would have agreed that Californian law was applicable. Yet the Californian courts on the whole apply their doctrine of comparative impairment in an even-handed way. In *Offshore Rental Co.* v. *Continental Oil Co.*[97] the plaintiff was a Californian corporation with its main place of business in California and places of business in other states, including Louisiana. A key employee of the plaintiff was injured in Louisiana owing to the defendant's negligence. The plaintiff sued for loss of services. Such an action was maintainable in California but not in Louisiana. The Supreme Court of California applied the law of Louisiana because it found that Louisiana's interest would be the more gravely impaired if its law was not applied.

Principles of preference

In 1965, Professor Cavers of Harvard published a book called *The Choice of Law Process* which was based on a course of lectures delivered the previous year in the University of Michigan. The central theme of the book is the presentation of seven "principles of preference" as guides for a court in cases where the conflict of laws is neither false nor readily avoidable.[98] Five of these principles relate to torts and two to contracts and conveyances. Professor Cavers disclaimed any idea that his seven principles were intended to form a complete system even in these two fields of law. He also emphasised that if a particular case did not fall within any of his principles, this does not mean that a contrary choice of law must be made: it simply meant that the case posed a different problem from that covered by the principle and therefore required further consideration.

---

[96] 16 Cal. 3d 313, 546 P. 2d 719 (1976).

[97] 22 Cal. 3d 157, 583 P. 2d 721 (1978).

[98] Cavers, Chaps. 5, 6, 7 and 8. For comments on his method, see Reese (1966) 35 Fordham L.Rev. 153; Ehrenzweig (1966) 80 Harv.L.Rev. 377; Baade (1967) 46 Tex.L.Rev. 141, 156–175; Scoles (1967) 20 Jo.Leg.Ed. 111; von Mehren (1975) 60 Cornell L.Rev. 927, 952–963; Westmoreland (1975) 40 Mo.L.Rev. 407, 423–427, 459–460; Leflar, s.95.

The five principles in the field of torts are as follows:

(1) Where the law of the state of injury sets a *higher* standard of condu
or of financial protection than the law of the state where the defenda
acted or had his home, the former law should be applied.[99]

(2) Where the law of the state in which the defendant acted and cause
an injury sets a *lower* standard of conduct or of financial protection tha
the law of the plaintiff's home state, the former law should be applied.[1]
sub-principle, not given a number, provides that if both plaintiff and defe
dant have their homes in a state or states other than the state of injury an
the law of the state of injury sets a lower standard of financial protectic
than that afforded by the law or laws of the parties' home state or state
the law of that home state which affords the lower degree of protectic
should be applied.[2]

(3) Where the state in which the defendant acted has established contro
(including civil liability) over the kind of conduct in which the defenda
was engaged when he caused a foreseeable injury to the plaintiff in anoth
state having no such controls, the law of the former state should b
applied.[3]

(4) Where the law of a state in which a relationship between tw
parties has its seat has imposed a standard of conduct or of financi
protection on one party for the benefit of the other which is *higher* tha
that of the state of injury, the law of the former state should b
applied.[4]

(5) Where the law of a state in which a relationship between tw
parties has its seat has imposed a standard of conduct or of financi
protection on one party for the benefit of the other which is *lower* tha
that of the state of injury, the law of the former state should b
applied.[5]

The two principles in the field of contracts and conveyances are as fo
lows:

(1) Where, for the purpose of providing protection from the conse
quences of incompetence, heedlessness, ignorance, or unequal bargainir
power, the law of a state has imposed restrictions on the power to contra
or to convey or encumber property, its protective provisions should b
applied if (a) the person protected has a home in that state and (b) th
affected transaction or protected property interest was centred there or (

---

[99] pp. 139–145. Lack of space precludes even a summary discussion of the illuminating cor
ment which accompanies each of the principles.

[1] pp. 146–157.

[2] pp. 157–159.

[3] pp. 159–166.

[4] pp. 166–177.

[5] pp. 177–180. But Cavers disapproves of this as a principle, and says that it would probab
not achieve general acceptance. The decisions of the New York Appellate Division in *Ke
v. Henderson* (1966) 270 N.Y.S. 2d 552, of the Supreme Court of Wisconsin in *Conklin
Horner*, 38 Wis. 2d 468, 157 N.W. 2d 579 (1968) and of the Supreme Court of Minnesota
Milkovich v. *Saari*, 295 Minn. 155, 203 N.W. 2d 408 (1973) (*ante*, p. 328) are inconsiste
with it.

if it were not, this was due to facts that were fortuitous or had been manipulated to evade the protective law.[6]

(2) If the parties expressly or presumably intend that the law of a particular state which is reasonably related to the transaction should be applied, that law should be applied if it validates the transaction, even though neither party has a home in that state and the transaction is not centred there. But this principle does not apply if it conflicts with principle (1) above, or if the transaction includes a conveyance of land and the mandatory rules of the *lex situs* invalidate the mode of conveyance or the interests created thereby. Nor does it affect third parties.[7]

Professor Cavers proposed no principles of preference for any fields of law other than torts and contracts and conveyances. But of course there are many other fields in which his method might be used—marriage, for example. He described his principles as "value judgments"[8]; and herein lies the chief difference between his method and that of Currie, though there is a great deal in common between the two.

Despite Cavers' own statement to the contrary,[9] it is difficult to believe that his theory will work in international situations any more than that of Currie. He has rendered articulate some of those choice-influencing factors which judges consciously or unconsciously resort to. But in an international case, how could a judge express a preference for the rules adopted by one country or another when those countries are not component parts of a federal system but are linked only by diplomatic relations or (perhaps) by a common cultural heritage?

Choice-influencing factors

In 1952, Professors Cheatham and Reese of Columbia University published an article[10] in which they listed and commented on a number of policies which they believed should guide the courts in deciding choice of law questions and in formulating rules for the choice of law. In the same year, Professor Reese was appointed Reporter of the Restatement Second of the Conflict of Laws. The enumerated policies are not meant to be exclusive, nor are they listed in the order of their relative importance. They are likely to point in different directions in all but the simplest case. Hence the choice of law rule will have to accommodate conflicting values.

The American Law Institute has now adopted these policies (with some modifications) in the Restatement Second of the Conflict of Laws. Section 6 says that in the absence of direct guidance from a relevant statute, the factors to be weighed by a court include the following:

[6] pp. 181–194. The type of laws included in this principle are envisaged as laws restricting the capacity of minors, married women and spendthrifts; laws protecting insured persons from harsh provisions in the fine print of insurance policies; laws limiting the creditor's right to repossess chattels sold on credit; and the statutes of frauds.
[7] pp. 194–198.
[8] p. 213.
[9] pp. viii, 117, 119 n.
[10] Cheatham and Reese (1952) 52 Col.L.Rev. 959. It was followed by two other publications by Reese: (1963) 28 *Law and Contemporary Problems* 679; (1964) *Recueil des Cours*, I, 315, 340–356. *Cf.* Yntema (1957) 35 Can.Bar.Rev. 721, esp. at p. 734.

(1) *The needs of the interstate and international systems.* Choice of law rules should seek to further harmonious relations between states and nations and to facilitate commercial intercourse between them. In the original article, *Cammell* v. *Sewell*[11] was cited as a good example of such a rule. In that case it was laid down that "if personal property is disposed of in a manner binding according to the law of the country where it is, that disposition is binding everywhere." The authors said that that rule "makes much good sense." They might also have cited *Goetschius* v. *Brightman*,[12] where the New York Court of Appeals gave a restrictive interpretation to a New York statute requiring the registration of hire-purchase contracts so as to protect a Californian owner against a New York bona fide purchaser.

(2) *The relevant policies of the forum.* Every rule of law, whether embodied in a statute or in judge-made law, was designed to achieve one or more purposes. Therefore a court should have regard for these purposes in determining whether to apply its own rule or the rule of another country in the decision of a particular issue. If those purposes would be furthered by the application of the rule to foreign facts, that is a weighty reason for doing so. It is only to be expected that a court will favour its own local policies over those of other countries.

(3) *The relevant policies of other interested states.* The forum, says the Restatement Second, should give consideration not only to its own relevant policies but also to those of all other interested states. It should seek to reach a result that will achieve the best possible accommodation of these policies. It is usually desirable that the state whose interests are most deeply affected should have its law applied. Which is the state of dominant interest may depend on the issue involved. So if a husband injures his wife in a state other than that of their domicile, the state of conduct and injury may have the dominant interest in determining whether his conduct was tortious or whether she was guilty of contributory negligence. But the state of their domicile is the state of dominant interest when the question is whether a husband is immune from tortious liability to his wife. The content of the relevant rule of law of a state may well be significant in determining whether that state is the one with the dominant interest. Thus, if the rule would absolve a defendant from liability, the state can have no interest in the welfare of the injured plaintiff.

(4) *The protection of justified expectations.* As a general rule, a man is entitled to expect that if he regulates his conduct in accordance with the law of one country (*e.g.* the country where he acts), it will not be called in question in another country. It is in furtherance of this policy that the parties are free, within limits, to select the law which shall govern their contract,[13] and that courts seek to apply a law which will sustain the validit

---

[11] (1860) 5 H. & N. 728; *ante,* p. 353.
[12] 245 N.Y. 186, 156 N.E. 660 (1927); *ante,* p. 355.
[13] *Ante,* pp. 270–274.

of a trust.[14] On the other hand, there are occasions, particularly in the field of negligence, when the parties act without giving thought to the legal consequences of their conduct or to the law which may be applied thereto. In such situations, the parties have no justified expectations to protect. Moreover, there are some rules of law which are frankly designed to defeat expectations, *e.g.* the Statute of Frauds and the rule against perpetuities. Then the policy for protecting justified expectations has no weight.

(5) *The basic policies underlying the particular field of law*. Situations sometimes arise where the policies of the interested states are largely the same but there are minor differences between their relevant local rules. In such instances, there is good reason for the court to apply the local law of that state which will best achieve the basic policy, or policies, underlying the particular field of law involved. Thus, in the law of trusts, American courts have gone to considerable lengths to apply a law that will uphold a trust against invalidity under the rule against perpetuities. But "this may be an acceptable result if the two laws agree in general policy and differ only in detail. It might well not be acceptable to an English court if a testator domiciled in some country where there is no rule against perpetuities attempted to create a trust of English property, to be administered in England, which infringed the rule."[15]

(6) *Certainty, predictability and uniformity of result*. These values, says the Restatement, are important in all areas of the law; and to the extent that they are attained in choice of law, forum-shopping will be discouraged. But these values can be purchased at too great a price. It may often be more important to experiment with new rules than that certainty, predictability and uniformity of result should be assured through continued adherence to existing rules of doubtful utility. But certainty, predictability and uniformity of result are of particular importance in areas where the parties are likely to give advance thought to the legal consequences of their transactions, *e.g.* in contracts and property. Uniformity of result is also important when an aggregate of movables situated in two or more countries is transferred, *e.g.* on marriage or on death.

(7) *Ease in the determination and application of the law to be applied*. Ideally, choice of law rules should be simple and easy to apply. Pushed to its logical conclusion, this policy would result in there being but one single rule, namely, that all cases should be decided in accordance with the *lex fori*. Hence, this policy should not be over-emphasised, since it is obviously of greater importance that choice of law rules should lead to desirable results. However, this policy does furnish the justification for applying the *lex fori* to questions of procedure.

It is significant that two policies listed in the original article have been abandoned in the Restatement Second, presumably because they did not

[14] *Ante*, p. 420.
[15] Morris and Leach, *The Rule against Perpetuities*, 2nd ed., p. 23.

find favour with the American Law Institute. These are (a) the principle that a court should apply its own law unless there is some good reason for not doing so; and (b) the policy of justice in the individual case. The article was very sceptical of (b); the authors pointed out that if this were the one and only value, it would be totally disruptive of all legal rules.

In 1966 Professor Leflar, formerly of the University of Arkansas and now of New York University, published two articles[16] in which he listed and discussed five choice-influencing factors. These are: (1) predictability of results; (2) maintenance of interstate and international order; (3) simplification of the judicial task; (4) advancement of the forum's governmental interests; (5) application of the better rule of law. It will be seen that, with one exception, all of these merely repeat some of the factors listed by the Restatement. The exception is the fifth of Leflar's factors, which he regarded as the "most controversial."[17] As might have been expected, it has been adopted by some American courts. Thus the Supreme Court of New Hampshire, in preferring its common law rule to the guest statute of Vermont, observed[18]:

> "We prefer to apply the better rule in conflicts cases just as is done in non-conflicts cases, when the choice is open to us. If the law of some other state is outmoded, an unrepealed remnant of a bygone age, 'a drag on the coat-tails of civilisation,' we will try to see our way clear to apply our own law instead. If it is our own law that is obsolete or senseless (and it could be) we will try to apply the other state's law. Courts have always done this in conflicts cases, but have usually covered up what they have done by employing manipulative techniques such as characterisation and renvoi."

But other commentators[19] frown on the application of the better rule of law, and with good reason. It is not the function of courts to reform the law of other countries (still less of their own country) by giving it the narrowest possible scope or refusing to apply it in a conflict of laws case. That is a task better left to legislatures or Law Commissions. As Cavers says, to ask the judge simply to express a preference between two rules of law on the ground of justice and convenience "is to abolish our centuries-old subject."[20]

False conflicts, dépéçage and foreign law as datum

As we have seen,[21] the great merit of the methods of Cavers and Currie is that they enable false problems to be identified and avoided. What are these false problems, or false conflicts as they are more usually called, and how can they be identified? The search for them in the United States is proceeding with such enthusiasm that it reminds one of the hunt for interpola-

---

[16] (1966) 41 N.Y.U.L.Rev. 267; (1966) 54 Calif.L.Rev. 1584. They are summarised in Leflar, ss.103–107.
[17] 54 Calif.L.Rev. 1584, 1587.
[18] *Clark* v. *Clark*, 107 N.H. 351, 355, 222 A. 2d 205, 209 (1966).
[19] *Ante*, p. 514, n. 61.
[20] Cavers, p. 86.
[21] *Ante*, pp. 516, 520.

tions in Justinian's Digest which was at one time fashionable on the continent of Europe. Already the literature on the subject is quite extensive.[22] The trouble is that no two writers agree on what constitutes a false conflict. Still, there is a large measure of agreement that false conflicts include the following:

(1) The first class consists of cases where two countries have different laws, but one of them was obviously not intended to apply to the case in hand. Examples are: *Milliken* v. *Pratt*[23] with the laws of the two states reversed (because the protective policy of Maine was not intended to apply to Massachusetts married women); the Englishman aged twenty who buys goods in a Ruritanian shop, minority ending in Ruritanian law at twenty-one[24]; *Babcock* v. *Jackson*[25] (because the Ontario statute was not intended to apply to New York hosts, guests and insurance companies); *Haumschild* v. *Continental Casualty Co.*[26] (because the Californian rule of interspousal immunity was not intended to apply to Wisconsin spouses). By contrast, the converse of each of these cases poses a true conflict: a married woman domiciled and resident in Massachusetts makes a contract in Maine which she is incapable of making by Massachusetts law (*Milliken* v. *Pratt*); a Ruritanian aged twenty buys goods in an English shop; an Ontario host negligently injures an Ontario guest in New York[27]; an Illinois husband negligently injures an Illinois wife in Wisconsin.[28] The difference between false and true conflicts of this class can easily be perceived even by those who are sceptical of governmental interest analysis. In this situation, to say that one country's law was not intended to apply is only another way of saying that it had no interest in applying its law to the case.

(2) The second class consists of cases where the laws of two countries are the same or would produce the same result. In an earlier chapter we have already noted some examples where a conflict of characterisation leads to the law of neither country being applied.[29] Here are some more examples, not dependent on any conflict of characterisation.

In *Scheer* v. *Rockne Motors Corporation*,[30] the defendant in New York lent his car to a person who took a lady for a ride into Ontario and negligently injured her there.[31] An Ontario statute provided that "the owner of a motor vehicle shall be liable for loss or damage sustained by any person by reason of negligence in the operation of such motor vehicle on a high-

---

[22] Perhaps the most comprehensive survey is that by Westen (1967) 55 Calif.L.Rev. 74, where copious references to the literature are given. For shorter statements, see Cavers, pp. 89–90; Leflar, s.93. The whole notion of false conflicts is criticised by Kahn-Freund (1974) *Recueil des Cours*, III, 259–268.

[23] 125 Mass. 374 (1878); *ante*, pp. 510, 513.

[24] *Ante*, p. 286.

[25] 12 N.Y. 2d 473, 191 N.E. 2d 279 (1963); *ante*, pp. 325–326.

[26] 7 Wis. 2d 130, 95 N.W. 2d 814 (1959); *ante*, p. 514.

[27] *Kell* v. *Henderson*, 270 N.Y.S. 2d 552 (1966).

[28] *Zelinger* v. *State Sand and Gravel Co.*, 38 Wis. 2d 98, 156 N.W. 2d 466 (1968); *cf. Johnson* v. *Johnson*, 107 N.H. 30, 216 A. 2d 781 (1966), where on similar facts an opposite result was reached.

[29] *Ante*, p. 487.

[30] 68 F. 2d 942 (1934). See Cavers (1950) 63 Harv.L.Rev. 822, 826–829; Morris (1951) 64 Harv.L.Rev. 881, 891–892.

[31] The accident happened a few years before the notorious guest statute was first enacted.

way unless such motor vehicle was without the owner's consent in the possession of some person other than the owner." New York had a similar statute which provided that "every owner of a motor vehicle operated upon a public highway shall be liable for injuries to person or property resulting from negligence in the operation of such motor vehicle by any person operating the same with the permission, express or implied, of such owner." A lower federal court in New York held the owner liable. But the federal Court of Appeals ordered a new trial on the ground that the owner did not give the driver permission to go into Canada merely by giving him possession of the car. There was perhaps a true conflict of laws here, because the jury's verdict was consistent with the owner having expressly prohibited the driver from going into Canada. By New York law, if the owner imposed a prohibition on where the driver should go, and the driver disregarded it, the owner was not liable. The law of Ontario was probably different. But if it was found that the owner merely gave the driver possession of the car, then there was no true conflict of laws at all, and the case should have been decided under the law that was common to both Ontario and New York. Otherwise, the accident of geography would be allowed to determine the result.

Again, in *Koop* v. *Bebb*[32] the infant plaintiffs brought an action in the Supreme Court of Victoria for damages for the death of their father, who was a passenger in a motor vehicle driven by the defendant and who was killed as a result of the defendant's negligence. The accident occurred in New South Wales (where all parties were resident) and the father died in hospital in Victoria. Both Victoria and New South Wales had enacted legislation based on Lord Campbell's Act which permitted specified dependants to recover damages for the loss of their breadwinner. The statutes of the two states did not differ in any relevant respect. Yet Dean J. held that the action failed because the Victorian statute did not apply to wrongful acts occurring outside Victoria. His decision was reversed by the High Court of Australia; but the judges were not unanimous in their reasoning, and they made heavy weather of what should have been a simple case.

(3) Both in England and the United States there is high authority for the proposition that in cases of tort the issues should be segregated and not necessarily resolved by reference to the same law.[33] Cases involving two or more issues naturally involve more complication than cases involving only one. If the issues are referred to different laws, this is called "*dépéçage*" by the French and "picking and choosing" by the Americans.[34] The question arises whether it is legitimate for a court to "pick and choose" between the two laws so as to reach a result which could not have been reached by applying only one of them. If the issues are unrelated except by the circumstance that they both arise in the same case, it would be perverse for a court to insist on applying the law of one country or the other to both the issues before it. If on the other hand the issues are related, there is a

---

[32] (1951) 84 C.L.R. 629.
[33] *Boys* v. *Chaplin* [1971] A.C. 356, 391F, *per* Lord Wilberforce; *Babcock* v. *Jackson*, 12 N.Y. 2d 473, 484, 191 N.E. 2d 279, 285 (1963), *per* Fuld J.
[34] See Wilde (1968) 41 So.Calif.L.Rev. 329; Reese (1973) 73 Col.L.Rev. 58.

danger that the purpose of either or both laws may be distorted if the court applies the laws of each country to different issues.

As an illustration of the first of these propositions, let us take a variation on *Babcock* v. *Jackson*[35] suggested by the minority in that case. Suppose that Miss Babcock's negligence had contributed to the accident, and that New York has retained the common law doctrine of contributory negligence, while Ontario has enacted an apportionment statute. If she sued her host in New York, and he pleaded the New York contributory negligence rule as a defence, presumably the New York court would allow her to recover reduced damages under Ontario law. If she sued her host in New York, and he pleaded the Ontario guest statute as a defence, we know from *Babcock* v. *Jackson* that she would recover. Thus, if the two issues had arisen in two separate cases, the plaintiff would have recovered damages in each. Does the fact that the two issues have arisen in the same case make it impossible for her to recover damages? Surely the answer must be no, because the enactment of the apportionment statute in Ontario was quite unrelated to the enactment of the guest statute.

But if the two issues are related the problem is different, and the problem may be false. There is a danger that an undiscriminating court may segregate the issues improperly and so produce an unjust result which distorts the laws of both the countries concerned. In *Maryland Casualty Co.* v. *Jacek*,[36] a husband, resident with his wife in New Jersey, negligently injured her while both were travelling in the husband's car in New York. The husband was insured under a policy issued in New Jersey which provided that the insurer would satisfy any claim which the husband might become "legally obligated to pay." By the law of New York, a wife could sue her husband in tort but could not recover on his insurance policy unless express provision to that effect was specifically included in the policy. By the law of New Jersey, the policy would be construed to cover the wife's injuries; but wives could not sue their husbands in tort. Thus, if all the facts had occurred in New Jersey, the wife would be unable to recover because she could not sue her husband in tort; if all the facts had occurred in New York, she would be unable to recover because the policy did not cover her injuries. Yet a lower federal court in New Jersey held that the wife could recover, because in its view the law of New Jersey governed the construction of the policy, and the law of New York governed the question whether the wife could sue her husband in tort.[37] The result seems wrong because the laws of both states were concerned with the danger of collusive suits by husbands or wives against insurance companies. The New York law permitting suits between spouses was enacted at the same time as the New York law restrictively interpreting insurance policies. There was a clear connection between the two laws, as the New York courts had observed[38]:

---

[35] 12 N.Y. 2d 473, 487, 191 N.E. 2d 279, 287 (1963).
[36] 156 F.Supp. 43 (1957). *Cf. Lillegraven* v. *Tengs*, 375 P. 2d 139 (1962).
[37] The case was decided two years before *Haumschild* v. *Continental Casualty Co.*, 7 Wis. 2d 130, 95 N.W. 2d 814 (1959), where the rule of the *lex loci delicti* in this situation was abandoned.
[38] *Fuchs* v. *London and Lancashire Indemnity Co.*, 14 N.Y.S. 2d 387, 389 (1940).

"The purpose and policy of the legislature in making these simultaneous amendments is unmistakably clear. The object was to authorise personal injury actions between spouses, and at the same time to guard against the mulcting of insurance companies by means of collusive suits between husband and wife."

The federal court in New Jersey thus exploited the interstate situation unfairly, to the detriment of the insurance company.[39] Although the laws of the two states were different, the conflict was false.

(4) Another type of false conflict is where foreign law is referred to not for a rule of decision but for a datum. Currie emphasised that his governmental interest analysis was confined to cases of the first class.[40] The notion of foreign law being referred to not to furnish the rule of decision but as datum is perfectly familiar to English law. Perhaps the simplest illustration is afforded by foreign rules of the road. These are not rules of decision but rules of conduct, non-compliance with which may amount to negligence. The foreign rules of conduct are incorporated in the English cause of action for negligence, just as the terms of a foreign statute may be incorporated in an English contract.[41]

But Currie's idea of foreign law being referred to as datum was very much wider than this. He said that if a widow claims workmen's compensation in New York for the death of her husband there, or claims to be entitled as his widow under a New York will or intestacy, and the validity of her marriage is governed by Italian law, then this is not a case in the conflict of laws at all, since New York law in both cases furnishes the rule of decision, and Italian law furnishes no more than a datum.[42] This extremely narrow conception of what constitutes a case in the conflict of laws is certainly not adopted in England. If it were, it would mean that our choice of law rules for the validity of marriage (and also, presumably, for legitimacy and legitimation) could only be treated as true choice of law rules in the context of petitions for a decree of nullity or for a declaration as to status, and not in any other context. Apparently Currie would regard *Simonin* v. *Mallac*[43] as a case in the conflict of laws, because the validity of the marriage was in issue in nullity proceedings brought by the wife against the husband. But he would not regard *Ogden* v. *Ogden*[44] as a case in the conflict of laws, because the invalidity of the marriage was asserted as a defence to the second husband's petition for nullity on the ground of bigamy. This distinction seems very artificial.

Conclusion

There are three points on which all the modern American conflicts

---

[39] *Contra*, Reese (1973) 73 Col.L.Rev. 58, 67–68, who approves of the result in this case.
[40] Currie, p. 178.
[41] See Dicey and Morris, pp. 950–951. *Cf. The Halley* (1868) L.R. 2 P.C. 193, 203.
[42] Currie, pp. 69–72, 177–178.
[43] (1860) 2 Sw. & Tr. 67; *ante*, p. 152.
[44] [1908] P. 46; *ante*, pp. 152–153.

experts are agreed: first, the vested rights theory is dead; secondly, the mechanical place of contracting and place of tort rules of the first Restatement have rightly been abandoned; and thirdly, conflicts problems must be resolved in a flexible manner, case by case and issue by issue. But there agreement stops. Each writer has his own theory, and each is apt to find support for his theory in every important new case that is decided.[45] This situation was amusingly exploited by Cavers in his *Choice of Law Process*,[46] where he assembled a "court" composed of five academics (including himself), each of whom gave "judgment" in accordance with his own theory in five hypothetical cases posed by Cavers.

As has been indicated in the previous pages, none of the new American methods (except the choice-influencing factors of the Restatement Second) is suitable for adoption by English courts in international cases. We would do better to build on what is good in the traditional system, as the Restatement Second seeks to do, rather than to abolish that system altogether and start again.[47] On the other hand, these methods have three lessons which we should do well to take to heart. The first is that choice of law rules should be flexible and should be flexibly applied. The second is that they should never be applied without some regard to the content of the foreign law referred to. The third is that we should be on the alert to identify and avoid the false conflicts, and not be afraid to decide such cases in accordance with the law that is common to both countries, rather than in accordance with traditional conflict rules.

---

[45] Perhaps the most striking instance of this is afforded by the comments on *Babcock* v. *Jackson* in (1963) 63 Col.L.Rev. 1212. *Cf.* Leflar, s.99.

[46] pp. 15–58.

[47] See Anton, pp. 33–42.

INDEX

TA681 BET

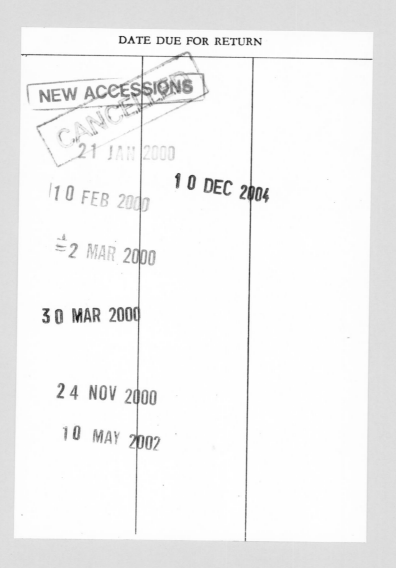

DATE DUE FOR RETURN

NEW ACCESSIONS
CANCELLED

21 JAN 2000

10 FEB 2000   1 0 DEC 2004

2 MAR 2000

3 0 MAR 2000

2 4 NOV 2000

1 0 MAY 2002

TA 681 BET